A Concise Introduction to World Religions

A Concise Introduction to World Religions

Third Edition

Edited by

Willard G. Oxtoby

Roy C. Amore

Amir Hussain

Alan F. Segal

OXFORD
UNIVERSITY PRESS

OXFORD
UNIVERSITY PRESS

Oxford University Press is a department of the University of Oxford.
It furthers the University's objective of excellence in research, scholarship, and education by publishing worldwide. Oxford is a registered trade mark of Oxford University Press in the UK and in certain other countries.

Published in Canada by
Oxford University Press
8 Sampson Mews, Suite 204,
Don Mills, Ontario M3C 0H5 Canada

www.oupcanada.com

First Edition published in 2007
Second Edition published in 2012

Library and Archives Canada Cataloguing in Publication

A concise introduction to world religions / edited by Willard G. Oxtoby, Roy C. Amore, Amir Hussain, Alan F. Segal. -- Third edition.

Includes bibliographical references and index.
ISBN 978-0-19-900855-1 (pbk.)

1. Religions--Textbooks. I. Oxtoby, Willard G. (Willard Gurdon), 1933-, editor II. Amore, Roy C., 1942-, author, editor III. Hussain, Amir, author, editor IV. Segal, Alan F., 1945-2011, editor V. Title: World religions.

BL80.3.C65 2015 200 C2014-907523-5

Cover image: Joey Chung/E+/Getty Images

Oxford University Press is committed to our environment. Wherever possible, our books are printed on paper which comes from responsible sources.

Printed and bound in the United States of America

3 4 — 18 17 16

Contents

5

6

7

8

9

10

11

12

Contributors

Roy C. Amore is a professor and an associate dean in the Faculty of Arts, Humanities, and Social Sciences at the University of Windsor in Ontario. His extensive research in the areas of comparative religion and Asia has enabled him to author *Two Masters, One Message*, a book comparing the lives and teachings of Christ and Buddha, and co-author *Lustful Maidens and Ascetic Kings: Buddhist and Hindu Stories of Life*.

Ken Derry received his PhD from the University of Toronto's Centre for the Study of Religion with a thesis on religion, violence, and First Nations literature. Since 1996 he has been teaching courses on religion, culture, literature, and film, and he is currently an instructor in the Department of Historical Studies at the University of Toronto.

Wendy L. Fletcher is a professor of the history of Christianity as well as the principal and vice-chancellor of Renison University College, University of Waterloo. She has published extensively in the areas of women and Christianity, spirituality, and religion and ethnicity.

Amir Hussain is a professor in the Department of Theological Studies at Loyola Marymount University in Los Angeles, where he teaches courses on Islam and world religions. A Canadian of Pakistani origin, he is the author of *Oil and Water: Two Faiths, One God*, an introduction to Islam for North Americans. He is also the editor of the *Journal of the American Academy of Religion* (*JAAR*).

Michele Murray is a professor in the Department of Religion at Bishop's University, where she holds the William and Nancy Turner chair in Christianity. She obtained her MA in Jewish history of the Second Temple period from the Hebrew University of Jerusalem, and her PhD in religion from the University of Toronto.

Vasudha Narayanan is a distinguished professor and the chair of the Department of Religion at the University of Florida as well as a past president of the American Academy of Religion. She is the author or editor of seven books and has written more than a hundred articles and chapters in books. Her current research focuses on Hindu traditions in Cambodia.

John K. Nelson is a professor in the Department of Theology and Religious Studies at the University of San Francisco. Trained as a cultural anthropologist, he is the author of *Experimental Buddhism: Innovation and Activism in Contemporary Japan* (2013) as well as two books on Shinto and a documentary film on the Yasukuni Shrine.

The late **Willard G. Oxtoby**, the original editor of the works on which this book is based, was a professor emeritus at the University of Toronto, where he launched the graduate program in the study of religion. His books include *Experiencing India: European Descriptions and Impressions* and *The Meaning of Other Faiths*.

The late **Alan F. Segal** was a professor of religion and an Ingeborg Rennert professor of Jewish studies at Barnard College, Columbia University. He wrote extensively in the fields of comparative religion, Judaism, and early Christianity. His books include *Rebecca's Children: Judaism and Christianity in the Roman World*, *Paul the Convert*, and *Life after Death: A History of the Afterlife in Western Religion*.

Pashaura Singh is a professor and the Dr Jasbir Singh Saini endowed chair in Sikh and Punjabi studies at the University of California, Riverside. He has authored three Oxford monographs, co-edited five conference volumes, and contributed articles to academic journals, books, and encyclopedias. His book *Life and Work of Guru Arjan: History, Memory, and Biography in the Sikh Tradition* (2006) was a bestseller in India.

Anne Vallely is an associate professor in the Department of Classics and Religious Studies at the University of Ottawa, where she teaches courses on South Asian traditions (especially Jainism and Hinduism), as well as nature and religion and death and dying. Her book *Guardians of the Transcendent: An Ethnography of a Jain Ascetic Community* (2002) is an anthropological study of Jain female ascetics. Her co-edited volume *Animals and the Human Imagination* was published in 2012.

Terry Tak-ling Woo teaches at York University and the University of Toronto Scarborough. She is involved with courses that introduce the study of religion and East Asian religions. Her research interests include women in Chinese religions and Chinese religions in diaspora.

Important Features of This Edition

This third edition of *A Concise Introduction to World Religions* is a significant revision, with three new contributors, four new chapters, a greater focus on women and contemporary issues, and an enhanced pedagogical program.

Based on the best-selling two-volume set *World Religions: Eastern Traditions* and *World Religions: Western Traditions*, fourth edition, these new chapters offer fresh perspectives and current research.

- **New introductory overview of the study of religion around the globe**, by Roy C. Amore and Amir Hussain
- **New "Indigenous Traditions" chapter** by Ken Derry, University of Toronto
- **New "Jewish Traditions" chapter** by Michele Murray, Bishop's University
- **New "Christian Traditions" chapter** by Wendy L. Fletcher, Renison University College, University of Waterloo
- **New content on the roles and experiences of women** in each chapter
- **New content on contemporary issues** in each chapter

Dynamic Pedagogical Program

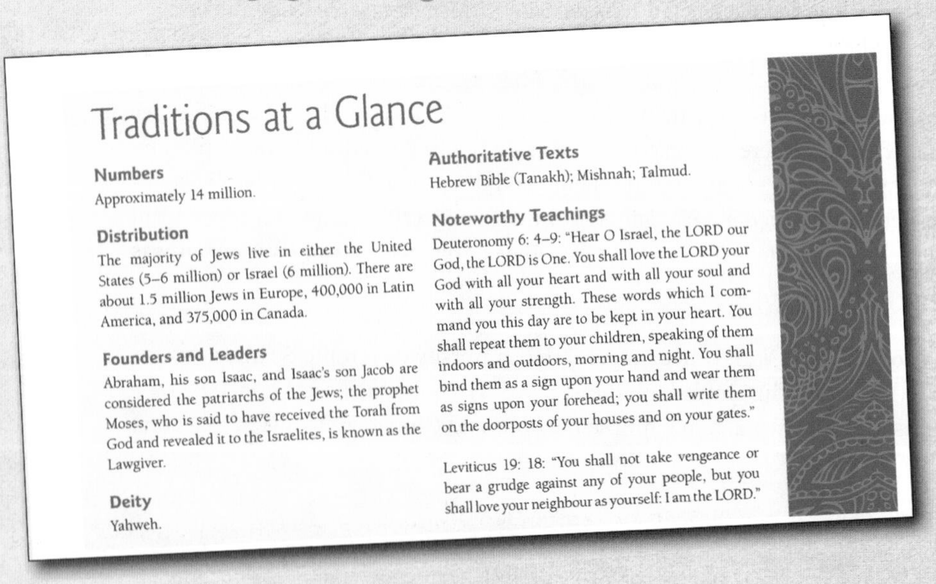
Traditions at a Glance

Numbers
Approximately 14 million.

Distribution
The majority of Jews live in either the United States (5–6 million) or Israel (6 million). There are about 1.5 million Jews in Europe, 400,000 in Latin America, and 375,000 in Canada.

Founders and Leaders
Abraham, his son Isaac, and Isaac's son Jacob are considered the patriarchs of the Jews; the prophet Moses, who is said to have received the Torah from God and revealed it to the Israelites, is known as the Lawgiver.

Deity
Yahweh.

Authoritative Texts
Hebrew Bible (Tanakh); Mishnah; Talmud.

Noteworthy Teachings
Deuteronomy 6: 4–9: "Hear O Israel, the LORD our God, the LORD is One. You shall love the LORD your God with all your heart and with all your soul and with all your strength. These words which I command you this day are to be kept in your heart. You shall repeat them to your children, speaking of them indoors and outdoors, morning and night. You shall bind them as a sign upon your hand and wear them as signs upon your forehead; you shall write them on the doorposts of your houses and on your gates."

Leviticus 19: 18: "You shall not take vengeance or bear a grudge against any of your people, but you shall love your neighbour as yourself: I am the LORD."

"Traditions at a Glance" boxes provide thumbnail summaries of numbers and distribution of participants, founders and leaders, deities, important texts, and noteworthy doctrines.

Timeline

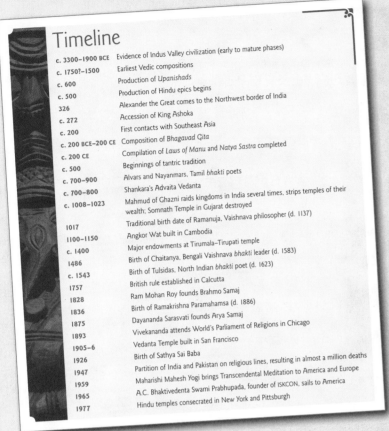

c. 3300–1900 BCE	Evidence of Indus Valley civilization (early to mature phases)
c. 1750?–1500	Earliest Vedic compositions
c. 600	Production of *Upanishads*
c. 500	Production of Hindu epics begins
326	Alexander the Great comes to the Northwest border of India
c. 272	Accession of King Ashoka
c. 200	First contacts with Southeast Asia
c. 200 BCE–200 CE	Composition of *Bhagavad Gita*
c. 200 CE	Compilation of *Laws of Manu* and *Natya Sastra* completed
c. 500	Beginnings of tantric tradition
c. 700–900	Alvars and Nayanmars, Tamil *bhakti* poets
c. 700–800	Shankara's Advaita Vedanta
c. 1008–1023	Mahmud of Ghazni raids kingdoms in India several times, strips temples of their wealth; Somnath Temple in Gujarat destroyed
1017	Traditional birth date of Ramanuja, Vaishnava philosopher (d. 1137)
1100–1150	Angkor Wat built in Cambodia
c. 1400	Major endowments at Tirumala-Tirupati temple
1486	Birth of Chaitanya, Bengali Vaishnava *bhakti* leader (d. 1583)
c. 1543	Birth of Tulsidas, North Indian *bhakti* poet (d. 1623)
1757	British rule established in Calcutta
1828	Ram Mohan Roy founds Brahmo Samaj
1836	Birth of Ramakrishna Paramahamsa (d. 1886)
1875	Dayananda Sarasvati founds Arya Samaj
1893	Vivekananda attends World's Parliament of Religions in Chicago
1905–6	Vedanta Temple built in San Francisco
1926	Birth of Sathya Sai Baba
1947	Partition of India and Pakistan on religious lines, resulting in almost a million deaths
1959	Maharishi Mahesh Yogi brings Transcendental Meditation to America and Europe
1965	A.C. Bhaktivedanta Swami Prabhupada, founder of ISKCON, sails to America
1977	Hindu temples consecrated in New York and Pittsburgh

Timelines help to place religious developments in historical context.

Map 4.1 The Spread of Christianity

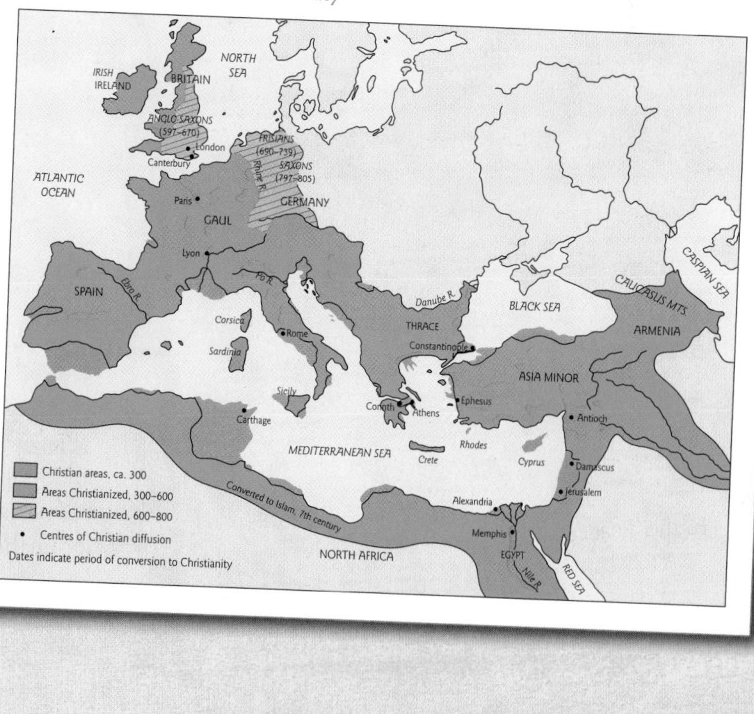

Informative maps provide useful reference points.

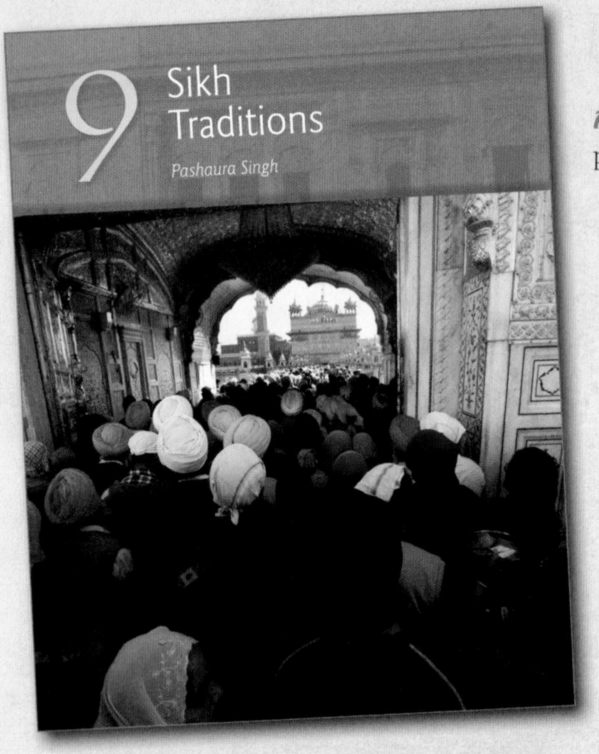

A vibrant art program highlights practitioners' lived experiences.

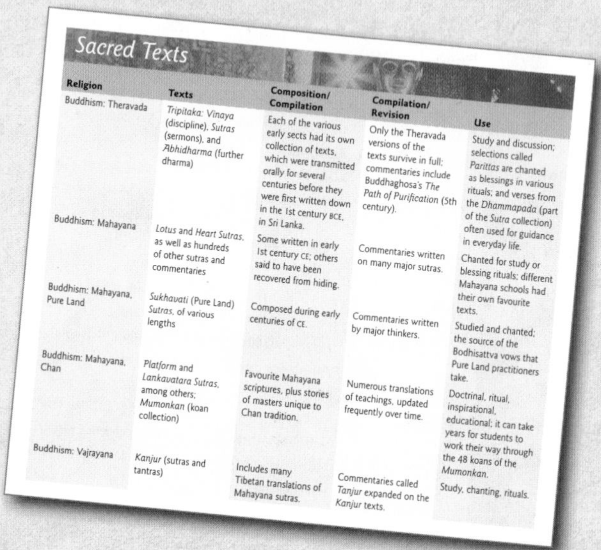

Sacred Texts

Religion	Texts	Composition/ Compilation	Compilation/ Revision	Use
Buddhism: Theravada	*Tripitaka: Vinaya* (discipline), *Sutras* (sermons), and *Abhidharma* (further dharma)	Each of the various early sects had its own collection of texts, which were transmitted orally for several centuries before they were first written down in the 1st century BCE, in Sri Lanka.	Only the Theravada versions of the texts survive in full; commentaries include Buddhaghosa's *The Path of Purification* (5th century).	Study and discussion; selections called *Parittas* are chanted as blessings in various rituals; and verses from the *Dhammapada* (part of the *Sutra* collection) often used for guidance in everyday life.
Buddhism: Mahayana	*Lotus* and *Heart Sutras*, as well as hundreds of other sutras and commentaries	Some written in early 1st century CE; others said to have been recovered from hiding.	Commentaries written on many major sutras.	Chanted for study or blessing rituals; different Mahayana schools had their own favourite texts.
Buddhism: Mahayana, Pure Land	*Sukhavati* (Pure Land) *Sutras*, of various lengths	Composed during early centuries of CE.	Commentaries written by major thinkers.	Studied and chanted; the source of the Bodhisattva vows that Pure Land practitioners take.
Buddhism: Mahayana, Chan	*Platform* and *Lankavatara Sutras*, among others; *Mumonkan* (koan collection)	Favourite Mahayana scriptures, plus stories of masters unique to Chan tradition.	Numerous translations of teachings, updated frequently over time.	Doctrinal, ritual, inspirational, educational; it can take years for students to work their way through the 48 koans of the *Mumonkan*.
Buddhism: Vajrayana	*Kanjur* (sutras and tantras)	Includes many Tibetan translations of Mahayana sutras.	Commentaries called *Tanjur* expanded on the *Kanjur* texts.	Study, chanting, rituals.

"Sacred Texts" tables give students a convenient summary of the most important texts in each tradition, how and when they were composed, and the uses made of them.

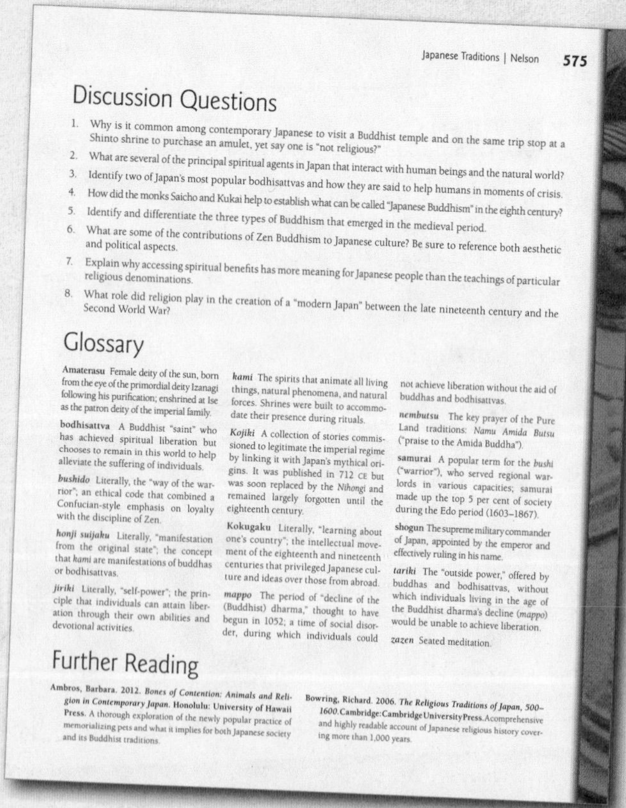

Japanese Traditions | Nelson 575

Discussion Questions

1. Why is it common among contemporary Japanese to visit a Buddhist temple and on the same trip stop at a Shinto shrine to purchase an amulet, yet say one is "not religious?"
2. What are several of the principal spiritual agents in Japan that interact with human beings and the natural world?
3. Identify two of Japan's most popular bodhisattvas and how they are said to help humans in moments of crisis.
4. How did the monks Saicho and Kukai help to establish what can be called "Japanese Buddhism" in the eighth century?
5. Identify and differentiate the three types of Buddhism that emerged in the medieval period.
6. What are some of the contributions of Zen Buddhism to Japanese culture? Be sure to reference both aesthetic and political aspects.
7. Explain why accessing spiritual benefits has more meaning for Japanese people than the teachings of particular religious denominations.
8. What role did religion play in the creation of a "modern Japan" between the late nineteenth century and the Second World War?

Glossary

Amaterasu Female deity of the sun, born from the eye of the primordial deity Izanagi following his purification; enshrined at Ise as the patron deity of the imperial family.

bodhisattva A Buddhist "saint" who has achieved spiritual liberation but chooses to remain in this world to help alleviate the suffering of individuals.

bushido Literally, the "way of the warrior"; an ethical code that combined a Confucian-style emphasis on loyalty with the discipline of Zen.

honji suijaku Literally, "manifestation from the original state"; the concept that *kami* are manifestations of buddhas or bodhisattvas.

jiriki Literally, "self-power"; the principle that individuals can attain liberation through their own abilities and devotional activities.

kami The spirits that animate all living things, natural phenomena, and natural forces. Shrines were built to accommodate their presence during rituals.

Kojiki A collection of stories commissioned to legitimate the imperial regime by linking it with Japan's mythical origins. It was published in 712 CE but was soon replaced by the *Nihongi* and remained largely forgotten until the eighteenth century.

Kokugaku Literally, "learning about one's country"; the intellectual movement of the eighteenth and nineteenth centuries that privileged Japanese culture and ideas over those from abroad.

mappo The period of "decline of the (Buddhist) dharma," thought to have begun in 1052; a time of social disorder, during which individuals could not achieve liberation without the aid of buddhas and bodhisattvas.

nembutsu The key prayer of the Pure Land traditions: *Namu Amida Butsu* ("praise to the Amida Buddha").

samurai A popular term for the *bushi* ("warrior"), who served regional warlords in various capacities; samurai made up the top 5 per cent of society during the Edo period (1603–1867).

shogun The supreme military commander of Japan, appointed by the emperor and effectively ruling in his name.

tariki The "outside power," offered by buddhas and bodhisattvas, without which individuals living in the age of the Buddhist dharma's decline (*mappo*) would be unable to achieve liberation.

zazen Seated meditation.

Further Reading

Ambros, Barbara. 2012. *Bones of Contention: Animals and Religion in Contemporary Japan*. Honolulu: University of Hawaii Press. A thorough exploration of the newly popular practice of memorializing pets and what it implies for both Japanese society and its Buddhist traditions.

Bowring, Richard. 2006. *The Religious Traditions of Japan, 500–1600*. Cambridge: Cambridge University Press. A comprehensive and highly readable account of Japanese religious history covering more than 1,000 years.

End-of-chapter discussion questions enhance students' critical understanding of key concepts; **glossaries** explain key terms; and lists of **further readings and recommended websites** provide excellent starting points for further research.

Document

"Document" boxes provide a generous selection of excerpts from scripture and other important writings.

Sites

"Sites" boxes draw attention to locations of special significance to each tradition.

Focus

"Focus" boxes give students greater understanding of certain aspects of each tradition.

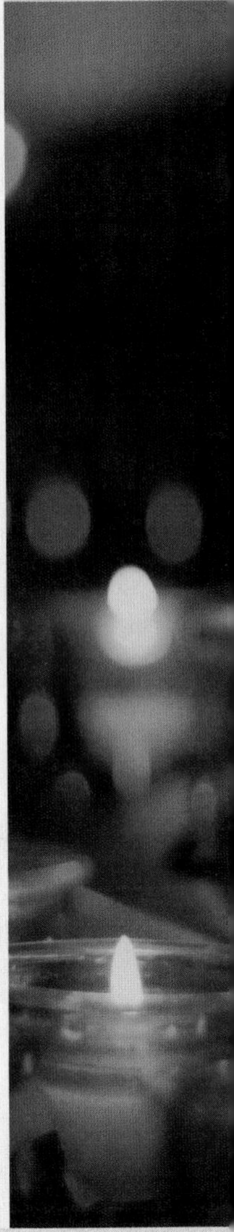

Extensive Ancillary Package

Online resources provide an outstanding array of teaching and learning tools for both instructors and students.

Instructors benefit from a suite of ancillaries designed to support their teaching goals.

- **An instructor's manual** contains chapter summaries, learning objectives, suggested lecture topics, class discussion topics, student activities, essay topics, and lists of multimedia resources for each chapter.
- **A test generator** includes multiple-choice, true/false, short answer, and essay questions, each with a difficulty ranking.
- **PowerPoint slides** cover all key concepts and are easily adapted to suit your course.
- NEW! **An image bank** provides all images and captions, maps, and boxed features.

Students have access to a wealth of additional information in the student study guide, which offers chapter summaries, learning objectives, short-answer questions (with answers), reflection questions, research paper topics, multimedia resources, fieldwork guidelines, and a bonus chapter on Zoroastrianism.

COMPANION WEBSITE

Edited by The late Willard G. Oxtoby and Alan F. Segal

A Concise Introduction to World Religions, Third Edition
ISBN 13: 9780199008551

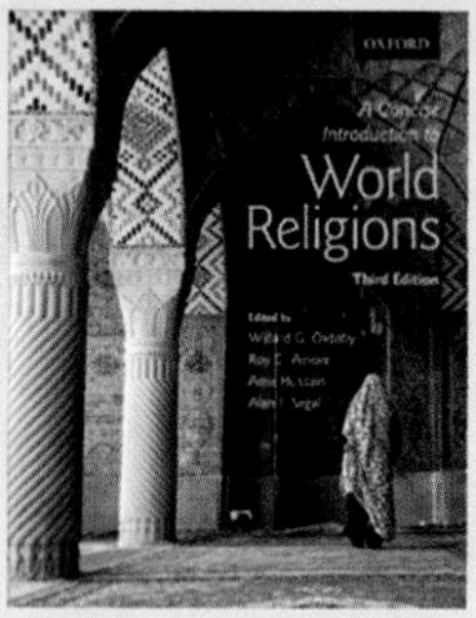

Inspection copy request

Ordering information

Contact & Comments

About the Book

The third edition of *A Concise Introduction to World Religions* is a comprehensive introduction to major faith traditions around the globe, designed for single-semester introductory courses. Written by experts on each tradition and building on the strong foundation provided by the two-volume *World Religions: Eastern and Western Traditions, A Concise Introduction* offers students an engaging, insightful overview of each tradition's history, teachings, practices, and interactions with the contemporary world.

Sample Material

Get Adobe PDF reader [US | UK]

Instructor Resources

You need a password to access these resources. Please contact your local Sales and Editorial Representative for more information.

Student Resources

www.oupcanada.com/OxtobyConcise3e

Preface

It has been an honour for us to edit this third edition of *A Concise Introduction to World Religions*. The late Will Oxtoby was an outstanding researcher, but his true excellence was as a teacher. It is no coincidence that the publications for which he will be remembered best are the textbooks *World Religions: Eastern Traditions* and *World Religions: Western Traditions*. It was also as a teacher that Will first met Alan Segal, who became a colleague, a close friend, and eventually a collaborator on those books. After Will's death, early in the planning of the first edition of *A Concise Introduction to World Religions* (2006), it was Alan who took over as general editor and saw the work through to completion. He also oversaw the development of the second edition of the present work, but just before it went to press, in 2011, he died—barely three months into his retirement from Barnard College.

With Alan's death, new authors were required for the chapters on Judaism and Christianity. In choosing his original contributors, Will Oxtoby looked for people who combined scholarship with sympathetic appreciation of the traditions in question. We have tried to be true to that vision in choosing our own contributors, the most recent of whom are Michele Murray and Wendy L. Fletcher. We are happy to include their chapters on Jewish and Christian traditions, respectively, in the present volume for the first time. This is also the first *Concise* edition to include Ken Derry's excellent work on indigenous traditions.

In his original foreword, Will wrote that people often used to ask him why he would waste his life on something as unimportant as religion, but that no one ever asked that question after the Islamic revolution in Iran. We have had the same experience: since the terrorist attacks of 9/11, not a single student has raised the issue of relevance. On the contrary, the study of world religions is more important today than ever before.

Acknowledgements

First, our thanks to the contributors without whom this book would not exist: Ken Derry, Wendy Fletcher, Michele Murray, Vasudha Narayanan, John Nelson, Pashaura Singh, Anne Vallely, and Terry Tak-ling Woo. At Oxford University Press we would like to thank Katherine Skene and Stephen Kotowych for their encouragement, Leah-Ann Lymer and Meg Patterson for their developmental guidance, and especially Sally Livingston for her hands-on editorial work, including abridgement of the two-volume material. Finally, we are grateful to all the reviewers whose comments helped to shape this volume, both those whose names are listed below and those who wished to remain anonymous:

Ernest P. Janzen, University of Winnipeg
David Perley, University of Toronto, Scarborough
Michelle Rebidoux, Memorial University of Newfoundland

We dedicate this volume to Will Oxtoby and Alan Segal.

Roy C. Amore, University of Windsor
Amir Hussain, Loyola Marymount University, Los Angeles
August 2014

A Concise Introduction to World Religions

1 About Religion

Roy C. Amore and Amir Hussain

Basic Human Religion: Looking Both Ways from Stonehenge

Standing on the west side of **Stonehenge**, we watch the sun rise through the circle of massive standing stones. Within the outer circle is a grouping of paired stones capped by lintels and arranged in a horseshoe pattern, opening towards the rising sun. At the centre of the horseshoe lies a flat stone that was once thought to have served as an altar for sacrifices. Today, however, it is believed that the centre stone originally stood upright, marking the spot where an observer would stand to watch the movements of the sun and stars.

The Stonehenge we know is what remains of a structure erected between 3,500 and 4,000 years ago. But the site had already been used as a burial ground for centuries before that time: researchers believe that the remains of as many as 240 people, probably from a single ruling family or clan, were interred there between roughly 3000 and 2500 BCE (Pearson 2012: 11–14). The structure itself is generally believed to have been used for ceremonial purposes, and its orientation—towards the point where the sun rises at the summer solstice—has led many to think it might have been designed to serve as a kind of astronomical observatory. Another recent theory, based on a similar arrangement of timber posts at an ancient settlement nearby called Durrington Walls, suggests that the two sites represented the living and the dead respectively, with Stonehenge serving as the permanent dwelling place of the ancestors. If so, there are parallels in other ancient cultures (Pearson 2012).

We position ourselves behind the central stone to note the position of the rising sun in relation to the "heel stone" on the horizon. Today, on the morning of the summer solstice, the sun rises just to the left of the heel stone. It's easy to imagine that in ancient times this day—the longest of the year, and the only one when the sun rises to the north of the heel stone—would have been the occasion for some kind of ceremony; that the entire community would have gathered at dawn to watch as someone with special authority—perhaps a priest, perhaps the local chief or ruler—confirmed the position of the rising sun. It's also easy to imagine the sense of order in the universe that would have come from knowing exactly when and where the sun would change course.

Tomorrow the sun will rise behind the heel stone, and it will continue its (apparent) journey towards the south for the next six months. Then in late December, at the winter solstice, the sun will appear to reverse course and begin travelling northwards again. Many centuries after people first gathered at Stonehenge, the Romans would celebrate this day as marking the annual "rebirth" of the sun—the high point of the festival they called Saturnalia. And in the fourth century CE, the Christians in Rome would choose the same time of year to celebrate the birth of their risen lord. Christmas would combine the unrestrained revelry of the Roman midwinter festival, marked by feasting, gift-giving, and general merriment, with the celebration of the coming to Earth of a deity incarnate.

Looking Back from Stonehenge

There are a few concepts, shared by virtually all human cultures, which seem fundamental to what we call religion: powerful gods, sacred places, a life of some kind after death, the presence in the physical world of spirits that interact with humans in various ways. These concepts are so old and so widespread that no one can say where or when they first emerged.

← Birds over Stonehenge (Tore Johannesen / Getty Images).

Three Worlds

Historically, it seems that humans around the globe have imagined the world to consist of three levels: sky, earth, and underworld. The uppermost level, the sky, has typically been considered the home of the greatest deities. Exactly how this concept developed is impossible to know, but we can guess that the awesome power of storms was one contributing factor. The apparent movement of the sun, the stars, and the planets across the sky was very likely another. Observing the varying patterns could well have led early humans to believe that the heavenly bodies were living entities animated by their own individual spirits—in effect, gods and goddesses.

The very highest level, in the heavens above the clouds and stars, was thought to be the home of the highest deity, typically referred to by a name such as Sky Father, Creator, or King of Heaven. This deity—invariably male—was the forerunner of the god of the monotheistic religions. Under the earth lived the spirits of serpents (surviving as the cobras, or ***nagas***, in the religions of India) or reptilian monsters (surviving in dragon lore); perhaps because they were associated with dark and hidden places, they were usually imagined as evil. Finally, between the sky and the underworld lay the earth: the intermediate level where humans lived.

Sacred Places

Around the world, there are certain types of places where humans tend to feel they are in the presence of some unusual energy or power. Such places are regarded as set apart from the everyday world and are treated with special respect. Among those sacred places ("sacred" means "set aside") are mountains and hilltops—the places closest to the sky-dwelling deities. In the ancient Middle East, for instance, worship was often conducted at ritual centres known simply as "**high places**." People gathered at these sites to win the favour of the deities by offering them food, drink, praise, and prayer. One widely known example is the altar area on the cliff above the ancient city of Petra in Jordan (familiar to many people from the Indiana Jones films).

Great rivers and waterfalls are often regarded as sacred as well. And in Japan virtually every feature of the natural landscape—from great mountains and waterfalls to trees and stones—was traditionally believed to be animated by its own god or spirit (*kami*).

Animal Spirits

Another common human tendency has been to attribute spirits to animals, either individually or as members of a family with a kind of collective guardian spirit. For this reason, traditional hunting societies have typically sought to ensure that the animals they kill for food are treated with the proper respect, lest other members of those species be frightened away or refuse to let themselves be caught.

In addition, body parts from the most impressive animals—bulls, bears, lions, eagles—have often been used as "power objects," to help make contact with the spirits of these animals. People in many cultures have attributed magical properties to objects such as bear claws or eagle feathers, wearing them as amulets or hanging them in the doorways of their homes as protection against evil spirits.

Death and Burial

From ancient times, humans have taken great care with the burial of their dead. The body might be positioned with the head facing east, the "first direction," where the sun rises, or placed in the fetal position, suggesting a hope for rebirth into a different realm. These burial positions in themselves would not be enough to prove a belief in an afterlife; however, most such graves have also contained, along with the remains of the dead, "grave goods" of various kinds. Some of these provisions for the afterlife likely belonged to the person in life; some appear to be specially made replicas; and some are rare, presumably costly items such as precious stones. Apparently the living were willing to sacrifice important resources to help the dead in the afterlife.

The belief that deceased ancestors can help to guide their living descendants appears to be especially widespread. Traditions such as the Japanese **Obon**, the Mexican **Day of the Dead**, and the Christian **All Saints Day** and **Hallowe'en** all reflect the belief that the souls of the dead return to earth once a year to share a ritual meal with the living.

Why Are Humans Religious?

The reasons behind human religiosity are complex and varied. All we can say with any certainty is that religion seems to grow out of human experiences: the fear of death, the hope for a good afterlife, the uncertainty surrounding natural events, the sense of control over nature provided by a priest who can predict the change of seasons and the movements of the planets. Religion emerges through the experience of good or bad powers that are sensed in dreams, in sacred spaces, and in certain humans and animals. But it also has emotional and intellectual dimensions, including curiosity about what causes things to happen, a sense of order in the universe that suggests the presence of a creator, and the drive to make sense out of human experience.

The nature of religious belief and practice has changed through the centuries, so we must be careful not to take the religion of any particular time and place as the norm. What we can safely say is that religion is such an ancient aspect of human experience that it has become part of human nature. For this reason some scholars have given our species, *Homo sapiens*, a second name: *Homo religiosus*.

Looking Forward from Stonehenge

Looking forward from ancient Stonehenge, we can see a number of patterns emerge in different parts of the world, some of them almost simultaneously. Since most of the chapters in this book focus on individual religions, it may be useful to begin with a broader perspective. What follows is a brief overview of some of the major developments in the history of what the late Canadian scholar Wilfred Cantwell Smith (1916–2000) called "religion in the singular," meaning the history of human religiosity in the most general sense.

Shamanism

One very early pattern involves a ritual specialist—in essence, a kind of priest—that we know today as a **shaman**. The word "shaman" comes from a specific central Asian culture, but it has become the generic term for a person who acts as an intermediary between humans and the spirit world. Other terms include "medicine man," "soul doctor," and "witchdoctor."

Hunting Rituals

Many ancient cave drawings depict hunting scenes in which a human figure seems to be performing a dance of some kind. Based on what we know of later hunting societies, we can guess that the

A replica of prehistoric animal images from the Chauvet cave in southern France, dated c. 30,000 BCE (© Arterra Picture Library / Alamy).

figure is a shaman performing a ritual either to ensure a successful hunt or to appease the spirits of the animals killed.

It's not hard to imagine why such societies would have sought ways to influence the outcome of the hunt. The more dangerous the endeavour, the more likely humans were to surround it with rituals. As the anthropologist Bronislaw Malinowski pointed out in his book *Magic, Science and Religion*, the Trobriand Islanders he studied did not perform any special ceremonies before fishing in the lagoon, but they never failed to perform rituals before setting out to fish in the open ocean. This suggests that religious behaviour is, at least in part, a way of coping with dangerous situations.

At the same time, as we have seen, many societies have believed that the spirits of the animals they hunt must be appeased. Thus a special ritual might be performed to mark the first goose kill of the season, in the hope that other geese would not be frightened away from the hunting grounds. Such rituals obviously reflect concern over the future food supply, but they also reveal something about the nature of belief in spirits. From very ancient times, it seems, people have believed that the spirit—whether of an animal killed for food or of a human being—survives death and can communicate with others of its kind.

Coping with Unfriendly Spirits

The spirits associated with natural phenomena—animals, storms, mountains, rivers—have typically been thought to behave towards humans in the same ways that humans behave towards one another. Strategies for dealing with unfriendly spirits, therefore, are usually based on what works with humans.

Many cultures have believed wild, uninhabited areas to be guarded by resident spirits. In some cases, these spirits have taken the form of monsters or mythical beasts; in others, of "little people" such as trolls (common in the folklore of Scandinavia, for example). Unfriendly spirits were of particular concern to those who ventured into the forest, but they were not confined to the wilderness. Pain and disease of all kinds were also attributed to possession by malevolent spirits or demons. In Sri Lanka, those suffering from certain illnesses were advised to have a shaman sacrifice a chicken as an offering to the "graveyard demon," effectively bribing him to go away; in such cases a second chicken, still alive, would be given as payment to the shaman who performed the ritual. Another approach was to frighten the demon away, either by threatening to invoke another, stronger spiritual power to drive him off, or by making threatening gestures or loud noises; that is the purpose of the firecrackers still used in some East Asian rituals.

The Shaman

The most important resources of all have been the shamans themselves. Shamans are still active in a number of cultures today. The way they operate varies, but certain patterns seem to be almost universal, which in itself suggests that the way of the shaman is very ancient. Sometimes the child of a shaman will follow in the parent's footsteps, but more often a shaman will be "called" to the role by his or her psychic abilities, as manifested in some extraordinary vision or revelation, or perhaps a near-death experience.

Candidates for the role of shaman face a long and rigorous apprenticeship that often includes a vision quest, in the course of which they are likely to confront terrifying apparitions. Typically the quester will acquire a guiding spirit, sometimes the spirit of a particular animal (perhaps a bear or an eagle, whose claws or feathers the shaman may wear to draw strength from its special powers) and sometimes a more human-like spirit (a god or goddess). That spirit then continues to serve as a guide and protector throughout the shaman's life.

To communicate with the spirit world, the shaman enters a trance state (often induced by rhythmic chanting or drumming). According to Mircea Eliade (1951/1964), contact is then made in one of two ways. In the first, the shaman's soul leaves his/her body and travels to the realm where the spirits live; this way is described as "ecstatic" (from a Greek root meaning to "stand outside"). In the second, the spirit is called into the shaman's body and possesses it; in such cases the shaman may take on the voice and personality of the spirit, or mimic its way of moving.

In either case, after regaining normal consciousness the shaman announces what has been learned about the problem at hand, which is typically traced to the anger of a particular spirit. The shaman then explains the reason for that anger and what must be done to appease the spirit: in most cases a ritual sacrifice of some kind is required.

Connecting to the Cosmos

A second pattern is the one that inspired the building of structures like Stonehenge. People of the Neolithic ("new rock") era created sacred areas by assembling huge stones in complex patterns. In some cases the motivation may have been to demonstrate a leader's power, but in others the main reason undoubtedly had something to do with religion: for instance, the need for a public space for rituals such as weddings, puberty rites, and funerals.

Discerning the Cosmic Cycles

Ritual centres such as Stonehenge may also have served purposes that we might think of as scientific or technical, but that their builders would have associated with religion. One important function of priests was to determine the best time for seasonal activities such as planting. In addition to tracking the north–south movements of the sun, the people of the Neolithic era paid careful attention to the phases of the moon and the rising positions of certain constellations. The horizon was divided into segments named after the planet or constellation associated with each one. What we now call astrology developed as a way of understanding the cycle of the seasons and how humans fitted into it, collectively and individually. In ancient times no important decision would have been made without consulting an expert in the movements of the sun, moon, planets, and constellations. Even today, many people, including political leaders, will consult an astrologer before making a major decision.

Hilltop Tombs

We suggested earlier that two powerful reasons behind human religion are the fear of death and the idea of an afterlife. Ancient cultures around the world appear to have favoured high places as burial sites. Where there were no hills, artificial ones were sometimes built, at least for the most important members of the society. The pyramids of Egypt and the stupas of Asia are both examples of this practice. In the pyramids, shafts extending from the burial chambers towards important stars connected the deceased with the cosmos. Similarly in Buddhist stupas, a wooden pole extended above the burial mound to connect the earth with the heavens. Scholars refer to this kind of symbolic link between earth and sky as an *axis mundi* ("world axis").

Animals and Gods

Another common feature of Neolithic religion was a tendency to associate certain animals with specific deities. One very early example comes from the ancient (c. 7000–5000 BCE) city of Catalhoyuk ("forked mound"), near Konya in modern Turkey, where a small sculpture was found of a woman flanked by two large felines. James Mellaart, the archaeologist who first excavated the site in the 1960s, believed she represented a mother goddess seated on a throne. Although this interpretation has been disputed, we know that the ancient Egyptians had a cat goddess named Bast who was revered as a symbol of both motherliness and hunting prowess. And the fierce Hindu goddess Durga is usually depicted riding a lion.

The Bull God

A similar pattern of association links the most powerful male deities with the strength and virility of the bull. In Greek mythology, the great god Zeus took the form of a white bull when he abducted the Phoenician princess Europa. A creature known as the minotaur—half man, half bull—was said to have been kept in a labyrinth beneath the ancient palace of Knossos, on the island of Crete, where frescos show people leaping over the horns of a bull. Greek temples often displayed bull horns near their altars. And in India a bull named Nandi is the sacred mount of the great god Shiva.

The association of the bull with the creator god can be seen even in Judaism, which strictly forbade the use of any image to represent its invisible deity. When the prophet Moses finds that his brother Aaron, the first high priest, has allowed the people to worship an image of a golden calf or bullock, he denounces this practice as idolatry. Centuries later, one of Solomon's sons is severely chastised for installing bull images in the temples he has built.

Temple Religion

A third pattern features larger temples, more elaborate sacrificial rituals, and the development of a priestly class endowed with unusual power, prestige, and wealth. This pattern, beginning at least 3,000 years ago, played an enormous role in shaping many traditions, including Hinduism, Judaism, and Chinese religion.

Indo-European Priests

"Indo-European" is a modern term referring to a language family and cultural system that eventually stretched from India all the way through Europe; it does not designate any particular ethnic group. The Indo-European (IE) cultural system may have originated in the region around the Black Sea, but that is only one of many theories that have been proposed. The vocabulary of "proto-IE," as reconstructed by linguists, indicates that the IE people practised metallurgy, drove chariots, and waged war, among other things. Yet farming does not appear to have been part of their culture: the fact that the IE vocabulary related to agriculture differs from one place to another suggests that in farming the Indo-Europeans simply adopted existing local practices.

Everywhere the IE warriors conquered, they set up a social system with four basic divisions, the top three of which consisted of priests, warriors, and middle-class "commoners." In India these groups are known respectively as the brahmins, kshatriyas, and vaishyas. The priests performed rituals, kept the calendar, taught the young, and advised the kings; within the warrior class, the top clans were the rulers; while the middle-class commoners earned their living as merchants or farmers. Finally, all people of local origin, no matter how wealthy or accomplished, were relegated to the servant (shudra) class.

The four-level social system was given mythic status in the *Rig Veda*, according to which the world came into being through the sacrifice of a "cosmic person" (*Purusha*). Out of his mouth came the brahmin priests, whose job was to chant the sacred hymns and syllables. The warriors came from his arms, the middle class from his thighs, and the servants from his feet. Even today, this ancient hymn continues to buttress the social class structure of India.

Beginning around 2500 BCE, the Indo-Europeans took control of the territories that are now Afghanistan, northwest India, Pakistan, Turkey, Greece, Rome, central Europe, and, for a while, even Egypt. Their religious culture was similar to most of its counterparts 4,000 to 5,000 years ago, with many deities, including a "sky father" (a name that survives in Greek Zeus Pater, Latin Jupiter, and Sanskrit Dyaus Pitar) and a storm god (Indra in India, Thor in Scandinavia); they sang hymns to female deities, such as the goddess of dawn; and they had a hereditary priesthood to offer sacrifices to the gods.

Document

The Sacrifice

When they divided the Man [*Purusha*, the primal Person sacrificed by the gods to create the world], into how many parts did they disperse him? What became of his mouth, what of his arms, what were his two thighs and his two feet called? His mouth was the brahmin, his arms were made into the nobles, his two thighs were the populace, and from his feet the servants were born (Doniger O'Flaherty 1975: 26).

Three times a year all your males shall appear before the Lord your God at the place which he will choose: at the feast of unleavened bread, at the feast of weeks, and at the feast of booths. They shall not appear before the Lord empty-handed: All shall give as they are able, according to the blessing of the Lord your God that he has given you (from Moses' instructions to the people of Israel; Deuteronomy 16: 16–17).

Although the IE people did not necessarily invent the system of hereditary priesthood, they certainly contributed to its spread. In addition to Hindu brahmins, examples include the ancient Roman priests and Celtic Druids. These priests enjoyed great power and prestige, and sometimes were resented by non-priests. One ancient Indian text includes a parody in which dogs, acting like priests, dance around a fire chanting "*Om* let us eat, *om* let us drink" (Chandogya Upanishad I, xii, in Zaehner 1966: 84).

Priests and Temples Elsewhere

The first Jewish temple was built in the mid-tenth century BCE by King Solomon, the son of the semi-legendary King David. Its priests soon made the temple the only site where sacrificial rituals could be performed.

The Jewish priesthood was hereditary. All those who served in the temple as assistants to the priests were required to be Levites (from the tribe of Levi), and priests themselves had to be not only Levites but direct descendants of Aaron, the original high priest.

Priests became a powerful social class in many other parts of the world as well, including Africa, Asia, and the Americas. Typically, the role of priest was reserved for males, females being considered impure because of the menstrual cycle; the Vestal Virgins of ancient Rome, who tended the sacred fires and performed rituals, were rare exceptions to the general rule.

Prophetic Religion

By 700 BCE, several new religious traditions had begun to form under the leadership of a great prophet or sage. The word "prophet" has two related meanings: a person who speaks on behalf of a deity, and one who foresees or predicts the future. The terms are often conflated because prophets delivering messages from the deity often warned of disasters to come if God's will was not obeyed. The site of the temple at Delphi, Greece, where a virgin priestess inspired by Apollo delivered prophecies, had been considered sacred for centuries, maybe millennia, before the glory

Document

Ritual Sacrifice in the Hebrew Bible

Long before priests began performing ritual sacrifices at the temple in Jerusalem, God commanded the Hebrew patriarch Abram (later renamed Abraham) to sacrifice several animals to mark the covenant that was about to be made between them.

Then [God] said to [Abram], "I am the Lord who brought you from Ur of the Chaldeans, to give you this land to possess." But he said, "O Lord God, how am I to know that I shall possess it?" He said to him, "Bring me a heifer three years old, a female goat three years old, a ram three years old, a turtledove, and a young pigeon." He brought him all these and cut them in two, laying each half over against the other; but he did not cut the birds in two. And when birds of prey came down on the carcasses, Abram drove them away.

As the sun was going down, a deep sleep fell upon Abram, and a deep and terrifying darkness descended upon him. Then the Lord said to Abram, "Know this for certain, that your offspring shall be aliens in a land that is not theirs, and shall be slaves there, and they shall be oppressed for four hundred years; but I will bring judgment on the nation that they serve, and afterward they shall come out with great possessions. As for yourself, you shall go to your ancestors in peace; you shall be buried in a good old age. . . ."

When the sun had gone down and it was dark, a smoking fire pot and a flaming torch passed between these pieces [the halved carcasses]. On that day the Lord made a covenant with Abram, saying, "To your descendants I give this land, from the river of Egypt to the great river, the river Euphrates, the land of the Kenites, the Kenizzites, the Kadmonites, the Hittites, the Perizzites, the Rephaim, the Amorites, the Canaanites, the Girgashites, and the Jebusites" (Genesis 15: 7–21).

days of classical Greece. It must have seemed a natural spot for making contact with the divine and receiving sacred knowledge: high up a mountainside, close to the gods, with a natural cave that resembled the entrance to a womb (*delphys* in Greek, representing the mysterious female energy) and a standing stone or *omphalos* (navel of the earth), representing the male energy and the connection between heaven and earth.

This sacred site dates back at least 3,000 years, to a time when the oracle was believed to be inspired not by Apollo but by the earth goddess Gaia. By the classical era males had taken control of the sacred site, but even then the virgin priestesses would prepare themselves to receive Apollo's message by bathing in an artesian spring and breathing intoxicating fumes from a fissure in the earth—both water and fumes issuing from Gaia, the earth.

Those wishing to consult the oracle had to climb the mountain, make their request known, pay a fee, and sacrifice a black goat before their question would be put to the oracle. The priestess would take her place over the fissure and, in an ecstatic trance, deliver Apollo's message, which was typically unintelligible and had to be translated into ordinary language by a male priest. Interpreting the real-world significance of a prophecy was not so simple, however. In one famous case, a Greek leader who asked what would happen if he went to war with another state was told that a great country would fall; accordingly, he went to war—but the country that fell was his own. Similarly in the Oedipus myth, the oracle's prophecy that the infant would grow up to kill his father and marry his mother was fulfilled despite the measures taken to avoid that fate.

Abrahamic Prophetic Traditions

In 586 BCE the people of Israel were forcibly removed from their homeland and exiled to Babylon. The centuries that followed the "Babylonian captivity" were the defining period for the concept of prophecy as it developed in the three monotheistic traditions that trace their origins to the prophet Abraham. Often, the Jewish prophets' messages were directed towards the people of Israel as a whole, warning of the disasters that loomed if they did not follow God's demands. Christianity saw Jesus and certain events surrounding his life as the fulfillment of Hebrew prophecies. And Islam in turn recognized the Hebrew prophets, beginning with Abraham and including Jesus, as the forerunners of the Prophet Muhammad, the last and greatest of all. Muslims understand Muhammad to have been the "seal of the prophets": no other prophet will follow him, since he has delivered the message of God in its entirety. As with earlier prophetic traditions, the Day of Judgment (or Day of Doom) and the concepts of heaven and hell are central to Islam.

Zarathustra, Prophet of the Wise Lord

Zarathustra (or Zoroaster) was a prophet figure who lived more than 2,500 years ago, probably in the region of eastern Iran or Afghanistan, and composed a collection of poems devoted to a "wise lord" called Ahura Mazda. The religion that developed around his teachings, Zoroastrianism, played an important part in the development of monotheism. The concepts of heaven and hell also owe a lot to the Zoroastrians, who believed that evil-doers were condemned to hell at their death, but that eventually a great day of judgment would come when the souls of all the dead would be made to pass through a fiery wall. Those who had been virtuous in life would pass through the fire without pain, while the rest would be cleansed of their remaining sin and permitted to enter paradise (a term believed to derive from a Persian word meaning garden). The threat of hell and the promise of heaven were powerful tools for prophets seeking to persuade people to behave as they believed the deity demanded.

The Energy God

Yet another important pattern emerged around 2,500 years ago. In it the divine is understood not as a human-like entity but as the energy of the cosmos. The Energy God does not issue commandments, answer prayers, or in any way interact with humans as a human. It does not create in the usual fashion of gods; it does not direct the course of history, or dictate the fate of individuals. In fact, some have suggested that this god may have more in common with the principles of modern physics than with the traditional gods of most religions. This divinity simply exists—or rather, "underlies" everything that exists. Among the traditions that developed around the Energy God concept were Chinese Daoism, the Upanishadic wisdom of India, and the pre-Socratic philosophy of the early Greek world.

Focus

Tell Megiddo, Israel

Tell Megiddo is an archeological mound in Israel, southeast of modern Haifa. The ancient city of Megiddo was strategically located near a pass used by the trade route connecting Egypt and Assyria. The site of a battle with Egypt in the sixteenth century BCE, Har ("Mount") Megiddo is mentioned numerous times in the Hebrew Bible, and is referred to by the Greek version of its name, "Armageddon," in the Book of Revelation 16: 16—a passage that some Christians interpret to mean that a final battle will be fought there at the end of time.

The remains of Har Megiddo, the site known to Christians as Armageddon. The circular rock structure is thought to have been an altar (© Richard T. Nowitz / Corbis).

Finding the Dao Within

The sage who became known as Laozi ("Master Lao") lived in northern China around 600 BCE. According to legend, he worked for the government as an archivist. At night students would visit him to hear his words of wisdom about life, especially how to live in harmony with one's inner

Document

Divine Energy

The Dao that can be told of
Is not the Absolute Dao;
The Names that can be given
Are not Absolute Names.
The Nameless is the origin of Heaven and Earth;
The Named is the Mother of All Things
(from Laozi in the *Daodejing*; Lin Yutang 1948: 41).

This finest essence, the whole universe has it as its Self: That is the Real: That is the Self: That *you* are, Svetaketu! (from the *Chandogya Upanishad* 6.9; Zaehner 1966: 110).

nature. But Lao had what we might call a mid-life crisis, which drove him to leave home and travel west, riding on a water buffalo. Apparently he had not even said goodbye to his students, but one of them happened to be working as a guard at the border, and he begged Lao to record his teachings before leaving China.

So Lao paused long enough to write down the fundamentals of his thought in a series of beautiful, if cryptic, verses that were eventually collected in a small volume called **Daodejing** (or *Tao De Ching*), meaning the book (*jing*) about the Dao and its power (*de*). It remains one of the world's most influential texts.

What did Laozi write that has spoken to so many through the millennia? He begins with what became one of the most famous opening lines in history: "The Dao that can be described is not the eternal Dao. The name that can be named is not the eternal name." In general usage the word Dao means "the way," but here it refers to the mysterious energy that underlies all things. Laozi is warning readers that words cannot adequately describe the Dao. Ogden Nash, a twentieth-century American poet noted for combining insight and humour, captured the same idea this way: "Whatever the mind comes at, God is not that."

In traditional cultures, people talk about the characteristics of various deities—their loving nature, or anger, or jealousy, or desire for a particular kind of behaviour. But the absolute, the eternal Dao, has no such attributes. Thus Laozi uses poetic imagery to give us some insights into its nature. Unlike Athena, Zeus, Yahweh, or Indra, the Dao does not have a "personality," and there is no reason for humans to fear, love, or appease it.

Rather, Laozi says, the Dao is like water: it will take on the shape of whatever container we pour it into. Falling from the sky, it may seem content to lie in the hollow made by the hoof of an ox in the muddy road. Raining on the rocky mountaintop, it tumbles all the way down. Water seems malleable, passive, without a will of its own. Yet a mountain will be worn down by the water over time. The water in the hoofprint will evaporate and return to the sky, to fall again when the time is right.

"That Is You": Sitting near the Sages of Old India

A worldview similar to that of Daoism took shape in northern India around the same time. It is reflected in the **Upanishads** (a Sanskrit term meaning "sitting-up-near" the master), a series of philosophical texts composed beginning around 600 BCE.

What the Daoist sages called the Dao the Upanishadic masters called *sat* (usually translated as "being," "truth," or "the real"). One Upanishad tells the story of a young man named Svetaketu who has just completed his studies with the brahmin priests. Back at home, his father, who is a king and therefore a member of the warrior class, asks Svetaketu what his priestly teachers have taught him about the original source of all things. When Svetaketu admits that he was not taught about that subject, his father instructs him in the secret wisdom.

The first lesson has to do with the need for sleep and food; then the real teaching begins. The father has Svetaketu bring a bowl of water and taste it. Then he tells him to put a lump of sea salt into the water. The next morning Svetaketu sees that the lump of salt is no longer visible; he tastes the water and finds it salty. We can imagine his impatience at being instructed in something he already knows. But his father has a bigger point in mind. He tells Svetaketu that just as the salt is invisible yet present in the water, so also there is a hidden essence present in the world. That hidden essence, the force that energizes everything, is the highest reality, the father says, and that reality is you (*tat tvam asi*: "that you are"). The Upanishadic master is initiating his son into a new religious worldview that understands "god" as an energy hidden within and sustaining everything. And that great energy, that ultimate reality, "*tat tvam asi*"—that is you.

The First Principle: Greek Philosophy before Socrates

Around 2,500 years ago, the Greek-speaking philosophers of what is now southwestern Turkey began to ask the same questions as Svetaketu's father: What is the first principle, the first cause, the source from which all else comes? Starting from the science of the day, which held there to be four primal elements—earth, air, fire, and water—they wanted to determine which of the four came first. Although their methods were those of philosophy rather than scientific experimentation, their attempt to understand the causal principle underlying all things—without bringing in a god as the final cause—marked a major advance towards the development of the scientific worldview.

Later Theistic Mysticism

European religious thought eventually reflected mysticism as well. German Christian mystics such as Jacob Böhme (1575–1624) would use terms such as *Ungrund* ("ungrounded") or *Urgrund* ("original ground") to refer to the divine as primal cause. Christian, Jewish, and Muslim mystics all believed in a god beyond human understanding.

Purity and Monasticism

At almost the same time that the "Energy God" worldview was establishing itself in China, India, and the Greek world, another spiritual movement of great importance was developing in northern India. The earliest historical records date from roughly 2,500 years ago, but the tradition itself claims to have much older roots. Its followers typically sought spiritual enlightenment through asceticism—intense bodily discipline. Their ethic was one of non-violence towards all creatures, and their goal was perfect purity of mind.

Ganges Spirituality

English has no specific term for the new type of religion that came into bloom in the region of the Ganges river around 500 BCE. By that time the Indo-European cultural system, including the religion of the brahmin priests, was firmly established. We can never know for certain what earlier traditions that religion displaced, since the written sources we rely on were the products of the brahmins themselves. However, linguistic and archaeological data lend support to the theory that two of the world's great living religions—Jainism and Buddhism—were rooted in the pre-brahminic traditions of the Ganges region.

Along the banks of the river were many camps where spiritual teachers operated what were in effect open-air seminaries. Though some were masters of the dominant brahmin tradition, others believed it was wrong to harm any living creature. Their followers rejected the killing of animals for food, and some even objected to farming, because hoeing and plowing would harm organisms living in the soil. While the brahmins continued to perform their animal sacrifices, those committed to the principle of non-harm (*ahimsa*) denounced that tradition, and some of them—such as the Jaina master Mahavira—went so far as to require their disciples to cover their mouths and noses and strain their drinking water, to avoid harming microscopic insects.

The students who gathered around these ascetic masters took vows of poverty and celibacy, and considered themselves to have "departed the world." The Buddhist and Jaina monastic traditions trace their roots to these ascetics, and it is possible that Indian monasticism played a role in the development of Western monasticism as well.

One more difference between the Indo-European and "Gangetic" cultural systems is worth mentioning here. In the IE system, priests were recruited only from the brahmin social class. In the Ganges tradition, by contrast, the notion of a hereditary priesthood was rejected entirely: anyone, however humble, could choose to lead the life of a holy person. As the Buddha would teach his followers, the status of the "true brahmin" is not a birthright, but must be earned through meritorious conduct.

Mystery Religion

"Mystery religion" refers to a type of Greek and Roman tradition in which the core teachings and rituals were revealed only to those who were prepared to undergo initiation in the hope of securing blessings during this life and a heavenly paradise in the afterlife. Such religions became so popular during the Roman period that they presented a threat to the power of the official Roman priesthood (not to be confused with the Roman Catholic priesthood).

The Eleusinian mystery tradition may be the oldest. Named for an ancient Greek town called Eleusis, it grew out of the myth of the young Persephone or Kore ("girl") who is abducted by the god of the dead (Hades) and taken down into the underworld. With the disappearance of this young girl—a potent symbol of fertility—everything on Earth begins to die. This imperils not only humans but the gods themselves, who depend on humans to feed them through sacrifices. The girl's mother, Demeter, is therefore allowed to descend into the underworld and bring her back. Scholars understand the Persephone myth to be based on the seasonal cycles of stagnation during the winter and renewal in the spring. Members of her cult believed that by identifying themselves with the dying and rising goddess through the celebration of seasonal rituals, they too would triumph over death.

Initiates into the mysteries associated with the god Dionysus were also following a very ancient tradition. Through rituals that included the drinking of wine, ecstatic dancing, and, perhaps, the consumption of mind-altering plants, participants entered ecstatic states of consciousness in which they believed that their god would ensure a pleasant afterlife. Another popular mystery cult, dedicated to the goddess Isis, had Egyptian origins.

Many scholars have suggested that mystery cults such as these may have influenced the development of Christianity. The early Christians were initiated by undergoing baptism. They then joined an inner circle of people who hoped that by following Christ they would secure blessings during this life and a place in heaven after death. Although Christianity developed out of Judaism, its theological structure does seem to have been influenced, however indirectly, by mystery religion.

Avatar: God on Earth

The Avatar

Long before anyone thought of an "avatar" as either a blue-skinned movie humanoid or the on-screen image representing a player in a computer game, *avatar(a)* was a Sanskrit theological term for the "coming down" to Earth of a god. By the first century of the Common Era, the idea of a god born in human form was taking root in many parts of the world. In the earlier stages of religion there were many stories of gods and goddesses who came down to Earth, but the avatar stories were different in two major respects.

First, whereas the ancient gods came down to Earth as gods, the avatar is a god in a truly human form—as a later Christian creed put it, "fully God and fully man." For example, in the ancient Indian story of Princess Dhamayanti, her father holds a party to which he invites all the marriageable princes from various kingdoms. Four gods also attend the party, however, all disguised as the handsome prince Nala, whom the princess has already decided to choose. At first she is disturbed to see five look-alikes, but then she finds that she can distinguish the four divine imposters because they do not sweat and are floating slightly above the ground. She marries the human prince, and they live happily ever after.

Unlike the gods at Dhamayanti's party, the avatar gods walk on the ground and are in every way human. They are incarnated in a human womb, are born, grow up, teach, save the world from evil, and eventually die. As a Christian layman once explained, "You have to understand that we Christians worship a god in diapers." His choice of words was unusual, but his theology was solid, and it

Document

Avatar Gods

For the protection of the good,
For the destruction of evildoers,
For the setting up of righteousness,
I come into being, age after age.
(Krishna to Arjuna in the *Bhagavad Gita*; Zaehner 1966: 267).

Have this mind among yourselves, which you have in Christ Jesus, who, though he was in the form of God, did not count equality with God a thing to be grasped, but emptied himself, taking the form of a servant, being born in the likeness of men. And being found in human form he humbled himself. . . . (St Paul to the Christians of Philippi: Philippians 2: 6–7).

The name Krishna means "dark one," and he is usually depicted as dark blue or black. In this scene (painted on the side of a truck in Jodhpur, India) the young Krishna is stealing ghee (Indian-style butter) from a storage pot—the escapade behind his nickname "The Butter Thief." He is both an avatar of God and a naughty human boy (© Floris Leeuwenberg / Corbis).

leads us to the second major innovation that came with the concept of the avatar god.

This second innovation is the idea that the avatar god is a saviour figure in at least two ways. Not only does he save the world from some evil power, such as Satan or a demonic king: he also saves from hell those who put their faith in him and secures them a place in heaven. In avatar religions, the ritual of sacrifice is replaced by the ritual of placing faith in the saviour god.

The biographies of saviour gods follow a well-known pattern. Typically, the avatar god has a special, non-sexual conception. His mother is chosen to bear him because she is exceptionally pure, and an angel or prophet tells her that the child she is carrying has a special destiny. The saviour's birth, usually in a rustic setting, is surrounded by miracles, which often include a fortuitous star or constellation pattern in the night sky. Sages foresee the child's greatness. An evil king tries to kill the baby, but kills another baby, or other babies, instead. The child has special powers, and as an adult is able to work miracles. He typically marries and has a child before embarking on his religious mission. His death represents a triumph over evil and the cosmos responds with natural signs such as earthquakes. Upon dying, he returns to the heavens to preside over a paradise in which his followers hope to join him after they die.

The avatar concept took root in Asia and the Middle East at least 2,000 years ago. Among Hindus its impact was reflected in the worship of Krishna; among Buddhists in the veneration of Amitabha Buddha (the figure who would become Amida in Japan); and among Jews in the rise of Christianity.

Krishna, Avatar of Vishnu

In some Hindu stories Vishnu is the ultimate deity, the god who lies at the origin of everything there is, including the creator god Brahman. Vishnu lies on his cosmic serpent, sometimes identified with the Milky Way, and out of his navel grows a lotus plant. From the lotus Brahman is born as the first of all creations; then the universe and all its material and spiritual energies follow. This is not exactly a mythic version of the big bang theory, but it comes close. Life evolves, over an unimaginable number of years, out of the divine energy at the centre of the universe. After the universe has run its allotted course, the process reverses from evolution to involution. Over an equally long period of time, eventually all things return into Vishnu, as if crossing the event horizon into a black hole. There all energy lies dormant as Vishnu sleeps, before the whole process begins again.

Another story about Vishnu sees him as the protector of the world. When Earth gets into trouble, he comes down to save us. The first five *avatars* of Vishnu take the form of animals that protect the world from natural disasters in its formative millennia. The next four avatars are humans, the most important of whom is Krishna. His exploits are narrated in several Hindu sources. The most famous is the *Bhagavad Gita*—the "Song of the Lord"—which tells of a great war between two houses of the royal family. Krishna is a relative of both houses and is recruited by both armies, but chooses to fight for neither. Instead, he drives the chariot of Arjuna, one of the five princes who lead one army.

Just before the battle, Arjuna asks Krishna to drive the chariot into the neutral zone between the two armies, so that he can get a better look at his adversaries. But when he sees that they include his cousins and former teachers, he loses his will to fight. Krishna tells him that, as a warrior, it is his duty to take up his bow. But Arjuna still has misgivings, and so they begin a long conversation about duty (dharma) and the eternal soul that cannot die even though the body may be killed in battle. Krishna teaches with such great authority that soon Arjuna asks how he knows so much. Krishna replies that he is a god of gods, that he is the energy behind all the categories of spirits and gods. When Arjuna asks for proof, Krishna grants him the eye of a god, with which he sees the splendours and mysteries of the universe as a god would.

In the end, Arjuna recognizes the divinity of Krishna, accepts his advice to fight, and wins the war. More important, however, is what Arjuna learns from Krishna about the many ways to lead a good religious life. These include the way (yoga) of good works (*karma yoga*), the way of deep spiritual wisdom (*jnana yoga*), and the way of faithful devotion to Krishna (*bhakti yoga*). Of these, the path of faithful devotion is the most highly recommended because it is the easiest and the most certain. The real saving power comes not from the wisdom or discipline of the individual, but from the saving power of the god. Krishna promises that those who practise devotion to him will go to his heaven when they die.

Amitabha, the Buddha of Saving Grace

The avatar concept gave Buddhism the story of Amitabha Buddha, in which a prince intent on achieving buddhahood makes 48 vows, some of which involve helping others towards the same goal. Among them is a promise to establish a paradise in which those who put their trust in Amitabha Buddha will be reborn after their death. His followers hope that if they sincerely profess their faith in his saving power, they will be rewarded with rebirth in that "Pure Land."

Jesus the Christ: God Come Down

The Christian doctrine of the trinity affirms that the one God exists in three persons: those of the father, the son, and the holy spirit. In formulating this doctrine, the Christians departed radically from the theology of Abraham and Moses. There is no room in Jewish thought for an avatar god, but that was the direction in which Christian thought developed. The prologue to the Gospel of John identifies Jesus with the divine Logos—the word of God that was present before creation. The apostle Paul says that Jesus "emptied himself" and came down for the salvation of the world. He is conceived in the womb of a virgin by the spirit of God. An angel announces the pregnancy and its significance to his mother. The birth is associated with a special star. Shepherds overhear the angels rejoicing and come to revere the infant, according to Luke's gospel. In Matthew's gospel, magi (wise men) from the East follow a special star to take gifts to the child.

For Christians, Jesus became the ultimate god who died on the cross on behalf of his followers and rose on the third day. By participating in the sacred rituals of baptism and the eucharist (in which consecrated bread and wine are consumed in commemoration of the "Last Supper" that Jesus shared with his disciples) and placing their trust in Jesus as Lord, Christians hoped to secure a place in heaven after their death.

So Christianity started with the Hebrew scriptures and the monotheism of Moses and incorporated into them the avatar pattern, along with elements of the mystery traditions, to form a new religion. Many Jews resisted these changes, but some accepted them in the belief that God had in fact offered the world a new dispensation.

Scriptural Religion

The beginning of scriptural religion is hard to date. The earliest scriptures we have are the compositions of Zarathustra (the core of the Zoroastrian Avesta), the Hindu Vedas, and the Torah of Judaism, all of which took shape approximately 3,000 years ago. Religions based primarily on scripture came much later, however, when different groups began to insist that their particular scriptures were the literal words of God, and to make adherence to those scriptures the focus of their religious life.

Scripturalism manifested itself in Rabbinic Judaism in the centuries that followed the destruction of the second Jerusalem temple in 70 CE. It then emerged in full force with the rise of Islam in the seventh century. It also played a large role in Protestant Christianity, starting in the sixteenth century, in which the authority of scripture replaced that of tradition and the papacy.

Living by Torah

During the Jews' exile in Babylon, the priests were not able to perform the traditional temple rituals, and so the Jews turned to the rabbis—scholars of the Torah with special expertise in Jewish

Document

The Word of God

In the beginning was the Word, and the Word was with God, and the Word was God. The same was in the beginning with God. All things were made by him, and without him was not any thing made that was made (John 1: 1–3, KJV).

And the Word was made flesh and dwelt among us (John 1: 14, KJV).

We have sent it [the revelation] down as an Arabic Qur'an, in order that you may learn wisdom (Qur'an 12: 2).

School children in Ibadan, Nigeria, learning to read the Arabic of the Qur'an (© Paul Almasy / Corbis).

law and ritual. In this way scripture began to play a more important role in Jewish life, a role that became even more important after the destruction of the second temple. Since that time, Jewish religious life has centred on interpretation of the scripture.

The Word of God

The gospels were not written until two or three generations after the death of Jesus, and the Christian canon did not take final shape until well into the third century CE. But once the books of the canon were fixed, the Church came to emphasize scripture as a divinely inspired source of faith and practice. The Bible became as central to Christianity as the Torah was to Judaism. Christians commonly refer to the scripture as the word of God, and some believe that the Bible was literally dictated by God to its human authors.

God's Final Prophet

The scriptural approach to religion reached its greatest height in Islam. The *surahs* that make up the Qur'an are believed to be the sacred words of God as revealed to the Prophet Muhammad by an angel, recorded by scribes, and compiled as a collection after his death. In essence, then, the

Qur'an is considered an oral text, meant to be recited—always in the original Arabic—rather than read. Nevertheless, the written Qur'an is treated with great respect. No other book is to be placed on top of it, and before opening the Qur'an, the reader is expected to be in the same state of ritual purity that is required for prayer.

The Lotus Sutra

The teachings of the Buddha were transmitted orally for centuries before they were written down, about 2,000 years ago. Although Buddhists revered these texts, their practice did not centre on them. In time, the Mahayana and Vajrayana schools would add many more texts to their respective canons. Yet no special properties were attributed to the scriptures themselves until the 1200s, when a Japanese monk named Nichiren taught his followers to place their faith in the power of his favourite scripture: Nichiren Buddhists chant their homage to the *Lotus Sutra* just as followers of the Pure Land school chant their homage to Amitabha/ Amida Buddha.

Creation through the Word of God

A number of scriptural traditions have maintained that their scriptures existed before the world was created. The medieval book of Jewish mysticism known as the *Zohar*, for example, teaches that the Torah played a role in the creation. The prologue to the Gospel of John talks about creation through the Word (*logos* in Greek). And Islam understands the Qur'an to have existed in the mind of God before the world itself was brought into existence.

This idea has very old roots. In ancient Israel, Egypt, India, and elsewhere, it was assumed that the deities would not have performed the physical work of creation themselves, like ordinary humans: rather, like kings, they would have commanded that the work be done: "Let there be light." Thus the divine word took on a special role in later theologies. In traditional Hindu thought, the goddess of speech, Vac, played this role. How could the scriptures—the actual words of the Torah, Bible, or Qur'an—be present in the mind of God at the time of creation, thousands of years before

Document

From *The Fundamentals*: on Scripture as the Inerrant Word of God

. . . objections [are] sometimes brought against the doctrine of inspiration—those, for example, associated with the question as to whether the Bible is the Word of God or only contains that Word. If by the former be meant that God spake every word in the Bible, and hence that every word is true, the answer must be no; but if it be meant that God caused every word in the Bible, true or false, to be recorded, the answer should be yes. There are words of Satan in the Bible, words of false prophets, words of the enemies of Christ, and yet they are God's words, not in the sense that He uttered them, but that He caused them to be recorded, infallibly and inerrantly recorded, for our profit. In this sense the Bible does not merely contain the Word of God, it is the Word of God (Torrey and Feinberg, eds, 1990: 139).

the historical events they describe? The answer for believers is that God knows the future. Outsiders might argue that this calls into question the concept of free will: if the deity knows everything in advance, how can humans be free to choose? What use is it to try to persuade people to do the right thing if the deity has already determined what each of them will do? Such questions have led to lively theological debates in many religious traditions.

Some followers of scriptural religions place such total authority in their scripture that outsiders have branded them **fundamentalists**. The term "fundamentalism" was first used in the early twentieth century to refer to an American Protestant movement characterized by a fervent belief in the literal truth of the Bible, but similar movements exist within most religious traditions.

What Is Religion?

Many scholars trace the derivation of the word "religion" to the Latin verb *religare*, "to bind." Yet others argue that the root is *relegere*, "to go over again." From the beginning, then, there has never been a universal definition of religion. We could say that religion is concerned with the divine, but even that simple description raises questions. Is the divine a single entity, or many? What about Theravada Buddhism, which is clearly a religion but doesn't worship the kind of god central to religions such as Judaism, Christianity, and Islam? The same problem arises with religious texts. Is there one text, or set of texts, that is particularly authoritative for a particular tradition? Is that "canon" closed, or can new materials be added to it? What are the distinctions between established religions and newer ones (sometimes referred to pejoratively as "cults")? We may accept the idea that one man (Moses) received revelations from God on Mount Sinai 3,200 years ago, or another (Muhammad) received similar revelations in Mecca 1,400 years ago, but reject the idea that a third (Joseph Smith) received revelations in upstate New York 200 years ago. There is some truth in the notion that today's cult is tomorrow's religion. Although this text focuses mainly on established traditions, it will discuss several newer religious movements in Chapter 12.

Another way of looking at religion is in terms of its functions. Thus a simple functional definition might be that religion is a way of creating community. For some people, "church" has less to do with piety or Sunday worship than with a community that offers a sense of belonging and activities to participate in. Karl Marx defined religion in terms of economics; Sigmund Freud, in terms of interior psychological states. Other scholars have approached the question from the perspective of sociology or anthropology, looking at religion as a social phenomenon or a cultural product. The academic study of religion is usually secular, undertaken without a particular faith commitment. One of the key scholars in this area is Jonathan Z. Smith at the University of Chicago. His work on the history of religions has had a profound impact on scholarly understanding of key terms such as "myth" and "ritual," and the way comparisons are made both within a single religious tradition and across different traditions.

Why Study Religion?

The first and most obvious reason to study religion is that it exists. Not all humans would lay claim to religious beliefs, but humans in general have been religious from time immemorial. A closely related reason is that religion has played such an important role in human affairs. People organize their communities around religious identities, go to war over religious beliefs, make great art in the service of religion, seek to change social norms, or to prevent change, out of religious conviction.

In short, religion so pervades the human world that it demands our attention regardless of whether it plays a direct role in our own lives.

It is also common to study religion for more personal reasons. You may want to know more about the tradition you, or someone close to you, grew up in. You may want to study other religions in order to understand other people's beliefs, or to look at your own beliefs from a different perspective. You may also want to arm yourself with knowledge in order to bring others around to your way of thinking, or to defend your beliefs against the arguments of those who might try to convert you to theirs.

Insider versus Outsider

Most people learn about their own religion from their parents, their teachers at religious schools, or other members of the same religious community. Naturally, we tend to accept the teachings of our own religion as true and assume that the teachings of other religions are false, or at least less true. As "insiders" we may find it disturbing when "outsiders" challenge our beliefs or suggest that the history of "our religion" may not be exactly as we have been taught. As Wilfred Cantwell Smith once noted, "Normally persons talk about other people's religions as they are, and about their own as it ought to be" (1962: 49).

One advantage of a book such as this is that it helps us appreciate our own traditions from both insider and outsider points of view. When approaching an unfamiliar tradition, outsiders must be sensitive to how it serves the needs of its followers. At the same time, insiders need to understand how their own tradition looks from the outside.

The insider–outsider matter is more complex than we might imagine, for there are many kinds of insiders. Is your Muslim friend a Sunni or a Shi'i? If a Shi'i, does she belong to the Twelver tradition, or one of the Sevener branches? Which variety of Buddhism does your classmate practise—Theravada, Mahayana, or Vajrayana? If Mahayana, which school? Is your Christian neighbour Protestant, Catholic, or Orthodox? A Protestant may well be an "outsider" to a member of another Protestant group, let alone to a Catholic Christian. A Zen Buddhist could have trouble seeing any connection between his practice and an elaborate Vajrayana ritual. Because each religion has many subdivisions, in this volume we will speak of traditions in the plural. We hope our readers will keep in mind the diversity behind the monolithic labels.

Religious Diversity

"Aren't all religions pretty much the same?" Most students of religion will be asked some version of this question more than once in their careers. Scholars might want to know what aspect of religion the questioner has in mind: teachings? practices? implications for society? Still, it would probably be safe to assume that he or she considers all religions to be of equal value and deserving of equal respect. And in twenty-first-century North America, many would agree. This was not the case 100 years ago, when North American society was overwhelmingly Christian and most of the Christian churches were actively engaged in missionary work. Missionary activity presumes a difference between one religion and all the rest—a difference so consequential that believers must spread the word.

Christianity began as a sect of Judaism, a religion focused almost exclusively on the relationship of one particular nation to God. But the early Christians decided that it was not necessary to

Focus

Missionary Religions

The fact that a mere three traditions—Buddhism, Christianity, and Islam—claim the allegiance of more than half the world's people reflects the success of their missionary activities. All three are "universal" rather than "ethnic" religions: that is, they direct their messages to all human beings, regardless of heredity or descent. And all three were strongly motivated from the start to spread their messages far and wide.

By the time Buddhism emerged, Indian society was already stratified into four broad social classes. Whether those distinctions had ethnic connotations in the time of the Buddha may be debated. What is clear is that Buddhism set caste and class status aside as irrelevant to the achievement of spiritual liberation. The early success of Theravada missionaries is credited to the influence of King Ashoka. We do not know enough about the indigenous traditions in all the regions where Theravada spread to determine why its teachings were accepted. In the case of Mahayana Buddhism, however, it seems that the Daoist interest in magic and healing techniques may have helped it to gain an initial foothold in China.

Document

Paul's Mission to the Athenians

While Paul was waiting for them in Athens, he was deeply distressed to see that the city was full of idols. So he argued in the synagogue with the Jews and the devout persons, and also in the marketplace every day with those who happened to be there. Also some Epicurean and Stoic philosophers debated with him. Some said, "What does this babbler want to say?" Others said, "He seems to be a proclaimer of foreign divinities" (Acts 17: 16–18; in Coogan et al., eds, 2010).

be a Jew in order to become a Christian. Early Christian teaching understood the new covenant to apply to all humans who accepted Jesus as their Lord, regardless of ethnicity. Once it became the religion of the Roman state, it converted several populations by converting their rulers. Its spread after the 1490s was closely associated with European colonialism: priests accompanied soldiers to the Americas, and in Mexico and Peru, the Spanish and Portuguese regimes took it as their responsibility to "save the souls" of the indigenous peoples whose bodies they enslaved. The cultural–religious imperialism of Catholic countries in the sixteenth century was matched in the nineteenth by that of Protestant England, notably in Africa.

Islam believes the Qur'an to incorporate the messages delivered to other groups by earlier prophets and to represent God's final revelation to humanity at large. In its early centuries it persuaded a significant number of nations to convert, perhaps partly because it offered improved legal status to Muslims. The first region where it did not succeed in converting the entire population was the Indian subcontinent. In the later centuries of its expansion, Islam grew not through military conquest, but through trade and the missionary activity of the mystic Sufi Muslims in particular. The devotional life of the Sufis resonated with the Hindu and Buddhist meditational traditions of Southeast Asia and gave Islam an entrée to that region, where it became dominant. Similarly in Africa south of the Sahara, traders and Sufis were the principal vehicles of Islam.

Dialogue in a Pluralistic Age

Today we often use the term "pluralism" to denote two things: the fact of diversity, and the evaluation of that diversity as desirable. But we need to be clear about what we mean by it. First, pluralism is not the same thing as diversity. People from many different religious and ethnic backgrounds may be present in one place, but unless they are constructively engaged with one another, there is no pluralism. Second, pluralism means more than simple tolerance of the other. It's quite possible to tolerate a neighbour about whom we know nothing; pluralism, however, demands an active effort to learn about others.

Third, pluralism is not the same thing as relativism, which can lead us to ignore profound differences. Pluralism is committed to engaging those differences in order to gain a deeper understanding both of others' commitments and of our own.

Fourth, we should distinguish pluralism from secularism. Secularism means the exclusion (in principle) of all religious groups, institutions, and identities from public support and public decision-making. Pluralism, by contrast, means equal support, acceptance, and participation in decision-making for multiple religious groups. Secularism and pluralism go hand in hand in the West to the extent that both seek to limit the role that Christianity can play in setting the society's standards. Where they differ is in what they propose as alternatives. Pluralism places a parallel and a positive value on the faith and practice of different communities. It often does so on the assumption that any religion is beneficial to society so long as it does no harm to other religions. It can also presume that the effort to understand a neighbour's religion—whatever it may be—is beneficial to society. Essentially, pluralism downplays the differences between religions and highlights the values they share. In its scale of priorities, harmony in the society as a whole is more important than the commitments of any particular religion. Finally, it is important to recognize that pluralism is happening not just in North America, but around the world,

Interfaith Dialogue

The word "dialogue" comes from a Greek root meaning to argue, reason, or contend. The Christian apostle Paul has sometimes been cited as an early proponent of interfaith dialogue because he is described as "arguing and pleading about the kingdom of God" with the Jews (Acts 19: 8–9). But Paul was a missionary, and missionary argumentation bears little resemblance to dialogue in the modern sense, which demands openness to other points of view.

Dialogue is also a literary form, almost always designed to advance the author's point of view. The Greek philosopher Plato was a master of that form, using questioners and objectors as foils to demonstrate the invincible logic of his own ideas and those of his mentor Socrates. The Hindu *Upanishads* also take the form of dialogues composed to advance specific arguments, with questioners serving as puppets whose only function is to bring out the views that the author is already committed to.

An early adventure in interfaith dialogue was the World's Parliament of Religions, convened in Chicago in 1893. Bringing together representatives of many—though not all—of the world's faiths, the conference offered many in the West their first introduction to Eastern traditions.

The World Council of Churches was formed in 1948, and among Christians the understanding of interfaith dialogue has grown considerably since then. Experienced dialogue participants emphasize that both parties must set aside their claims to exclusivity and work to understand the other on his or her own terms. Both participants must also be open to the possibility of revising their views in the light of what they learn—though this is easier said than done. Even the best-intentioned participants may be tempted to read their own views into others'. Thus the Roman Catholic theologian Karl Rahner (1904–84) referred to people of other faiths as "anonymous Christians"—Christians who simply did not recognize the fact. By the same token, couldn't Rahner himself have been an anonymous Buddhist?

The goal of dialogue in the modern sense is understanding. But "understanding" can be a slippery term in the religious context. Academic students of religion may understand very well what a particular tradition requires of its adherents and how it has developed, but that understanding is not the same as participation or identification. Similarly, participants in dialogue can identify one another's commitments, but that is not to say that they identify with those commitments. Particularly in the area of Jewish–Christian–Muslim dialogue, there have been calls for complete solidarity on complex and hotly debated issues, characterized by one critic as "ecumenical blackmail." Does true understanding of Judaism require uncritical endorsement of Israel's policies towards the Palestinians? If one truly "understands" Islam, must one agree with Iran's theocratic government and its suppression of democracy? Does understanding Hinduism mean accepting polytheism or animal sacrifice? No. Real understanding is not a matter of agreement or acquiescence, but a quest for a patient and appreciative relationship that can persist despite disagreement.

Religions are not all the same, but many may be humanly acceptable if they benefit human beings. On some occasions, when they have lived up to their ideals, all the major traditions have passed that test; on other occasions, when they have fallen short of their ideals, the same traditions have failed. Typically, though, the various traditions see their distinguishing features as eminently valuable in themselves. If all religions were of equal worth, if there were no fundamentally important differences, why would anyone choose one of them over another? Pluralism may be socially desirable, but it poses a serious theological challenge. Does it really require us to modify our own doctrinal claims?

Affirmations of religious "truth" that used to be understood as statements of fact are now increasingly regarded as perspectival—true "for me"—rather than universal claims. Today, thinkers from various backgrounds are presenting their traditions as symbolic accounts of the world and metaphorical narratives of the past. What's more, they argue that this is the way the various traditions should have been seen all along, and that literal interpretation has always been a mistake.

Pluralism demands that religious traditions adapt to a world that is becoming ever more interconnected. Here we think again of Wilfred Cantwell Smith. In his book *Towards a World Theology: Faith and the Comparative History of Religion* (1981) he argued that our various religious traditions are best understood in comparative context, "as strands in a . . . complex whole":

> What those traditions have in common is that the history of each has been what it has been in significant part because the histories of the others have been what *they* have been. This truth is newly discovered; yet truth it has always been. Things proceeded in this

> interrelated way for many centuries without humanity's being aware of it; certainly not fully aware of it. A new, and itself interconnected, development is that currently humankind *is* becoming aware of it, in various communities (Smith 1981: 6).

In a world where the differences that separate the world's religions are painfully clear, it is more crucial today than ever to appreciate the complex connections they share. We hope that this book will help to deepen your understanding of our interconnected religious worlds.

Discussion Questions

1. What are some concepts that are fundamental to what we call religion?
2. What are some of the major developments or patterns in the history of human religiosity?
3. What is an avatar? Give an example from both an Eastern and a Western tradition to illustrate your answer.

Glossary

All Saints Day A Christian festival honouring all the departed saints; held in the West on 1 November.

Daodejing The Daoist "Classic of the Way and Power," compiled roughly 2,500 years ago and traditionally attributed to Laozi.

Day of the Dead A Mexican festival honouring the dead.

fundamentalists Believers who ascribe total authority to their tradition's scriptures or doctrines, and reject any conflicting secular or religious alternatives.

Hallowe'en Now a popular secular holiday, held on 31 October; originally celebrated as the "Eve" of All Saints Day.

high places Sacred areas located on hill- or mountain tops; such places existed throughout the ancient Near East.

naga A mythical cobra living in the underworld, often associated with water and fertility in Indian religions.

Obon A Japanese festival honouring ancestors.

shaman A type of priest, widespread among hunter–gatherer societies, who communicates with the spirit world on behalf of the people.

Stonehenge One of several ancient rock structures thought to have been constructed for ritual purposes.

Upanishads Hindu religious texts thought to have been composed around 600 BCE.

References

Ballter, Michael. 2005. *The Goddess and the Bull: Catalhoyuk: An Archaeological Journey to the Dawn of Civilization*. New York: Free Press.

Coogan, Michael D., et al., eds. 2010. *New Oxford Annotated Bible with Apocrypha*. 4th edn. New York: Oxford University Press.

Doniger O'Flaherty, Wendy. 1975. *Hindu Myths: A Source Book*. Translated from the Sanskrit. Harmondsworth: Penguin Classics.

Eliade, Mircea. [1951] 1964. *Shamanism: Archaic Techniques of Ecstasy*. Translated by Willard R. Trask. Princeton: Princeton University Press.

Lin, Yutang. 1948. *The Wisdom of Laotse*. New York: The Modern Library.

Malinowski, Bronislaw. 1948. *Magic, Science and Religion*. Boston: Beacon Press.

Pearson, Mike Parker. 2012. *Stonehenge: Exploring the Greatest Stone Age Mystery*. London: Simon and Shuster.

Smith, Wilfred Cantwell. 1962. *The Meaning and End of Religion*. New York: Mentor Books.

———. 1981. *Towards a World Theology: Faith and the Comparative History of Religion*. Philadelphia: Westminster Press.

Torrey, R.A., and Charles L. Feinberg, eds. 1990. *The Fundamentals: The Classic Sourcebook of Foundational Biblical Truths*. Grand Rapids, MI: Kregel Academic and Professional.

Zaehner, R.C., ed. 1966. *Hindu Scriptures*. London: Everyman's Library.

2 Indigenous Traditions

Ken Derry

Traditions at a Glance

Numbers

Reliable statistical information is virtually non-existent, but the United Nations estimates that there are approximately 370 million Indigenous people in the world. On average perhaps 15 to 20 per cent practise their ancestral traditions, but the figures are much higher in some communities and much lower in others.

Distribution

There are more than 5,000 distinct Indigenous cultures in some 90 countries around the world. By far the largest populations are in Asia and Africa; fewer than 10 per cent are in Central and South America, approximately 2 per cent in North America and Oceania, and just a small fraction in Europe.

Recent Historical Periods

Written records of most Indigenous traditions do not begin until after first contact with non-Indigenous people, so the only developments we can trace with any certainty are relatively recent. However, Indigenous religions had been evolving for millennia before that time.

600–700 CE	First contact between Muslims and Indigenous Africans
1450–1850	First contact between Europeans and Indigenous people of Africa, North America, and Oceania; development of Atlantic slave trade and other colonial practices that devastated Indigenous populations
1930–1960	Several governments begin to reduce restrictions on Indigenous people and religion
1960–present	Revival of many traditions around the world; development of global pan-Indigenous movements

Founders and Leaders

Few pre-contact traditions identify a human founder, although most attribute key elements of their religious life to superhuman ancestors. Virtually all of them recognize religious authority figures such as elders, and rely on ritual specialists such as diviners and healers who invoke spiritual powers to aid their communities. In response to colonialism, several new movements were founded by specific people, such as Wovoka (Paiute) or Nongqawuse (Xhosa).

Deities

Indigenous conceptions of gods vary widely. Some traditions recognize a single supreme deity as the source of all life and power. Others attribute creation to a series of gods, spirits, or ancestors. Almost all believe that personal deities (or spirits or ancestors) have ongoing influence in the world.

Authoritative Texts

Most pre-contact Indigenous religions passed along their sacred stories orally. These stories often include accounts of the creation of the world and/or the origins of the community. Many also recount the ongoing activity of personal spiritual forces in the world. New tales continue to be told (and written), particularly about trickster figures, and some post-contact movements (such as the Handsome Lake religion of the Iroquois) have their own sacred texts.

Noteworthy Teachings

Indigenous traditions are typically bound to specific places where important spiritual forces have manifested themselves (e.g., where acts of creation occurred). They also tend to be more concerned with what happens during life than after death; therefore

← An **Aymara** priest prepares to celebrate the new Aymara year 5520 on 21 June 2012 in the sacred pre-Columbian city of Tiwanaku, Bolivia (© Martin Alipaz / epa / Corbis).

they place greater emphasis on behaviour than on belief, and assess actions in terms of their impact on the community. Many Indigenous traditions understand time as rhythmic rather than linear; in this conception, the sacred interacts with the world on an ongoing basis, responding to changing circumstances.

> So.
> In the beginning, there was nothing. Just the water.
> Coyote was there, but Coyote was asleep. That Coyote was asleep and that Coyote was dreaming. When that Coyote dreams, anything can happen.
> I can tell you that.
>
> —Thomas King (1993: 1), **Cherokee**/Greek

Anything can happen. The possibilities, the complexities, of religions seem to be endless. This is particularly true of Indigenous traditions, which constitute the majority of the world's religions. They are interwoven with the entire history of humanity, they encompass the whole Earth. And they are almost unimaginably diverse. So where to begin?

Perhaps it's best to start with ourselves. Let us approach the task of generalizing about Indigenous traditions with humility, recognizing that there are exceptions to every rule. We should also keep in mind that many past interpretations have been deeply mistaken. Looking through the lenses of their own assumptions and cultural biases, scholars can easily see things that aren't there, or miss what is right in front of them.

Coyote would not be surprised.

"Indigenous Religion"

Definitions

> There is a shared sense of Aboriginality nationally (and internationally with other Indigenous peoples), regardless of the geographical location or socio-economic experience of the individual.
>
> —Anita Heiss (2001: 207), **Wiradjuri**

There is no definitive understanding of "Indigenous religion." In fact, the meanings of the words "Indigenous" and "religion" themselves are open to debate, and it's possible to question whether they mean anything at all. You might think that any effort to define such a phenomenon is doomed to fail. But we are going to try.

"Religion"

Many of the difficulties surrounding the word "religion" stem from the variety of human practices. Are religions always about gods? (No.) Do all religions have a sacred text, believe in life after death, or promote the same basic values? (No again.) So what are we talking about when we refer to "religion"? Although scholars generally agree that no definition is likely to please everyone, they also point out that all definitions are themselves constructs. In other words, often we simply need to be clear about which construct we are using.

The view of religion underlying this chapter focuses on the beliefs, experiences, and practices of specific communities with respect to *non-falsifiable* realities (Cox 2007: 88). A proposition that is falsifiable is one that can be scientifically proven untrue. Religious propositions are of a different kind. It may not be possible to prove them true, but it is equally impossible to prove them false. Religious propositions traffic in the unseeable, the untouchable, the un-measurable. Whenever we step outside material reality to address questions of spirit, meaning, or divinity, I would say, we are dealing with religion.

This definition is not perfect, of course. Among other potential weaknesses, it implies a distinction between religion and science—as if religion had no scientific components, or science could not function as a religion for some people. This is not a reasonable distinction: religion and science may often overlap. Nor do I mean to imply that scientific knowledge supersedes other forms or ways of knowing. Scientists have been proven wrong about aspects of our world that some Indigenous cultures have long been right about.

Still, a focus on "non-falsifiable realities" can work quite well as a basis for defining religion. In particular, it is a good fit for the examples of Indigenous religion that follow.

"Indigenous"

The term "Indigenous" is also problematic, for it obliges us to ask which cultures and people are "Indigenous" and which are not. This question is loaded with legal and political implications, and so how it is answered has a direct and lasting impact on the lives of people around the world. If we cannot identify a particular group as Indigenous, for example, how can its members assert their treaty rights, or see their land claims settled fairly?

Unfortunately, it is usually non-Indigenous governments that impose the definitions, and those definitions themselves tend to change over time. In Canada, for instance, for many years a "status Indian" woman who married a "non-status" man was no longer legally Indigenous; she automatically forfeited all the rights that the (legally defined) Indigenous people of Canada are entitled to. When this law was overturned, in 1985, these women and their children "became" Indigenous virtually overnight.

Other definitions are also problematic. Almost invariably, "Indigenous" is understood to mean "original to the land." Yet places such as India and Africa have very ancient histories of migration and interaction between various groups. How could anyone possibly determine the "original" inhabitants of such lands?

It's also hard to find patterns among "Indigenous" religious beliefs and practices. Some cultures recognize a single supreme being; some recognize a variety of deities; and some don't bother at all with such things. Among the peoples who do believe in one or more gods, there are some who pray to those higher powers and some who do not. How reasonable is it to group such diverse traditions together?

That said, there are two elements of central importance to cultures that have typically been considered Indigenous: kinship and location. Thus we might say that an "Indigenous" (or "Aboriginal") community is one that is defined both by its members' *genealogical* relations to one another and by its connection to a particular *place*. The people who make up this community may or may not be the first or "original" inhabitants of this place. They may not even inhabit it now. Yet they see themselves as belonging to it, and they distinguish themselves from people who do not share this connection.

Timeline

The events listed here relate only to the cultures discussed in this chapter—a tiny fraction of the thousands that have existed. Although most of the dates relate to events since contact with non-Indigenous people, the histories in question began many millennia earlier.

c. 190,000 BCE	Earliest evidence of Indigenous people in Africa
c. 70,000 BCE	Earliest evidence of Indigenous people in Australia, Europe, and Asia
c. 12,500 BCE	Earliest evidence of Indigenous people in the Americas
616 CE	First Muslims arrive in Africa (Ethiopia)
c. 1250	First contact between the Ainu and the Japanese
c. 1300	First Indigenous settlers arrive in New Zealand (from Polynesia)
1444	Portuguese exploration of sub-Saharan Africa begins
c. 1480	Atlantic slave trade begins
1492	Christopher Columbus (Italian) arrives in the West Indies, initiating Spanish colonization of the Americas
1642	Dutch explorer Abel Janszoon Tasman arrives in New Zealand
1788	British First Fleet arrives in Sydney, Australia
1799	Handsome Lake experiences his first vision
1819	British and Xhosa (led by Nxele) fight Battle of Grahamstown
c. 1840	Canada establishes residential school system
1856–7	Nongqawuse's vision leads to Xhosa cattle massacre
1869	Australia begins taking Aboriginal children from their families, producing the first of many "Stolen Generations"
1883	Pauline Johnson (Mohawk) publishes first poems; US bans Sun Dance
1884	Canada bans potlatch
1885	European powers partition Africa at Congress of Berlin; intensive Christian missionary efforts begin in non-Muslim areas of Africa; earliest recorded "cargo cult" begins in Fiji
1889	Wovoka revives the Ghost Dance
1890	US Cavalry massacres more than 300 Lakota Sioux at Wounded Knee, North Dakota
1899	Japan appropriates Ainu lands, denies Ainu status as Indigenous people
1934	US lifts ban on Sun Dance and potlatch
1951	Canada lifts ban on potlatch
1956–65	Beginning of African post-independence era
1958	Chinua Achebe (Igbo) publishes *Things Fall Apart*
1969	Kiowa novelist N. Scott Momaday's *House Made of Dawn* wins Pulitzer Prize for Fiction

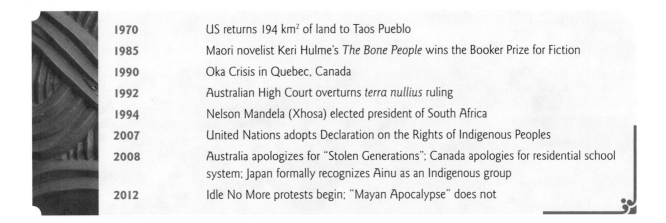

1970	US returns 194 km^2 of land to Taos Pueblo
1985	Maori novelist Keri Hulme's *The Bone People* wins the Booker Prize for Fiction
1990	Oka Crisis in Quebec, Canada
1992	Australian High Court overturns *terra nullius* ruling
1994	Nelson Mandela (Xhosa) elected president of South Africa
2007	United Nations adopts Declaration on the Rights of Indigenous Peoples
2008	Australia apologizes for "Stolen Generations"; Canada apologies for residential school system; Japan formally recognizes Ainu as an Indigenous group
2012	Idle No More protests begin; "Mayan Apocalypse" does not

Putting our two terms together, then, "Indigenous religion" refers to the beliefs, experiences, and practices concerning non-falsifiable realities of peoples who (a) identify themselves as Indigenous and (b) rely (at least in part) on kinship and location to define their place in the world.

Change and Syncretism

It's important to keep in mind that Indigenous religions no longer exist as they did before contact with the "outside" world. This situation is partly the result of **syncretism**: the merging of elements from different cultures. Many Native North American religions have been deeply affected by Christianity; some African rituals have incorporated elements of Islam; the sacred oral stories of Japanese Shinto became written texts under the influence of Chinese Buddhism. Does this mean that "real" Indigenous religions have disappeared?

Definitely not. Indigenous people and their religions may be connected to history, but they are not bound (or buried) by it. It is true that Indigenous religions today are not the same as they were 100, or 500, or 10,000 years ago. But the traditions as they exist now are no less authentic than they were in the past. Change and syncretism have taken place among *all* religions throughout history. The forms of Christianity practised in the contemporary United States have likewise been influenced by the beliefs and practices of many cultures, including African and Native American. These American forms in turn are quite different from the European Christianity that Martin Luther knew in the 1500s, or the Hellenized Christianity that Paul taught in the first century—a tradition that of course began as the Palestinian Judaism practised by Jesus. Like everything else in the world, religions change, and none of them is ever exactly what it used to be.

The "Patterns" section below will offer an overview of additional features that seem to be common to many, if not all, Indigenous religions. Before we can say much more about what Indigenous religions are, however, we first need to consider what they are not. That means breaking down some common non-Indigenous misconceptions.

Map 2.1 North American Indigenous Language Families

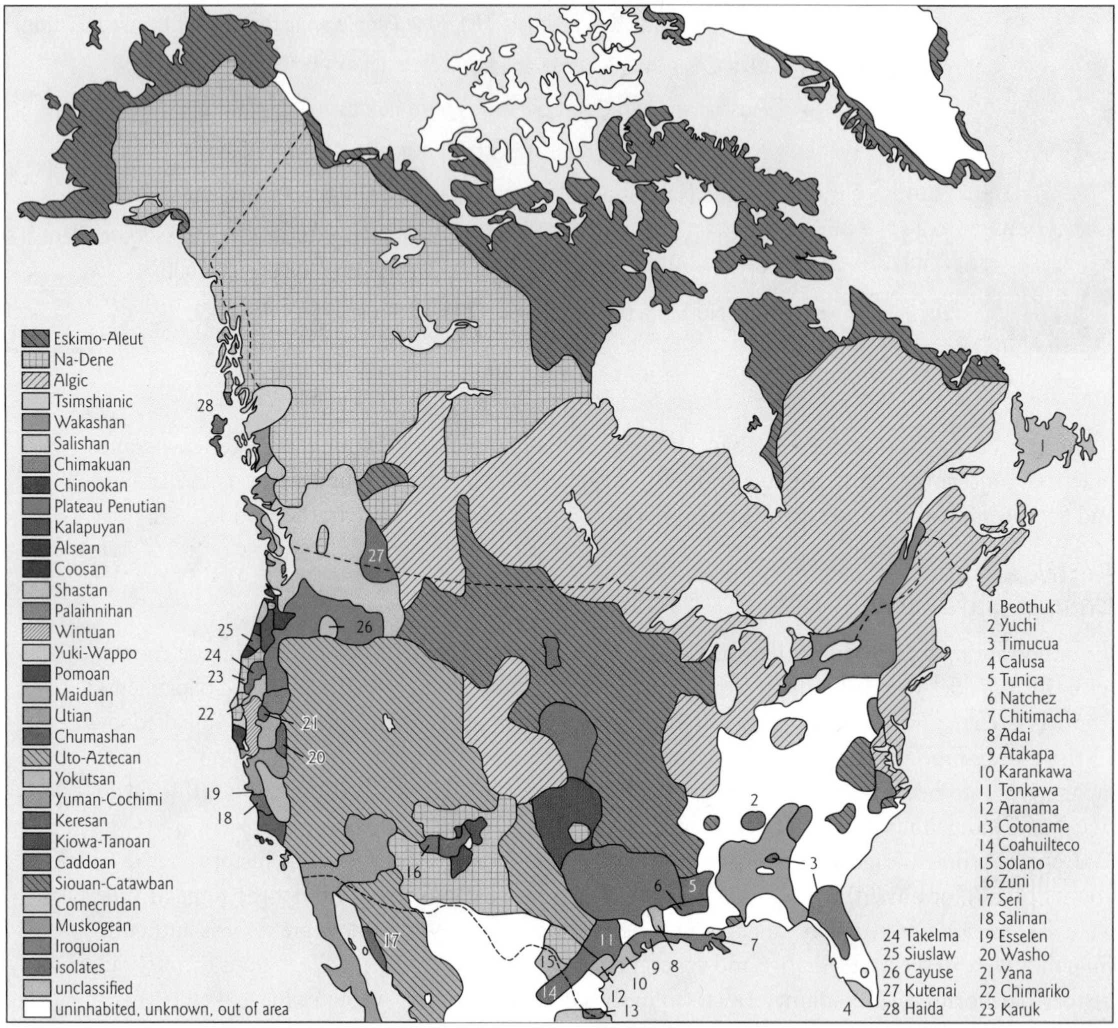

This map shows the distribution of North American language families north of Mexico at the time of European contact (to the extent that scholars can determine). Language borders were in reality much fuzzier than this image suggests. The map points to the tremendous diversity of Native North American cultures, since each *language family* may contain dozens of distinct *languages*.

"Us" and "Them"

> The people who have control of your stories, control of your voice, also have control of your destiny, your culture.
>
> —Lenore Keeshig-Tobias, **Anishinaubae** (in Lutz 1991: 81)

Most of what most people know, or think they know, about Indigenous cultures has come from non-Indigenous people. This reality points to one further element common to Indigenous traditions: **colonialism**. Although the effects of colonialism will be discussed later, it's important to say a few words now about one facet of it: namely, academic work on Indigenous people and cultures.

Scholars with Weapons

Recent decades have seen some opposition to the efforts of non-Indigenous scholars to "explain" Indigenous people. The main concern is that even unfounded theories can have significant social and political influence. The recent confusion about the "**Mayan** Apocalypse" stems from an academic misunderstanding about Indigenous people. Early discoveries indicated that the Mayans had identified a 5,000-year age of the gods ending in 3114 BCE. Scholars then assumed the next age would also last 5,000 years and therefore end on 21 December 2012. In fact, the Mayans understood the next age to be composed of entirely different time periods; thus the identification of 2012 as the end of *any* Mayan-related phenomenon was meaningless.

A more harmful example of academic impact was outlined by the **Oglala Sioux** lawyer, historian, and activist Vine Deloria, Jr (see Document box). Anthropologists seeking to explain the social ills plaguing the Oglala community ignored the "real issue, white control of the reservation," and theorized that the people were simply "warriors without weapons" (Deloria, Jr, 1988 [1969]: 90). In this view, the Oglala were incapable of adapting to a market-economy lifestyle because, deep in their souls, they remained violently primitive. Accordingly, attention was diverted away from the pressing needs of the people—credit, employment, housing, medical services—and focused instead on figuring out how to make "modern Indians" out of them (Deloria, Jr, 1988 [1969]: 92).

Document

From *Custer Died for Your Sins*, by Vine Deloria, Jr (Oglala Sioux)

Published in the early days of the American Indian Movement, Custer Died for Your Sins *(1969) remains one of the most influential works of Indigenous non-fiction ever written.*

From lack of roads to unshined shoes, Sioux problems were generated, so the anthros discovered, by the refusal of the white man to recognize the great desire of the Oglala to go to war. Why expect an Oglala to become a small businessman, when he was only waiting for that wagon train to come around the bend?

The very real and human problems of the reservation were considered to be merely by-products of the failure of a warrior people to become domesticated. . . . What use would roads, houses, schools, businesses, and income be to a people who, everyone expected, would soon depart on the hunt or warpath? . . .

The question of the Oglala Sioux is one that plagues every Indian tribe in the nation, if it will closely examine itself. Tribes have been defined as one thing, the definition has been completely explored, test scores have been advanced promoting and deriding the thesis, and finally the conclusion has been reached—Indians must be redefined in terms that white men will accept, even if that means re-Indianizing them according to the white man's idea of what they were like in the past and should logically become in the future (Deloria, Jr, 1988 [1969]: 92).

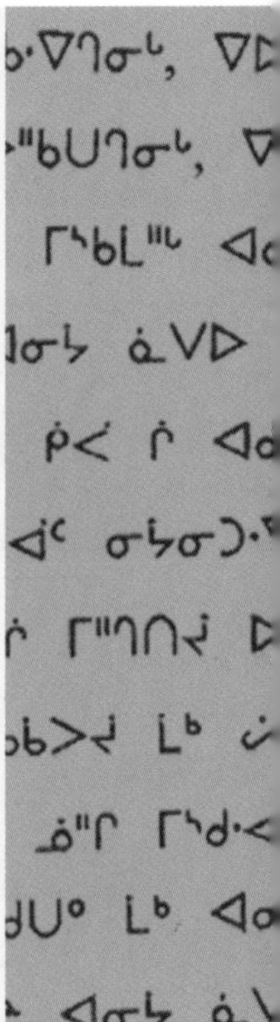

Today concern is often expressed when non-Indigenous scholars speak about Indigenous people. The main objection might seem to be that "outsiders" lack the necessary "insider" knowledge and insight. As Deloria suggests, however, the real problem is one of *power* and *control*. The fact is that, historically, such scholars have had the authority to define Indigenous people not only to non-Natives, but even to Native people themselves.

Unacceptable Terms

Another important problem with academic work about Indigenous people is that it tends to reinforce the idea that "they" are different from "us." Thus the study of Indigenous religions has produced many terms and concepts that typically are applied only to those traditions, and not to "world" religions more broadly—terms such as "animism," "fetish," "mana," "myth," "shaman," "taboo," and "totem." This chapter will rarely use any of those terms, in part because they are not necessary for an introductory understanding of Indigenous religions, but also because they are not used in reference to the other religions discussed in this book, even when they might be relevant. For example, Indigenous origin stories are usually labelled "myth," while similar stories in the Hebrew Bible or the *Mahabharata* are considered "sacred literature." Similarly, the rule that prohibits an African mask carver from having contact with a woman during his work would normally be called a "taboo"; yet that term is not applied to the rule that forbids a Christian priest from pouring unused communion wine down the drain. In short, it's important not to perpetuate the notion that Indigenous religions are of a different order from non-Indigenous religions.

"Primitives" and the Problem of History

> If I press any anthros . . . on exactly why they study Indians and other tribal peoples and why they study anthropology at all, I am almost always informed that tribal people represent an earlier stage of human accomplishment and that we can learn about our past by studying the way existing tribal peoples live.
>
> —Vine Deloria, Jr (1997: 214), Oglala Sioux

The More Things Change

For many years non-Indigenous people assumed that Indigenous people and cultures had changed very little before colonization began. In fact, until quite recently anthropologists were the only ones who studied Aboriginal people: historians did not think there was any Aboriginal history to look at.

The development of anthropology can be traced to the seventeenth and eighteenth centuries, when "explorers" began describing their encounters with previously unknown cultures that were primarily oral in nature, for example, and that used simpler technology.

Assuming that such cultures had remained essentially unchanged from their beginnings, the Europeans called them "primitive" (from Latin *primus*, "first") and supposed that for them history began only when they encountered "modern/civilized" cultures. This notion was supported by the fact that the majority of Europeans at the time were Christians who believed both in the (God-given) superiority of their own culture and in the divine imperative to spread their religion to those who had not yet heard the gospel. Indigenous cultures were seen as blank slates with no real religion of their own. This missionary worldview often went hand in hand with academic inquiry, and tended to colour the scholars' interpretation (in some cases, fabrication) of the details of Indigenous lives.

We know now that those assumptions about Indigenous cultures as static and ahistorical were completely untrue. All the available evidence shows that Indigenous peoples had dynamic, eventful histories full of change long before they were "discovered." They have also been quite conscious of their histories, using stories, songs, or physical markings to record past events, changes in the culture or the land, family genealogies, and so on.

A Persistent Problem

One example of the persistent notion that Indigenous cultures are "primitive" is the tendency to think of them as non-literate. This belief is deeply problematic in several ways, which will be discussed in the next section ("Transmission"). For now I simply wish to state three points. First, writing is not inherently more "advanced" than orality. Second, many Indigenous cultures did use a form of writing before contact with non-Indigenous people (see, for example, the Mayan glyphs below). Third, of course, the vast majority of contemporary Indigenous cultures are fully literate; to ignore this is to think of these cultures only in the past tense.

Another example of the tendency to regard Indigenous people as "primitive" is the belief that they do not distinguish between the "religious" and "non-religious" aspects of their lives—that they consider everything to be sacred. Thus some commentators have claimed that the Navajo "Blessingway" ceremony, which is performed before a new dwelling is occupied, transforms the home into a sacred site in which every activity is equally sacred. This notion is both inaccurate and patronizing. Essentially, it likens Indigenous people to children who believe that their stuffed animals are alive and sentient.

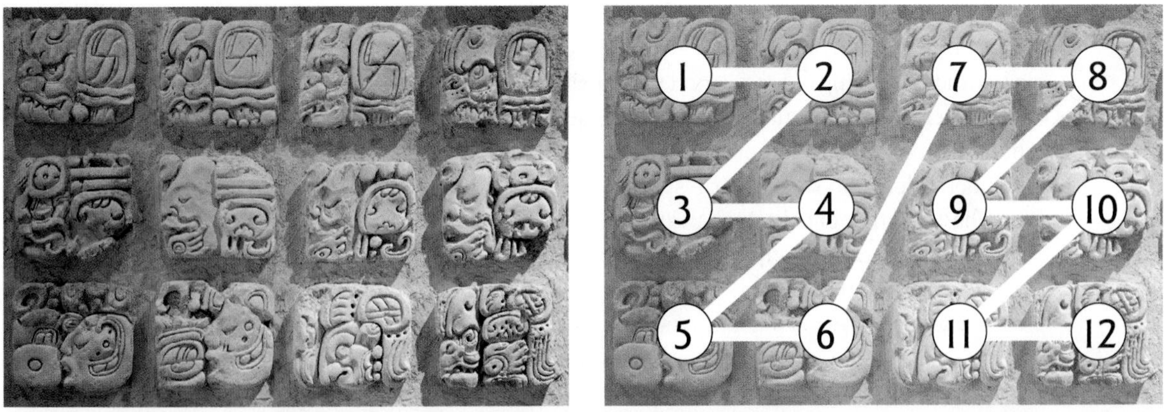

Mayan writing consisted of elaborate images, or glyphs, which were "logosyllabic" (each image represents either a word or a syllable). These images were painted on ceramics, carved in wood, or—as here—moulded in stucco. Most often they were arranged in blocks of two columns, each one to be read from left to right, top to bottom (© Ariadne Van Zandbergen / Alamy).

The fact is that Indigenous cultures are no less able than non-Indigenous ones to form distinctions in relation to the category of religion. Observant Muslims may take their prayer mats wherever they go, but they use the mats only at specified times. Similarly, an Australian **Aborigine** knows that certain acts are performed only in particular ritual contexts.

Many non-Indigenous scholars now realize that Indigenous cultures were (and are) just as complex and innovative as their own, and that the idea of the "primitive" typically suggests a belief in one's own superiority that justifies the "improvement" of Indigenous cultures. In a similar fashion, those who romanticize "primitive" cultures often do so in the belief that their own "civilized" culture has alienated people from themselves, or from the natural world. The concept of the "primitive" tells us more about the people who hold it than it does about the people they apply it to.

The idea of the "primitive" is one reason why many world religions courses still exclude Indigenous traditions. It also helps to explain why literary scholars often ignore modern Indigenous writers, while anthropologists continue to pore over transcriptions of ancient tales. As the Anishinaubae author Daniel David Moses has commented: "This image of traditional Native storytelling places Native people in the museum with all the other extinct species" (Moses and Goldie 1992: xiii).

Patterns

> The knowledge imposes a pattern, and falsifies . . .
> The only wisdom we can hope to acquire
> Is the wisdom of humility: humility is endless.
>
> —T.S. Eliot (1959: 23–4), Euro-American

Eating and Seeing

Dr Clare Brant, a **Mohawk** from southern Ontario, has recounted an experience from the 1970s when his band invited a group of James Bay **Cree** to a sporting tournament they were hosting (Ross 1992: 2–3). The Mohawk—who developed agriculture long before meeting Europeans—had a tradition of setting out more food than their guests could eat, in order to demonstrate their wealth and generosity. Unfortunately, the Cree had a very different tradition. Coming from a culture of hunting and gathering, they were accustomed to living with scarcity; therefore they would eat all the food offered, to show their respect for the skill and generosity of those who provided it.

The Cree thought the Mohawk were deliberately forcing them to overeat, while the Mohawk thought the Cree were grossly self-indulgent and bizarrely determined to insult their hosts. Thus each group saw the other as intentionally disrespectful, even though both were simply trying to be polite.

This story highlights two important points. First, even people who live very close to one another may think or behave very differently. (The greatest ethnographic diversity on Earth is contained within the region of New Guinea and its surrounding islands: approximately one-quarter of all the world's cultures—and languages and religions.) Second, anyone attempting to understand another culture is in a position similar to that of the Mohawk and Cree. The eyes we see through are the ones we have inherited from our own cultures: therefore we must use them with caution and humility.

Common Elements

The rest of this chapter will try to identify some elements common to many (if not necessarily all) Indigenous religions. Among them are the following:

- orality
- connection to specific places
- emphasis on community and relationship
- sense of time as rhythmic
- greater emphasis on what happens in life than after death
- behaviour more important than belief
- authority of **elders**
- **complementary dualism**
- a view of the sacred as ongoing process rather than static revelation
- gendered roles

This last point requires some comment. Traditionally, all members of an Indigenous community had clearly defined roles that were often gendered. In general, hunting and warfare were male occupations, while food preparation and healing were the responsibility of women. **Maori** carvers were men, and Maori weavers were women. The **Bunu Yoruba** men were responsible for growing cotton, and the women for turning it into cloth. Men and women depended on one another, and yet were also independent in important ways.

A similar balancing can often be seen in regard to political and social power. The heads of most Indigenous societies have typically been male. Yet in many instances women have been inherently involved with any decision affecting the entire community. And in some cases such decisions have normally been made by women, then carried out by men.

It is also important to note that gender classification could be somewhat fluid. Sometimes women might participate in men's work, and vice versa. Sexual roles and orientations could also be fluid. Accounts of men identifying as women, wearing female clothes, and taking on women's roles are not unusual. There are also accounts of Indigenous women identifying as men and becoming hunters or warriors.

There is no definitive gender pattern with respect to kinship. Some Indigenous societies are matrilineal, tracing ancestry primarily through the mother, while others are patrilineal, focusing on the father. Similarly, important spirits and gods—including the supreme being—may be either male or female.

It was also not uncommon for Indigenous societies to separate the religious activities of women and men. Yet most studies have looked only at male practices—whether because male scholars were unaware that women had their own practices, or because they were not permitted to study the women, or because they assumed that the men were the most important members of their communities and hence that their practices were the only ones worth investigating. It is only relatively recently that scholars have begun to examine what Indigenous women think and do in the context of religion.

Final Concerns

Most of the examples examined in this chapter come from Africa, Oceania, and North America. It's important to emphasize that the very idea of such regions was a European invention: their

Indigenous inhabitants thought in much more local terms. Still, this European (mis-)perception can serve a useful political purpose for Indigenous people: for example, it can give them a stronger voice on issues such as land claims or self-government. These and many other matters of general concern were set out in the 2007 United Nations Declaration on the Rights of Indigenous Peoples, which would not have been possible without a global understanding of what it means to be Indigenous.

Finally, please note that the aspects of Indigenous religious life discussed in the next three sections—"Transmission," "Practice," and "Cultural Expressions"—are in reality not as cleanly demarcated as those headings might suggest. As with all religions, there is a good deal of overlap. Oral stories are also ritual performances, for example, while rituals may involve works of art, which in turn may evoke stories central to a community's religious tradition.

The last point to keep in mind is that the examples in this chapter represent only a tiny sample of the world's Indigenous religious traditions. They represent what I know and what I think is important, arranged into the patterns that I see. An author with different views, experience, or knowledge might have constructed quite a different picture. All this is true in any context, of course, which is why nothing should be taken at face value. Still, this point is especially important in relation to Indigenous people, who have consistently been misrepresented, often with harmful results. I have done my best to avoid grievous errors, and I apologize upfront for any mistakes I may have made.

Transmission

The Power of Speech

> When you dig in the earth, you find stone and earthen implements, but not words—not the words of our ancestors. Words aren't buried in the ground. They aren't hanging from the branches of trees. They're only transmitted from one mouth to the next.
>
> —**Ainu** elder (in Shigeru 1994: 154–5)

Orality may not be a defining characteristic of Indigenous religions, but it remains a vital one for the vast majority of them. Even cultures that have long had writing have usually passed on critical values and beliefs orally, through stories.

Writing versus Speaking

Unfortunately, many non-Indigenous people continue to think of orality as "primitive" and writing as a defining characteristic of "civilization." To them, writing represents a key evolutionary advance, permitting abstract philosophical thought, while oral cultures remain attached to the present and the material world, incapable of sophisticated analysis or extended self-reflection. Writing frees us to develop science, according to this view, whereas reliance on speech limits us to magic.

Such beliefs are both incorrect and self-interested, and they contribute to the construction of Indigenous cultures as primitive. Furthermore, all cultures—including all other world religions—have many crucial oral dimensions. Both the Qur'an and the stories of the Buddha were transmitted in oral form for many years before they were written down.

In addition, there are contexts in which things that are *said* still have a power that the written word does not. Shakespeare's plays literally come alive when the words are voiced, and the preaching of Martin Luther King, Jr, affected the course of history in a way that no book of his sermons could have.

There is also the obvious fact that many non-Indigenous people today are abandoning books and newspapers for video, film, and television—media that in many ways have more in common with Indigenous storytelling than they do with written texts. Although this trend is often lamented as proof of civilization's decline, it may be that we are more easily engaged by narratives that are performed than by those that just sit on a page. If so, perhaps modern communications technology is letting non-Indigenous people experience stories in their full power once again, as Indigenous people have been experiencing them all along.

Stories

> I can recall lying on the earth and wondering what it was all about. The stars were a beautiful mystery and so was the place where the eagle went when he soared out of sight. Many of these questions were answered in story form by the older people. How we got our pipestone, where corn came from and why lightning flashed in the sky, were all answered in stories.
>
> —Luther Standing Bear, **Lakota** (in Beck et al. 1992 [1977]: 59)

In many cultures, stories serve as vehicles for the transmission of beliefs and values. Yet it is not always easy to determine what is being passed along. This is as true for Indigenous tales as it is for the parables of Jesus. There are many factors that may undermine our ability to interpret a particular story.

The Afterlife

Stories about the afterlife often appear to reveal a culture's beliefs about what literally happens following death, but the truth may be more complex. In a **Kewa** tale from Papua New Guinea, for instance, a young man finds a tunnel that leads to the underworld, where he recognizes his dead kinsmen. The men give him many valuable items to distribute among the living, but warn him not to say where these things came from. The young man gives everything away but breaks his promise not to speak, and when he returns to the tunnel he finds it sealed.

An Anishinaubae story tells of a man whose beloved dies just before they are to be married. Distraught, he sets out in search of the Path of Souls, hoping to see his love one last time. When he finds the path, the guardian of the land of the dead lets him enter only after he promises to return to his regular life once his wish is fulfilled. The man agrees, journeys through a misty forest and across a turbulent river, and finds the woman he loved. Then he turns his canoe around and returns home, heartbroken but prepared now to continue with his life.

What do these stories tell us about the Kewa and the Anishinaubae? Do they believe that their dead reside underground, or on the other side of a forest? Perhaps. Yet both stories seem to have more to do with relationships than with metaphysics. In the Kewa tale, ancestors help their descendants, and the young man helps his community but breaks his promise to his dead kinsmen; as a result, life becomes a little harder for everyone. Similarly, the Anishinaubae story depicts the necessity of pushing through loss and returning to life after tragedy.

In short, these stories may tell us more about how we should live than about what happens when we die. Even the places where the dead reside have a this-worldly quality to them: our ancestors have not disappeared into some inaccessible other dimension, but are (relatively) nearby, and can affect our lives in direct, material ways.

Truth in Storytelling

Thus we should not assume that the literal meaning of a story is its most important aspect. Some stories may well be understood to be fiction, or true only in a figurative or symbolic sense. The Kewa, for example, clearly distinguish between true stories called *ramani* (oral *history*) and fictional tales called *lidi* (oral *literature*). Similarly, the **Nyanga** of Zaire contrast *nganuriro* (true stories) with *karisi* (epic poems).

We must also be careful not to assume that a given story is a reflection of a culture. It may be only a single storyteller's version, and the narrative details may reflect the teller's own preferences as much as they do the values or worldview of his or her culture. In other words, the story may be "true" only to the person who is telling it.

Context

Perhaps the most important point to remember is that we almost never encounter Indigenous stories in their natural form: spoken to a group in their original language. Instead, most of us read them silently, to ourselves, in our own colonial language, in a time and a place far removed from the circumstances in which they would normally have been performed. The difference is significant—akin to the difference between reading "Close your eyes and I'll kiss you . . ." and being part of the shrieking studio audience in February 1964 when the Beatles opened their first American television appearance, on *The Ed Sullivan Show*, with "All My Loving."

The act of storytelling is itself a ritual: many stories are told only in a particular place and time, and only by certain people. Similarly, not all stories are for everyone: some may be just for women, some for men, and some for children. When we lose all this context, what else is lost?

Writing the Spoken

Writing also diminishes the capacity of an oral story to change with the teller and the time. A story told by a cheerful woman on a sunny day will seem different if it is told by an angry man on a rainy night. And the stories can alter or evolve in response to changing circumstances or needs. So what happens when a story is committed to ink on paper? Is it fixed in place forever?

Perhaps, in certain ways. But writing may be less "fixed in place" than we think. This fact becomes evident when we look at different written versions of the same oral story. In various collections of Anishinaubae tales, for example, Basil Johnston has several times recounted the fight between the **trickster** Nanabush and his father Epingishmook (the spirit being who represents the West, old age, and death). In one version, the two appear equally matched, and the battle ends only when Nanabush cuts his father with a piece of flint; in another, Epingishmook wins, stopping the fight when Nanabush falls to the ground, exhausted and expecting to die at his father's hands. Together, the two versions of the story emphasize that Nanabush is both a brave, strong warrior and a weak, cowardly one. In addition, the stories together raise the question of what is true about them.

Generally speaking, every Indigenous culture has thousands of stories, and every story may have many variations. It is impossible to do justice to such variety here. We will simply consider a few examples of two types of stories: those that in some way explain origins, and those that feature "trickster" figures. With luck, this will demonstrate both the challenges and the rewards of trying to understand what such stories may be saying to—and about—the people who tell them.

Origin Stories

> No matter if they are fish, birds, men, women, animals, wind or rain. . . . All things in our country here have Law, they have ceremony and song, and they have people who are related to them.
>
> —Mussolini Harvey, **Yanyuwa** elder (in Swain and Trompf 1995: 24)

North America

Among the best-known origin stories in North America are "Earth Diver" tales. Several of their key elements are common to cultures across the eastern woodlands. Typically, the story begins with the world destroyed by flooding; then an animal or deity brings some earth up from beneath the waters to begin rebuilding the land.

In one version, Sky Woman, a spirit being, descends to earth during the flood. Seeing that she is pregnant, the giant turtle offers to let her rest on his back. She then asks the other animals to dive for some soil. Many try but fail, and they drown. In the end, it is the lowly muskrat—who has been ridiculed by the others—that succeeds. Sky Woman breathes into the soil, which spreads across the turtle's back to become what is now called North America. Her breath infuses the earth with life. She gives birth to twins (the ancestors of the people who tell this story) and awards joint stewardship of the land to all the beings who live there—human, animal, and spirit.

Africa

The African **Dogon** people also refer to a form of pregnancy in their origin stories, which tell how the supreme being, Amma, created the world (and humanity) essentially by accident. Out of loneliness, Amma transformed himself into a womb holding four new beings called Nummo; two of these were mostly male but partly female, and the other two were mostly female but partly male. Before their 60-year gestation period was complete, one of the males became so impatient to be with his sister that he tore away part of the womb searching for her. This torn part of the womb became the earth.

Life began when Amma sacrificed the sister and scattered the pieces of her body on the ground to purify the earth. The two remaining Nummo clothed the earth with vegetation and infused it with a creative, universal life force called *nyama*. Amma and the Nummo also created eight beings who were placed in separate celestial chambers and prohibited from eating a certain type of grain. They became lonely, however, and when their food ran out, they gathered together and cooked the forbidden grain. When they were expelled from the heavens and crashed to earth, the world as we know it was created.

Australia

The origin stories of the Australian Aborigines centre around events that occurred in a time that nineteenth-century anthropologists famously mis-translated as "**The Dreaming**"; a more accurate translation might be "The Uncreated." Although anthropologists understand The Dreaming as archaic time, Aborigines have usually referred to the events of The Dreaming as if they had occurred not long before their own time. In other words, those events are out of reach of living memory, but recent enough to remain vital and meaningful to the communities that speak of them.

Unlike most Africans and Native North Americans, Australian Aborigines generally do not recognize a single divine authority from whom all life, values, rules, and so on derive. Instead, stories of origin usually concern the first ancestors, whose actions shaped both the physical world and the cultural practices of their descendants. There are countless stories of The Dreaming, but many tales reflect some basic patterns. For example, "Love Magic" (in the document box) explains how the love magic ritual and a specific sacred site originated in the actions of two ancestors, while reinforcing the community's prohibitions on incest and rape. The metamorphosis of the ancestors into physical formations on the land is typical of Dreaming tales.

Meanings

What do origin stories mean? It's certainly possible that they were understood to be straightforward historical accounts. I have met many Native people in Canada who refer to North America as "Turtle Island" and regard it as sacred. But to my knowledge none of them think that the continent was actually formed from a clump of mud on the back of a giant reptile.

In any case, we should also consider what other aspects of these stories might be important. First, as in the "afterlife" stories above, relationships are central. In each case, creation results from a desire for community or companionship, and the central beings are the ancestors of the people who tell the story. Second, the stories typically underline the relatedness of all aspects of existence. Just as the Aborigines are related to ancestors from The Dreaming who remain connected to the landscape, all of existence is connected. The world in its entirety is infused with the spirit of the ancestors. Third, origin stories typically do not imagine the beginning of time: they presuppose the existence of the universe and focus on the origin of certain elements—language, culture, landscape—that still exist, connecting us to the actions of our ancestors. Past and present are forever linked.

Document

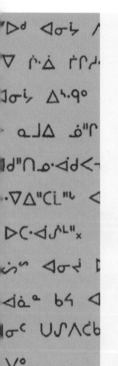

"Love Magic" (Australian Aborigine)

"Ngarlu" *has three meanings in this story from central Australia. It is the flower of the ngarlkirdi (witchetty grub tree) as well as the name of a sacred site and of the ceremonies performed there. A "subsection" is a kinship group, while "hairstring" is string made from human hair.*

There was a Dreaming man named Linjiplinjipi of the Jungari subsection at this site. He had adorned his body with *Ngarlu* and was spinning hairstring. The whirling sound of his spinning tool [made of crossed sticks] attracted a woman of the Ngapangardi subsection [and therefore his mother-in-law]. He climbed the hill and as he was watching her she stopped to urinate. Sexually aroused, he continued to attract her with the noise. Finally, he caught her, forced her legs apart and raped her. Upon ejaculation, however, she closed her legs and her tight vagina dismembered his penis.

Today, at Ngarlu her vagina remains transformed into rock and the severed stone-penis is still embedded in it. *Linjiplinjipi* himself, in agony, went to the other side of the hill where he turned into a large boulder which has paintings upon it depicting his hairstring cross and his erect penis. *Yilpinji* ["love magic"] is performed modelled on *Linjiplinjipi's* methods of attracting his mother-in-law, using sticks from *Ngarlu* and adorning the torso with the flowers of the witchetty grub tree (Swain and Trompf 1995: 22–3).

Finally, it's worth noting that these stories rarely present a simple, idealized picture of the world. They tell us that it is (at least in part) the product of violence: a torn womb, a rape, a devastating flood. The Dogon tradition associates the creation of humans with loneliness and disobedience, while in North America many animals sacrifice themselves to help Sky Woman and her baby. Order, creation, and life are almost always connected to chaos, destruction, and death.

And speaking of chaos . . .

Contemporary Yolngu artist David Malangi in 1997, painting the Milmildjark Dreaming on bark. When the Australian government eventually compensated Malangi for using his work "Gurrmirringu's Mortuary Feast" on the one-dollar note, the payment marked the first recognition of Aboriginal copyright (© Penny Tweedie / Alamy).

Tricksters

> "You know what I noticed? Nobody panics when things go according to plan, even if the plan is horrifying. If tomorrow I tell the press that, like, a gang-banger will get shot, or a truckload of soldiers will be blown up, nobody panics. Because it's all part of the plan. But when I say that one little old mayor will die, well then *everyone loses their minds*."
>
> —Joker, in *The Dark Knight* (2008)

The concept of the trickster was developed by scholars to categorize a certain type of character that appears in the stories of many cultures, including the Norse (Loki) and the ancient Greeks (Hermes). Tricksters are sometimes referred to as "culture heroes," typically because they are the central figures in many of the community's stories, and also because they often teach important lessons.

Shape-Changers

As their name implies, tricksters are hard to pin down. They can usually shape-shift, and many take the form of animals. In North America, for example, the raven and the coyote are often tricksters. In addition, many tricksters are able to change their gender (always from male to female).

Tricksters are typically more than human but less than gods. They can be selfless or greedy, kind or cruel, funny or deadly serious. And while their behaviour often violates the social order, this is not always a bad thing. Sometimes the social order *needs* to be violated, and sometimes the most effective way to do that is through laughter.

Self and Others

So how do we know when to follow the trickster's example and when to shun it? Often the main clue is the motivation behind the action: is it self-interest, or the desire to help others? In such cases our judgment depends on understanding what is good for the community. A common scenario centres on the disastrous results of the male trickster's efforts to satisfy his enormous sexual appetite. Such stories testify to the understanding that unrestrained (male) sexuality poses a serious threat to society.

By contrast, in the Anishinaubae story "Red Willows," Nanabush displays consideration for his mother. However, he is also extremely self-indulgent and shows no restraint when eating the bear—a transgression for which he pays a painful price.

Like many trickster stories, "Red Willows" explains the origins of certain elements of the community's physical world, from the river at Sault Ste Marie to the rugged terrain around Sudbury. And since those (colonial) towns are named, we know that this is either a modern retelling of an old

Document

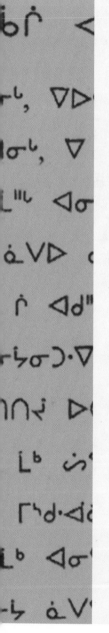

"Red Willows" (Anishinaubae)

Nanabush was wandering in the far north. He was hungry. Nanabush was always hungry.

He was with his mother at the time. That old lady is known by many names. Some call her "Dodomum" or "Dodum"; others call her "Gushiwun" or "Gushih."

They wandered until Nanabush chanced to meet a bear. "Ha!" he announced. "I'm going to eat you!" "Oh no you don't," replied the bear. "I will fight back if you try to kill me. Get out of here, Nanabush."

Nanabush would not leave. "Listen," he pleaded, "I'm hungry. Can't you see that? I'm hungry. I've eaten next to nothing for about three days. Maybe four days! I'm going to kill you."

They started fighting somewhere over there, somewhere near Kenora. They battled tooth and nail. They fought in a number of different places along the way, even where Sault Ste Marie now stands. At the rapids. That really happened. That was all land then. At that time there was no channel of water flowing there.

First, Nanabush would hit the bear; then the bear would hit Nanabush. One time, Nanabush threw the bear so hard against the ground he broke the earth, and water began to flow through. That in fact is the reason the water now flows past Sault Ste Marie.

Finally, Nanabush said to his mother, "You go on ahead and stay there. When I get there too, I will kill this bear." As soon as the word was given, she was gone.

She could hear them battling in the distance. At one point, the bear sent Nanabush flying with such force that he landed on his mother, causing her to fall backwards onto her rump. That is why the lake there is called "The Old Lady Sat Down."

They fought all along the way. The evidence of it is still there. At the place that is now called Sudbury they hurled rocks at one another.

Where they pulled boulders up from the earth, ore was later found. Where they dragged each other along the ground, depressions were made in the land.

Eventually, Nanabush killed the bear, in the general vicinity of Parry Sound.

Meanwhile, his mother came along behind, carrying supplies. She made a fire and put a pot of water over it. Nanabush butchered the bear. When it was cooked, he ate and ate. But he ate too much and very soon suffered the runs.

"Oh!" He ran over there. "Ah!" Such discomfort. He could not stop going to the toilet. When he sat down to defecate, blood also flowed. He couldn't find anything to use to wipe himself, so he grabbed a sapling and used that. Then he stuck the sapling—with the blood and feces on it—into the earth, somewhere near Parry Sound.

A red willow grew at that spot. Its colour came from the blood of Nanabush.

That is how the red willows came to be (Johnston 1995: 33–7).

tale or one of the new stories of Nanabush that continue to appear. Finally, we learn that the red willows got their colour from Nanabush's bloody feces. This is a wonderful example of a view of nature that recognizes holistic connections between the beautiful and the ugly or painful.

Chaos and Order

Like origin stories, trickster tales often attribute aspects of our world to destructive activity. And so the trickster invents the bow and arrow, breaks the teeth in women's vaginas to make intercourse possible, and introduces death. Despite his association with chaos, then, the trickster also brings a kind of order to the world.

The Yoruba trickster Eshu, for example, is constantly playing pranks in the hope that disorder will result. But his tricks work only when the people forget the importance of community stability and become greedy or lazy, or behave stupidly. In one story Eshu wears a special hat, black on one side and red on the other, while walking between two friends who, each seeing only one side of the hat, fight over what colour it is and wind up bitter enemies for no good reason.

"Red Willows," by contemporary Anishinaubae artist David Johnson (with permission of the Royal Ontario Museum).

Thus trickster stories can play many roles: they can show us how we *should* behave, or should *not*; they can help to explain the origins of the world, and connect a community more deeply to its place; and they are almost always entertaining and provocative. They embody the contradictions of humanity: our weaknesses and strengths, selfishness and compassion, humiliations and triumphs.

It's also worth noting again that almost all the traditional trickster figures we know of are male. One reason could be the fact that until recently the academics who recorded the stories were invariably male: perhaps they had no interest in female trickster stories; or perhaps such stories were the preserve of women and the male scholars never inquired about them. On the other hand, it may be that in some communities the trickster's typical activities—hunting, travelling, unrestrained sex—were in fact associated only with men.

Practice

Ritual

If you ask what is the greatest thing
I will tell you
It is people, people, people.

—Maori proverb (in Webber-Dreadon 2002: 258)

Rituals perform the same functions in every culture. To an extent, they identify and remind us of what is important to the community we live in. In religious terms, their purpose is to communicate in some way with gods, ancestors, or spirits. At the same time, rituals remain rooted in *human* needs and relationships.

Varieties

Around the world, people affirm their faith through daily domestic rituals, many of which involve food. Thus Jews and Muslims observe kosher and halal regulations; many Buddhists set aside a portion of each meal for their ancestors; and the Anishinaubae traditionally put a small amount of food in a dish for the spirits. To maintain the animal species they rely on for food, some Australian Aborigines sing the song of the ancestor while rubbing a pile of stones.

More complex rituals mark critical moments in the life of individuals (birth, marriage, death), the community (departure of a powerful leader, liberation from slavery, completion of a great project), or the natural world (annual cycles, great disasters, rich harvests). Sometimes these rituals mark transformations, and sometimes they help to bring transformation about. It is this less frequent, more dramatic type of ritual that will be discussed here.

Meaning and Structure

When someone who has been ill recovers after a ritual healer asks an ancestor spirit to remove the illness, does the healer (or the patient, or the community) believe that the illness has actually been removed by the spirit? Similar questions may be asked about non-Indigenous rituals. To what extent does a young Jewish girl change, at the moment of her Bat Mitzvah, into an adult woman? How many Catholics believe they drink the literal blood of Christ when they take communion?

Many people, past and present, have believed in the literal truth of their religious stories and rituals. Once again, though, we often separate Indigenous traditions from other world religions by treating their ritual practices as "magic" rather than "religion," implying that "they" believe in things that obviously are not true, whereas "we" do not. In fact, many people, Indigenous and non-Indigenous, believe at least some of their religious traditions to be literally true, while many others in both groups take a more figurative approach.

In either case, when we look closely at the rituals of any Indigenous culture, what we find is a system of formal activities through which community members relate to the world and to one another. Such activities tap into their deepest beliefs about the origins of the world, the existence of order, and the beginnings of life. Repeating them therefore serves in some way to recreate key aspects of the world, of order, of life. In this sense, we can see ritual as an indicator both of the human need for meaning and structure in a world that is often random and frightening, and of the human capacity to create such meaning and structure.

Rites of Passage

> All people who go to the sacred bush benefit from it. They may be observers; they may be priests; they may be the initiate. Only we concentrate on the initiate most. Yet everybody is involved, particularly the priests, for there is a belief . . . that we are reborning ourselves. Even we priests, we are getting another rebirth.
>
> —Ositola, **Yoruba** (in Drewal 2002: 133)

The Journey

Many cultures regard life as a journey or quest; this perspective forms the central metaphor of a huge number of popular songs ("Like a Rolling Stone," "Proud Mary," "Born to Run," "Road to Nowhere"), and can also be seen in the sacred Yoruba text in the box below. Rituals highlight points along the way, but they also constitute journeys on their own. This understanding is most evident in rites of passage, which explicitly mark a change of state and often involve *literal* journeys.

Typically, such rituals take participants away from their community to a new place with unfamiliar rules, where some sort of transformation occurs. For males this place is often outside, in the forest or the bush or the desert, whereas for females it is often a domestic space of some sort. Once the ritual is complete the participants return home, often with a physical change, such as a tattoo or scar, to symbolize their new mode of being. While away, they exist in a kind of in-between or "liminal" state, after the death of the old self but before the birth of the new.

In South Africa, young **Pondos** preparing to become sacred healers are moved into a special hut. If they go into town before the ritual is completed, their faces and bodies must be covered in white—the colour of transformation in many parts of Africa—to indicate that they are in the midst of a journey between the realms of the living and the ancestors. This initiation is most often undertaken by women, and is complete only when the initiates receive a dream of a particular animal, the incarnation of the ancestor who will authorize them to become healers.

Many Anishinaubae undertake a similar initiation, known as a **vision quest**. After years of preparation, a boy on the verge of adulthood travels far from home to a designated site in the wilderness where the spirits dwell. Typically, this is the first time he has ever been completely alone. He has no food, only water. He endures cold, hunger, and fear. With luck, the spirits will give him dreams or visions that reveal his true self and the role he is to play in his community. After several days, an adult male will arrive and take the initiate home. If the religious leader determines that the boy experienced true spirit visions during the quest, the ritual is complete and the boy is recognized as an adult man.

Document

Yoruba Verse

This verse from the sacred literature of the Yoruba (known as the Odu Ifa) describes life as a quest.

A small child works his way off the edge of his sleeping mat.
A bird soars high above it all.
They divined for our elderly people,
When they were preparing to leave heaven to go to the world. They said, what are we going to do?
They asked themselves, where are we going?
We are going in search of knowledge, truth, and justice.
In accordance with our destiny,
At the peak of the hill
We were delayed.
We are going to meet success.
We will arrive on earth knowledgeable.
We will arrive on earth in beauty.
We are searching for knowledge continuously.
Knowledge has no end (Drewal 2002: 129).

Young Pondo women from Transkei in South Africa during their initiation to become sacred healers (Daniel Lainé).

Behind the Curtain

The rite of passage for Wiradjuri males in eastern Australia also involves a journey, along with fear and pain. At the appointed time, the women and children of the village are covered with branches and blankets. They hear a roaring sound, identified as the voice of the spirit being Daramulun, who takes the boys away to the bush, where he will devour them and regurgitate them back as men. The boys are led away and each one has an incisor tooth knocked out. Then fires appear and the boys are told that Daramulun is coming to burn them.

At the height of their terror, however, the boys receive a shock. Their blankets are removed and the men of the village reveal that they have been acting as Daramulun all along. It was the men who took the boys' teeth, set the fires, and made the voice of the spirit being. It's much like Toto pulling aside the curtain to show Dorothy that the Great and Powerful Oz is just an old man, except that in this case the deceivers reveal themselves.

When the boys return to the village, therefore, they are truly transformed. They have been initiated into a secret (male) knowledge about the spirit world, and have formed bonds with one another through their shared experience. Returning to the village as men, they are given new adult names and take up residence outside their parents' homes.

But doesn't this ritual expose the community's religious beliefs as false? Not necessarily. According to Sam Gill, its point is to demonstrate that what is genuinely meaningful lies beyond the surface of reality. By exposing their trickery, the men produce "a disenchantment with a naive view of reality, that is, with the view that things are what they appear to be" (Gill 1982: 81). In this way, the boys experience a true death of their youthful selves.

Sacrifice

> We are imitating what the gods or holy people have done. It is a return to the beginning.
>
> —Blackhorse Mitchell, Navajo (in Beck et al. 1992 [1977]: 76)

In Mel Gibson's film *Apocalypto* (2006), Mayan priests cut out the beating hearts of captured villagers and make offerings of them to appease the gods and end the famine that is afflicting the people. Although it is true that some Indigenous cultures did perform human sacrifices, *Apocalypto* perpetuates common misunderstandings about the nature of sacrifice.

Bears, Men, and Cows

Sacrificial rituals are extremely common. At one time the central religious ceremony of the Ainu of northern Japan, for example, was bear sacrifice. They would capture a cub, raise it for two or three years, shoot it with ceremonial arrows, and finally kill it. The carcass was specially prepared—often the head was emptied out and filled with flowers—and then cooked and eaten by the entire village.

Among the Aboriginal peoples of the North American plains, the **Sun Dance** is an annual ritual lasting several days. Inside a specially created lodge, participants dance to the point of exhaustion while the community provides support. The Sioux Sun Dance includes a kind of self-sacrifice: male dancers fast, pierce their chests and backs, and attach themselves to a central pole with ropes tied to sticks that are inserted through the piercings. They may be partially or entirely suspended off the ground, and they dance until they pass out or their fastenings tear loose.

In Africa, the **Nuer** regularly sacrifice an ox to celebrate, to heal, and to atone for moral transgressions. The **Xhosa** perform a similar but more complex ritual when a young woman falls ill and a **diviner** determines that she is being punished by an ancestor spirit. To restore good relations between the woman's home and the ancestor, a cow is consecrated and then speared. The animal's cry opens up the path of communication with the spirit world. Inside the woman's home, a special part of the animal is cooked. One piece of the meat is given to the woman, who sucks it and throws it to the back of the house as a sign that she is throwing away her illness. She is then given a second piece, which she holds while being chastised for behaving in a manner displeasing to the ancestor(s). She consumes the meat and is congratulated for having "eaten the ancestor." Then the rest of the cow is cooked and eaten by the entire community in celebration.

Community and Ritual Action

When we compare these rituals to the sacrifice in *Apocalypto*, two major differences become clear. First, there is no communal participation in the film's ritual. Yet communal participation is crucial for the Ainu, the Sioux, and the Xhosa. Everyone becomes involved in some way, whether by providing support or simply by sharing in the group meal. The ritual ultimately brings people together. By contrast, in the film the ritual helps to tear the community apart.

The second difference is that *Apocalypto* presents the sacrifice as a simple offering made in return for some reward. The Mayans in the film want food, and apparently the gods want human hearts—it's a simple exchange. Yet in many cultures, the object of sacrifice itself is clearly not of central importance. When necessary, the Nuer can replace the ox with a cucumber, and if the Xhosa have no suitable cow, they can use beer instead.

The fact that such substitutions are possible suggests that, in some cases at least, the materials involved are far less meaningful than the ritual actions themselves. When the Xhosa sacrifice a cow, why don't they just kill and eat it? Why go through all the complex stages? What appears to be primarily at stake here is the woman's behaviour in relation to notions of social order set down by the ancestors and reinforced by (male) ritual elders. The community thus shares both in naming the transgression that led to her illness and in the meal generated by the ritual that heals her.

Why is a special lodge built for the Sun Dance? Its creation replicates the creation of the world, and is accompanied by songs that tell of this creation. The pole used in the dance is a newly cut tree; in its state between life and death and its physical positioning at the centre of the lodge, it links the material world to the world of the spirits. Physically attached to this tree, the dancers are thus also tied to the spirits and to the earliest times.

Why did the Ainu fill the bear's head with flowers? Because the animal was the mountain god in disguise, and the ritual killing of his bear form was necessary to release the god's spirit back to his own realm. The Ainu were not offering a bear to the god; rather, from primordial times onward the god became a bear, over and over again, as a gift to the Ainu. The flowers were an expression of the community's gratitude.

In each case, the ritual actions relate to the spiritual and sometimes physical establishment of the community, or of the world itself. Sacrificial practices thus play a key role in (re-)creating order and meaning. In re-enacting ancient events, these rituals join people to the past, and yet they also respond to current situations and needs. Thus they reflect the common Indigenous sense of time as rhythmic, neither purely linear nor entirely cyclical. Individuals and communities are always changing; nothing ever repeats exactly. But in the course of their journeys, people do need to be replenished, and through ritual they return to a source that sustains them.

Cultural Expressions

Among the art forms traditionally produced by Indigenous cultures are architecture, songs, baskets, clothing, statues, paintings, drums, pipes, mats, headdresses, amulets, masks, and tapestries. In each community, some art forms will exist almost entirely for religious purposes, some will be entwined with religion only at specific times, and others may have very little to do with religion.

What You See

> If you don't live the things that go with it, then it's only a design. It's not a ***moko***.
>
> —George Tamihana Nuku, Maori (in Mitchell 2003)

With a good deal of Indigenous creative work, what you see is not what you get. In some cases, you don't see anything at all when the work is done, because the piece has been consumed by the same process that brought it into being.

A key element of some death rituals in Papua New Guinea, for example, is the creation and burning of delicate sculptures made from fibre, wood, bark, and feathers. Likewise, Navajo sand paintings must be erased the day they are made if they are to perform their healing function; through ceremony, the cosmic pictures become identified with the patient's sickness, and it is only through its destruction that health can be restored.

Other works, such as those discussed below, are created from materials that decay over time. These works are often understood as living things, which can—and should—dissolve back into the earth when their time is done. Even when the work remains, it may be relatively bereft of meaning (and life) when we look at it, especially if it is completely removed from its native context. If we don't know what an African mask or Native American basket is used for, and why, we can't understand what it represents.

In this respect, Indigenous "art" is fundamentally about relationships. There is a network that connects an object to the person(s) who created it, the ritual in which it is used, the people it is made to serve, and the stories that underlie their worldview. These relationships are vital to the culture in question, and some or all aspects of the network—object, creation, ritual, stories—may be considered religious. To illustrate the complex ways in which Indigenous art forms are related to Indigenous religion, we will consider three examples: weaving, carving, and building.

Weaving

> It all starts from the beginning with roots. How the basket makes itself. Like two people meeting. . . . What I'm talking about when I'm talking about my baskets is my life, the stories, the rules, how this things is living, what they do to you.
>
> —Mabel McKay, **Pomo** (in Sarris 1992: 23–4)

To weave is to intertwine, to connect. Even in modern English, we speak of the "social fabric," the "warp and weft" of history, friendships, or community life. In most cultures, weaving is a social activity; weavers work together, helping (and watching) one another, sharing stories, passing on their skills to younger generations, and the products of their work often have both a religious meaning and a practical purpose. These functions reflect and reinforce the bonds among community members, as well as the bonds between them and their environment, ancestors, and gods.

Sacred Thread

In Maori tradition, all weavers are female. A prospective weaver is selected as a baby and a special prayer is spoken over her. As she grows up, she learns from her mother, aunts, and grandmothers, until the art becomes a natural part of her. But her destiny is not fixed. The more she learns, the more the women *discourage* her from weaving. This is a test. The girl must demonstrate her commitment. When her elders are satisfied, she is at last initiated into the collective of weavers. Only then does she come to understand why the weft used to create the pattern and design in Maori weaving is called "sacred thread."

Maori weaving traditions include not only physical techniques but rituals. The materials used must be specially prepared; sex is prohibited the night before dyeing fibres; no food may be consumed while weaving; and no strangers can view any work until it is completed.

Maori weaving patterns and techniques were given to humanity by Niwareka, daughter of the lightning god Uetonga. The goddess of weaving is Hine-te-iwaiwa, who also presides over healing and childbirth and is often associated with the moon and menstruation. The colours used—black, red, and white—symbolize the forces of creation. Black represents the realm of potential being, the darkness from which the Earth emerged; white represents the process of coming into being, the energies that make life possible; and red represents the realm of being and light, the physical world itself. The sacred thread thus runs not only through the people's garments but also through time and the various realms of existence, entwining the Maori in the cosmos itself.

Undying Cloth

The final product of weaving also has religious significance. Around the world, a key function of clothing is to declare who we are—Muslim or Hindu, artist or lawyer, man or woman—and how we fit into the "social fabric." Yet clothing can hide as much as it reveals, helping us to construct a public face while obscuring certain aspects of ourselves.

Many people think of African textiles as colourful, but the most common traditional cloth is actually white. Among the Bunu Yoruba, white may represent anything from human secretions (milk, semen) to aspects of nature (air, water) and religious phenomena (spirits, heaven). White cloth—traditionally woven by Bunu women only—is thus often used to bridge the gap between the physical and spirit worlds, between living people and their ancestors. It is worn to remedy disorders caused by destructive spirits (miscarriage, anger, illness); wrapped around the trunks of sacred trees to appease the spirits living inside them; wound around a pot of objects to help bring rain; and used for burial shrouds to facilitate the deceased's rebirth as an ancestor. In short, white cloth helps members of the Bunu community cope with pain, disruption, and loss.

Spirit Baskets

Baskets figure in the sacred stories of many cultures. The Hebrew Bible tells how the infant Moses' mother put him in a basket and set it in the river, to be found by Pharaoh's daughter (Exodus 2: 3–5). Tane, the Maori god of light and wisdom, brought three baskets of knowledge from heaven to earth (knowledge of ritual matters; of acts of harm and aggression among people; and of peace and well-being). A Navajo story describes the origin of small birds: a woman plucked the feathers of several winged monsters and put them in her basket, but when she passed through a forbidden territory filled with sunflowers, the feathers were transformed into tiny birds and flew out of the basket.

Mabel McKay (1907–91) was a traditional Pomo healer whose practice was interwoven with basket-making: she gave each of her patients a miniature basket (sometimes the size of a pea), or instruction in making one. In Pomo communities, men traditionally wove the heavy baskets used for purposes such as fishing; baskets that had explicitly religious purposes were woven by women. As in most Indigenous communities, rituals were prescribed for obtaining and preparing the materials, and the weaving process was surrounded by restrictions. Thus weavers were forbidden to make baskets at all when menstruating or consuming alcohol. They were also forbidden to include representations of humans in their designs, or to reproduce the designs of medicine weavers such as Mabel.

This last rule reflected the fact that those designs were the product of personal spiritual visions. Such visions were for the weaver alone, and were relevant to particular situations. Although Mabel followed the traditions of her culture, everything she produced was unique. Even more than usual, then, her baskets were living things that both reflected and communicated her sacred visions. When asked if she had been taught to weave by her grandmother or mother, she replied: "No, spirit teach me, since I was small child" (Sarris 1992: 25).

Carvings

> What annoys me is that a lot of totem poles that go up have no plaque or information. People who come by wonder, "Who did this? What's it all about?" Every time I carve a totem pole, there's always a kind of signature to identify my family or my nation, the Nisga'a.
>
> —Norman Tait (1993: 11), **Nisga'a**

Masks

The difference that context makes in understanding the meaning of cultural objects is well illustrated by African masks. In the museums where non-Africans usually see them, they are mere shadows of themselves, but they come alive when used as intended, in ritual activities. Some aspects of a mask's meaning may be apparent even to outsiders, but we must be cautious in our interpretations. Although masks are typically meant to bring a spirit into the community, in African traditions the supreme being is never represented by any physical object: therefore masks can relate only to lesser deities. Also, the fact that certain masks clearly represent certain animals does not mean (as was once assumed) that the people who use them worship those animals. In Mali, both the Dogon and Bamana cultures use antelope masks in agricultural ceremonies that have little to do with actual antelopes, but the symbolic meanings are not identical: for the Dogon the antelope represents hard work, whereas for the Bamana its horns symbolize tall sprouts of grain.

When we focus only on the form of a mask, without reference to its use, we can easily miss the meaning of certain critical elements. For example, the fact that the intricately carved Epa masks of the Yoruba are extremely heavy reflects their function in rituals celebrating the male passage into adulthood. The strength required to dance with such a mask is a literal representation of the wearer's ability to take on his responsibilities as an adult member of the community.

Another unseen but equally important aspect of the mask is the process of its creation. Carvers have traditionally been male, trained as apprentices to master carvers. Ritual is no less central in the creation of a mask than in the ceremony for which it is made. Typically, for example, carvers must work in isolation while fasting, abstaining from any sexual activity, and avoiding contact both with women and with anything connected to death.

Totem Poles

The **totem poles** produced by the Aboriginal peoples of the Pacific Northwest Coast pose similar challenges of context and symbolism. The various markings and carving styles are specific to particular communities and locations; those familiar with these traditions would immediately know, on encountering a totem pole, whose territory they had entered.

Yet for many years now, totem poles have been removed from their homes. Poles from different cultures, and with different functions, are often displayed together in places such as Stanley Park in Vancouver. Some groups have fought this trend—in 2006 the **Haisla** of northern British Columbia successfully retrieved from Sweden's Museum of Ethnography a sacred totem pole that had been stolen from them almost 80 years earlier.

Ironically, the word "totem" is derived from the Anishinaubae word *dodaem*, which has been variously translated as "heart," "nourishment," and "kinship group." But the Anishinaubae (who live thousands of kilometres to the east) never made totem poles, and the cultures of the Pacific Northwest themselves never used the word "totem." The **Tsimshian** people—to pick just one example—call such a pole a *ptsan*.

Normally carved from a single cedar tree, a pole can survive for a century or so. It is traditionally regarded as a living thing and is allowed to rot naturally; some believe that to physically preserve a totem pole is to interfere with the natural order of the world. Certain communities even forbid the "preservation" of poles in drawings or photographs.

The meaning of a particular pole depends on its intended use. Some were designed primarily to serve as supporting structures or grave markers; others, as symbols of status or power. Most, however, tell stories. Some stories are mainly historical, recounting achievements, murders, arguments, victories, defeats, marriages, ancestral lineages, and so on. But other stories are explicitly religious, relating to particular beliefs, or to the tales of supernatural figures such as Raven or Thunderbird (responsible for great storms).

The photos below show two totem poles. The pole on the left may appear more ornate than the other but is actually much simpler, depicting only two main figures. Grizzly Bear is at the base, holding a human, which usually represents self-preservation or survival. Thunderbird, a symbol of strength, is at the top. The pole's relative simplicity reflects the fact that it was one of a pair created primarily to support the roof beam of a house.

The pole on the right, carved by Norman Tait (with Robert and Isaac Tait), tells a more complicated story. The family is represented by the man at the top, who is holding Eagle to signify their clan. Five disembodied faces represent five ancestral brothers who once saw two beavers emerge from their home, remove their skin, and become men. The figures told the five brothers that they were being slaughtered by the humans, so the brothers sang a sad song that froze the river, protecting the beavers (who can be seen climbing the pole). This is how the Tait ancestors came to adopt the Beaver for their crest.

Totem poles in Vancouver's Stanley Park reflect different creative ends: to support a roof (left), and to tell the story of the Tait family crest (right) (© imagebroker / Alamy; © Douglas Lander / Alamy).

Moko

Maori carvings are rarely displayed outside their original physical context. This is because many of them are an integral part of the ancestral meeting house, or *whare whakairo* ("carved house"), for which they were created. The figures that decorate these houses are ancestors such as Tihori, of the Ngati Awa in Bay of Plenty, New Zealand. The carving of Tihori in the Bay of Plenty meeting house holds a weapon used in hand-to-hand combat, which symbolizes his role as a warrior. Tihori is also covered with traditional Maori tattoos, or **moko** (literally, "to strike" or "to tap"). The same markings can be seen on some contemporary Maori men and women, including the famous **Tuhoe** activist Tame Iti.

Originally chiselled (not just inked) into the skin, these markings identify both the individual and his or her relationship to the community. Some *moko* elements may signify education level, personal and family rank, tribal history, or ancestral connections; others may simply be marks of beauty or ferocity in battle. Traditionally, women were allowed tattoos only on or around their lips and chin, while men could receive markings on their entire face.

A key design that is repeated on Iti's face is the *koru*, or frond/spiral, the most common (and important) of all *moko* elements. A Maori proverb—"As one fern frond dies, another is born to

Tame Iti, an outspoken and sometimes controversial Maori activist who is well known for his full facial *moko* (© George Steinmetz / Corbis).

take its place"—suggests that the *koru*'s primary meaning has to do with birth, regeneration, and sustainability, but that it can also represent the ancestors who gave birth to the Maori and continue to sustain them.

Beyond this symbolism, the art of *moko* itself is directly linked to the Maori ancestors. Uetonga, the god of lightning, developed *moko* in imitation of the marks that his grandfather Ru, god of earthquakes, had left on the face of the primal parent, the Earth. One day Uetonga's daughter Niwareka (who brought weaving to humanity) fell in love with the Maori ancestral chief Mataora. The two married and lived together until Mataora, in a jealous rage, hit Niwareka and she fled home to the underworld. In sorrow, Mataora followed her and came upon Uetonga tattooing a man by cutting deep patterns into his flesh. When Mataora asked to have his own story marked on his face in the same way, Uetonga agreed.

To ease the pain of the carving, Mataora sang of his loss and regret, and the sound reached Niwareka, who forgave him. The couple reunited and received permission to return to the surface world. But Mataora neglected to leave an appropriate offering for the guardian of the portal between the two realms, and so from then on living humans were forbidden to enter the underworld. *Moko*—in fact, all traditional carvings—thus remind Maori people of their ancestors, the importance of meeting one's obligations, the need to treat one another with respect, the power of the natural world, and the boundaries between life and death.

Buildings

> The way into the shrine was a round hole at the side of a hill, just a little bigger than the round opening into a henhouse. Worshippers and those who came to seek knowledge from the god crawled on their belly through the hole and found themselves in a dark, endless space in the presence of Agbala.
>
> —Chinua Achebe (1996 [1958]: 12), **Igbo**

Ancestral Houses

The *whare whakairo* is part of a larger complex called a **marae**, a cleared area containing structures such as a dining room, shelters, and a site where the recently deceased are placed to lie in state. The *marae* is the religious and social home of a Maori person, the site of ritual ceremonies such as weddings, funerals, family celebrations, and formal welcomes for visitors. Authority on the *marae* is held by the community's elders, who use the space to pass on traditions, stories, and arts such as weaving and carving.

As in the case of African masks, the builders and carvers of the *whare whakairo* were traditionally male; the rest of the community was banned from the site until the work was officially declared complete. The workers operated under ritual restrictions and obligations from the moment the first trees for the building were cut down. Traditionally, *marae* artists could be put to death if the community did not judge their work to be acceptable.

The location of the *marae* is critical: it must be a place where previous generations carried out the religious and social activities that continue to define and restore the world itself. This connection to the land is not merely metaphorical: it is Maori custom to bury the placenta in the ground at birth, as well as the bones after death. The *marae* is also identified with a single common ancestor to whom all members of the community are ostensibly connected.

This identification is given physical form in the *whare whakairo*, which represents the body of the ancestor. On the front of the house, where the roof slopes meet, is the mask-head of the ancestor; the boards along the front of each side of the roof are his arms; the central ridge of the roof is his spine, with ribs/rafters spreading out from it; the front door is his mouth; and the window is his eye. Non-Maori cannot grasp what such a building truly means to a community without understanding its cultural roots.

Three Points, and a Shrine

That said, the attention to detail in the *whare whakairo* is so great that even a casual observer might recognize that such a building has great significance. Many other Indigenous religious structures—including most of those in Africa and North America—are so plain that it may be difficult for outsiders to understand how they could have any deeper meaning.

There are three points at issue here. First, the majority of Indigenous people throughout history have performed all or most of their rituals outdoors, in the natural world. Specific locations can be crucial; when the purpose of a ritual is to make contact with particular entities, for example, the ritual must generally be performed where they dwell or intersect with our world. Although some communities may erect a simple structure to mark such sites, to do anything more elaborate would in many instances not be in keeping with their religious worldview.

Second, it may be helpful to think about the functions of the elaborate religious structures erected by various non-Indigenous groups. One reason the Catholic Church blanketed Europe with grand cathedrals was the simple fact that for a long time it was the ultimate authority in that part of the world. Such buildings symbolized the Church's political power. Small Indigenous communities that did not rule entire continents had no occasion for such displays.

Finally, we come back to the point that what you see is often not what you get. An African shrine may contain nothing more than a couple of small, plain, human-shaped carvings, but if the community understands that from time to time they are inhabited by particular ancestors or spirits, then at those times the figures become visible manifestations of the gods.

Other shrine statues may have quite a different meaning, however. Consider the **mbari** shrine in the photo on the right. How would you interpret these figures? Are they gods? Which one is the most important? Who is the man sitting in front of the statues, and why is he there?

A *mbari* shrine in southeastern Nigeria (Daniel Lainé).

The figure in the lower middle represents the founder of the community, with his wife above and servants on either side. He was renowned as a great healer some two centuries ago, but was attacked by another community and forced to flee across the marshes, carrying his wife on his shoulders. Relics of the healer, kept with the statues, protect the community from disease. Because most of the *mbari* shrines in this region have been destroyed, an elder stands guard at all times. But this is a modern development. Traditionally, *mbari*—like totem poles—were never repaired; after several rains, they would simply dissolve back into the earth.

Hogans

The Navajo **hogan** is our final example of a structure that is much more than it appears. It is also the only one that is not "explicitly" religious: although many ceremonies are performed there, a hogan is also simply a traditional dwelling in which any Navajo family might live. As such it is the site of all the daily activities that go on in a home, some of which are religious and some of which are not.

Before a newly constructed hogan is occupied, the community will perform the Blessingway ritual, which includes a song that refers to "a holy home" (Gill 1982: 10), although this term merely hints at what the hogan represents. The point becomes clearer when we learn that the Blessingway is in many ways the foundation of Navajo religious thought and practice. Before any other ritual can be conducted, some version of the Blessingway must be performed.

The Blessingway song names four divine beings: Earth, Mountain Woman, Water Woman, and Corn Woman. But it also speaks of everyday things: vegetation, fabrics, long life, happiness. In this way it represents a joining of perspectives, the cosmic with the mundane.

Document

From the Nightway Prayer (Navajo)

Like the Blessingway song performed as part of the creation of a new hogan, the first part of this prayer connects the ordinary with the extraordinary through the central symbol of the home. And like the Yoruba verse in the box on page 51, its concluding section envisions life as a journey.

In Tse 'gíhi
In the house made of the dawn
In the house made of the evening twilight
In the house made of the dark cloud
In the house made of the he-rain
In the house made of the dark mist
In the house made of the she-rain
In the house made of pollen
In the house made of grasshoppers
Where the dark mist curtains the doorway
The path to which is on the rainbow . . .
In beauty (happily) I walk
With beauty before me, I walk
With beauty behind me, I walk
With beauty below me, I walk
With beauty above me, I walk
With beauty all around me, I walk
It is finished (again) in beauty
It is finished in beauty
It is finished in beauty
It is finished in beauty
(Matthews 1995 [1902]: 143–5)

The cosmic–mundane connection is furthered by the song's identification of the four deities with the four supporting poles of the Hogan; in Navajo cosmology, the same deities provide support for the world itself. In fact, the Navajo understand the creation of the world to have begun with the building of a structure; which is to say that the world *is* a structure—a hogan. It should come as no surprise that creation was accompanied by the first performance of the Blessingway ritual. Thus to build a hogan is to reproduce the origin of all things, and to fulfill one's ongoing (sacred) responsibility to continually make and re-make the world.

Despite its apparent simplicity, then, the Navajo hogan—like Pomo baskets and Nisga'a totem poles, like Yoruba white cloth and Dogon shrines, like Maori tattoos and *whare whakairo*—is a vital link between present and past, between community and place, between our world and that of the spirits.

Colonialism

"Colonialism" refers both to the process in which people from one place establish and maintain a settlement in another, and to the effects of this process on any people already living there. Typically, those effects include their subjugation, if not removal, and the imposition of new laws, economies, and social practices that are often modelled on those of the colonists' home territory.

An enormous amount of colonial activity occurred between the fifteenth and twentieth centuries, when western Europeans were exploring parts of the world such as Africa, North and South America, Australia, and the islands of the Pacific Ocean. Until this activity began, western Europe was a relatively insignificant region in terms of global influence; afterwards, it was the centre of the world.

The quests for power and profit have often been the key factors driving colonialism. Religion has also played a critical role, however, both as a motivating factor and as a justification. The consequences for the religious traditions of the conquered peoples have been profound. It is not possible to understand Indigenous traditions today, therefore, without understanding colonialism.

Invasion

> They do not bear arms, and do not know them, for I showed them a sword, they took it by the edge and cut themselves out of ignorance. . . . They would make fine servants. . . . With fifty men we could subjugate them and make them do whatever we want.
>
> —Christopher Columbus, Italian (in Zinn 1995: 1)

Columbus

The journals of Christopher Columbus record the start of the most devastating colonial project in history. His first contact with the **Arawaks** foretells much of what happened later: "[O]n the first Island which I found, I took some of the natives by force in order that they might . . . give me information of whatever there is in these parts" (Zinn 1995: 1).

What Columbus most wanted to know was where the gold was. Unfortunately for the Arawaks, there was very little gold to find, but Columbus was not deterred. Those who managed to bring him a specified amount of gold were given a copper token to hang around their necks; those who were then found without a token had their hands cut off and were left to bleed to death.

Eventually Columbus came to see that the islands' most valuable "resources" were the people themselves, and he shipped them back to Europe by the boatload. Thus he exclaimed: "Let us in the name of the Holy Trinity go on sending all the slaves that can be sold" (Zinn 1995: 4). Within two years of his arrival, roughly half of the estimated original population of 250,000 had been either exported or killed. A century later, all of the Arawaks on the islands were gone.

Genocides

Colonial efforts elsewhere—in Africa, Australia, New Zealand, the Americas—were similarly catastrophic. Millions of people, representing thousands of distinct cultures, were wiped out.

In Africa, as in the West Indies, the chief source of wealth for the Europeans was the population itself. By the late nineteenth century, upwards of 20 million Africans had been taken from their homes and sent to the Americas as slaves, though only about 11 million made it there alive. Scholars estimate that by the time the trans-Atlantic slave trade ended, the population of Africa had been reduced by half.

In Australia, less than half of the original population of about 500,000 remained after just a few years of contact with Europeans. The southeast—where the First Fleet arrived in 1788—was hit the hardest. During the first year of colonization, approximately two-thirds of the estimated 250,000 Aboriginals in the region were killed by a smallpox epidemic. By 1850, 96 per cent were dead.

In the Americas, records suggest that by 1600 as many as 90 million Indigenous people—more than 90 per cent of the original population—had died as a direct result of the Europeans' presence. More people had been killed than existed in all of Europe at the time (approximately 60 to 80 million). The destruction of the original inhabitants of the Americas was genocide on a scale that has not been seen before or since. The biggest single cause of the depopulation of both Australia and the Americas was disease, but other factors included military action, slavery, mistreatment, starvation or malnutrition, and loss of will to live. And the destruction has not ended yet. Indigenous citizens are still expendable, for instance, when governments want more land.

"Masters of the Continent"

In many parts of North America, European occupation was initially accomplished through relatively peaceful negotiations with the original inhabitants. After all, the first settlers were greatly outnumbered, and the Indigenous people possessed valuable knowledge and skills. As the settler population grew, however, and the Indigenous population declined, negotiation became less important; eventually it ceased entirely in most instances, and Native people living on land that Europeans wanted were either forcibly removed or simply killed.

Colonists justified this behaviour in many ways, some of which were explicitly religious. Many equated their situation with that of the Jews who were ordered by God to destroy the native inhabitants of Canaan. Only then could they inherit the Promised Land.

The notion of ***terra nullius*** ("no one's land") was also invoked by European settlers. Colonists argued variously that Indigenous people were not "really" using the land; or that they could not own the land because they did not have any concept of ownership; or that because of their "primitive" nature, they did not count as people and therefore the land on which they lived was technically unoccupied. All these arguments were, of course, specious, self-serving, and inherently racist.

By the late nineteenth century, it was widely assumed that the Indigenous people of North America were on the way to extinction. A newspaper editor in South Dakota named L. Frank Baum—the future author of *The Wizard of Oz*—wrote an editorial in December 1890 that carried the theory of the "vanishing Indian" to a brutally logical conclusion:

> The Whites, by law of conquest, by justice of civilization, are masters of the American continent, and the best safety of the frontier settlements will be secured by the total annihilation of the few remaining Indians. Why not annihilation? Their glory has fled, their spirit broken, their manhood effaced; better that they die than live the miserable wretches that they are (Baum 1890).

In effect, Baum was calling for his fellow Euro-Americans to complete the genocide begun by Columbus.

Just nine days after Baum's editorial, the US Calvary moved to relocate an encampment of Lakota Sioux near Wounded Knee Creek, South Dakota, in order to free up the land for colonial settlers. The result was a massacre. More than 300 Sioux were killed, among them unarmed women and children; some were shot as they tried to run away.

Around the world, Wounded Knee remains a powerful symbol of colonialism and its consequences for Indigenous people. A similar conjunction of land acquisition and extreme violence can be found at some point in the history of virtually every encounter between colonial interests and Indigenous people.

Conversion

> I thought I was being taken just for a few days. I can recall seeing my mother standing on the side of the road with her head in her hands, crying, and me in the black FJ Holden wondering why she was so upset. . . . I see myself as that little girl, crying myself to sleep at night, crying and wishing I could go home to my family. Everything's gone, the loss of your culture, the loss of your family, all these things have a big impact.
>
> —Lyn Austin, Australian Aborigine (in Cooke 2008)

As a result of colonialism, the majority of the world's Indigenous peoples were converted to the religion of one colonial power or another. That religion was usually some form of Christianity, but other missionary religions took hold in some areas of the world, notably Islam in parts of Africa and Buddhism throughout Asia.

Accurate information on adherence to Indigenous religions is virtually non-existent. Such data are normally obtained from national censuses. On the topic of religion, however, many countries have had trouble either with their census questions or with the answer choices they offer. In Indonesia, for example, Indigenous religions are not recognized by law; thus Indigenous people are counted as members of the dominant tradition (Islam) by default. As well, Indigenous people in many parts of the world may give the answers they think are desired, to avoid possible reprisals or repercussions.

That said, approximately 70 per cent of Indigenous people in the world today identify with a colonial religion; only 15 to 20 per cent report that they practise an Indigenous religion. The rest declare adherence either to an alternative tradition or to none at all.

Loss of Religion

Some early European missionaries tried to persuade Indigenous communities that Christianity made more sense than their own traditions, but that approach was rarely successful. A more effective strategy was to demonstrate the "superiority" of Christian beliefs in practical terms. In many cases, that task was accomplished through the association of military strength with religious authority. The message was simple: Our people are stronger than your people because our god is stronger than yours.

Another major factor in the decline of Indigenous religions was the people's belief that they needed the education available only through missionaries. Then, as colonial abuses accumulated, many oppressed Native people looked to the missionaries for *protection* from the new system. In both situations, Christianity flourished at the expense of traditional beliefs and practices.

Document

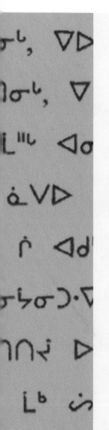

From *Things Fall Apart*, by Chinua Achebe (Igbo)

Achebe's 1958 novel—which focuses on an Igbo man named Okonkwo from a fictional village in Nigeria in the late 1800s—is the most influential work of African literature ever written. In this passage Okonkwo has just returned home after a seven-year exile, and his best friend Obierika is explaining the dramatic changes that colonialism has brought during his absence.

"Perhaps I have been away too long," Okonkwo said, almost to himself. "But I cannot understand these things you tell me. What is it that has happened to our people? Why have they lost the power to fight?"

"Have you not heard how the white man wiped out Abame?" asked Obierika.

"I have heard," said Okonkwo. "But I have also heard that Abame people were weak and foolish. Why did they not fight back? Had they no guns and machetes? We would be cowards to compare ourselves with the men of Abame. Their fathers had never dared to stand before our ancestors. We must fight these men and drive them from the land."

"It is already too late," said Obierika sadly. "Our own men and our sons have joined the ranks of the stranger. They have joined his religion and they help to uphold his government. If we should try to drive out the white men in Umuofia we should find it easy. There are only two of them. But what of our own people who are following their way and have been given power? They would go to Umuru and bring the soldiers, and we would be like Abame." He paused for a long time and then said: "I told you on my last visit to Mbanta how they hanged Aneto."

"What has happened to that piece of land in dispute?" asked Okonkwo.

"The white man's court has decided that it should belong to Nnama's family, who had given much money to the white man's messengers and interpreter."

"Does the white man understand our custom about land?"

"How can he when he does not even speak our tongue? But he says that our customs are bad, and our own brothers who have taken up his religion also say that our customs are bad. How do you think we can fight when our own brothers have turned against us? The white man is very clever. He came quietly and peaceably with his religion. We were amused at his foolishness and allowed him to stay. Now he has won our brothers, and our clan can no longer act like one. He has put a knife on the things that held us together and we have fallen apart" (Achebe 1996 [1958]: 124–5).

Some colonial governments outlawed the practice of Indigenous religions. This was invariably the case whenever such religions were suspected of involvement with anti-colonial resistance. And sometimes such laws were put into effect in a more pre-emptive manner.

In 1883, for example, the United States banned many Native ceremonies, including the Sun Dance. The next year, Canada amended its **Indian Act** and criminalized the **potlatch**. In both cases the declared motive was not to regulate religion but to protect Aboriginal citizens—from physical harm in the case of the Sun Dance, and from economic hardship in the case of the potlatch, which the government depicted as driving people into poverty.

Finally, the conversion of Indigenous people had an enormous impact on gender relations, which in turn has had repercussions in all areas of life. Most colonial powers brought a form of patriarchy with them that resulted in the gendered stratification of local societies, and the devaluation of women and their roles. As the Métis author Maria Campbell has pointed out, this devaluation was often supported by colonial religious teachings:

> The missionaries had impressed upon us the feeling that women were a source of evil. This belief, combined with the ancient Indian recognition of the power of women, is still holding back the progress of our people today (Campbell 1973: 168).

Loss of Language

As a result of colonialism, an untold number of Indigenous languages have disappeared forever. It has been estimated that Australia had almost 300 distinct Aboriginal languages at first contact; today all but 20 are either extinct or endangered. According to the United Nations, as many as 90 per cent of all existing languages are in danger of dying out within 100 years; the vast majority of these languages are Indigenous.

Focus

The Potlatch

The potlatch is practised by many peoples of the Pacific Northwest, including the Haida, Kwakwaka'wakw, Salish, Tlingit, and Tsimshian. A way of demonstrating hospitality and redistributing wealth, it takes the form of a feast at which the hosting family presents the guests with gifts.

A potlatch is typically held to mark important moments such as marriage, childbirth, or death, and may include music, theatre, and ceremonial dancing. It may also serve to indicate social status: families demonstrate their wealth and importance by giving away (or even destroying) more resources than other families.

Recognizing the potlatch as a central element of many Native cultures, Christian missionaries thought that banning it would facilitate assimilation. Their governments agreed: the potlatch was made illegal in Canada in 1884, and in the US a few years later. But the law was hard to enforce (Indigenous communities were large enough that they could often hold potlatches in secret), and many non-Natives—including the government agents tasked with enforcing the ban—considered it harsh and unnecessary. The ban was finally lifted in the US in 1934 and in Canada in 1951.

For cultures that rely heavily on oral traditions to transmit their beliefs and values, the loss of language constitutes a devastating blow to their religion. In his memoir *Our Land Was a Forest*, Kayano Shigeru tells a story about the last three fluent Ainu-speakers in his town, one of whom was his father. The three agreed that the first among them to die would be the luckiest, because the other two would be able to perform the death ritual for him in the Ainu language and thereby ensure that he would "return to the realm of the gods" (Shigeru 1994: 107).

What has caused this situation? In many cases, as communities died their languages died with them. In others, the process of language loss was accelerated by government programs designed specifically to promote assimilation. Thus in Canada Aboriginal children were taken from their families, often by force, and placed in church-run **residential schools** where they were forbidden to speak their own languages. In Australia children were sent either to foster homes or (more often) to government- or church-run institutions, where they remained as wards of the state until they reached the age of 18. Record-keeping was often either inadequate or non-existent, with the result that some children could never return to their families.

In both countries, many agents of the institutions involved inflicted physical, psychological, and/or sexual abuse on the children in their care. Taken from their families and told they were worthless, heathen, primitive, these children grew up with no knowledge of their language and culture; at the same time they were deprived of the social knowledge required to establish healthy relationships and raise their own families. It is no wonder that in Australia the victims of this system have been termed the "**Stolen Generations**."

Loss of Land

We have already noted how closely Indigenous religions are tied to specific locations: the sacred places where gods, spirits, and ancestors become present in the lives of each community. Limiting or preventing access to such locations, therefore, undermines the very foundations of Indigenous religion.

Thousands of Indigenous religious sites have been taken over or destroyed as a result of colonialism; no doubt there are many more such sites that we know nothing of, because the people who held them sacred have been destroyed. Yet even where both the people and the land survive, gaining recognition of land rights is an ongoing problem.

Canada and Australia have particularly poor track records. When they became independent from Great Britain, they essentially refused to recognize any titles granted to Indigenous people by the British. In 1971, an Australian judge upholding the concept of *terra nullius* ruled that Aborigines had no land rights at all—a decision that was not overturned until 1992. The situation in Canada remains in many ways very poor. As recently as 2012 the federal government amended the Navigable Waters Protection Act to offer "protection" only for corporate projects such as oil pipelines; the new "Navigation Protection Act" (NPA) specifically deregulated many waterways that pass through First Nations territory.

In the US, more than 90 per cent of the land had been taken from its Indigenous inhabitants by 1890. A key (negative) moment in the Native Americans' struggle to reclaim some of this territory came almost a century later, when the Forest Service proposed putting a paved road through the Six Rivers National Forest in northern California, to open the space for commercial logging. The project would effectively destroy the centre of religious existence for two Native communities, the **Yurok** and the **Karuk**.

The case was brought to the Supreme Court. The Native people were not asking that the land be returned to them—only that they retain access to it. Yet the court found that their attachment to the territory was no different from the attachment that any individual might feel for any space. Thus to agree to their request would set a precedent allowing anyone to request protection of any site on religious grounds. The petition was denied.

This case highlights two central problems in the understanding that many non-Indigenous people have of Indigenous religions. The first is that religion in general is often seen primarily as an individual commitment to a set of beliefs. Indigenous religions, by contrast, are communal and are as much about practice as belief.

The second problem is the difficulty that non-Indigenous people have in understanding why Indigenous practices often depend on access to particular sites—unlike, say, Muslim prayer or Buddhist meditation, which can be performed anywhere. If the Vatican were destroyed, Catholics would be upset, but they would not be separated from God or the sacraments. There is an important difference between religions that see the world as a unity—all people are loved equally by Allah; all have equal access to the Four Noble Truths—and religions that see the world in more particular, or locative, terms. For most Indigenous people, specific places are sacred to specific people, not to everyone in the world. For such people, one might say that the place itself *is* the religion; without it, the religion is fundamentally different.

Appropriation

> We lost most of our land, most of our "Aboriginal" rights, many of our languages, most of our traditional cultural ways, our religion, our relationship to the land and the spirits of the land, and, it seems, that we've even lost control of much of our identity through the process of "trade-marking" images of us, and elements of our culture.
>
> —Philip Bellfy (2005: 30), Chippewa

Identity

For some people, a match between the Cleveland Indians and the Atlanta Braves is not just a baseball game: it's a stark reminder of the ongoing legacy of colonialism, of all that has been and that continues to be taken from them. Adding insult to injury, the Braves' fans are known for doing the "tomahawk chop," while the Indians' mascot is a caricature named "Chief Wahoo."

This phenomenon is not limited to baseball. Many North American sports teams—including the Chicago Blackhawks and Washington Redskins—have taken Indigenous-oriented names. And many other businesses have used "Indigenous" names or logos to market their products, from Eskimo Pie ice cream to the Ford Thunderbird. In effect, the dominant colonial culture has appropriated Indigenous identities and reconstructed them to evoke whatever "primitive" stereotype is best suited to the product in question: the primal "warrior" for a sports team, the noble "chief" for tobacco, or the pure, natural "Indian maiden" for a line of dairy products or even beer.

Such appropriation is thus not simply arrogant, impolite, or politically incorrect. It perpetuates an image of Indigenous people that is far removed from current reality and thus helps to blind non-Indigenous people to ongoing injustices. People who see Indigenous cultures as primitive and uncivilized, as vanished or vanishing, will have difficulty recognizing the reality of modern communities and their concerns. Whether they are celebrating or protesting, laughing or grieving, practising Indigenous traditions or Christianity, Indigenous people should at least have the right to own and control their own identity.

The Washington Redskins are the only major professional sports team named after a racial slur. The name, logo, and mascot "Chief Zee" have been the subject of ongoing legal action. Some Native Americans have proposed that, if the team will not change its name, it could at least change its mascot—to a red-skinned potato (© Chris Szagola / NewSport / Corbis).

Religion in the Movies

From the "Indian burial ground" of Stephen King's *Pet Sematary* to the baboon "shaman" Rafiki in *The Lion King*, to Betty White's "tribal" chanting in *The Proposal*, American films are filled with false ideas about Indigenous religious life. The best-known portrayals of Native culture likely remain those from the classic Hollywood westerns—most of which used Italian or Spanish actors to play the "Indians." Again and again, Indigenous people are portrayed either as fierce/savage warriors or as the noble/dying people of a lost age.

Similar patterns are evident in movies from Oceania and Africa. In the Australian film *Crocodile Dundee*, Dundee's Aboriginal friend Neville is repeatedly shown to have left his roots behind ("God, I hate the bush," he mutters). More disturbingly, Dundee himself proclaims that "Aborigines don't own the land. They belong to it." It is precisely this view of traditional Aboriginal conceptions of place that the Australian government used to help deprive people of their land rights.

The Gods Must Be Crazy remains the most commercially successful movie about Indigenous people ever made. Released in 1980, it focused directly on the (imagined) religious beliefs of the (real) **Ju/'hoansi** people, in the Kalahari Desert of southern Africa. The movie presents them as "noble savages" living in a simple, idyllic society whose peace is shattered when a Coke bottle falls out of a plane and upsets the balance of Indigenous life, prompting the film's hero, Xi, to set off for the end of the world in order to return the offending object to the gods who sent it. In other words, the movie presents the Ju/'hoansi as naive, superstitious, and innocent, and then uses them to criticize modern non-Indigenous culture.

Catching Dreams and Burning Men

Around the world, sacred Indigenous items are still turned into souvenirs for cultural tourists. There is a lot of money to be made by selling cheap versions of African masks to non-Africans. Imitation Maori *moko* are popular among non-Indigenous tattoo enthusiasts, and were even used on fashion models for a 2007 Jean-Paul Gaultier collection. Even more striking is the proliferation of dream catchers. Originally used in Anishinaubae culture to help protect children from nightmares, they are now sold by the thousands for use as decorative knick-knacks. Often they can be seen hanging from a rearview mirror like a pair of fuzzy dice.

Indigenous opinion concerning the commercial use of religious objects and symbols is divided. Some people see it as disrespectful and damaging; others argue that it has some value, not only in economic terms but in educating the public about Indigenous culture. Still, there are forms of appropriation that almost all agree are inappropriate. Some of these are part of what is often called the **New Age** movement.

Many New Age teachings that seem to reflect Indigenous religions in fact turn them upside down. Thus elements of a locative and communal tradition are co-opted to promote notions of universal truth and individual fulfillment. Non-Indigenous people are often willing to pay New Age "shamans" lots of money for the opportunity to get in touch with a "primal" part of themselves and overcome their own psychological and emotional problems. To this end they practise all manner of pseudo-Indigenous rituals: telling stories, chanting, passing around a talking stick, banging drums, dancing, and yelling in a forest.

These imitative practices can actually be quite dangerous. In October 2009, three people died and 18 more were hospitalized when self-help guru James Arthur Ray conducted a New Age **sweat lodge** ceremony in Arizona. In the traditional practice, participants sit in an enclosed space and water is poured over rocks heated in a fire to create steam. The ritual is used for various medicinal and religious purposes, including purification and reconnection to the spirits. Many Native communities, including the Anishinaubae, Lakota, **Crow**, and **Chumash**, conduct sweat lodge ceremonies safely in enclosures covered with hides, dirt, or blankets, but it seems that Ray's lodge was covered with plastic sheeting. On 3 February 2010, Ray was charged with manslaughter for the three deaths.

The largest Indigenous-themed New Age event is the annual Burning Man festival in northern Nevada. Taking its name from its central ceremony, when a large wooden effigy is set aflame, since 2007 it has attracted well over 40,000 people each year. Some have complained about the festival's appropriation of Indigenous cultures. In April 2009 organizers of an offshoot party in Oakland, California, circulated an online flyer encouraging participants to "GO NATIVE" and offering a discount to those "in Native costume." Given the immense popularity of Burning Man, it is impossible to overestimate the degree to which such appropriation influences the views of non-Natives about Native people—and thereby affects the lives of the latter.

Recent Developments

> There are references to Gen. Custer and the US Cavalry, to John Wayne and to US policies toward Indians over the years, but *Smoke Signals* is free of the oppressive weight of victim culture; these characters don't live in the past and define themselves by the crimes committed against their people.
>
> —Roger Ebert (1998), Euro-American

Given that Indigenous traditions are the world's oldest religions, the changes that have taken place since the 1500s certainly qualify as "recent developments." Also, as a result of colonialism, the religious traditions of Indigenous people have arguably changed more dramatically over the last centuries than the traditions of any other cultures in the world. That said, it's important to bear two points in mind.

First, there is a critical difference between recognizing that awful things have been done to Indigenous people and defining them as "victims"—a label that robs them of full humanity. Second, and relatedly, Indigenous people were never simply the passive objects of colonialism: they engaged with it at every step, and they have remained active agents in the developments that have shaped their histories, including recent developments in their religions.

Interaction and Adaptation

> I picture oppressors . . . coming into our garden of Eden like a snake. Satan used the snake as his instrument to tempt God's people and to try to destroy God's plan for his people. The bad influence came in breaking our relationship with God, with man, and the Land. We never dreamed that one day the bulldozers would come in.
>
> —Djiniyini Gondarra, **Yolngu** (in Swain and Trompf 1995: 107)

Dualisms

Soon after contact with Europeans, many Indigenous people began to incorporate elements of the colonial religion into their own traditions. An important example was the shift that sometimes took place from the more typically Indigenous worldview of **complementary dualism** (seeing the universe as necessarily including both creative and destructive forces, which can work together), to the "Western" worldview of **conflict dualism** (seeing the universe as divided between good and evil forces that are in constant battle with one another).

Such a shift occurred around 1600 among many of the Indigenous people of Peru, who previously had no real concept of "evil." In certain regions, local populations were demonized as enemies of Christ, giving the Spanish invaders licence to use extreme violence to subjugate and convert them. The plan worked: many Indigenous Peruvians did adopt Christian beliefs, including good–evil dualism. While they came to regard Jesus as a positive and humane figure, however, they saw the Spanish as the true embodiments of evil.

A similar change took place among the **Iroquois** in the late 1700s. A man named Ganioda'yo, or Handsome Lake, experienced a series of visions in which he met Jesus as well as four angels sent by the creator, Tarachiawagon. As a result of these visions, he taught the Iroquois to publicly confess their sins, avoid evil (including witchcraft and alcohol), and worship only Tarachiawagon, not his malevolent brother, Tawiskaron. This division of the world between the good and evil brothers represented a potent fusion of Indigenous religion with Christian conflict dualism. Today approximately a third of all Iroquois practise what came to be called the Handsome Lake or Longhouse religion.

The Diaspora and the Diviner

The Atlantic slave trade carried African traditions to the Americas, where they mixed with elements of both Christianity and Native American religions. Many relocated Africans continued to worship Yoruba gods under the guise of Christian saints, but in time elements of the two traditions often merged in fact, giving rise to new religions such as Macumba (in Brazil), Voudou (in Haiti), and Santeria (in Cuba).

Many Africans also moved towards conflict dualism. In the early 1800s, in the region that became South Africa, a Xhosa diviner named Nxele experienced what he understood to be an intervention by Christ. Although he continued to practise divination, he also began preaching a message that echoed the teachings of the nearby Christian missionaries.

Like the Indigenous Peruvians, however, Nxele came to see the Europeans as Christ's betrayers. Preaching that the god Mdalidiphu was on the Xhosa's side, Nxele led 10,000 warriors against the British at Grahamstown. The attack failed and Nxele was imprisoned. He later drowned off the Cape coast while attempting to escape.

Cargo Cults

A famous recent example of an Indigenous religion changing in response to contact with outsiders is the **cargo cult**. Most cargo cults developed in the southwest Pacific region, although a few similar groups have also appeared in Africa and the Americas. The cargos in question were the supplies and manufactured goods that regularly arrived for the foreigners.

A young man worships at Saut d'Eau, Haiti, in July 2008 as part of the annual Voudou pilgrimage to the site (© Aurora Photos / Alamy).

Colonists and missionaries first appeared on many Pacific islands in the late nineteenth and early twentieth centuries, but activity intensified during the Second World War when military forces established bases on them. The local people believed that the goods arriving for the forces were provided by deities or ancestors, and that in order to receive similar shipments they should imitate the newcomers. Thus they painted military insignia on their bodies, marched like soldiers, made guns from wood and radios from coconuts. Some even built replicas of airplanes, control towers, and headphones, waved landing signals, and lit torches along runways at night.

Their hopes were fuelled by the belief that acquiring the desired goods would allow for reciprocal exchanges with the Europeans—a practice that for many Indigenous cultures was central to establishing relationships—and help bring about a new age of social harmony, healing the wounds caused by the arrival of the colonists.

Unfortunately, the focus on obtaining cargo eclipsed other elements of the local religions. Even though the cults reflected the content of their tradition (which explained the cargo as originating with gods or ancestors), they radically changed its form (their ritual behaviour). In the end, many of those local traditions completely disappeared.

Paths of Resistance

Not all Indigenous religions changed so dramatically or quickly. Several Australian communities neither merged their tradition with the colonial one nor rejected one or the other. Instead, they declared the contradictory truth of both. Some have suggested that the Aborigines were better able than most to entertain two radically different cosmologies because their cultural heritage had accustomed them to paradoxes and non-linear thinking.

In a number of instances Christianity was subsumed by the Indigenous tradition. The Warlpiri of Central Australia, for example, used ritual song and dance to tell Bible stories, just as they did with Dreaming tales. They also tended to conflate events, as if Adam, Abraham, and Jesus had lived at the same time as the Warlpiri's own ancestors. In effect, by telling the biblical stories in their own way, they reconfigured them to focus on place rather than the sequence of events.

This emphasis on place is a clear indication that the Aboriginal worldview took precedence over the Christian. To most Christians, it is theologically critical to understand the sequence in which the stories of Adam, Abraham, and Jesus occur. For the Aborigines, however, this sequence was irrelevant; the biblical figures were thus easily incorporated into their universe. In other words, unlike the cargo cult practitioners, they kept the form of their traditional religion (how stories were told), even as they altered its content to include biblical references. It's possible that this approach allowed them to resist conversion longer than many other communities.

"The End Is Near"

> They [the Ghost Dancers] danced in rings, the men outside circling to the right, the women and children inside circling to the left. Some of the songs came from Siletz [a community in Oregon], others were dreamed by the people when they were in a trance. All the songs were wordless. The dancers wore the old-time dress. Most of them went crazy and then they would see the dead.
>
> —Robert Spott, Yurok (in Beck et al. 1992 [1977]: 176)

In the wake of the destruction wrought by Europeans, many Indigenous cultures experienced a religious crisis. One response was to understand colonialism as punishment for inadequate observance of Native traditions. Among the people who took this view were some who reasoned that repentance might help to usher in a new golden age. In some cases this view may have reflected the influence of Christian eschatology—the idea that the end of the world was near and the kingdom of God would soon arrive. Of course, it may also have reflected the fact that the world as Indigenous people had known it really was coming to an end.

The Cattle Massacre

In the mid-1800s—a time when the Xhosa were suffering greatly under the British—a young woman named Nongqawuse had a vision in which her ancestors told her that, because some of her people had practised witchcraft, the British had been sent to punish them all. If the Xhosa renounced witchcraft and destroyed their food supplies, then the Europeans would be destroyed, the ancestors would return, their food would be replaced, and their land would be restored to them.

Many Xhosa responded by burning their granaries and slaughtering their cows—ultimately, almost half a million were killed. The result was starvation. The Xhosa population fell from 105,000 to 27,000 in a year. Many blamed the tragedy on those who had failed to heed Nongqawuse's prophecy, although there was a later backlash against Nongqawuse herself. In the end, most of the survivors turned to Christianity.

The Ghost Dance

Nongqawuse's vision shares some basic similarities with a vision promoted in 1889 by a **Paiute** religious leader named Wovoka in the region that is now Nevada. Reviving a movement from two decades earlier, he prophesied that in a few years the ancestors would return, the buffalo herds would be restored, and the settlers would disappear. To hasten this renewal, Wovoka urged his people to live peacefully and perform a ritual focused on the spirits of their ancestors. The Lakota Sioux termed this ritual the "spirit dance," which the Euro-Americans translated as "**Ghost Dance**."

Delegates from various Native communities were sent to hear Wovoka. The Navajo, who were enjoying a period of relative stability, were not convinced. But the Lakota were on the verge of starvation after the US government had broken a treaty and given away their fertile reservation lands to white settlers. With the bison gone, crops scarce, and government supplies running low, the Lakota were strongly attracted to Wovoka's message, in particular the idea that the whites could be made to disappear. They danced with greater urgency as their situation deteriorated, and many took to wearing "Ghost Shirts," which they believed would repel bullets. Alarmed, the Bureau of Indian Affairs dispatched thousands of US Army troops to the Lakota territory. Among the consequences were the death of Sitting Bull and the massacre at Wounded Knee.

From Earth to Sky

The British arrived in Australia in 1788 at the site that would become Sydney. They then appropriated the original inhabitants' territories so efficiently that, within a decade, the people were practising special rituals to drive them out, appealing to the serpent Mindi to destroy them with (fittingly) smallpox.

But these efforts failed, and a religious crisis developed. Some Aborigines came to believe not only that the world would soon end, but also that the source of sacred power and authority had moved from the earth to a heavenly utopia in the sky. Evidence suggests that these beliefs were a direct result of exposure to Christianity.

Traditionally, the Aborigines had understood that after death their spirits would return to their homelands. Now, in a sad irony, they found comfort in the colonizers' promise that their spirits would journey to a paradise in the sky. The only difference was that, for the Aborigines, that paradise would be free of Europeans.

Autonomy and Equality

> "If God be for us, who can be against us?"
>
> —Archbishop Desmond Tutu, Xhosa (quoting Romans 8:31; in Allen 2008: 334)

Unable to prevent colonialism, many Indigenous people eventually found other ways of pursuing autonomy, equality, and fair treatment. In many cases, religion has been at the heart of these efforts.

Non-Indigenous Religions

Often the religion involved in the quest for equity has been Indigenous, but not always. Many Indigenous Christians have fought passionately against colonial (and Christian) abuses using ideas from the imported religion itself. Like Archbishop Tutu, they have drawn on biblical notions of justice, sympathy for the oppressed, and deliverance from evil to support their campaigns for equality and redress.

By the same token, some Indigenous Christians have incorporated Indigenous views into their critiques of colonial attitudes and practices. To this end Desmond Tutu has frequently cited the African concept of ***Ubuntu***, according to which all human beings are interconnected and therefore to harm others is to harm oneself. Stan McKay (Cree), an ordained minister and former moderator of the United Church—the first Native person in Canada to head up a mainline denomination—similarly draws on Aboriginal notions of the inter-relatedness of all life in his censure of Christianity's contributions to current environmental problems through its denial of "the integrity of creation" (McKay 1996: 55).

Land Claims

McKay's position combines a general concern for the environment with more specific concerns related to sacred Indigenous lands. Some efforts to reclaim such lands have failed completely, some have done well, and others have had more complex results. One early success came in 1970, when 194 square kilometres (48,000 acres) of land in New Mexico were returned to the Taos **Pueblo** by President Richard Nixon. Originally confiscated by President Theodore Roosevelt and designated the Carson National Forest, the region includes Blue Lake, which Taos tradition holds to be the site of creation.

In Canada, a major land dispute erupted in 1990 between the Mohawk community of Kanesatake and the town of Oka, Quebec. At issue was Oka's plan to expand a golf course onto land sacred to the Mohawk. After a court ruling allowed construction to proceed, some Kanesatake people erected a barricade denying access to the disputed territory. The 78-day standoff eventually pitted

Native people from across North America against the Canadian army. Ultimately, the federal government purchased the land and stopped the golf course development. But the victory was only partial for the Mohawk, since ownership of the land still did not rest with them.

Australian Aborigines have perhaps had more success at reclaiming land than any other Indigenous group. Since a High Court case in 1992 overturned the idea of Australia as *terra nullius*, Aborigines have successfully negotiated approximately 3,000 land claims. In the Northern Territory, most of the coastline and more than 40 per cent of the land area is now (once again) owned by Indigenous people.

Other Victories

Most countries have also repealed their laws inhibiting the practice of Indigenous religions. The bans on the Sun Dance and potlatch were lifted decades ago. Much more recently, when a local government in Florida outlawed animal sacrifice in an effort to stop the practice of Santeria and Voudou, the US Supreme Court ruled the legislation unconstitutional.

On a much larger scale, South Africa's apartheid laws were eliminated and its colonial regime overturned in 1994, and in 2008 Australia's Prime Minister Kevin Rudd officially apologized to the Aboriginal people for the policies that had created the Stolen Generations. Later the same year,

More than 2,000 people marched on Ottawa's Parliament Hill for the Idle No More protest in December 2012 (ANDRE FORGET / QMI AGENCY).

Canada's prime minister, Stephen Harper, issued an official apology for the residential school system, acknowledging that "it was wrong . . . to separate children from rich and vibrant traditions."

Such victories are reflected in changes in attitude. School teams around the world have replaced their Indigenous-themed names or mascots. An especially imaginative solution was devised in 2006 for the Syracuse Chiefs baseball team in New York State, which kept its name but changed its logo from an "Indian chief" to a silver locomotive (with a "chief engineer"). The change actually made the team's name more relevant to the town's history as a railway hub.

In April 2009, when several Native people got wind of the "GO NATIVE" party promoting the Burning Man festival, they decided to attend and explain why they believed the event was harmful. After they had lectured the participants about colonialism and the history of invasion, genocide, and appropriation associated with it, most of those present apologized, and several broke down sobbing.

In Canada in the fall of 2012, four Saskatchewan women (Jessica Gordon, Sylvia McAdam, Sheelah Mclean, and Nina Wilson), outraged by the implications for Aboriginal treaty rights and the environment of the omnibus budget bill (C-45) that included the new Navigation Protection Act, organized a protest that sparked similar demonstrations across Canada. Two days after the first "Idle No More" rally, **Attawapiskat** Chief Theresa Spence began what was to become a six-week hunger strike. As a result of these actions, Prime Minister Stephen Harper met with First Nations leaders in January 2013.

Contemporary Indigenous Traditions

> The people nowadays . . . think the ceremonies must be performed exactly as they have always been done. . . . But long ago when the people were given these ceremonies, the changing began, if only in the aging of the yellow gourd rattle or the shrinking of the skin around the eagle's claw, if only in the different voices from generation to generation, singing the chants. You see, in many ways, the ceremonies have always been changing.
>
> —Betonie, a character in the novel *Ceremony* by Leslie Marmon Silko (1977: 132), Laguna Pueblo

Resurgence

With increasing legal and social recognition has come a rise in the actual practice of Indigenous traditions. Most of the religious traditions discussed in this chapter have recently experienced revivals, from carving masks in Africa to telling Dreamtime stories in Australia to performing the Sun Dance in North America. The resurgence of the Maori *moko* tradition may be especially significant, symbolically. As we saw, *moko* is said to have originated in the underworld and been brought to the surface. When the practice was abolished by colonial rulers, the tradition returned underground in a political and figurative way; and thus its modern "resurfacing" can be seen as a re-enactment of the ancestral story.

The revival of Indigenous religions is understood, at least in part, as a way of coping with the cultural damage done by colonialism. At the same time some people—Indigenous and non-Indigenous—have pointed out that the more material consequences of colonialism must be addressed as well. For many Indigenous people, these consequences include extreme poverty and deprivation; therefore it is important to channel the positive effects of religious revitalization in ways that will also contribute to the improvement of Indigenous living conditions.

It's important to recognize that Indigenous people themselves are not of one mind on the revival of traditional religions. Many want no part of them, whether because they do not find value in them or because they now practise another religion. Nevertheless, growing numbers of Indigenous people do seem eager to incorporate traditional beliefs and practices into their lives.

Always Been Changing

The ways in which Indigenous traditions are practised today are rarely identical to the ways in which they were practised in the past, for several reasons. First, all religions change over time. Second, colonial disruptions have been so severe that in many instances it is not possible to recover pre-colonial traditions. Third, Indigenous traditions are typically interested in the manifestation of the sacred in the here and now; the intersection of spirits and ancestors with the world is an ongoing reality that necessitates adaptation.

Among the Yoruba, for example, the god of iron and war, Ogun, has come to be associated with the protection of welders, mechanics, and chauffeurs. Also, as a result of lifestyle upheavals, very little cloth is now woven by hand, and younger people in particular often wear American clothing even to ceremonial events. Yet the Bunu still ascribe great value to hand-woven cloth, and so continue to produce it for the most important religious occasions.

New trickster stories frequently embody the ways in which Indigenous religions have responded to historical developments. When colonization began, some tricksters used their powers to get the better of the newcomers; others imitated colonizing practices—for example, negotiating worthless agreements—to fool the Indigenous people into giving them things they wanted. Tricksters in modern stories appear in many non-traditional guises, as politicians, bartenders, or university teachers. In addition, there are now many female tricksters.

Gender shifts are evident in other areas of Indigenous life as well. In the past, men and women often had quite different, though interdependent, functions; but because of disruptions to traditional lifestyles, the same role differentiation is often not possible. For example, if at one time in a community women were responsible for preparing the food that the men killed or grew, that arrangement fell apart once their land was taken. This dissolution combined with the advent of colonial patriarchies to put severe stress on Indigenous gender relations.

Some communities are now moving towards more balanced gender representation, many of them related to religious practices. Thus increasing numbers of Native American men are weaving ritual baskets. Similarly, there are now several female *moko* artists, and it is no longer uncommon for women to receive full *moko* themselves. Such changes are among the ways in which Indigenous people are working to overcome the gender hierarchies that developed under colonialism.

Cultural Expressions

One especially notable recent development is the presence of Indigenous religions in art forms that originated in non-Indigenous cultures, including film, written literature, oil painting, and electronic music. Works *by* Indigenous people *about* Indigenous people are receiving much attention and acclaim. Religion has been employed in some of these works both to engage issues arising from colonialism (past or present) and to explore aspects of Indigenous life on their own terms.

An example of the latter approach is the painting "Red Willows" by David Johnson (p. 49). The work is clearly modern, produced in the mid-1990s to accompany Basil Johnston's retelling of the traditional story. The pairing of art and text adds meaning to both, often in a way that highlights the religious aspects of the tale. Thus the significance of the colour red in the painting is revealed only by the text, while the branch that appears both inside and outside the man suggests the interrelatedness of all things, a theme that readers of the story—distracted by its vivid, humorous physicality—could easily miss.

Prominent recent films that focus primarily on Indigenous religion include *Atanarjuat: The Fast Runner* (Canada, 2001), *Whale Rider* (New Zealand, 2002), and *Ten Canoes* (Australia, 2006). Two notable documentaries that consider the appropriation of Indigenous religion are *White Shamans and Plastic Medicine Men* (US, 1996), on the theft and commercialization of Native American traditions by non-Natives, and *Reel Injun* (Canada, 2009), on the depictions of Native people in movies.

Several other films refer to Indigenous religion while focusing primarily on the consequences of colonialism, among them *Dance Me Outside* (Canada, 1994), *Rabbit-Proof Fence* (Australia, 2002), *Moolaadé* (Senegal/France/Burkina Faso/Cameroon/Morocco/Tunisia, 2004), and, perhaps most famously, *Once Were Warriors* (New Zealand, 1994). Directed by Lee Tamahori (Maori) and starring mostly Maori actors, *Once Were Warriors* presents a complex picture of the return to Indigenous traditions. For some key female characters, this return is beneficial, helping them to regain a sense of community and self-worth in the wake of the havoc wreaked by colonialism. For a number of male characters, however, the return is clouded by anger and misunderstanding, and sadly perpetuates the violence resulting from colonialism.

Literature

One of the first Indigenous writers to be recognized internationally was the poet Pauline Johnson (Mohawk), who began publishing in 1883 and was described by critics of her time as "perhaps the most unique figure in the literary world on this continent," even "the greatest living poetess" (Francis 1992: 113). Her poetry very often returned to the sacred theme of place, as in her most famous work, "The Song My Paddle Sings."

The modern era of Indigenous literature began in earnest in 1958 with the appearance of Chinua Achebe's *Things Fall Apart* (see p. 66), which depicts the effects of British colonialism, and particularly Christian missionaries, on the life and religion of the Indigenous people of Africa. *Things Fall Apart* was a landmark, and regularly appears high on the lists of the top 100 books of all time.

Indigenous authors have since produced a huge variety of compelling works of fiction, poetry, autobiography, and drama. Among those authors are

- José María Arguedas (Quechua)
- Maria Campbell (Métis)
- Jack Davis (Noongar)
- Louise Erdrich (Anishinaubae)
- Tomson Highway (Cree)
- Keri Hulme (Maori)

Document

From *The Bone People*, by Keri Hulme (Maori)

Published in 1983, this Booker Prize–winning novel follows three interconnected characters—Simon, Joe, and Kerewin—whose experiences are symbolically linked to Maori religious beliefs and practices. These characters are briefly introduced in the book's prologue.

He walks down the street. The asphalt reels by him.
It is all silence.
The silence is music.
He is the singer.
The people passing smile and shake their heads.
He holds a hand out to them.
They open their hands like flowers, shyly.
He smiles with them.
The light is blinding: he loves the light.
They are the light.
. . .
He walks down the street. The asphalt is hot and soft with sun.
The people passing smile, and call out greetings.
He smiles and calls back.
His mind is full of change and curve and hope, and he knows it is being lightly tapped. He laughs.
Maybe there is the dance, as she says. Creation and change, destruction and change.
New marae from the old marae, a beginning from the end.
His mind weaves it into a spiral fretted with stars.
He holds out his hand, and it is gently taken.
. . .
She walks down the street. The asphalt sinks beneath her muscled feet.
She whistles softly as she walks. Sometimes she smiles.
The people passing smile too, but duck their heads in a deferential way as though her smile is too sharp.
She grins more at the lowered heads. She can dig out each thought, each reaction, out from the grey brains, out through the bones. She knows a lot.
She is eager to know more.
But for now there is the sun at her back, and home here, and free wind all round.
And them, shuffling ahead in the strange-paced dance. She quickens her steps until she has reached them.
And she sings as she takes their hands.
. . .
They were nothing more than people, by themselves. Even paired, any pairing, they would have been nothing more than people by themselves. But all together, they have become the heart and muscles and mind of something perilous and new, something strange and growing and great. Together, all together, they are the instruments of change (Hulme 1983: 3–4).

- Thomas King (Cherokee)
- N. Scott Momaday (Kiowa)
- Sally Morgan (Palku)
- Leslie Marmon Silko (Laguna Pueblo)
- Wole Soyinka (Yoruba)

Religion is a central issue in the works of most Indigenous authors. The very title of Momaday's breakthrough novel *House Made of Dawn*—winner of the 1969 Pulitzer Prize for Fiction—is taken from the Navajo Nightway Prayer.

Keri Hulme's novel *The Bone People* similarly displays elements characteristic of the resurgence of Indigenous traditions in general and Maori traditions in particular. Many of these elements are evident even in the book's brief prologue:

- a rhythmic sense of time, the past connected to the present;
- complementary dualism (the "dance" of "creation and change, destruction and change");
- allusion to the central *koru* (frond/spiral) element of Maori *moko*; and
- the importance of community, of rebuilding the *marae*.

Like other works of contemporary Indigenous art, *The Bone People* applies traditional religious views and practices to current situations. With both pathos and humour, it shows us characters struggling with their place in the world as individuals and as members of a community. Some of them manage better than others; some make terrible mistakes. But nothing is forever, and (as in many Indigenous stories, past and present) when we get to the end, we are also at a beginning. For there are always new stories to tell.

Summary

A key problem in understanding Indigenous people and their religions is that they have long been defined, regulated, altered, and in many instances destroyed by non-Indigenous people. In the process, many incorrect and damaging views of Indigenous people and their traditions have been passed along, among them the belief that, before colonialism, Indigenous cultures were unchanging and illiterate—which is to say, "primitive."

There is enormous diversity among Indigenous cultures, but many of them share certain broad beliefs and social structures (recall the list on p. 41). In addition, although some were literate long before colonialism, orality remains important to virtually all of them. Stories continue to transmit beliefs and values, although interpretation remains tricky. As with all religious texts, for example, it is difficult to know which stories people understand to be objectively true, and which ones they think about in a more figurative way. Different communities may perform similar rituals but attribute entirely different meanings to them. There is also, as we have noted, great diversity among Indigenous religions. Despite the harmful changes that have taken place in Indigenous communities over the past several hundred years, many of these communities are reviving and recreating their religious traditions in various ways. Not only are elements of religious traditions being presented in new forms or contexts—novels, paintings, films—but, perhaps most important, religious activity is increasingly linked with political activism. Indigenous people are working passionately to reclaim the lands and rights taken from them, and religion continues to be a critical component of those efforts.

Sites

Bandiagara Escarpment, Western Africa

In the Dogon creation story, the supreme being Amma sacrificed one of his four children and scattered the remains on the earth. The Bandiagara escarpment in Mali is one of the sites where the Dogon people erected shrines to house the pieces.

Uluru, Central Australia

An enormous sandstone formation that is sacred to the local Pitjantjatjara and Yankunytjatjara people. In 1985 the Australian government finally agreed to transfer title to them in exchange for a 99-year lease arrangement and tourist access, but the latter continues to be a point of contention.

Bighorn Medicine Wheel, Wyoming, US

A circular arrangement of stones with radial lines from the centre to the rim, designed to facilitate communication with spirits, located in Wyoming. It is still used by Blackfoot, Crow, Cheyenne, Sioux, and Arapahoe communities for vision quests, healing rituals, and prayer.

Ife, Nigeria

The ancient site where the Yoruba deities Oduduwa and Obatala began the creation of the world—an event that is celebrated at the annual Itapa festival in Ife.

Nibutani, Japan

The site on the northern island of Hokkaido where the Ainu god Okikurmikamuy arrived on Earth; now home to the Nibutani Museum of Ainu Cultural Resources, established by the Ainu author Kayano Shigeru.

Tiwanaku, Bolivia

The most sacred place for the Aymara people. Located roughly 70 km (45 miles) west of La Paz, it is the centre of the world, the site of humanity's creation, and the place where the Aymara go to communicate with their ancestors.

Kanesatake, Quebec, Canada

The Mohawk community that objected when the neighbouring town of Oka planned to expand a golf course onto land that contains a Mohawk cemetery. After a 78-day standoff in the summer of 1990, the government of Canada bought the site and stopped the development.

Saut d'Eau, Haiti

A group of waterfalls where Yoruba spirits are understood to dwell along with several Catholic saints. Voudou adherents make an annual pilgrimage to Saut d'Eau in June.

Tanna, Vanuatu

An island in the South Pacific that is home to one of the last cargo cults. The Jon Frum movement began in the 1930s urging a return to traditional practices, and became a cargo cult during the Second World War, when approximately 300,000 American troops were stationed in Vanuatu. Its followers still hold a military-style parade every year.

Blue Lake, New Mexico, US

The site of the most sacred rituals and stories of the Taos Pueblo, confiscated in 1906. After more than 60 years of campaigning, they regained their title to it in 1970. Juan de Jésus Romero, the Pueblo's religious leader in the late 1960s and 1970s, once said: "The story of my people and the story of this place are one single story. No man can think of us without also thinking of this place. We are always joined together."

Discussion Questions

1. Are all Indigenous religions essentially the same? Why or why not?
2. Why was the colonial appropriation of land so harmful to Indigenous religions?
3. What are some elements of contemporary non-Indigenous culture that Indigenous people have used for their own purposes?
4. How do some trickster tales use chaos to promote social order in a community?
5. What is the literal and symbolic significance of a "journey" in Indigenous rites of passage?
6. What meaning is lost when Indigenous art is examined in a museum?
7. With reference to religious beliefs and practices, how did Indigenous gender relations become more unequal because of colonialism? What are some instances in which gender relations have recently become more equitable?

Glossary

Aborigine An Indigenous person; often specifies an Indigenous person of Australia.

Ainu The Indigenous people of northern Japan; not officially recognized as such by the government of Japan until 2008. Current population estimates range from 25,000 to 200,000.

Anishinaubae The term (roughly translating as "the people") traditionally used by the Odawa, Ojibwe, and Algonkin peoples to refer to themselves; located mainly around the Great Lakes in Canada and the US.

Arawak The Indigenous people encountered by Columbus in the West Indies in 1492. Most were killed by the Spanish, but a few small populations remain in northeastern South America.

Attawapiskat An isolated Cree community on James Bay in northern Ontario. In December 2012 Attawapiskat's chief, Theresa Spence, began a hunger strike to protest the treatment of Aboriginal people by the government of Canada.

Aymara South American Indigenous people from the Andes and Altiplano regions, initially colonized by the Inca and then by the Spanish. The current population is about 2 million in Bolivia, Chile, and Peru.

Bunu A Yoruba group in central Nigeria.

cargo cults Religious movements, mainly in Melanesia, inspired by the shipments of goods arriving for foreigners; founded on the belief that one day the spirits would send similar shipments to the Indigenous people initiating a new age of peace and social harmony.

Cherokee The largest federally recognized Native American group, with more than 300,000 members. Most currently live in the southeastern US, with band headquarters in Oklahoma and North Carolina.

Chumash A Native American people traditionally based along the southern California coast. Although only about 200 remained in 1900, recent estimates put their numbers at around 5,000.

colonialism The process in which people from one place establish and maintain a settlement in another, and its consequences for the Indigenous people.

complementary dualism A worldview in which the universe necessarily comprises both creative and destructive forces, which can work together; a feature of many Indigenous religions.

conflict dualism A worldview in which the universe is divided between good and evil forces that are in constant battle with one another; a feature of many Western religions.

Cree The largest Aboriginal group in Canada, numbering more than 200,000. Formerly based in central Canada, Cree populations are now well established in every province from Alberta to Quebec, as well as parts of the northern US.

Crow A Siouan-speaking Native American people historically based in the Yellowstone River valley, and now concentrated in Montana.

diviner A religious specialist who uses various ritual tools and practices to gain insight into the hidden or spiritual aspects of particular circumstances, events, problems, etc.

Dogon A West African people living mainly in central Mali, with a population of about half a million. Their first contact with Europeans was in 1857, but the Dogon have been more successful at preserving their traditional religion than many other Indigenous Africans.

The Dreaming The term that anthropologists gave to the time and place of Australian Aboriginal origin stories. Although often assumed to represent the archaic past, The Dreaming is understood by many traditional Aborigines to lie just out of reach of living memory.

elders Men or women whose wisdom and authority in cultural matters are recognized by their community. Elders are not necessarily old, but are understood to possess greater knowledge of tradition than others, and often to be more closely in touch with spiritual forces.

Ghost Dance A religious movement that emerged in the western US in response to colonialism. Launched in 1869 and revived in 1889, the Ghost Dance was performed in an effort to hasten the removal of the settlers and the restoration of what Native people had lost. Smaller revivals occurred periodically throughout the twentieth century.

Haisla First Nation on the North Coast of British Columbia; The population of the Haisla reserve in Kitimaat Village is less than 2,000.

hogan A traditional Navajo home. The first hogan was the Earth itself, and so building a new home reproduces the creation. This structure is at the centre of the community's domestic, social, and religious life.

Igbo One of the largest Indigenous groups in Nigeria, based in the southeast; worldwide population estimates range between 20 million and 40 million.

Indian Act Canadian federal legislation created in 1876 that defines and regulates Native people and their lands and outlines the federal government's responsibilities towards them. The act is administered by the Department of Indian and Northern Affairs and has undergone several amendments and revisions.

Iroquois Also known as the Six Nations; a North American Native confederacy based in the northeastern US and southeastern Canada, originally composed of five Iroquoian-speaking groups (Mohawk, Oneida, Onondaga, Cayuga, and Seneca) and joined in 1722 by the Tuscarora.

Ju/'hoansi Indigenous African group with a population of about 30,000 in northeast Namibia and 5,000 in northwest Botswana. Until 50 years ago, the Ju/'hoansi were nomadic hunters and gatherers, but since then most of them have adopted settled lives and occupations.

Karuk A community in northwestern California, with a population of about 3,500. "Karuk" translates as "upstream people," in contrast to their downstream neighbours, the Yurok.

Kewa Indigenous people from the Southern Highlands of Papua New Guinea, with a current estimated population of about 65,000.

Lakota The largest of the three Native American groups that make up the Sioux Nation (the others are the Eastern and Western Dakota); originally based near the Great Lakes, but moved to the Great Plains in response to the influx of European settlers.

Maori The Indigenous people of New Zealand, who appear to have arrived there in the late thirteenth century from elsewhere in Polynesia. Current estimates put the Maori population at around 700,000.

marae The religious and social home of a Maori community: a cleared area bordered with stones or wooden posts and containing several structures including the *whare whakairo* ("carved house").

Maya A Mesoamerican civilization (c. 2000 BCE–late 1600s), noted for their highly developed written language, art, architecture, mathematics, and astronomy. Despite the Spanish conquest, Maya people today make up a large portion of the population throughout the region, and millions continue to speak Mayan languages.

mbari A mode or style of cultural practice, especially architecture; principally identified with the Owerri Igbo of Nigeria.

Mohawk The most easterly of the Iroquoian Six Nations, based near Lake Ontario and the St Lawrence River.

moko Traditional Maori tattoos, originally chiselled into the skin, that identify the individual and his or her relationship to the community. Said to have been brought to Earth from the underworld by the ancestors, *Moko* was prohibited by colonial rulers but has resurfaced with the revival of other Maori practices.

Navajo The second-largest Native group in the US (after the Cherokee), with an estimated population of almost 300,000. The Navajo occupy extensive territories in Arizona, New Mexico, and Utah.

New Age A common term for Western spiritual movements concerned with universal truths and individual potential that draw from a wide range of religions and philosophies, including astrology, Buddhism, metaphysics, environmentalism, and Indigenous traditions.

Nisga'a Indigenous people of the Nass River valley in northwestern British Columbia. In 1998 the provincial and federal governments acknowledged Nisga'a sovereignty over 2,000 square km of land; the Nisga'a agreement was the first formal Native treaty signed in BC since 1854.

Nuer A confederation of peoples in southern Sudan and western Ethiopia; the largest Indigenous group in East Africa, with a population of about 33 million. The Nuer successfully fought off colonial forces in the early 1900s and have largely resisted conversion to Christianity.

Nyanga Indigenous people from the highlands of east-central Zaire, near the borders of Rwanda and Uganda. Part of the larger Bantu group, their current population is about 35,000.

Oglala One of seven groups that make up the Lakota Sioux; based at the Pine Ridge Indian Reservation in South Dakota, the second-largest reservation in the US.

Paiute Two related groups, the Northern Paiute (based in California, Nevada, and Oregon) and the Southern Paiute (based in Arizona, California, Nevada, and Utah). Wovoka, the leader of the 1889 Ghost Dance movement, was a member of the Northern group.

Pomo Native people of the northern California coast who, though connected by geography and marriage, traditionally lived in small separate bands. The Pomo linguistic family once comprised seven distinct languages, but few Pomo speakers now remain.

Pondo South African group who speak the Xhosa language and live along the southeastern coast of Cape Province.

potlatch A ritual practised by many Indigenous groups of the Pacific Northwest (e.g., Haida, Salish, Tlingit, Tsimshian), in which a family hosts a feast and offers guests gifts. The ritual typically marks important moments such as marriage, childbirth, or death, and may include music, theatre, and ceremonial dancing.

Pueblo Native people from the southwestern US, particularly New Mexico and Arizona, who traditionally lived in small villages ("pueblos" in Spanish). Approximately 25 Pueblo communities remain, including the Hopi, Taos, and Zuni.

residential schools Church-run schools, funded by the Canadian federal government, designed to facilitate assimilation and Christian conversion. Indigenous families were forced to send their children to the schools, where they were forbidden to speak their own languages and often subjected to neglect or abuse. The system was established in the 1840s and the last school did not close until 1996.

Sioux Native people with reserves in the Dakotas, Minnesota, Montana, Nebraska, Manitoba, and southern Saskatchewan, comprised of three main groups: Lakota, Eastern Dakota, and Western Dakota. The Sioux have been central to many key moments of American colonial history, including the Battle of the Little Bighorn, and Sioux writers and political leaders remain among the most influential members of the Native North American community.

Stolen Generations The generations of Australian Aborigines who as children were taken from their families and sent either to foster homes or to government- or church-run institutions. Because records were frequently lost (or not kept), many children were never able to reconnect with their families. The practice continued from approximately 1869 to the early 1970s.

Sun Dance Annual summer ritual practised by peoples of the North American plains (e.g., Blackfoot, Cheyenne, Crow, Kiowa, Sioux). The details of the ritual vary from one community to the next, as does the meaning of the solar symbolism. In the late nineteenth century the Sun Dance was severely discouraged by the Canadian government and outlawed in the US; it has experienced a revival since the 1960s.

sweat lodge A structure traditionally covered with skins, blankets, or dirt, used to induce sweating by pouring water over heated stones to create steam. Sweat lodge ceremonies are performed by several Native North American communities for medicinal and religious purposes, including purification and reconnection to the spirits.

syncretism The combination of elements from two or more religious traditions. Too often the term is used negatively to suggest that the "purity" of a particular religion has been compromised or contaminated.

terra nullius Latin for "no one's land," referring to territory over which no person or state has ownership or sovereignty; a concept invoked in several instances by European colonists to claim land occupied by Indigenous people. In Australia, the High Court invalidated this justification in a 1992 ruling.

totem pole A tall pole traditionally carved from a single cedar tree by an Indigenous community of the Pacific Northwest Coast (e.g., Haisla, Nisga'a, Tsimshian) to record historical events, indicate social status, represent ancestral lineage, support a physical structure, etc. Markings are often highly symbolic and specific to particular communities and locations.

trickster Term coined by scholars to classify a variety of usually superhuman figures who appear in the stories of cultures around the world; tricksters disrupt the norms of society and/or nature and often serve to teach important lessons about what is and is not acceptable in a particular community.

Tsimshian Indigenous people of the Pacific Northwest from British Columbia to southeast Alaska. The current population is approximately 10,000.

Tuhoe A Maori community of about 40,000, named for the ancestral figure Tuhoe-pọtiki. The Tuhoe are known for their dedication to Maori identity and heritage: about 20 per cent continue to live on their traditional lands on the steep eastern North Island of New Zealand, and 40 per cent still speak their native language.

Ubuntu The African concept that all human beings are interconnected, employed most famously by Nelson Mandela and Archbishop Desmond Tutu as one of the founding principles of the new South Africa. *Ubuntu* has since gained prominence in the US as well.

vision quest Fasting ritual undertaken to induce visions through contact with spirits; typically involving a solitary journey into the wilderness, it may be undertaken as a rite of passage to adulthood or during other key life events, such as preparation for war.

Wiradjuri The largest Indigenous group in New South Wales, Australia, who have lived in the central region of the state for more than 40,000 years. No known native speakers of the Wiradjuri language remain.

Xhosa Indigenous people living mainly in southeast South Africa. There are currently about 8 million Xhosa, and their language is the second most common in South Africa after Zulu. Nelson Mandela and Archbishop Desmond Tutu are both Xhosa.

Yanyuwa A small group located mainly in the Northern Territory of Australia. Fewer than ten speakers of the Yanyuwa language currently remain.

Yolngu Aboriginal community from northeastern Arnhem Land in Australia's Northern Territory. For more than fifty years, Yolngu leaders have been centrally involved with land claims.

Yoruba One of the largest Indigenous groups in west Africa, with a population of approximately 30 million based mainly in Nigeria. Yoruba traditions have had an enormous influence on African communities around the world; because so many African slaves were Yoruba, their impact has been especially significant in the Americas.

Yurok Native American community, with a population of about 6,000, who have lived near the northern California coast for more than 10,000 years. Yurok translates as "downstream people," in contrast to their upstream neighbours, the Karuk.

Further Reading

Ballinger, Franchot. 2004. *Living Sideways: Tricksters in American Indian Oral Traditions*. Norman: University of Oklahoma Press. An excellent, engaging introduction to Native American trickster figures; focuses on traditional (oral) stories but also includes references to contemporary literature.

Baum, Robert M. 1999. *Shrines of the Slave Trade: Diola Religion and Society in Precolonial Senegambia*. New York: Oxford University Press. This detailed study is one of the few to examine the pre-contact history of any African Indigenous religion.

Bell, Diane. 1983. *Daughters of the Dreaming*. Melbourne: McPhee-Gribble. An accessible (and bestselling) work of groundbreaking scholarship on the religious lives of Aboriginal women in central Australia.

Bockle, Simon. 1993. *Death and the Invisible Powers: The World of Kongo Belief*. Bloomington: Indiana University Press. An insider's introduction to the religious life of the Kongo people of Lower Zaire and to African religions generally, focusing on views and behaviours concerning death.

Deloria, Vine, Jr. 1994 (1972). *God Is Red: A Native View of Religion*. 2nd ed. Golden: Fulcrum. Indispensable overview of Native American religious perspectives, particularly regarding the importance of sacred places and the effects of colonialism.

Francis, Daniel. 1992. *The Imaginary Indian: The Image of the Indian in Canadian Culture*. Vancouver: Arsenal Pulp. A detailed, accessible discussion of the ways in which non-Natives in Canada have appropriated Native identity.

Gill, Sam D. 1982. *Beyond the "Primitive": The Religions of Nonliterate Peoples*. Englewood Cliffs, NJ: Prentice-Hall. Still one of the best general introductions to Indigenous traditions; especially useful on what religious practices mean to their communities.

Jacobs, Sue-Ellen, Wesley Thomas, and Sabine Lang, eds. 1997. *Two-Spirit People: Native American Gender Identity, Sexuality, and Spirituality*. Urbana and Chicago: University of Illinois Press. A vital collection of essays examining the connections between Native North American religions and constructions of gender and sexuality, from the traditional acceptance of diversity in many communities to current efforts to reclaim that acceptance.

LeRoy, John, ed. 1985. *Kewa Tales*. Vancouver: University of British Columbia Press. A valuable collection of traditional oral narratives from Papua New Guinea, catalogued to highlight various story patterns.

Mead, Hirini Moko. 2003. *Tikanga Maori: Living by Maori Values*. Wellington, NZ: Huia. A useful overview of Maori *tikanga* ("way of doing things"), especially the connections between religion and the creative arts; promotes *tikanga* as a guide for non-Maori people.

Olajubu, Oyeronke. 2003. *Women in the Yoruba Religious Sphere*. New York: State University of New York Press. Examines women's roles—along with issues of gender and power relations—in both traditional and contemporary Yoruba thought and practice.

Olupona, Jacob K., ed. 2004. *Beyond Primitivism: Indigenous Religious Traditions and Modernity*. New York: Routledge. One of the very few works to look at the contemporary situation of Indigenous religions; contributors from a broad range of backgrounds consider traditions from across America, Africa, Asia, and the Pacific.

Renne, Elisha P. 1995. *Cloth That Does Not Die: The Meaning of Cloth in Bùnú Social Life*. Seattle: University of Washington Press. A clear, insightful look at the role of a key material object in the culture (and especially religion) of the Bunu Yoruba people.

Rosaldo, Renato. 1980. *Ilongot Headhunting 1883–1974: A Study in Society and History*. Stanford: Stanford University Press. An influential analysis of the meaning and function of headhunting for the Ilongot people in the Philippines; discredits the notion that Indigenous societies were/are static, as opposed to European societies that changed over time.

Ryan, Allan. 1999. *The Trickster Shift: Humour and Irony in Contemporary Native Art*. Vancouver: University of British Columbia Press. The first book-length study of the influence of trickster conceptions in modern Native art, with photos of recent work alongside commentaries from the artists.

Shigeru, Kayano. 1994. *Our Land Was a Forest: An Ainu Memoir*. Trans. Kyoko Selden and Lili Selden. Boulder: Westview. A moving personal account by an Ainu man who has spent much of his life documenting his people's culture and history, as well as creating a school to ensure the continuation of the Ainu language.

Smith, Jonathan Z., et al., eds. 1995. *The HarperCollins Dictionary of Religion*. San Francisco: Harper-Collins. The following entries provide excellent brief introductions to topics relevant to Indigenous religions: "Africa, traditional religions in"; "Australian and Pacific traditional religions"; "circumpolar religions"; "Mesoamerican religion"; "Native Americans (Central and South America), new religions among"; "Native Americans (North America), new religions among"; "non-literacy"; "North America, traditional religions in"; "Religions of Traditional Peoples"; "South American religions, traditional"; "traditional religions, Western influence on."

Swain, Tony, and Garry Trompf. 1995. *The Religions of Oceania*. London: Routledge. The first (and possibly best) book in English on the religions of the southwest Pacific as a whole; provides clear interpretive tools and general information on the history and content of these traditions, from before colonialism through to modernity.

Wright, Ronald. 1992. *Stolen Continents: The "New World" through Indian Eyes*. Boston: Houghton Mifflin. A powerful, accessible account of the colonization and survival of the Aztec, Maya, Inca, Cherokee, and Iroquois civilizations; includes much Indigenous testimony.

Recommended Websites

http://cwis.org

Center for World Indigenous Studies Virtual Library: a list of websites offering further information on Indigenous cultures and current issues, organized by region.

www.everyculture.com

Countries and Their Cultures: brief but substantive information on most Indigenous cultures, including an overview of religious beliefs and practices, and a bibliography for each group.

http://indigenouspeoplesissues.com

Indigenous Peoples Issues and Resources: articles, updates, and information on current issues affecting Indigenous communities around the world, provided by a global network of scholars, activists, and organizations.

www.hanksville.org/sand/index.html

A Line in the Sand: information and resources about (and critiques of) the appropriation of Indigenous cultural property, particularly religious images and practices.

www.nativeweb.org

NativeWeb: news and information from and about Indigenous people and organizations around the world. Initiated the NativeWiki project, a library of Indigenous data to which users can also contribute.

www.peoplesoftheworld.org

Peoples of the World: education for and about Indigenous people; includes lists of resources such as documentaries and volunteer programs, as well as detailed information about Indigenous people organized by language, country, and name.

References

Achebe, Chinua. 1996 (1958). *Things Fall Apart*. Oxford: Heinemann.

Allen, John. 2008. *Desmond Tutu: Rabble-Rouser for Peace: The Authorized Biography*. Chicago: Lawrence Hill.

Baum, L. Frank. 1890. *Aberdeen* (South Dakota) *Saturday Pioneer*, 20 December.

Beck, Peggy V., Anne Lee Walters, and Nia Francisco. 1992 (1977). *The Sacred: Ways of Knowledge, Sources of Life*. Redesigned ed. Tsaile: Navajo Community College Press.

Bellfy, Philip. 2005. "Permission and Possession: The Identity Tightrope." In Ute Lischke and David T. McNab, eds. *Walking* a Tightrope: Aboriginal People and Their Representations, 29–44. Waterloo: Wilfrid Laurier University Press.

Campbell, Maria. 1973. *Halfbreed*. Halifax: Goodread.

Cooke, Dewi. 2008. "'Sorry' Statement Should Acknowledge Cultural Loss, Says State Leader." *The Age* (1 February). Accessed 11 Oct. 2009 at www.theage.com.au/articles/2008/01/31/1201714153311.html.

Cox, James L. 2007. *From Primitive to Indigenous: The Academic Study of Indigenous Religions*. Aldershot: Ashgate.

Deloria, Vine, Jr. 1988 (1969). *Custer Died for Your Sins: An Indian Manifesto*. Norman and Lincoln: University of Oklahoma Press.

———. 1997. "Conclusion: Anthros, Indians, and Planetary Reality." In Thomas Biolsi and Larry J. Zimmerman, eds. *Indians and Anthropologists: Vine Deloria, Jr., and the Critique of Anthropology*, 209–21. Tucson: University of Arizona Press.

Drewal, Margaret Thompson. 2002. "The Ontological Journey." In Graham Harvey, ed. *Readings in Indigenous Religions*, 123–48. London: Continuum.

Ebert, Roger. 1998. Review of *Smoke Signals*. rogerebert.com (3 July). Accessed 17 Jan. 2010 at http://rogerebert.suntimes.com/apps/pbcs.dll/article? AID=/19980703/REVIEWS/807030303/1023.

Eliot, T.S. 1959. *Four Quartets*. London: Faber and Faber.

Francis, Daniel. 1992. *The Imaginary Indian: The Image of the Indian in Canadian Culture*. Vancouver: Arsenal Pulp.

Gill, Sam D. 1982. *Beyond the "Primitive": The Religions of Nonliterate Peoples*. Englewood Cliffs: Prentice-Hall.

Heiss, Anita. 2001. "Aboriginal Identity and Its Effects on Writing." In Armand Garnet Ruffo, ed. *(Ad)dressing Our Words: Aboriginal Perspectives on Aboriginal Literatures*, 205–32. Penticton, BC: Theytus.

Hulme, Keri. 1983. *The Bone People*. Wellington: Spiral.

Johnston, Basil. 1995. *The Bear-Walker and Other Stories*. Illustrated by David Johnson. Toronto: Royal Ontario Museum.

King, Thomas. 1993. *Green Grass, Running Water*. Toronto: HarperCollins.

Lutz, Hartmut. 1991. *Contemporary Challenges: Conversations with Canadian Native Authors*. Saskatoon: Fifth House.

McKay, Stan. 1996. "An Aboriginal Christian Perspective on the Integrity of Creation." In James Treat, ed. *Native and Christian: Indigenous Voices on Religious Identity in the United States and Canada*, 51–5. New York: Routledge.

Matthews, Washington. 1995 (1902). *The Night Chant: A Navaho Ceremony*. Salt Lake City: University of Utah Press.

Mitchell, Ryan. 2003. "Maori Chief on Facial Tattoos and Tribal Pride." *National Geographic News* (14 Oct.). Accessed 21 Mar. 2009 at http://news.nationalgeographic.com/news/pf/84577710.html. 2009.

Moses, Daniel David, and Terry Goldie. 1992. "Preface: Two Voices." In Daniel David Moses and Terry Goldie, eds. *An Anthology of Canadian Native Literature in English*, xii-xxii. Toronto: Oxford University Press.

Ross, Rupert. 1992. *Dancing with a Ghost: Exploring Indian Reality*. Markham: Octopus.

Sarris, Greg. 1992. ""What I'm Talking about When I'm Talking about My Baskets": Conversations with Mabel McKay." In Sidonie Smith and Julia Watson, eds. *De/Colonizing the Subject: The Politics of Gender in Women's Autobiography*, 20–33. Minneapolis: University of Minnesota Press.

Shigeru, Kayano. 1994. *Our Land Was a Forest: An Ainu Memoir*. Trans. Kyoko Selden and Lili Selden. Boulder: Westview.

Silko, Leslie Marmon. 1977. *Ceremony*. New York: Penguin.

Swain, Tony, and Garry Trompf. 1995. *The Religions of Oceania*. London: Routledge.

Tait, Norman. 1993. Foreword to Hilary Stewart, *Looking at Totem Poles*, 9–11. Vancouver: Douglas & McIntyre.

Webber-Dreadon, Emma. 2002. "He Taonga Tuku Iho, Hei Ara: A Gift Handed Down as a Pathway." In Graham Harvey, ed. *Readings in Indigenous Religions*, 250–9. London: Continuum.

Zinn, Howard. 1995. *A People's History of the United States: 1492–Present*. New York: HarperPerennial.

Note

I would like to express my very great thanks to all those who read, commented upon, or inspired any part of this chapter: Meagan Carlsson, Ted Chamberlin, Michel Desjardins, Graham Harvey, Amir Hussain, Agnes Jay, Kelly Jay, Daniel Heath Justice, Sarah King, Sally Livingston, Jennifer Mueller, Michael Ostling, Keren Rice, and Mark Ruml. I also wish to dedicate this chapter to Willard Oxtoby, who defined much of my time at the University of Toronto and who was always generous with both his scholarship and his humour.

3 Jewish Traditions

Michele Murray

Traditions at a Glance

Numbers

Approximately 14 million.

Distribution

The majority of Jews live in either the United States (5–6 million) or Israel (6 million). There are about 1.5 million Jews in Europe, 400,000 in Latin America, and 375,000 in Canada.

Founders and Leaders

Abraham, his son Isaac, and Isaac's son Jacob are considered the patriarchs of the Jews; the prophet Moses, who is said to have received the Torah from God and revealed it to the Israelites, is known as the Lawgiver.

Deity

Yahweh.

Authoritative Texts

Hebrew Bible (Tanakh); Mishnah; Talmud.

Noteworthy Teachings

Deuteronomy 6: 4–9: "Hear O Israel, the LORD our God, the LORD is One. You shall love the LORD your God with all your heart and with all your soul and with all your strength. These words which I command you this day are to be kept in your heart. You shall repeat them to your children, speaking of them indoors and outdoors, morning and night. You shall bind them as a sign upon your hand and wear them as signs upon your forehead; you shall write them on the doorposts of your houses and on your gates."

Leviticus 19: 18: "You shall not take vengeance or bear a grudge against any of your people, but you shall love your neighbour as yourself: I am the LORD."

Jewish Identity as Ethnicity and Religion

Introducing Three Jews

Having removed the ornately wrapped Torah scroll from the Holy Ark, the rabbi carefully slid the velvet curtains closed. As she turned to face her congregation, she placed the scroll gently on the table before her and began to recite the first blessing.

*

Normally it was not so blustery in Jerusalem, but the weather had been stormy all day. The young man was thankful for the warmth of his long black coat and vest as he hurried along the narrow pathway to his Talmud study class. The wind tossed his curly sidelocks wildly behind him as he dipped his head low against the wind, one hand grasping his wide-brimmed black hat.

*

Rashel walked into her favourite greasy spoon in downtown Montreal and sat down at her usual table. Every Saturday morning she came here for breakfast, with the local paper in hand to read

← Jerusalem: view from the Old City over the Western Wall and the Dome of the Rock (© FredFroese / Getty Images).

as she ate. She didn't even need to put in her order, because it was the same every time: a ham and cheese omelette with a side order of bacon.

*

Each of the three people described above is Jewish. And Judaism has room for all three. Some Jews, including the first two, feel their Jewishness to be inseparable from Jewish religious practices and customs. Others—in fact, the majority of Jews in North America and Israel—are more like Rashel in that they rarely if ever attend **synagogue** (the place of congregational worship) and make no attempt to follow the rules set down by **Halakhah** (Jewish law). They consider themselves to be ethnically Jewish because they were born to Jewish parents, and they may or may not identify with aspects of secular Jewish culture (music, literature, food, and so on), but the religious dimension is not important to them. Thus Jewishness can be grounded in religious, ethnic, or cultural elements, or any combination of them.

Alina Treiger—the first female Rabbi to be installed in Germany since the Holocaust—introduces herself to her parish at the synagogue in Oldenburg on 1 February 2011 (© Ingo Wagner / dpa / Corbis).

For some Jews the mere idea of a female **rabbi** ("teacher") is preposterous and contrary to Halakhah. They believe that women have important roles in the Jewish community, but that the role of rabbi is reserved for men alone. For others, a female rabbi is completely natural; in fact, some might be attracted to a particular synagogue precisely because it has a female rabbi. Similarly, some Jews might perceive the dress and lifestyle of the young man described above—a member of a rigorously observant sub-group of Orthodox Jews known as **Haredim**—to be antiquated and unnecessary, while others would consider the devotion of such men, whose lives revolve around the study of ancient Jewish texts, to be one of the reasons for the survival of Judaism, and therefore worthy of deep respect. Jews holding the latter perspective would likely maintain that eating pork and consuming meat and dairy together—as Rashel does—are serious transgressions of Jewish law. Yet if you asked Rashel if she identified herself as Jewish, she would respond fervently in the affirmative. And there are many Jews (particularly in Canada, the United States, and Israel) who would say the same.

Timeline

c. 1850 BCE	Abraham (Abram) arrives in Canaan
c. 1260	Moses leads the Exodus from Egypt and Yahweh reveals the Torah to the Israelites
c. 1000	David takes Jerusalem and makes it his capital
921	Northern kingdom separates following Solomon's death
722	Assyrians conquer northern kingdom and disperse its people
586	Babylonians conquer Jerusalem and deport its leaders
539	Persians conquer Babylonia, permitting exiles to return in 538 BCE
c. 515	Rededication of the Second Temple
c. 333	Alexander the Great's conquests in the eastern Mediterranean begin the process of Hellenization
c. 200	The Torah is translated from Hebrew into Greek; the translation is called the Septuagint
167–164	Maccabean Revolt
70 CE	Romans lay siege to Jerusalem and destroy the Second Temple
132–135	Bar Kochba Revolt
c. 220	The Mishnah of Rabbi Judah ha-Nasi
c. 400	The Palestinian (or Jerusalem) Talmud
c. 500	The Babylonian Talmud
1135	Birth of Moses Maimonides, author of *The Guide of the Perplexed* (d. 1204)
1492	Jews expelled from Spain
1569	Kabbalah scholar Isaac Luria establishes a centre of Jewish mysticism in the northern Palestinian city of Safed
1666	Sabbatai Zvi is promoted as the messiah
1698	Birth of Israel ben Eliezer, the Baal Shem Tov, in Poland (d. 1760)
1729	Birth of Moses Mendelssohn, pioneer of Reform Judaism in Germany (d. 1786)
1881	Severe pogroms in Russia spur Jewish emigration
1889	Conservative Judaism separates from Reform Judaism in the United States
1897	Theodor Herzl organizes the first Zionist Congress
1935	Nuremberg Laws revoke many rights of Jews in Germany
1938	9–10 November *Kristallnacht*, the "Night of Broken Glass": Jewish businesses and synagogues attacked across Germany in prelude to the Holocaust
1939–45	Second World War (including the Holocaust)
1947	Discovery of the Dead Sea Scrolls
1948	Establishment of the state of Israel

The spectrum of Jewish identity is broad, and what one Jew considers an essential part of that identity may not hold any significance for another. Who ought to be called Jewish and what constitutes acceptable Jewish behaviour are subjects of ongoing debate among Jews themselves.

Earliest Jewish History: The Biblical Story

Any discussion of Jewish history must begin with the **Hebrew Bible**, also known to Jews as the **Tanakh** and to Christians as the Old Testament (Jews do not use the latter term, which reflects the Christian idea that the Hebrew Bible was superseded by the New Testament). Although often referred to as a book, the Hebrew Bible is in fact an anthology of 24 books, many of which were initially separate. They represent an assortment of literary forms, including poems, songs, legal prose, and vivid narratives full of drama and supernatural events. Most scholars believe they were composed by a variety of authors from different segments of society from approximately the tenth to the second century BCE. Eventually the separate books were assembled in a single canonical collection. There were many additional writings that could have been selected, but the Jewish community had come to recognize only a certain set of documents as theologically meaningful and authoritative.

The Hebrew Bible is divided into three sections: Torah, Nevi'im, and Ketuvim. ("TaNaKh" is an acronym based on the first letters of the three section names, separated by the vowel "a"; the "h" indicates that the final "k" is pronounced with a guttural sound). "Torah" is a Hebrew word that has two meanings. In its broad sense it designates the law or instruction of God, and as such is another way of referring to the Hebrew Bible as a whole. In its narrow sense it refers specifically to the first five books (Genesis, Exodus, Leviticus, Numbers, and Deuteronomy), which recount the history of the **Israelites** from the creation of the world until the entry into the Promised Land, and tell them how to live moral and ritually acceptable lives. Also known collectively as the **Pentateuch** (Greek for "five books"), they are considered the most sacred part of the entire Hebrew Bible. "Nevi'im" is the Hebrew word for "prophets": men such as Moses, who were believed to speak for God to the Israelites. The third section, "Ketuvim" ("writings") includes songs, prayers, and wisdom literature (i.e., the books of Job, Proverbs, and Ecclesiastes, which offer practical advice for dealing with common human concerns) as well as historical texts.

The Biblical Narrative as Sacred History

The biblical people of Israel, the Israelites, were the precursors of modern Jews, and the majority of Jewish festivals, rituals, and customs are derived from biblical stories. Yet the accuracy of those stories is a matter of debate, since in most cases there is no extra-biblical evidence that the events they describe ever occurred, or even that the people involved in them actually existed. But it was not the goal of the stories' human authors to record an objective account of historical events. Rather, they sought to convey a theological message and teach the Israelites how to live a devout life. Although some of the Tanakh stories do contain accurate historical information, we should not assume any of them to be entirely factual.

The biblical narrative is more properly understood as "sacred" history: it was because the stories served a theological agenda that they were valued and incorporated in the Tanakh. What the Hebrew Bible does is provide insight into the characters and events that came to be considered

Document

The Tanakh

The books comprising the three sections of the Tanakh are as follows:

I. Torah (תּוֹרָה, "Law"):

1. (בְּרֵאשִׁית / Bərē'shît) Genesis
2. (שמות / Shemot) Exodus
3. (ויקרא / Vayikra) Leviticus
4. (במדבר / Bəmidbar) Numbers
5. (דְּבָרִים / Dəbhārîm) Deuteronomy

II. Nevi'im (נְבִיאִים, "Prophets"):

6. (יְהוֹשֻׁעַ / Yĕhôshúa') Joshua
7. (שופטים / Shophtim) Judges
8. (שְׁמוּאֵל / Shĕmû'ēl) Samuel (I & II)
9. (מלכים / M'lakhim) Kings (I & II)
10. (יְשַׁעְיָהוּ / Yĕsha'ăyāhû) Isaiah
11. (יִרְמְיָהוּ / Yirmĕyāhû) Jeremiah
12. (יְחֶזְקֵיאל / Yĕkhezqiēl) Ezekiel
13. (תרי עשר) The Twelve Prophets
    a. (הוֹשֵׁעַ / Hôshēa') Hosea
    b. (יוֹאֵל / Yô'ēl) Joel
    c. (עָמוֹס / 'Āmôs) Amos
    d. (עֹבַדְיָה / 'Ōbhadhyāh) Obadiah
    e. (יוֹנָה / Yônāh) Jonah
    f. (מִיכָה / Mîkhāh) Micah
    g. (נַחוּם / Naḥûm) Nahum
    h. (חֲבַקּוּק / Ḥăbhaqqûq) Habakkuk
    i. (צְפַנְיָה / Ṣĕphanyāh) Zephaniah
    j. (חַגַּי / Ḥaggai) Haggai
    k. (זְכַרְיָה / Zĕkharyāh) Zechariah
    l. (מַלְאָכִי / Mal'ākhî) Malachi

III. Ketuvim (כְּתוּבִים, "Writings"):

14. (תהלים / Tehillim) Psalms
15. (משלי / Mishlei) Proverbs
16. (אִיּוֹב / Iyyōbh) Job
17. (שִׁיר הַשִּׁירִים / Shīr Hashīrīm) Song of Songs
18. (רות / Rūth) Ruth
19. (איכה / Eikhah) Lamentations
20. (קֹהֶלֶת / Qōheleth) Ecclesiastes
21. (אֶסְתֵר / Estēr) Esther
22. (דָּנִיֵּאל / Dānī'ēl) Daniel
23. (עזרא ונחמיה / Ezra v'Nechemia) Ezra-Nehemiah
24. (דברי הימים / Divrei Hayamim) Chronicles (I & II)

theologically meaningful for the Jewish community. Among the characters whose existence cannot be confirmed are Abraham, his son Isaac, Isaac's son Jacob, and Moses. The earliest biblical figure for whom we may have archaeological evidence is David, the lowly shepherd-turned-king of Israel. Yet even this evidence—an inscription on a monumental stela—is disputed by a few scholars.

The Creation of Humanity

There are two different accounts of the creation of humans in the Hebrew Bible, and each of them has its own repercussions for gender relations. The first one is found in the Book of Genesis 1: 26–7:

> Then God said, "Let us make humankind in our image, according to our likeness; and let them have dominion over the fish of the sea, and over the birds of the air, and over the cattle, and over all the wild animals of the earth, and over every creeping thing that creeps

> upon the earth." So God created humankind in his image, in the image of God he created them; male and female he created them.

In this account, man and woman are created at exactly the same time in "the image of God": thus they are equals. Yet in the second creation story, man is created first, out of the earth, and woman is created later, out of one of his ribs, as a "helper" for him (Genesis 2: 7, 18, 21–4):

> Then the Lord God formed man from the dust of the ground, and breathed into his nostrils the breath of life; and the man became a living being. . . . Then the Lord God said, "It is not good that the man should be alone; I will make him a helper as his partner." . . . So the Lord God caused a deep sleep to fall upon the man, and he slept; then he took one of his ribs and closed up its place with flesh. And the rib that the Lord God had taken from the man he made into a woman and brought her to the man. Then the man said, "This at last is bone of my bones and flesh of my flesh; this one shall be called Woman, for out of Man this one was taken." Therefore a man leaves his father and his mother and clings to his wife, and they become one flesh.

This second account, in which Eve is a secondary creation, is by far the better known of the two, and many people assume that it is the only creation story. Rabbis through the centuries have tried to explain the significance of the rib. One **midrash** (rabbinic commentary or interpretation) proposes that because "the rib is a hidden part of the body, . . . it was chosen to teach women modesty" (*Bereshit Rabbah* 18). This is an example of circular reasoning: the rabbinic account of why God chose to create the woman out of a rib (so that she will be modest) is used to justify the rabbinic view of the way women ought to behave (modestly). Rabbinic literature excludes women from numerous leadership roles on the grounds that it would be immodest for a woman to perform a public role of any kind. In fact, this creation story has been used throughout history to justify the dominance of men over women. Some interpretations suggest that because the female was created from a bone rather than from the earth, women were "lesser" creations whose central obligation was to serve men, not God. This understanding has shaped everything from the tasks of a married woman to the imagery used to express the relationship between God and Israel, in which God is the husband and Israel the wife.

So where was the first woman, made together with Adam in Chapter 1 of Genesis, when Eve was created in Chapter 2? The rabbis devised a creative answer with the midrash of Lilith, the original female being. In early rabbinic references, Lilith appears as a long-haired, winged succubus: a female demon who has sexual relations with sleeping men. Later, succubae were said to be envious of human wives, and to hate the children born of ordinary human relations. Thus Lilith became known as an enemy of women, and all problems related to childbearing, including infertility and miscarriage, were blamed on her.

The earliest reference to the people of Israel outside the Bible is found on an Egyptian stela, from approximately 1208 BCE, inscribed with a hymn recording the pharaoh's triumphs. In a verse that reads "Israel is wasted, its seed is not . . ." (Hallo 2003: 41), "Israel" almost certainly refers to an ethnic group or people. By the end of the thirteenth century BCE, then, it seems that a people calling itself "Israel" existed in Canaan (roughly the region of modern Israel, the Palestinian territories, Lebanon, and part of Syria).

The Origins of "Israel," "Hebrew," "Jew," and "Semitic"

The origins of the term "Israel" are not certain, although one interpretation ("the one who struggled with God") links it with a story in which Abraham's grandson Jacob wrestled with a divine being and was then renamed "Israel." Two other terms used on occasion in the Tanakh are "Hebrew(s)" and "Jew(s)." Abraham, for example, is called a Hebrew, and the prophet Jonah identifies himself as a Hebrew. In modern usage, "Hebrew" is reserved for languages: the ancient Hebrew of the Bible and the modern Hebrew that is one of the two official languages of the modern state of Israel (the other is Arabic). The word "Jew" is derived from "Judah," the name of the territory that in ancient times was considered the Jewish homeland. "Semitic" is derived from "Shem": the name of the man from whom both Jews and Arabs were said to have descended. (According to the biblical story, Shem was one of three sons of the legendary Noah, builder of the Ark that survived the great flood sent by God to destroy the creation.)

When Was the Torah Written Down?

Traditional Jews (for example, those belonging to the Orthodox branch of Judaism) hold that the Torah was divinely revealed to the legendary prophet Moses at Mount Sinai and written down by him as a single document. As we have seen, however, most contemporary biblical scholars believe the Torah to be a composite of texts composed at different times by human beings. The theory that still dominates modern discussions of the Torah question is the **Documentary Hypothesis**, proposed in 1883 by the German scholar Julius Wellhausen, which argues that the Five Books of Moses consist of material from four different authors (or schools of authors) that can be identified through their differences in style and vocabulary as well as theological viewpoint. The basic assumption that the Bible is a human rather than a divine creation has drawn vigorous criticism from traditional Jews, Christians, and Muslims alike. More liberal-minded scholars have also been critical of the Documentary Hypothesis, in particular regarding the composition of the documents. Nevertheless, it is now widely accepted that the Torah texts represent multiple voices. The second book of the Torah, Exodus, tells how Moses, with divine help, led the Israelites out of slavery in Egypt and eventually, after 40 years of wandering in the desert, to the Promised Land of Canaan. Some scholars suggest that part of Exodus may have been written as early as the thirteenth century BCE.

Other scholars suggest that the writing process may have begun during a time of crisis when it was feared that the oral traditions might be lost if they were not recorded. Two such periods were the eighth century BCE, after the northern kingdom of Israel fell to the Assyrians, and the sixth century BCE, after Jerusalem fell to the Babylonians and the leaders of the Israelites were sent into exile in Babylonia.

It is probably safe to assume that the earliest material to have been written down was the Torah. The first five books likely took their final form in the post-exilic period, sometime between the sixth and fourth centuries BCE. The Nevi'im were probably finalized around 200 BCE, and the Ketuvim by the second century CE. The most recent book in the Hebrew Bible is that of Daniel, whose final chapters (7–12) were composed after 167 BCE (even though the narrative is written as if the events it describes took place during the time of the exile).

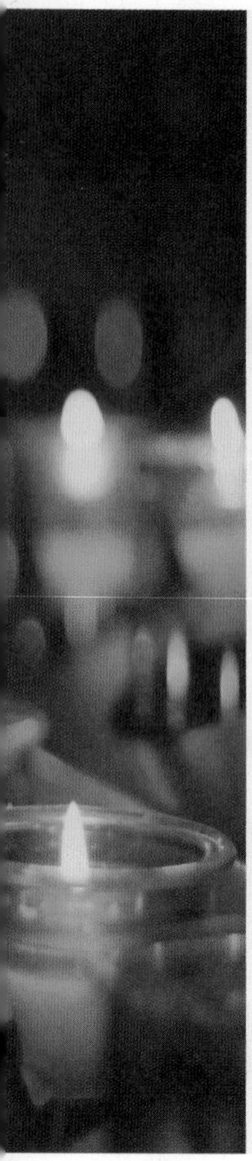

Focus

Passover

Passover (*Pesach* in Hebrew) commemorates the supposed liberation of the Israelites from slavery in Egypt. It falls in the spring and its focal point is the ritual meal called the **Seder** ("order"), during which a text called the **Haggadah** is read aloud. Relating the story of the **Exodus** from Egypt, it celebrates the fact that death passed over the Israelites when God sent a plague to destroy the Egyptian firstborn. During Passover Jews eat only unleavened bread (without yeast), to remind them that the Israelites had to flee Egypt so quickly that they could not wait for their bread to rise. In fact, all cereal products are forbidden over the holiday, because they could ferment: only the unleavened bread called matsoh is allowed.

The Seder is a joyous occasion, a gathering of family and friends that should include a spirited discussion of the holiday's meaning. The centrepiece of the Seder table is a plate of five or six symbolic foods. The *karpas* (vegetable), typically a piece of parsley or celery, represents spring or hope and before it is eaten it is dipped in salt water, which symbolizes the tears of the Israelites. *Maror* (bitter herb), usually represented by horseradish, recalls the bitterness of slavery, while *kharoset*—a mixture of fruit, nuts, wine, and spices, recalls the mortar from which the Israelite slaves made bricks for the pharaoh. The *zeroa* (shankbone) echoes the lamb's blood with which Israelites marked their doorways, signalling their presence to God so that he would "pass over" without taking their firstborn. The *baytzah* (hard-boiled egg) symbolizes either fertility or mourning for the loss of the two historic Temples in Jerusalem (because hard-boiled eggs are relatively easy to digest, they were often eaten during periods of mourning). Finally, *hazeret* (bitter vegetable; often a piece of romaine lettuce) is an optional second symbol of the harsh life of a slave. Jews retell the story of the Exodus as if all those present had been liberated from slavery in Egypt themselves.

Relationship as Covenant: The Israelites and their God

The Bible identifies the Israelites as God's chosen people. On the one hand, they were chosen by Yahweh: "For you are a people holy to the LORD your God; the LORD your God has chosen you out of all the peoples on earth to be his people, his treasured possession" (Deuteronomy 7: 6). On the other hand, the Israelites themselves chose Yahweh: "Then Joshua said to the people, 'You are witnesses against yourselves that you have chosen the LORD, to serve him.' And they said, 'We are witnesses'" (Joshua 24: 22). It is unlikely that the Israelites understood their selection by Yahweh to mark them out as superior to other peoples; rather, it obliged them to assume the responsibilities of serving God. Nor was the notion of being a "chosen people" unique to the Israelites; other peoples in the ancient world also understood themselves to have been chosen by their deities.

One of the central themes in the Bible's account of the relationship between the Israelites and their God is that of the **covenant**. The Hebrew word for "covenant" is ***brit***, which can also be translated as "treaty," "alliance," or "pact." A *brit* is an agreement in which promises are made under oath either to carry out or to abstain from certain specified actions; marriage is a modern example of this type of agreement. The first biblical covenant, described in Genesis 9: 8–17, is made when God promises Noah that he will never again send a flood to destroy the world.

It is the custom to reserve some wine in a special cup for the prophet Elijah, whose return to Earth will herald the coming of the Messianic Age, a time of peace and prosperity for all. At one point in the evening the door to the house is even held open for him to come in and partake of the Passover meal.

According to the Torah, *Pesach* lasts seven days, but Conservative and Orthodox Jews living outside Israel typically observe the holiday for eight days. The reason for the two-day celebration is that in antiquity the beginning of a new month was not established until two witnesses had seen the new moon; the sighting was then communicated by lighting signal fires. Because this system of communication took some time, Jews living outside Israel could not always be sure exactly when *Pesach* began, so to be on the safe side they added an extra day to the celebrations. Even though the Jewish calendar is now fixed and there is no longer any risk of missing the correct festival day, the tradition has been maintained by most Jews outside Israel (the exceptions are members of the Reform branch and some Reconstructionist congregations).

Passover is the first of three major festivals known collectively as the *Shalosh Regalim* ("Three Pilgrimages"), for which the Torah commanded the ancient Israelites to make a pilgrimage to Jerusalem; the other two are Shavuot and Sukkot.

A Seder plate makes a colourful centrepiece for the Passover table. Clockwise from the top, the six symbolic foods are a hard-boiled egg, a shankbone, a "mortar" mixture made of apples, nuts, wine, and spices, a piece of lettuce, parsley, and horseradish (© ZUMA Press, Inc. / Alamy).

Covenants played an important part in the governance of ancient Near Eastern societies. Typically they were made between two parties of unequal power: thus a powerful ruler would promise protection to a less powerful one on condition that the latter fulfilled certain obligations. One way of ritualistically sealing such a treaty was to have a number of animals cut in half and their carcasses lined up in rows. The two parties would then walk between the bodies, symbolically indicating their understanding of the contract: if either party did not fulfill its obligations, it would suffer the same fate as the animals.

What was unusual about the Israelites' covenants was that, in exchange for the deity's protection and presence in their lives, they required the humans involved to live in accordance with a moral code. Other Near Eastern peoples offered sacrifices to their national or tribal deities in hopes of receiving rainfall, fertility, and prosperity, as well as protection, but they did not promise to behave in an ethical manner as part of the pact.

The Book of Genesis traces Israelite ancestry back to a single patriarch, a descendant of Noah (through his son Shem) named Abraham, who has left his birthplace in Mesopotamia (present-day Iraq and Syria) and been travelling with his extended family towards the land of Canaan. Although much of the family decides to stay at a midway point called Haran, God tells Abraham to continue on to Canaan, where they make a covenant that shares many of the elements outlined above.

God, who is obviously the more powerful of the two parties, promises that he will give the land of Canaan to Abraham's still unborn offspring, on condition that Abraham shows perfect obedience to God. When Abraham asks for a guarantee that God will keep his promise, the ceremonial splitting of animal carcasses is performed, and God, whose presence is symbolized by a smoking fire pot and flaming torch, "passe[s] between these pieces" (Genesis 15: 17–18).

Many years later, Abraham agrees to God's request that he undergo circumcision (removal of the foreskin of the penis) as a sign of their covenant (Genesis 17). Then, in fulfillment of another promise that God makes to Abraham, his wife Sarah miraculously produces a son, Isaac, even though she is now well past childbearing age. A few chapters later, in Genesis 22, God asks Abraham to sacrifice the young Isaac as a burnt offering, and Abraham prepares to fulfill his part of the bargain. But just as he is about to plunge the knife into his son's body, an angel intervenes, instructing him to free Isaac and sacrifice a ram instead. Abraham, who has now shown that he was willing to obey God even if it meant sacrificing his beloved son, becomes the ultimate model of obedience for the Israelite people.

Abraham's son Isaac and Isaac's son Jacob in turn make further covenants with God, but it is only centuries later that Moses makes a covenant with God on behalf of the Israelites. The Decalogue—Latin for "ten words"; also known as the Ten Commandments—which Moses transmits to the Israelites at Mount Sinai, stipulates the people's duties both to God and to one another. This

Focus

Circumcision

Judaism, like other religious traditions, uses rituals to commemorate important transitional moments in a person's life. Circumcision is one of the best-known of these rituals, and the first one performed on a Jewish male, usually eight days after birth. Just as Abraham underwent circumcision as a sign of the covenant between him and God, so too does every male born into a Jewish family. Known as a *Brit milah* ("covenant of circumcision") in Hebrew, in **Yiddish** (the vernacular language of Central and Eastern European Jews) it is called a "**Bris**." It involves the removal of the foreskin from the penis by a ritual circumciser called a **mohel**. Usually the ceremony is conducted at home in the presence of family members and friends, although it can also take place in a synagogue. The only people who are required to be present are the father, the mohel, and the *sandek*, the person who holds the baby while the circumcision is performed. Traditionally, the baby is then named and a celebratory meal is served that connects the presence of a new life with the joy of sharing food with family and friends. Blessings for the child and his parents are recited as part of the ritual.

Nowadays, many Jewish families are finding formal ways of expressing their joy on the birth of daughters as well. The more liberal branches of Judaism hold a naming ceremony called a **Simchat Bat** ("joy of a daughter") that celebrates the bringing of a daughter both into the family and into the covenant with God. Since there is no explicit ritual formula to follow, families tend to create their own traditions: some invite relatives and friends simply to share a meal, while others make the event more of a traditional ceremony, including various prayers and blessings.

aspect of the Torah confirms that ethical behaviour was an obligatory component of the Israelites' covenant with God.

The second book of the Torah, Exodus, is called *Shemot* ("Names") in Hebrew, from its first sentence, "These are the names of . . ." It describes how God, through Moses, led the Israelites out of Egypt to Mount Sinai, where he revealed his commandments, beginning with the Decalogue. Then Moses went up the mountain and stayed there for 40 days and 40 nights.

Lost without Moses, the Israelites persuaded his brother Aaron to make a god to lead them. Aaron collected the people's gold earrings, melted them down, and used the gold to create an idol in the form of a golden calf. They were worshipping the calf when Moses descended from the mountain with the stone tablets on which God had engraved his commandments—the second of which forbade the making of idols. Enraged, Moses hurled the Tablets of the Law to the ground, shattering

Document

The Decalogue (Ten Commandments)

The terms of the covenant into which Yahweh and the Israelites enter are presented in the Decalogue or Ten Commandments. The Decalogue appears twice in the Torah: in the second book, Exodus (20: 2–17) and in the fifth, Deuteronomy (5: 6–21). The first five commandments concern responsibilities to God; the second, to fellow human beings.

I am the LORD your God who brought you out of Egypt, out of the land of slavery.

You shall have no other god to set against me.

You shall not make a carved image for yourself nor the likeness of anything in the heavens above, or on the earth below, or in the waters under the earth. You shall not bow down to them or worship them; for I, the LORD your God, am a jealous god. I punish the children for the sins of the fathers to the third and fourth generations of those who hate me. But I keep faith with thousands, with those who love me and keep my commandments.

You shall not make wrong use of the name of the LORD your God: The LORD will not leave unpunished the man who misuses his name.

Remember to keep the sabbath day holy. You have six days to labour and do all your work. But the seventh day is a sabbath of the LORD your God; that day you shall not do any work, you, your son or your daughter, your slave or your slave-girl, your cattle or the alien within your gates; for in six days the LORD made heaven and earth, the sea, and all that is in them, and on the seventh day he rested. Therefore the LORD blessed the sabbath day and declared it holy.

Honour your father and mother, that you may live long in the land which the LORD your God is giving you.

You shall not commit murder.

You shall not commit adultery.

You shall not steal.

You shall not give false evidence against your neighbour.

You shall not covet your neighbour's house; you shall not covet your neighbour's wife, his slave, his slave-girl, his ox, his ass, or anything that belongs to him (Exodus 20: 2–17.)

Focus

Shavuot

Shavuot celebrates God's revelation of the Torah to Moses, although its origins can be traced to the barley harvest in the ancient Land of Israel. Also known as the Festival of Weeks, it is the second of the *Shalosh Regalim*.

By the mid-second century CE, Shavuot was marked by reading the Decalogue (a crucial part of the Law) and the Book of Ruth (set during the barley harvest). Another tradition, still observed today by religious Jews, is to stay up the entire night of Shavuot reading from a special volume that contains passages from every book of the Bible and every section of the rabbinic commentary on it (the Mishnah); this ritual, introduced by sixteenth-century mystics, represents devotion to the Torah. A third tradition is to eat sweet dairy foods such as cheesecake and cheese blintzes, possibly because they recall the description of the Torah as "honey and milk . . . under your tongue" (Song of Songs 4: 11). Usually falling in late May or early June, Shavuot is celebrated for just one day in Israel, but for two days by most Jews living elsewhere.

them; he then destroyed the golden idol, and, with help of those who had not taken part in the idol worship, put to death 3,000 who had. According to the Bible, the Israelites spent the next 40 years wandering in the desert; then, within sight of the Promised Land of Canaan, Moses died. Leadership of the people of Israel was transferred to Joshua, who guided them across the Jordan River to take possession of Canaan.

According to the book of Joshua, the Israelites annihilated the people of Canaan. But there is no archaeological evidence to support this account, and many biblical scholars argue that it was constructed to convey the theologically important idea of the Israelites' taking full possession of the land that had been promised to their ancestor Abraham. Archaeological findings reveal that the earliest Israelite communities were not built on the ruins of Canaanite settlements, but on formerly uninhabited land in the central highlands. As a result, most scholars now understand the acquisition of Canaan to have been accomplished through settlement rather than military conquest.

Focus

Sukkot

Sukkot commemorates the Israelites' wanderings in the wilderness. It is an eight-day holiday during which—weather permitting—Jews eat and sleep in the open air in a temporary structure called a *sukkah* ("booth" or "tabernacle"; *sukkot* is the plural form). The *sukkah* should have a roof made of organic material such as palm leaves, bamboo sticks, or pine branches, and it must be possible to see the sky through the gaps in the roof. This symbolizes the Israelites' willingness to put themselves directly under divine protection. Usually falling in September or October, Sukkot is said to have taken its name from the temporary shelters that farmers used in autumn to guard their ripening crops. It is the third and last of the *Shalosh Regalim*.

The Personal Name of God

The God with whom all these biblical figures made their covenants has a personal name, which is represented in Hebrew by four consonants: YHWH. Although this **Tetragrammaton** ("four-letter word") is conventionally written as "Yahweh," no one knows how it ought to be pronounced, since there are no vowels between the consonants. In Exodus 3: 14 YHWH tells Moses, "I am who I am," which suggests a possible linkage with the Hebrew verb *hayah*, "to be," but there is no strong consensus on this interpretation. In any case, many Jews consider the Tetragrammaton too sacred to ever be pronounced. Indeed, the Decalogue commands that God's name not be taken in vain. Modern Jews reading the Tanakh aloud substitute "Adonai" ("Lord") or "haShem" ("the Name") for "YHWH." English translations normally use capital letters (the LORD or GOD).

In the sixteenth century, a mistaken belief that the vowels of "Adonai" were those belonging to the Tetragrammaton, YHWH, produced the name "Jehovah." Protestants were in a power struggle against the Church of Rome at that time, and to buttress their arguments they turned to the original Hebrew and Aramaic texts. But they were not well-versed in these languages, and did not realize that the vowels they were combining with the Tetragrammaton were in fact those of another word altogether. To this day, certain Christians (in particular, Jehovah's Witnesses) continue to use the name "Jehovah," but it has never been used by Jews.

Of Kings and Messiahs

It is possible that the biblical David—an obscure shepherd who, according to one tradition, killed the giant Goliath with his slingshot and became king—is based on a historical figure. David, whose reign is said to have begun around 1000 BCE, is identified as the Israelites' greatest king, the ruler against whom every future leader of Judah is compared. As part of the inauguration ritual, the new king was anointed with oil. The Hebrew term *mashiach*, from which the English **messiah** is derived—as is the Greek form "Christos," hence "Christ"—is directly related to this ritual, as it means "anointed [one]." Thus David was a messiah. He was also a warrior king credited with conquering an impressive number of neighbouring peoples and establishing an empire of sorts that his son Solomon inherited.

Solomon built the first Temple in Jerusalem as a focal point for national identity and worship, the latter primarily in the form of sacrifices. After his death, in the second half of the tenth century BCE, the kingdom split in two: Israel in the north and Judah in the south. From this point on, the historicity of events described in the Hebrew Bible is on firmer ground.

The Exile in Babylonia

Some two centuries later (c. 722 BCE), the northern kingdom fell to the superpower of the region, the Assyrians. The victors deported some of the Israelites to other parts of their empire, and imported people from elsewhere into Israel, destroying its national cohesion. The Israelites remaining in the south fell to a later superpower, the Babylonians, in 586 BCE, at which time the Temple in Jerusalem was destroyed and the Israelites' political and religious leaders were deported to Babylonia (modern-day Iraq) to prevent them from stirring up trouble in their homeland. Thus began the Babylonian captivity or "**Exile**."

The Exile is of paramount importance in Israelite–Jewish history. Marking the beginning of the **Diaspora**—the dispersion of Jews outside Israel—it reverberates throughout the Hebrew Bible in passages evoking the trauma of alienation from their homeland, which Jews have dealt with throughout their history (see Document box). One important theological development associated with the Exile was the first unambiguous statement of monotheism: the belief in a single god,

Focus

Samaritans

The Samaritans are an ancient people who still inhabit the region of Samaria, in the centre of modern Israel. Although they identify themselves as Jews, some believe they were the product of intermarriage between the people who were not deported by the Assyrians and those brought to the region from elsewhere. In any event, the Samaritans broke away from mainstream Jewish beliefs and practices in about the fifth century BCE. The Jerusalem Temple was never their holy place—they had their own temple on Mount Gerizim in Samaria, although it was destroyed in the second century BCE and was never rebuilt—and their Bible consists of the Torah or Pentateuch alone. Although they number only about 600 today, during Passover they still offer sacrifices at the foot of Mount Gerizim.

Samaritan priests prepare a fire pit for their Passover sacrifices, held at the foot of Mount Gerizim in Samaria (© www.BibleLandPictures.com / Alamy).

Document

From Psalm 137: 1–4

Although tradition attributes the poetic prayers called the Psalms to King David, modern scholars believe they were composed by a multitude of post-exilic authors. Indeed, the exile is a frequent theme. Psalm 137, for example, expresses an exile's longing for his home, Jerusalem.

By the rivers of Babylon,
    there we sat,
    sat and wept,
    as we thought of Zion.
There on the poplars
    we hung up our lyres,
    for our captors asked us there for songs,
    our tormentors, for amusement,
    "Sing us one of the songs of Zion."
How can we sing a song of the Lord on alien soil? . . .

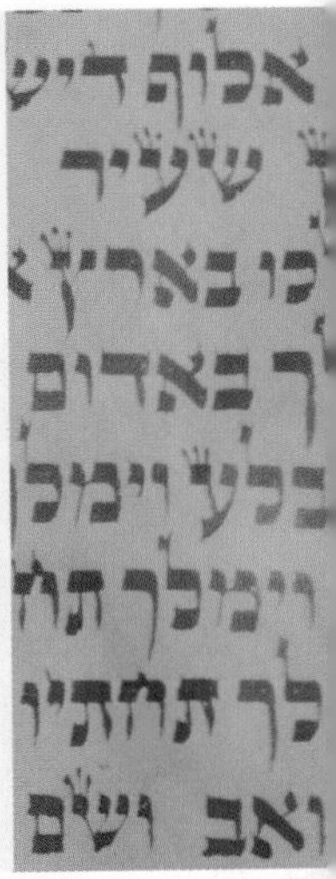

creator of the universe. Scholars theorize that, far from their homeland, the exiles recast their national deity as universal. The earliest writer to describe Yahweh as the only god is the unnamed prophet who is believed to have composed chapters 40 to 55 of the Book of Isaiah: in Isaiah 45: 21, for example, he has Yahweh declare that "There is no other god besides me, a righteous God and a Saviour; there is no one besides me."

The Exile came to an end in 539 BCE, when Cyrus of Persia (modern-day Iran) conquered the Babylonians and freed their captives. Many Judeans then returned to their homeland, but after nearly five decades in Babylonia, a sizeable number had put down roots there, and they decided to stay. In time, Babylonia would become one of Judaism's most vibrant intellectual centres. It was the Babylonian Jewish community that produced one of the central texts in the history of Judaism: the Babylonian Talmud, completed in the sixth century CE.

The Second Temple Period (515–70 CE)

Those who did return found that their ancestral homeland had been reduced to the area immediately around Jerusalem. Nevertheless, they rebuilt the Temple and (with the help of the Persians) furnished it with many of the gold and silver items that the Babylonians had taken. Rededicated in 515 BCE, the "Second Temple" would endure until 70 CE.

The Impact of Alexander the Great

Alexander the Great (356–323 BCE) brought major cultural shifts to the ancient Near East. The son of the king of Macedon, as a youth Alexander had been tutored by the Greek philosopher Aristotle, and he had no doubt that Greek culture surpassed all others. When his father died, the 20-year-old Alexander set out to become the master of the then known world.

Across Asia Minor (modern-day Turkey) and down into the eastern Mediterranean basin, Alexander established more than 30 cities (20 named after himself), in each of which he established institutions central to Greek civilization, such as theatres and gymnasia. Before long, Greek became

Focus

The Septuagint

The arrangement of the books in the Christian "Old Testament" is based on the Greek version of the Hebrew text, which was translated around 200 BCE to serve the Greek-speaking Jewish community in Alexandria, Egypt. The Greek text is known as the **Septuagint** (Latin for "seventy") because legend had it that the Torah was translated by 70 (or 72) Jewish sages who, although they had worked independently, all produced exactly the same text. This was taken as evidence that their work was divinely sanctioned.

the new lingua franca of the region. In this way Alexander laid the foundations for the *cosmopolis* ("world city") and made possible a new sense of interconnectedness among formerly disparate peoples.

Hellenization and the Jews

Jewish responses to the introduction of Greek culture ("Hellenization") varied widely. Some Jews so admired Greek culture that they even underwent surgery to hide the evidence of circumcision, so that they would blend in with the uncircumcised Greeks when they exercised in the nude at the gymnasium. Yet many other Jews, particularly in non-urban areas, staunchly rejected all Greek ideas and customs.

The Maccabean Revolt

For over a century, Judea was controlled by the Ptolemies, the Greek dynasty that had ruled Egypt since 305 BCE. In 198 BCE, however, a rival Greek dynasty named the Seleucids, who already ruled Syria, took control of Judea. The territory around Jerusalem became known in Greek as *Ioudaia*, and a person from there was a *Ioudaios*.

Antiochus IV Epiphanes (r. 175–163 BCE) was a Seleucid who strongly advocated assimilation to Greek culture in the territories he ruled. He prohibited the reading and teaching of the Mosaic Law, commanded that Torah scrolls be burned, and made observation of the **Sabbath** (the seventh day) a crime punishable by death. He also ordered that women who had had their sons circumcised be put to death; the First Book of Maccabees (one of several texts excluded from the Hebrew and Protestant canons but included in Catholic and Eastern Orthodox Bibles) contains gruesome stories of mothers executed with their sons' bodies tied around their necks (e.g., I Macc. 1: 60–1).

All this was extremely painful for Jews, but the most egregious actions of all were directed against the Temple, where Antiochus erected altars to other gods, placed a statue of Zeus in the sanctuary courtyard, and even sacrificed pigs—animals that Israelites were forbidden to eat, let alone offer to their deity—on Yahweh's altar. Antiochus also intervened in the selection of the Temple's high priest and, when Jews objected, imposed further restrictions on them. His ultimate goal might well have been to promote political unity, but since religion was intertwined with all aspects of life in that era, the Judeans interpreted his actions as a comprehensive attack on their way of life.

Jews who refused to transgress the laws of their faith were often tortured and put to death. The graphic descriptions in 1 and 2 Maccabees suggest that some Jews interpreted the persecution as a sign that the end of the world was imminent. This **apocalyptic** perspective is also reflected in the later chapters of the Book of Daniel, which describe the toppling of Antiochus from his throne; as we have noted, chapters 7–12 are thought to have been written in this period.

The Hasmonean Family

In 167 BCE, a family of priests known as the Hasmoneans mounted a successful uprising against Antiochus and Hellenized Jews. Judah and his brothers coordinated a band of fighters whose guerilla-style warfare proved unexpectedly effective. Judah's prowess as a fighter and leader earned him the nickname "Maccabee" ("the Hammer"), from which the revolt as a whole derives its name. The Maccabeans recaptured the Temple, purged it of foreign idols and impure animals, and rededicated it to its rightful deity in 164 BCE. It is this rededication that is recalled by the annual Hanukkah holiday (see Focus box).

Establishing themselves as client kings of the Seleucids, the Hasmoneans ruled from 164 to 63 BCE in precarious semi-independence during a time of profound sectarian discord and civil war. Eventually many of them willingly adopted Hellenistic culture. In 63 BCE, however, the Roman general Pompey secured Jerusalem and made the state a vassal of Rome, bringing Jewish self-rule to an end.

A Variety of Judaisms

An astonishing variety of Jewish groups emerged during the Hasmonean period. Then as now, there were competing views about who was a Jew, what it meant to be a Jew, and how Jews should relate to non-Jews. Because of this diversity, it is more accurate to refer to "Judaisms" than "Judaism" in the Second Temple period.

Focus

Hanukkah

Hanukkah, the festival of lights, commemorates the return of the Temple to the Jews by Judah the Maccabee and his brothers. According to the legend, when the Temple was purified, only one vial of oil could be found to light the seven-branched oil lamp called the **menorah**. This amount of oil should have run out after one day, but—miraculously—it lasted for eight days. For this reason Hanukkah is celebrated by lighting a candle on a special menorah for eight consecutive days and eating foods cooked in oil, such as potato latkes (pancakes) and *sufganiot* (doughnuts filled with jam or caramel).

Sadducees and Pharisees

The Sadducees came primarily from the wealthy upper echelons of society. They made up most of the membership of the Sanhedrin, the local Jewish council, and were responsible for the running of the Temple, in particular the sacrificial system. Considering the Torah to be the only authoritative text, they demanded a narrow, literal interpretation of it, and focused on cultic worship as Jews' primary obligation.

By contrast, the Pharisees sought to apply Halakhah to everyday life. Although the early Christians interpreted this focus as narrow and legalistic, we should not accept that portrayal at face value: after all, the Pharisees were their rivals. Rather, the Pharisees were concerned with what it meant to live their daily lives in accordance with the Torah. In contrast to the Sadducees, the Pharisees tended to interpret the scriptural text broadly. They had a social conscience, practised alms-giving, prayer, and fasting, and believed in the resurrection and future day of judgment. For them, the entire Tanakh was sacred and worthy of study.

Among their concerns were the Torah's instructions regarding matters such as food purity, Sabbath observance, and family issues. For example, the Decalogue called on Jews to keep the Sabbath day holy. But what did that mean in practical terms? If it meant refraining from work on the Sabbath, how did one define "work"? The Pharisees formulated answers to such questions; they also established rules and instructions to help Jews observe the law. In time, these teachings attained the status of divinely revealed law, and came to be known as the Oral Law or Oral Torah. In developing their interpretations and regulations, the Pharisees were not trying to split hairs: their goal was to understand what God had commanded so that they could obey and help other Jews do likewise.

Essenes

The Essenes are generally held to have been the authors of the Dead Sea Scrolls: a collection of texts produced between the second and first centuries BCE that were discovered in 1947. These manuscripts shed light on the worldview of the Essenes—a monastic community of meticulously observant priests. They also include the earliest manuscripts of every book of the Hebrew Bible (some in fragmented form only) except, for unknown reasons, the Book of Esther.

Cultic purity—a bodily state in which one is sufficiently pure to be acceptable in the sacred spaces of God—was of the utmost importance for the Essenes. Like the Pharisees, they sought to apply the Bible to daily life, but in a much more rigorous manner. They established their community at Qumran in the Judean desert after expressing disapproval of the way the Hasmoneans were running the Temple cult. They held an apocalyptic worldview, believing that the world was under the control of evil forces and that God would soon intervene to defeat the powers of darkness. The Essenes thought of themselves as the new children of Israel, biding their time until the day when, with God's help, they would take back the Promised Land from the corrupt leadership of Hellenized Jews.

Therapeutae

The Therapeutae were a monastic group living near Lake Mareotis in Egypt. In sharp contrast to the monastic Essenes of Qumran, the Therapeutae included women as well as men in their community, and although the sexes lived and ate separately, they would meet to worship, sing

Focus

Purim

Purim is a joyful minor holiday that falls around March. The Book of Esther tells how the Jews of Persia were saved from the evil plot of a Persian official named Haman, who sought to exterminate them ("purim" means "lots," a reference to the lottery by which Haman determined the date of his attack on the Jews). At the centre of the story are Esther, a wise and beautiful Jewish woman, and her uncle Mordecai, who together prevent the destruction of the Jews. Since the holiday celebrates deliverance from a physical threat, it focuses on material rather than spiritual things. When the Book of Esther is read in the synagogue, members of the congregation use noise-makers or bang pots and pans to drown out every mention of Haman's name. There is also a festive meal, at which guests are expected to drink enough wine that they cannot distinguish between "Blessed be Mordecai" and "Cursed be Haman." As in the North American celebration of Halloween, there are costume parties and gifts of food, especially *hamantashen*: cookies (traditionally filled with poppy seeds) that are supposed to resemble the ears of Haman.

hymns, and dance together. Members of the community renounced private property and family life, lived their lives in devotion to God, prayed at sunrise and sunset, and spent the rest of their time in study or worship.

Zealots

The Zealots did not exist as an organized group until well into the first century CE. In contrast to the Sadducees, the Zealots vehemently refused to cooperate with Rome, and they encouraged their fellow Jews to engage in violent rebellion. The result was the First Jewish Revolt (66–73 CE), in the course of which most of Jerusalem, including the Temple, was destroyed and much of the Jewish population either killed or forced into slavery.

Other Visions of the Future

Further expressions of diversity can be seen in the varied expectations for the future held by Jews in this period. Some hoped for a messiah to lead them out from under Roman oppression. Until the end of Judean monarchic rule in 586 BCE, the term *mashiach*, "anointed one," referred exclusively to the current Hebrew king. But by Hellenistic times the idea of an "anointed" king had moved out of the world of current possibility and into the realm of anticipation: now the *mashiach* was the ideal future king whom God would empower to defeat Israel's enemies. The Essenes awaited two messiahs: one a king and one a priest.

Not all expectations centred on a messiah, however. Some Jews hoped for a new covenant between God and his people; others, a new era of justice and equality. There were also some who looked forward to a time when Jerusalem would become central to the world, and all peoples would worship God at Mount **Zion**. The range of thought regarding the future is similarly broad among modern Jews.

Focus

Monotheism

Monotheism—the belief in and worship of a single god, creator of the universe—is a central feature of Judaism, and is one of the fundamental teachings of the Torah. Yet there is evidence in the Hebrew Bible that the pre-exilic Israelites did practise polytheism, worshipping fertility gods such as Ba'al and Asherah along with Yahweh, who was initially perceived as a national deity. Eventually, through their battles with other peoples and their gods, as well as their internal struggles, the Israelites became persuaded that Yahweh was the sole god of the universe. The belief in one god is a central tenet today not only for Jews, but also for Christians and Muslims.

Points of Consensus

Diversity of expectations notwithstanding, a degree of consensus did exist concerning certain fundamental factors. The majority of Jews, regardless of sect, believed in:

1. The oneness of God. By the Second Temple period, Judaism was a monotheistic tradition centred on the idea of a single, all-powerful creator God.
2. The authority and sacred nature of the Torah.
3. The special status of Israel as the chosen "people of God." Who exactly was included in the "people of God" was a point of contention (as it continues to be in the modern state of Israel). But there was a general belief in both a "people of God" and a "land of God."
4. The status of the Temple in Jerusalem as the place where God and his people met.

Finally, it is important to note that most Jews in late antiquity did not belong to any of the sects discussed above. They simply continued to observe the aspects of the Torah law that their parents, and their parents' parents before them, had observed.

Enter the Romans (63 BCE)

In time, conflicts among the Hasmonean leaders led to a bloody civil war. In 63 BCE the Roman general Pompey was called to Judea settle the rivalry among the various contenders for the Hasmonean throne. Instead, he took control of the land. Thus began approximately four centuries of repressive Roman rule over Judea.

Herod the Great

In 37 BCE the Romans put an end to the Hasmonean dynasty by naming Herod the Great king of Israel. Herod's governance style was one of extravagant self-indulgence, brutality, and deception; yet he was one of the most vibrant and successful leaders in all of Jewish history, cleverly balancing Roman and Jewish interests. Nevertheless, because he was not of Judean descent—his ancestors were Idumeans, converts to Judaism who inhabited the territory just south of Judea—many Jews did not accept his rule as legitimate.

Herod was indeed devoted to Rome and Hellenistic culture, but he made many advances on behalf of Judean culture and religion. He also greatly improved life for the peasantry by extending irrigation and reducing lawlessness and banditry. At the same time, he was pathologically suspicious, prepared to kill any member of the former Hasmonean dynasty who might possibly threaten his power, including his wife Mariamme and three of his sons. After their murders he was frequently tormented with guilt. Perhaps it is no wonder that the Roman emperor Augustus, who was a friend of Herod's, is said to have declared that he "would rather be Herod's pig than Herod's son."

Herod built many impressive public structures, including temples, aqueducts, and theatres, but his most famous project was the renovation of the Temple in Jerusalem. He replaced what had been a rather modest building, more than four centuries old, with a stunningly beautiful structure on a much-enlarged site.

The Rabbinic Period (70–700 CE)

In 70 CE the Romans destroyed the Second Temple, which was never rebuilt. Among the only groups to survive were the Pharisees; by the second century CE, however, those who would have been called Pharisees in an earlier time were referred to as **rabbis** (from *rav*, "teacher" in Hebrew). The Pharisees' oral tradition likewise survived, and was developed further under the rabbis, who added their own interpretations to those they inherited. According to rabbinic tradition, God gave Moses the Oral Torah at the same time as the written version. Finally, the Oral Torah was written down and codified around the year 220 CE, by Judah haNasi ("Judah the Prince") and in this written form is called the **Mishnah**.

A model of Jerusalem in Herod's day (the late first century BCE), including the refurbished Second Temple (above; scale 1:50) was constructed in the 1960s and is now located at the Israel Museum in Jerusalem (© Vladimir Khirman / Alamy).

A woman deep in prayer on the women's side of the Western Wall (see p. 146). Also visible are some of the many prayer requests that, by tradition, the faithful have placed in the cracks (© Michele Murray).

The interpretations developed by the **rabbinic movement** have defined Jewish belief and practice for the past 2,000 years. The teachers and religious leaders who helped to steer Jewish communities after the loss of the Temple replaced sacrificial worship—never practised again—with liturgical prayer and a new emphasis on ethical behaviour.

Synagogues (the term comes from the Greek for "gathering together") already existed while the Temple still stood, but they gained in importance once it was gone. Communal gathering places in which Jews met to read the Torah, to pray, and to study, by the first century CE synagogues were scattered across the Roman Empire.

The fact that texts and interpretations, rather than a particular place, became the focus of Judaism helped isolated Jewish communities maintain a sense of unity. Because of the centrality of Torah study to Judaism, literacy rates tended to be higher among Jewish males than among their non-Jewish counterparts. If most Jewish boys learned to read, however, it seems that girls and women were generally excluded from Torah study on the grounds that women's primary domain was the home.

The limiting of Torah study to males was not unusual for the era in which the rabbis were writing (between roughly the second and sixth centuries CE). What may be surprising is that the rabbis outlined a set of laws (based on Exodus 21: 10) according to which a wife is entitled to three things from her husband: food, clothing, and "marital rights" (i.e., sexual relations). The Talmud specifies how often a man must provide sex for his wife based on his profession, since what he does for a living will affect how long he is away from her and how physically tired he is: "Men of independent means: every day; workmen: twice a week; ass drivers: once a week; camel drivers: once a month, and sailors: at least once every six months" (BT, Ketubbot 5: 6). If a husband does not fulfill his duty, he must divorce his wife so that she can find a different husband to meet her sexual needs. Given the period in which the Talmud was composed, this acknowledgement of women's sexual needs seems rather progressive. On the other hand, these laws may have been based on the idea that women's sexuality was so passive that they were not capable of asking for sex, or perhaps that women were not capable of controlling their sexuality and therefore had to be satisfied. The same laws, by prohibiting men from taking vows of abstinence, increased the likelihood that Jews would obey what the rabbis of the Talmudic period considered the first **mitzvah** (commandment) in the Bible: "Be fruitful and multiply, and fill the earth. . . ." (Genesis 1: 28).

By the end of the first century CE, most Jews were living outside Judea. The total Jewish population was probably between 5 and 6 million, and Jewish communities could be found in every major city of the Roman Empire.

Another Clash with Rome

The last major Jewish revolt against Roman rule took place between 132 and 135 CE. It is associated with a messianic figure named Shimon Bar Kosiba, whom his supporters called Bar Cochba ("son of the Star") but who was known to his critics as Bar Koziba ("son of the Lie" or "Liar"). The revolt was likely prompted by the emperor Hadrian's plan to establish a Roman city on the remains of Jerusalem, and a temple to Jupiter on what had been the site of the Temple. The revolt failed miserably. Those Jews who had been living in Jerusalem were driven out, and faced death if they tried to return. It was at this time that the Romans renamed Judea—a Roman province since 6 CE—"Syria-Palestina." Until the establishment of the state of Israel in 1948, Judaism would be mainly a religion of the Diaspora.

Rabbi Hillel

Rabbi Hillel was a popular teacher who was active between 30 BCE and 10 CE, hence an older contemporary of Jesus of Nazareth. He was a humble woodworker who became the leader of a religious school (**yeshiva**) and was renowned for his piety. According to a famous story, an impertinent non-Jew once came to Hillel and said that he would convert to Judaism if the Rabbi could recite all of the Torah while standing on one foot. Hillel reportedly told him: "What is hateful to you, do not do to your neighbour: that is the entire Torah. The rest is commentary; go and learn it!" Whereas Hillel was said to have been lenient in his interpretation of the Torah, his compatriot and rival, Rabbi Shammai, took a stricter, more literal view. More than 300 arguments between the House of Hillel and the House of Shammai are recorded in the Talmud, and in most cases it was Hillel's interpretation that the rabbinic scholars followed.

The Androcentric Perspectives of the Rabbis

The foundational literature of rabbinic Judaism reflects the interests and concerns of the male rabbis. Women generally were excluded from the rabbinic hierarchies of achievement, and exempt from the rituals and activities considered most meritorious, such as the study of Torah and the performance of mitzvot ("commandments," the plural of "mitzvah"). Women were typically expected to fulfill only those commandments that were negative ("you shall not . . .") and did not have to be performed at a specific time. While rabbinic Halakhah gave women more freedom and protection than biblical law did, and the rabbis made it possible for some women to inherit, control, and dispose of property, the status of most women—in particular wives and unmarried minor daughters—was clearly subordinate to that of men in all areas of life: judicial, religious, sexual, and economic.

On the other hand, non-rabbinic evidence (such as inscriptions) demonstrates that some women did serve as heads of synagogues, particularly in the Greco-Roman Diaspora, and that others were patrons and benefactors of both civic and religious institutions. While it is true that these women would have belonged to the elite, and so had opportunities that most women did not, they remind us of how important it is to differentiate between the idealized life of the Jewish woman that the rabbis prescribed and the realities of the lives that Jewish women actually lived in antiquity. It was—alas—the idealized image, not the flesh and blood reality, that would determine the norms, roles, and expectations for Jewish women in subsequent centuries.

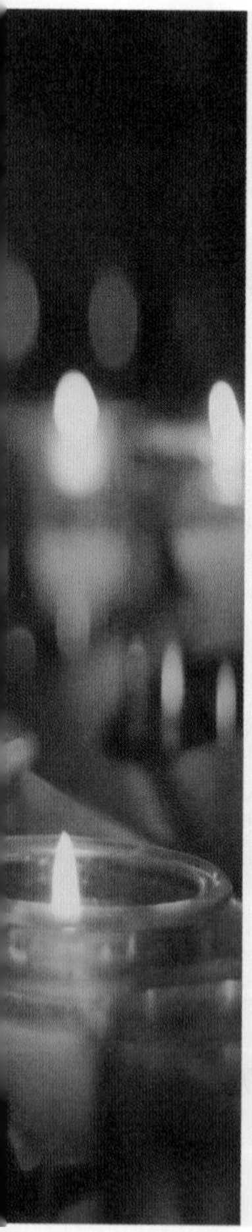

Focus

Mishnah and Gemarah: The Talmud

The written version of the Oral Torah, the Mishnah, is divided into six "orders," each of which deals with a particular sphere of life and the laws that govern it, although some also address other subjects. The names of the orders reveal their central topics: Seeds (laws of agriculture); Appointed Seasons (laws governing festivals, fast days, and the Sabbath); Women (laws governing marriage, divorce, betrothal, and adultery; this section also includes Vows); Damages (civil and criminal law, and the most commonly read section of the Mishnah, the "Sayings of the Fathers," a collection of ethical maxims); Holy Things (temple-related matters such as sacrifices, ritual slaughter, and the priesthood rituals); and Purities (issues of ritual purity and impurity).

The writing of the Mishnah in the early third century CE did not mark the end of rabbinic commentary, however. Over the next few centuries, rabbis in both Babylonia and the Land of Israel continued to study and interpret traditional teachings, including the Mishnah. Their commentaries, called **Gemarah** (from an Aramaic root that means "teaching"), were transmitted orally from teacher to student, just as the Oral Law had been. The Gemarah contains both Halakhah (legal material) and **Aggadah** (narrative material). Aggadah includes historical material, biblical commentaries, philosophy, theology, and wisdom literature.

Eventually, this commentary also was written down. The Gemarah produced in Palestine was put into writing in the early fifth century, and in that form is called the Palestinian (or Jerusalem) Talmud. The Gemarah produced by Babylonian rabbis was written down about a century later, and it was this "Babylonian Talmud" that gained predominance in the Jewish world, so that any general reference to "the Talmud" is understood to refer to it. Both Talmuds are compendia of law, interpretation, and argument that offer what may be described as a "slice of life" from the rabbinic academies of the time, since the discussions they present (in stream-of-consciousness fashion) often go round and round before reaching a conclusion.

Two Main Rabbinic Centres: Palestine and Babylonia

After the Bar Kochba revolt, Judaism developed under the guidance of the rabbis, the successors of the priestly leaders of the previous period. There were two main centres of development: in the Galilee region of northern Palestine, and in Babylonia, which was now ruled by the Parthians. Relations between Palestinian Jews and the Romans eventually calmed, and the Jews were granted the same treatment as other minorities in the empire, with the extra privilege of exemption from pagan cultic observances. Roman leaders recognized the Jewish Patriarch, a descendant of Rabbi Hillel, as the central political leader of the Jewish community. But the situation for Jews deteriorated as the third century progressed, primarily because of a general decline in economic and political circumstances across the Roman Empire that left Palestine relatively impoverished.

In general, conditions were better for Babylonian Jews in that era. When the Persian Sassanids replaced the Parthians in 226 CE, Jews experienced some persecution as a result of the Sassanids' efforts to promote their own religion (Zoroastrianism), but by the middle of the century the Persian rulers allowed the Jews extensive autonomy under their communal leader in exile, the exilarch. Intellectual activity flourished at two Babylonian academies, in Nehardea (later moved to Pumbeditha) and Sura, that rivalled and eventually surpassed in prestige the rabbinic schools of Palestine, thriving as centres of Jewish scholarship until the eleventh century.

The Rise of Christianity

When the Roman emperor Constantine I gave Christians the liberty to practise their faith in 313, he began a process that led to Christianity's becoming the official religion of the Roman Empire in 380. Henceforth all inhabitants of the Byzantine Empire would be expected to follow the Christian faith. This did not bode well for Jews.

Christian attitudes towards Jews had been shaped in large part by the fact that Christianity had begun as a Jewish sect. Jesus was Jewish, as were his earliest disciples, but his message had had only modest success among Jews. By the end of the second century, most new Christians were Gentiles (non-Jews). In time, as Christian leaders sought to differentiate their movement from Judaism, tensions developed, especially with certain Gentiles who identified themselves as Christians but chose to adopt Jewish practices such as circumcision, observe Jewish dietary laws, and attend synagogue. Since these "Judaizers" were undermining Christian efforts at differentiation, Christian leaders such as Paul sought to dissuade them. In his letter to the Galatians (c. 50 CE), for example, he urged Gentile Christians not to tie themselves to "a yoke of slavery" (5: 1) by observing Jewish law. Other Christians argued that their movement had superseded Judaism. According to Justin Martyr in the mid-second century, Christians had replaced Jews as "the true and spiritual Israelite nation, and the race of Judah and of Jacob and Isaac and Abraham" (*Dialogue with Trypho* 11: 5); elsewhere he asserted that circumcision was commanded of the Jews to set them apart for suffering. In response to Christians in Syria, who were still attending synagogue services in the fourth century, the bishop of Antioch, John Chrysostom, preached some of the most vehement anti-Jewish sermons in Christian history, condemning the synagogue as "a whorehouse and a theatre . . . a den of thieves and a haunt of wild animals" (*Against the Judaizers* 1.3). Although this rhetoric was directed at Christian Judaizers, it would eventually be repurposed for use against Jews.

Other early Christian literature, such as the Gospel of Matthew, explicitly blamed the Jews for the death of Jesus (e.g., 24: 26); this charge would be recycled in later centuries whenever tensions between Jews and Christians were high. The same gospel contains a diatribe against Jewish leaders that has unfortunately been influential in the formation of anti-Jewish attitudes: "Woe to you scribes and Pharisees, hypocrites! for you are like whitewashed tombs, which outwardly appear beautiful, but within they are full of dead men's bones and all uncleanness. . . . You serpents, you brood of vipers, how are you to escape being sentenced to hell?" (Matthew 23: 27, 32).

By the early fifth century the continuing vitality of Judaism was seen by some as contrary to Christian interests. Now the Roman Empire introduced laws restricting Jewish religious and commercial activities. Jews were forbidden to hold public office, build new synagogues, or marry Christians. They were also prohibited from owning Christian slaves. Biblical law offered certain protections to Jewish slaves (including the possibility of manumission), and although masters were forbidden to force their slaves to convert, the fact that many slaves voluntarily converted to Judaism may have been one of the reasons behind the prohibition. At a time when slavery was an integral part of the agricultural system, this injunction meant that Jews had no hope of competing economically with Christian farmers (Efron et al. 2009: 134). It also represented a first step in the alienation of Jews from the land, a process that by the Middle Ages would transform them into an almost entirely urban people.

Certain Christian leaders favoured banning Judaism entirely and presenting Jews with the choice that the Romans had given Christians themselves in the third century CE: renunciation of their faith or death. King Sisebut, the Visigothic ruler of Spain from 612 to 621, forced Jews to choose between conversion to Christianity, exile, and death. The Church's approach, formulated

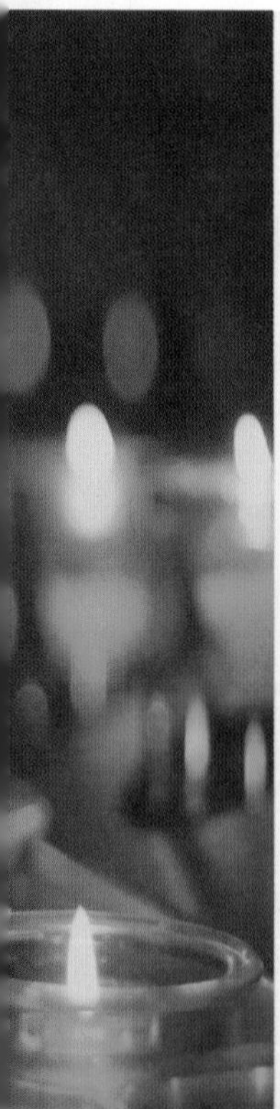

Focus

The Jewish Calendar

The Gregorian calendar, used in the Western world, is based on the solar year of 365¼ days. The Jewish calendar is a lunar calendar, based on 12 months of 29½ days. Since this adds up to 354 days for a lunar year—about 11 days less than a solar year—any given date in the lunar calendar will move backwards each year by 11 days. In order to ensure that holidays and festivals consistently fall around the same time of the year, the Jewish calendar adds a thirteenth "leap month" on a fixed schedule of 7 years out of every 19. Today the astronomical calculations are made by experts, and festival dates and leap months are established far in advance.

According to the Gregorian calendar, a new day begins at midnight—the first moment of the morning. By contrast, the Jewish day begins at nightfall, defined as the time when at least three stars can be seen in one glimpse of the sky. Thus the Sabbath begins at nightfall on Friday evening and ends at nightfall on Saturday. This is in accordance with the description of the first day of creation in Genesis 1: 5—"And there was evening and there was morning, the first day"—in which evening precedes the day.

By convention, the Jewish calendar counts the years from the creation of the universe, based on the life spans and time periods mentioned in the biblical text. But this number is not taken too literally, since even people who believe the creation story in Genesis to be factual acknowledge that the biblical references to time periods may not be reliable. The system is accepted, however, as a matter of convenience. The Gregorian calendar year "2015–16" is the year "5776 since the Creation" in the Jewish calendar (Wylen 1989: 67).

in the fifth century by Augustine of Hippo in his *City of God* and later accepted by Pope Gregory I (r. 590–604), was less radical but nonetheless devastating for Jews. Augustine wished Jews to serve as an example of the consequences of not accepting Jesus as messiah. To that end, he proposed that Jews should not be eradicated, but rather allowed to live in suffering. To justify his position, Augustine quoted a verse from Psalms 59: 11, in which David, the ancient king of the Israelites, says of his enemies: "Do not destroy them, lest my people forget."

Jewish Life under Islam: Seventh–Twelfth Century

Islam emerged in the early seventh century, and would soon have a deep impact on Jewish history. Within a few short decades, Islam had seized Palestine and Egypt from the Christian Byzantine Empire, and Persia from the Persian Empire, and by the end of that century most of the world's Jews resided in a unified Islamic empire encompassing territory from the Iberian Peninsula in the west to India in the east. As a consequence, Jews in Palestine, Egypt, and Spain were liberated from the injustice and oppression they had known under antagonistic Christian rulers. Muslims considered Judaism and Christianity their partners in monotheism and respected them for possessing, as did Islam, a divinely revealed book. Thus Jews and Christians living under Islam were defined as *dhimmis* ("protected peoples") and guaranteed protection of their lives and property, as well as the right to practise their religion, as long as they paid special taxes and adhered to certain rules stipulated in a document called the Pact of Umar.

For Jews, life under Muslim rule was considerably better than it had been under Christian Rome. Without the complicated history shared by Christianity and Judaism, Jewish–Muslim relations were less fraught with tension. In addition, Muslims understood that with Jews they shared not only belief in a single god, but opposition to the use of images in the worship of Yahweh/Allah. Hence they tended to be less suspicious of Jews than of Christians, whose doctrine of the Trinity, and pervasive use of crucifixes, overtly contradicted Islamic principles.

The period of European decline often called the "Dark Ages," from the seventh to the thirteenth century, was a time of great advances for Islam. And since the majority of the world's Jews lived in the Islamic empire, they benefited from its prosperity. By the end of the eighth century, more Jews in the Muslim world were active in urban trade and commerce than in agriculture. Arabic, originally the language of a small tribal population, was now the language of a vast culture, and it replaced Aramaic as the Jewish lingua franca.

The Gaonic Period

In 750 CE the Abbasid dynasty overthrew the Umayyads, and as a result the capital of the Muslim Caliphate moved from Damascus to Baghdad. The academies of Pumbeditha and Sura likewise moved to Baghdad in the ninth and tenth centuries respectively, and attracted Jewish students from all over the Muslim world. They also attracted letters from rabbis seeking advice from the academies' leaders, the **Gaonim**, on problematic cases involving matters that ranged from divorce and inheritance to commercial affairs. The answers to the rabbis' questions, called **responsa**, reflected the Gaonim's interpretations of Talmudic laws, and provided the foundation for later legal and philosophical developments.

The main opposition to the Gaonim came from the **Karaites** ("scripturalists"), a movement founded in Iraq in the eighth century by Anan ben David. Rejecting the principle that the rabbinic interpretations of the Oral Torah/Talmud had the status of divinely revealed truth, and arguing that the Tanakh was the exclusive source of legal authority, Ben David encouraged individual Jews to interpret the (written) Torah for themselves, and to favour the plain meaning of the words in their context over the creative explanations of the rabbis. Because of its emphasis on individual interpretation, the Karaite movement was characterized by division and disunity. Nevertheless, it enjoyed significant popular support and its impact on the rabbinic world was important: the Karaites were the first Jews to make an intensive study of Hebrew grammar and the manuscript traditions of the Bible, and they influenced the codification of the Hebrew text in the tenth century. Although the rabbinic tradition eventually prevailed, largely because the Muslim authorities recognized the rabbis as the official representatives of Judaism, small communities of Karaites still exist today in Israel, Turkey, and elsewhere in the Diaspora.

Maimonides

By the beginning of the eleventh century Iraq no longer dominated the Muslim world. At the same time the influence of the Gaonim was waning, and instability in Babylonia prompted many Jews to leave for more promising lands.

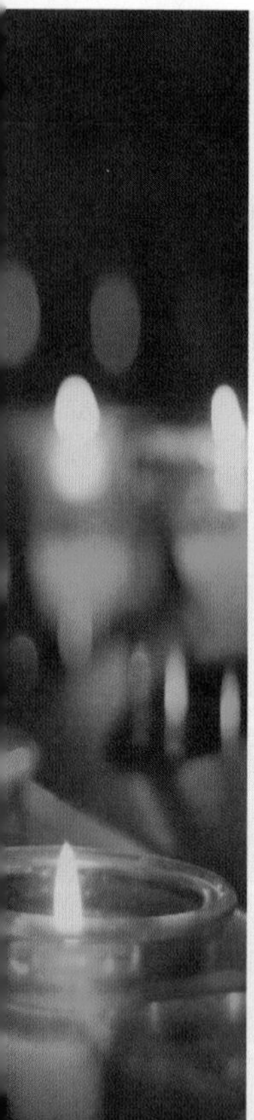

Focus

Ashkenazim, Sephardim, and Mizrahim

Over time, three distinct Jewish cultural traditions took shape. The oldest by far originated in Babylonia with the exiles who did not return to Judea in the sixth century BCE—the first members of the Diaspora. These Jews, and all the others whose ancestors remained in the general region of the Middle East, eventually came to be known as **Mizrahim** (from the Hebrew meaning "East"). Since many Mizrahi Jews come from Arab countries, the language most closely associated with them is Arabic, but some speak languages such as Persian and Kurdish. Other Jews made their way west to Europe. Those who settled on the Iberian Peninsula (modern Spain and Portugal) came to be known as **Sephardim** (from the Hebrew for "Spain"), while those who turned north towards France and Germany became the **Ashkenazim** (from the Hebrew for "Germany"). From the eighth century until the fifteenth, the Sephardic communities fared significantly better under the Muslim rulers of Al-Andalus than did the Ashkenazic communities of Christian-dominated Europe.

These two groups are distinct from one another in language, food, and certain religious rituals. **Ladino** (a blend of medieval Spanish and Hebrew that is written in Hebrew characters) is traditionally associated with Sephardic Jews, while Yiddish (German-based, with influences from Hebrew and other languages, written in Hebrew characters) is the lingua franca of the Ashkenazic community. At Passover Sephardic Jews eat rice, corn, and beans—all of which comply with the Passover prohibition on foods made with yeast (such as bread)—but Ashkenazic Jews avoid such foods because when they are cooked they rise and expand just as leavened foods do. In addition to lighting two candles on Sabbath eve, Sephardic Jews light candles in honour of family members who have died. Mizrahi Jews tend to follow Sephardic religious practices.

Some Babylonian Jews headed to Spain, where Jewish culture was blossoming under the Umayyads. But that period too came to an end in the twelfth century, when a puritanical Muslim sect from Morocco called the Almohads took power and banned both Judaism and Christianity. Many Jews fled Spain as a result.

Among the latter was the family of a judge named Maimon. His son, Moses ben Maimon, better known as **Moses Maimonides** (1135–1204), would become one of the most famous Jewish philosophers and legal scholars of the Islamic age, identified in religious texts as "Rambam" (R-M-B-M, the acronym of "Rabbi Moses ben Maimon").

As an adult Maimonides ultimately established himself in Egypt—a central hub of Jewish life, at that time under the control of the renowned Salah al-Din (Saladin). Jews were generally treated well at his court, and Maimonides became the personal physician to a high official.

Maimonides was a prolific writer, producing the famous 14-volume code of Jewish law called **Mishneh Torah** as well as various treatises on medicine and logic, but his most important work was philosophical. *The Guide of the Perplexed*, originally written in Arabic, was directed to Jews "perplexed" by the challenges of living in a cosmopolitan and philosophically sophisticated environment that tested their faith. Using Greek philosophy, particularly that of Aristotle, Maimonides sought to diminish the tension between faith and knowledge and emphasized that learning ought not to undermine faith. He believed that all the biblical commandments were rational, although some were easier to understand than others, and he argued against the literal interpretation of scripture. As he explains in the boxed excerpt below, biblical language that attributes human qualities to God is intended only to make God understandable to humans and should not be interpreted literally.

Document

From Maimonides, *Guide of the Perplexed: On Image* (tzelem) *and Likeness* (demut)

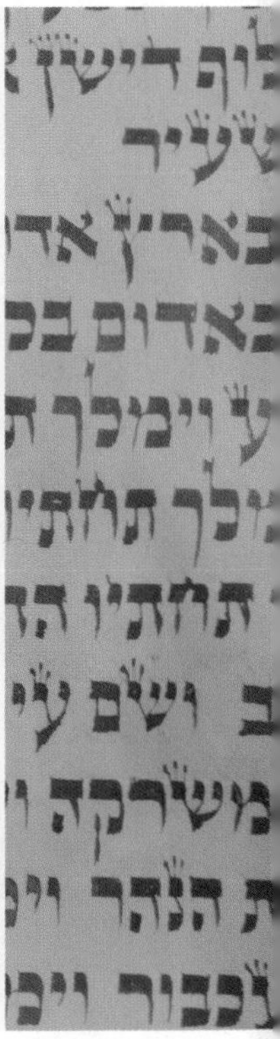

People have thought that in the Hebrew language *image* [*tzelem*] denotes the shape and configuration of a thing. This supposition led them to the pure doctrine of the corporeality of God, on account of His saying: "Let us make man in our image, after our likeness" (Gen. 1: 26). . . . [They] deemed that if they abandoned this belief, they would give the lie to the biblical text. . . .

As for the term *likeness* (*demut*), . . . it too signifies likeness in respect of a notion. For the Scriptural dictum, "I am like a pelican in the wilderness" (Ps. 102: 7), does not signify that its author resembled the pelican with regard to its wings and feathers, but that his sadness was like that of the bird. . . . Now man possesses as his proprium something in him that is very strange as it is not found in anything else that exists under the sphere of the moon, namely, intellectual apprehension. In the exercise of this, no sense, no part of the body, none of the extremities are used; and therefore this apprehension was likened to the apprehension of the Deity. . . . It was because of this something, I mean because of the divine intellect conjoined with man, that it is said of the latter that he is "in the image of God and in His likeness" (Gen. 1: 26–7), not that God, may He be exalted, is a body and possesses a shape (*Guide of the Perplexed*, Part I, Chapter 1; I. Twersky [1972]: 246–7).

Medieval Jewish thought was deeply influenced by Islam. Muslim writers and thinkers had translated the scientific and philosophical works of Greeks such as Plato and Aristotle into Arabic—works that emphasized rational thought and human reason over revelation. Muslims considered Greek philosophy to be part of their culture and did not see it as alien or threatening to the revelatory foundation of Islam. Jewish intellectuals such as Maimonides, inspired by Muslim thinkers to undertake the challenge of connecting philosophy to religion, in turn influenced Jewish thought in Christian Europe.

Jews in the Christian World: Seventh to Fifteenth Century

Christian Europe between the seventh and twelfth centuries was largely a feudal agricultural society in which peasants farmed land owned by the wealthy in exchange for their protection. Jews, however, belonged mainly to the urban merchant class and relied on government for protection. Jewish intellectual life flourished in France and Germany, but elsewhere in Europe Jews faced undercurrents of hostility that at times would surge into waves of persecution, expulsion, or both.

Perhaps the best-known expulsion was the one ordered by the Christian monarchs of Spain, Ferdinand and Isabella, in 1492. Having finally taken the last Muslim stronghold, they completed their "reconquest" by commanding that the Jewish population either convert to Christianity or leave the country that had been their home for centuries. When Christopher Columbus embarked on the voyage that would take him to the "new world," in August 1492, he was forced to set sail from a small port in southern Spain because all the major ports were so congested with departing Jews. Of the tens of thousands who left, most sought refuge in the Ottoman Turkish Empire. There they were welcomed by Sultan Bayazid II, who recognized the potential value of the refugees, many of whom were highly skilled. To this day, some Turkish Jews still speak Ladino.

The Spanish Inquisition

In order to avoid expulsion, other Spanish Jews did convert to Christianity, but some of these "Conversos" (and their descendants) would continue to practise Jewish rites in secret. They were not the first. As early as 1481, Ferdinand and Isabella had petitioned the Pope for permission to establish an Inquisition to root out and punish such heresy. Known for its ruthlessness, the Spanish Inquisition established tribunals in many cities with the goal of finding and executing those Conversos (also referred to as Marranos, "swine") who had not abandoned all Jewish traditions. More than 13,000 Conversos were put on trial during the first 12 years of the Spanish Inquisition.

The Kabbalah

Perhaps in response to the pain of expulsion, many Jews took a renewed interest in mysticism, particularly the tradition known as **Kabbalah** (from the Hebrew meaning "to receive"). Although Kabbalah itself appears to date from the twelfth century, some of its teachings are said to have

Map 3.1 Expulsion and Migration of Jews from Europe, c. 1000–1500 CE

been passed from teacher to student from as far back as Moses, and perhaps earlier. Certainly the biblical Book of Ezekiel abounds in prophecies and mystical visions of the divine, and there was a long tradition of literature recounting visionary ascents into the heavenly palaces of the divine. In the Jewish mystical tradition, the devout can experience direct revelation of God, usually through meditation or ecstatic prayer. This tradition developed in new ways in the Middle Ages, influenced in part by the Islamic mystical tradition of Sufism.

The most authoritative Kabbalah text (actually a collection of texts) is a commentary on the Five Books of Moses called the Zohar ("splendour" or "radiance"). Though written in the voice of the second-century rabbinic sage Shimon bar Yochai, it is generally thought to have been written (in Aramaic) by Moses de Leon, a thirteenth-century Spanish–Jewish mystic who was immersed in the great Jewish thinkers of the Islamic world, including Maimonides.

Kabbalists refer to God as the *Ayn Sof* ("Without End" or "Infinite"), for God is considered to be beyond thought, beyond form, beyond gender—in effect, the unknowable creator. What *can* be known about God are the aspects of his being that connect the created world with its unknowable divine source, and through which the powers of the *Ayn Sof* flow, revealing him to the world. Kabbalists call these aspects—of which there are 10—Sefirot, which literally means "numbers" but is usually translated as "emanations" or "channels" of God's creative energy and power. The Sefirot are *Keter*/Crown, *Hokhmah*/Wisdom, *Binah*/Understanding, *Hesed*/Loving kindness, *Gevurah*/Might, *Tiferet*/Beauty, *Hod*/Splendor, *Netzakh*/Victory, *Yesod*/Foundation, and *Malkhut*/Sovereignty. Each is an aspect of the *Ayn Sof* that radiates from the divine sphere into the created, material realm, and each one is interlinked with the others. Kabbalists seek not only to understand the Sefirot and their interrelations, but also (through the Kabbalists' own actions, thoughts, and words) to modify these interrelations.

But why should humans intervene in such divine matters? And how can they possibly do so? The Zohar explains that at the beginning of creation (in the Garden of Eden), the powers of the Sefirot were perfectly in balance, but this balance was disturbed when Adam and Eve disobeyed God by eating of the forbidden fruit. According to the Zohar, the Torah was given to Israel to provide a way of restoring the Sefirot to their original harmony. Each time a Jew fulfills a commandment, a small positive shift occurs that helps to bring the Sefirot into balanced alignment. Likewise, every time a commandment is not fulfilled, the Sefirot are pushed into further disarray. When perfect balance is achieved, the divine powers will flow unhindered, just as they did at the beginning of creation.

Isaac Luria

An enormously influential later scholar of the Kabbalah was **Isaac Luria** (1534–72), who was born in Jerusalem and moved to the northern Palestinian city of Safed in 1569. Although he died just three years later, at the age of 38, he and his disciples transformed the city into the centre of Jewish mysticism that it remains to this day. Unfortunately, Luria did not write his teachings down, but his students' writings indicate that they were extremely complicated and creative.

One of the better-known components of Lurianic mysticism is the concept of *tikkun* ("mending" or "restoration"). The basis of this idea is Luria's understanding of how the universe was created. First, since the Ayn Sof was everywhere, he had to contract himself in order to make room for the world. Luria interpreted this *tzimtzum* ("contraction") as a type of divine exile. Next, divine light surged from God into the empty space, taking the form of the 10 Sefirot as well as the first man: Adam Kadmon ("primal man"). Out of the eyes, nose, and mouth of Adam Kadmon the light streamed, and this created vessels that held the light. But the vessels were unable to contain such divine power, and so they exploded into luminous fragments that became trapped in the created world. In this way, thought Luria, evil entered creation.

Like the Zohar, Luria held that Jews had the capacity to reverse this dismal situation, for the divine sparks longed to be liberated from their material abode and returned to their original state; through prayer, study, and the performance of mitzvot, Jews could assist in the process of "restoring the world," or ***tikkun olam***. For Jews struggling with the aftermath of the expulsion from Spain, the idea that individual religious acts made a difference was empowering. At the same time, the concept of the Ayn Sof's fragmentation during the creation process, resulting in the introduction of evil into the world, offered a way of understanding the Jews' suffering.

Sabbatai Zvi

Messianic expectations swelled when a student of Lurianic Kabbalah named **Sabbatai Zvi** was declared the messiah in Turkey in 1666. A number of mystically oriented Jews aligned themselves with him, and together they marched on Istanbul. The sultan eventually put Zvi in prison and offered him the choice of conversion to Islam or death. Zvi chose to convert, and although the majority of his followers abandoned him, some of them believed his choice was divinely sanctioned: therefore they too converted to Islam, but continued their Jewish mystical practice in secret. Descendants of this sect still live in modern Turkey, where they are known as the Dönmeh ("returners" in Turkish).

Eastern Europe

For centuries, Ashkenazic Jews had tended to live in their own (largely urban) communities, separated to some extent from the Christian mainstream of European life. By the early 1500s, however, many places were beginning to enforce segregation. Among them was the Republic of Venice, which called its Jewish quarter the "ghetto." Meanwhile, persecution had been pushing many Jews farther east. The feudal leaders in Poland welcomed them, and several areas of Eastern Europe became home to a vibrant Ashkenazic culture,

In 1648, however, a revolt against the Polish nobles by Ukrainian peasants brought this peaceful period to an end. Jews, who had developed ties with the nobility through their commercial activities, were also targeted by the rebels. This prompted many Ashkenazim to leave Poland and move west, back into the regions their ancestors had fled.

Hasidism

In the mid-eighteenth century, in southeastern Poland, a movement emerged to counter the scholarly rabbinic leaders who dismissed uneducated Jews as incapable of knowing God. The charismatic founder of **Hasidism** (from the Hebrew word for "piety"), Israel ben Eliezer (1698–1760), came to be known as the **Baal Shem Tov** ("Master of the good name") or "Besht" (an acronym). An itinerant healer and teacher, the Besht encouraged his fellow Jews to worship God with joy and delight, from the heart rather than the head. The little that is known about his personal life comes from the stories of his disciples, who claimed that he had supernatural powers, including the ability to heal illness and even revive the dead. A collection of those stories, entitled *In Praise of the Baal Shem Tov* (1815), is an early example of the storytelling tradition that is one of the most valuable legacies of Hasidic culture. Today the movement continues to flourish in certain Jewish communities. Hasidic men in particular are easily identified by their long black coats, black hats, and substantial beards and sidelocks.

In keeping with the Besht's emphasis on deep religious feeling rather than scholarship, Hasidic leaders are not rabbinic scholars but charismatic individuals known as Tzaddikim ("righteous men") whose authority is based on what are believed to be their supernatural powers; Hasidic teaching goes so far as to assert that "Whatever God does, it is also within the capacity of the tzaddik to do" (Efron et al. 2009: 264). Hasidim believe that through a personal relationship with a **Tzaddik** it is possible for an ordinary person to attain attachment to God. Thus the relationship between a Tzaddik and his disciples tends to be very close, and Hasidim address their Tzaddikim by the Yiddish title Rebbe instead of the more formal "Rabbi."

Document

A Rabbi for a Day

Jacob ben Wolf Kranz, the famous "Preacher of Dubno," was born in Lithuania around 1740 and died in 1804. Although he does not appear to have been a Hasid himself, his down-to-earth, often humorous, stories, subverting conventional assumptions, recall the Hasidic storytelling tradition. In the following tale, for example, one might assume that the distinguished rabbi would be more clever than his driver . . .

The famous Preacher of Dubno was once journeying from one town to another delivering his learned sermons. Wherever he went he was received with enthusiasm and accorded the greatest honours. His driver, who accompanied him on this tour, was very much impressed by all this welcome.

One day, as they were on the road, the driver said, "Rabbi, I have a great favour to ask of you. Wherever we go people heap honours on you. Although I am only an ignorant driver I'd like to know how it feels to receive so much attention. Would you mind if we were to exchange clothes for one day? Then they'll think I am the great preacher and you the driver, so they'll honour me instead!"

Now the Preacher of Dubno was a man of the people and a merry soul, but he saw the pitfalls awaiting his driver in such an arrangement.

"Suppose I agreed—what then? You know the rabbi's clothes don't make a rabbi! What would you do for learning? If they were to ask you to explain some difficult passage in the Law, you'd only make a fool of yourself, wouldn't you?"

"Don't you worry, Rabbi—I am willing to take that chance."

"In that case," said the preacher, "here are my clothes."

And the two men undressed and exchanged clothes as well as their callings.

As they entered the town all the Jewish inhabitants turned out to greet the great preacher. They conducted him into the synagogue while the assumed driver followed discreetly at a distance.

Each man came up to the "rabbi" to shake hands and to say the customary: *Sholom Aleichem*, learned Rabbi!"

The "rabbi" was thrilled with his reception. He sat down in the seat of honour surrounded by all the scholars and dignitaries of the town. In the meantime the preacher from his corner kept his merry eyes on the driver to see what would happen.

"Learned Rabbi," suddenly asked a local scholar, "would you be good enough to explain to us this passage in the Law we don't understand?"

The preacher in his corner chuckled, for the passage was indeed a difficult one. "Now he's sunk!" he said to himself.

With knitted brows the "rabbi" peered into the sacred book placed before him, although he could not understand one word. Then, impatiently pushing it away from him, he addressed himself sarcastically to the learned men of the town, "A fine lot of scholars you are! Is this the most difficult question you could ask me? Why, this passage is so simple even my driver could explain it to you!"

Then he called the Preacher of Dubno: "Driver, come here for a moment and explain the Law to these 'scholars'!" (Ausubel 1961: 21–2).

With the passage of time, many subgroups developed, of which the largest and best-known today is Chabad. Named for three concepts that it considers central—*chokhmah* (wisdom), *binah* (reason), and *da'at* (knowledge)—it was founded by Rebbe Shneur Zalman (1745–1813) and today is widely known as Chabad–Lubavitch, after the Russian town that was its base for many years. Chabad's adherents, often referred to as Lubavitchers, follow many Lurianic traditions. For example, they attribute human suffering to the fragmentation of the Godhead, and their prayer book follows the same arrangement as Luria's. In 1940 the community fled wartime Europe and set up a synagogue in New York. Menachem Mendel Schneerson (1902–94), who assumed the leadership in 1951, significantly expanded its international activities and founded a worldwide organization whose goal is to reach out to Jews and, in so doing, hasten the coming of the Messianic Age. In fact, some of his followers believed Schneerson was the Jewish messiah (although he denied it). All Lubavitcher homes displayed his portrait, followers regularly sought his blessing, and some devotees still consider him the messiah. The reverence with which he was treated by his followers led many Jewish critics, from both the right and the left, to decry what they saw as the personality cult that had developed around him. Despite the criticism, and the fact that no successor has yet emerged to replace Schneerson, Chabad continues to grow: it now claims more than 200,000 adherents, and up to a million Jews attend Chabad services at least once a year.

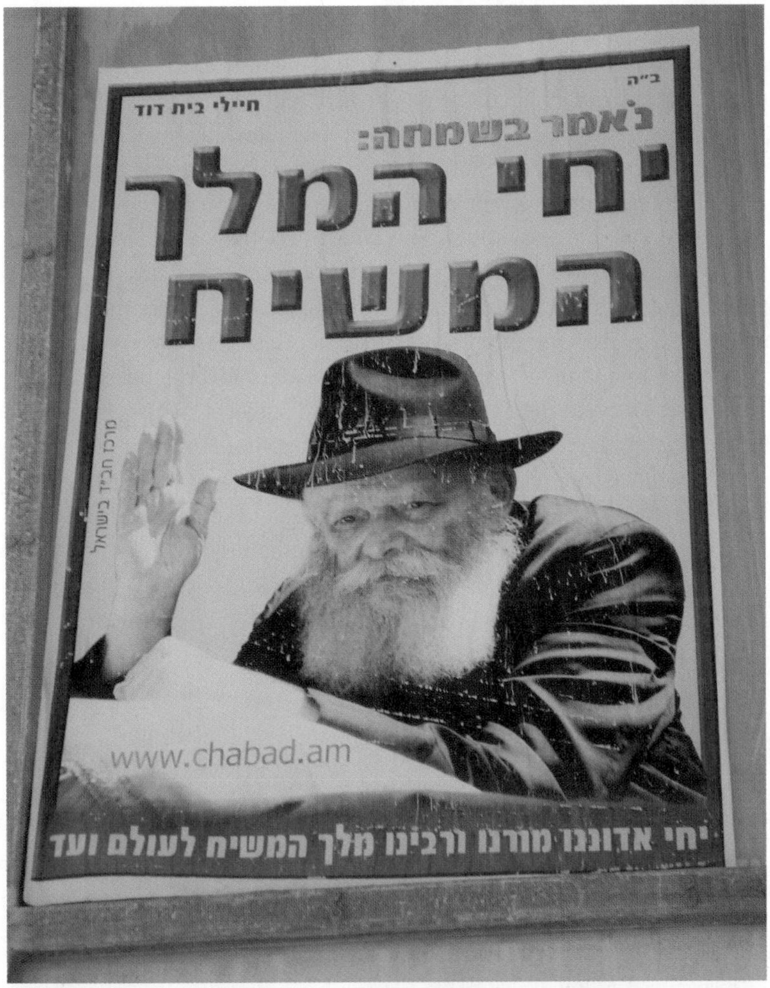

A poster in Jerusalem shows the "Lubavitcher Rebbe," the late Menachem Mendel Schneerson (1902–94), and proclaims that "The King, the Messiah Lives!" (© Michele Murray).

Hasidim vs Mitnagdim

The eighteenth century was a dark time for Eastern European Jews. Poor, downtrodden, and politically disenfranchised, they needed reasons for hope, and Hasidism provided them. The Baal Shem Tov taught that everyone, no matter how impoverished or uneducated, could commune with God, for God was everywhere. The Hasidic emphasis on community and equality also struck a chord. Hasidic worship was marked by swaying prayer, ecstatic dancing, and joyous singing to melodies that would eventually shape Jewish music across denominational lines. By the early nineteenth century almost two-thirds of Eastern European Jewry had joined the movement, and today Hasidim make up an important component of Orthodox Judaism (see below).

The Modern Period

Haskalah: The Jewish Enlightenment

In the eighteenth century, a number of European philosophers articulated a program for the radical freedom of individual thought. Enlightenment thinkers argued that individuals should be able to judge for themselves what was right and wrong. The French Revolution (1789–99) ended feudalism and overturned the Catholic alliance with the French monarchy in favour of freedom, equality, and brotherhood. As the Enlightenment swept Western Europe, Jews benefited from its emphasis on reason, tolerance, and material progress. Restrictions were lifted, the walls that surrounded many ghettos fell, and Jews were free to live where they wished. Some countries gave Jews citizenship, which opened up opportunities for them to vote, attend universities, and choose their own occupations.

It was in response to these developments that the **Haskalah** (Jewish Enlightenment) was launched. As doors began opening for Jews, Haskalah leaders advocated a restructuring of Jewish education to devote less time to the Talmud and more to subjects such as modern languages and practical skills, which would help Jews integrate (without assimilating) into European society. The philosopher Moses Mendelssohn (1729–86) recognized that, after so many years behind ghetto walls, his fellow German Jews had become inward-looking and segregated from the rest of society. Encouraging them to speak German rather than Yiddish, he urged them to be Jews at home and Germans on the street. The "new Jew" would be both a committed adherent of Judaism and a full participant in modern culture.

Modern Branches of Judaism

The adaptation of traditional Jewish thought and practice to the modern world laid the foundation for the emergence of what we know today as the Reform, Orthodox, Conservative, Reconstructionist, and Humanistic branches of Judaism. Each of these diverse movements originated in an effort to reconcile centuries-old traditions with the new ways of thinking and living promoted by the European Enlightenment.

Reform

Reform Judaism began with the goal of making Jewish practice meaningful for Jews living in eighteenth-century Germany. Its pioneers explicitly supported Enlightenment ideals and drew attention to their compatibility with Judaism. The father of Reform was Israel Jacobson (1768–1828), who in

1815 opened his Berlin home for worship services with sermons by other leaders of the movement. Three years later the Hamburg Temple was established for Sabbath services that used the everyday German of the community rather than Hebrew, eliminated the traditional references to the hoped-for restoration of the Temple in Jerusalem, and featured choral music with organ accompaniment. (This was quite a daring innovation: although instrumental as well as vocal music had been a part of Jewish worship in the Temple, it had been banned after the Temple's destruction, as a sign of mourning.) It took two generations for Reform Judaism to find its niche among German congregations, however. Reform synagogues did not have a meaningful presence in Germany until the 1830s, and a German-language prayer book was not introduced until 1848.

The spiritual leader of the Reform movement was Abraham Geiger (1810–74), a scholar of Near Eastern languages and philosophy who argued that Judaism had been adapting to its surroundings throughout history, and hence that reform was natural to it. Geiger used critical textual analysis to argue that the Hebrew Bible reflected the concerns and perspectives of post-biblical Jewish movements. He also demonstrated the connections among Judaism, Christianity, and Islam.

Today Reform Jews do not generally observe the dietary laws (see p. 129) although growing numbers are now becoming more observant. They understand Judaism to be a flexible, living

In April 2013, while attending the monthly women's prayer service at the Western Wall, this woman was arrested for wearing a tallit (prayer shawl), which the Haredi community insists is reserved for men. Four other women were also detained (AP Photo / Michal Fattal).

religion that remains relevant because it evolves as the realities of human life change. Reform encourages interfaith dialogue. It also allows women to serve as rabbis; it was a Reform seminary that ordained Sally Priesand, the first female rabbi in North America, in 1972.

Orthodox Judaism

The spread of Reform Judaism stimulated the establishment of the Orthodox branch, a traditionalist reaction that was largely spearheaded by Samson Raphael Hirsch (1808–88). Hirsch sought to prove that traditional Judaism was compatible with modernity, and promoted the application of Torah in all aspects of everyday life.

Orthodox Jews believe that the Hebrew Bible is the revealed word of God, and understand the Mishnah and Talmud to be written forms of Oral Law that originated with Moses; they follow rabbinic Halakhah and observe the laws of Torah. While the more liberal Orthodox Jews participate to some degree in non-Jewish society the most conservative, the Haredim, "trembling ones" (from Isaiah 66: 5: "Hear the word of the Lord, you who tremble at his word"), tend to live and work in segregated communities, and every part of their lives is governed by Halakhah. The Hasidim are a subgroup of the Haredim.

Conservative

The third branch of Judaism was founded by Zacharias Frankel (1801–75) under the name "Positive-Historical Judaism." An attempt to find middle ground between rigid Orthodoxy and the radical liberalism of Reform, it eventually developed into what is known today as Conservative Judaism. Frankel argued that core teachings such as the oneness of God were divinely revealed, but also acknowledged that Judaism had developed within history, and therefore that its traditions were open to moderate reinterpretation and modification. Conservatives interpret the text more literally than Reform Jews do, but more liberally than the Orthodox, though typically they do follow the dietary laws. Since they are not Orthodox, however, they also allow for some restructuring in order to stay relevant in modern times. Conservative synagogues vary in their attitudes towards women's roles: more liberal congregations allow female rabbis and full female participation in synagogue services, whereas more traditional ones do not.

Reconstructionism

Whereas the Reform, Orthodox, and Conservative movements all originated in Germany, the Reconstructionist movement was created in North America. Its founder, Mordechai Kaplan (1881–1983), began his career as an Orthodox rabbi, but soon grew uncomfortable with Orthodoxy. He then obtained a teaching position at the Jewish Theological Seminary (a Conservative institution) and in 1922 established a Reconstructionist synagogue called the Society for the Advancement of Judaism. In his book *Judaism as a Civilization* (1934), he argues that Judaism was not supernaturally revealed, but is an ever-changing religious civilization involving language, literature, art, social organization, and symbols as well as beliefs and practices. Kaplan called for the synagogue to be a social and cultural centre (rather than a religious one), and he introduced the idea of the Jewish Community Centre—an institution that has become a regular part of the North American Jewish environment. He also argued that the scriptures were not divinely revealed, but created

Focus

Dietary Laws

Some Jews jokingly suggest that Judaism is a way of eating. That may not be far from the truth. Food is an essential part of Jewish observance. Jewish dietary laws (*kashrut*) stipulate the foods that are acceptable and those that must be avoided, as well as how to cook the acceptable foods, and the types of food that can be eaten together in the same meal. Food is considered **kosher** if it is "fit" or "proper" in accordance with Jewish law.

Leviticus 11 and Deuteronomy 14: 2–21 instruct that, among land animals, only those that have split hooves and chew their own cud are acceptable (thus cows and goats can be eaten, but pigs and rabbits cannot). Among sea creatures, only those with both scales and fins are permitted; thus mussels and crustaceans such as shrimp are prohibited. Among birds, the chicken, turkey, goose, and duck are acceptable, but birds of prey such as the vulture, owl, and hawk are not. The products of non-acceptable animals are likewise considered unkosher (except for honey, which is understood to derive from flowers rather than bees, which fall into the forbidden category of "winged swarming things").

Even a permitted meat must be prepared and cooked correctly to qualify as kosher. For example, an animal that has died a natural death is not to be eaten; only animals that have been slaughtered in accordance with the law are acceptable. This means that an animal must be put to death humanely, by slitting the throat with a sharp knife. There are also rules about how food is to be eaten. For example, meat must not be consumed at the same time as dairy. Thus cheeseburgers are never on the menu for observant Jews. This stipulation is drawn from an instruction that appears twice in the Torah: "you shall not boil a kid in its mother's milk" (Exodus 23: 19 and Deuteronomy 14: 21). The rabbis interpreted this to forbid the combination of meat and dairy, and from it they derived a number of additional laws: thus one must wait between one and six hours, depending on the cultural tradition, after eating meat before having (for example) ice cream for dessert. Some Jews consider it so important to keep meat and dairy separate that they have not only two sets of dishes and cutlery (one for meat, one for dairy), but two sinks and two dishwashers.

Kosher manufacturers use various symbols to inform consumers of their products' status. One of the most common is a capital U (for "Union of Orthodox Jewish Congregations") inside a circle, which indicates that a body of rabbis has inspected the plant at which the product was prepared and deemed it to be kosher.

by the Jewish people themselves; and that the traditions existed for the people, not the other way around, and so could be modified. As an example, in 1922 Kaplan conducted the world's first bat mitzvah for his daughter Judith: this ceremonial equivalent to the **bar mitzvah** for boys is now practised regularly not only by Reconstructionists, but by Reform and Conservative Jews as well. Thus Kaplan's influence is felt well beyond the movement he established.

Since Reconstructionism developed primarily out of the Conservative movement (Kaplan had aspired to change Conservative Judaism from within rather than launch an entirely new movement), it preserved a number of traditional features, such as the dietary laws and the custom of wearing the **kippah** (skullcap) for men, as well as a significant amount of Hebrew in the liturgy. As a consequence, its practice resembles that of Conservative Judaism, although the two traditions are clearly distinguished by Reconstructionism's rejection of the idea of the Jews as the chosen people, its gender-neutral prayer book, and the fact that some of its adherents may well describe themselves as atheists. What matters to Reconstructionists more than individual faith is active participation in a community and the effort to honour Jewish history by retaining meaningful symbols and customs.

Humanistic Judaism

The American rabbi Sherwin Wine (1929–2007) took Kaplan's ideas several steps further, removing God from the picture altogether. He initially served as a rabbi in a Reform synagogue, but as his belief in the existence of God waned, he looked for a more congenial community. Finding none, in 1963 he established a secular congregation called the Birmingham Temple, which continues today with some 400 members in Farmington Hills, Michigan. In 1969 this congregation united with several like-minded others to form the Society for Humanistic Judaism (SHJ), which now includes congregations from across North America. According to the society's website, its goal is "to foster a positive Jewish identity, intellectual integrity, and ethical behaviour."

Over the years Wine developed a new liturgy, in both Hebrew and English, which makes no reference to God. He also found new focal points for the various Jewish holidays (for example, at Passover Humanists read from a new haggadah that links aspects of the Exodus story to contemporary social concerns). Humanistic Jews welcome everyone to participate in their services, regardless of gender, sexual orientation, or religious background. From the perspective of Humanists, Jewish identity is largely a personal decision. Not surprisingly, Humanist rabbis will officiate at marriages between Jews and non-Jews.

The Modern Synagogue

The synagogue is at the heart of the Jewish religious community: it is a place for prayer and study of sacred texts, a venue for communal worship and a place to learn. It also functions as a centre for social interaction and charitable activity (many synagogues run soup kitchens and offer beds for the homeless). In Hebrew it is called a Beit K'nesset (literally, "house of assembly); "synagogue" is the Greek equivalent. Orthodox and Hasidic Jews typically use the Yiddish term "Shul" (from the German for "school") and emphasizes the synagogue's role as an intellectual hub. Whereas Conservative Jews tend to use the term "synagogue," Reform Jews call their local place of assembly a "temple" because in their view it has definitively replaced the Temple in Jerusalem.

Typically, the synagogue is run by a board of directors made up of laypeople. Although most synagogues have a rabbi, some do not: instead, they invite different members of the community to lead the service. Synagogues tend to derive most of their income from annual membership dues, voluntary donations, fees for memorial plaques honouring deceased relatives, and the sale of tickets for seats at services during the High Holidays (see box).

The Holy Ark (or Ark of the Covenant) in which the Torah scrolls are kept symbolizes the place in which the tablets given to Moses were stored. Once the scrolls have been opened, a pointer is used to aid in the reading; often in the shape of a hand, it is called a *yad* ("hand" in Hebrew). Human hands never touch the parchment, since sweat contains acids that could damage it. The scrolls are stored in a fabric cover that may be ornately decorated with silver or gold.

The Great Synagogue of Aleppo, above, was the storage place of the Aleppo Codex, the earliest manuscript containing the entirety of the Tanakh, for approximately six centuries (c. 1400–1947). The synagogue was burned in 1947 by anti-Zionist groups but the codex was rescued. It remained hidden until 1958, when it was smuggled out of Aleppo and given to the president of Israel. Several pages, however, remain missing. The fate of the synagogue since the outbreak of civil war in Syria is not known (© Michele Murray).

Prayer Services

Jewish prayers take two forms: pre-set (typically from the ancient period) and spontaneous (created on the spot by the individual Jew). Prayer services revolve around the former type. Three times a day, in the evening, morning, and afternoon, practising Jews daven (Yiddish for "pray") in communal worship services that correspond to the three daily sacrifices performed at the Temple in Jerusalem. Prayers are also recited during mundane activities, such as on getting up in the morning and before washing one's hands, as well as before and after eating.

Every Sabbath morning service includes readings from the Torah and the Prophets. The Torah has 54 sections, each of which is read and studied for a week, so that the entire Torah is covered in an annual cycle. Every section is further divided into seven parts, all of which are read during the Sabbath morning service. The only other days when the Torah is read are Monday and Thursday.

Tradition teaches that it is better to pray in a group than alone. Thus in Orthodox practice at least 10 adult males are needed to make up a quorum for public prayer; this group of 10 is called a **minyan** ("number" in Hebrew). Certain Conservative synagogues allow women to be part of the minyan, and Reform Judaism does not require a minyan at all.

In most Conservative and Orthodox synagogues, males wear the skullcap known as a kippah in Hebrew and a **yarmulke** in Yiddish. The **tallit** is a fringed prayer shawl, typically worn by

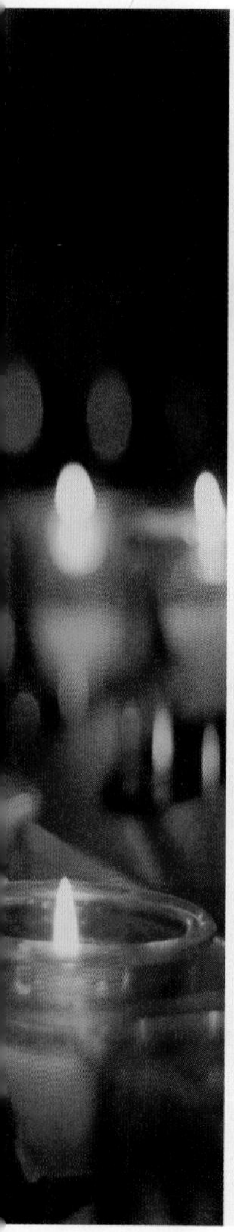

Focus

The High Holidays

The High Holidays, also called the High Holy Days or Days of Awe, encompass ten days that usually fall in September or October. The first day, **Rosh Hashanah**, is considered the Jewish New Year: on it God is said to open the "Book of Life" in which he will inscribe the individual's fate for the year on the Day of Atonement, **Yom Kippur**. This is the time of the year when Jews are supposed to examine their consciences. Historically, it was also the only time when the Divine Name of God was pronounced—by the high priest before the ark in the Jerusalem Temple's most sacred place, the Holy of Holies—in order to make atonement for the people. Apples dipped in honey are customarily eaten at Rosh Hashanah as an expression of the hope for a "sweet" new year.

Nowadays Yom Kippur is spent at the synagogue in prayer and supplication, asking for God's forgiveness. Fasting—no eating or drinking from sundown on the evening of Yom Kippur until the following nightfall—is compulsory for all adults except pregnant women, the elderly, and the ill. Although God is understood to forgive sins against himself, a person who has been wronged must be asked for forgiveness. The word for "sin" is *chet*, which means "missing the mark" (as in archery). Thus one can think of a sin as a missed opportunity for a kind word or a righteous act. The liturgy during the High Holy Days makes frequent references to the many ways in which human beings hurt each other, both in speech and in action. The time between Rosh Hashanah and Yom Kippur is meant for contemplative reflection on one's own words and behaviour. Yet these "days of penitence" should not be sad, because Jews are supposed to have confidence in the power of repentance and the mercy of God.

Most members of the Jewish community mark Yom Kippur to some degree, and many attend synagogue even if they do not go again for the rest of the year. At intervals throughout the service, the shofar (usually a ram's horn) is sounded. This tradition has been ascribed many symbolic meanings, including a "wake up" call to reflect on one's sins and the need for repentance, a summons to war against evil inclinations, and a reminder of the ram that God told Abraham to sacrifice instead of his son Isaac. Whatever the interpretation, the plaintive sound of the shofar is one of the most stirring aspects of Yom Kippur.

Document

The Shema

Among the prayers recited daily, the oldest and most highly revered is the Shema *(from its first word: "Shema," "Hear"). The first section (reprinted here) comes from Deuteronomy 6: 4–9) and is followed by sections from Deuteronomy 11: 13–21 and Numbers 15: 37–41.*

Hear, O Israel: The Lord is our God, the Lord alone. You shall love the Lord your God with all your heart, and with all your soul, and with all your might. Keep these words that I am commanding you today in your heart. Recite them to your children and talk about them when you are at home and when you are away, when you lie down and when you rise. Bind them as a sign on your hand, fix them as an emblem on your forehead, and write them on the doorposts of your house and on your gates.

men during the morning prayers (the only time it is worn in the evening is on Yom Kippur). The tallit fulfills the commandment to the Israelites to "make fringes on the corners of their garments throughout their generations and to put a blue cord on the fringe at each corner" so that they will "remember all the commandments of the Lord and do them" (Numbers 15: 37–41). Likewise, for weekday morning prayer men put on **tefillin** (or **phylacteries**): small black leather boxes containing words of scripture from Exodus and Deuteronomy, which are tied to the forehead and upper arm. Worn in literal fulfillment of the instruction in the Shema to "Bind them [these words] as a sign on your hand, fix them as an emblem on your forehead," the tefillin must be wrapped onto the forehead and arm in a particular way, in order to concentrate the mind, and the box on the arm is then held toward the heart during prayer. Traditionally, only men have worn the tallit and tefillin, but in modern times some Conservative women have begun wearing them as well. In Reform congregations, more and more women are now wearing the tallit and kippah, although the tefillin ritual is not generally practised by either sex. This could change, however, if the recent trend towards increasing ritual observance continues.

As this storefront display in Jerusalem shows, the kippah (skullcap; literally: "dome" in Hebrew) can be a colourful and creative vehicle for personal expression, including expressions of support for favourite sports teams (© Michele Murray).

In Reform and Conservative synagogues, all members of the congregation sit together, but Orthodox men are not permitted to pray in the presence of women, lest they be distracted from their prayers. Thus Orthodox women sit in their own section at the back or side of the room, or in a balcony. Language is another area of difference. In Orthodox and many Conservative synagogues, every part of the service is in Hebrew, but Reform services in North America are conducted mainly in English—although the use of Hebrew has been increasing in the last decade or so.

Finally, it is interesting to note that Conservative and Reform services are more tightly organized than their Orthodox counterparts. This might seem odd, but in Orthodox synagogues people arrive on their own schedule and catch up to the group at their own pace, so there tends to be a loud din of both prayer and talk. Still, some find it more natural to pray this way than to try for unison.

Anti-Semitism

In the aftermath of the Enlightenment, the nineteenth century seemed to offer Jews the opportunity to participate more fully in Western European culture and society. But a new debate arose over what came to be known as "the Jewish Question." In an 1843 essay, a German Protestant theologian named Bruno Bauer claimed that Jews as a group were scheming against the rest of the world, and that they were to blame for the hostility they encountered in modern society because they refused to abandon their ancestral culture. Underpinning these accusations was the long-standing Christian view of Jews as "Christ killers." In fact, European society was undergoing major changes in the later 1800s, and with those changes came severe tensions. Workers were beginning to demand more rights, while middle-class shopkeepers and skilled workers were watching the growth of department stores and factories with mounting concern. Competition among England, France, and Germany was increasing, and nationalism and racism added to the tensions leading up to the outbreak of the First World War.

At a time of anxiety and division, politicians used opposition to Jews to bring disparate social groups together. In Central and Western Europe, parties from across the political spectrum exploited anxieties to gain votes and popular support. No matter how illogical and contradictory the charges, Jews were to blame, whether for Marxism, liberalism, communism, or rampant capitalism. Even when they were not blamed for the unsettling shifts in European society, Jews were said to be undeserving of the benefits of emancipation.

Political parties were established specifically to promote anti-Semitism; Jews were openly derided in cartoons, posters, and pamphlets all over Europe. Germany produced more of this propaganda than any other country, and the organizations that distributed it were located at the very centre of society. In this way anti-Semitic attitudes were made respectable.

The central difference between ancient anti-Judaism and modern anti-Semitism was the racial dimension associated with the latter. In the modern world, Jews were publicly attacked for being racially "other": whereas ancient writers had focused on Jews' religious practices and customs, nineteenth-century propaganda portrayed them as racially alien. Even when they converted to Christianity, they remained racially tainted.

The German writer credited with coining the term "anti-Semitism" was Wilhelm Marr (1819–1904). Noting that Jewish financial investors emerged from the economic depression of 1873 in better shape than non-Jewish investors, he suggested that the problem was not that Jews lacked connection with European society, but rather that they were so well integrated that they were taking over. These views were promoted at the First International Anti-Semites' Congress held in Dresden in 1882.

The Dreyfus Affair

In France, hostility towards the changes brought about by the Revolution of 1789 was reflected in anti-Semitic attitudes. French Jews, who had been granted legal equality in 1791, came to be seen as symbols of all that was wrong with post-revolutionary France, and anti-Semitism served as a rallying point for the discontented. In 1894 a Jewish army officer named Alfred Dreyfus (1859–1935) was falsely accused of spying for Germany, based on forged documents and a military cover-up. The "Dreyfus Affair" was motivated by overt anti-Semitism. Four years after Dreyfus was found guilty and sentenced to life imprisonment, his cause was taken up by the novelist Émile Zola, who charged ("J'accuse!") the French army with a cover-up. The army tried Dreyfus again, and again he was found guilty, but this time under "extenuating circumstances" (Efron et al. 2009: 378). In 1899, after the details of the army cover-up were made public, he was pardoned, and eventually he was awarded the Legion of Honour.

The Russian Context

In Tsarist Russia, both church and state labelled Jews as outsiders to Russian society and enemies of Christianity. Jews became targets of violent popular persecutions called **pogroms**, in which their houses were burned, their businesses ransacked, and Jews themselves were beaten, tortured, and killed. Although the government did not organize these pogroms, it did nothing to stop them. Russia's most lasting contribution to modern anti-Semitism, however, was *The Protocols of the Elders of Zion*, a fiction created by the Russian secret police in the late 1890s, which purported to be the minutes of a meeting at which members of a Jewish conspiracy had discussed a secret plan for global domination. It enjoyed widespread distribution in Western Europe, especially in the years after the First World War, and was published in the United States by the automobile entrepreneur Henry Ford. Although it was exposed as fraudulent not long after its composition, the document resonated with anti-Semites around the world and is still in circulation today.

Zionism

The pogroms and poverty faced by Jews in Eastern Europe, and the growth of political and racial anti-Semitism in Western Europe, triggered the development of the movement called **Zionism**, which sought to return Jews to the ancient land of Israel to establish a nation there. The idea was not new: the words of the Passover Seder, "Next year in Jerusalem," indicate an enduring desire for return to the ancient Land of Israel, whether in the present or in some future messianic age. Zion is the biblical name of a hilltop in Jerusalem that is described as God's dwelling place and is known today as the Temple Mount. In ancient times the name "Zion" had a variety of associations and could be used to refer to the land around Jerusalem, the people, or their religious and political traditions.

Jewish Nationalism

Zionism as a political movement was formally established by the Austro-Hungarian journalist and playwright Theodor Herzl (1860–1904). Herzl had become persuaded that a Zionist movement was necessary during the Dreyfus affair and the resulting rise in anti-Jewish sentiment. In August

1897 he spearheaded the first Zionist Congress, held in Basel, Switzerland, which attracted 200 people. Out of that meeting came a platform calling for a Jewish national home in what was then Ottoman-controlled Palestine. Other places, including Uganda, Australia, and Canada, were also considered. But Herzl insisted that Palestine was the only suitable location, and that the future state would have to be recognized by international law. It would be half a century before that state—Israel—was established, by which time the need for it could no longer be disputed.

The Holocaust (1933–1945)

Of all the adversities that the Jewish people have experienced in their long history, the most shattering took place between 1933 and 1945 under Adolf Hitler's National Socialist German Workers' Party, better known as the "Nazis" (from the German for "National," *Nazional*). By the end of the Second World War at least 6 million Jews were dead, and the vibrant Ashkenazic and Sephardic cultures established on European soil over the previous millennia had been all but eradicated. Now widely known as the **Holocaust** (from the Greek meaning "whole" and "burnt"), the Nazi program of genocide is referred to in Hebrew as the **Shoah** ("catastrophe").

The Rise of Hitler

In the grim economic conditions that followed Germany's defeat in 1918, the Nazi party attracted enthusiastic popular support. Hitler placed the blame for Germany's defeat squarely on the Jews. In the account of his life and thought entitled *Mein Kampf* ("My Struggle"; 1925) Hitler tells how, as a young man, he learned of a Jewish conspiracy to infiltrate German politics in order to destroy the "Aryan" world. "Aryan" was in fact a linguistic term referring to the Indo-European family of languages, but it had already been given a racial meaning and used to argue the supremacy of Aryans over people of Semitic stock ("Semitic" too originally referred to a group of languages, including Hebrew, Arabic, and Aramaic). Hitler associated "Aryan" with purity and "Semitic" with impurity. His goal was first to reveal the threat that the Jews posed to Aryans, and then to destroy that threat. He cast his project as a service to God: "In standing guard against the Jew I am defending the handiwork of the Lord" (cited in Gilbert 1985: 28).

As soon as Hitler became chancellor of Germany, in January 1933, he began enacting legislation designed to overturn the emancipation of Germany's Jews, eliminate them from public life, and divest them of their citizenship. On 11 March Jewish-owned department stores in Braunschweig were ransacked, and two days later all Jewish lawyers in Breslau were expelled from court. On 1 April the government orchestrated a day-long boycott of Jewish-owned stores and businesses, during which Storm troopers stood with signs advising "Germans" not to enter shops owned by Jews, and wrote *Jude* ("Jew") across their windows, often with a Star of David (the six-pointed Jewish star symbol). New discriminatory laws were introduced almost daily thereafter: on 4 April the German Boxing Association excluded all Jewish boxers; on 5 April the systematic dismissal of Jewish faculty and teaching assistants at the universities began; on 7 April the government announced the "retirement" of all civil servants who were "not of Aryan descent" (Gilbert 1985: 36); and on 10 May books written by Jews were publicly burned at universities across the country (Efron et al. 2009: 377–8).

Some Jews began planning to leave the country, but as yet there was no widespread panic: of the roughly 525,000 Jews in Germany in 1933 only 37,000 left in that year (ibid.: 378). Those who remained hoped that the wave of persecution would subside. Given *Mein Kampf*'s references to Jews as "cockroaches," "maggots," and *Untermenschen* ("subhumans"), they hoped in vain.

A new phase in Hitler's offensive against the Jews was introduced in September 1935, when the Nuremberg Laws revoked Jews' German citizenship, deprived them of legal and economic rights, and prohibited marriage between Jews and people of allegedly "pure" Nordic blood. On 20 October 1935, the *New York Times* reported that a Jewish doctor named Hans Serelman, who had transfused his own blood to save the life of a non-Jew, had been charged with "race defilement" and sent to a concentration camp for seven months (Gilbert 1985: 50).

Jewish businesses were taken over by members of the Aryan "master race" in two stages. From 1933 to 1938 Jews could "voluntarily" transfer their businesses; then after November 1938 they were compelled to hand them over. Again, many Jews left Germany, but many others stayed. Although the Nazis also targeted gays and lesbians, Roma (Gypsy) people, communists, and the disabled, Germany's hardships were blamed on the Jews alone.

The first burning of a synagogue took place in Munich on 9 June 1938; afterwards, more than 2,000 Jews were incarcerated throughout Germany. In October approximately 17,000 Polish Jews were expelled from German territory; Poland then refused them entry, leaving them in a no-man's land. Barely a week later, on 6 November, 17-year-old Hershel Grynszpan, whose parents had been among the deported Polish Jews, assassinated the third secretary at the German Embassy in Paris. In response, Hitler ordered that free rein be given to "spontaneous" anti-Jewish demonstrations, and on the night of 9 November a series of riots took place that came to be known as *Kristallnacht*, the "Night of Broken Glass." More than 1,000 synagogues were plundered and some 300 burned; Jewish homes and businesses were destroyed by storm troopers and ordinary German citizens. Ninety-one Jews were killed, and approximately 26,000 were rounded up and placed in concentration camps (Efron et al. 2009: 384).

The S.S. St. Louis

Thousands of Jews left Germany over the months that followed. In May 1939, the German passenger ship *St Louis* left Hamburg for Cuba with 936 Jews aboard seeking asylum. Although all had paid $150 for a tourist visa, the Cuban government refused them entry unless they paid an additional fee of $500 each—money that most of them did not have. Captain Gustav Schröder, the ship's non-Jewish commander, hoped that the United States would accept his passengers, but ultimately it too refused, having enacted quotas on immigrants from eastern and southern Europe in 1924.

A group of academics and clergy in Canada tried to persuade Prime Minister Mackenzie King to offer the passengers sanctuary. But Canadian immigration officials and cabinet ministers opposed to Jewish immigration persuaded King not to intervene. Among the officials was Frederick Charles Blair, director of the Immigration Branch, who argued that Canada "had already done too much for the Jews" and that "'the line must be drawn somewhere'" (Abella and Troper 1991: 8, 64).

Thus the ship returned to Europe, docking at Antwerp, Belgium, in June 1939. The United Kingdom, France, Belgium, and Holland granted the passengers refuge, but in 1940 Germany invaded Belgium and France, putting the lives of all the Jews in those countries in jeopardy. Of the 936 refugees who returned to Europe it is estimated that 227 were killed in concentration camps (G. Thomas and M.M. Witts 1974: 135–217).

The Second World War

The Second World War began on 1 September 1939, when German forces invaded Poland. Immediately Poland's Jews were subjected to random public humiliation. By the end of September they were being herded into ghettos surrounded by fences or walls that were locked from the outside by German guards. Overcrowding led to rampant typhus, tuberculosis, and dysentery, which, along with starvation, killed many inhabitants.

In Germany the enactment of anti-Semitic laws continued. Jews increasingly were moved into separate apartment buildings; Germans writing Ph.D. dissertations were permitted to quote Jews only when unavoidable, and Jewish authors had to be listed in a separate bibliography. In November 1939 all Polish Jews over the age of ten were ordered to wear a yellow badge in the shape of the star of David, and on 1 September 1941 German Jews were required to follow suit.

The Death Camps

To facilitate what they called the "final solution to the Jewish problem," the Nazis built a network of large-scale death camps in Poland. The gassing of Jews began at the Chelmno camp in December 1941. One after another, groups of Jewish and Roma prisoners were placed in a sealed

During the two-minute siren that sounds throughout Israel on Holocaust Memorial Day, people cease whatever they are doing—including driving—to stand at attention and honour those who died during the Holocaust (© Reuters / Corbis).

van and driven away to be gassed by the exhaust fumes that were channelled back into the compartment where they were held. The first camp to use gas chambers was Belzec, in south-eastern Poland, in March 1942. But the largest extermination camp was Auschwitz-Birkenau, where more than 1 million Jews as well as tens of thousands of Roma, Poles, and Soviet prisoners of war were killed using a cyanide-based insecticide. Up to 7,000 Jews were gassed each day at Auschwitz-Birkenau alone. When it became clear that the allied forces were advancing on Poland in the winter of 1944, prisoners were removed from the Polish camps and sent to Germany both by train and on foot; such "death marches" killed approximately 250,000 prisoners. British and American forces liberated the rest of the camps between April and May 1945 (Efron et al. 2009: 385–405).

The State of Israel

When the horrors perpetrated against the Jews of Europe came to light, the United Nations voted to create a Jewish state in Palestine. The decision gave hope to Jews around the world. Yet it created a new refugee problem for the indigenous Arab people of Palestine, many of whom would be forced out of their homes. The original UN plan partitioned the land between the Jews and the Arabs, with Jerusalem to be administered by a UN Trusteeship Council for the first decade, after which the city's fate would be negotiated. Neither the Palestinian Arab community nor the Arab League accepted the partition plan, and Jewish leaders themselves had reservations, although they accepted it because the need for a Jewish homeland was so great.

The Jewish state of Israel came into being on 14 May 1948 and was attacked the following day by Egypt, Jordan, Syria, and Iraq. This was the start of decades of battles between Israel and the Palestinians, as well as neighbouring Arab countries. While peace treaties have been signed with Egypt and Jordan, and some of the territory that Israelis gained in later conflicts has been given back, the region continues to be extremely volatile. Most residents, whether Israeli or Palestinian, now support a two-state solution, but negotiating the boundaries continues to be inordinately difficult.

Focus

Holocaust Memorial Day

Holocaust Memorial Day, or Yom HaShoah, was inaugurated in 1953. It falls on the 27th of the Hebrew month of Nisan (usually in March or April). In Israel, Yom HaShoah begins at sundown with a state ceremony at Yad Vashem, Israel's official Holocaust memorial, in Jerusalem. The national flag is lowered to half-mast, the President and Prime Minister deliver speeches, Holocaust survivors light six torches symbolizing the 6 million, and the Chief Rabbis recite prayers. At 10 the next morning sirens are sounded throughout Israel for two minutes, during which people cease whatever they are doing and stand in silent tribute to the dead. Ceremonies and services are held at schools, military bases, and other community institutions. Places of public entertainment are closed by law, television broadcasters air Holocaust-related documentaries and talk shows, and subdued songs are played on the radio.

The Israeli electoral system is based on proportional representation, which means that even the most popular parties never win a clear majority of seats. Thus to form a government, the party with the most votes must gain the support of one or more smaller parties, usually in return for promises of special treatment. This tends to give religious parties influence well beyond their size.

In 1950 the Israeli government adopted the Law of Return, which granted "Every Jew . . . the right to immigrate to the country." The Israel Central Bureau of Statistics put the country's 2013 population at approximately 8 million, of whom perhaps 75 per cent are Jews and just over 20 per cent Arabs. In the early years most Jewish Israelis were of European Ashkenazi descent, but now the majority are of Middle Eastern origin (termed "Mizrachi" since the 1990s). Just over a million Israeli Jews are immigrants from the former Soviet Union, who now have their own political parties and Russian-language media. Another 130,000 are Beta Israel ("House of Israel"): Ethiopian Jews, many of whom were evacuated to Israel by the Israeli government between the late 1970s and 1991. Although the process of integration has not been easy, especially for older people, the community now has a strong presence in Israeli society—a presence that is reflected in the fact that popular entertainers such as the Idan Raichel Project now include songs in the Ethiopian language, Amharic, in their repertoire.

Idan Raichel is an Israeli singer-songwriter and musician whose group, the Idan Raichel Project, sings in Amharic, Arabic, Spanish, and Swahili as well as Hebrew (AP Photo / Dan Balilty / CP).

Map 3.2 Jewish Populations around the World

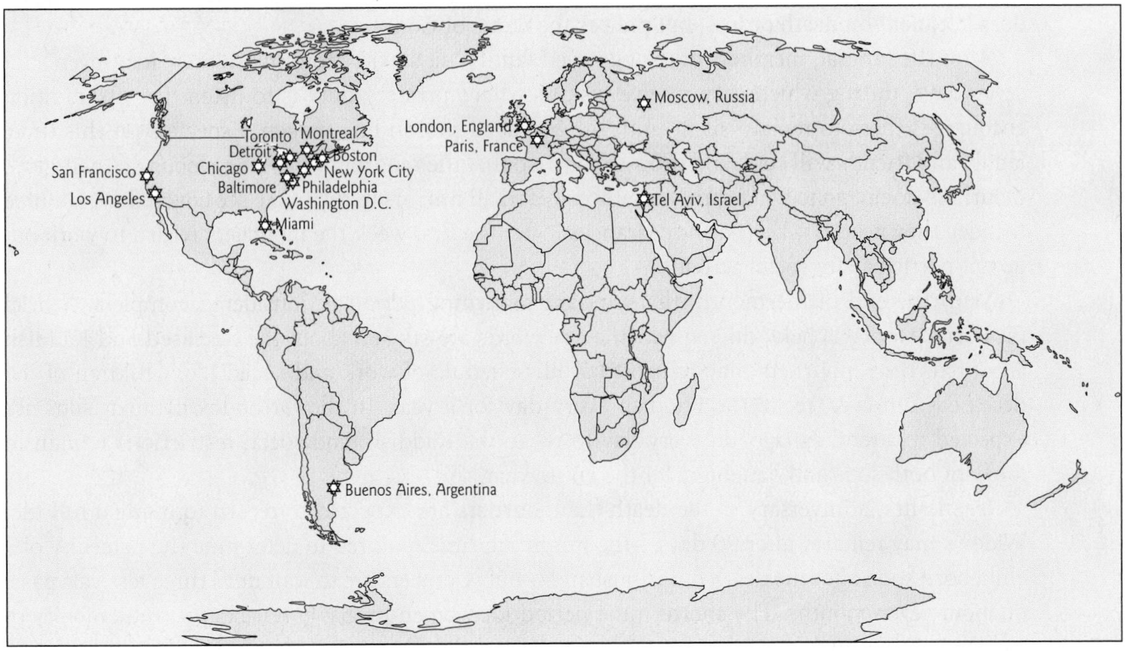

Life-Cycle Events

How Jews Deal with Death

Jews consider death to be a natural part of the life cycle. As the Book of Ecclesiastes 3: 1–2 says, "To everything there is a season, and a time to every purpose under heaven—a time to be born, and a time to die. . . ." Death is to be faced head-on, with unflinching realism. If possible, members of the immediate family should maintain a constant presence in the room of a dying person. The reasoning behind this custom is that we do not enter the world alone, and therefore ought not to depart it alone.

Jewish customs associated with the bereavement process allow mourners to express their grief and facilitate their return to regular life. Friends and relatives outside the deceased person's immediate family are expected to comfort the latter and provide for their needs.

Jewish law and tradition require that the body be buried as soon as possible after death, preferably within 24 hours. Members of the local burial society wash and dry the body while reciting prayers and psalms, and then wrap it in a simple white shroud. Candles, symbolic of the resplendent soul, are lit and placed at the head of the body, and an attendant is hired to stand by and read psalms continuously; Psalm 91, which refers to God taking humans "under the shelter of his wings," is considered particularly appropriate.

No consolation visits are made before the funeral, and there is no public viewing of the body. The deceased is simply buried in the ground, in accordance with Genesis 3: 19: "you are dust, and to dust you shall return." The corpse is not embalmed, and if a coffin is used, it is expected to be simple, in plain wood. But coffins are rare in Israel: in most cases the body is simply lowered into the ground on a stretcher or a bed of reeds. After the burial, the children of the deceased (in Orthodox families, only the sons) recite the Kaddish: a prayer that is part of every synagogue service, but that since the Middle Ages has also been used as a mourner's prayer. Intriguingly, it does not mention death or loss, but praises the name of God.

After the funeral, members of the bereaved family "sit shiva" (from the Hebrew for "seven") for seven days, during which they receive visitors whose primary duty is to listen: Jewish tradition encourages them to remain silent until the bereaved person has spoken. Especially at this time, family and friends will cook and drop off food, so that the mourners are free to focus on their grief. Mourners do not go to work during that week, and all mirrors in the home are covered to reinforce the idea they need not keep up appearances. After the first week the mourners return to work but do not participate in social activities.

With the end of the month, the standard mourning period is considered complete. A brief memorial service is held, during which a few words are spoken about the deceased and Kaddish is recited; then mourners may return to a full schedule of work and social life. Children of the deceased, however, recite the Kaddish every day for a year. In the Orthodox context, sons are expected to attend synagogue every day to recite the Kaddish, and social restrictions remain in force for both sons and daughters for the entire year.

By the first anniversary of the death the mourners are expected to return to living a full life. Widows may remarry after 90 days—the minimum time required to determine the paternity of a child born soon after the death of the husband—but widowers are to wait until three festivals pass, or about seven months. The shorter time period for women probably reflects the vulnerability of women without husbands in ancient times.

Marriage

Marriage in Judaism is regarded as a natural and highly desirable state for human beings. Indeed, as we have seen, the rabbis held "Be fruitful and multiply . . ." to be Yahweh's first mitzvah: thus

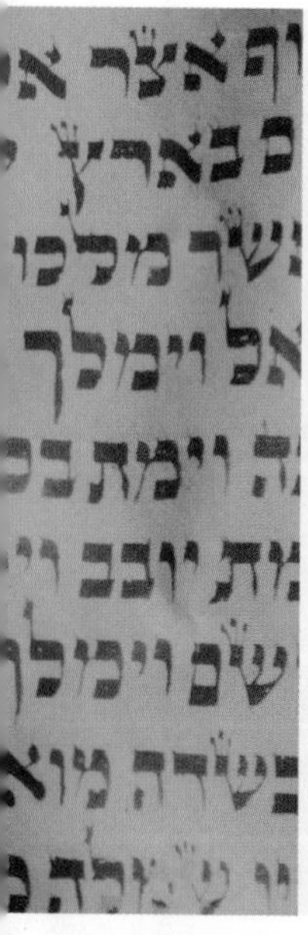

Document

The Kaddish Prayer

Reader: Hallowed and enhanced may He be throughout the world of His own creation. May He cause His sovereignty soon to be accepted, during our life and the life of all Israel. And let us say: Amen.

Congregation and Reader: May He be praised throughout all time.

Reader: Glorified and celebrated, lauded and worshipped, acclaimed and honoured, extolled and exalted may the Holy One be, praised beyond all song and psalm, beyond all tributes that mortals can utter. And let us say: Amen.

May the prayers and praise of the whole House of Israel be accepted by our Father in Heaven. And let us say: Amen.

Let there be abundant peace from Heaven, with life's goodness for us and for all the people Israel. And let us say: Amen.

He who brings peace to His universe will bring peace to us and to all the people Israel. And let us say: Amen.

everyone is encouraged to marry and raise children. Sexual relations within the sanctified bounds of marriage are encouraged both for reproduction and for the pleasure they bring to the couple; as we noted earlier, a husband is generally considered to owe his wife sexual fulfillment.

The Ketubah

Jewish marriages are occasions for happy celebration in a framework of religious seriousness and sanctity. A wedding can take place almost anywhere: in a home, a synagogue, a hotel, or outdoors. A rabbi is present in a legal capacity, to make sure that the marriage contract, the ketubah, is properly prepared and the appropriate procedures are followed. The early rabbis introduced this contract mainly to protect the economic rights of wives. To provide for a woman in the event of divorce or widowhood, it would stipulate a "bride price" to be paid to her from the husband's estate. The contract also established the dowry (such as bedding and linens) that the bride's family would provide to help the young couple set up a home. Today the dowry and bride-price customs are no longer observed, and the ketubah does not have much official power in North America, since the legal obligations of spouses are set by law. However, traditional Jews continue to sign a ketubah written in Aramaic (the lingua franca in the era when the ketubah was created), while liberal Jews sign a modern version.

Under the Chuppah

For the marriage ceremony, the couple stands under a chuppah, a wedding canopy supported by four poles that may be either free-standing or held by family or friends. Its origins are not certain, but the chuppah is most often understood to symbolize the home that the couple will create. The canopy itself can be plain or ornately decorated, and is sometimes made of a tallit. At Orthodox and Conservative weddings, the bride and her family circle the groom under the chuppah several times; this custom derives from the instruction in Jeremiah 31: 22 that "A woman shall court a man," which the rabbis interpreted to mean that she should "go around" him.

Traditionally the ring is placed on the index finger of the bride's right hand, where it can be seen by the official witnesses to the wedding, and moved to the third finger of the left hand after the ceremony. The rabbi, **cantor**, or friends then recite seven blessings, which include a blessing over a cup of wine and expressions of hope for the future happiness of the couple; then the bride and groom drink from the cup.

The conclusion of the wedding comes with one of the best-known rituals associated with Jewish weddings: the breaking of the glass. At Orthodox and some Conservative weddings the glass is broken under the foot of the groom, while at Reform, Reconstructionist, and Humanistic weddings both of the newlyweds typically step on a glass (or sometimes a light bulb) wrapped in a napkin. The sound of the shattering glass is greeted with joyful shouts of "Mazel tov!" ("Congratulations!"). The glass-breaking ritual has multiple interpretations: some understand it to be a reminder of the destruction of the Jewish Temple—and the realization that even in happy times one must be aware that life also brings sadness and pain; others suggest that it reminds the couple how fragile life and love are. At Orthodox and some Conservative weddings, the newlyweds spend a few minutes alone after the ceremony, sharing some bread and wine before joining their family and friends at the reception.

Many Jewish homes have a mezuzah ("doorpost") affixed beside the front entrance as a reminder of God's presence and commandments. Inside the decorative container is a piece of rolled parchment with handwritten verses from the Shema prayer. Religiously observant Jews touch the mezuzah and then kiss their fingers as they pass through the doorway (© Pascal Deloche / Godong / Corbis).

Divorce

Divorce is mentioned several times in the Bible (particularly in Deuteronomy 24: 1–4) and Judaism accepts it as a legal institution. The Bible gives the power of divorce to the husband, and even today a divorce must be initiated by him. The husband presents the divorce decree, called a get, to the wife. Obtaining a divorce was traditionally rather easy under Jewish law; on the other hand, no woman can be divorced against her will, as mutual consent is required. In practice, divorce is strongly discouraged, and this is one reason that in North America divorce rates are lower among Jews than in the general population.

The text of the get often stipulates a financial settlement and provisions for the return of property that rightfully belongs to the wife. Among non-religious and many liberal Jews, civil divorce is deemed sufficient, but Orthodox and certain Conservative Jews must obtain a get if either party wishes to remarry; however, it is not provided until the civil divorce is completed.

Recent Developments

In the course of its history, Judaism became the foundation for two other major monotheistic religions. Christianity and Islam, like Judaism, are referred to as "Abrahamic traditions" because they too trace their spiritual lineage back to the biblical Abraham. Judaism is by far the smallest of the three, with only 1 to 2 per cent of the adherents that Christianity and Islam have. In total, there are approximately 14 million Jews in the world, the vast majority of whom live in either the United States or Israel, each of which is home to roughly 6 million Jews. There are about 1.5 million Jews in Europe (including more than 100,000 in Germany), 400,000 in Latin America, and 375,000 in Canada, which has the fourth-largest Jewish population after Israel, the US, and France. Toronto, Montreal, and Vancouver are home to the largest Canadian Jewish communities.

The Jewish Bloodline

One issue of concern in Jewish communities today is patrilineal versus matrilineal descent. According to Halakhah, it is the mother's status as a Jew that determines the status of her children: to be a Jew by birth, one must be born to a Jewish mother. Orthodox and Conservative Jews accept a child as Jewish only if the mother is Jewish by either birth or conversion in an Orthodox or Conservative synagogue. Reform and Reconstructionist Jews do not consider the Halakhic rules binding. They accept a child as Jewish if either parent is Jewish, as long as the child is raised as a Jew and adopts a Jewish identity. Because different branches of Judaism follow different conversion processes, conversions performed by more liberal denominations are not accepted by rigorously observant groups.

Attitudes towards Gays and Lesbians

Traditionally, male homosexual intercourse has been considered unacceptable (based on Leviticus 18: 22; 20: 13), and this is still the Orthodox position. The Reform and Reconstructionist branches, however, advocate full equality and accept both same-sex marriage and ordination of gays and lesbians as rabbis. The Conservative branch's Committee on Jewish Law and Standards took the same view as the Orthodox branch until recently, but since 2006 has recognized multiple positions in support of its pluralistic philosophy. One position upholds the Orthodox view but another is significantly more relaxed regarding homosexual relationships, although it continues to regard certain sexual acts as prohibited.

The Hebrew Bible makes no reference to lesbianism, and rabbinic tradition considers it a minor offence: an example of immoral behaviour, but nowhere near as serious a transgression as male homosexuality. This reflects the androcentric perspective of rabbinic law, which defines a sexual act as penetration by the male member; hence sexual activity between women cannot violate the law.

Gender Equality: A Distance Yet to Go

Finally, extraordinary strides have been taken in recent decades towards full gender egalitarianism. The Conservative, Reform, and Reconstructionist branches now ordain women to the rabbinate and allow full female participation in synagogue worship. Orthodox women, by contrast, cannot become rabbis; they do not count as members of a minyan, and they cannot be called to read from the Torah in synagogue services. Yet increasing numbers are studying Torah with other women—an activity formerly limited to males. As Jewish feminists point out, gender equality means that gendered traditions, images, regulations, rites, and rituals deeply embedded in Judaism must be recreated in the spirit of gender equality. This process of transformation is underway in all branches of Judaism, and is far from finished.

Summary

In this chapter you have learned about the development of Judaism from its sacred beginnings as recorded in the Bible through its varied expressions during the Second Temple period to the innovations introduced in late antiquity by the rabbis. The importance of both oral and written texts was discussed, as well as the diverse types of literature produced through the centuries by Jewish communities. You have also learned about the history of the Jewish people, and their often creative responses to difficult times. Finally, you have seen how the challenges of the Enlightenment and modernity were reflected in the development of the multiple, frequently incompatible, approaches to Jewish law, practice, and identity that are manifest in the various branches of Judaism that exist today.

Sites

Jerusalem

Within Jerusalem's boundaries are monuments sacred to all three Abrahamic faiths. It was this city that, according to the Bible, King David made his capital, and in which his son Solomon built the First Temple. It became a centre of worship for Christians with the construction of the Church of the Holy Sepulchre (begun in 326). Then in 637 it became part of the new Islamic world; the Muslim shrine known as the Dome of the Rock was completed on the Temple Mount in 691.

The city's status remains one of the most contentious issues in the Israeli–Palestinian conflict. During the 1948 War, West Jerusalem was among the areas captured and later annexed by Israel, while East Jerusalem, including the Old City, was captured by Jordan. But Israel annexed East Jerusalem after the 1967 Six-Day War, and although Israelis call the city Israel's "undivided capital," the international community considers East Jerusalem to be Palestinian territory held under military occupation.

The Western Wall

The "Western Wall" (*kotel* in Hebrew) is the last remnant of Herod's temple, and since antiquity Jews have gathered before it to mourn on the ninth day of the month of Av—the day on which, according to legend, both the First and Second Temples were destroyed. In 1967, the wall area was designated an open-air synagogue, and since then it has been sex-segregated, with men praying on the left and women on the right.

Aleppo, Syria

Aleppo was once one of Judaism's most important intellectual and spiritual centres. After 1948, Jews in Syria were banned from government employment and political office, and were virtually forbidden to leave the country (for fear they would immigrate to Israel, and in hope that their presence in Syria would prevent Israel from attacking it). When the travel restriction was finally lifted in 1992, an estimated 4,000 Jews left immediately, and by 2011 the Jewish population had fallen to no more than 150.

Sacred Texts

Religion	Text	Composition/ Compilation	Compilation/ Revision	Use
Judaism	Hebrew Bible (Tanakh): 24 books organized in three sections: Teaching or Law (Torah), the Prophets (*Nevi'im*), and sacred Writings (*Ketuvim*).	Written in the first millennium BCE.	Canon fixed sometime between 200 BCE and 100 CE.	Doctrinal, inspirational, educational, liturgical.
	Mishnah	Teachings of rabbis in the land of Israel between 100 BCE and 220 CE.	Compiled by Rabbi Judah the Prince c. 220 CE.	One of the foundations of Jewish law; the object of ongoing study.
	Babylonian Talmud	Teachings of rabbis in the land of Israel and in Babylonia between 100 BCE and 500 BCE.	Compiled in Babylonia in 6th century CE.	Another foundation of the law; also the object of ongoing study.
	Zohar	Mystical teachings of various rabbis.	Composed/edited in the 13th century.	Study, inspiration, contemplation.

Discussion Questions

1. Explain how Jewish identity can be based on religious, ethnic, or cultural elements—or any combination of them.
2. The Jewish Exile in Babylonia is of paramount importance in Israelite–Jewish history, reverberating in Hebrew literature and providing a framework for dealing with the displacement and feeling of alienation from their homelands that Jews have dealt with throughout their history. How so?
3. How did the Enlightenment affect Jews living in Europe?
4. What is anti-Semitism, and how does it differ from anti-Judaism? What were some of the circumstances in Europe in the nineteenth and early twentieth centuries that gave rise to anti-Semitism?
5. Describe the life-cycle rituals that provide a "framework of meaning" for Jews as they pass through different stages of their lives.
6. What are some of the religious traditions that Jewish women today are challenging?
7. How do different Jewish rituals and practices reflect the importance that Judaism attributes to its historic past?

Glossary

Aggadah Anecdotal or narrative material in the Talmud; see also **Halakhah**.

apocalyptic Refers to the belief that the world is under the control of evil forces, but that God will intervene and defeat the powers of darkness at the end of time; from "apocalypse," a Greek term meaning "unveiling" (the Latin equivalent is "revelation"). Apocalyptic literature flourished in the Hellenistic era.

Ashkenazim Jews of Central and Eastern European ancestry, as distinguished from **Sephardim** and **Mizrahim**.

Baal Shem Tov (Hebrew, "Master of the good name") Rabbi Israel ben Eliezer (1698–1760), the founder of **Hasidism**; also known as "the Besht" (an acronym).

bar mitzvah "Son of the commandment;" the title given to a 13-year-old boy when he is initiated into adult ritual responsibilities; some branches of Judaism also celebrate a **bat mitzvah** for girls.

bris The Yiddish form of the Hebrew **brit**.

brit "Treaty" or (most commonly) "covenant" in Hebrew; the special relationship between God and the Jewish people. **Brit milah** is the covenant of circumcision.

cantor The liturgical specialist who leads the musical chants in synagogue services; *hazzan* in Hebrew.

covenant See **brit**.

Diaspora A collective term for Jews living outside the land of ancient Israel; from the Greek meaning "dispersal." The Diaspora began with the Babylonian Exile, from which not all Jews returned to Judea.

Documentary Hypothesis The theory that the Pentateuch was not written by one person (Moses) but was compiled over a long period of time from multiple sources; proposed by the German scholar Julius Wellhausen in 1883.

Exile The deportation of Jewish leaders from Jerusalem to Mesopotamia by the conquering Babylonians in 586 BCE; disrupting local Israelite political, ritual, and agricultural institutions, it marked the transition from Israelite religion to Judaism.

Exodus The migration of Hebrews from Egypt under the leadership of Moses, understood in later Hebrew thought as marking the birth of the Israelite nation.

Gaonim The senior rabbinical authorities in Mesopotamia under Persian and Muslim rule; singular "Gaon."

Gemarah The body of Aramaic commentary attached to the Hebrew text of the Mishnah, which together make up the Talmud (both the Jerusalem Talmud and the Babylonian Talmud).

Haggadah The liturgy for the ritual Passover dinner.

Halakhah Material in the Talmud of a legal nature; see also **Aggadah**.

Haredim A rigorously observant subgroup of Orthodox Judaism.

Hasidism Movement founded in Eastern Europe by the eighteenth-century mystic known as the **Baal Shem Tov**. Today the movement encompasses many subgroups, each of which has its own charismatic leader. The Hasidim ("pious ones") make up a significant part of Orthodox Judaism.

Haskalah The Jewish Enlightenment.

Hebrew Bible The sacred canon of Jewish texts, known to Jews as the **Tanakh** and to Christians as the Old Testament.

Holocaust The mass murder of approximately 6 million European Jews by the Nazi regime of Adolf Hitler during the Second World War; from the Greek words meaning "whole" and "burnt." The Hebrew term is **Shoah** ("catastrophe").

Israelites The biblical people of Israel.

Kabbalah The medieval Jewish mystical tradition; its central text is a commentary on scripture called the *Zohar*, which is thought to have been written by Moses of León (d. 1305) but is attributed to Rabbi Shimon bar Yohai, a famous second-century rabbinic mystic and wonder-worker.

Karaites "Scripturalists"; an eighth century anti-rabbinic movement that rejected the Talmud, taking only the Bible as authoritative.

kippah "Dome" or "cap;" the Hebrew word for the skullcap that Jewish men wear; see also **yarmulke**.

kosher Term for food that is ritually acceptable, indicating that all rabbinic regulations regarding animal slaughter and the like have been observed in its preparation.

Ladino A language composed mainly of old Spanish and Hebrew, spoken by some Sephardic Jews.

Luria, Isaac (1534–72) Influential Kabbalah scholar.

Maimonides, Moses Latinized name of Moses ben Maimon (1135–1204), one of the most famous Jewish philosophers and legal scholars of the Islamic age, identified in religious texts as "Rambam" (from R-M-B-M, the acronym of "Rabbi Moses ben Maimon").

menorah The seven-branched oil lamp that has been a Jewish symbol since ancient times, well before the widespread adoption of the six-pointed star; the nine-branched menorah used at Hanukkah is sometimes called a hannukiah.

messiah From the Hebrew *Mashiach*, "anointed [one]." The Greek translation is "Christos," from which the English term "Christ" is derived.

midrash Rabbinic commentary on scripture.

minyan The quorum of ten required for a prayer service. In more rigorously observant synagogues, only adult males qualify; in more liberal synagogues adult women may also participate in the minyan.

Mishnah The Oral Law—inherited from Pharisaism and ascribed to Moses—written down and codified by topic; edited by Rabbi Judah haNasi around 220 CE, it has an authority paralleling that of the written Torah.

Mishneh Torah A topically arranged code of Jewish law written in the twelfth century by **Maimonides**.

mitzvah A commandment (plural "mitzvot"); in the Roman era, the rabbinic movement identified exactly 613 specific commandments contained within the Torah.

Mizrahim Jews of Middle Eastern ancestry, as distinguished from **Ashkenazim** and **Sephardim**.

mohel A ritual circumciser.

Passover A major spring festival that began as a celebration of agricultural rebirth, but came to commemorate the supposed liberation of the Israelites from slavery in Egypt under Moses' leadership.

Pentateuch The Greek name for the first five books of the Hebrew Bible, ascribed by tradition to Moses but regarded by modern scholars as the product of several centuries of later literary activity.

phylacteries The usual English term for **tefillin**.

Purim Literally "lots"; the holiday commemorating the escape of the Jews of Persia from an evil plot of a Persian official named Haman, as described in the Book of Esther. Haman used a lottery system to determine the date for the destruction of the Jews, hence the name of this holiday.

rabbi Literally "teacher," but by the second century CE the official title of an expert on the interpretation of Torah; once priestly sacrifices had ended with the destruction of the Temple in 70 CE, the rabbi became the scholarly and spiritual leader of a Jewish congregation.

rabbinic movement Legal teachers and leaders who inherited the teachings of the Pharisees and became the dominant voices in Judaism after the destruction of the Temple in 70 CE.

responsa From the Latin for "answers"; accumulated rulings on issues of legal interpretation issued by rabbinical authorities in response to questions from rabbis.

Rosh Hashanah The new year festival, generally falling in September; the day when God is said to open the Book of Life in which he will inscribe the individual's fate for the year on Yom Kippur.

Sabbath The seventh day of the week, observed since ancient times as a day of rest from ordinary activity.

Seder "Order"; the term used for the ritual Passover dinner celebrated in the home; the six divisions of the **Mishnah** are also called orders or seders.

Sephardim Jews of Spanish–Portuguese ancestry, as distinguished from **Ashkenazim** and **Mizrahim**.

Septuagint The Greek translation of the Hebrew scriptures, made in Alexandria during the Hellenistic period, beginning in the third century BCE.

Shavuot A one-day festival (two days in the Diaspora, except for Reform and Reconstructionist Jews) in late May or early June that celebrates the revelation of the Torah by God to Moses on Mount Sinai; also known as the Festival of Weeks for the seven weeks that separate the second day of Passover and the day before Shavuot.

Shema, the The oldest and most sacred fixed daily prayer in Judaism, found in Deuteronomy 6: 4–9; and 11: 13–21, and Numbers 15: 37–41. "Shema" ("Hear") is its first word.

Shoah "Catastrophe"; the Hebrew term for the **Holocaust**.

Simchat Bat ("Joy of a daughter"); the naming ceremony for girls that more liberal branches of Judaism have adopted as an equivalent to the Brit ceremony conducted for boys.

Sukkot The Feast of "Tabernacles" or "Booths"; probably named for the temporary shelters that were constructed by farmers in autumn to protect their ripening crops and later given a historical interpretation commemorating the wanderings of the Israelites in the wilderness after the Exodus.

synagogue From the Greek for "gathering together"; the local place of assembly for congregational worship, which became central to the tradition after the destruction of the Jerusalem Temple.

tallit A shawl with fringes at the corners, worn for prayer; usually white with blue stripes.

Tanakh The entire Hebrew Bible, consisting of Torah (Law), Nevi'im (Prophets), and Ketuvim (Sacred writings); the name is an acronym of the initial letters of those three terms.

tefillin Small black leather boxes, also termed **phylacteries**, containing parchment scrolls on which the words of four paragraphs from the Torah are written, tied to the forehead and upper arm by leather thongs.

Tetragrammaton "Four-letter" word, the personal name of the Jewish deity, consisting of the four Hebrew letters *yod, hay, vav, hay* (YHWH); conventionally written as "Yahweh."

tikkun olam "Restoration of the world": the Kabbalistic concept, introduced by Isaac Luria, that the world can be restored through prayer, study, meditation, and the observance of commandments.

Tzaddik "Righteous person," a title conveying the Hasidic ideal for a teacher or spiritual leader; plural "Tzaddikim."

yarmulke The Yiddish word for the **kippah** or skullcap worn by Orthodox males.

yeshiva A traditional school for the study of the scriptures and Jewish law.

Yiddish The language spoken by many Central and Eastern European Jews in recent centuries; although it is written in Hebrew characters and contains some words derived from Hebrew, it is essentially German in its structure and vocabulary.

Yom Kippur The "Day of Atonement," dedicated to solemn reflection and examination of one's conduct; falls ten days after Rosh Hashanah, usually in September.

Zion In biblical times, the hill in Jerusalem where the Temple stood as God's dwelling place; by extension, the land of the Israelites; in modern times, the goal of Jewish migration and nation-state settlement (Zionism).

Zionism The modern movement, initiated by Theodor Herzl in 1897, for a Jewish nation-state in the ancient land of Israel.

Zvi, Sabbatai A student of Lurianic Kabbalah who was declared the messiah in the year 1666; given the choice between death and conversion to Islam, he chose to convert.

Further Readings

Abella, Irving, and Harold Troper. 1991. *None Is Too Many: Canada and the Jews of Europe 1933–1948*. Toronto: Lester Publishing. An eye-opening must-read for Canadians.

Ausubel, Nathan, ed. 1961. *A Treasury of Jewish Folklore: The Stories, Legends, Humor, Wisdom and Folk Songs of the Jewish People*. New York: Crown Publishers. To get a sense of the Jewish penchant for story-telling, read this book.

Baskin, Judith, ed. 1999. *Jewish Women in Historical Perspective*. Detroit: Wayne State University Press. A collection of insightful research.

Berlin, Adele, and Marc Zvi Brettler, eds. 2004. *The Jewish Study Bible*. Oxford: Oxford University Press. The best translation of the Hebrew scriptures currently available.

Biale, Rachel. 1984. *Women and Jewish Law: The Essential Texts, Their History and Their Relevance for Today*. New York: Schocken Books. An excellent source of insight into issues of concern to observant Jewish women.

Brooten, Bernadette J. 1982. *Women Leaders in the Ancient Synagogue: Inscriptional Evidence and Background Issues*. Chico, CA: Scholars Press. Ground-breaking research findings argue against the long-standing assumption that women could not have held leadership roles in the Judaism of late antiquity.

Diamant, Anita. 1997. *The Red Tent*. New York: Wyatt Books for St Martin's Press. A historical novel that centres on a minor female character in the Book of Genesis; a fascinating glimpse into what life might have been like for girls and women in the time of the ancient Israelites.

Diamant, Anita, and Howard Cooper. 1991. *Living a Jewish Life: Jewish Traditions, Customs and Values for Today's Families*. New York: HarperCollins. An easy-to-read guide written from a liberal perspective.

Goldstein, Elyse. 1998. *ReVisions: Seeing Torah Through a Feminist Lens*. Toronto: Key Porter Books. An insightful, accessible analysis of biblical writings by a female Reform rabbi.

———, ed. 2009. *New Jewish Feminism: Probing the Past, Forging the Future*. Woodstock, VT: Jewish Lights. An excellent anthology of feminist writings from a variety of denominational perspectives.

Greenberg, Irving. 1988. ***The Jewish Way: Living the Holidays.*** **New York: Simon & Schuster.** A comprehensive exploration of Judaism through its holy days.

Magness, Jodi. 2012. ***The Archaeology of the Holy Land: From the Destruction of Solomon's Temple to the Muslim Conquest.*** **Cambridge: Cambridge University Press.** A lucid, engaging overview of the archaeology of ancient Palestine by a specialist.

De Lange, Nicholas. 2003. ***Judaism.*** **2nd edn. Oxford: Oxford University Press.** An accessible overview of Jewish history.

Plaskow, Judith. 1991. ***Standing Again at Sinai: Judaism from a Feminist Perspective.*** **New York: Harper One.** A classic of Jewish feminism.

Scholem, Gershom G. 1974. ***Kabbalah.*** **Jerusalem: Keter.** A survey of the medieval mystical tradition by one of its most respected modern interpreters.

Spiegelman, Art. 1986, 1992. ***Maus I and II.*** **New York: Pantheon Books.** A powerful graphic novel that tells the story of Spiegelman's father, a survivor of the Holocaust.

Steinsaltz, A. 1989. ***The Talmud, the Steinsaltz Edition: A Reference Guide.*** The "go-to" source for understanding the Talmud.

Wiesel, Elie. 1960. ***Night.*** **New York: Bantam.** A short, compelling memoir by a writer who, as a teenager, survived the concentration camps at Auschwitz, Buna, and Buchenwald.

Recommended Websites

www.centuryone.com/hstjrslm.html

A chronological history of Jerusalem

www.ushmm.com

United States Holocaust Memorial Museum

www.idanraichelproject.com/en/

Idan Raichel's group performs in multiple languages, including Arabic, Amharic, and Swahili as well as Hebrew, and has been described as providing a "window into the young, tolerant, multi-ethnic Israel taking shape away from the headlines" (*Boston Globe*)

www.jbooks.com

The Online Jewish Book Community

www.jewishfilm.com

Publishes an annual list of films concerning Jewish themes and issues

www.tikkun.orgTikkun Magazine

An excellent source of articles on politics, religion, and creating a meaningful life from a progressive Jewish perspective.

http://jwa.org

A comprehensive archive of Jewish women's issues

www.myjewishlearning.com

Useful information on Jewish life

www.jewishvirtuallibrary.org

A vast collection of information and resources, with more than 13,000 entries and 6,000 photos.

References

Abella, Irving, and Harold Troper. 1991. *None Is Too Many: Canada and the Jews of Europe 1933–1948*. Toronto: Lester Publishing.

Ausubel, Nathan, ed. 1961. *A Treasury of Jewish Folklore: The Stories, Legends, Humor, Wisdom and Folk Songs of the Jewish People*. New York: Crown Publishers.

Efron, John, Steven Weitzman, Matthias Lehmann, Joshua Holo. 2009. *The Jews: A History*. Upper Saddle River, NJ: Pearson Education.

Gilbert, Martin. 1985. *The Holocaust: A History of the Jews of Europe during the Second World War*. New York: Holt, Rinehart and Winston.

Goldstein, Elyse. 1998. *ReVisions: Seeing Torah Through a Feminist Lens*. Toronto: Key Porter Books.

Hallo, William W., ed. 2003. *The Context of Scripture*. Vol. 2. *Monumental Inscriptions from the Biblical World*. Leiden: Brill.

Hertz, Joseph H. 1960. *The Authorised Daily Prayer Book*. New York: Bloch Publishing Company.

Manning, Christel, and Phil Zuckerman. 2005. *Sex & Religion*. Belmont, CA: Thomson Wadsworth.

Marcus, Ralph, trans. Josephus, *Jewish Antiquities*. Book 13: 1927–65.

Murray, Michele. 2004. *Playing a Jewish Game: Gentile Christian Judaizing in the First and Second Centuries CE*. Waterloo, ON: Wilfrid Laurier University Press.

Robinson, George. 2000. *Essential Judaism: A Complete Guide to Beliefs, Customs, and Rituals*. New York: Pocket Books.

Segal, Alan F. 2012. "Jewish Traditions." Pp. 80–139 in Willard G. Oxtoby and Alan F. Segal, eds. *A Concise Introduction to World Religions*, 2nd edn. Toronto: Oxford University Press.

Thomas, Gordon, and Max Morgan-Witts. 1974. *Voyage of the Damned*. London: Hodder & Stoughton.

Twersky, Isadore. 1972. *A Maimonides Reader*. New York: Behrman House.

Wylen, Stephen M. 1989. *Settings of Silver: An Introduction to Judaism*. New York: Paulist Press.

4 Christian Traditions

Wendy L. Fletcher

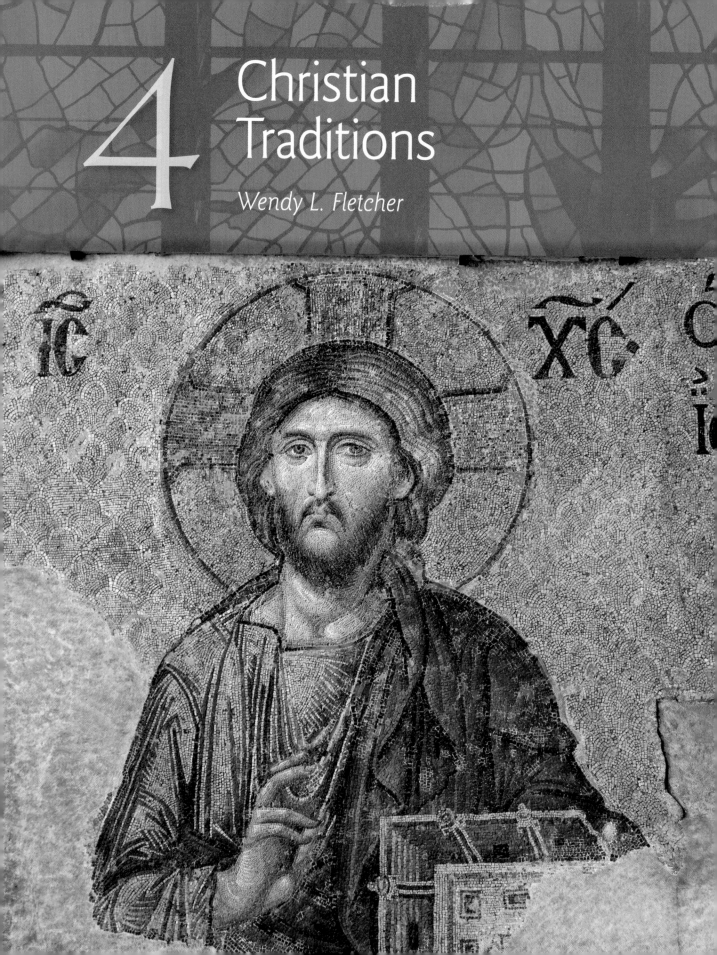

Traditions at a Glance

Numbers
2.2 billion around the world.

Distribution
Christians constitute the majority of the population in Europe and the Americas, Oceania, sub-Saharan Africa, Russia, and the Philippines, and nearly a quarter of the population of Asia.

Founders and Leaders
Founded by the followers of Jesus of Nazareth, called the **Christ**, on the basis of his teachings and resurrection. Among the early founders, the Apostles Peter and Paul were especially important.

Deity
One, called "God" or "Lord."

Authoritative Texts
The Christian Bible consists of the Old Testament (the Hebrew Bible) and the New Testament. The Roman Catholic and Orthodox churches include as part of the Old Testament a number of books from the Septuagint (the Greek translation of the Hebrew Bible) that Protestants set apart as Apocrypha.

Noteworthy Teachings
According to the doctrine of the Trinity, the One God exists in three persons, as Father, Son, and Holy Spirit. Jesus, the second person of the Trinity, is truly God as well as truly man, and his resurrection is the sign that those who believe in him will have eternal life. The authority of the Church has been passed down from the Apostles.

From its beginnings as a small movement within Palestinian Judaism, Christianity has grown to become the world's largest religion. Comprising more than 25,000 distinct denominational groups, whose ethnic and cultural diversity reflects its wide geographic distribution, today's Christianity is a study in complexity and adaptation. This is not a new thing. From the beginning, Christianity has evolved through negotiation of differences in belief, practice, and ecclesiastical form.

Christians profess the faith commitment that Jesus of Nazareth was the Son of God, both human and divine; that he died on a cross for the sins of all; and that he was resurrected two days later, demonstrating the power of God over death. From these propositions an "atonement theology" was developed, according to which Jesus' suffering and death atoned for the sins of the world and reconciled humanity with God, thus assuring the possibility of what Christians call salvation: going home to God after death. What that faith commitment means and how it is expressed vary widely, depending on time, place, socio-political context, theological perspective, and cultural–ethnic identity.

Origins

There is very little that we can say definitively about the historical Jesus. However, it is generally agreed that he was born in Palestine around the year 3 BCE, was raised as a Jew in an Aramaic-speaking family, and began his public ministry around the age of 30. From the **Gospels** written after his death, it seems he was an itinerant teacher in the prophetic tradition of his day. Accompanied by a growing group of followers, he moved from place to place, teaching and preaching, healing,

← Christ in Majesty: detail of a thirteenth-century mosaic in Hagia Sophia, Istanbul (© Cultura Creative (RF) / Alamy).

casting out demons, and on occasion raising the dead. At the age of about 33, he was arrested by the Romans and sentenced to death by crucifixion. The nature of his crime is unclear. Pontius Pilate, the Roman official who presided over his trial, found him guilty of nothing. But those who had handed him over to Pilate insisted he be put to death for the blasphemy of claiming to be the son of God. What distinguished Jesus from other prophetic leaders of his time was his followers' claim that, two days after his execution, he rose from the dead and commissioned them to carry on his work.

The main sources of information on Jesus are the four Gospels of Matthew, Mark, Luke, and John, and the **Pauline Epistles** (a series of letters written by the Apostle Paul to various early Christian communities). The first Gospel, Mark, was likely written at least 30 years after Jesus' death, and overlapping themes, words, and phrases indicate that it served as the basis for Matthew and Luke. As a consequence, these three books are known as the "**synoptic**" Gospels (from the Greek *syn*, "together," and *optic*, "seen"). Although they were named after three followers of Jesus, their actual authors are not known. They were written not to record an actual life, but to sustain and inform a later generation of Christian believers. Nevertheless, scholars agree that some of the material they contain does go back to Jesus of Nazareth: sayings, **parables** (simple stories illustrating a moral or spiritual lesson), and accounts of his miracles, as well as stories of his death and resurrection. The fact that the sayings and parables recur, often in differing contexts, in Matthew and Luke has led scholars to hypothesize that both drew on a single earlier source referred to as Q (from *Quelle*, German for "source").

Compared with these narratives, the Gospel of John is a major theological essay proclaiming Jesus' identity as messiah and saviour. The opening passage makes the author's purpose clear: "In the beginning," he writes (recalling the opening words of the Hebrew Bible) "was the **logos**, and the logos was with God, and the logos was God; all things were made through him" (John 1: 1). This logos is the "word" with a capital W, used by John to declare Jesus the **incarnation** of that divine Word: "The logos became flesh and dwelt among us, full of grace and truth; we have beheld his glory, glory as of the only Son from the Father" (John 1: 14). As John's Gospel unfolds, Jesus and his followers are continually challenged by Jewish opponents, and Jesus prophesies that his followers will be expelled from synagogues. These details draw attention to Christianity's origins as a movement within Judaism. For John, the true inheritors of Abraham's faith are those who believe that the Word became flesh in Jesus, that the risen Jesus lives among them, and that it is their mission to declare those beliefs to the world.

The Gospels' authors selected certain teachings and events from the life of Jesus to give the early Christian community a context in which to understand the events it professed to have experienced. They took particular care to situate Jesus amid conflict and tell stories that foreshadowed his death and resurrection.

The Pauline Epistles discuss issues of theology, practice, and discipline. **Paul** (d. c. 65) had a profound influence on the shape that early Christian life took. He never met the historical Jesus; in fact, he had persecuted Christians on behalf of the Pharisees. But one day on the road to Damascus he was overcome with an experience of the risen Christ, which led him to believe that Jesus was the Messiah that many Jews had been waiting for, the Son of God who had been raised from the dead to extend to all the promises that God had first made to Israel.

Not all the Epistles called Pauline are believed to have been written by Paul. The undisputed letters—Romans, I and II Corinthians, Galatians, Philippians, 1 Thessalonians, Philemon—emphasize Paul's understanding of Jesus as the Jewish Messiah whose death and resurrection were

Timeline

c. 3 BCE	Birth of Jesus
c. 30 CE	Death of Jesus
c. 65	Death of Paul
312	Constantine's vision of the cross
325	First Council of Nicaea
c. 384	Augustine's conversion experience
529	Benedict establishes monastery
842	Iconoclast controversy ends
862	Cyril and Methodius in Moravia
c. 1033	Birth of Anselm (d. 1109)
1054	Break between Rome and Constantinople
1095	Urban II calls for the first crusade
c. 1225	Birth of Thomas Aquinas (*Summa Theologiae*) (d. 1274)
1517	Luther posts his 95 theses
1534	Henry VIII proclaims himself head of the Church of England
1536	Calvin's *Institutes*
1563	Council of Trent concludes
1738	John Wesley's conversion experience
1781	Immanuel Kant's *Critique of Pure Reason*
1830	*Book of Mormon*
1859	Charles Darwin's *On the Origin of Species*
1870	First Vatican Council concludes
1910	Publication of *The Fundamentals*
1944	Florence Li Tim-Oi becomes the first woman ordained as a priest in the Anglican Church
1948	First assembly of the World Council of Churches
1965	Second Vatican Council concludes
1980	Roman Catholic Archbishop Oscar Romero is killed in El Salvador
1982	"Baptism, Eucharist and Ministry" (BEM) document published
1984	Archbishop Desmond Tutu is awarded the Nobel Peace Prize for his role in opposing apartheid in South Africa
1988	United Church of Canada declares that homosexuality in itself is not an impediment to ordination
1992	Porvoo Common Statement is signed, facilitating cooperation between a number of Lutheran and Anglican churches
2013	Benedict XVI becomes the first pope in 600 years to resign.

ordained by God. By contrast, the disputed Epistles—Ephesians, Colossians, 2 Thessalonians, and the Pastorals (1 and 2 Timothy and Titus)—focus on life in the Church and the Church's place in the larger world, and were most likely written by followers of Paul. Contemporary with the Gospels, they testify to the institutionalization of beliefs, practices, and emerging leadership structures. Whereas Paul believed the end of the world to be imminent, the later letters suggest a longer, less urgent perspective.

The Epistles give clear instructions as to the shape that a Christian life should take. Paul did not write a systematic treatise on his thought: rather, he wrote to the congregations he had founded to instruct and admonish them. Since these letters address conflicts related to Paul's teachings, we know that opinions regarding the meaning of Jesus' life, death, and resurrection varied. Although Paul's beliefs became normative, it seems that this early period was marked by disagreements over Jesus' message and intentions, and differences in both ethics and religious practices.

Internal Conflicts in the Early Church

It took approximately four centuries for Christianity to become an organized religion in its own right. The process involved fundamental questions of identity, authority, belief, and organizational

An Easter procession along the Via Dolorosa in Jerusalem, where Jesus is said to have carried the cross to his crucifixion (© Mahmoud illean / Demotix / Corbis).

Focus

Christian Sacraments

From the beginning, members of the Christian community gathered regularly for worship, prayer, and instruction from community leaders. The rituals that they called "**sacraments**" also developed very early on. A sacrament is defined as an outward and visible sign of an inward and spiritual grace—something in the physical world that demonstrates the love and action of God. All Christians accept the sacraments of **baptism** (the rite of initiation) and the **Eucharist** (which commemorates the last meal that Jesus shared with his disciples before his death) as essential, but the Roman Catholic and Anglican churches also recognize five more: ordination (the setting apart of some individuals for particular work or positions of authority); unction (the anointing of people who are sick or dying); confirmation (the public confession of faith by adults who were baptized as infants or children); marriage; and penance (the confession of sins and receiving of forgiveness). Most sacraments must be administered by an ordained minister, and each church has its own laws regulating them.

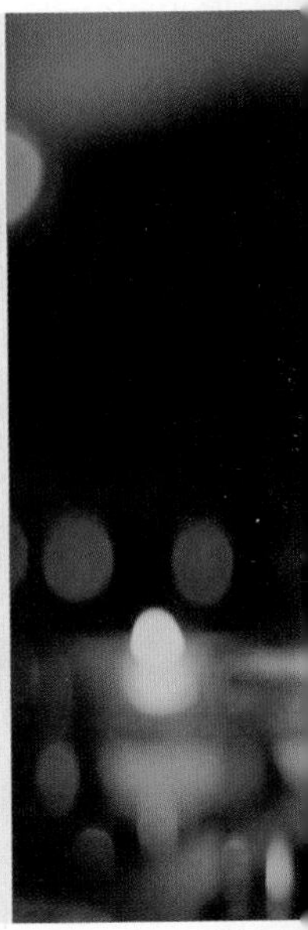

structure. For example, was the Jesus movement only for Jews, or could it accommodate Gentiles? Jesus of Nazareth probably conceived of himself as an emissary sent to Israel alone (Matthew 10: 6; Mark 7: 19–29). But his reinterpretation of the Torah resulted in a radical reformulation of the idea that God's covenant applied only to Jews. Paul dramatically expanded Jesus' teachings by interpreting them as part of a universalizing plan whereby membership in the community of the faithful would depend not on adherence to laws, but on faith in Jesus (Romans 3: 21–31). In Matthew (28: 19) Jesus commands his disciples to baptize Gentiles and teach them what he taught; in Acts (1: 6–9) they are commissioned to be his witnesses "to the ends of the earth." A movement that began with a message directed solely to Israel expanded to embrace all the earth's peoples as potential followers.

A second question was whether, if Gentiles were to be included, they should conform to Jewish norms regarding circumcision, food, and ritual purity. Eventually Gentiles were forbidden to adopt the markers of Jewish identity. Perhaps it is not surprising that a movement that explicitly separated itself from Judaism has, tragically, often been actively hostile to Jews.

Relations between Church and Society

The religious climate of the age into which Jesus was born was, to a significant degree, otherworldly and escapist. Greco-Roman religion was an amalgam of beliefs and cults from many lands and stages of cultural development. Religious practice was largely unorganized, and people were free to worship the gods they chose. However, at the head of the pagan pantheon stood the state gods of Rome, most notably the Emperor himself. The imperial cult made loyalty to the empire a primary social and religious duty.

As monotheists, Jews and Christians could not acknowledge any god but theirs. Thus they refused to offer sacrifices to the Emperor, and it was this refusal, above all, that led to their

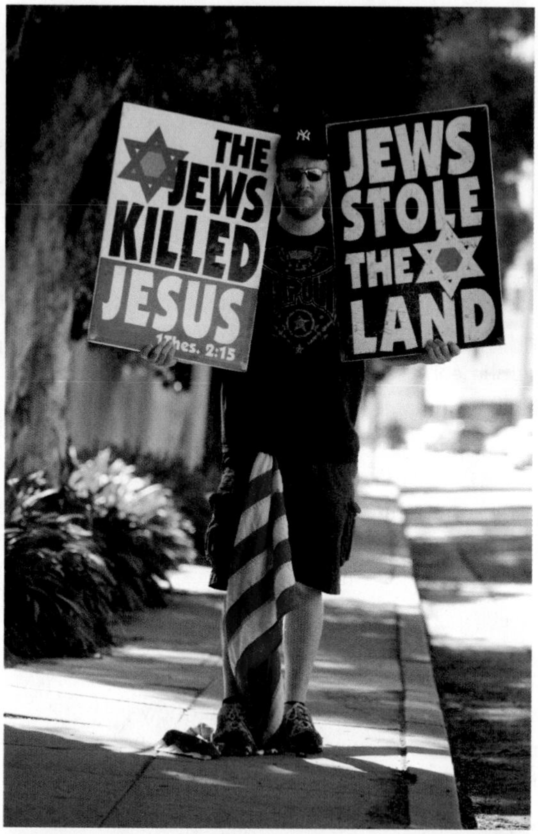

A member of the Westboro Baptist Church, a Kansas-based independent Baptist group that is notorious for its protests against homosexuals and Jews, pickets a Jewish high school for girls in Los Angeles (Todd Bigelow / Aurora Photos / GetStock).

persecution, particularly after 250, when the Emperor Decius ordered that all inhabitants of the empire prove they had made the required sacrifices. Some Christians converted to paganism, others went into hiding, and still others were **martyred**. Seven years later, in 257, the Emperor Valerian ordered first the deportation and then the execution of many Christian clergy. The result was a serious loss of leadership for the young Church.

Valerian's death was followed by 40 years of peace during which Christianity, though technically illegal, was tolerated. This made possible a consolidation of the Church's organization, and regular meetings of regional leaders promoted greater unity, although one last great persecution was launched in 298 by the Emperor Diocletian.

Constantine

The external fortunes of Christianity changed significantly in 312, after the Emperor of the Western segment of the Roman Empire, **Constantine** (c. 272–337), won a major battle at a bridge over the Tiber. According to legend, he had seen a cross symbol over his head before the battle and taken this as a portent of victory. With the realization of that victory, Constantine confirmed his loyalty to the Christian God. Although he was not baptized until shortly before his death, Constantine's policies became increasingly favourable to the Christians. Beginning in 313, he exempted North African clergy from taxation and used imperial money to enlarge churches, laying the foundation for the accumulation of vast ecclesiastical fortunes. As well, he gave bishops the same power as magistrates, and a significant number of Christians were called to upper-level posts in his administration.

Between 320 and 330 Constantine thrust the Church to the forefront of public life, guaranteed religious toleration, and forbade both the erection and the worship of statues of himself, thus undermining the political function of the pagan religious system. Later Constantine declared that the Church had the right to emancipate slaves belonging to Christians, and empowered its bishops to exercise juridical authority in disputes among its adherents.

With Constantine Christianity began its journey from persecuted sect to power-holder in Western culture. No longer did affiliation with Christianity come with a negative stigma: now it promised status and opportunity. Membership expanded accordingly, with troubling implications for a community that until then had been characterized by its capacity for self-sacrifice. In retrospect, many have asked what it meant for Christianity to become a partner of the state rather than a humble servant of the world.

Authority in the Early Church

The earliest Christian worship was conducted in the privacy of the household. Although there were public spaces dedicated to religious expression—temples for pagans and synagogues for Jews—devotional activity was still largely centred in the home. It was only when Christianity grew large enough to move into the public realm that formal authority structures began to develop.

From the beginning, to be a follower of Jesus was to live out God's commandment to love one's neighbour as oneself. This concrete expression of an internal faith was called ministry. Baptism signalled the Christian's entry into the ministry of Christ himself; thus joining the community of Christians meant living a life of self-giving love. During the lifetimes of the **Apostles** (those who had seen the risen Christ and received his commission to continue his work), ministry was largely a matter of **charism**: a spiritual gift that surfaced in the context of the local community. By the end of the first century, however, the need for a more structured system of ministry and a recognized chain of authority was evident.

The early Christians believed that the end times and "second coming" of Jesus were imminent, and lived accordingly, but a broader vision was required once it became clear that Jesus was not returning in the expected timeframe, especially as the numbers of Christians continued to grow. Together, the external threat of persecution and the internal threat of theological division made it essential for the early Christians to standardize their institutional structures, as well as their doctrine.

The foundational office was the **episcopacy** (literally, "oversight"). As the twelve disciples (the list of names varies slightly between the Gospels and the Book of Acts) became travelling evangelists, carrying the good news of his resurrection from one place to the next, they appointed local people to oversee the nascent communities of believers. These local leaders, or *episcopoi*, were what the early Church came to call "**bishops**." Although there is no record of formal ordination, this was the beginning of the Church's structure of authority. The role of the bishop is to preach the Word, preside at sacraments, and administer discipline, providing oversight for the continuity and unity of the Church.

As the numbers of Christians and Christian communities grew, individual *episcopoi* found that they needed to delegate the authority to administer sacraments to others. Those others, appointed for their particular spiritual gifts, were known as **presbyters** (literally, "elders"). Over time, the role of presbyter evolved to become the role of the priest as we understand it today. A third office that dates from the earliest days of the Church is that of the **deacon** (from Greek *diakonia*, service). The deacon's work supported that of the bishops and often took the form of service to the poor and the destitute.

Centralized Authority

With regional expansion, it became necessary to decide how authorities in different parts of the Christian world should relate to one another. Five major episcopal areas or **sees** developed—Rome, Constantinople, Alexandria, Antioch, and Jerusalem—whose authority reflected both their place in the development of the Church and the administrative structure of the Roman Empire. From the time of the Emperor Justinian I (r. 527–565), the Eastern sees generally accepted this division of authority; however, Rome insisted on its own primacy from very early on. Conflict was particularly intense between Rome and Constantinople. Both theological and institutional, it eventually led to a permanent schism between Eastern and Western Christianity.

In the East, a system of oversight developed in which the secular emperor was invested with both secular and religious authority. This led to the concept of a single society in which the sacred and the secular lived in harmony, guided by the Holy Spirit and presided over by an emperor who was the earthly counterpart of the divine monarch, God. In the ancient Eastern Church, the term pope (*papae*) was reserved for the bishop of Alexandria, but today it applies to all Orthodox priests.

Over time, the bishop of Rome, whom we identify today as the **pope**, the head of the Western (Roman Catholic) Church, assumed primary authority over all churches in the West. As in the East, however, the word *papae* ("pope") originally referred to any bishop. When the Bishop of Rome rebuked another bishop for using the title, in 988, his peers generally assumed that he had the right to object, but it was not until 1073 that Pope Gregory VII formally prohibited use of the title by anyone other than the bishop of Rome. Rome's claim to primary authority in Western Christianity was accepted on the grounds that its bishop was the direct successor of **Peter**, the "prince of Apostles," who was said to have arrived in Rome as early as the year 42. Although there is little or no evidence to support that tradition, we do know that when Paul wrote his Epistle to the Romans, around the year 58, there was already a large Christian community in the city.

St Peter's Basilica is said to sit on the burial site of St Peter. Its square was designed by the great Baroque sculptor and architect Gian Lorenzo Bernini between 1656 and 1667 (© Günter Lenz / imagebroker / Corbis).

The model of Church–state relations that developed in this period was strikingly different from its Eastern counterpart. In the West a fundamental dualism between sacred and secular set the stage for constant antagonism between religious leaders and secular princes.

Women in Ministry

As the centre of Christianity shifted from the private household to the public square, the place of women in the Church also shifted. Women held significant authority in the household, and some were the heads of their households in every sense. Thus gatherings of early Christians were sometimes presided over by the female head of the house in which they met. As the Church became more deeply embedded in the public world, however, the roles that women could fill in and for it were increasingly restricted, and the function of presiding over worship gatherings was lost.

In the gospels we see Jesus welcoming women as followers. Paul wrote about the equality of all before God, including male and female, and his letters indicate that women as well as men performed diaconal (service) roles for the early community. Individual women were also acknowledged as prophets and identified as co-preachers with men in the work of evangelization (Acts 2: 17–18). Yet by the end of the apostolic age, the letters known as the Pastoral Epistles were admonishing women to be silent in church. And as the three orders of ministry (bishop, priest, deacon) developed, women were excluded from all of them. Only two lesser offices were open to women: those of **widow** and **deaconess**.

The order of widows originated in response to the needs of poor widows in the community. Because the Church supported them, only a limited number of women were granted the official designation of widow. To qualify for it, a woman had to be at least 60 years of age, have no other means of support, have had only one husband, and be known for her domesticity, compassion, and abstinence from sexual activity. In return for support, the widows lived lives of contemplation and intercession, praying for the Church.

Although they too took their title from the concept of *diakonia*, deaconesses were not female equivalents of deacons, and it was only over time that their role developed into an ecclesiastical office. Different regions had different practices, but it is known that by the third century women (like men) were ordained through the laying on of hands during the service of the Eucharist. Beyond this, we know only that deaconesses helped to prepare female candidates for baptism, visited sick women and children, and prayed for the suffering, as well as the Church. By the sixth century the office of deaconess had died out almost entirely, and the idea of women in ordained ministry would not surface again until the nineteenth century.

Ecclesiastical Virgins

In the third and fourth centuries several upper-class Christian women—some widowed, some never married—used their wealth to establish spiritual communities of female relatives and friends, orphaned girls, and poor women. The "*mater familias*" was the head of the household, setting the schedule for common prayer and determining what kinds of charitable work the women would perform. These women voluntarily withdrew from society and their consecration to the religious life was informal, but their asceticism was often rigorous.

The Development of Orthodoxy

By the end of the second century the Church was developing an institutional form, but it did not yet have a clearly defined system of doctrine and belief. Passions ran high for centuries as Church leaders and theologians disputed what would eventually become the Church's normative theological positions, including its **Christology** (understanding of who Jesus was). Early controversies were addressed through the compilation of "Rules of Faith" based on bishops' teachings, the establishment of a scriptural canon, and the use of councils to settle disputes.

The Scriptural Canon

To preserve its legitimacy as the successor to the Church of the Apostles, the early Church decided to recognize as "**scripture**" only writings that were associated with an Apostle and "orthodox in doctrine" (although **orthodoxy** itself was still in the process of being defined). Eventually, 27 books were recognized as constituting the official **canon** of **New Testament** scriptures. From the fourth century in the West and the fifth in the East, there was a general consensus on the canon. As well, both traditions considered the sacred texts of the Jewish people—in the form of the Greek translation known as the Septuagint—authoritative.

Councils of the Church

Very early in the Church's history, bishops began to meet in councils known as synods to discuss common problems and work out solutions. Four councils held between 325 and 451 are called "ecumenical" ("worldwide") because they were accepted by both the Eastern and Western branches of Christianity.

The Council of Nicaea, 325

The first significant agreements as to the nature of Christ were reached at the **Council of Nicaea**, convened by the Emperor Constantine in 325. **Athanasius** and **Arius** represented the opposing sides of a debate over whether Jesus was of the same substance (*homoousious*) as God the Father or of similar substance (*homoiousious*). The debate was resolved in favour of the Athanasians and a statement of belief was formulated that came to be called the **Nicene Creed**.

The Councils of Antioch, 341, and Constantinople, 381

Although it had seemed that the question of Jesus' nature was settled at Nicaea, debates continued to rage, particularly in the Eastern churches. The Council of Antioch was summoned in an attempt to reverse the decision made at Nicaea and produce a creedal statement more reflective of the Arian position, but the result was further division in the Eastern churches. Four decades later, the Council of Constantinople also failed to resolve the matter.

Document

The Nicene Creed

The Nicene Creed affirms the humanity and the divinity of Jesus in one person, as the second person of the Trinity. It expresses the understanding of his nature that is shared by all Christian traditions. However, the text was modified more than once after the Council of Nicaea, and the version that follows includes three words—"and the Son"—that have never been accepted by the Eastern churches. At issue is the nature of the relationship of the Holy Spirit to the Father and the Son *(see also p. 167).*

We believe in one God, the Father almighty, maker of heaven and earth, and of all things visible and invisible; and in one Lord Jesus Christ, the only-begotten Son of God, begotten of the Father before all worlds, God of God, light of light, very God of very God, begotten not made, being of one substance with the Father, by whom all things were made, who for us men and for our salvation came down from heaven, and was incarnate by the Holy Spirit of the Virgin Mary, and was made man, and was crucified for us under Pontius Pilate. He suffered and was buried, and the third day he rose again according to the scriptures, and ascended into heaven, and sits on the right hand of the Father, and he shall come again with glory to judge both the living and the dead; whose kingdom shall have no end. And we believe in the Holy Spirit, the Lord and giver of life, who proceeds from the Father *and the Son*, who with the Father and Son together is worshipped and glorified, who spoke by the prophets. And we believe in one holy catholic and apostolic church. We acknowledge one baptism for the remission of sins. And we look for the resurrection of the dead, and the life of the world to come.

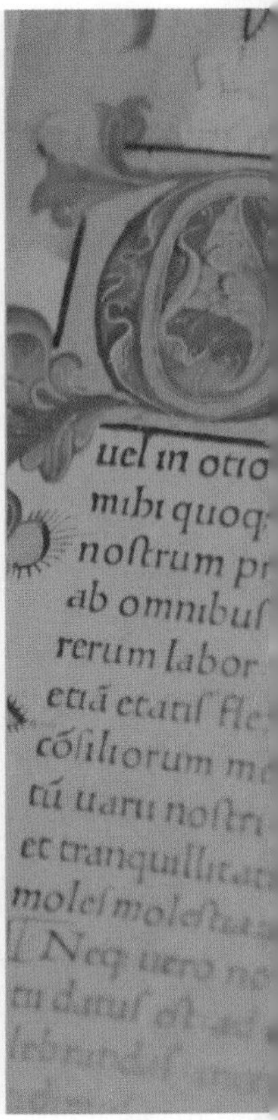

The Council of Ephesus, 431 CE

The Council of Ephesus was convened in response to a theological movement called **Nestorianism**, which was eventually declared a **heresy** (a belief or practice contrary to the accepted doctrine of the Church). Nestorius and his followers argued that the incarnate Christ had two natures, one fully divine (Christ) and one fully human (Jesus), and that the human Mary—the mother of the human Jesus—could not be the mother of God (the divine Christ). The Council of Ephesus decided against Nestorius, and Mary was affirmed as *Theotokos* ("God bearer").

The Council of Chalcedon, 451 CE

Disputes over the nature of Jesus were finally resolved at the **Council of Chalcedon** in response to the argument that Christ had two natures (human and divine) before the incarnation but only one divine nature after it. This view was a variation on a position known as **monophysitism**, according to which Christ had only one nature (divine). The Council of Chalcedon affirmed the decisions of both Nicaea and Ephesus and adopted as orthodoxy for both branches the position known as **dyophysitism**: that the two natures of Jesus, human and divine, are united in the second person of the Trinity. Although monophysitism persisted in breakaway branches such as the Coptic Church, the dyophysite belief affirmed at Chalcedon became normative thereafter.

Focus

Christianity in Egypt, Ethiopia, and Armenia

The indigenous Christians of Egypt, the Copts, believe that their faith was taken to Egypt by the gospel writer Mark, and that their ancestors were pioneers in the development of monasticism (see p. 169). After the Islamic conquest in the seventh century, Egyptians who remained Christian were a minority, but a significant one. The Copts have retained a sense of cultural pride as "original" Egyptians.

By the fourth century, Coptic influence had extended to Ethiopia. A few centuries later, Ethiopia gave asylum to Muslim emigrants but remained Christian, recognizing the authority of the Coptic **patriarch** in Cairo and maintaining its own priests and monks in Jerusalem. The Ethiopian Church has remained essentially Coptic, though it has been formally independent of Cairo since the mid-twentieth century.

In Armenia, legend traces the introduction of Christianity to the missionary activity of the Apostles Thaddeus and Bartholomew. Armenian Christians maintain that their king Tiridates III, who was baptized around 301, was the first ruler anywhere to establish Christianity as a state religion.

One of 11 rock-hewn churches on UNESCO'S World Heritage list, Bieta Ghiorghis (Saint George's House) in Lalibela, Ethiopia, was carved from volcanic rock in the thirteenth century. It is an important pilgrimage site for members of the Ethiopian Orthodox Tewahedo Church (© Philippe Lissac / Godong / Corbis).

Other Early Heresies

Nestorianism was not the only movement defined as heretical. Among the others were Gnosticism and Pelagianism.

Gnosticism (from *gnosis*, "knowledge") was a worldview that influenced many ancient religions, including Christianity. Based on a radical dualism that gave priority to reason and spirit over the physical, Gnosticism took Neoplatonic metaphysics as its point of departure for interpreting the relationship between God the Father and Jesus the Son. Gnostics separated God the creator from God the supreme being, positing that the creator was a lower being or "demi-urge." This idea contradicted the developing Christian orthodoxy of the **Trinity**, which conceived of God as three co-equal persons of one divine substance: Father, Son, and Holy Spirit. Among the texts generally considered Gnostic gospels today is the "Gospel of Mary": an incomplete document, discovered in 1896, recounting a conversation with Jesus that a female disciple had in a vision, and the opposition she encountered when she told some male disciples about it.

The heresy of **Pelagianism** centred on the concept of **original sin**: the teaching that the sin of the first humans, Adam and Eve—disobedience of God's command not to eat of the tree of knowledge of good and evil—was passed down to all their descendants, and that for this reason no human being could live a moral life without God's grace. The British theologian Pelagius (354–c. 420) argued that humans were not so tainted as to be unable to choose the good of their own free will. His opponents, most notably Augustine of Hippo, declared him a heretic on the grounds that he attributed too much autonomous agency to humans and too little dependence on God's grace.

St Augustine of Hippo

The theologian who argued against Pelagius was **Augustine** (354–430), Bishop of Hippo Regius in North Africa and author of (among others) ***The City of God*** and *De Trinitate*. Augustine's thought in the areas of original sin, grace, suffering, and just war shaped the emerging scholastic tradition, which would reach its full flower in the thirteenth century with Thomas Aquinas.

Gregory the Great

The papacy of Gregory the Great (540–604) was a watershed in the development of the Western Church. In a sense, Gregory embodied the transitional character of the late sixth century, drawing on the traditions of late antiquity while heralding the Rome-centred clerical culture of the medieval West. His letters reveal efforts to strengthen Christian authority over secular rulers, to establish bishops as leaders of Christian communities at every level, to eradicate the superstition and idolatry retained from antiquity, and to bolster the authority of Rome by promoting the cults of St Peter and St Paul.

Gregory's measures did not constitute a master strategy to achieve Roman supremacy, but his strong stance against temporal authority, his assertion of Roman authority against Byzantium (the tradition of the four Eastern sees), his internal consolidation of the bureaucracy, and his careful oversight of internal Church life served as foundations for the medieval papacy.

Map 4.1 The Spread of Christianity

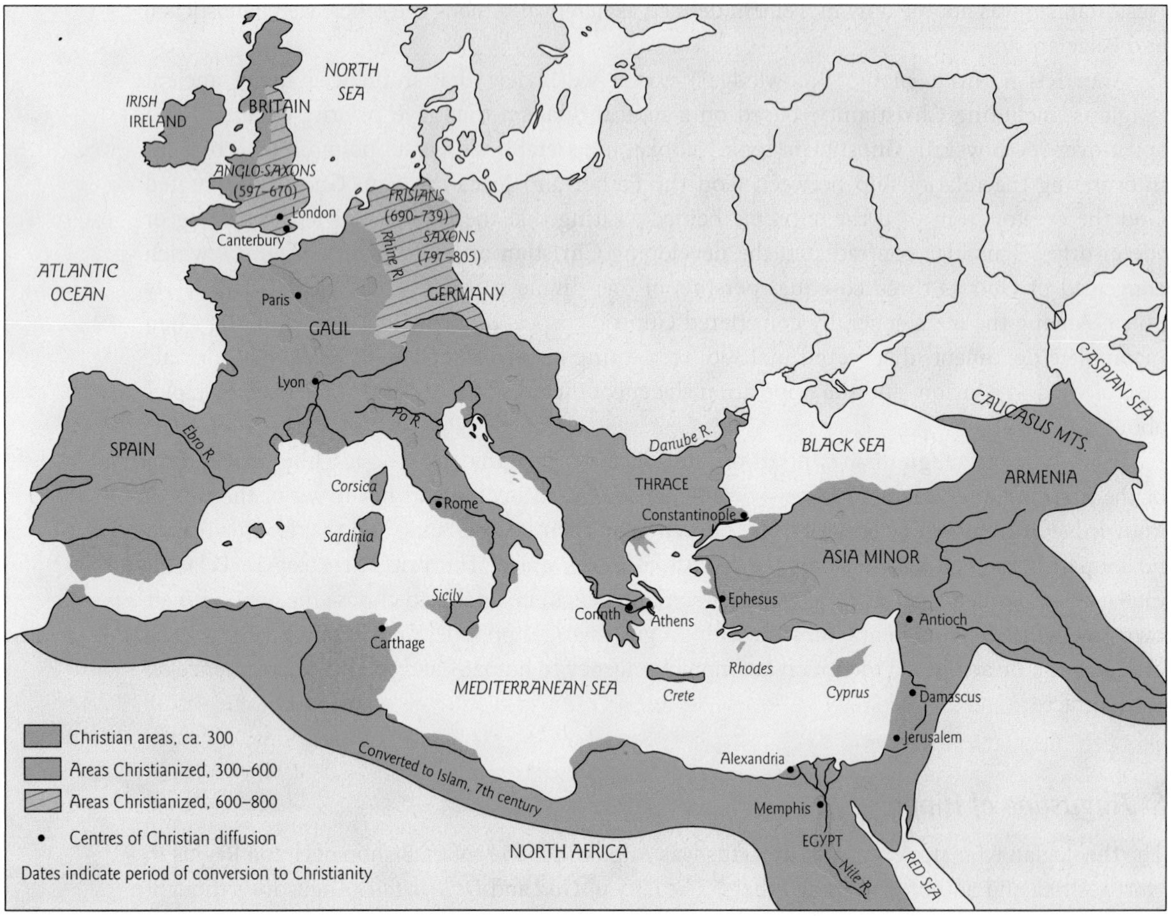

Relations between East and West

Although the Council of Chalcedon upheld a non-Arian Christology, the Arian controversy persisted, leading to a schism between Rome and Constantinople that lasted from 486 to 518. After the breach was closed, the bishops of Rome were under the thumb of Byzantium, deprived of the liberty they had enjoyed during the schism.

The Lombard invasion of Italy in 586 served to limit Byzantium's control of Rome, but it also inaugurated a long period during which the Roman Church had to negotiate power with secular rulers from the north and west. This meant that by the early seventh century the Western Church was less stable than its Eastern counterpart and had not developed its infrastructure, theology, art, institutions, and social mission to the degree that the East had.

Constantinople and Rome

After Chalcedon, Greek and Latin Christianity grew further and further apart. The underlying reasons probably had more to do with politics and cultural differences, but once again a theological formulation provided a rallying point. At issue was the word *filioque* (Latin, "and the son"). Did the Holy Spirit "proceed" from God the father alone, as the original Nicene Creed had it, and as the Greek Church continued to hold, or from the father "and the son," as the Latin church came to maintain in the ninth century? Photius, the patriarch of Constantinople, in 867 denounced the insertion of *filioque* into the creed. For the next two decades, one party in Constantinople repudiated the term and condemned the pope, while another supported the term and condemned Photius. Behind the theological niceties lay the basic issue of authority, for Rome had added *filioque* to the creed without the consent of a universal Church council. In so doing, Rome had staked its claim to be the centre of authority against the Greek view of it as just one among five equally important patriarchates, and the Roman notion of papal authority against the Greek notion of authority as vested in councils of bishops. The final break is conventionally dated to 1054, though it was in the making before then and attempts were made after that date to heal it.

The *filioque* was not the only issue that separated the Orthodox and Roman traditions. In addition, the Orthodox tradition venerated icons (see p. 173), permitted married clergy, used languages other than Latin in Bible readings and **liturgy**, and—most important—refused to recognize the Roman pontiff as supreme.

Eastern-Rite Catholic Churches

Rome's efforts to recruit new adherents among Eastern Orthodox Christians led to the formation of new churches that, even though they were aligned with Rome, retained important elements of the Eastern tradition, from the use of local languages (rather than Latin) to immersion baptism. They also continued to have married priests, although their higher ecclesiastical officers were generally celibate. Since most of the Eastern Catholic churches had Orthodox roots, most of them continue to have Orthodox counterparts today. The exception is the Maronite Church of Lebanon, which has been part of the Roman Catholic world since its founding in the fifth century.

Practice

Worship Spaces

Because Christianity began as a small movement, private dwellings were the logical places to gather for worship. Such gatherings usually took place in the larger homes of the group's wealthiest members, although poorer urban Christians met on the upper levels of multi-family dwelling spaces. This kind of domestic worship continued well into the Constantinian era, but from that time on the worship spaces used by Christians became more diverse.

From the mid-second century, some houses used for Christian worship were re-modelled to accommodate as many as 75 people in a single room. This type of building is known as a house church (*domus ecclesiae*). As well, rooms known as baptisteries provided space for full-immersion baptism rituals. The house church at Dura Europos in Syria, built in the third century, is the earliest known example.

Constantine's pro-Christian initiatives led to the construction of much larger and grander worship spaces called basilicas. Constantine had several of these buildings—in the shape of long

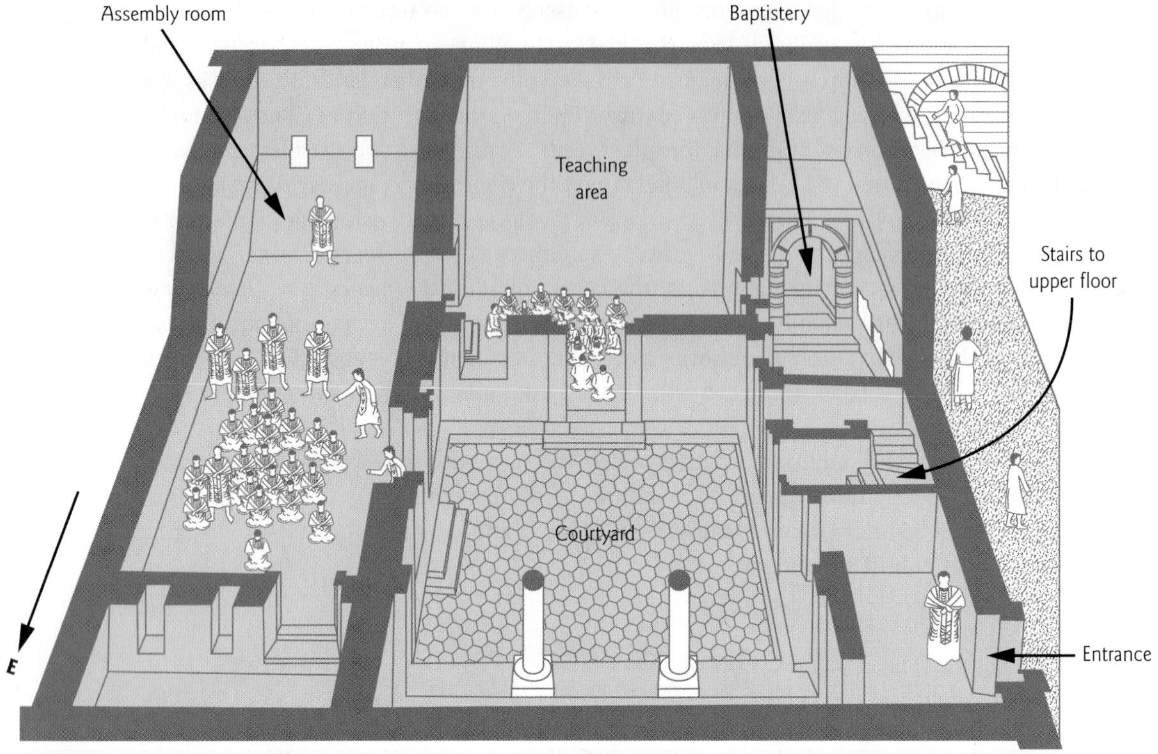

Diagram of the Dura-Europos house church.
Source: Adapted from www.deeperstudy.com/link/dura_church.html.

rectangles with side aisles—constructed as spaces for Christian worship, usually adorned with wall paintings and gilded mosaics.

The earliest records suggest that two rituals with their roots in Judaism were critical to the identity of the first communities: baptism, the rite of initiation into the Christian community, and the Eucharist, the shared symbolic meal, which became part of the weekly worship life of the community.

Baptism

In the Jewish world of the first century there were several rituals involving the use of water. Some were designed to wash away impurities and restore the worshipper to fitness for contact with God. In Jewish communities outside Palestine, conversion to Judaism required a water bath, along with instruction and male circumcision, and although the early Christians abandoned the latter, they retained the ideas of instruction and immersion in water as a symbolic purification in preparation for initiation into the faith.

In the Synoptic Gospels, the story of Jesus' baptism by his cousin, a holy man known as John the Baptist, is generally understood to signal the beginning of his public ministry. Early Christians developed their baptism ritual in keeping with the story of Jesus' own baptism. It is in the act of baptism that the Christian life begins and the path of discipleship is undertaken.

The Eucharist

We know that the early Christians usually gathered around a shared meal at which scripture was read, prayers were offered, and the consecrated bread and wine of the Eucharist were distributed. This structure was modelled on that of Jewish gatherings for prayer and worship.

The idea of the Eucharist drew on the Synoptic Gospels' accounts of the night before Jesus was arrested. At supper with his friends, he took bread, gave thanks to God, blessed the bread, broke it, and shared it with them. He then took a cup of wine, gave thanks, blessed it, and shared it with his followers. As Jesus shared the wine and bread he said, "Do this in memory of me." This ritual act of remembering Jesus' life and death became central to Christian life and worship. The Synoptics reflect the assumption that the last supper was a Passover meal, although it does not follow the pattern of a Seder. Over time, the form of the Eucharist became fairly predictable, and that form was then established as liturgical practice.

Early Christian Art

The earliest art of the Christian community reflects the influence of classical Greco-Roman models. Most of what has survived is funerary art: sarcophagi (coffins) decorated with scenes from Jesus' life, biblical stories, and images of the deceased; statues representing Jesus as the good shepherd carrying a lamb across his shoulders; wall and funerary plaque inscriptions with Christian symbols; portraits of the deceased with their arms raised in prayer; representations of early Christian martyrs; and scenes depicting both the last supper and the symbolic heavenly banquet at which Jesus' followers would gather after the second coming. These symbols suggest the frame of meaning that early Christians placed around their practice.

The Rise of Monasticism

In time, many churches became substantial landowners and bishops became influential patrons, often interceding with the state on behalf of individuals. From the third century forward, some Christians became concerned about the implications of this worldly activity. Could the Church exercise influence in places of social power without losing some of its moral agency and independence?

Such questions contributed to the rise of the monastic movement. The idea of living under an ascetic discipline was not unique to Christianity: in the Jewish tradition, the Essenes were ascetics with a rigorous communal lifestyle, and the Theraputae practised a severe discipline. Pagan religious traditions had their own versions of ascetic discipline: many philosophers embraced solitude and a strictly celibate life.

External societal factors also contributed to the rise of monasticism. As the Empire fragmented, social, political, and economic chaos combined with serious epidemics to create a climate of instability that called for new ways of both surviving and living in community. Among them were two streams of monastic life: **anchoritic** and **cenobitic**.

A fourth-century mosaic in the basilica of Santa Pudenziana in Rome shows Jesus teaching the Apostles in the heavenly Jerusalem (© jozef sedmak / Alamy).

Anchoritic and Cenobitic Monasticism

The term "anchorite" was commonly used to refer to hermits, people who devoted their lives to silence, prayer, and sometimes mortification of the flesh. The first significant Christian anchorite was Anthony of Egypt (251–356), who at the age of 18 gave up all his possessions and retired to the desert, where he attracted disciples who joined him in the ascetic life.

Thousands of others, including some women, followed suit. Through a life of silence, refusal of attachments (both material and spiritual), continual prayer, and self-supporting work, the "desert fathers and mothers" sought to move more deeply into communion with God.

"Cenobitic" means "communal." The founder of cenobitic monasticism is understood to be St Pachomius (290–346), a pagan who was converted to Christianity and lived for a time as a hermit, but felt himself drawn toward community life. Accordingly, he built a monastery, or community house, and many came to join him. By the time of his death the movement or "order" he founded counted nine monasteries and two nunneries: large communities that supported themselves by practising a variety of trades and occupations, they became models for the religious communities to follow.

Communal monasticism developed further in the East under the influence of St Basil, Bishop of Caesarea (358–384) and in the West under St Benedict of Nursia in Italy (480–550). Basil wrote a rule (code of discipline) that still forms the basis of Eastern monasticism. Basilian monasteries tended to be small (no more than 40 people) and all property was held in common. No excesses of asceticism were allowed, local bishops maintained control over orders in their area, and each Basilian community was expected to be of service to the larger community around it.

Document

The Desert Fathers and Mothers

Although the desert fathers and mothers lived mainly as recluses, they would share their wisdom with pilgrims who sought them out, often in the form of anecdotal stories designed to help the petitioners find their own way forward.

Someone asked Abba [Father] Anthony, "What must one do in order to please God?" The old man replied, "Pay attention to what I tell you: whoever you may be, always have God before your eyes; whatever you do, do it according to the testimony of the holy Scriptures; in whatever place you live, do not easily leave it. Keep these three precepts and you will be saved" (Anthony the Great in Ward 1975: 2).

One of the old men said, "When Saint Basil came to the monastery one day, he said to the abbot, after the customary exhortation, "Have you a brother here who is obedient?" The other replied, "They are all your servants, master, and strive for their salvation." But he repeated, "Have you a brother who is really obedient?" Then the abbot led a brother to him and Saint Basil used him to serve during the meal. When the meal was ended, the brother brought him some water for rinsing his hands and Saint Basil said to him, "When I enter the sanctuary, come, that I may ordain you deacon." When this was done, he ordained him priest and took him with him to the bishop's palace because of his obedience (Basil the Great in Ward 1975: 39–40).

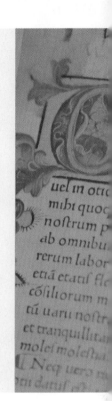

More than a century later, Benedict began as a hermit, but after twelve monks had gathered around him, he developed the prototype for Western monastic life. **Benedict's Rule** was grounded in the principle that the community's central activity was the divine office: the devotional services held at specified hours throughout the day and the night. As in the East, all possessions were held in common, and moderation and balance were key aspects of the religious life.

Eastern Orthodoxy

The eastern Mediterranean was comparatively stable and prosperous in the seventh and eighth centuries, and thus more conducive to intellectual life than its Western counterpart, which was still struggling after the barbarian invasions. Byzantium lasted more than 1,000 years after Constantine. Even the slow but steady spread of the Ottoman Turks, who took control of Constantinople in 1453, did not mean the end of the Greek Church. Formally tolerated under Islam, though now forbidden to proselytize, Orthodox Christians became a self-governing religious community with the patriarch as their civil ruler.

Theology

Representative of the eastern Mediterranean's cultural sophistication was the Greek theologian John of Damascus (c. 675–c. 749). His most important work, *The Fountain of Wisdom*, is a comprehensive treatise on theological topics. Medieval Byzantine theology included a rich vein of devotional practice and mysticism, exemplified in the writings of St Simeon the New Theologian (see Document box).

Document

St Simeon

St Simeon the New Theologian (949–1022), who headed a monastery in Constantinople, wrote of God's closeness to the faithful:

I know that the Immovable comes down;
I know that the Invisible appears to me;
I know that he who is far outside the whole creation
Takes me into himself and hides me in his arms. . . .
I know that I shall not die, for I am within the Life,
I have the whole of Life springing up as a fountain within me.
He is in my heart, he is in heaven (McManners 1990: 147–8).

By the fourteenth century a group calling themselves the Hesychasts (from a Greek word meaning "inner stillness") had developed a devotional practice centred on repetition of a mantra-like formula known as the Jesus Prayer: "Lord Jesus Christ, son of God, have mercy on me, a sinner." When their practical spiritual discipline was challenged by Barlaam the Calabrian on the grounds that one could know God directly only in the next life, another great Byzantine theologian came to their defence. Gregory Palamas agreed with Barlaam that God transcends this realm, but argued that God's energies come through to humans like the radiance of the transfigured Christ:

> He is being and not being; he is everywhere and nowhere; he has many names and cannot be named; he is both in perpetual movement and immovable; he is absolutely everything and nothing of that which is (Meyendorff 1964: 209).

Christianizing the Slavs

Eastern Orthodoxy was carried from Byzantium to various peoples in Eastern Europe. Orthodox missionaries to the Slavic peoples made significant headway in the ninth century. Language played an important part in the success of the Orthodox missionaries, who used local vernaculars rather than Greek; this encouraged the development of independent local churches with a strong sense of national identity. The missionary effort was pioneered by two brothers, Cyril (826–869) and Methodius (c. 815–885). In 862 they travelled to Moravia (the region of today's Czech Republic), where they preached in the vernacular and translated the Bible and liturgy into Slavonic. When a new alphabet (based on the Greek) was later created for Slavic languages such as Bulgarian, Serbian, Ukrainian, and Russian, it was named Cyrillic in his honour. Romania, which was originally colonized by Rome as the province of Dacia, was Christian from the fourth century and adopted the Latin alphabet, but its church was eventually brought into the Eastern Orthodox orbit during a period of Bulgarian rule. Other parts of Eastern Europe were converted by Roman Catholic missionaries, who instituted a Latin liturgy and more centralized Church control. Thus the languages of mainly Catholic peoples such as the Croats, Slovenes, Czechs, Slovaks, Poles, Lithuanians, and Hungarians use the Latin alphabet.

The early centre of Russian Orthodoxy was Kiev, in Ukraine, whose pagan people were forcibly converted to Christianity following the marriage of their ruler Vladimir to the sister of the Byzantine emperor around the year 987. It was only after Kiev fell to Mongol invaders in 1237 that Moscow replaced it as the centre of Russian religion and politics.

Worship in the Greek Church

In the first centuries of Christianity, religious services must have included chanting. The evidence is only fragmentary, but similarities in medieval Roman Catholic, Greek Orthodox, Muslim, and Jewish melodies and harmonies point to a common background, and the signs used for musical notation in the Byzantine era are virtually identical to those used in medieval Hebrew manuscripts.

Many Christians celebrate the eve of **Easter** with a vigil service in which members of the congregation pass a flame symbolizing Jesus' resurrection from candle to candle. The ceremony is particularly spectacular at the Greek Orthodox Church of the Holy Sepulchre in Jerusalem. Hundreds of worshippers, each carrying a candle, pack the church's rotunda. A priest is ritually searched to ensure that he is not carrying any matches. He then enters the chamber at the centre of the rotunda—the traditional site of Jesus' tomb. After a time he extends his arm from the chamber with a miraculously burning taper. The people closest to him light their candles from his and then share the fire with others, so that within moments the vast rotunda is a sea of flame. Outside the church, the fire is carried by runners to Orthodox congregations elsewhere. This ritual symbolizes the spreading of the Easter light and the gospel message.

Byzantine Art

The influence of the Byzantine imperial tradition can be seen in images of Jesus. After Constantine made Christianity mainstream, Jesus began to appear in art not as the young shepherd of the early centuries, but as a distinguished older man dressed in the robes of a king or a judge. It was also around this time that he began to be depicted with a halo representing the radiance of the sun. (Third- to seventh-century Sasanian kings were also portrayed with halos, and similar imagery was used throughout Asia in representations of the Buddha.) By the sixth century, Byzantine mosaics were showing Christ enthroned in heaven as the ruler of creation.

Icons in the Orthodox Church

The Orthodox churches developed a distinctive form of portraiture for depicting religious figures. An **icon** (from Greek, "image") might be an entirely two-dimensional painting, often on a piece of wood, or it might be overlaid in low relief, in wood or precious metal and ornamented with jewels. While the robes clothing the figure were executed in relief, the hands and face were typically two-dimensional, so that the parts of the image representing flesh appeared to exist on a different plane from the material world around them. Nevertheless, in the seventh and eighth centuries these images became the subject of a heated dispute known as the iconoclastic controversy.

Pitting a faction called the iconoclasts ("icon breakers") against one called the iconodules ("icon worshippers"), the controversy served in part as a vehicle for other antagonisms (political, regional, etc.). But points of principle were also at stake, and Byzantine intellectuals engaged in serious theological discussions concerning the role of images in worship. In the end the Second Council of Nicaea in 787 decided that icons were permissible as long as the faithful did not actually worship them.

A shop selling religious icons in Monastiraki, Athens (© Mike Kemp / In Pictures / Corbis).

Some historians wonder whether the dispute might also have reflected the success of Islam, which rejects any kind of iconography, since the iconoclastic movement seems to have been particularly strong in the regions bordering Syria. In any event, their opponents prevailed, and Eastern Christendom retained its distinctive tradition. In Orthodox sanctuaries today, a massive screen in front of the altar holds a row of large icons. Smaller icons are hung in private homes.

Medieval Christianity

Decline and Expansion

The first widespread decline in Christian influence began about the year 600 and continued until the mid-tenth century. Internally, the Western Church was weakened by poor leadership and corruption. External factors included the decline of the Roman Empire, the ensuing socio-political and economic turmoil, and Islam's rise to power in various parts of the Euro-Mediterranean theatre.

The rapid spread of Islam changed the religious map. After only three centuries it was as geographically widespread as Christianity and was the official faith of states much more powerful than many that professed to be Christian. And then the tide turned. Near the end of the tenth century, the invasions that had racked Western Europe for 500 years simply ceased, even though Muslim populations were well established on the Iberian peninsula. The resulting stability was conducive to urban growth, the development of commerce and wealth, and the emergence of modern states.

Between 950 and 1050 CE, Christianity made the greatest geographic advances in its history. Scandinavia, which had been a passionate enemy of Christianity, was converted. Czechs, Poles, and Hungarians were Christianized, and Sicily and northern Spain were "recovered" from Islam. Christians co-existed with Muslims, Jews, and occasional enclaves of paganism. By 1350, however, most of Europe had converted to Christianity.

In Western Europe, nascent nations were emerging from feudalism. In 911 Germanic tribal princes elected a king; in 987 feudal princes chose a king of France; and in 1066 William the Conqueror began establishing a strong state in England. Across territories previously conquered by Islam, political power shifted from Muslim to Christian rulers.

The Crusades

After the Arab Muslims captured Jerusalem in 637, the Christians who lived there were tolerated, and Christian pilgrims were still allowed to visit. In 1071, however, the city was captured by the Seljuq Turks, who were less accommodating than the Arabs had been. The Byzantine emperors appealed to the West for help, and in 1095 Pope Urban II proclaimed the first in what would become a series of "**crusades**" to liberate the holy places of Palestine. Participation was framed as a sacred pilgrimage and encouraged by promises that those who died in the attempt to free the Holy Land would be honoured as martyrs. At the same time, the prospects of worldly adventure and profit encouraged peasants and nobles alike to "take the cross."

In all, the Crusades spanned nearly four centuries, but the most significant period ended in 1204, when crusaders attacked the Christian city of Constantinople, plundering it and placing a ruler from Flanders on the throne. Although the Byzantines recaptured the city in 1261, relations between Western and Eastern Christians did not recover.

Punishing Heresy

Beginning in the thirteenth century, the Church undertook to discover and punish Christians whose views differed from Church teaching. Until the twelfth century the punishment for heresy was **excommunication** (exclusion from participation in the Christian community), but by the early thirteenth century the Church had access to state power to enforce its decisions.

The first Inquisition was established in 1232, after the Emperor Frederick II entrusted the hunt for heretics to state officials. Pope Gregory IX, fearing Frederick's ambitions, claimed this responsibility for the Church and appointed papal inquisitors to travel the countryside in search of heretics. After a grace period during which accused heretics were given the opportunity to confess and do penance, those who had not confessed were put on trial. The Inquisitor was assisted by a jury, and evidence was heard from at least two witnesses. (The famous Spanish Inquisition had a different character, as it was established by the state specifically to investigate Jewish and Muslim converts to Christianity. Its grand inquisitor, Tomás de Torquemada, ordered more than 2,000 executions and was a major force behind the expulsion of the Jews and Muslims from Spain in 1492.) Penalties for those found guilty ranged from confiscation of goods to imprisonment to execution; those sentenced to death were handed over to secular authorities and burned at the stake.

When the pope who appointed Torquemada, Innocent VIII, called for the eradication of witchcraft, a German **Dominican** named Heinrich Kraemer produced a handbook for Christian witch-hunters entitled the *Malleus Maleficarum* ("Hammer of Witches"; 1486).

The Development of Papal Authority

Innocent III

After several weak predecessors, Innocent III (c. 1160–1216) asserted the authority of the papacy over secular princes and promoted the development of ecclesiastical government. The papacy became a consultative focal point for the Church, maintaining communication with churchmen all over Europe, Byzantium, and Russia.

By the later Middle Ages, however, the pope and the councils of the Church were competing for power. This also implied a contest with the secular authority as councils allowed opportunities for secular challenges to papal authority.

Boniface VIII

Some of the strongest claims for papal authority in the temporal realm were made by Pope Boniface VIII (1235–1303), who in 1302, in the bull *Unam Sanctam*, proclaimed it "absolutely necessary for salvation that every human creature be subject to the Roman pontiff."

During this period the monarchs of Europe were competing for power, and the kings of both England and France decreed that Church revenues in their countries should be used to support their respective governments (and help pay for their wars against one another). Boniface issued the bull *Clericos Laicos* (1296) in an effort to prevent such appropriation, but both Philip IV of France and Edward I of England asserted their higher authority to exact tax from the Church. In response to *Clericos Laicos*, Philip prohibited the export of gold, silver, precious stones, or food from France to the Papal states, which cut off major revenue sources for the papacy. In 1297 a more moderate bull, *Etsi de Statu*, decreed that kings could tax the Church in an emergency.

The Avignon Papacy

When Boniface's successor died, the conclave to choose his successor was deadlocked for nearly a year before electing Clement V in 1305. Clement, who was French, had the papal court moved to Avignon in southern France. The Avignon period continued for 67 years, during which papal administration was increasingly influenced by the French Crown.

Finally in 1377 Pope Gregory XI chose to return the papacy to Rome. On his death, however, division emerged between his successor, Urban VI, and the cardinals (senior clergy), who established a second line of popes in Avignon while Urban remained in Rome. Although the Church considered them illegitimate, the Avignon pope and his successor remained in power until 1398, when the latter lost the support of the French king. The "Western schism" was not officially brought to an end until 1417, at the Council of Constance.

The Conciliar Movement

The Avignon years gave rise to a critique of papal authority in the Church. A theologian named Marsilius of Padua (1290–1343) held that the pope could teach salvation but had no right to command obedience. He argued that power flowed from God to the people and from the people to the king in the realm of worldly affairs, and to the pope with reference to spiritual matters. With Marsilius we see the kernel of medieval conciliar theory, according to which the councils of the Church represented the people and the popes depended on the councils for their power. In the old model, God invested both spiritual and worldly authority in the pope, who in turn invested worldly power in the secular ruler; then the two of them, each in his own sphere, ruled the people.

It was the Council of Constance that, with the decree *Sacrosancta* (1415), declared the council itself the supreme authority within the Church. It then used its new power to demonstrate conciliar authority over the papacy, deposing the competing popes and electing a single successor. The Constance council also decreed that a new council should be called within five to seven years and every ten years thereafter.

The conciliar theory did not mean lay enfranchisement, but it did provide for a broader sharing of power. The relationship between the councils and the Pope after the investiture of authority was not clear; the theory was never fully developed as a working model of power sharing and accountability; and by the mid-fifteenth century the movement had been crushed by a revived papal monarchy. Nevertheless, the Council of Constance would influence both the development of representative governments in emerging nation-states and the thinking of religious reformers, both inside and outside the Catholic Church.

Reason and Revelation

The most critical intellectual issue of the Middle Ages was framed as an epistemological question: how do we know what we know? That question was answered by two competing (or complementary) perspectives: scholasticism and mysticism.

Scholasticism

Scholasticism was the product of an effort to reconcile the philosophy of ancient Greece and, later, Rome with Christian theology. In effect, it was a method of philosophical and theological speculation that came to characterize medieval learning.

Institutionally, "scholasticism" is defined as the teaching of the clergy in the "schools"—that is, the emerging universities of Paris, Bologna, and Oxford, where theology was a central part of the curriculum. (The clerical foundations of the university are reflected in the academic hoods and gowns, similar to monks' robes, that are still common today.) Intellectually, scholasticism is defined in terms of its assumptions and goals. For the scholastics, who saw philosophy as the "handmaid" of theology, faith and reason were mutually confirming, and by the fifth century Augustine was describing theology as "faith seeking understanding."

John Scotus Erigena, who was born in Ireland around 810 and taught in Paris, expanded on Augustine's understanding of the relationship between reason and scriptural revelation. For Erigena, scripture was the source of authority, but it was the duty of reason to examine and expound it. While scholastic teaching was initially based on the reading of scripture in an effort to arrive at a rational grasp of its meaning, in time it developed a dialectical structure in which a proposition of doctrine was stated and then objections to it were raised and systematically addressed.

Some two centuries later, **Anselm** (c. 1033–1109) moved away from the principle of scriptural authority, asserting that faith itself has a kind of rationality. One of the formulations for which he is famous is the statement "I believe so that I may understand." The most tantalizing of the medieval proofs for the existence of God is Anselm's "**ontological argument**." Unlike later proofs that infer God's existence from inspection of the universe, Anselm's argument finds it implied in the very idea of God.

Thomas Aquinas

The tradition on which the early scholastics relied was based on the thought of Plato and dominated by abstract ideas. In the twelfth century, however, Latin Christianity discovered the thought of Plato's contemporary Aristotle, who had developed a model of rational argument that provided more scope for examination of the material world. The greatest of the Aristotelian scholastics was the Dominican **Thomas Aquinas** (1225–74).

In writings such as the *Summa Theologiae* ("Summation of Theology") Aquinas sharpened the distinction between reason and faith. Although he believed some Christian doctrines, such as those of the Trinity and the incarnation of God in Christ, to lie beyond reason in the realm of faith (though that did not mean they were contrary to reason), he thought others, such as the existence of God, were provable by reason. Aquinas identified five "ways" of proving God's existence, most of which involved describing some feature of the material world and arguing that such a world could not exist without a God. For example, in his second proof he argued that the pattern of cause and effect necessarily implies the existence of a First Cause that itself is uncaused, and that that First Cause must be God.

Because the new rational approach was based on logic rather than faith, its exponents were sometimes suspect in the eyes of Church authorities. Nevertheless, it was used to explore the key theological questions of the age: How can reason be present in the soul? What is the right relationship between reason and revelation? What is the basis of knowledge?

Mysticism

While Thomas's views sparked further discussion of the limits of reason in matters of faith, another development rendered those limits to some extent irrelevant. The late Middle Ages saw a remarkable flowering of mysticism.

To describe something as "mystical" is not simply to say that it involves mystery. **Mysticism** is a specific tradition that emphasizes the certainty of profound personal experience. Typically, mystics are certain of God not because of some logical proof but because they have experienced a moment of intense, vivid awareness. One characteristic of that experience is a sense of union with the divine through a temporary dissolving or bridging of the gulf that normally separates the human person from God. The mystic then re-engages ordinary time with new perspectives.

Accounts of mystic experience are inevitably written after the moment of ecstasy has passed. A number of medieval Christian mystics nevertheless described their experiences in vivid detail. Medieval mysticism was part of a long tradition of cultivation of the interior life, or "spirituality," in which the heart or conscience opens itself to the divine through prayer and contemplation.

For many Christians, spirituality reflects the action of the Holy Spirit on the soul. Christian spirituality had roots in the Jewish tradition, was cultivated by the desert fathers and mothers, and was central to the monastic life.

In medieval Europe, one of the most notable systematizers of mystical thought was the German Dominican Johannes ("Meister") Eckhart (c. 1260–1327). Eckhart believed that although human beings are created in the image of God, our divine nature is obscured because our life is finite and creaturely. However, the mind of the spiritual person permits actualization of the divine nature that the soul contains. Eckhart's mysticism seeks to dissolve distinctions between self and God.

Whereas Eckhart sought to identify the self with the image of God, the French Cistercian **Bernard of Clairvaux** likened the awareness of God to the awareness of one's beloved. Like the ecstasy of love, this union is fleeting, but no less intensely experienced:

> To lose yourself so that you are as though you were not, to be unaware of yourself and emptied of yourself, to be, as it were, brought to nothing—this pertains to heavenly exchanges, not to human affection (O'Brien 1964: 122).

Female Mystics

A striking feature of late medieval mysticism was the scope it afforded women. Although they were forbidden to participate fully in clerical activities, and were limited to supporting roles even in female religious orders, there was no limit to the experiential depth that women could attain in their devotion.

Hildegard of Bingen (1098–1179) was a Benedictine abbess who had a creative life in writing and music but was also involved in politics and diplomacy: feudal nobles as well as clergy sought her advice. When she became abbess in 1141, she had a vision of tongues of flame from the heavens settling on her, and over the next ten years she wrote a book of visions entitled *Scivias* ("Know the ways [of God]").

Catherine of Siena (1347–80 or 1333–80) in Italy was a member of a Dominican lay order. She was actively involved in the religious politics of the day, but her *Dialogue* records her mystical visions.

The English mystic Julian of Norwich (c. 1342–c. 1413) was 30 when she experienced a series of visions during a severe illness. After two decades of reflection, she wrote an analysis of those visions in her *Showings*, or *Sixteen Revelations of Divine Love*. To Julian, evil was a distortion, introduced by the human will, that served to reveal the divine love of God all the more clearly.

Document

Julian of Norwich

Julian has attracted new attention in recent years, as she speaks to the anxiety so prevalent in the world today. Her revelations assured her that all that is created is known, loved, and held by God. The following text uses the image of the hazelnut to express this understanding.

And at the same time I saw this corporeal sight, our Lord showed me a spiritual sight of his familiar love. I saw that he is to us everything which is good and comforting in our help. He is our clothing, for he is that love which wraps and enfolds us, embraces us and guides us, surrounds us for his love, which is so tender that he may never desert us. And so in this sight I saw truly that he is everything which is good, as I understand. And in this he showed me something small, no bigger than a hazelnut, lying in the palm of his hand, and I perceived that it was as round as a ball. I looked at it and thought: What can this be? And I was given this general answer: It is everything which is made. . . . In this little thing I saw three properties. The first is that God made it, the second that he loves it, the third is that God preserves it. It is that God is the Creator and the lover and the protector (Colledge and Walsh, ed. and trans., 1978: 130–1).

Medieval Religious Communities

Monastic Orders

Monastic communities developed a highly structured religious discipline. Monks (male) and **nuns** (female) were required to take solemn vows of poverty, chastity, and obedience, to stay within the physical precincts of the community, and to follow its rule.

Monks played an important part in both the Greek and Latin traditions. Technically, since monasticism had begun as an alternative to established religion, monks were laymen rather than priests, but followed a demanding schedule of prayer and worship. A distinction was drawn between "religious" (or "regular") clergy, who followed a monastic rule, and "secular" clergy, who worked in the world and in the Greek Church (though not the Roman) were even permitted to marry; members of the ecclesiastical hierarchy were always celibate, however.

Cluniac Fathers

Founded in 910, the monastery at Cluny in France became the centre of a movement to bring Benedictine monastic institutions under the control of religious rather than secular authorities. Cluny became a centre of revitalization that inspired other efforts at renewal. Nevertheless, within a century of its founding Cluny itself was growing rich and abandoning the rigorous simplicity that Benedict had called for.

Cistercians

In response to the changes at Cluny, an austere new order was founded at Cîteaux, north of Cluny, in 1098. The Cistercians (from the Latin for Cîteaux) wore simple undyed wool habits, ate no meat, and worshipped in sparsely decorated churches. By 1100 there were 500 Cistercian abbeys. One group of Cistercians in particular became known for their rule of silence. The Cistercians of the Strict Observance, or Trappists, were founded in the 1600s at the monastery of La Trappe in Normandy. The best known Trappist of the twentieth century was the mystic Thomas Merton (1915–68), who explored Asian spirituality, especially Zen Buddhism, and was active in social protest in the 1960s. Other Cistercians helped to found spiritual orders of knights such as the Knights Templar, the Knights of St John, and the Teutonic order. Their members made pilgrimages to the Holy Land and took as their biblical model the Maccabees, the Jewish patriots of the second century BCE.

Carthusians

Founded in 1084, the austere Carthusian order (named after its base at La Grande Chartreuse in France) demanded a vow of silence from its members. Like the Benedictine abbey of Fécamp, near the English Channel, the Chartreuse abbey supported itself in part by making and selling a famous drink, in this instance the brilliant green liqueur that gave its name to the colour chartreuse.

Mendicant Orders

The monastic response to the secular world had been to withdraw from it, but with urban growth some monastics felt the need to respond to the needs of the urban poor. Thus a new type of religious order emerged whose members—called **friars**, from the Latin *frater* ("brother")—dedicated themselves to pastoral work. These "**mendicants**" either worked or begged for their living, and were not bound to a particular convent.

Franciscans

Francis of Assisi (1182–1226) grew up as the privileged son of a wealthy cloth merchant in central Italy, but a serious illness in his twenties led him to rethink his life. On a pilgrimage to Rome, he was so moved by the beggars outside St Peter's Basilica that he exchanged clothes with one of them and spent the day begging for alms. When he returned to Assisi, he dedicated his life to serving the poor. Gradually attracting a small group of like-minded companions, he established a rule of life emphasizing poverty, which received papal approval in 1209. Within a few years, Clara of Assisi had formed a Franciscan women's order known as the Poor Clares. An offshoot of the Franciscans called the Capuchins drew up their own rule in 1529 and are still known today for their soup kitchens, which offer free meals in impoverished neighbourhoods.

In 1224 Francis experienced a vision of an angel from whom he received the "stigmata": wounds in his own body that replicated those suffered by Christ on the cross. Proclaimed a saint in 1228—just two years after his death—he quickly became a beloved figure and the subject of many legends, among them several that emphasized his love of the natural world. In one of the most famous tales, he preaches to a flock of birds, telling them how fortunate they are that God provides for them.

Founded in 1929 by Capuchin friars, the Capuchin Soup Kitchen in Detroit now serves 2,000 people a day in some of the city's poorest neighbourhoods. In 1997 the friars founded a farm that in 2011 harvested nearly 3,000 kilograms (6,000 pounds) of produce for the soup kitchen (© Jim West / Alamy).

Dominicans

In 1216–17 a priest from northern Spain named Dominic Guzmán received a papal mandate to establish a preaching order dedicated to combatting the "Albigensian heresy." (Named for the city of Albi in southwestern France, Albigensianism was a dualistic doctrine, not unlike **Manichaeism**, centred on a view of existence as a struggle between light and darkness, and was highly critical of Roman Catholicism.) Dominicans such as Aquinas rapidly established their influence as itinerant preachers of doctrine in university towns such as Paris.

Carmelites

The hermits of Mount Carmel were organized in Palestine in 1154, during the Crusades, and given a rule by the patriarch of Jerusalem. As the numbers of crusaders in the Holy Land declined, the **Carmelites** established themselves in Europe and England, where they were termed "White Friars."

Celibacy

The insistence that priests be celibate became stronger in the Middle Ages. Rationales included the spiritual benefit of surmounting worldly desires and the practical benefit of freedom from the responsibilities of marriage and parenthood. In addition, since it made a hereditary priesthood impossible, celibacy worked against the tendency for institutional influence to become concentrated in particular families.

Women in Medieval Catholicism

The tradition of women in a consecrated religious life had roots in the early Church, but its most significant period of development was in the Middle Ages. Various forms of religious life for women flourished throughout the period.

The Vita Canonica

We have already seen that informal groups of women living a religious life were organized in the time of the early Church. Eventually this way of life came to be known as the Vita Canonica. In response to women's requests for direction on how to order a common religious life, local bishops would write rules ("canons") for them. Communities of "canonesses" were characterized by their diversity, lack of formal structure, and relative autonomy.

Nuns

The rules governing female monastic communities paralleled those for male communities. Normally, each woman entering the convent was required to furnish a dowry and relinquish all private property. Nuns lived together under one roof and took vows of poverty, continence, and obedience that reflected a permanent commitment to the religious life. The formal consecration ended with the vow to live always as the bride of Christ.

Over time, it became common for women's communities to separate themselves entirely from the world; by the thirteenth century, the male hierarchy of the Church had imposed this "cloistering" on all women's communities. The **abbesses** who presided over these communities were quite powerful. In addition to making and enforcing the convent's laws, the abbess was responsible for its landholdings, and so played a significant role in the feudal system. She administered the financial affairs of the estate and also oversaw the lives of tenants who farmed it.

Nevertheless, the power of the female monastic community declined by the later Middle Ages. Secular princes anxious to limit the autonomy of the Church claimed an interest in Church-owned lands, and in the twelfth century, *Gratium's Decretum* enforced the legal principle that no layperson could exercise control over a cleric. Since no woman could be ordained, even an abbess was by definition a layperson and therefore forbidden to exercise authority over a male cleric, however junior. Increased strictures around cloistering also meant that abbesses could not leave their convents to conduct business.

Beguines and Beghards

Beguines were unconsecrated women who lived a freer type of communal religious life. They did not live under the authority of local bishops and did not follow any of the traditional monastic rules, but came together in small groups, mainly in urban environments, to live in poverty, celibacy, prayer, and service, after the model of the gospel. This new style of religious life also attracted some men, known as **Beghards**, though in smaller numbers.

A number of Beguines are known for their writing in the tradition of love mysticism. Among them are Mechthild of Magdeburg in Saxony (1207–97), and Hadjewich, a Beguine from Flanders who wrote many letters as well as poems and accounts of visions. A common theme in their work was the ecstatic union of the soul with God. A third notable female mystic who is widely thought to have been a Beguine was Marguerite Porete, who was burned at the stake for heresy in 1310. Though condemned by Church authorities, her book *The Mirror of Simple Souls* influenced Christian mystics for centuries.

Document

Mechthild of Magdeburg, "Of the Nine Choirs and How They Sing"

The nine orders or "choirs" of angels were a standard part of the religious imagery of Mechtild's day. The idea of a hierarchy of angels was well established from the fifth century.

Now listen, my love. Hear with spiritual ears what the nine choirs sing.

We praise You, O Lord.
For you have sought us in your humility,
Saved us by your compassion,
Honoured us by your humanity,
Led us by your gentleness,
Ordered us by your wisdom,
Protected us by your power,
Sanctified us by your holiness,
Illumined us by your intimacy,
Raised us by your love (Madigan, 1998: 138).

Saints

Expansion into Africa, Asia, and Eastern Europe was facilitated by Christianity's emphasis on the miraculous power of **saints**.

Sainthood

Over the centuries the Church developed criteria for sainthood (including the performance of attested miracles), a canonical list of saints, and a rigorous procedure for screening candidates. The first person to be declared a saint was a German bishop, in 993.

The saints collectively came to be regarded as a kind of heavenly senate composed of individuals thought to possess a special merit or virtue, a personal credit in the economy of blessedness that could be drawn on by believers who wanted them to intercede with God on their behalf. By praying to certain saints or making pilgrimages to their shrines, one might win release from punishment in the next existence. Particular saints came to be associated with specific conditions or occupations. St Christopher, for example, who was said to have carried the child Jesus across a dangerous river, is one of several patron saints of travellers, and St Cecilia is the patron of musicians because she sang to God on her deathbed.

The Virgin Mary

Pre-eminent among the saints was **Mary**, the virgin chosen by God to become the mother of Jesus. By the later Middle Ages it was thought that someone so close to Christ must share in his redeeming work, and that she would be willing to plead with her son on behalf of sinners. The resulting increase in devotion to Mary reflected a broader theological shift towards a greater concern with the humanity of Jesus.

In Latin Europe, artistic depictions of Mary followed a particular set of conventions. Although some of them can be traced to the cult of the pre-Christian goddess Isis, Mary's role is not limited to that of the devoted young mother. She is also the mature woman who grieves at the martyrdom of her adult son, the model of purity and incorruptibility, devotion and fidelity, sorrow and compassion.

Worship in the Medieval Church

Liturgical reforms in the early medieval period limited the opportunities for ordinary people to participate. Portions of the liturgy that had been spoken in the vernacular were increasingly performed in Latin, and the rules governing the Eucharist were tightened to require a complex process of confession and penitence before the sacrament could be received. This meant that priests could take communion frequently, but laypeople perhaps only once a year. In addition, only the clergy were allowed to receive the wine (the blood of Christ); laypeople were given only the bread (the body).

Church music also became less accessible to the average person. Gregorian chant or plainsong had been simple and easy for congregations to learn by rote, but as musical forms became more complex, using several voices, participation was increasingly restricted to formal choirs made up of monks and clergy.

Church architecture contributed to the distancing of lay people. Between the nave (the main body of the church, where the worshippers gathered) and the altar, another section of seats was added for the choir, and by the later medieval period worshippers' view of the altar had been further obstructed by rood screens erected between the nave and the chancel. Finally, the altar was pushed up against the wall, so that instead of standing behind it, facing the people, while celebrating the Eucharist, the priest now turned his back on them. This change had a theological basis: now the priest was offering the sacrifice on behalf of the people rather than presiding at the Eucharistic banquet of the whole people of God.

The Early Modern Era

Humanism

In the 1300s Europe crossed the watershed that divided the medieval from the early modern world. After centuries that one of the first Renaissance humanists, the poet Petrarch, described as the "dark ages," Western culture began to rediscover the philosophy, science, art, and poetry of Greek and Roman antiquity. Among the consequences was a renewed emphasis on life in this world, the celebration of beauty, and the capacity of human beings to govern themselves. This put the humanists in conflict with a Church that had traditionally understood itself to be the primary interpreter and mediator of human experience.

Erasmus (1466–1536)

Much of the groundwork for later reformers was laid by **Erasmus** of Rotterdam in the Netherlands. After his ordination as an Augustinian priest he had studied at a college of the University of Paris that favoured reform of some traditional Catholic teachings. He was critical of the Church's abuses and called for demanding new standards of scholarship in theology, based on new translations of the original sources.

In itself, humanism posed no real threat to the Church, but the external force of humanism was met with a push towards reform from within the Church itself. Together, these external and internal forces for change led to the schism within Western Christianity that came to be known as the Protestant Reformation.

The Protestant Reformation

The English Reformation, though not unrelated to the reforming activity on the continent, was uniquely linked to the British political context; therefore it will be discussed separately (see p. 191).

The Continental Reformation

The influence of the Church in Europe was all-pervasive in the early sixteenth century. It was Europe's largest landholder. Clergy played more than one role in society, not only dispensing the sacraments but providing medical care and education. The religious enthusiasm of the laity was reflected in pilgrimages, ostentatious public devotions, and huge investments in the Church, through paid funeral **masses** and the purchase of **indulgences** (releases from the time that the soul was required to spend in purgatory—a kind of holding area for the departed on their way to the next existence). Yet there were concerns about the Church, particularly in Germany: while many German clergymen were penniless and ill-educated, bishops often came from very affluent families and used their ecclesiastical positions to reinforce their wealth, social status, and political power. At the same time, this period was one of unprecedented advances in lay literacy, which reformers such as **Martin Luther** promoted by translating the scripture into vernacular languages. The combination of a changing intellectual world, dissatisfaction with the Church, and direct access to scripture for ordinary people (a development facilitated by the invention of the printing press) set the stage for the Reformation.

Martin Luther (1483–1546)

Widely considered to be the father of the Protestant Reformation, Luther was the son of a German miner. He became an Augustinian friar in 1505, and in 1512 was made a doctor of theology and professor of Scripture at the University of Wittenberg.

Luther struggled with the theological issues of salvation. In the complex system of clerical mediation between God and sinner, he feared that he would not be found worthy, until a sudden revelation convinced him that humans are justified (set right with God) only by faith, which itself is a gift of God's grace; there are no "works" we can do to earn that justification. His anxieties relieved, from this point forward he argued that if we have faith, then we are assured of salvation.

This bronze statue by Johann Gottfried Schadow, erected in Wittenberg's town square in 1821, was the first public monument to Luther (© typographics / iStockphoto).

In October 1517 Luther posted a list of "95 Theses" against indulgences on the door of the church at Wittenberg. This public protest eventually led to his excommunication and emergence as the primary agent of the Protestant Reformation, a schism that split the Church into many differing groups, among them one named for Luther himself.

Although Luther's core doctrine was justification by faith alone, through grace alone, the Lutheran tradition also emphasizes the idea of the priesthood of all believers, whereby all have direct access to God without mediation by a priest. This notion led to the development of a church that is much less dependent than its Catholic counterpart on ministers, particularly bishops.

Jean Calvin (1509–1564)

Jean Calvin represents the second stage of the Reformation. A French Protestant theologian, trained as a lawyer, he was unwelcome in Catholic France and so took refuge in Geneva between 1536 and 1538. Although his first attempt to establish his version of Christianity in Geneva failed, in 1541 he returned and became the undisputed master of the Genevan reformation.

Calvin's theology was not expressly innovative. Like Luther, he attributed primary authority to scripture—the

Word of God—rather than clergy, and affirmed the justification of the sinner by faith alone. Where Calvin differed was in his theology of sin and salvation. He believed that, since the fall of Adam, no human could freely choose faith and thereby realize his own salvation: only God could bring that about, and even before the creation he had predestined some of his creatures for damnation and some for salvation. By contrast, Luther believed that the death and resurrection of Christ made the gift of faith by grace available to all. Calvin's notion of **predestination**, which echoes Augustine's, emphasizes the omnipotence of God. After his death, his teachings were developed in a number of emerging Protestant traditions.

Calvin's Geneva reflected his vision of a reform community, with regular preaching, religious instruction for adults and children, and close Church regulation of the business and moral life of the community. In effect, it was a **theocracy**: a state ruled by God through religious authorities. The Genevans hoped to convert France, but in 1562 the first in a series of "Wars of Religion" broke out between French Roman Catholics and Protestants (Huguenots), who were heavily influenced by Calvin. Under persecution in the seventeenth and eighteenth centuries, the Huguenots sought refuge in Protestant lands throughout Europe and as far afield as the present-day US and South Africa. As we will see, a variety of denominations, usually identified as "Reformed" or "Presbyterian," resulted from this diaspora.

Ulrich Zwingli (1484–1531)

The father of the Swiss Reformation, Ulrich Zwingli, had been ordained a Roman Catholic priest in 1506. His rupture with Rome came gradually, with early critiques of the Church that were influenced by Erasmus. Inspired by Luther, Zwingli argued that the gospel is the sole basis of truth, and in so doing rejected the authority of the pope. Until 1522 he accepted the traditional Roman Catholic view of the Eucharist as a ritual of **transubstantiation** in which the bread and wine became the literal body and blood of Jesus. But by 1524 he was arguing that the Eucharist was strictly symbolic. This stance made union with other Protestant churches impossible, as most accepted the idea of the real presence of Christ in some form.

Sixteenth-Century Denominations

The Reformation was marked by division. Many early reformers were no less authoritarian than the Church they had rejected, and their competition for adherents led to redundancy and confusion. Denominational fragmentation has continued to the present day. In continental Europe, two main theological directions emerged in the sixteenth century—Lutheran and Calvinist—although there were also several more radical movements.

Lutherans

Lutheranism flourished in Germany and Scandinavia. Stressing the authority of scripture and the guidance of the Holy Spirit, it allowed ample scope for rational argument, but it also encouraged a deep personal piety. Images of God as friend and companion are just as frequent in Lutheran hymns as images of God as warrior or judge.

In worship and ecclesiastical organization, Lutherans departed in only some respects from the Roman Church. They retained a Eucharist-like sacrament, although they celebrated it in the vernacular and held that Christ's body was present along with the bread and wine but was not produced out of them. Lutheran priests continued to be governed by bishops, but were permitted to marry. (Only in recent years have Lutheran women been ordained.)

In most parts of Germany and Scandinavia, Lutheran Christianity became the state religion. The **Evangelical** Church, as it is called in Germany, is dominant in the north of the country, while Catholicism is stronger in the south (to this day, Germany provides basic funding for both churches out of tax revenues). Lutheranism was carried to North America by Germans who settled in places such as Pennsylvania, Ohio, Missouri, and Ontario, and by Scandinavians, most of whom settled in Minnesota and Wisconsin.

Reformed Churches

In the mid-1500s reformers in and around Switzerland departed from Luther's position on several points. While Zwingli in Zürich disputed Luther's Eucharistic theology, Martin Bucer in Strasbourg promoted a more active role for lay people as ministers, elders, deacons, and teachers.

From Geneva the ideas of the Swiss Reformation spread to France, the Netherlands, Hungary, England, and Scotland. In the Netherlands, Calvinist predestination was challenged by Jacobus Arminius, who believed that God's sovereignty was compatible with human free will. Arminian views were condemned by an assembly in Dordrecht (Dort) in 1518, which sentenced their supporter, the scholar and jurist Hugo Grotius, to life imprisonment (he escaped in a box of books being shipped to his wife). In the Netherlands and Hungary, the Calvinist churches are known as **Reformed churches**.

In England the Reformed tradition is called Presbyterian because it is governed by lay elders or "presbyters"; for the same reason, the established Church of Scotland is termed Presbyterian. Reformed churches do not have bishops; instead, the presbyters corporately perform the tasks of a bishop. Presbyterians from England and Scotland settled in eastern Canada and the middle Atlantic American states, as well as in New Zealand and Australia. Dutch Reformed settlers carried their tradition to South Africa, New York, and Michigan. In the nineteenth and twentieth centuries, Presbyterian missionaries reached many parts of Asia and Africa, but in most cases the churches they founded remained small, and in Islamic regions they found most of their recruits among Eastern Orthodox Christians. The Presbyterians did become a sizable minority in Korea, however.

Anabaptists

The "radical Reformation" rejected the broader Protestant movements' affiliations with secular power. Groups such as the Anabaptists shunned politics, military service, and even the taking of oaths. Believing that baptism should be actively sought on the basis of mature personal commitment, the Anabaptists practised adult rather than infant baptism. Essentially anti-establishment in orientation, the Anabaptist movement emerged in the 1520s, when some of the more radical followers of Zwingli began administering adult baptism in defiance of Zwingli himself. A decade later, in Münster, Germany, Anabaptist efforts to establish the kingdom of God by force prompted a crackdown by both Catholic and Protestant authorities.

Thereafter a former Dutch priest named Menno Simons led the movement into a largely otherworldly and non-violent path. Since there was no chance of removing the authorities, he urged his followers to remove themselves from society. Some of his followers—the Mennonites—settled in the Netherlands, where they were tolerated and in time largely assimilated to the secular climate of the Enlightenment. As the movement spread eastward to the Ukraine, however, persecution led some to leave Europe altogether.

Mennonites who migrated to the Americas settled mainly in Pennsylvania, where they came to be known as Pennsylvania Dutch (from *Deutsch*, "German"), and, later, Ontario and the Canadian prairies.

Today most Mennonites are fully part of the modern world, though branches such as the Old Order Amish continue to live a strictly traditional life, using only the simple tools of a century ago because they associate modern technology with the moral temptations and corruption of the secular world.

Unitarians

Unitarians took their name from their understanding of God as a single person rather than the three persons of the Trinity. Among the first to express this view was the German Martin Cellarius (1499–1564), but Unitarian communities also emerged in Poland and Hungary. In England, John Biddle began to publish Unitarian tracts in 1652, and a Unitarian congregation was organized in London in 1773–4. In the US, William Ellery Channing preached a sermon in 1819 that American Unitarians have taken as a kind of denominational manifesto.

In North America, Unitarianism has appealed mainly to people of a humanist and rationalist bent, often in university circles. Because of its minimal creedal demands (from early on, some Unitarians even dispensed with the idea of a divinity), it has become the denomination of choice for many Jewish–Christian couples.

Women and the Continental Reformation

Although the reformers did not see women as equal to men, their emphasis on the individual believer's direct relationship with God would have huge significance for women over time. Eventually, many Protestant churches would allow women to participate fully in their leadership. But that is a story for the modern era.

In the sixteenth century, one of the more consequential reform arguments was against celibacy. In the course of the Reformation, many convents and monasteries were closed, and although most nuns did not renounce their vocations, some did leave and marry. Martin Luther himself married a former nun, Katherine Von Bora, and together they made their home a centre for the new movement. In addition, Luther's commitment to the principle that ordinary people should have unmediated access to scripture led him to advocate public education for girls as well as boys.

The Counter-Reformation

The Protestant Reformation had the effect of stimulating reform from within the Roman Catholic Church, which led to its revitalization as an institution. This phenomenon is known as the Counter-Reformation. From the mid-1500s to the Thirty Years War (1618–48), the reforming Church was reinvigorated by the development of new religious orders, the Council of Trent, and a revitalized spirituality.

The defining religious order of the Counter Reformation was the Society of Jesus (Jesuits). Its founder, Ignatius Loyola (1491–1563), was a knight from a noble Spanish family who had a conversion experience after being wounded in battle. After several years as a hermit, in 1534 he joined with six companions to form the Society of Jesus. Characterized by a rigorous discipline that reflected Loyola's military background, the Jesuits became the spearhead of the missionary forces that carried Christianity to both the Americas and Asia. The Council of Trent (1545–63), was the first ecumenical council to be convened since the Council of Constance. Meeting in three sessions over 18 years, it laid a solid foundation for renewal of both the discipline and the spiritual life of the Church. It would be three centuries before another council was convened. Thus Trent was a watershed that marked the beginning of early modern Roman Catholicism.

Counter-Reformation Mysticism

During the Counter-Reformation many religious orders experienced a revitalization of spiritual life. The most notable figures in this renewal were the Spanish mystics Teresa of Avila and John of the Cross.

Teresa of Avila (1515–1582)

Teresa lived in what has come to be known as the golden age of Spanish mysticism. Educated by Augustinian nuns, she entered a Carmelite convent in 1535. Her personal experience of God fired her with reforming zeal to establish several houses within her order. Teresa wrote extensively about her religious experience. All her teachings were grounded in intense personal experience of revelation: she experienced the immediacy of God's presence in a physical as well as a spiritual sense. Significantly, her writings were received with enthusiasm even though her time was one of extreme repression for women.

Teresa's primary themes were self-knowledge, the need for awareness of one's weakness and vulnerability, the reality of God's presence, and the certainty of forgiveness and transformation through Christ. For Teresa mysticism was not an escape from reality. Rather, the experience of divine illumination set humanity free to be for God and others. From suffering came compassion, and through prayer the person who practised looking inward would be transfigured, released to live a life of active love.

In her most famous work, *The Way of Perfection*, she describes the path to union with God. She writes of being inundated with spiritual sweetness as the soul joins with God, and describes the marriage of the soul to its divine love as two candlesticks joining in one flame. Ten years later, in *The Interior Castle*, she described the path towards the unitive state as a journey through seven "dwelling places," the last of which is the interior castle where God resides in the self. Such an encounter fundamentally changes perceptions of reality: priorities shift, the soul knows peace, and understanding both of God and the self in relation to God expands.

John of the Cross (1542–1591)

John of the Cross was also a Carmelite, and with Teresa he founded a reform order called the Discalced ("Barefoot") Carmelites. He is best known for the beauty of his writings, which are considered the summit of Spanish mystical literature. Like Teresa, John experienced the movement

Document

Teresa of Avila' from *The Interior Castle*

Now let us come to imaginative visions, for they say the devil meddles more in these than in the ones mentioned, and it must be so. But when these imaginative visions are from our Lord, they in some way seem to me more beneficial because they are in greater conformity with our nature. I'm excluding from that comparison the visions the Lord shows in the last dwelling place. No other visions are comparable to these (Madigan 1998: 250).

Document

St John of the Cross

From his commentary on the poem "The Dark Night of the Soul":

[H]owever greatly the soul itself labours, it cannot actively purify itself so as to be in the least degree prepared for the Divine union of perfection of love, if God takes not its hand and purges it not in that dark fire (John of the Cross, 1990: 22).

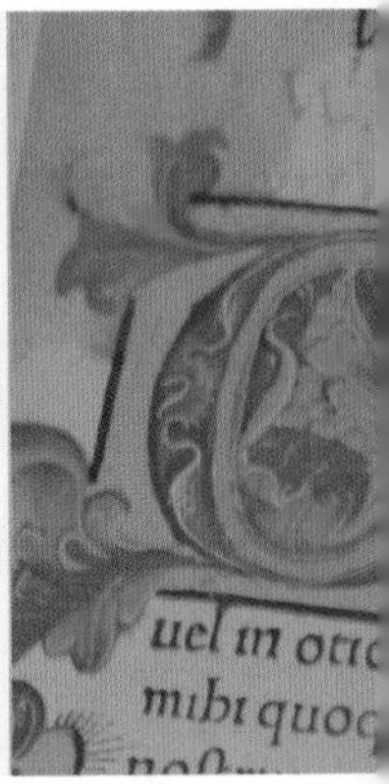

toward God as a journey of many stages. His most famous poem, "The Dark Night of the Soul," describes the stage when the soul, longing for God, becomes disoriented and loses its way. As he later explained in a commentary on the poem, this part of the journey is painful and can last for years, but it is a necessary stage on the way to union with God.

The English Reformation

The relationship of the English Reformation to the Continental Reformation is complex. England had been acquainted with Christianity since the fourth century, and by the seventh century it was fully embedded in the Roman ecclesiastical system. However, it was predisposed to the principles behind the Continental Reformation.

A century and a half before Luther posted his 95 Theses, John Wycliffe (1320–84) had written against indulgences as well as the wealth and power of the papacy. He also advocated the use of the vernacular in both scripture and worship, and promoted an early translation of the Bible into the language of ordinary people. Today it is generally believed that the English translation from the Latin Vulgate known as "Wycliffe's Bible" was not made by Wycliffe himself, although he was the main force behind its production. Even though possession of Wycliffe's Bible could lead to a death sentence, many copies were made between the 1380s and 1530s, when it was superseded by a new translation, from the original Hebrew and Greek, that had the benefit of the printing press (as did Luther's German Bible). The main author of that work was William Tyndale (1492–1536). Having left the still-Catholic England of Henry VIII in the 1520s for the continent, Tyndale was arrested in the Netherlands and put to death as a heretic before he could complete it. Yet just three years later, Henry himself authorized a different English translation. What had changed?

The English Reformation was as much political as it was theological. When the Continental Reformation began, Henry VIII defended the papacy, put his name on an anti-Lutheran tract, sentenced priests with reform sympathies to death, and, through his Lord Chancellor Sir Thomas More, actively suppressed Protestant heresies. But things changed when Henry needed a divorce from his wife Catherine of Aragon so that he could marry Anne Boleyn, who herself was significantly influenced by Protestant thinking. The pope's refusal to grant the divorce eventually led to a schism between England and Rome. The Church of England was established as an autonomous entity in 1534, no longer subject to the authority of the bishop of Rome.

The concept of Church–state relations that developed in England was different from the concept that prevailed in Roman Catholic lands. In England, Henry declared himself the head of the church as well as the head of state. This model was based on the idea that temporal and spiritual authority were united in the person of the monarch. Religion in this system was "established" as the official religion of the state, supported by the state in all ways, including economically, and any changes to it would have to be passed into law by the country's parliament.

To demonstrate his authority in ecclesiastical matters (and appropriate their wealth for the Crown), Henry suppressed the monasteries in two waves. First the smaller monasteries were dissolved and their properties confiscated. Then, after an act of Parliament had invested the Crown with all monastic possessions, the larger monasteries began to dissolve themselves; the last house surrendered in 1540.

England remained Protestant under Henry's young son, Edward VI, but with the succession of Edward's half-sister Mary I (r. 1553–8) it once again became officially Catholic. The contest for power was violent. Not until Elizabeth I (r. 1558–1603) negotiated what came to be known as the Elizabethan Settlement did the situation begin to stabilize. The Act of Supremacy (1559) re-established the English Church's independence from Rome and made Elizabeth the "Supreme Governor of the Church of England." It also re-established the liturgy contained in the *Book of Common Prayer* (BCP) as the standard for the new Church.

First published in 1549 and revised several times in its first decade, the BCP was produced under the direction of Thomas Cranmer, who had been appointed Archbishop of Canterbury (the senior Episcopal seat in England) by Henry VIII. Mary had Cranmer burned at the stake for treason and heresy. Nevertheless, the BCP reflects his commitment to negotiated compromise between varying theological positions. Thus many strains of theology, Catholic as well as Protestant, became foundation texts in the BCP. Indeed, Anglicanism itself represents a middle way between Roman Catholic and Protestant theologies and worship forms.

Puritans

The Puritans embraced a more extreme purification of the Church along Calvinist lines. They were never a majority, but they held considerable economic and political power. They condemned all forms of church ornamentation, the elaborate robes worn by clergy, and the use of organ music, while calling for an emphasis on preaching rather than sacraments, and strict observance of Sunday as the Sabbath. As well, Puritans insisted on the Calvinist principle of predestination. Their most problematic commitment, however, was their insistence, following Calvin, that the state should be subject to the Church. This would eventually lead to charges of treason against the Puritans.

Seventeenth-Century Denominations

Quakers

Also significantly at odds with the established Church of England was the Religious Society of Friends, better known as the Quakers, a group founded almost spontaneously as people came to adopt the principles and practices of George Fox (1624–91). Coming of age during the upheaval of the English civil war, Fox developed a pacifist approach to life as a Christian. Opposing the established religion, he travelled the countryside as a dissenting (non-Church of England) preacher advocating a Christianity stripped of non-essential trappings, including clergy, ceremonial rites, church buildings, and special holy days.

The name "Quaker" referred to the Friends' tendency to tremble when overflowing with the spirit within. Friends worshipped together without paid clergy, and sat in silence unless the spirit moved a member to speak. They refused to pay tithes to support the established Church, to take legal oaths (because one should always tell the truth), and to serve in the military (because we should love our enemies). Embracing simplicity and love of neighbour, the Quakers cultivated a practical mysticism in which union with God was meaningful only in so far as it furthered the goal of service to others.

Congregationalists

The Congregational churches trace their roots to "separatist" clergy in the time of Elizabeth I, but they did not become a significant force in England until the mid-1600s. Doctrinally, there is little to distinguish Congregationalism from Presbyterian Calvinism. Where they differ is in their form of governance. Carrying the notion of the priesthood of all believers to its logical conclusion, Congregationalists reject the idea of elders and accord every congregation the authority to manage its own theological and institutional affairs: for them, the only higher power is God.

In England, Congregational churches formed a Union in 1832 and were active in political and missionary causes throughout the nineteenth century. But the tradition's stronghold was Massachusetts, where Congregationalists founded Harvard University in 1637 in order not "to leave an illiterate ministry to the churches, when our present ministers shall lie in the dust." Yale University (1701) was also founded by Congregationalists.

Baptists

Like the Anabaptists on the continent, the English Baptists practised the baptism of mature believers rather than infants. But they were much more intimately connected with the Puritans than with the Anabaptists. By the 1640s, the English Baptist movement had two branches. Calvinist, or "Particular," Baptists reserved redemption for a particular sector of humanity, whereas "General" Baptists proclaimed a general redemption for humanity.

The first Baptist churches in the US were established as early as 1639, but the Baptist presence remained small until the revival movement of 1740–3 known as the Great Awakening. Though the Baptists were not among its principal protagonists, they made massive numerical gains in its wake. They positioned themselves to become the largest American Protestant denomination partly through their successful appeal to the black population; by the mid-1950s, two out of every three African-American Christians were Baptists.

Pietism

The term "**Pietism**" designates not a denomination but a movement that rippled through various Protestant denominations, including the Lutherans in Germany and the Reformed (Calvinist) churches in the Netherlands, beginning in the late 1600s. Dissatisfied with the rigidity they perceived in the Protestant churches, Pietists sought a spontaneous renewal of faith accompanied by a feeling of certainty of divine forgiveness and acceptance. For many, that feeling of certainty was all the evidence they needed to validate their faith. This position set Pietists against the emerging rationalism of the Enlightenment, but would find intellectual expansion in the emphasis laid on feeling by the German philosopher Friedrich Schleiermacher (1768–1834). Pietism spread in Lutheran circles both in Europe and in the Americas. In the form articulated by the Moravian Brethren—who traced their origins to the early Czech reformer John Hus—it also contributed to the development of Methodism.

Worship and the Protestant Reformation

Protestant reformers such as Luther, Zwingli, and Calvin all called for less mediation by clergy, to give the faithful more direct access to God. Although each denomination developed its own new worship forms, all emphasized the use of the vernacular. New forms of music were designed for full congregational participation, the frequency of communion increased, and in the Lutheran and Anglican traditions clergy and congregation alike shared in both the bread and the wine. As well, worship spaces were reconfigured, especially in the traditions influenced by Calvin, putting clergy and people together in a less hierarchical arrangement that allowed full participation for all. Some traditions placed their altars away from the wall; others introduced a movable communion table. These changes were designed to communicate the theological point that all the baptized have direct access to God, without mediation by clergy.

The Modern Era

The Enlightenment

By the end of the eighteenth century Christianity was no longer at the centre of Western civilization, and the ties between Church and state had been significantly loosened. The intellectual movement responsible for those changes is generally known as the Enlightenment.

The precise beginning of the Enlightenment is hard to identify, but a crucial early moment came in 1543, when the Polish astronomer Nicolaus Copernicus proposed that the universe revolved around the sun rather than the Earth. Half a century later, the Italian mathematician Galileo Galilei confirmed that theory through observation. The Church responded by adding Copernicus's book to its list of prohibited writings and, in 1633, bringing Galileo to trial before the Inquisition. Found guilty of heresy, he was forced to "abjure, curse, and detest" his supposed errors, and lived the rest of his life under house arrest.

Deism

The growing importance of science was reflected in the rise of Deism, a philosophical position that gained a considerable following in England in the seventeenth and eighteenth centuries. Recognizing that the universe manifests regular patterns or "laws of nature," the Deists did not believe that those laws could be suspended by divine intervention, but they could envision the universe as the product of a divine intelligence. They saw their creator God as a divine clockmaker, who assembled the universe and then left it to run on its own. The idea that if one can observe a design, then one can infer the existence of a designer goes back to ancient Greece and is known as the **teleological argument**, or argument from design.

The English philosopher William Paley offered the following example of the teleological argument from design for the existence of God in his *Natural Theology* (1802). If we found a watch on a desert island, we would not need to have seen any other watch in order to posit the existence of a maker; the watch would not even have to work perfectly, nor would we have to understand the function of every part. The same is true of the universe as evidence for God: even if the creation is imperfect, or not fully comprehensible, humans can still reasonably posit the existence of a perfect creator deity.

Philosophy

At the same time, Enlightenment philosophers such as the Scotsman David Hume and the German Immanuel Kant were questioning Christian claims for the transcendent. According to Kant, Thomas Aquinas's argument for God as the First Cause cannot be proved. But what Kant showed to be in principle unprovable is by the same token not disprovable. Whereas earlier thinkers sought to prove the existence of the transcendent itself, many philosophers of religion since Kant have focused instead on experience and feeling—that is, the human response to the transcendent. In the early nineteenth century, Schleiermacher characterized religion as an "intuitive sense of absolute dependence": if we cannot prove the existence of what we intuitively feel that we depend on, at least we can describe that intuition.

Schleiermacher also contributed to a "subjective" understanding of Christ's atonement. In the traditional Christian understanding, it is through Christ's sacrifice that humanity is saved and restored to its proper relationship with God, but for Schleiermacher Jesus functions as a moral example, an embodiment of human awareness of God; salvation comes first as a change in spiritual awareness and then atonement follows as a divine–human reconciliation. It was from Schleiermacher "liberal" theology developed.

Evolution

At the beginning of the nineteenth century, scientists held that every species on Earth had been created by God with specific characteristics. This view was challenged by Charles Darwin, whose theory of evolution proposed that new types of organisms were not created by a deity but developed over time through a process he called natural selection. Darwin's epoch-making study *On the Origin of Species* was published in 1859, more than 20 years after he had worked out the basics of his theory. Having studied theology, Darwin was well aware of the resistance his theory would encounter. He needed not merely to make a credible case for evolution, but to refute the basic tenets of biological creationism. He also knew that natural selection was antithetical to the teleological argument from design. If the natural world was completely self-regulating, there was no need for a supervising deity.

Because of Darwin, modern Christian theologians have tended to locate human distinctiveness not in a special physical creation but in a unique intellectual and spiritual capacity for transcendence. For religious thinkers persuaded by Darwin's discoveries, what matters is not so much where we came from as where we are going.

Socio-political Context

Following the Enlightenment, social, political, and economic revolutions precipitated a fundamental shift in the relationship between Church and society, which in turn meant significant internal changes for Christianity. The French Revolution (1789) represents a watershed between the past and modern political systems. The violent overthrow of the French monarchy left the Church without a partner in political power. Meanwhile, the Thirteen Colonies had already thrown off the control of Britain and established themselves as a sovereign nation, without an established Church. From that point on, religion would be a choice. Running parallel to these political revolutions was the economic revolution whereby a land-based economy became a money-based one. This shift precipitated several other changes that also affected the role of the churches in society.

Anti-evolution literature for sale in 1925 in Dayton, Tennessee—the site of the famous "monkey trial" in which John Scopes was convicted of violating a Tennessee law that prohibited the teaching of evolution in state-funded schools. The conviction was later overturned, but only on technical grounds, and the law remained in place until 1967. The creation-vs-evolution debate continues to rage, particularly where school curricula are concerned (© AP Photo / CP).

Rural-to-urban migration and the breakdown of the extended family helped to displace the Church from its position as the focal point of community and social norms. The exploitation of the industrial working class led to the development of labour unions, which became its primary champions, reducing workers' reliance on the churches. At the same time, organized religion was increasingly becoming the preserve of the emerging middle class. All these contextual changes contributed to the declining significance of Christianity in Western culture.

Evangelical Great Awakenings

In the face of that decline, Christianity paradoxically experienced several waves of revival in the early years of the modern era. The first "Great Awakening" swept Protestant Europe and British America in the 1730s and 1740s. Focusing mainly on people who were already believers, it summoned them to participate actively in proclaiming the Word of God and setting hearts on fire with love of his gospel. The second Great Awakening, beginning around 1800, was slightly different in its goals, focused on bringing non-believers to Christ. Many significant missionary organizations trace their origins to this time.

The third Great Awakening spans the period from 1858 to 1914. In 1858, after two centuries of self-imposed isolation, Japan allowed the first Christian missionary of modern times to enter the country, and the publication of David Livingstone's *Missionary Travels and Researches in South Africa* fuelled enthusiasm for global mission. The principle of the priesthood of all believers summoned all Christians to become active agents of God's saving work. This time the emphasis was on social engagement, whether through religious education, distribution of the Bible, or social reform. Both the movement for women's suffrage and the modern ecumenical movement had their roots in this period.

John Wesley (1703–91)

The primary catalyst of the first Great Awakening was John Wesley. Ordained an Anglican priest at the age of 25, he formed a small study group that was nicknamed the "Methodists" for their methodical pursuit of holiness. Wesley spent some time in the mission field in Georgia in 1735, but on the return voyage his life was changed by an encounter with a group of German Moravians. Heavily influenced by Pietism, they reflected a lively and heartfelt faith that Wesley had not experienced in the Anglican world.

Back in England, Wesley had a transformative religious experience that he described as a moment when his heart "was strangely warmed." From then on it was his mission to summon lukewarm believers to an engaged experience with the living Christ. Wesley's theology reflected his Anglican heritage in that (like Luther) he rejected the Calvinist theory of predestination in favour of the Arminian view that all who believed would be saved by grace. Unlike Luther, however, Wesley also believed that all who had been saved by faith would become progressively more holy. According to this notion of "sanctification," the transfiguration of the heart by the saving grace of God would be reflected in one's works.

Wesley had not intended to break with the Church of England, but his new way of preaching and teaching was not welcome there. In his commitment to theology as experience, Wesley developed a new expression of Christianity that became known as Methodism. Giving priority to preaching of the Word and lay involvement, the Methodists emphasized engagement with the world as the place where the Kingdom of God was to be made real. The notion of progressive sanctification became central to the denomination.

Jonathan Edwards (1703–58)

Edwards was an American-born revivalist preacher from Puritan Calvinist roots who sparked enthusiasm for the gospel throughout the Thirteen Colonies. An itinerant preacher, like most in the revivalist mode, he inspired new enthusiasm for his faith with a dramatic and emotional style. Where Edwards and Wesley differed was in their primary theological commitment. While Wesley was an Arminian, Edwards was grounded in the Calvinist assumptions that only some were predestined to be saved, and that God alone knew who they were. He made a major contribution to American revivalism through both his preaching and his writings, which inspired thousands to pursue a missionary vocation.

Holiness Churches

In time the main Methodist bodies in America became more sedate and conventional, but new independent groups continued to spring from Methodism's revivalist roots. Because of their emphasis on the conversion experience in which the gift of holiness or sanctification was received, these congregations have often been described as **Holiness Churches**. Like the early Methodists, they believed in progressive sanctification. Converts broke away from their more mainstream denominations to form their own Holiness congregations.

Women and Revivalism

In emphasizing the ministry of all the baptized, the Great Awakenings created openings for women to participate more actively in their churches. Although the majority of revivalist preachers were men, most of the people who attended their meetings were women, and once the visiting preachers had moved on, it was those women who found new ways to live their faith. This openness to the revival experience was reinforced by the prevailing gender assumption that while men toiled in the often corrupt public world, women would make the private world of the family a haven of virtue and tenderness.

Led mainly by middle-class women who could afford time away from their household responsibilities, voluntary associations were formed that promoted the development of Sunday Schools and missionary societies (which sent both male and female missionaries into the field), supported the paid employment of single laywomen in various Church contexts, and maintained connections with other women's groups, both nationally and globally. These activities laid the groundwork for the recognition of women's right to vote in Church matters and, eventually, to ordination. As the women of the revival era learned the skills required for organization-building, fund-raising, and so on, their churches gradually became accustomed to the idea of women in leadership roles.

Missions

From its beginnings, Christianity has been a missionary religion: evangelization in the time of the Apostles; the Christianization of the Roman Empire; the age of exploration, when European powers began expanding their empires, taking Christianity with them. What was new in the era of the awakenings was that now the missionary organizations included Protestants as well as Catholics. Although the mission societies reflected their varied denominational traditions, they shared a strong adherence to the exclusive claims of Christianity; a tendency to see the religions of missionized people as the work of the "devil"; and an emphasis on conversion and the distribution of bibles, with little social outreach.

By the third awakening, both Protestant and Catholic missionaries were also actively promoting the Christianization of their own societies. This led various colonial churches to work with government on projects of cultural assimilation. In the case of new immigrants, conversion to Christianity and cultural assimilation were often presented as one and the same thing. As well, in places such as Canada, the US, and Australia, the colonial churches collaborated with government to promote the assimilation of indigenous people. The most disturbing examples of collaboration were the residential school systems in which governments paid the churches to

Focus

Black Elk (1863–1950)

In North America, some now argue that the harm done by Christianity in the process of colonization means that it has no value for indigenous people today. Yet there have been Aboriginal leaders who believed that indigenous wisdom and Christian belief were complementary. An Oglala Lakota man by the name of Black Elk was perhaps the most significant example. During a childhood illness he experienced a vision that led him to become a healer. As an adult he was converted to Christianity by Roman Catholic missionaries, but continued to receive visions that confirmed the experience of his youth, and in time he came to see parallels between Lakota and Christian teachings. Thus the "Great Spirit" or Creator of the Lakota tradition was analogous to the Creator God of the Christian Trinity, and the traditional pipe given to the Lakota people was a way of knowing God before the arrival of Christianity. He understood that the path of all creation, the "Red Road" in Lakota teaching, was the Christ he had met when he was converted to Christianity. Today his visions and theology continue to play a significant part in conversations between indigenous elders and Christian theologians.

strip indigenous children of their culture and assimilate them to Euro-descent norms. Together, the loss of culture and the abuse suffered by those children have harmed several generations of indigenous people.

Theological Controversies and Denominational Splitting

The development of historical biblical criticism and "modernist" theology led to the splitting of denominations and the creation of new traditions. Three schools of thought shaped the drama of denominational splitting: liberalism, evangelicalism, and fundamentalism.

The term "modernist" was first used to refer to a group of Roman Catholic theologians who, in the late nineteenth century, adopted a critical and skeptical attitude towards traditional Christian doctrines, especially with reference to Christology and salvation. This movement fostered a positive attitude towards radical biblical criticism and stressed the ethical rather than the doctrinal dimensions of faith. The term migrated into North American Protestantism fairly rapidly. By the turn of the twentieth century, mainstream Protestant denominations were increasingly influenced by "modernist attitudes," as reflected in a rethinking of the doctrine of creation, an emphasis on God's presence in creation rather than his transcendence, and a shift in atonement theology towards Schleiermacher's view, in which the emphasis is less on Christ's sacrifice as the means to human salvation and more on the moral example he set for humanity ("what would Jesus do?").

Historical Biblical Criticism

In the nineteenth century the Bible came to be studied as a historical document. Historical criticism is a method of biblical interpretation in which understanding the true meaning of a biblical passage

Focus

Christianity in Nazi Germany

When the National Socialist (Nazi) party took power in 1932, the Christian churches were pressured to welcome Hitler as their Führer. Although most of them bowed to this pressure, a significant number of Protestant ministers resisted. They banded together to form what they called the Confessing Church, and in 1934 they produced the Barmen Declaration, proclaiming that Jesus Christ alone was the Lord of the Church—an act of resistance to Hitler's insistence that the church should be subject to him. The influential theologian Karl Barth (1886–1968) was a leader in the Confessing Church movement, and Dietrich Bonhoeffer, a Lutheran pastor and theologian, was among the signatories of the declaration. Bonhoeffer was arrested by the Nazis in 1942, and would be executed in 1944, at the age of 39, but he continued to write from prison, arguing that to say "Jesus is Lord" with words was insufficient: all Christians are called to live the meaning of "Jesus is Lord," even to the point of self-sacrifice for love of the other.

requires knowledge not of Christian doctrine but rather of the historical and social conditions in which it was composed. Many scholars saw historical criticism as the enemy of Christianity, as it undermined the "absolute truth" claims of Christian doctrine and appeared to make faith conditional on historical circumstance.

The Historical Jesus

Yet many theologians saw in history a means of freeing Christianity from developments that, in their view, Jesus never intended. They used historical methods to write biographies of him that were free of Christian dogma. When the German theologian and humanist Albert Schweitzer (1875–1965) noticed that these "lives" coincidentally affirmed the values of Jesus' biographers, he condemned "The Quest for the Historical Jesus" based on modern notions, while himself constructing a Jesus, based on the gospels, who thought the end time was coming within the current generation. The historical quest was largely abandoned until after the Second World War, when new archaeological discoveries began to shed new light on the Judaism of Jesus' day. In 1985 150 scholars formed the Jesus Seminar to study the sayings and deeds attributed to Jesus and debate whether they originated with Jesus or were attributed to him by later followers. Like the earlier questers, they have been criticized for "discovering" a Jesus who conforms to the ideals of liberal democracy.

Reactions to Modernism

Evangelicalism

Reactions against modernism and its impact on theology were expressed in two primary forms: evangelicalism and fundamentalism. Evangelical Protestants' position is reflected in their emphasis on the necessity of personal conversion, the goal of personal sanctification, and the pre-eminence of scripture and preaching (the ministry of the Word). In the twentieth century, evangelicalism influenced many Protestant denominations, but was most significant among the Reformed churches.

Fundamentalism

The term "**fundamentalism**" derives from "The Fundamentals": a series of 12 tracts by eminent Evangelical leaders that were widely distributed in the English-speaking world beginning in 1909. In reaction against historical criticism and the theory of evolution, fundamentalists sponsored a series of Bible conferences at which they developed a statement of belief based on what came to be known as the "Five Points" or "Fundamentals": the inerrancy of scripture, the divinity of Jesus Christ, the virgin birth, the substitutionary theory of the atonement (the idea that Christ died in our place, and in so doing paid the debt we owe God for our sins), and the physical resurrection and second coming of Christ. Fundamentalism affected a variety of denominations, inspiring theological conflicts so intense that they led to denominational splitting.

Pentecostalism

Pentecostalism should not be confused with fundamentalism: it has more in common with the Holiness movement of the nineteenth century. It takes its name from an episode in the Book of Acts in which the Holy Spirit visits a gathering of the Apostles and some others on the Feast of the **Pentecost** (the fiftieth day after Easter) and bestows on them the gift of **glossolalia**, or "speaking in tongues."

Focus

Aimee Semple McPherson (1890–1944)

Spirit-based movements such as Pentecostalism have been more likely than more mainstream denominations to offer women opportunities as preachers and leaders. This unusual openness stems from the idea that if God has given someone a gift for a particular kind of ministry, then the Church should affirm that gift.

Aimee Semple McPherson was an important example of this phenomenon. Born in Ontario and converted to Pentecostalism in her teens, she followed her passion for preaching all the way to Los Angeles, where she became the most famous evangelist of her generation. Unlike other early Pentecostals, she quickly realized the potential of modern media as vehicles for evangelization. She became renowned both for her preaching and for the healings that were reported to take place at her revival meetings. Eventually she built a large church that was filled by the thousands for every worship service. She also founded a Pentecostal denomination known as the Four Square Gospel Church, which still exists today. The media-based ministry that she pioneered served as a prototype for later forms of North American Pentecostalism.

Aimee Semple McPherson prays enthusiastically with her congregation at Tom Noonan's Chinatown mission in New York in 1933 (© Hulton-Deutsch Collection / Corbis).

The renewal movement that gave rise to Pentecostalism was led by an American evangelist named Charles Parham, who taught that speaking in tongues was evidence of the "baptism of the spirit" described in Acts. One of his students, an African-American pastor named William J. Seymour (1870–1922) adapted Parham's message to be inclusive across racial and gender lines, then began preaching the imminent return of Jesus to mixed-race crowds in Los Angeles in 1906. The popularity of Seymour's "Azusa Street Revival" sparked similar gatherings across the US and around the world. Speaking in tongues, divine healing, and prophecy were interpreted as signs that God was with the community. Many new denominations were born from this renewal movement, including the Assemblies of God, the Pentecostal Fellowship, and the Church of God.

Of the more than 2 billion Christians in the world today, more than one-quarter are Pentecostal or "charismatic." While Latin Americans, Native Americans, Africans, and Asians say that Pentecostal interpretations of Christianity are more in keeping with their cultural worldviews than other forms of Christianity, current studies indicate that the single most important reason for the growth of Pentecostalism is the experience of divine healing—a significant attraction in places where access to health care is difficult for most people. A second attraction is the fact that Pentecostal churches (unlike the historic colonial churches) offer their congregations help with everyday problems.

The social activist Dorothy Day (1887–1980), co-founder of the Catholic Worker movement. A convert to Roman Catholicism, Day is currently under consideration for canonization (© Brian Nicholas Tsai).

The Social Gospel

Early in the twentieth century, an American Baptist minister named Walter Rauschenbusch (1861–1918) argued that Christianity is by nature revolutionary, that realizing the Kingdom of God was not a matter of getting to heaven but of transforming life on earth into the harmony of heaven. This perspective inspired a new emphasis on social engagement. The social gospel was enthusiastically embraced in Canada as well as the US, although the two nations developed the theology differently. Whereas the American movement had a political dimension that led it to side with labour against big business, in Canada the churches focused on urging business people to treat their workers fairly and humanely. Although this strategy was largely unsuccessful in effecting social change, several Canadian churchmen carried the social gospel message into the political arena. The best-known was Tommy Douglas (1904–86), a Baptist minister who left the ministry to enter politics. As premier of Saskatchewan, he led the way to socialized medicine, and the Saskatchewan plan for universal health care was eventually mirrored across Canada.

Theological Diversity in the Modern/Postmodern Era

Particularly in North America, liberal theologians developed new forms of theological expression. These included the application of existential philosophy to theology, as in the work of Paul Tillich (1886–1995); the development, by Alfred North Whitehead (1861–1947), Charles Hartshorne (1897–2000) and others, of process theology, which drew on physics to argue for a God who is in some respects changeable, in ongoing relationship with the unfolding universe; and the rise of liberation theologies focused on the particular concerns of oppressed groups including women, indigenous people, African-Americans, and, in Latin America, the poor and politically violated.

In response to this explosion of liberal theologies, an opposing "neo-orthodoxy" emerged in the interwar years. Its primary architect was Karl Barth, who emphasized the transcendence of God and the inability of human beings to work out their own salvation. Barth's radical doctrine of sin and grace found resonance among the Reformed churches in particular.

The Changing Place of Women

Even today, only a minority of Christians belong to a church that allows women to participate fully in leadership roles. More than half of the world's Christian population is Roman Catholic, another significant segment is Eastern Orthodox, and yet another is conservative Protestant. With minor variations, women in these churches do not have full ecclesiastical voting rights and are not eligible for ordination. Although most historic colonial or mainline Protestant denominations, as well as some evangelical churches, do ordain women today, some of them have had difficulty expanding the roles that women can play. For example, while the Anglican Church of Canada has permitted ordination of women as bishops, priests, and deacons since 1976, it took the Church of England nearly four decades longer to allow women to serve as bishops. Finally, in July 2014 the General Synod voted overwhelmingly to open the House of Bishops to women. The required two-thirds majority in each house (bishops, clergy, and laity) was achieved easily, with 351 votes in favour, only 72 against, and 10 abstentions.

Bishop Barbara Harris of the Episcopal Diocese of Massachusetts at her ordination as the first female bishop in the Anglican Communion, in 1989 (© Reuters / Corbis).

Several denominations have had women as presiding officers. The first female bishop in the Anglican Communion was Barbara Harris, who served as an Episcopalian bishop in Massachusetts from 1989 to 2003. Lois Wilson was the first female moderator (head) of the United Church of Canada and from 1983 to 1991 served as co-president of the World Council of Churches, a position held from 1954 to 1960 by Madeleine Barot of France.

The fact that the Roman Catholic and Eastern Orthodox churches, some conservative evangelical denominations, and some Indigenous denominations in Africa, Asia, and Latin America refuse to ordain women at all can be traced back to the early Church, though in some cases it also reflects current views on gender. Both Roman Catholic and Orthodox theologians have argued that women cannot represent Christ because Christ was male.

Twentieth-Century Movements for Social Change

In the twentieth century, Christians played an active part in several grassroots movements for social change, including the anti-apartheid movement in South Africa, the grassroots *Communidades de Base* movement in Latin America, and the civil rights movement in the US. However, in each case there were Christians on both sides of the debate. While some demanded an end to injustice and oppression, particularly of the poor, others defended the status quo.

In South Africa, the Afrikaners who justified the seizure of land from Indigenous Africans were generally members of the Dutch Reformed Church. They argued that they had been chosen by God to administer South Africa and prevent the mixing of races through intermarriage. South African Anglicans for the most part opposed apartheid, and black Anglican clergy such as Desmond Tutu became very public political figures. However, individual church members disagreed as to tactics, and some Anglicans of European descent vigorously opposed their Church's involvement in politics. Methodism quickly became an overwhelmingly black denomination with a strong anti-apartheid stance, which cost it support from those who feared the power of the apartheid state. The Roman Catholic Church in South Africa opposed apartheid as well, although a group calling itself the South African Catholic Defence League condemned the Church's political involvement and denounced school integration.

In Latin America the Roman Catholic Church was an agent both of change and of resistance to change. As the official Church of Spain in the colonial era, it allied itself with the state in regimes of control and repression, but with decolonization the Church–state relationship shifted. When economic crises from the 1960s to the 1990s permitted the rise of military dictatorships, the poor faced crushing poverty and extreme violations of human rights. Although some local Church leaders stood with the military regimes, most positioned themselves in solidarity with the poor and suffering. In 1968, at the second conference of Latin American bishops, three important documents were generated. Entitled "Justice," "Peace," and "Poverty of the Church," they shattered the centuries-old alliance between the Church, the military, and the wealthy. The key words that emerged as blueprints for the future were "liberation" and "participation." The Church pledged to participate in the dynamic action of an awakened community in resistance to the forces that oppressed and denied life. This consciousness-raising was reflected in the *Communidades de Base*. Offering Bible study, prayer, and fellowship in the poorest *barrios* and slums, they became focal points of resistance and renewal, expressions of the Church's theological commitment to the dignity of all human beings. Many Church leaders paid with their lives for their commitment to the poor. The most notable example was Bishop Oscar Romero of El Salvador. Although before his appointment he had been a mild-mannered academic, as bishop he became a recognized leader of the non-violent resistance to the military dictatorship of the day. His assassination, while presiding at worship in March 1980, inspired many others to take up the defence of the human rights of political resistors and the poor.

In the United States, the civil rights movement was largely driven by the black churches. Historically, through the era of slavery and beyond, black churches had served as focal points for communal life and empowerment. Thus when the time came for resistance to white repression, the black clergy played a pivotal role in gathering the community and providing both inspiration and strategy. Most notable of all was the Reverend Dr Martin Luther King, Jr (1929–68), a Baptist pastor whose skills as an orator and insistence on non-violence made him the movement's principal spokesman until he was murdered at the age of 39. The Christian principle that all people are made in the image of God animated social action in a world where a significant proportion of the population was not accorded the most basic human rights.

Vatican II

The election of Pope John XXIII in 1958 sparked significant change in the Roman Catholic Church. Though already in his late seventies he had a fearless openness to change. Calling for *aggiornamento* ("updating"), John XXIII convoked the Second Vatican Council, which met from 1962 to 1965.

The changes set in motion at the council ushered in a new era for Catholicism. Latin was replaced by the vernacular as the language of the mass, and the priest now turned to face the congregation (although the doctrine of transubstantiation was retained). Whereas the First Vatican Council (1869–70) had emphasized the monarchical aspect of the pope's role, Vatican II emphasized the more collegial nature of his work in council with the bishops. Efforts were also made to improve relations both with other Christians and with people of other religions, especially Jews.

A major breach developed in the Church shortly after the council, in 1968, when John's successor, Pope Paul VI, in his encyclical *Humanae Vitae* ("On human life") prohibited the use of artificial birth control. The gap between the Church's official stand on sexuality and the actual practice of the faithful has only widened in the intervening decades. Many Catholics have ceased to follow some of the teachings they consider out of date. At the same time *Humanae Vitae* intensified the theological tension between the reform-minded and traditionalist wings in the Church's hierarchy.

The Church of Rome Today

More than fifty years after Vatican II, its agenda still has not been completed, and pressing problems remain. The numbers of candidates for the priesthood are in serious decline. A variety of factors have contributed to this reality, most notably rising secularism in Western culture generally and an increasing disinclination to choose celibacy as a way of life. The challenges to the Church's authority and credibility resulting from a tide of sexual abuse charges may also be affecting the numbers of men offering themselves for leadership as clergy. The sexual abuse of children by religious professionals is not solely a phenomenon of the modern era or of the Roman Church. However, in recent years the latter has been shaken by widespread sexual abuse cases involving priests. Criminal trials received significant media attention in Canada, the United States, and Ireland in particular, and thousands of civil lawsuits have been filed against the Church seeking compensation. Restitution payments made between 1950 and 2012 have been estimated at more than $3 billion.

In February 2013 Pope Benedict XVI became the first pope since 1415 to resign from the papal office. At the age of 86, he said he no longer had the physical strength to perform his duties adequately. His successor, Cardinal Jorge Bergoglio of Argentina, who took the name Francis I, is the first pope from the Global South and well known for his commitment to social justice and his solidarity with the poor. His election has sparked hope that positive change for the Church is not only possible but imminent.

Recent Developments

For several decades the mainline denominations in Europe and North America have been declining, even as Christianity grows rapidly in the Global South. In response, the traditional churches have been re-evaluating the forms and structures of their worship and organizational life. Meanwhile, new groups such as the Emergent Church Movement are experimenting with innovative forms of urban monastic community, house churches, and participation in environmental and social projects as an expression of faith. Although continuing immigration from Asia and the Global South is likely to slow the decline to some degree, it will also lead to changes in Church life in the next generation.

Ecumenism

For more than a century the mainline Protestant denominations have been working to overcome their historic divisions. Part of this movement was rooted in the 1910 decision by denominational mission boards to reduce competition by dividing overseas territories among the various denominations. Also significant was collaboration in youth work through organizations such as the interdenominational Student Christian Movement.

By mid-century, a generation of leaders who had grown up with interdenominationalism had moved into positions of responsibility in their own churches. The time was ripe for worldwide collaboration, and in 1948 the World Council of Churches was formed, with representation from most major Protestant and Orthodox bodies. **Ecumenism** (from the Greek meaning "inhabited world") offered a climate of mutual acceptance and common purpose, although Protestants agreed to continue disagreeing on issues such as Eucharistic theology.

One of the first denominational mergers of the twentieth century took place in 1925, when Canadian Methodists, Congregationalists, and a majority of the country's Presbyterians formed the United Church of Canada. In Australia, a similar group of churches joined to form the Uniting Church in 1977. In England, the Presbyterians and Congregationalists merged to form the United Reformed Church in 1972, and in the US a multiple merger in 1961 produced the United Church of Christ.

But more ambitious attempts at union remain unconsummated. In the US and New Zealand, Anglicans, Presbyterians, and others were unable to resolve differences over ordination and the Eucharist. Anglicans hesitated to rush into union with Reformed Churches, partly because they also wanted to conduct conversations with the Lutheran and Roman Catholic churches. However, a variety of Protestant denominations, including Anglicans, formed the Church of South India in 1947, and a number of regionally defined unions followed in North India, Pakistan, and Bangladesh. Episcopalians and Lutherans in the US moved part of the way towards union in 1999.

Among the most significant advances have been the theological agreements reached between various churches. In 1982 the Faith and Order Commission of the World Council of Churches produced a document entitled "Baptism, Eucharist and Ministry" ("BEM") which reflects a significant degree of consensus on these issues, while identifying areas of ongoing difference. In 1992 the Anglican churches of England and Ireland; the Church in Wales and the Episcopal Church of Scotland; the Churches of Denmark, Norway, and Sweden; and the Evangelical Lutheran churches of Estonia, Finland, Iceland, Latvia, and Lithuania ratified the Porvoo Common Statement, allowing for co-operation and sharing in areas such as communion and clergy.

Rome's move into ecumenism is associated primarily with the papacy of John XXIII. A permanent Secretariat for the Promotion of Christian Unity was established in 1960, and rapprochement with other Christians was an important item at Vatican II. By the end of the 1960s, Protestant and Catholic institutions for the study of theology and the training of clergy were making collaborative arrangements, while their students were attending the same lectures and reading the same books.

Fission and Fusion

Reflecting the explosion of theological diversity and the rapid global expansion of Christianity, historic colonial denominations seeded new churches that developed in their own ways. There are now more than 20,000 distinct denominational families in the world, most of which have come into being in the last century (Barrett et al. 2001). Perhaps ironically, the ecumenical movement has contributed to division when complicated union negotiations have left some parties behind, as in the case of the United Church of Canada.

Currently, as we have noted, the single largest Christian denomination in the world is Roman Catholicism and the fastest growing dimension of Christianity is Pentecostalism (not as a denomination in itself but as a way of being Christian). These two factors have led the demographer Philip Jenkins to conclude that eventually only two basic forms of Christianity will remain: Roman Catholicism and Pentecostalism.

Together, the rapid expansion of Christianity in the Global South and its rapid decline in the North and West have re-shaped the face of Christian missions. In prior centuries, European and North American denominations sent missionaries to the Far East and the Global South, but today the largest numbers of missionaries are being sent from Africa, Latin America, and Korea to convert the largely de-Christianized societies of Europe and North America (Jenkins 2007: 214–20).

Christianity and Pluralism

By the beginning of the third millennium, diversity had become part of the national fabric not only of societies built on immigration, like Canada, the US, and Australia, but also of European societies where until recently the great majority of citizens shared a common cultural background, including the Christian faith.

One of the great opportunities and challenges of this generation is the fact that Christians now live side by side with people of many faiths. Opportunities abound for people of differing religious commitments to work together for the well-being of local and global communities. Of course, religious diversity can fuel division and violence. Yet traditional commitments to compassion, love of neighbour, and mutual respect impel Christian communities, in their best moments, towards new ways of authentically Christian living in partnership with non-Christian neighbours. To learn this discipline well will be one of the most significant projects for Christians in the next centuries.

Table 4.1 Professing Christians Worldwide, 2011

Total Christians as % of world population: 33%	
Affiliated Christians (church members)	**2,187,138,999**
Church attenders	1,523,229,000
Evangelicals	965,400,000*
Pentecostals/Charismatics/Neocharismatics	612,472,000
Membership by six ecclesiastical megablocs	
Roman Catholic	1,160,880,000
Protestant	426,450,000
Independent	378,281,000
Orthodox	271,316,000
Anglican	87,520,000
Marginal Christian	35,539,000

* Includes Great Commission Christians

Source: Adapted from Johnson, Barrett, and Crossing 2011: 28–9.

The Major Branches of Christianity

Christianity has seven major branches comprising 156 distinct traditions and more than 21,000 denominations.

1. **Orthodox**

   Greek
   Russian
   Syrian
   Bulgarian; Serbian; Romanian (offshoots: Monophysites such as Nestorians and Coptic Christians)
   Armenians

2. **Roman Catholic**
3. **Catholic (Non-Roman or Eastern)**

   Old Catholic
   Russian and Ukrainian

4. **Protestant**

   Sixteenth century

   Lutheran; Reformed (Presbyterian); Anabaptist

   Seventeenth and eighteenth centuries

   Pietist; Congregationalist; Baptist; Methodist

   Nineteenth century

   Holiness Churches; Salvationists

   Twentieth century

   Pentecostal; Uniting Churches

5. **Anglican** (from the sixteenth century)
6. **Non-White Indigenous Protestant** (from the seventeenth century, but mainly the nineteenth and twentieth)
7. **Marginal Protestant**

   Unitarian; Mormon; Jehovah's Witnesses

Source: adapted from Barrett 1982: 34–45.

Summary

This short overview has suggested both the complexity and the consistency of Christianity. Originating as a Jewish reform movement, it grew to embrace the globe, incorporating philosophical perspectives that produced diverse schools of theology and a wide range of ecclesiastical forms and practices. Today it continues to expand, but rather than looking back to Europe, it now looks to the Global South as the location of its most pressing concern. As it carries the gospel of Jesus Christ into the future, it will fashion its next becoming with the tools it has honed in the workshop of negotiated difference.

Sites

Jerusalem

Jerusalem, a holy city for all three Abrahamic traditions, is sacred to Christians as the place where Jesus died. Tradition holds that he carried the cross along the Via Dolorosa to the hill where he was to be crucified.

St Peter's Basilica

A late-Renaissance church in Vatican City that is one of the most sacred places in the Roman Catholic tradition. The tradition that it sits on the burial site of St Peter—the disciple said to have been martyred, along with Paul, during the persecution of 64—makes it a pilgrimage site for Catholics from around the world.

Wittenberg, Germany

It was on the doors of what is now All Saints' Lutheran Church in Wittenberg that Luther nailed his 95 Theses. Today the church houses Luther's tomb.

Sacred Texts

Religion	Text	Composition/ Compilation	Compilation/ Revision	Use
Christianity	Old Testament (Genesis, Exodus, Leviticus, Numbers, Deuteronomy, Joshua, Judges, Ruth, 1 Samuel, 2 Samuel, 1 Kings, 2 Kings, 1 Chronicles, 2 Chronicles, Ezra, Nehemiah, Esther, Job, Psalms, Proverbs, Ecclesiastes, Song of Solomon, Isaiah, Jeremiah, Lamentations, Ezekiel, Daniel, Hosea, Joel, Amos, Obadiah, Jonah, Micah, Nahum, Habakkuk, Zephaniah, Haggai, Zechariah, Malachi)	Composed by various individuals and schools, from approximately 625 BCE to the 1st century BCE.	Individual books and sections revised from the 6th to 1st century BCE. At the Council of Yavne (70–90 CE) these writings were brought together and the canon reached final form. However, later writings suggest that debates were ongoing as to which texts belonged in the canon.	Doctrinal, ritual, inspirational, educational

Continued

Sacred Texts (Continued)

Religion	Text	Composition/ Compilation	Compilation/ Revision	Use
Christianity	New Testament: Undisputed Pauline Epistles (1 Thessalonians, Galatians, Philippians, 1 Corinthians, 2 Corinthians, Romans, Philemon)	Composed between approximately 51 and 63 CE, over the course of Paul's career in Ephesus, Corinth, Philippi, Macedonia, and Rome.		Doctrinal, ritual, inspirational, educational
	New Testament: Disputed Pauline Epistles (2 Thessalonians, Colossians, Ephesians)	Composed in Macedonia and Asia Minor between approximately 60 and 85 CE. Scholars doubt that they were actually written by Paul.		Doctrinal, ritual, inspirational, educational
	New Testament: Pastoral Epistles (1 Timothy, 2 Timothy, Titus)	Composed in Asia Minor and perhaps Crete between approximately 90 and 140 CE. These letters are named after the people to whom they were addressed and traditionally attributed to Paul, but their actual authors are unknown.		Doctrinal, ritual, inspirational, educational
	New Testament: Additional Epistolary Writings (1 Peter, 2 Peter, James, Jude, 1 John, 2 John, 3 John)	Composed in Asia Minor and Rome between 64 and 150, and attributed to the disciples after whom the texts are named. Their real authors are unknown, however.		Doctrinal, ritual, inspirational, educational
	New Testament: Hebrews	Composed in either Rome or Alexandria in 63 CE, by an anonymous author.		Doctrinal, ritual, inspirational, educational
	New Testament: Synoptic Gospels (Matthew, Mark, Luke)	Composed in Antioch, Southern Syria or possibly Galilee, and Ephesus between 65 and 85 CE; attributed to the disciples for whom they are named, but their actual authors are unknown.		Doctrinal, ritual, inspirational, educational

Sacred Texts (Continued)

Religion	Text	Composition/ Compilation	Compilation/ Revision	Use
Christianity	New Testament: Gospel of John	Composed in Ephesus or possibly Alexandria in 90 CE and traditionally attributed to Jesus' disciple John, son of Zebedee; actual author unknown.		Doctrinal, ritual, inspirational, educational
	New Testament: Acts of the Apostles	Composed in western Asia Minor, perhaps Ephesus, between 85 and 140 CE; attributed to Luke the Evangelist, the same disciple named as the author of the Gospel of Luke; the actual author is unknown.		Doctrinal, ritual, inspirational, educational
	New Testament: Revelation	Dated to between 64 and 96 CE and traditionally attributed to John the Evangelist, writing on the Greek island of Patmos, but the actual author is unknown.		Doctrinal, ritual, inspirational, educational

Discussion Questions

1. How has local culture shaped Christian thought and practice?
2. How did the shift from private to public worship affect Christianity?
3. What are some examples of changes in Christian thinking that reflect the changing world in which Christianity has lived?
4. In what contexts has Christianity been a reform movement? How has it served as a stabilizing influence within society?
5. Even though Christianity suffered persecution in its own early days, it has acted as persecutor in other contexts. Discuss.
6. What factors have influenced the place of women in Christianity?
7. How do you imagine the future of Christianity will unfold, based on its past?

Glossary

abbesses Powerful nuns who oversaw the lands owned by their communities; they played a significant role in the feudal landholding system.

anchoritic monasticism The form of monasticism practised by the "desert fathers and mothers," who withdrew from society; anchorites may also be known as hermits.

Anselm Eleventh-century Archbishop of Canterbury who moved away from the principle of scriptural authority. His most notable contribution was the **ontological argument** for the existence of God.

Apostles The early followers of Jesus who witnessed his return as the risen Lord and were sent out into the world to proclaim him.

Aquinas, Thomas Dominican theologian considered the greatest of the scholastics, author of the *Summa Theologiae*.

Arius The early theologian who argued (against Athanasius) that Jesus was of like substance with God rather than the same substance.

Athanasius The Bishop of Alexandria who argued (against Arius) that Jesus was of the same substance as God.

atonement Christ's restoration of humanity to a right relationship with God, variously interpreted as divine victory over demonic power, satisfaction of divine justice, or demonstration of a moral example.

Augustine Bishop of Hippo Regius in North Africa, whose theological writings shaped much of the theological tradition of Western Christianity.

baptism The ritual of initiation into the Christian faith; one of the two key sacraments. The details vary from one tradition to another, but the ritual typically involves either immersion in water or pouring of water over the head and the recitation of a Trinitarian formula recognizing the Father, Son, and Holy Spirit.

Beghards, Beguines Lay men and women respectively who lived together in semi-monastic communities that were usually not under the authority of a local bishop.

Bernard of Clairvaux Twelfth-century founder of a Cistercian monastery at Clairvaux.

Benedict's Rule The prototype for Western monastic life, written in the sixth century by St Benedict.

bishop The supervising priest of an ecclesiastical district called a diocese.

Calvin, Jean The French Protestant theologian, seen as the father of the Reformed churches, who emphasized a radical doctrine of sin and grace.

canon A standard; a scriptural canon is the list of books acknowledged as scripture; the list of acknowledged saints is likewise a canon. Canon law is the accumulated body of Church regulations and discipline.

Carmelites An ascetic monastic order of hermits established on Mount Carmel in Palestine. After the failure of the Crusades, many members migrated to Europe and reorganized themselves as a mendicant order.

Carthusians A monastic order that demanded a vow of silence and considerable austerity from its members.

cenobitic monasticism The form of monasticism practised by religious who live in community with one another.

charism A spiritual gift such as preaching, healing, speaking in tongues (glossolalia), and prophesying, which surfaced in local worshipping communities in the period of the early Church. Movements that emphasize such gifts are described as "charismatic."

Christ From *Christos*, the Greek translation of the Hebrew *mashiach* (messiah), "anointed one."

Christology A theory of who Jesus was, by nature and in substance.

Cistercians An austere monastic order, founded in France in 1098; a particularly strict branch of Cistercians, known as Trappists, observe a rule of silence.

City of God Work by Augustine of Hippo, which articulated a vision for the relationship between sacred and secular in the age of the encroaching decline of the Roman Empire.

Cluniac Fathers An order, founded in 910, at the centre of a movement to reform monasticism by bringing its institutions under the control of religious rather than secular authorities.

Constantine The first Christian emperor, who convened the Council of Nicaea in 325 CE.

Council of Chalcedon The fifth-century Church council where the controversies over the nature of Jesus' humanity and divinity were finally resolved.

Council of Nicaea The fourth-century Church council, convened by **Constantine**, that formally established many beliefs about Christ.

creeds Brief formal statements of doctrinal belief, often recited in unison by congregations.

Crusades A series of military actions (1095–late 1200s) undertaken by European Christians to drive Islam out of the Holy Land.

deacon From Greek *diakonia* "service"; the third order of (male) ministry in the early Church.

deaconess The female counterpart of the deacon's office in the early Church, devoted to serving women and children in the community.

Dominicans A **mendicant** preaching order formed in the early 1200s to combat the "Albigensian heresy."

dyophysitism The belief that the two natures of Jesus, human and divine, are united in the second person of the Trinity; affirmed at both Nicaea and Ephesus and proclaimed as orthodoxy for both the Western and Eastern Christian churches.

Easter The festival, held in March or April, celebrating the resurrection of Jesus.

ecumenism The movement for reunion or collaboration between previously separate branches of Christianity.

episcopacy Literally, "oversight"; the foundational office of authority in early Christianity; see also **bishop**.

Erasmus The humanist thinker who laid the groundwork for Reformation theologians such as Luther.

Eucharist The sacramental meal of bread and wine that recalls Jesus' last supper before his crucifixion; a standard part of Christian worship.

Evangelical In Germany, a name for the Lutheran Church. In the English-speaking world, "evangelical" refers to conservative Protestants with a confident sense of the assurance of divine grace and the obligation to preach it.

excommunication Formal censure or expulsion from a church, particularly the Roman Catholic Church, for doctrinal error or moral misconduct.

Franciscans Mendicant order whose monks live by a rule based on the life and example of St Francis of Assisi.

friar A member of a **mendicant** order such as the Carmelites, Dominicans, or Franciscans.

fundamentalism A twentieth-century reaction to modernity, originally among Protestants who maintained the infallibility of scripture and doctrine.

glossolalia Speaking in "tongues"; a distinguishing feature of charismatic groups such as **Pentecostals**, in which people who feel filled with the spirit begin speaking in what they believe is a special heavenly language. The ability to interpret such speech is also considered a spiritual gift.

Gnosticism A worldview based on a radical dualism, which prioritized reason and spirit over the physical.

gospel "Good news" (*evangelion* in Greek); the news of redemption that the Hebrew prophets had promised. The Gospels are the accounts of Jesus' life attributed to his disciples Mark, Matthew, Luke, and John.

heresy A belief or practice that is contrary to the accepted orthodoxy.

Holiness Churches Protestant churches that believe their members have already received "holiness" (spiritual perfection) as a gift from God.

icon From the Greek for "image"; a distinctive Byzantine form of portraiture used to depict Jesus, Mary, and the saints.

humanism The intellectual movement that is seen as a necessary precursor of the Protestant Reformation.

incarnation The embodiment of the divine in human form; the Christian teaching that God became human in the person of Jesus.

indulgences Releases from time in **purgatory**; the selling of indulgences by the Church was one of the abuses that led to the Protestant Reformation.

liturgy A prescribed form for public worship.

logos "Word" in the sense of eternal divine intelligence and purpose.

Luther, Martin The father of the Protestant Reformation.

Manichaeism An intensely dualistic religion, founded in the third century, that grew out of Syrian Christianity under the influence of Gnosticism.

martyrs Christians who have died for their faith.

Mary The mother of Jesus; a major saint, deeply venerated by Roman Catholics in particular.

mass The Roman Catholic name for the Eucharist.

mendicant orders Orders that, instead of withdrawing from the world and living predominantly in closed communities, dedicate themselves to pastoral work, serving the people; examples include Carmelites, Dominicans, and Franciscans.

monophysitism The belief that Christ had only one nature, either divine or a synthesis of divine and human; abandoned in favour of **dyophysitism** which is the classical teaching of the church.

mysticism The pursuit of intensely experienced spiritual union with the divine.

Nestorianism The position that there was one (divine) nature in Christ and it was separate from the human Jesus.

New Testament The collection of 27 books—accounts of Gospels, Acts of the Apostles, Epistles, and Revelation—written by various authors in the first and early second centuries and determined to be authoritative for the early Christian Church.

Nicene Creed The statement of faith agreed on at the Council of Nicaea.

nuns Women living a common life under vows in a monastic community.

ontological argument Anselm's argument for the existence of God based not on observation but on the logic that such a being must necessarily exist.

original sin The idea that human beings are inherently sinful because our earliest ancestors, Adam and Eve, chose to disobey God.

orthodoxy Literally, the "straight way," meaning correct belief; in any church, the accepted doctrine.

parables Simple stories told to illustrate a lesson.

patriarchs In the early Church, the five bishops who held primacy of authority by geographical region: Rome, Constantinople, Alexandria, Antioch, and Jerusalem. Today the term refers to those bishops in the Eastern Orthodox churches who preside over specific geographical regions and/or historical forms of the churches.

Paul, St The Jewish convert to Christianity (originally known as Saul of Tarsus) who founded a number of Christian communities and wrote them letters of instruction and guidance.

Pauline Epistles Letters attributed to Paul in the New Testament, some of which were probably written by others.

Peter, St The "prince of Apostles" who was said to have become the first bishop of Rome.

Pelagianism A heresy according to which human nature was not so tainted by **original sin** as to be incapable of choosing good or evil without divine assistance.

Pentecost The fiftieth day after Easter, commemorated as the dramatic occasion when Jesus' followers experienced the presence of the Holy Spirit.

Pentecostals Modern Protestant groups that emphasize **glossolalia** as a sign of the presence of the Holy Spirit and hence of the individual's holiness or spiritual perfection.

Pietism A movement that originated in late seventeenth-century Lutheran Germany, expressing spontaneous devotion to God and a confident certainty of forgiveness gained through religious experience.

pope The head of the Roman Catholic Church.

predestination The notion that God anticipates or controls human actions and foreordains every individual to either salvation or damnation.

presbyter Literally, "elder"; a key office that developed in the post-Apostolic period.

Reformed Churches Churches that are Calvinist in doctrine and often Presbyterian in governance; strong in the Netherlands and Scotland and also found in France, Switzerland, Hungary, and North America.

sacrament A ritual action seen as signifying divine grace. The most widely accepted sacraments are baptism and the Eucharist, although the Catholic and Anglican churches also recognize five others.

saints People recognized by the Church for their faith and virtue. Most saints are believed to have worked at least one miracle.

scriptures The holy writings of Christianity, consisting of the Hebrew Bible in Greek translation (the Septuagint), which Christians call the "Old Testament," and the "New Testament" accounts of Jesus' life and the early years of the Christian community.

see One of the five major episcopal areas: Rome, Constantinople, Alexandria, Antioch, and Jerusalem.

Synoptic Gospels The Gospels of Matthew, Mark, and Luke, called "synoptic" ("seen together") because of their many overlapping stories and themes.

teleological argument From Greek *telos*, "end" or "purpose"; an argument inferring the existence of God from the perception of purpose or design in the universe.

theocracy A state in which all of society is controlled by the Church or religious leaders.

transubstantiation The view, held mainly by Roman Catholics, that during the mass the bread and wine of the Eucharist become the literal body and blood of Jesus.

Trinity The doctrine that God exists in three "persons" or manifestations: as Father, as Son, and as Holy Spirit.

widows The earliest known order for women in Christianity, originally a response to the social problem of providing support for poor widows in the community.

Zwingli, Ulrich The father of the Swiss Reformation.

Note

My appreciation to Harry O. Maier for his assistance with the preparation of the New Testament materials. I am also grateful to have been able to incorporate portions of the late Willard Oxtoby's original chapter here.

Further Reading

Beilby, James, ed. 2009. *The Historic Jesus: Five Views*. Downers Grove, IL: IVP Academic. Five scholars present their views of the historic Jesus.

Bettenson, Henry S., and Maunder, Chris, eds. 1999. *Documents of the Christian Church*. 3rd edn. London: Oxford University Press. Strong on the early Church and Anglicanism.

Cross, F.L., and Livingstone, E.A., eds. 2005. *The Oxford Dictionary of the Christian Church*. 3rd edn. New York: Oxford University Press. The best general one-volume reference handbook.

Ehrman, Bart. 2011. *The New Testament: An Historical Introduction to Early Christian Writings*. New York/Toronto: Oxford University Press. An overview of the Christian scriptures in their historical, social, and literary contexts within the Greco-Roman world.

Farmer, David Hugh. 2004. *The Oxford Dictionary of Saints*. New York: Oxford University Press. A comprehensive guide.

Hastings, Adrian. 2000, 2007. *A World History of Christianity*. Grand Rapids: Eerdmans Publishing. A detailed history including Orthodox, Asian, African, Latin American, and North American Christianity.

Holder, Arthur (editor). 2005. *Blackwell Companion to Christian Spirituality*. Oxford, UK; Malden, MA: Blackwell. Essays by various scholars, each of whom represents a different perspective on Christian spirituality and its forms.

Jenkins, Philip. 2007. *The Next Christendom: The Coming of Global Christianity*. New York: Oxford University Press. Explores the implications of the shift in Christianity's centre of gravity from Europe and North America to South America, Africa, and Asia.

Kraemer, Ross. *Maenads, Martyrs, Matrons, Monastics: A Sourcebook on Women's Religions in the Greco-Roman World*. 1988. Philadelphia: Fortress Press. A collection of primary texts relating to women's religion in antiquity.

MacCulloch, Diarmaid. 2010. *Christianity: The First Three Thousand Years*. New York: Viking Adult. A large recent work by a noted Reformation historian.

McGinn, Bernard. 2006. *The Essential Writings of Christian Mysticism*. New York: Modern Library. A wide-ranging anthology.

McManners, John. 2002. *The Oxford Illustrated History of Christianity*. Oxford/Toronto: Oxford University Press. A comprehensive volume detailing the development of Christianity.

Murray, Peter, and Linda Murray. 1998. *The Oxford Companion to Christian Art and Architecture*. New York: Oxford University Press. An illustrated guide.

Sakenfeld, Katharine Doob. 2009. *New Interpreter's Dictionary of the Bible*. 5 vols. Nashville: Abingdon Press. A good reference work on biblical topics.

Schussler-Fiorenza, Elisabeth. 1994. *In Memory of Her: A Feminist Theological Reconstruction of Christian Origins*. New York: Crossroad. Explores the role of women in the development of Christianity; a classic.

Skinner Keller, Rosemary, and Rosemary Radford Ruether. 2006. *Encyclopedia of Women and Religion in North America*. 3 vols. Bloomington: Indiana University Press. A three-volume collection of essays on women's religious experience in North America, past and present.

White, James. 2001. *Introduction to Christian Worship*. 3rd edn. Nashville: Abingdon. The liturgical history of the Christian Church.

Wilson-Dickson, Andrew. 1997. *The Story of Christian Music: From Gregorian Chant to Black Gospel: An Authoritative Illustrated Guide to All the Major Traditions of Music for Worship*. Oxford: Lion Publishing. Traces the development of Christian worship music.

Recommended Websites

www.ccel.org

Links to many classic Christian texts.

www.newadvent.org

A Catholic site with links to many primary texts from the time of the early Church.

http://biblos.com

A tool for Bible study, containing many different translations of the Bible.

www.christianity.com

A comprehensive source of articles, videos, and audio resources on Christian history, theology, and living, as well as Bible study tools.

www.ncccusa.org

Site of the National Council of Churches USA.

www.oikoumene.org

Site of the World Council of Churches.

www.religionfacts.com/christianity/index.htm

A wide-ranging source of information on Christianity as well as other religions.

www.vatican.va/phome_en.htm

The English-language version of the official Vatican site.

http://virtualreligion.net/forum/index.html

Site of the Jesus Seminar.

www.wicc.org

Site of the Women's Inter-Church Council of Canada.

www.worldevangelicals.org

A global association of evangelical Christians.

References

Barrett, David B. 1982. *World Christian Encyclopedia: A Comparative Survey of Churches and Religions in the Modern World*. Oxford: Oxford University Press.

———, George T. Currian, and Todd M. Johnson. 2001. *World Christian Encyclopedia: A Comparative Survey of Churches and Religions in the Modern World*. 2nd edn. 2 vols. Oxford: Oxford University Press.

Bettenson, Henry, ed. 1967. *Documents of the Christian Church*. 2nd edn. Oxford: Oxford University Press.

Bonhoeffer, Dietrich. 2012. *Collected Works V.1-8*. Minneapolis: Fortress.

Brown, Candy Gunther, ed. 2011. *Global Pentecostal and Charismatic Healing*. New York: Oxford University Press.

Colgrave, Bertram, and R.A.B. Mynors. 1969. *Bede's Ecclesiastical History of the English People*. Oxford: Clarendon Press.

Colledge, Edmund, and James Walsh, eds and trans. 1978. *Julian of Norwich: Showings*. Western Classics of Spirituality. New York: Paulist Press.

Day, Dorothy. 2012. *All the Way to Heaven: The Selected Letters of Dorothy Day*. Random House.

Epstein, Daniel Mark. 1993. *Sister Aimee: The Life of Aimee Semple McPherson*. New York: Harcourt Brace.

Fletcher-Marsh, Wendy. 1995. *Beyond the Walled Garden*. Dundas, ON: Artemis.

Frend, W.H.C. 1965. *The Early Church*. Oxford: Blackwell.

Jenkins, Philip. 2007. *The Next Christendom: The Coming of Global Christianity*. New York: Oxford University Press.

John of the Cross. 1990. *The Dark Night of the Soul*. Trans. E. Allison Peers. Ed. P. Silverio de Santa Teresa, C.D. New York: Doubleday.

Johnson, Todd M., David B. Barrett, and Peter F. Crossing. 2011. "Christianity 2011: Martyrs and the Resurgence of Religion." *International Bulletin of Missionary Research* 35, 1 (January): 28–9.

Kavanaugh, Kieran. 1987. *John of the Cross: Selected Writings*. New York: Paulist Press.

King, Martin Luther, Jr. 1964. *Why We Can't Wait*. New York: New American Library.

Lamm, Julia. 2013. *The Wiley–Blackwell Companion to Christian Mysticism*. Hoboken, NJ: Wiley.

Livingstone, David. 1858. *Cambridge Lectures*. Cambridge: Deighton.

McManners, John, ed. 1990. *The Oxford Illustrated History of Christianity*. Oxford: Oxford University Press.

Madigan, Shawn, ed. 1998. *Mystics, Visionaries and Prophets: A Historical Anthology of Women's Spiritual Writings*. Minneapolis: Fortress Press.

Martos, Joseph, and Pierre Hegy. 1998. *Equal at the Creation: Sexism, Society and Christian Thought*. Toronto: University of Toronto Press.

Meyer, Robert T., trans. 1950. *Athanasius, Life of St. Anthony*. Westminster, MD: Newman Press.

Neill, Stephen. 1965. *A History of Christian Missions*. Grand Rapids, MI: Eerdmans.

O'Brien, Elmer. 1964. *Varieties of Mystic Experience*. New York: Holt, Rinehart and Winston.

Petroff, Elizabeth Alvilda, ed. 1986. *Medieval Women's Visionary Literature*. New York: Oxford University Press.

Smith, Wilfred Cantwell. 1963. *The Faith of Other Men*. New York: New American Library.

Steletenkamp, Michael F. 2009. *Nicholas Black Elk: Medicine Man, Missionary, Mystic*. University of Oklahoma Press.

Stevenson, J., ed. 1957. *A New Eusebius*. London: SPCK.

Stokes, Francis G., trans. 1909. *Epistolae obscurorum virorum*. London: Chatto & Windus.

Sykes, Stephen, Jonathan Knight, and John Booty, eds. 1998. *The Study of Anglicanism*. Philadelphia: Fortress Press.

Teresa of Avila. 1979. *The Interior Castle*. Translated by Kieran Kavanaugh and Otilio Rodriguez. New York: Paulist Press.

Von Gebler, Karl. 1879. "Letter to Castelli (excerpt)." Accessed 26 Feb. 2010 at www.law.umkc.edu/faculty/projects/ftrials/galileo/lettercastelli.html.

Ward, Benedicta. 1975. *The Sayings of the Desert Fathers*. Translated and foreword by Benedicta Ward. Trappist, KY: Cistercian Publications.

Whitehead, Alfred North. 1929. *Process and Reality*. Cambridge: Cambridge University Press; New York: Macmillan.

5 Muslim Traditions

Amir Hussain

Traditions at a Glance

Numbers

There are approximately 1.6 billion Muslims around the world, including more than 1 million in Canada, nearly 3 million in Great Britain, and 6 to 7 million in the United States.

Distribution

Although Islam originated in Arabia, the largest Muslim populations today are in Indonesia, Pakistan, India, and Bangladesh. Muslims are the second largest religious community, after Christians, in many Western countries, including Canada, Great Britain, France, and Germany.

Principal Historical Periods

570–632	Lifetime of the Prophet Muhammad
632–661	The time of the four caliphs
661–750	Umayyad caliphate
750–1258	'Abbasid caliphate
1517–1924	Ottoman caliphate

Founder and Principal Leaders

There are two major branches of Islam: Sunni and Shi'a. All Muslims place authority in Muhammad as the last prophet, but the Shi'a give special authority after Muhammad to his son-in-law 'Ali and 'Ali's descendants (the Imams).

Deity

Allah is Arabic for "the God" and is cognate with the Hebrew *'Eloh*, "deity." Muslims believe Allah to be the same God worshipped by Christians, Jews, and other monotheists.

Authoritative Texts

The essential text is the Qur'an (literally, "The Recitation"), believed to have been revealed by God to Muhammad between 610 and 632 CE. Second in importance are the sayings of Muhammad, known collectively as the *hadith* (literally, "narrative").

Noteworthy Doctrines

Islam, like Judaism and Christianity, is based on ethical monotheism. Its prophetic tradition begins with the first human being (Adam) and ends with the Prophet Muhammad. Muslims believe that the first place of worship dedicated to the one true God is the Ka'ba in Mecca, built by Abraham and his son Ishmael.

Before the terrorist attacks of September 2001, many courses on Islam would begin with a standard historical introduction to the life of Muhammad and the beginnings of Islam. The students often knew little about Islam or the religious lives of Muslims before signing up; and even for Muslim students, such a course was often their first formal introduction to their faith. After 9/11, however, some instructors found that students were coming in with preconceptions about Islam that came from the popular media and were at odds with Muslims' own understandings of their faith. As a result, those instructors decided that they had to begin with a crash course on media literacy, underlining how TV news in particular privileges the controversial and provocative over the thoughtful and accurate. How many of us come to the study of Islam with our minds already made up, convinced either that it is a religion of peace that can help modern Western society, or that it is a religion of violence and intolerance, incapable of co-existing with that society?

"Islam" means "submission" in Arabic: the name signifies the commitment to live in total submission to God. A person who professes Islam is called a Muslim, meaning "one who submits to God." An older term, rarely used today, is "Mohammedan," which misleadingly—and to Muslims offensively—suggests that Muslims worship the Prophet Muhammad himself.

← An imam at the Imamzadeh Helal-ebne Ali Shrine in Kashan, Iran (© ZUMA Press, Inc. / Alamy).

Document

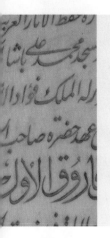

A *Hadith* (Saying) of the Prophet Muhammad

A man sinned greatly, and when death came to him he charged his sons, saying: "When I have died, burn me, then crush me and scatter my ashes into the sea. For, by God, if the Lord takes possession of me, God will punish me in a manner in which God has punished no one else." So they did that to their father. Then God said to the earth "Produce what you have taken!"—and there was the man. God said to the man, "What induced you to do what you did?" The man replied, "Being afraid of you, O my Lord." Because of that, God forgave the man (from the earliest *Hadith* collections of al-Bukhari and Muslim ibn al-Hajjaj).

The Qur'an, the Islamic scripture, presents Islam as the universal and primordial faith of all the prophets from Adam to Muhammad, and of all those who have faith in the one sovereign Lord, creator, and sustainer of all things. According to the Qur'an, Islam is God's eternal way for the universe.

Who is a Muslim? Inanimate things, plants and animals, even the angels: all are *muslims* to God by nature or instinct. Only human *islam* is an *islam* of choice. Human beings may accept or reject God, but on the Day of Judgment they will be either rewarded for their faith or punished for their rejection of it.

Most Muslims are born into Muslim families. But one can also become a Muslim simply by repeating before two Muslim witnesses the ***shahadah***, or profession of faith: "I bear witness that there is no god except God, and I bear witness that Muhammad is the messenger of God." Anyone who does this becomes a Muslim, with all the rights and responsibilities that this new identity entails.

Beginnings

Pre-Islamic Arabia

The Qur'an refers to Arab history before Islam as the age of "foolishness" or "ignorance." The term designates not so much a lack of knowledge as it does a lack of moral consciousness. The Arabs before Islam (like the ancient Hebrews) did not believe in an afterlife. Since time would spare no one, they believed that humans ought to make the most of this life while they could. Arab society was thus focused on earthly accomplishments and pleasures, praising the man who made a good name for his tribe while drowning his existential sorrows in wine, women, and sentimental verse.

The Arabs before Islam recognized Allah (Arabic for "the God") as the supreme creator god, but they worshipped many other deities as well, including a god named Hubal ("vapour"), who may originally have been a rain god, and three goddesses who were said to be the daughters of Allah (one of them may have been a version of the Greco-Roman goddess of love Aphrodite or Venus). Although the three goddesses were worshipped as intermediaries who might bring devotees closer

Timeline

622 CE	Muhammad's *hijrah* from Mecca to Medina
632	Muhammad dies; leadership passes to the caliph
642	Birth of al-Hasan al-Basri, early Sufi ascetic (d. 728)
661	Damascus established as capital of Umayyad caliphate
680	Death of Husayn at Karbala, commemorated as martyrdom by Shi'as
711	Arab armies reach Spain
762	Baghdad established as 'Abbasid capital
801	Death of Rabi'a al-'Adawiyah of Basra, a famous female Sufi
1058	Birth of al-Ghazali, theological synthesizer of faith and reason (d. 1111)
1071	Seljuq Turks defeat Byzantines in eastern Anatolia
1165	Birth of Ibn 'Arabi, philosopher of the mystical unity of being (d. 1240)
1207	Birth of Jalal al-Din Rumi, Persian mystical poet (d. 1273)
1258	Baghdad falls to Mongol invaders
1492	Christian forces take Granada, the last Muslim stronghold in Spain
1529	Ottoman Turks reach Vienna (again in 1683)
1602	Muslims officially expelled from Spain
1703	Birth of Ibn 'Abd al-Wahhab, leader of traditionalist revival in Arabia (d. 1792)
1924	Atatürk, Turkish modernizer and secularizer, abolishes the caliphate
1930	Muhammad Iqbal proposes a Muslim state in India
1947	Pakistan established as an Islamic state
1979	Ayatollah Khomeini establishes a revolutionary Islamic regime in Iran
2001	Osama bin Laden (d. 2011) launches terrorist attacks on America
2006	Orhan Pamuk becomes the second Muslim (after Naguib Mahfouz in 1988) to win the Nobel Prize for Literature
2010	Islamic scholars at the Mardin Conference in Turkey issue a ruling against terrorism
2011	The "Arab Spring"; the governments of Tunisia, Egypt, Yemen, and Libya are overthrown. Tawakkul Karman, a leader of the movement in Yemen, becomes the second Muslim woman (after Shirin Ebadi in 2003) to win the Nobel Peace Prize

to their father (see Q. 39: 3), the Qur'an repudiates them as mere "names which you [the Arabs] and your fathers named; God sent down no authority concerning them" (Q. 53: 20–3).

Arabs shared the general Semitic idea of a sacred place (*haram*) where no living thing—plant, animal, or human—could be harmed. For the people of Mecca (Makkah) and most of Arabia, the chief *haram* was the shrine called the Ka'ba: an ancient square building that contained many idols or images of gods and goddesses (among them some figures that may represent Jesus and his virgin mother Mary) and still contains an unusual black stone (perhaps a meteorite) that has been revered since pre-Islamic times. The Ka'ba was believed to have been built by the biblical patriarch Abraham and his son Ishmael (Isaac's brother), who had settled with his mother, Hagar, in the valley of Makkah (Q. 14:37). Before Islam, then, the Ka'ba was already a major pilgrimage site.

When Islam emerged in the seventh century CE, Arabia was bordered to the west by the Christian Byzantine empire and to the east by the Zoroastrian empire of the Sasanians (Iran/Persia). The city of Mecca, some 70 kilometres (40 miles) inland from the Red Sea, was dominated mainly by the Quraysh tribe, but it was open to many cultural and religious influences, including those of the Jewish and Christian communities that had been present in the territory for centuries. There were desert hermits who practised holiness and healing, and a group of Meccan Arabs known as *hanifs* ("pious ones") who shared the ethical monotheism of Judaism and Christianity.

During the *hajj*, as many as 500,000 pilgrims gather in the inner courtyard of the Great Mosque of Mecca and circumambulate the Ka'ba. Outside the courtyard but still within the mosque there may be almost 2 million more pilgrims. (© Jamal Nasrallah / epa / Corbis).

The Life of Muhammad (570–632 CE)

Muhammad was born into the Quraysh tribe around the year 570. His father died before his birth and his mother a few years later. In the tribal society of pre-Islamic Arabia, to be without a family was to be on the margins of society, but the orphaned Muhammad was taken in first by his paternal grandfather, 'Abd al-Muttalib, and later by his uncle Abu Talib.

The young Muhammad worked with his uncle in the caravan trade. By his mid-twenties, however, he was employed as a merchant for a rich widow named Khadijah, and when she proposed marriage to him, he accepted. He was called al-Amin ("the faithful" or "trustworthy"), and early biographies describe him as a contemplative, honest, and mild-mannered young man. Once a year, during the month of **Ramadan**, Muhammad spent days in seclusion in a cave a short distance from Mecca. Tradition reports that it was during one of those retreats that he received the call to prophethood and the first revelation of the Qur'an.

As Muhammad was sitting one night in his retreat, an angel—later identified as Gabriel (Jibril in Arabic)—appeared. Taking hold of him, the angel commanded, "Recite [or read]!" Muhammad answered, "I cannot read." After repeating the command a second and third time, the angel continued:

> Recite in the name of your Lord who created, created the human being from a blood clot. Recite, for your Lord is most magnanimous—who taught by the pen, taught the human being that which s/he did not know (Q. 96: 1–5).

Shivering with fear, Muhammad ran home and asked the people of his household to protect him. Khadijah was the first to believe his story of the encounter with Gabriel, but his young cousin 'Ali (the son of Abu Talib) also supported him.

The angel returned to him often, saying, "O Muhammad, I am Gabriel, and you are the Messenger of God." Eventually, Khadijah took Muhammad to her cousin, a learned Christian named Waraqah ibn Nawfal, who declared him to be a Prophet for the Arabs, chosen by God to deliver a sacred law to his people just as Moses had to the Jews.

The idea of a prophet—*nabi* in both Arabic and Hebrew—was not unfamiliar to the Meccans, but for 12 years most of them resisted Muhammad's message. They did not want to abandon the gods of their ancestors, and they feared the implications of the new faith both for their way of life and for the status of the Ka'ba, which as a pilgrimage centre brought significant income to their city. Muhammad's message was not only religious but also moral and social. He instructed the Meccans to give alms, care for the orphaned, feed the hungry, and assist the oppressed, and warned of impending doom on the day of the last judgment. The first to accept the new faith, after Khadijah, were his cousin (and future son-in-law) 'Ali ibn Abu Talib, his slave Zayd ibn Harithah (whom he later freed and adopted), and his faithful companion Abu Bakr.

Like Jesus and his disciples, Muhammad and his followers were often vilified. Around 615, one group of Muslims faced such severe persecution from the Meccans that the Prophet advised them to migrate across the Red Sea to Christian Abyssinia (Ethiopia), where they were well received. And in 619 the Prophet himself was left without support or protection when both his wife and his uncle died. Although he later entered into a number of polygamous marriages (as was the custom in his society), the loss of Khadijah must have been particularly hard: they had been married for almost half his life, she was the mother of their four daughters, and she had been the first person to believe in him. But the death of Abu Talib, his protector and surrogate father, must have been almost equally hard. It was soon after these losses that Muhammad experienced what came to be known as the "night journey," travelling from Mecca to Jerusalem on his horse Buraq in the course of a single night, and the ***mi'raj***: a miraculous ascent to heaven, where he met some of the earlier prophets and was granted an audience with God. For the Muslims, these miraculous events confirmed that their Prophet still had the support of God. Even so, it would be another three years before he found a place for the Muslims to establish their own community, free of the persecution they suffered in Mecca.

The First Muslim Community

Finally, in 622, an invitation was offered by the city of Yathrib, about 400 kilometres (250 miles) north of Mecca. The migration (***hijrah***) to Yathrib, which thereafter came to be known as "the city of the Prophet" or Medina ("the city"), marked the beginning of community life under Islam, and thus of Islamic history. In Medina Muhammad established the first Islamic commonwealth: a theocracy led by a prophet who was believed to be guided by a divine scripture.

Medina's social structure was far more diverse than Mecca's, for it included a substantial Jewish community as well as two feuding Arab tribes who kept the city in a continuous state of civil strife. Muhammad succeeded in welding these disparate elements into a cohesive social unit. In a brief constitutional document known as the covenant of Medina, he stipulated that all the people of the city should form a single Muslim commonwealth. Jews were granted full religious freedom and equality with the Muslims, on condition that they avoid any action against the state.

The Qur'an's worldview is closely akin to the prophetic view of history laid out in the Hebrew Bible. The Prophet expected the Jews of Medina, recognizing this kinship, to be natural allies, and he adopted several Jewish practices, including the fast of the Day of Atonement (Yom Kippur). But the Medinan Jews rejected both Muhammad's claim to be a prophet and the Qur'an's claim to be a sacred book. The resulting tension is reflected in the Qur'an's treatment of the Jews. Some references are clearly positive; for example, "Among the People of the Book are an upright community who recite God's revelations in the night, prostrate themselves in adoration, believing in God and the Last Day . . . these are of the righteous . . . " (Q. 3: 113–15). Others are just as clearly negative: "Take not the Jews and Christians for friends" (Q. 5: 51). Increasingly, Islam began to distinguish itself from Judaism, so that the fast of Ramadan soon took precedence over the Yom Kippur fast and the ***qiblah*** (direction of prayer) was changed from Jerusalem to the Ka'ba in Mecca.

Focus

Islamic Dates

The migration to Mecca was the starting-point for the dating system used throughout the Muslim world. Years are counted backwards or forwards from the *hijrah* and accompanied by the abbreviation AH, from the Latin for "year of the *hijrah*." Because Muslims use the lunar year—which is 11 days shorter than the solar year—*hijri* dates gain one year approximately every 33 solar years. Thus the year 1400 AH was reached in 1979 CE, and the new year of 1440 AH will be celebrated in 2019 CE.

The Conversion of Mecca

The Muslims who had fled Mecca for Medina had left all their property behind; thus to support themselves they began raiding the caravans of Meccan traders. In 624, when the Meccans sent an army of roughly 1,000 to Medina, they were met at the well of Badr by a 300-man detachment of Muslims. Though poorly equipped and far outnumbered, the Muslims inflicted a crushing defeat on the Meccans. Thus the Battle of Badr is celebrated in the Qur'an as a miraculous proof of the truth of Islam: "You [Muhammad] did not shoot the first arrow when you did shoot it; rather God shot it" (Q. 8: 17). To avenge their defeat, the Meccans met the Muslims the following year by Mount Uhud, not far from Medina, and this time they prevailed. Following that battle, the Jews were expelled from Medina on the grounds that they had formed alliances with the Meccans against the Muslims. But the real reason may have been to free the Muslim state of external influences at a critical stage in its development.

Meanwhile, the Muslims continued to raid the caravans of the Quraysh, and before long they learned that the Meccans were planning to attack Medina itself. On the advice of Salman the Persian, a former slave, the Prophet had a trench dug around the city, to prevent the Meccan cavalry from entering. Thus when the Quraysh and their allies tried to invade Medina in 627, they failed. The "Battle of the Trench" marked a tipping point, and in 628 the Meccans were impelled to seek a truce. Two years later, when the Quraysh breached the truce, the Prophet set out for Mecca at the head of a large army. But there was no need to fight. When the Muslims arrived, the Meccans surrendered to them and accepted Islam en masse.

Whenever an individual or tribe accepted Islam, all hostilities were to cease. Therefore the Prophet granted amnesty to all in the city. He attributed the victory solely to God, as prescribed in the Qur'an: "When support from God comes, and victory, and you see people enter into the religion of God in throngs, proclaim the praise of your Lord . . ." (Q. 110). He returned to Medina, where he died two years later, in 632. Muhammad was always known as "the Messenger of God" rather than as a ruler or military leader. But he was all of these. He waged war and made peace. He laid the foundations of a community (**ummah**) based on Islamic principles. He established Islam in Arabia and sent expeditions to Syria. Within 80 years the Muslims would administer the largest empire the world had ever known, stretching from the southern borders of France through North Africa and the Middle East into Central Asia and India.

No one could have foreseen that future at the time of his death. The majority of Muslims—the **Sunni**, meaning those who follow the ***sunnah*** (traditions) of the Prophet—believed that he had not even designated a successor or specified how one should be chosen. But a minority community, known as the **Shi'a** (from the Arabic meaning "party"), believed that Muhammad had in fact appointed his cousin and son-in-law 'Ali to succeed him. Muhammad's death therefore precipitated a crisis that would grow into a permanent ideological rift.

A *khalifah* is one who represents or acts on behalf of another. Thus after Muhammad's death, his close companion Abu Bakr became the *khalifat rasul Allah*—the "successor" or "representative" of the Messenger of God—and Abu Bakr's successor, 'Umar ibn al-Khattab, was at first referred to as the "successor of the successor of the Messenger of God."

From the beginning, the institution of the caliphate had a worldly dimension as well as a religious one. As a successor of the Prophet, the **caliph** was a religious leader, but as the chief or administrative head of the community, he was also the *amir* or commander of the Muslims. Perhaps conscious of this temporal role, 'Umar is said to have chosen the title "commander of the faithful." Nevertheless, the caliph continued to function as the religious leader ("imam") of the community. In all four caliphs ruled from 632 to 661. From 661 to 750, the Muslim world was ruled by a hereditary dynasty known as the Umayyads. Then the Umayyads in turn were defeated by the 'Abbasid dynasty, which ruled from 750 to 1258.

Foundations

Prophets and Messengers

According to the Qur'an, God operates through prophets and messengers who convey God's will in revealed scriptures and seek to establish God's law in their communities. From the Islamic perspective, therefore, human history is prophetic history. Tradition maintains that, from the time of Adam to the time of Muhammad, God sent 124,000 prophets into the world to remind people of every community of their obligations to the one Lord and warn them against disobedience: "There is not a nation but that a warner was sent to it" (Q. 26: 207). Among the 25 prophets that the Qur'an names are the biblical figures Abraham, Moses, David, Solomon, Elijah, John the Baptist, and Jesus. Islamic tradition distinguishes between prophets and messengers. A prophet (*nabi*) is one who conveys a message from God to a specific people at a specific time. A messenger (*rasul*) is sent to a specific community, but the message he delivers is a universally binding sacred law (***shari'ah***). The Torah given to Moses was an example of the latter: though delivered to the ancient Hebrews, it was binding on all who knew it, Hebrews and others, until the arrival of the next revelation—the gospel of Jesus. In other words, every messenger is a prophet, but not every prophet is a messenger. Among the messenger-prophets, five—Noah, Abraham, Moses, Jesus, and Muhammad—are called "prophets of power" (Q. 46: 35) because their revelations were universally binding.

Abraham

In the Qur'an, it is the innate reasoning capacity of Abraham—Ibrahim in Arabic—that leads him away from the Hebrews' tradition of idol worship and towards the knowledge of God. Even as a youth he recognizes that idols cannot hear the supplications of their worshippers and therefore can do them neither good nor harm.

One night, gazing at the full moon, Abraham thinks that it must be God. But he changes his mind when it sets. He then gazes at the bright sun and thinks that, since it is so much larger, it must be the real God. But that night the sun too sets, leading Abraham to declare: "I turn my face to the One who originated the heavens and the earth . . . I am not one of the Associators [those who associate other things or beings with God]" (Q. 6: 77–9).

Jesus

Muslims believe that all the major prophets' claims to be sent by God are supported by evidentiary miracles. The Qur'an presents Jesus as a miracle in himself. His virgin birth, his ability to heal the sick, feed the hungry, even raise the dead: these miracles affirm God's creative and life-giving power against all those who deny the reality of the resurrection and life to come. Furthermore, he performed his miracles at a time when Greek medicine, science, and philosophy were challenging

Document

From the Qur'an: Abraham Destroys the Idols

When [Abraham] said to his father and his people, "What are these idols that you so fervently worship?" they said, "We found our fathers worshipping them."

He said, "Both you and your fathers are in manifest error." They said, "Have you come to us with the truth, or are you one of those who jest?"

He said, "Your Lord is indeed the Lord of the heavens and the earth, for your Lord originated them; and to this I am one of those who bear witness. By God, I shall confound your idols as soon as you turn your backs."

He thus destroyed them utterly except for the chief one, so that the people might turn to it [for petition].

They said, "Who did this to our gods? He is surely a wrongdoer."

Some said, "We heard a youth called Abraham speaking of them."

Others said, "Bring him here in the sight of the people, so that they may all witness."

They said, "Did you do this to our gods, O Abraham?"

He said, "No, it was their chief who did it. Question them—if they could speak."

The people then turned on one another, saying, "Indeed you are the wrongdoers!" Then they bowed their heads in humiliation, saying, "You know well, [O Abraham], that these do not speak."

He [Abraham] said, "Would you then worship instead of God a thing that can do you neither good nor harm? Shame on you and on what you worship instead of God; do you not reason?"

They said, "Burn him and stand up for your gods, if you would do anything."

We [God] said, "O fire, be coolness and peace for Abraham."

They wished evil for him, but We turned them into utter losers. And We delivered him and Lot to a land that We blessed for all beings. We also granted him Isaac and Jacob as added favour, and We made them both righteous. We made them all leaders guiding others by our command. We inspired them to do good deeds, perform regular worship, and give the obligatory alms; and they were true worshippers of Us alone (Q. 21: 51–73).

the sovereignty of God as the sole creator and Lord of the universe. The miracles of Jesus therefore assert God's power over human learning and wisdom.

The Qur'an presents Jesus as delivering this message to the children of Israel: "God is surely my Lord and your Lord. Worship him, therefore; this is the straight way" (Q. 3:51). For Muslims, particularly the mystics, Jesus is a world-renouncing ascetic, a wandering prophet of stern piety but deep compassion for the poor, suffering, and oppressed, whoever they might be. Although the Qur'an categorically denies that Jesus is the divine son of God (Q. 5: 116, 19: 34–5, and 5: 17 and 72), it sees his role as extending far beyond his earthly existence, insisting that he did not die, but was lifted up to heaven by God (Q. 4: 157–8) and will return at the end of time to kill the anti-Christ and establish true Islam on Earth.

Each prophet prepares for and supports the prophet to come after him. Thus Jesus in the Qur'an announces the coming of Muhammad: "O children of Israel, I am the messenger of God to you, confirming the Torah that was before me, and announcing a messenger who shall come after me whose name is Ahmad [Muhammad]" (Q. 61: 6).

Muhammad

For Muslims, Muhammad is "the Prophet of the end of time." Just as the sacred book that he receives from God, the Qur'an, is God's final revelation for humanity, confirming and supplanting all previous revelations (see Q. 5:48), so Muhammad himself is "the seal of the prophets," and his life-example (*sunnah*) is the prophetic model that will guide history until it comes to an end on the Day of Judgment.

For the early Muslims, whatever the Prophet said or did was on God's behalf and by his command: therefore obedience to the *sunnah* of the Prophet was the same as obedience to God. When the Qur'an says that God has sent his Messenger with "the Book and wisdom" (Q. 62: 2), Muslims understand "the Book" to be the Qur'an and the "wisdom" to be the *sunnah*. Thus Muslims believe the Prophet's actions and sayings to be no less divinely inspired than the Qur'an itself.

The spiritual pre-eminence that Muslims accord Muhammad is reflected in the story of the night journey and *mi'raj*, which is elaborated in a ***hadith*** (tradition) based on the following short passage from the Qur'an: "Glory be to him who carried his servant by night from the Holy Mosque to the Further Mosque, the precincts of which we have blessed, that we might show him some of our signs" (Q. 17:1). The experience of the *mi'raj* ("ladder") parallels the heavenly ascents of prophetic figures described in visionary terms in Jewish religious literature.

To show their respect for Muhammad, Muslims speak (or write) the phrase "peace [and blessings of God] be upon him" every time his name or title is mentioned. In writing, the formula is often abbreviated as PBUH. When the prophets as a group, culminating in Muhammad, are mentioned, the formula changes to "peace be on them all."

The Qur'an

The *ayahs* (verses) and ***surahs*** (chapters) that make up the Qur'an were revealed to Muhammad by the angel Gabriel over a period of 23 years. The Prophet's role as transmitter is reflected in the Qur'an's characteristic phrasing: God ("We") instructs the Prophet ("you") to "say" something to the people (that is, to deliver a particular message to them). Yet the first instruction, as we have seen, was the command that Muhammad himself "recite" or "read." The term "Qur'an" is derived from the same root: *q–r–'*, meaning "to read" or "recite."

The Qur'an is nearly as long as the New Testament. Its contents range from short verses on a single theme or idea to fairly lengthy chapters. The early Meccan *surahs* are generally brief admonitions couched in terse and powerful verses, while the later ones are didactic tales of earlier prophets and their communities. Through stories, parables, and exhortations, the Qur'an aims to create an *ummah*: a "community" united by faith. The *surahs* revealed in Medina are fewer but longer, presenting didactic arguments, discourses, and legal pronouncements, often in response to situations arising in the life of the community.

The Status of the Qur'an

Muslims believe that the Qur'an contains the eternal Word of God. In fact, there is a theological parallel with Christian understandings of Jesus, who in the prologue to John's gospel is proclaimed to be the eternal Word of God made incarnate at a certain moment in history. For Christians Christ is the Word of God made flesh, while for Muslims the Qur'an is the Word of God made into a book.

Document

From the Qur'an: On the Day of Judgment

This short surah (chapter) is known by the title "The Earthquake."

In the name of God, the All-merciful, the Compassionate. When the earth shall be shaken with a great quake, and the earth yields up her burdens, and the human being exclaims, "What has happened to her!" On that day the earth shall recount her tidings—as her Lord had inspired her. Whoever does an atom's weight of good shall then see it, and whoever does an atom's weight of evil shall then see it (Q. 99).

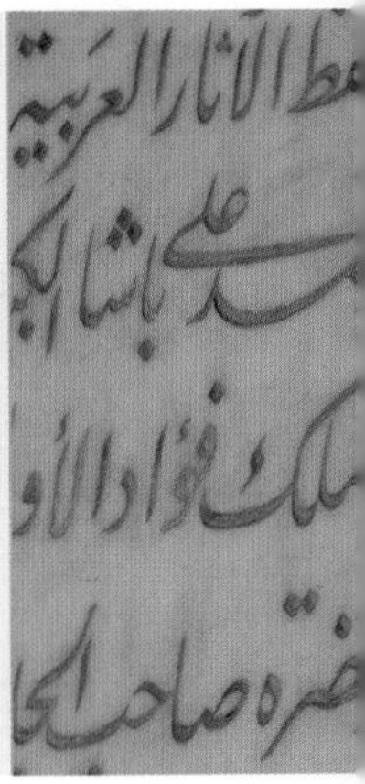

Muslims understand the Qur'an to have been revealed specifically in Arabic—the language of its first audience. Hence any translation is considered an interpretation, not the Qur'an itself. Even in places where few if any Muslims speak the language, the Qur'an is always recited in Arabic. Of course, each passage is usually followed by a translation in the appropriate language.

The words of the Qur'an are spoken in a newborn's ear as a blessing. They are also recited to seal a marriage contract or a business deal, to celebrate a successful venture, or to give solace. They are broadcast daily on radio and television throughout the Muslim world, and in the form of calligraphy they have also been a central motif in Islamic art.

Compiling the Qur'an

When the Prophet died in 632, there were many people who had committed the Qur'an to memory, but the only physical records were fragments written on stones, bones, palm leaves, and animal parchment. In some cases the same material existed in several versions, and since the vowel marks were not added until later, certain words or phrases could be read in more than one way. These variants came to be identified with specific readers through the generations of Muslim scholars. Tradition maintains that the verses within each *surah* were arranged by the Prophet at Gabriel's instruction, but that the order of the *surahs* in relation to one another—roughly in decreasing order of length—was fixed by the committee appointed to compile an official version. When it was completed, within 20 years of the Prophet's death, one of the first copies was given to his widow Hafsah.

Qur'anic Commentary (Tafsir)

The term for commentary on the Qur'an, ***tafsir***, means "unveiling" or elucidating the meaning of a text. Any such interpretation is based on one of three authoritative sources: the Qur'an itself, Prophetic *hadith*, and the opinions of the Prophet's companions and their successors. Like the Qur'an and the *hadith*, the earliest commentaries were transmitted orally, but by the tenth century Qur'anic interpretation had become a science with several ancillary fields of study. Since every legal or theological school and religious or political movement in Muslim history has looked to the Qur'an as its primary support, a wide range of interpretations emerged over time.

The Qur'an's Concept of God

The Qur'an speaks of the deity as the one and only God, creator, sustainer, judge, and sovereign Lord over all creation. For Muslims, it is a sin to associate any other being with God; this sin is called "*shirk*."

As we noted earlier, "Allah" is not the name of a particular deity: it means "the God," "the Lord of all beings" (Q. 1: 2) who demands faith and worship of all rational creatures. It was used in the same sense by the pagan Arabs before Islam, and is still used in that sense by Arab Jews and Christians today.

Islamic theology holds that God's essence is unknowable, inconceivable, and above all categories of time, space, form, and number. Materiality and temporality cannot be attributed to God. Nor can any gender, although references to God use masculine pronouns, verbs, and adjectives. God is known through the attributes known as the "most beautiful names" (sometimes translated as "wonderful names"):

> God is God other than whom there is no god, knower of the unknown and the visible. God is the All-merciful, the Compassionate. God is God other than whom there is no god, the King, the Holy One, Peace, the Faithful, the Guardian, the Majestic, the Compeller, the Lofty One (Q. 59: 22–3).

Faith and Action

Righteousness in the Qur'an has several components. In addition to faith in God, God's angels, books, prophets, and the last judgment, it includes good works: Muslims should give of their wealth to orphans and the needy, and for the ransoming of slaves and war captives. Righteousness also includes steadfastness in times of misfortune and war, and integrity in one's dealings with others.

Because all men and women are part of one humanity, they are all equal before God, regardless of race, colour, or social status. They may surpass one another only in righteousness: "Humankind, We have created you all of one male and one female and made you different peoples and tribes in order that you may know one another. Surely, the noblest of you in God's sight is the one who is most aware of God" (Q. 49: 13).

The Arabic word *iman* means faith, trust, and a personal sense of well-being in God's providential care, mercy, and justice. On this level of inner personal commitment, *iman* is a deeper level of *islam*: total surrender of the human will and destiny to the will of God. The opposite of *iman* is ***kufr***: knowing the truth but wilfully denying or obscuring it. The Qur'an also makes an important distinction between Islam and faith. Islam is a religious, social, and legal institution, while faith, *iman*, is an inner conviction whose sincerity God alone can judge, a commitment to a way of life. This is described beautifully in the Qur'an (49: 14), where the Bedouin come to Muhammad and say, "we have faith." Muhammad responds: "Do not say that you have faith, rather, say that you have submitted [you have *islam*], for faith has not yet entered your hearts." When asked "What is faith?" the Prophet is said to have answered, "Faith is seventy-odd branches, the highest of which is to say 'There is no god except God' and the lowest is to remove a harmful object from the road." In short, faith is a comprehensive framework of worship and moral conduct.

Above Islam and *iman* stands *ihsan* (doing good or creating beauty). On the level of human interrelations, *ihsan* is a concrete manifestation of both Islam and *iman*. On the level of the Muslim's personal relationship with God, *ihsan* constitutes the highest form of worship, expressed in this *hadith*: "*Ihsan* is to worship God as though you see God, for even if you do not see God, God sees you."

Practice

The Five Pillars of Islam

Individual faith and institutional Islam converge in the worship of God and service to others. According to tradition, the Prophet himself said that Islam was built on five "pillars." With the exception of the first (the *shahadah*, the profession of faith), these pillars are all rites of worship:

- to declare, or bear witness, that there is no god except God, and that Muhammad is the Messenger of God;
- to establish regular worship;
- to pay the ***zakat*** alms;
- to observe the fast of Ramadan; and
- to perform the ***hajj*** (pilgrimage to Mecca) once in one's life.

These are the foundations of Islam as a religious system of faith and social responsibility, worship, and piety. Each one has both an outer or public obligatory dimension and an inner or private voluntary dimension.

Bearing Witness

The first pillar is the *shahadah*: "I bear witness that there is no god except God, and I bear witness that Muhammad is the messenger of God." The first part, affirming the oneness of God, expresses the primordial state of faith in which every child is born. The Prophet is said to have declared, "Every child is born in this original state of faith; then his parents turn him into a Jew, Christian, or Zoroastrian, and if they are Muslims, into a Muslim." The second part, affirming Muhammad's role as messenger, signifies acceptance of his claim to prophethood, and hence the truth of his message.

Prayer

The obligatory prayers (***salat***) are distinguished from voluntary meditations and personal prayers (which may be offered at any time), in that they must be performed five times in a day and a night: at dawn, noon, mid-afternoon, sunset, and after dark. They were the first Islamic rituals, and must always be preceded by ritual washing. *Wudu'* ("making pure or radiant") includes washing the face, rinsing the mouth and nostrils, washing the hands and forearms to the elbows, passing one's wet hands over the head, and washing the feet to the heels.

Five times a day—on radio and television, through loudspeakers, and from high minarets—the melodious voice of a ***mu'adhdhin*** chants the call to prayer. Whether praying alone at home or at the mosque, as a member of the congregation, every Muslim is always conscious of countless other

Women in Fez, Morocco, performing ablutions at the Zawiya (shrine) of Moulay Idris II, who ruled Morocco from 807 to 828 (© Charles O. Cecil / Alamy).

men and women engaged in the same act of worship at the same time. Each phrase of the call to prayer is repeated at least twice for emphasis:

> God is greater. I bear witness that there is no god except God, and I bear witness that Muhammad is the Messenger of God. Hasten to the prayers! Hasten to success (or prosperity)! (Shi'as add: Hasten to the best action!) God is greater. There is no god except God.

The prayers consist of cycles or units called *rak'ahs*, with bowing, kneeling, and prostration. The dawn prayers consist of two cycles, the noon and mid-afternoon prayers of four each, the sunset prayer of three, and the night prayers of four. Apart from some moments of contemplation and personal supplication at the end of the *salat*, these prayers are fixed formulas consisting largely of passages from the Qur'an, especially the opening *surah* (*al-Fatihah*):

> In the name of God, the All-merciful, the Compassionate:
>
> Praise be to God, the All-merciful, the Compassionate, King of the Day of Judgment. You alone do we worship, and to you alone do we turn for help. Guide us to the straight way,

the way of those upon whom you have bestowed your grace, not those who have incurred your wrath, nor those who have gone astray (Q. 1: 1–7).

The ***Fatihah*** is repeated in every *rak'ah*—at least 17 times in every 24-hour period.

Unlike Judaism and Christianity, Islam has no Sabbath specified for rest, but Friday is the day designated for congregational assembly and prayers. On Friday the first two *rak'ahs* of the noon prayers are replaced by two short sermons, followed by two *rak'ahs*. The place of worship is called the *masjid* ("place of prostration in prayer") or *jami'* (literally, "gatherer"). The English term "mosque" is derived from *masjid*. Other congregational prayers are performed on the first days of the two major festivals, **'Id al-Fitr** and 'Id al-Adha, which mark the end of Ramadan and the *hajj* pilgrimage, respectively.

Faithful Muslims see all things, good or evil, as contingent on God's will. Hence many preface any statement about hopes for the future with the phrase *in-sha' Allah*, "if God wills."

Almsgiving

The third pillar reflects the close relationship between worship of God and service to the needy. Traditionally, all adult Muslims who had wealth were expected to "give alms" through payment of an obligatory tax called the *zakat*. Offering alms in this way served to purify the donor, purging greed and attachment to material possessions.

The *zakat* obligation was 2.5 per cent of the value of all one's wealth (savings, financial gains of any kind, livestock, agricultural produce, real estate, etc.). During the early centuries of Islam, when the community was controlled by a central authority, the *zakat* revenues were kept in a

Focus

A Muslim Ritual: The Call to Prayer

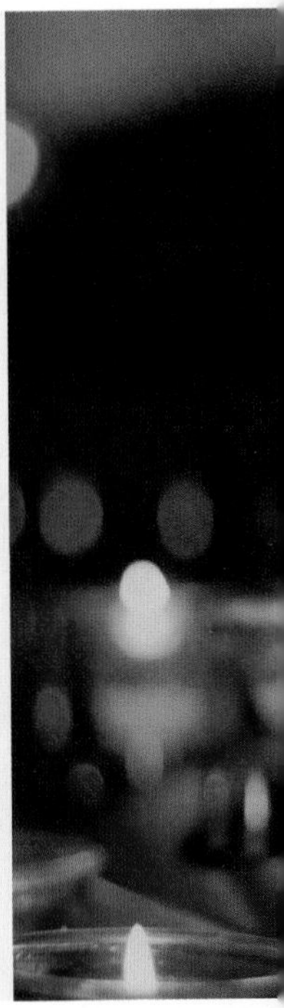

It is Friday afternoon, a few minutes before the start of the weekly congregational prayer. In this mosque in Southern California, perhaps 1,000 men and 100 women are gathered; the difference in numbers reflects the fact that this prayer is obligatory for men but optional for women. A young man walks to the front of the men's section (the women are seated in a second-floor gallery), raises his hands to his ears, and begins the call to prayer: "*Allahu akbar*, God is greater. . . ." When he has finished, the people behind him line up in rows and wait for the imam—the person who will lead the prayer—to begin.

Were this service in a different location, the call to prayer might already have been sounded in the traditional way, broadcast from minarets (towers) beside the mosque. But there are no minarets here, as the mostly non-Muslim neighbours wanted the building to "fit in" with its surroundings. Nor does this mosque have the characteristic dome: it is a two-storey building that looks more like a school than a mosque. In this non-traditional context, the function of the call to prayer has changed. Instead of being broadcast outside, to let the community know that it is time to pray, the call is broadcast inside to those already assembled for the prayer. This is one of the ways in which this congregation has adapted to its surroundings.

central treasury and disbursed for public projects, education, care of orphans and the needy, and the ransoming of Muslim war captives. Now the Muslim world is divided into nation-states, most of which collect some form of income tax, and the *zakat* obligation has become largely voluntary. However, Muslims are also expected to practise voluntary almsgiving (***sadaqah***). The Qur'an calls *sadaqah* a loan given to God, which will be repaid on the Day of Resurrection (Q. 57: 11).

The Ramadan Fast

The fourth pillar of Islam is the fast of Ramadan, which extends from daybreak till sundown each day for a month. It is mandated in this passage of the Qur'an:

> O you who have faith, fasting is ordained for you as it was ordained for those before you, that you may become aware of God. . . . Ramadan is the month in which the Qur'an was sent down as a guidance to humankind, manifestations of guidance and the Criterion. Therefore whosoever among you witnesses the moon, let them fast [the month], but whosoever is sick or on a journey, an equal number of other days (Q. 2: 183, 185).

Named for the month in which the Qur'an was revealed to the Prophet, the Ramadan fast requires complete abstention from food, drink, smoking, and sexual relations. The fast is broken at sunset, and another light meal is eaten at the end of the night, just before the next day's fast begins at dawn. Since, as the Qur'an notes, "God desires ease for you, not hardship" (Q. 2: 185), children, the sick, travellers, and women who are pregnant, nursing, or menstruating are exempted from the fast, either altogether or until they are able to make up the missed days.

Before Islam, the Arabs followed a lunar calendar in which the year consisted of only 354 days. To keep festivals and sacred months in their proper seasons, they (like the Jews) added an extra month every three years. The Qur'an abolished this custom, allowing Islamic festivals to rotate throughout the year. When Ramadan comes in the summer, abstaining from water in particular

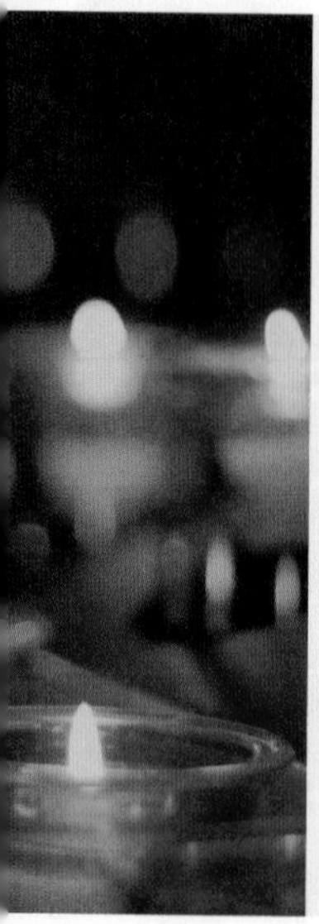

Focus

Beginning the Fast

Ms Becker teaches fourth grade in a public elementary school. Eleven of the school's pupils are Muslim, and one of them is in Ms Becker's class. This year, seven of the Muslim students have decided that they will fast during Ramadan. Some of them have fasted before, but for the nine-year-old in Ms Becker's class this will be the first time.

There is no set age at which Muslim children are expected to begin observing the fast. It may be as early as eight or nine, or as late as adolescence. In certain Muslim cultures, girls begin at an earlier age than boys, who are usually exempted on the grounds that they "aren't strong enough." While their non-Muslim classmates have lunch, those who are fasting gather in Ms Becker's classroom to work quietly on school projects. They are also excused from their physical education classes, and instead do a writing assignment about physical fitness. In this way, a public school accommodates the needs of its Muslim students.

can be a real hardship, especially in hot climates. But when it comes in winter, as it did in the 1990s in the northern hemisphere, it can be relatively tolerable.

Ramadan ends with a three-day festival called 'Id al-Fitr. Children receive gifts and wear brightly coloured new clothes, people visit the graves of loved ones, and special sweet dishes are distributed to the poor. Before the first breakfast after the long fast, the head of the household gives special alms on behalf of the family. Those who are exempted from fasting because of old age or chronic illness must feed a poor person for every day they miss.

The fast becomes a true act of worship when a person shares God's bounty with those who have no food with which to break their fast. True fasting also means abstaining from gossip, lying, or anger, and turning the heart and mind to God in devotional prayer and meditation.

The Pilgrimage to Mecca

The fifth pillar of Islam is the *hajj* pilgrimage, instituted by Abraham at God's command after he and his son Ishmael were ordered to build the Ka'ba. Thus most of its ritual elements are understood to re-enact the experiences of Abraham, whom the Qur'an declares to be the first true Muslim.

Before the pilgrims reach Mecca, they exchange their regular clothes for two pieces of white linen, symbolic of the shrouds in which Muslims are wrapped for burial. With this act they enter the state of consecration required to enter the city. The Great Mosque is the world's largest, covering more than 35 hectares (88 acres) of land that features in the Abrahamic narrative. The first ritual, the "lesser *hajj*," is performed there: after circumambulating the Ka'ba seven times, pilgrims run seven times between the two small hills (al-Safa and al-Marwa) contained within the mosque's walls. This part of the ritual recalls how Hagar, the mother of Abraham's son Ishmael, is said to have run between these hills in search of water for her dying child. After the seventh run, water gushed out by the child's feet, and Hagar contained it with sand. According to tradition, the place is marked by the well of Zamzam ("the contained water"). Its water is considered holy, and pilgrims often take some of it home for family and friends.

The *hajj* proper begins on the eighth of Dhu al-Hijjah, the twelfth month of the Islamic calendar, when throngs of pilgrims set out for the plain of 'Arafat, about 20 kilometres (13 miles) east of Mecca, on which stands the Mount of Mercy (Jabal al-Rahmah). As the sun passes the noon meridian, all the pilgrims gather for the central rite of the pilgrimage: standing till sunset on the Mount of Mercy as though standing before God on the judgment day. At sundown the pilgrims leave 'Arafat for Muzdalifah, a sacred spot a short distance along the road back to Mecca. There they observe the combined sunset and evening prayers and gather pebbles for the ritual lapidation (throwing of stones) at Mina the next day.

Tradition says that it was as Abraham was on his way from 'Arafat to Mina that God commanded him to sacrifice that which was dearest to him—his son Ishmael. Satan whispered to him three times, tempting him to disobey God's command. Abraham responded by hurling stones to drive him away. Thus pilgrims gather early in the morning at a spot called al-'Aqabah, meaning the hard or steep road, to throw seven stones at a pillar representing Satan. Three other pillars in Mina, representing the three temptations, are also stoned.

Following the stoning ritual, the head of each pilgrim family or group offers a blood sacrifice—a lamb, goat, cow, or camel—to symbolize the animal sent from heaven with which God ransomed Abraham's son (Q. 27: 107). Part of the meat is eaten by the pilgrims and the rest is distributed to

Pilgrims throw stones at one of the pillars representing Satan. This ritual is a key part of the pilgrimage (© AP Photo / Hassan Ammar / CP).

the poor. Then, to mark the end of their state of consecration, pilgrims clip a minimum of three hairs from their heads (some shave their heads completely). The *hajj* ends with a final circumambulation of the Ka'ba and the completion of the rites of the lesser *hajj* (*'umrah*) for those who have not done so.

Tradition asserts that Muslims return from a sincerely performed *hajj* free of all sin, as on the day when they were born. Thus the *hajj* represents a form of resurrection or rebirth, and its completion marks a new stage in one's life. Every pilgrim is henceforth distinguished by the title *hajjah* or *hajji* before her or his name.

Religious Sciences

In Arabic a learned person is termed an *'alim*. The plural, *'ulama'*, refers to the religio-legal scholars, or religious intellectuals, of the Islamic world as a whole. The "religious sciences" were part of a comprehensive cultural package—including theology, philosophy, literature, and science—that developed as Islam expanded far beyond the religio-political framework of its Arabian homeland. Cosmopolitan, pluralistic Islamic cultural centres like Baghdad, Cordoba, and Cairo offered ideal settings for intellectual growth.

Islam is a religion more of action than of abstract speculation about right belief. Hence the first and most important of the religious sciences, Islamic law, stresses that the essence of faith is right living. For Muslims, inner submission to the will of God means living within the framework of divine law, the *shari'ah*.

Islamic Law (Shari'ah) and Its Sources

The Qur'an

The Qur'an and hence the *shari'ah* are centrally concerned with relationships among individuals in society and between individuals and God. The most intimate human relationship is the one between husband and wife; the second is the relationship between parent and child. The circle then broadens to include the extended family, the tribe, the *ummah*, and the world.

Islam has no priesthood. Every Muslim is responsible both for his or her own morality and for the morality of the entire *ummah*: "Let there be of you a community that calls to the good, enjoins honourable conduct, and dissuades from evil conduct" (Q. 3: 104).

The Qur'an places kindness and respect for parents next in importance to the worship of God. These are followed by caring for the poor and needy. But renunciation of material possessions is no more desirable than total attachment to them. Rather, the Qur'an enjoins the faithful to "Seek amidst that which God has given you, the last abode, but do not forget your portion of the present world" (Q. 28: 77). In short, the Qur'an is primarily concerned with moral issues in actual situations. It is not a legal manual: of its 6,236 verses no more than 200 are explicitly legislative.

The Sunnah

The life-example of the Prophet includes not only his actions and sayings but also his tacit consent. His actions are reported in anecdotes about events he participated in or situations to which he reacted. In cases where he expressed neither approval nor objection, his silence is taken to signify consent. Thus the *sunnah* of consent became a normative source of Islamic law.

Accounts of the Prophet's *hadiths* must go back to an eyewitness. The *hadith* literature is the most important component of *sunnah* because it is the most direct expression of his judgments regarding the community's conduct.

To qualify as a *hadith*, a text must be accompanied by its chain of transmission, beginning with the compiler or last transmitter and going back to the Prophet. The aim of *hadith* study is to ascertain the authenticity of a particular text by establishing the completeness of the chain of its transmission and the veracity of its transmitters.

There are six canonical *hadith* collections. The earliest and most important collectors were Muhammad ibn Isma'il al-Bukhari (810–70) and Muslim ibn al-Hajjaj al-Nisaburi (c. 817–75). As their names suggest, the former came from the city of Bukhara in Central Asia and the latter from Nishapur in northeastern Iran. Although they did not know one another, both spent many years travelling across the Muslim world in search of *hadiths*. The fact that their independent quests produced very similar results suggests that a unified *hadith* tradition was already well established.

Both men are said to have collected hundreds of thousands of *hadiths*, out of which each selected about 3,000, discounting repetitions. Their two collections, *Sahih* (literally, "sound") *al-Bukhari* and *Sahih Muslim*, soon achieved canonical status, second in authority only to the Qur'an. Within less than half a century, four other collections were produced. It's worth noting that their compilers also came from Central Asia and Iran. Each of these collections is entitled simply *Sunan* (the plural of *sunnah*). As legal manuals, all six collections are organized topically, beginning with the laws governing worship and continuing with the laws regulating social, political, and economic life.

The Scope of Islamic Law

The *shari'ah* is sacred law, "the law of God." It consists of the maxims, admonitions, and legal sanctions and prohibitions enshrined in the Qur'an and explained, elaborated, and realized in the Prophetic tradition.

Shari'ah originally signified the way to a source of water. Metaphorically it came to mean the way to the good in this world and the next. It is "the straight way" that leads the faithful to paradise in the hereafter. Muslims believe the *shari'ah* to be God's plan for the ordering of human society. Within the framework of the divine law, human actions range from those that are absolutely obligatory and will bring rewards on the Day of Judgment to those that are absolutely forbidden and will bring harsh punishment. Actions are classified in five categories:

- lawful (***halal***), and therefore obligatory;
- commendable, and therefore recommended;
- neutral, and therefore permitted;
- reprehensible, and therefore disliked; and
- unlawful (***haram***), and therefore forbidden.

These categories govern all human actions. The correctness of an action and the intention that lies behind it together determine its consequences for the person who performs it.

Jurisprudence

Jurisprudence, or ***fiqh***, is the theoretical and systematic aspect of Islamic law, consisting of the interpretation and codification of the *shari'ah*. Islamic jurisprudence is based on four sources, of which the Qur'an and *sunnah* are primary. The two secondary sources are the personal reasoning (***ijtihad***) of the scholars and the general consensus (***ijma'***) of the community. The four schools of Islamic law (Hanafi, Maliki, Shafi'i, and Hanbali) differed in the degree of emphasis or acceptance that they gave to each source.

Personal reasoning is the process through which legal scholars deduced from the Qur'an and *sunnah* the laws that are the foundations of their various schools of thought. *Ijtihad* represents a scholar's best effort in this endeavour, which is based on reasoning from analogous situations in the past: thus modern software piracy would be considered analogous to theft.

Finally, the principle of consensus (*ijma'*) is meant to ensure the continuing authenticity and truth of the three other sources. In the broadest sense, it refers to the community's acceptance of applied *shari'ah*. More narrowly, it has encouraged an active exchange of ideas among the various schools, at least during the formative period of Islamic law. Consensus has remained the final arbiter of truth and error, expressed in the Prophet's declaration that "my community will not agree on an error."

Yet even this important principle has been the subject of debate and dissension. Among the questions at issue are whether the consensus of earlier generations is binding on the present one, and whether the necessary consensus can be reached by the scholars alone, without the participation of the community at large.

Early Jurisprudence

The Qur'an calls on Muslims to choose a number of individuals to dedicate themselves to the acquisition of religious knowledge so that they can provide instruction when the people ask for it (Q. 9: 122). The need for such a group was felt from the beginning when some pilgrims visiting Mecca from Medina accepted Islam and on returning took with them some Muslims with the necessary knowledge to teach the Medinans. As Islam spread across Arabia, the Prophet sent governors with special religious knowledge to administer the new Muslim communities and instruct their people in Islam.

Among those governors was Mu'adh ibn Jabal. Before sending him to Yemen, the Prophet is said to have asked him how he would deal with the People of the Book (Jews and Christians), who made up the majority of the region's population. Mu'adh supposedly answered that he would deal with them in accordance with the Book of God and the *sunnah* of his Prophet. Muhammad then asked what would happen if he did not find the answer to a problem in either of the two sources. Mu'adh is said to have answered, "I would then use my reason, and would spare no effort."

This pious tale no doubt was invoked to bestow on a developing discipline an aura of Prophetic blessing and authority. Nevertheless, the anecdote aptly illustrates the development of Islamic law in its early stages. A number of the companions were known for their ability to deduce judgments from Qur'anic principles, together with the actions and instructions of the Prophet.

As the Muslim domains expanded, the need for a uniform body of religious law was filled for a time by Muslims of the first and second generations (the Companions and their successors), who laid the foundations for subsequent legal traditions. Until the eighth century, these traditions were centred in western Arabia, particularly in Medina and Mecca, and Iraq, especially in Kufah and Basrah. It was in these centres that the "living tradition" of jurisprudence was transformed from an oral to a written science, with an ever-growing body of literature.

The Sunni Legal Schools

The earliest Sunni legal schools were founded in the eighth and ninth centuries. After a period of often violent conflict, they gained universal acceptance as equally valid interpretations of the *shari'ah* in different regions of the Muslim world.

Some less important legal schools died out: for example, the Yahiri school ceased with the end of Muslim rule in Spain. Others survived, but only in isolated communities: among them is the Ibadi school, which was established during the first century of Islam and is still represented in small communities in North Africa and Oman.

Hanafi Law

The most famous jurist of Iraq was Abu Hanifah (699–767), the son of a Persian slave. Although he left no writings that can be ascribed to him with certainty, two disciples developed his system into the most widespread Sunni legal school. The Hanafi school was for centuries accorded state patronage, first by the 'Abbasid caliphate and then by the Ottoman Empire, and spread to all the domains influenced by them: Egypt, Jordan, Lebanon, Syria, Iraq, Central Asia, the Indian subcontinent, Turkey, and the Balkans.

Maliki Law

Malik b. Anas (c. 715–95), the leading scholar of Medina and founder of the Maliki school, developed his system in the framework of the *hadith* and legal traditions he collected in his book *The*

Levelled Path. The first such collection to be made, it reflects the early development of legal thought in Islam.

Unlike later jurists and *hadith* collectors, Malik gave equal weight to the *sunnah* of the Prophet and the "practice," or living tradition, of the people of Medina. He also relied much more on *ijtihad*—the personal effort to deduce legal opinions—than did later scholars. He was guided in this effort by the principle of common good (*maslahah*).

Abu Hanifah had also relied greatly on living tradition, along with the principles of deductive analogical reasoning (*qiyas*; for example, deciding that software piracy is analogous to theft) and rational preference (*istihsan*, according to which one may prefer one particular ruling over other possibilities). The work of both Malik and Abu Hanifah indicates that the principle of reliance on the *sunnah* as a source of jurisprudence was still in the process of development. It went hand in hand with the "living traditions" of major cities or centres of learning. Both ultimately traced their judgments back to the Prophet or the first generation of Muslims. The Maliki school was carried early to Egypt, the Gulf region, and North Africa and from there to Spain, West Africa, and the Sudan.

Shafi'i Law

A decisive stage in the development of Islamic jurisprudence came in the ninth century with the work of Muhammad ibn Idris al-Shafi'i (767–820). He studied in several different centres, without clearly allying himself with any school, before writing the first systematic treatise on Islamic jurisprudence. Shafi'i advocated absolute dependence on the Qur'an and *sunnah*. He based his own system on a vast collection of *hadith* and legal tradition, which he compiled for that purpose.

Shafi'i restricted the use of *qiyas* or analogical reasoning, and rejected both the Hanafi principle of rational preference (*istihsan*) and the Maliki principle of common good (*maslahah*). He insisted that all juridical judgments be based on the Qur'an and the *sunnah*, and (unlike most jurists of his time) preferred *hadiths* transmitted by single authorities to personal opinion. Although Shafi'i's system later became the foundation of the school bearing his name, he expressly opposed the idea. He saw himself not as the founder of a new legal school, but as the reformer of Islamic law. The Shafi'i school spread from Egypt, where Shafi'i lived and died, to southern Arabia and then followed the maritime trade routes to East Africa and to Southeast Asia, where it remains the dominant school.

Hanbali Law

The well-known *hadith* collector Ahmad ibn Hanbal (780–855), a strict conservative, founded the Hanbali school in conformity with Shafi'i's position. The *hadith* collection he produced, the *Musnad*, was arranged not by subject, as other standard collections were, but by the names of primary transmitters, often the Prophet's Companions. Though the *Musnad* was not the first work of this genre, it was by far the largest and most important, and it became the foundation of the Hanbali legal system.

The Hanbali school has had a smaller following than its rivals, but also a disproportionately great influence, especially in modern times. Although it exists almost exclusively in central Arabia (the present Saudi kingdom), its conservative ideology has been championed by revolutionaries and reformers since the thirteenth century.

The End of Ijtihad

The Prophet is reported to have declared that "The best generation is my generation, then the one that follows it, and then the one that follows that." The idea that Muslim society grew increasingly corrupt after the normative period of first four "rightly guided" caliphs was widely held. Yet there were people who modelled their lives on the examples of scholars, jurists, and *hadith* collectors of that formative period.

With the establishment of the major Sunni legal schools by the tenth century, there was a sort of undeclared consensus that the gate of *ijtihad* had closed. This did not mean that the development of Islamic legal thinking ceased altogether, but it did mean that no new legal systems would henceforth be tolerated. In fact, the process of exclusion had already begun through the awarding of political patronage to some schools and the denial of it to others. From this time on, only the experts in religious law (*muftis*) of each city or country were empowered to issue legal opinions (*fatwas*), in accordance with the principles of their respective legal schools. Various collections of famous *fatwas* have served as manuals for less able or less creative *muftis*.

Ja'fari (Shi'i) Law

The Shi'i legal and religious system is named after the man regarded as its founder, Ja'far al-Sadiq (c. 700–65). The sixth in the line of Imams that began with 'Ali—the cousin and son-in-law of the Prophet whom the Shi'a believed to be his only legitimate successor—Ja'far was revered as a descendant of the Prophet's family, and, with his father Muhammad al-Baqir (the fifth Imam), was among the leading scholars of Medina. They left no written works, but a rich oral tradition was codified in the tenth and eleventh centuries as the foundation of the legal system that governs **Imami** or **Twelver** Shi'ism (see Focus box). In the Ja'fari school, Twelver Shi'ism possesses the Shi'i legal school closest to Sunni orthodoxy.

Focus

The Twelfth Imam

According to the Shi'i doctrine of *imamah*, the Prophet appointed 'Ali as his vice-regent. 'Ali in turn appointed his son Hasan to succeed him as Imam, and Hasan appointed his brother Husayn. Thereafter, each Imam designated his successor, usually his eldest son.

Mainstream Shi'as believe that the line of Imams descended from Husayn continued until 874, when the twelfth Imam, the four-year-old Muhammad ibn Hasan al-'Askari, disappeared; it is for this reason that they are also known as "Twelvers." They maintain that he went into hiding ("occultation"), but continued to communicate with his followers until 941, when he entered a new phase—known as the "greater occultation"—that will continue until the end of the world. At that time, before the Day of Resurrection, he will return as the **Mahdi**, "the rightly guided one," who with Jesus will establish universal justice and true Islam on Earth. In short, Twelver Shi'ism understands the *sunnah* to include not only the life-example of the Prophet and his generation, but the life-examples of the twelve Imams—the men they believe to be his rightful successors. Hence for Twelvers the period of the *sunnah* extends over three centuries, until the end of the "lesser occultation" of the twelfth Imam in 941.

In contrast to Sunni legal schools, which developed first a science of jurisprudence and then a canonical *hadith* tradition to buttress it, the Ja'fari school based its legal system on a vast body of *hadith* centred on the traditions of the Imams descended from 'Ali. The first of what would become four collections of Imami *hadith* was compiled by Muhammad al-Kulayni (d. 941): entitled "The Sufficient," it resembles Sunni *hadith* collections in that it begins with the fundamentals of doctrine and worship and then addresses ancillary legal matters.

Where it diverges from the Sunni model is in the section dealing with the imamate. The essential point of difference is the Shi'i belief that the Imam is the proof or argument (*hujjah*) of God to his human creatures, and hence that the world cannot be without one, whether he be present and active in the community or hidden from human perception (see Focus Box on previous page).

Following al-Kulayni, important *hadith* collections were compiled by Ibn Babawayh (c. 923–91) of the Iranian holy city of Qom, who was known as "the truthful ***shaykh***," and Abu Ja'far al-Tusi (d. 1067), "the jurist doctor of the community."

With Tusi the foundations of the Imami *hadith* and legal traditions were virtually fixed. In the absence of the Imam, his role as guardian of the *shari'ah* had to be filled, however imperfectly, by scholars of the community. This meant that *ijtihad*, personal reasoning, had to continue, albeit in a limited way, in the form of scholarly efforts to interpret the Imams' rulings in ways that would apply to new situations, and consensus must be limited to the *ijma'* of the scholars alone (as opposed to the community as a whole).

For this reason the Imami legal school rejected analogical reasoning as an instrument of *ijtihad*. This does not mean that reason played a secondary role in the development of Shi'i jurisprudence. On the contrary, the primary sources of law were identified early on as the transmitted tradition, including the Qur'an, and human reason. Furthermore, where transmitted tradition and reason come into conflict, reason takes priority over tradition.

Ijtihad remains in principle a primary source of Shi'i law today. But the risk of error, in the absence of the Imam, has meant that its use has been circumscribed by the principle of precaution. This has tended to limit the use of personal reasoning to the point that original thinking is rare.

Taqlid means following the *ijtihad* of a particular jurist. For the Sunni, it meant following the founder of one of the recognized legal schools, which implied strict adherence to a traditional system with no room for innovation. For the Shi'a, the absence of the Imam made *taqlid* of a living jurist a legal necessity. This emphasis has had the same effect on the Shi'i community that the closing of the gate of *ijtihad* has had on the Sunni. The development of courageous and sensitive new approaches to the interpretation and application of the *shari'ah* is therefore imperative in both communities today.

Islamic Philosophy and Theology

An important subset of the religious sciences consisted of the "rational" sciences of philosophy and theology. Theology is discourse about God, but also human free will and predestination, moral and religious obligations, and the return to God on the Day of Resurrection for the final judgment. Insofar as theology addresses human faith and conduct, it is part of the science of *fiqh*, jurisprudence.

In time, however, Islamic theology also addressed more philosophical questions about the existence of God, creation, and the problems of evil and suffering. In these areas it reflects the influence of Hellenistic philosophy, whose principles and rationalistic methodology it adopted.

The rapid spread of Islam into Syria and Mesopotamia brought Muslims into contact with people of other faiths, including Hellenized Jews and Christians. By the mid-eighth century, interest in Greek philosophy, science, and medicine was increasing, and Arabic translations of Greek works began to appear.

The quest for knowledge reached its peak in the next century under the caliph al-Ma'mun (r. 813–33), whose "House of Wisdom" in Baghdad was the first institution of higher learning anywhere in the West. Christian scholars had already translated many Greek medical, philosophical, and theological treatises into Syriac and commented on them, but the House of Wisdom, which housed an impressive library of Greek manuscripts, provided additional support for their work. Smaller centres of philosophical and medical studies in Syria and Iran also made notable contributions.

The Early Period

Early Islamic philosophy was Aristotelian in its logic, physics, and metaphysics, Platonic in its political and social aspects, and Neoplatonic in its mysticism and theology. Two figures stand out in this period. The first was the Iraqi theologian-philosopher Abu Yusuf Ya'qub al-Kindi (d. 870), who used philosophical principles and methods of reasoning to defend fundamental Islamic teachings such as the existence and oneness of God, the creation of the universe out of nothing, and the necessity of prophets. In his argument for the latter, Al-Kindi distinguished between the philosopher, who acquires his knowledge through rational investigation, and the prophet, who receives his knowledge through divine revelation.

In sharp contrast to al-Kindi, the Iranian Abu Bakr Zakariyah al-Razi (c. 865–926) was a Platonist who rejected the doctrine of creation out of nothing. Rather, drawing on Plato, he argued that the universe evolved from primal matter, floating gas atoms in an absolute void. The universe came into being when God imposed order on the primeval chaos, but it will return to chaos at some distant point in the future, because matter will revert to its primeval state.

The Flowering of Islamic Philosophy

Abu Nasr al-Farabi (c. 878–950), who moved to Baghdad from Turkestan, was not only a great philosopher but an important musician and musical theorist. According to his Platonic system, God is pure intellect and the highest good. From God's self-knowledge or contemplation emanates the first intellect, which generates the heavenly spheres, and a second intellect, which then repeats the process. Each subsequent intellect generates another sphere and another intellect.

Al-Farabi agreed with al-Kindi that a prophet has intellect capable of receiving philosophical verities and without mental exertion. He then communicates these truths to the masses, who are incapable of comprehending them on the philosophical level.

Although al-Farabi was called "the second teacher," after Aristotle, even he was excelled by "the great master" Ibn Sina (known in Latin as Avicenna, 980–1037). Born in Bukhara, Central Asia, he was a self-taught genius who mastered the religious sciences at the age of 10 and by 18 had become a leading physician, philosopher, and astronomer. Ibn Sina built on al-Farabi's Neoplatonic ideas to produce a comprehensive system of mystical philosophy and theology. He developed al-Farabi's theory of emanations, placing it in a more precise logical and philosophical framework. Although he affirmed the prophethood of Muhammad, the revelation of the Qur'an, and the immortality of the soul, he rejected the Qur'anic traditions of the resurrection of the body, the reward of paradise, and the punishment of hell.

According to a widely accepted Prophetic tradition, at the beginning of every century God raises a scholar to renew the faith of the Muslim community. For the sixth Islamic century, that scholar was Abu Hamid Muhammad al-Ghazali (1058–1111) of Tus, in Iran. His work went far beyond theology and philosophy to encompass mysticism and all the religious sciences.

As a professor of theology and law in Baghdad, he defended mainstream Sunni Islam against the innovations of the theologians and the heresies of the philosophers. But in 1095 he suffered a psychological crisis and gave up teaching. After a long quest, he determined that one cannot attain true knowledge through either the senses or the rational sciences, but only through a divine light that God casts into one's heart. His reason thus enlightened, al-Ghazali produced *The Revivification of the Religious Sciences*, in which he examines all religious learning from a deeply mystical point of view.

In his book *The Incoherence* [or "Collapse"] *of the Philosophers*, al-Ghazali rejected the philosophical principle of causality, in which created things could be the efficient causes of events, and in its place proposed a theory of occasionalism, in which the only cause of anything in the universe is God. But Al-Ghazali's critique itself would become the subject of a critique by the Aristotelian philosopher Ibn Rushd.

Ibn Rushd (1126–98), who was born in Cordoba, Spain, came from a long line of jurists, and was himself a noted scholar of Islamic law. His legal training decisively influenced his philosophy. In *The Incoherence of the Incoherence* Ibn Rushd methodically criticizes both al-Ghazali for misunderstanding philosophy and Ibn Sina for misunderstanding Aristotle. The first to construct a true Aristotelian philosophical system, Ibn Rushd essentially shared his Eastern predecessors' belief in the primacy of philosophy over religion. In his famous double-truth theory, however, he argued that both were valid ways of arriving at truth: the difference was that philosophy was the way of the intellectual elite, while religion was the way of the masses.

The great "renovator" of the thirteenth century, Ibn 'Arabi, will be discussed below, in the context of Sufism. He was followed by a more empirical philosopher, the Tunisian-born 'Abd al-Rahman Ibn Khaldun (1332–1406). Through his extensive travels and his work as a jurist and political theorist, Ibn Khaldun gained insight into the workings both of nations and of political and religious institutions. This led him to write a universal history that is most notable for its introduction, in which he presented the first social philosophy of history in the Western world.

Islamic philosophy had a lasting influence on medieval and Renaissance thought in Europe, particularly through its interpretation of Aristotelianism. Europeans came to know many Muslim philosophers by Latinized forms of their names: Rhazes for al-Razi, Alpharabius or Avennasar for al-Farabi, Avicenna for Ibn Sina, Algazel for al-Ghazali, Averroës for Ibn Rushd. Among the Europeans who were influenced by the latter in particular was the great medieval Catholic philosopher and theologian Thomas Aquinas. It is impossible to properly understand his thought without appreciating its roots in the Muslim philosophy of Ibn Rushd and the Jewish philosophy of Maimonides.

Variations

Shi'ism

As we have seen, for all Muslims an "imam" is someone who serves as the leader of prayer at the mosque; but for Shi'as "Imam" is also the title of the one individual divinely mandated to lead the Muslim community because he is descended from the Prophet's cousin, son-in-law, and rightful successor 'Ali.

Devotion to the family of the Prophet ("the people of the house," usually meaning his daughter Fatimah, her husband 'Ali, and their sons, Hasan and Husayn) has always been a central characteristic of Shi'ism. Its source is a *hadith* according to which the Prophet, on his way back from Mecca to Medina, stopped at a place called Ghadir Khumm, took 'Ali by the hand, and made the following declaration:

> O people, hear my words, and let him who is present inform him who is absent: Anyone of whom I am the master, 'Ali, too, is his master. O God, be a friend to those who befriend him and an enemy to those who show hostility to him, support those who support him and abandon those who desert him.

On the basis of this and other sayings in which they believe the Prophet directly or indirectly designated 'Ali as his successor, Shi'i scholars constructed an elaborate legal and theological system supporting the doctrine of *imamah*, according to which the source of all legitimate authority is the Imam.

Ashura

In the year 680 the Prophet's grandson Husayn ('Ali's son) was leading an uprising against the Umayyad Caliph Yazid when he was killed in battle at Karbala in Iraq. The anniversary of his death, on the tenth day of the month of Muharram, has become a focal point for the Shi'i community's hopes and frustrations, messianic expectations, and highly eschatological view of history.

In the Iranian city of Isfahan, actors perform a *tazieh*, or "passion play," re-enacting the events surrounding the death of Husayn at Karbala in 680. This is part of the Shi'a commemoration of Ashura (© CAREN FIROUZ / Reuters / Corbis).

"Ashura" ("ten"), as the anniversary came to be known, is still commemorated by Shi'as around the world. Blending sorrow, blessing, and mystery, it has inspired a rich devotional literature, and is observed by the Shi'a as a day of suffering and martyrdom that is marked by devotional activities that include solemn processions, public readings, and passion plays. The Sunni community commemorates "Ashura" with a day of fasting.

Divisions within Shi'ism

The Shi'a share a general allegiance to the right of 'Ali and his descendants to authority in the Muslim community after Muhammad. But "Shi'ism" is a broad term that covers a variety of religio-political movements, sects, and ideologies.

The majority of Shi'as accepted the line of Husaynid Imams down to Ja'far al-Sadiq, the legal scholar who was sixth in the succession. But a major schism occurred when Ja'far's oldest son and successor, Isma'il, predeceased him. Ja'far then appointed a younger son, Musa al-Kazim, as his own successor. The Shi'a who accepted this appointment and went on to revere Musa as the seventh Imam eventually came to be known as Imamis or Twelvers (see Focus Box p. 241 above).

Others, though, considered the appointment irregular and insisted that the seventh Imam should be Isma'il's son Ahmad. For this reason they came to be known as **Isma'ilis** or "**Seveners**," The largest faction, called Nizaris, carried on the line of Imams through Ahmad and his descendants down to the present. Over the centuries Isma'ili philosophers and theologians developed the doctrine of the divine mandate of the Imam into an impressive esoteric system of prophetology. The Isma'ilis have played very conspicuous intellectual and political roles in Muslim history.

For centuries they lived as an obscure sect in Iran, Syria, East Africa, and the Indian subcontinent. Since 1818 their leader (Imam) has been known as the Agha Khan, an Indo-Iranian title signifying nobility. The third Agha Khan (1877–1957) initiated a movement for reconciliation with the larger Muslim community, and efforts to resolve differences have continued under his Harvard-educated successor, Karim Agha Khan (b. 1936). In modern times Isma'ilis have migrated in large numbers to the West. Prosperous and well-organized, they now number roughly 15 million and are the best-integrated Muslim community in the West.

Sufism: The Mystical Tradition

The early Muslim mystics were said to wear a garment of coarse wool over their bare skin in emulation of Jesus, who is represented in Islamic hagiography as a model of ascetic piety. For this reason they became known as Sufis (from the Arabic meaning "wool"). Asceticism was only one element in the development of Sufism, however.

At least as important was the Islamic tradition of devotional piety. Since the ultimate purpose of all creation is to worship God and sing his praises (Q. 17: 44 and 51: 56), the pious are urged to "remember God much" (Q. 33: 41). The Prophet's night vigils and other devotions (Q. 73: 1–8), embellished by hagiographical tradition, have served as a living example for pious Muslims across the centuries. *Hadith* traditions, particularly the "divine sayings" in which the speaker is God, have also provided a rich source of mystical piety. Above all, the *mi'raj*—the Prophet's miraculous journey to heaven—has been a guide for mystics on their own spiritual ascent to God. One early champion of the ascetic movement was a theologian and *hadith* collector named al-Hasan al-Basri, who was born in Medina in 642 and lived through both the crises and the rise to glory of the Muslim *ummah*. Hasan once likened the world to a snake: soft to the touch, but full of venom.

The early ascetics were sometimes called weepers, for the tears they shed in fear of God's punishment and in yearning for God's reward. Significantly, the movement emerged in areas of mixed populations, where other forms of asceticism had existed for centuries: places such as Kufa and Basra in Iraq (long the home of Eastern Christian asceticism); northeastern Iran, particularly the region of Balkh (an ancient centre of Buddhist asceticism, now part of Afghanistan); and Egypt (the home of Christian monasticism as well as Gnostic asceticism).

The Agha Khan, spiritual leader of the world's 15 million Isma'ili Muslims, addressing the Parliament of Canada in February 2014 (Photo by Jason Ransom. Source: © Office of the Prime Minister, 2014).

Asceticism for its own sake, however, was frowned on by many advocates of mystical piety. Among the critics was the sixth Imam, Ja'far al-Sadiq, who argued that when God bestows a favour on a servant, God wishes to see that favour manifested in the servant's clothing and way of life. Ja'far's grandfather 'Ali Zayn al-'Abidin is said to have argued that God should be worshipped not out of fear of hell or desire for paradise, but in humble gratitude for the gift of the capacity to worship God.

What transformed ascetic piety into mysticism was the all-consuming love of the divine exemplified by an early woman mystic named Rabi'a al-'Adawiyah of Basra (c. 713–801). Born into a poor family, Rabi'a was orphaned and sold into slavery as a child, but her master was so impressed with her piety that he set her free. She lived the rest of her life in mystical contemplation, loving God with no motive other than love itself:

> My Lord, if I worship you in fear of the fire, burn me in hell. If I worship you in desire for paradise, deprive me of it. But if I worship you in love of you, then deprive me not of your eternal beauty (Smith 1928).

Mystics of all religious traditions have used the language of erotic love to express their love for God. Rabi'a was perhaps the first to introduce this language into Islamic mysticism. She loved God with both the love of passion and the devotional love of the worshipful servant for her Lord. A more controversial tradition within Sufism pursued absolute union with God. Among the proponents of this ecstatic or "intoxicated" Sufism was Husayn ibn Mansur al-Hallaj (c. 858–922), whose identification with the divine was so intense as to suggest that he made no distinction between God and himself. For this apparent blasphemy he was brutally executed by the 'Abbasid authorities.

Al-Hallaj had travelled widely, studying with the best-known Sufi masters of his time. But eventually he broke away from his teachers and embarked on a long quest for self-realization.

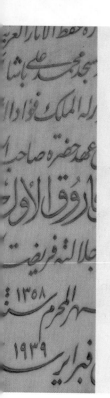

Document

Rabi'a al-'Adawiyah

When Rabi'a's fellow Sufis urged her to marry, she consented in principle, but only on the condition that the prospective husband—a devout man named Hasan—answer four questions. In the end she remained unmarried, free to devote all her thoughts to God.

"What will the Judge of the world say when I die? That I have come forth from the world a Muslim, or an unbeliever?"

Hasan answered, "This is among the hidden things known only to God. . . ."

Then she said, "When I am put in the grave and Munkar and Nakir [the angels who question the dead] question me, shall I be able to answer them [satisfactorily] or not?" He replied, "This is also hidden."

"When people are assembled at the Resurrection and the books are distributed, shall I be given mine in my right hand or my left?" . . . "This also is among the hidden things."

Finally she asked, "When mankind is summoned (at the Judgment), some to Paradise and some to Hell, in which group shall I be?" He answered, "This too is hidden, and none knows what is hidden save God—His is the glory and the majesty."

Then she said to him, "Since this is so, and I have these four questions with which to concern myself, how should I need a husband, with whom to be occupied?" (Smith 1928: 11).

It began when he went to see his teacher and, when asked who was at the door, answered, "I, the absolute divine truth"—calling himself by one of the 99 "wonderful names" of God. His teacher reprimanded him and warned against such apparent blasphemy. At its core, al-Hallaj's message was moral and intensely spiritual, but it was interpreted as suggesting that God takes the form of a human person (as Christians believe of Jesus)—a deeply shocking claim for most Muslims of his time. Whereas a less extreme predecessor, Bayazid Bistami, had preached annihilation of the mystic in God, al-Hallaj preached total identification of the lover with the beloved:

> I am He whom I love, and He whom I love is I.
> We are two spirits dwelling in one body.
> If thou seest me, you see Him; and if thou seest Him, you see us both (Nicholson 1931: 210–38).

After eight years in prison, al-Hallaj danced to the gallows, where he begged his executioners to "Kill me, O my trusted friends, for in my death is my life, and in my life is my death."

The Development of Sufism

The mystical life is a spiritual journey to God. The novice who wishes to embark on such an arduous journey must be guided by a master who becomes his or her spiritual parent. But as Sufism grew, many well-recognized masters attracted too many disciples to allow for a one-to-one relationship.

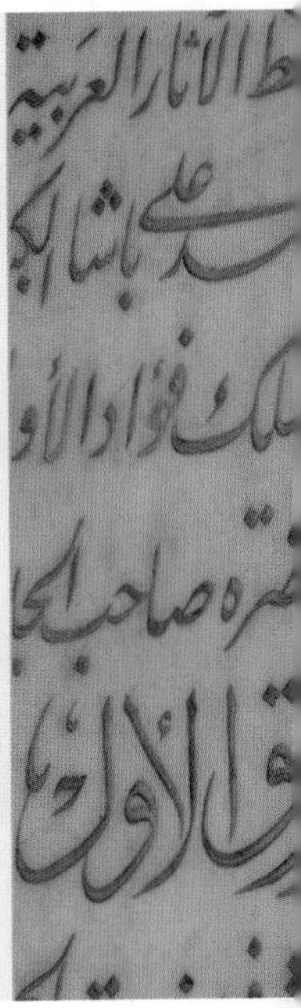

Document

Farid al-Din ‘Attar

*Farid al-Din ‘Attar lived in Iran at the turn of the thirteenth century. In this extract, the words “Ask not” echo a phrase that theologians use to express paradox—*bila kayf*, “without asking how”—but here they evoke the mystic’s sense of ineffability.*

His beauty if it thrill my heart
If thou a man of passion art
Of time and of eternity,
Of being and non-entity,
Ask not.

When thou hast passed the bases four,
Behold the sanctuary door;
And having satisfied thine eyes,
What in the sanctuary lies
Ask not. . . .
When unto the sublime degree
Thou hast attained, desist to be;
But lost to self in nothingness
And, being not, of more and less
Ask not.
(Arberry 1948: 32–3)

By the eleventh century, therefore, the ideas of the masters were being recorded and transmitted in writing. Perhaps the greatest work of the period was al-Ghazali’s *Revivification of the Religious Sciences*.

Roughly half a century after al-Ghazali, Shihab al-Din Suhrawardi (c. 1155–91) became known as the great master of illumination. Drawing on a verse in the Qur’an (24: 35) that speaks of God as the light of the heavens and the earth, he described a cosmos of light and darkness populated by countless angelic spirits.

The most important Sufi master of the thirteenth century was Muhyi al-Din Ibn ‘Arabi (1165–1240), who was born and educated in Muslim Spain and travelled widely in the Middle East before finally settling in Damascus. The central theme of his numerous writings is the “unity of being.” According to Ibn ‘Arabi, God’s essence remains in “blind obscurity,” but is manifested in the creation through an eternal process of self-disclosure. Thus even as human beings need God for their very existence, God also needs them in order to be known. Ibn ‘Arabi’s doctrine of the unity of being had many implications, among them the idea that, if God alone really is, then all ways ultimately lead to God. This means that all the world’s religions are in reality one. Ibn ‘Arabi says:

> My heart has become capable of every form: it is a pasture for gazelles and a convent for Christian monks,
> And a temple for idols, and the pilgrim’s Ka’ba, and the tables of the Torah and the book of the Koran.
> I follow the religion of Love, whichever way his camels take. My religion and my faith is the true religion (Nicholson 2002 [1914]: 75).

Ibn ‘Arabi remains one of the greatest mystic geniuses of all time.

Rumi

The most creative poet of the Persian language was Jalal al-Din Rumi (1207–73). Like Ibn 'Arabi, he was the product of a multicultural, multi-religious environment. Rumi was born in Balkh, Afghanistan, but as a child fled with his parents from the advancing Mongols. At last they settled in the city of Konya in central Anatolia (Turkey), a region that had been part of the Roman Empire.

In 1244 Rumi met a wandering Sufi named Shams of Tabriz. The two men developed a relationship so intimate that Rumi neglected his teaching duties because he could not bear to be separated from his friend. Yet in the end Shams disappeared, leaving Rumi to pour out his soul in heart-rending verses expressing his love for the "Sun" ("Shams" means "sun" in Arabic) of Tabriz.

Rumi's masterpiece is his *Mathnawi* ("Couplets"), a collection whose opening verses evoke the haunting melodies of the reed flute lamenting its separation from its reed bed. In stories, lyrical couplets, and at times even coarse tales of sexual impropriety, the *Mathnawi* depicts the longing of the human soul for God.

Sufi Orders and Saints

By the thirteenth century a number of Sufi fraternities were becoming institutionalized as religious orders, usually under the leadership of a famous *shaykh* (master). The validity of a *shaykh*'s claim to leadership depended on his or her spiritual genealogy, which had to lead back in an unbroken chain from the *shaykh*'s own master to an authority such as 'Ali, a Companion of the Prophet, or one of their successors. The *shaykhs* are similar to Christian saints in that the faithful pray to them for assistance and ascribe miracles to them, although they are recognized through popular acclaim rather than official canonization.

Devotional Practices

Although Sufis also perform the five daily prayers, their most characteristic practice is a ritual called the ***dhikr*** ("remembrance") of God, which may be private or congregational. The latter type is usually held before the dawn or evening prayers. It consists of the repetition of the name

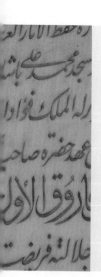

Document

Jalal al-Din Rumi

In this excerpt from the Mathnawi *(Book 3, 3901–3906) Rumi expresses the mystic's experience of union with God in terms of the dissolution of individual identity.*

I died as mineral and became a plant
I died as plant and rose to animal,
I died as animal and I was Man.
Why should I fear? When was I less by dying?
Yet once more I shall die as Man, to soar
With angels blest; but even from angelhood
I must pass on: all except God doth perish [Q. 28: 88].
When I have sacrificed my angel-soul,
I shall become what no mind e'er conceived.
Oh, let me not exist! for Non-existence
Proclaims in organ tones, "To him we shall return"
[Q. 2: 151] (Nicholson 1950: 103).

Document

Jalal al-Din Rumi, *Diwan*

Ghazal no. 1827

If anyone asks you about *houris* [heavenly beings], show your face and say, "Like this."
If anyone speaks to you about the moon, rise up beyond the roof and say, "Like this."
When someone looks for a fairy princess, show your face to him.
When someone talks of musk, let loose your tresses and say, "Like this."
If someone says to you, "How do clouds part from the moon?"
Undo your robe, button by button, and say, "Like this."
If he asks you about the Messiah, "How could he bring the dead to life?"
Kiss my lips before him and say, "Like this."
When someone says, "Tell me, what does it mean to be killed by love?"
Show my soul to him and say, "Like this."
If someone in concern asks you about my state,
Show him your eyebrow, bent over double, and say, "Like this."
The spirit breaks away from the body, then again it enters within.
Come, show the deniers, enter the house and say, "Like this."
In whatever direction you hear the complaint of a lover,
That is my story, all of it, by God, like this.
I am the house of every angel, my breast has turned blue like the sky—
Lift up your eyes and look with joy at heaven, like this.
I told the secret of union with the Beloved to the east wind alone.
Then, through the purity of its own mystery, the east wind whispered, "Like this."
Those are blind who say, "How can the servant reach God?"
Place the candle of purity in the hand of each and say, "Like this."
I said, "How can the fragrance of Joseph go from one city to the next?"
The fragrance of God blew from the world of his Essence and said, "Like this."
I said, "How can the fragrance of Joseph give sight back to the blind?"
Your breeze came and gave light to my eye: "Like this."
Perhaps Shams al-Din in Tabriz will show his generosity, and in his kindness display his good faith, like this (Chittick 2000: 89–90).

of Allah, or the *shahadah*, "There is no god except God" (*la ilaha illa Allah*). The *dhikr* is often accompanied by special bodily movements and, in some Sufi orders, by elaborate breathing techniques. Often the performance of the *dhikr* is what distinguishes the various Sufi orders from one another. In some popular orders it is a highly emotional ritual intended to stir devotees into a state of frenzy. By contrast, in the sober Naqshbandi order the *dhikr* is silent, an inward prayer of the heart.

Another distinctly Sufi practice is the *sama'* ("hearing" or "audition"), in which devotees simply listen to the hypnotic chanting of mystical poetry, accompanied by various musical instruments. As instrumental music is not allowed in the mosque, *sama'* sessions are usually held in a nearby hall, or at the shrine of a famous *shaykh*.

Dervishes at the Dervish Festival in Konya, Turkey (© Bruno Morandi / Robert Harding World Imagery / Corbis).

Music and dance are vital elements of devotional life for members of the Mevlevi (Mawlawi) order, named after Mawlana ("our master") Rumi. As practised by the Mevlevis—also known as the "Whirling Dervishes"—dance symbolizes the perfect motion of the stars, while the melodies that accompany the chanting echo the melodies of the heavenly spheres.

Sufism has always shown an amazing capacity for self-reform and regeneration. It was the Sufis who preserved Islamic learning and spirituality after 1258, when Baghdad fell to Mongol invaders, and Sufis who carried Islam to Africa and Asia. Today in the West it is primarily Sufi piety that is attracting non-Muslims to Islam.

Women and Sufism

Women have played an important role in the Sufi tradition, often serving as role models and teachers for men as well as women. This may help to explain part of the historical tension between orthodox Islam and Sufism. One of the most beloved stories about Rabi'a has her roaming the streets of Basra carrying a bucket of water and a flaming torch, ready to put out the fires of Hell and set fire to the gardens of Paradise so that people would worship God out of Love alone.

The Sufi tradition provided a rare outlet for Muslim women to be recognized as leaders. After Rabi'a, Sufi women could serve as *shaykahs* for mixed congregations, even though they were barred from the role of imam in such groups (women did serve as imams for other women, however). It's also worth noting that the shrines of Sufi saints, male or female, tend to attract more women than men, inverting the usual gender breakdown at mosques. It isn't hard to imagine how some men could feel threatened by a public space in which women are the dominant presence. Thus they might categorize Sufism as "un-Islamic" not because of its doctrines, but because of the power and privilege it accords to women.

Sufi women in Srinagar, Kashmir, pray outside the shrine of their order's founder, Shaikh Abdul Qadir Jilani, on the anniversary of his death (© FAYAZ KABLI / Reuters / Corbis).

The Spread of Islam

Islam, like Christianity, is a missionary religion. Muslims believe that their faith is intended for all humankind, and that the Qur'an confirms the scriptures that preceded it, notably the Torah and the Gospels. From the beginning, they interacted with people of other faiths, particularly Christians and Jews. As a religio-political power, therefore, Islam had to regulate its relations with non-Muslim citizens.

As People of the Book, Jews and Christians living in Muslim lands were free to practise their faith as long as they paid a tax that also guaranteed them physical and economic protection and exemption from military service. Legally such communities came to be known as ***dhimmis*** ("protected people"). The same designation was later extended to other communities with sacred scriptures, including Zoroastrians in Iran and Hindus in India.

In its first century Islam spread through conquest and military occupation. Much of the Byzantine and Roman world and all of the Sasanian domains came under Umayyad rule. In later centuries, politico-military regimes continued to contribute to Islam's dominance, especially in regions under Arab, Iranian, or Turkish rule.

Over time, however, the influence of mystics, teachers, and traders has reached farther and endured longer than the power of caliphs and conquerors. It was mainly through the efforts of individual Muslims that Islam spread to China, Southeast Asia, and East and West Africa. In modern times, migration and missionary activity have carried Islam to the Western hemisphere as well.

North Africa

After conquering Syria, Egypt, and Iran, the Muslims moved into North Africa in the second half of the seventh century. Before that time North Africa had been first an important Roman province and then an equally important home of Latin Christianity. With its indigenous Berber, Phoenician,

Map 5.1 Language and Culture in the Spread of Islam

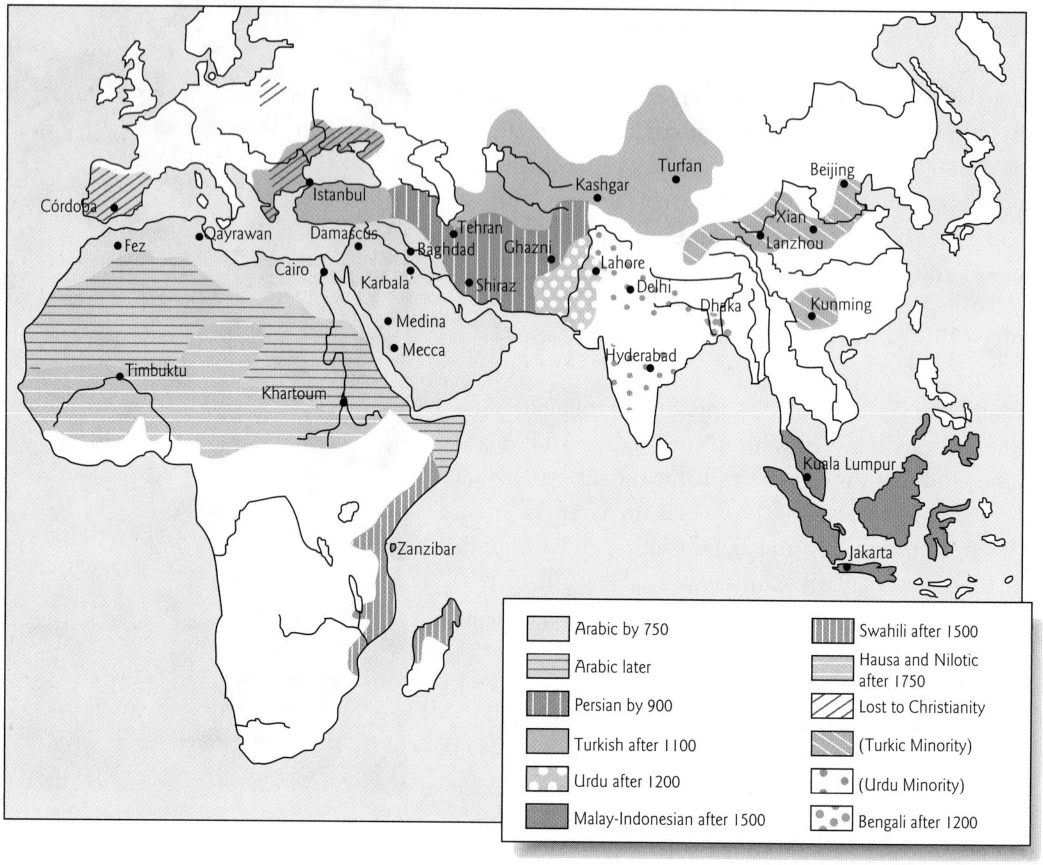

Roman, and Byzantine populations, the region has always maintained a distinct religious and cultural identity that reflects its ancient diversity.

The Umayyads established their capital in Damascus in 661. With the shift of the capital to Baghdad under the 'Abbasids in 762, the main orientation of the eastern Islamic domains became more Persian than Arab, more Asian than Mediterranean. Meanwhile, the centre of Arab Islamic culture shifted from Syria to the western Mediterranean: to Qayrawan in what is today Tunisia and to Cordoba in Spain, which rivalled Baghdad and Cairo in its cultural splendour. North African mystics, religious scholars, and philosophers were all instrumental in this achievement, and in the nineteenth and twentieth centuries, North African Sufi masters in particular played a crucial role in the struggle for independence, mobilizing resistance to the colonial regimes in Libya (Italian) and Algeria (French). Despite the deep influence of the French language and secular culture, North African popular piety still reflects the classical Islamic heritage.

Spain

When Arab forces arrived on the Iberian Peninsula in 711, Jews who had lived there for centuries were facing harsh restrictions imposed by rulers recently converted to Christianity. They welcomed the Arabs as liberators.

Document

María Rosa Menocal on *Convivencia*

An excerpt from Menocal's essay "Ten Years After: The Virtues of Exile":

In the destruction of the whole of the magnificent National Library . . . in Sarajevo in 1992, it now appears one very significant book was rescued, the famous manuscript called the Sarajevo Haggada. A Haggada is of course a prayer book that is, appropriately, the collection of prayers to be said on Passover, on the eve of exodus, but despite its name this gorgeous and elaborately illuminated manuscript . . . is not "Sarajevan" at all, nor "merely" Jewish, but rather "Spanish." And what can "Spanish" possibly mean . . . that is so different from what it seems to be in most other uses of this and other "identity" tags? Made in Spain in the late thirteenth century, it is, to put it most reductively, one of the many reflections of a Jewish culture that flourished . . . precisely because it adopted the virtues of exile and found its distinctly impure voice within an Arabic culture that was expansive and promiscuous and often exilic itself. It was thus altogether fitting that the precious object, the book that inscribes the story of the exile from Egypt, was carried out of Spain by members of the exiled Sephardic community in 1492: and remained, for the better part of the subsequent five hundred years, well-protected and cherished inside the Ottoman Empire, itself a remarkable example of the great good of empires, which learn how to absorb and tolerate and intermarry "identities," and which became, after 1492, the place of refuge of most Sephardic Jews and of many Andalusian Muslims. But the manuscript had to be rescued once again, during World War II, and it was when a Muslim curator in Sarajevo, attached as most Muslims are to the memory of Spain, saved that Spanish Haggada from Nazi butchers.

Surely, the morals of the story are perfectly clear: to understand the richness of our heritage we must be the guardians of the Haggada—the Muslim librarian who was not an Arab, of course, but who in saving the manuscript was fulfilling the best of the promises of Islamic Spain and Europe—and we must be the translators who reveal the exquisite ambivalence and sometimes painful conflict of identity of Judah Halevi, whose poetry is sung in so heavy an Arabic accent, and we must be the guardians and defenders of the interfaith marriage between the Christian girls who sang in corrupt Romance and the refined poets of the Arab courts. . . . We must, in other words, reject the falsehoods of nations in our work, and reveal, with the exquisite Ibn 'Arabi, the virtues of what he more simply calls love. "My heart can take on any form," he tells us, and then he simply names those temples at which he prays, the temples that inhabit him: the gazelle's meadow, the monks' cloister, the Torah, the Ka'ba. These are the temples whose priests we need to be, if we are to understand what any of this history is about, and it is only in them that there can be any future understanding of the complex "identity" of Europe in the Middle Ages. And almost undoubtedly in its present and future as well (Menocal 2003: 269–70).

With astonishing speed, Umayyad forces conquered al-Andalus, as they called southern Spain, and laid the foundations for an extraordinary culture. Arab men married local women, and a mixed but harmonious society developed that was Arab in language and expression and Arabo-Hispanic in spirit. Muslims, Christians, and Jews lived together in mutual tolerance for centuries before fanatical forces on all sides stifled one of the most creative experiments in interfaith living in human history. One of the greatest scholars of the *convivencia* ("shared life") between Muslims, Jews, and Christians in medieval Spain was the late María Rosa Menocal (see Document box).

Arab Spain produced some of the world's greatest minds, including not only Ibn 'Arabi and Ibn Rushd but the jurist and writer Ibn Hazm (994–1064) and the mystic-philosopher Ibn Masarrah (d. 931). Students came from as far away as Scotland to study Islamic theology, philosophy, and science in Cordoba and Toledo. It was in these centres of higher learning that the European Renaissance was conceived, and the great universities in which it was nurtured were inspired by their Arabo-Hispanic counterparts.

In Muslim Spain the Jews enjoyed a golden age of philosophy and science, mysticism, and general prosperity. Jewish scholars, court physicians, and administrators occupied high state offices and served as political and cultural liaisons between Islamic Spain and the rest of Europe. Arab learning penetrated deep into Western Europe and contributed directly to the rise of the West. In addition to symbiotic creativity, however, the 900-year history of Arab Spain (711–1609) included the tensions and conflicts typical of any multi-religious, multicultural society ruled by a minority regime. In the end, Islamic faith and civilization were driven out of Spain and failed to establish themselves anywhere else in Europe.

The Mosque–Cathedral of Cordoba began as a Visigoth church, was transformed into a medieval Muslim mosque, and is now a Catholic cathedral. Spanish Muslims have been lobbying the Spanish government and the Vatican to be allowed to perform prayers inside its walls (© Bettina Strenske / Alamy).

Sub-Saharan Africa

Islam may have arrived in sub-Saharan Africa as early as the eighth century, spread first by traders and then on a much larger scale by preachers. Finally jurists established the new faith as a religious and legal system. Sufi orders played an important part both in the spread of Islam and in its use as a motivation and framework for social and political reform.

To compete with traditional African religion, Muslim prayers had to prove themselves no less potent than Indigenous rain-making prayers or rituals of the Indigenous traditions. In the fourteenth century, the Moroccan Muslim traveller Ibn Battutah wrote a vivid account of the efforts of Muslim converts in the Mali Empire of West Africa to adapt their new faith to local traditions.

In East Africa Islam spread along the coast, carried mainly by mariners from Arabia and the Gulf trading in commodities and slaves. From the sixteenth century on, after Portuguese navigators rounded the southern cape of Africa, the cultural and political development of East African Islam was directly affected by European colonialism as well.

Unlike the populations of Syria, Iraq, Egypt, and North Africa, the peoples of East Africa did not adopt the Arabic language. But so much Arabic vocabulary penetrated the local languages that at least one-third of the Swahili vocabulary today is Arabic, and until recently most of the major African languages were written in the Arabic script.

An important element of East African society has been the Khoja community. Including both Sevener (Isma'ili) and Twelver (Imami) Shi'as, the Khojas emigrated from India to Africa in the mid-1800s. They have on the whole been successful business people with Western education and close relationships with Europe and North America. These relationships have been strengthened by the migration of many Khojas to Britain, the United States, and Canada.

Central Asia and Iran

Before the arrival of Islam, Central Asia had been a cosmopolitan culture in which Buddhism, Gnosticism, Judaism, and Christianity existed side by side in mutual tolerance with the Zoroastrianism of its Iranian rulers. The Arab conquest took more than a century, from 649 to 752.

In Iran itself, Persian culture flourished under the Samanid dynasty in the ninth and tenth centuries, as did *hadith* collectors, historians, philosophers, and religious scholars working in Arabic. Important centres of learning developed in the cities of Bukhara and Samarkand (in what is now Uzbekistan). While the Buyids promoted Shi'i Islam in the region that is now Iraq, the Samanids established the Sunni tradition in Central Asia. Among the great Sunni minds of tenth- and eleventh-century Central Asia were the philosopher Ibn Sina, the theologian al-Maturidi, the historian of religion Abu Rayhan al-Biruni, and the famous Persian poet Ferdowsi. In this intellectual environment, Islam was spread by persuasion rather than propaganda and war.

Early in the eleventh century, however, the Karakhanid Mongols conquered both Iran and Central Asia. The devastating consequences of the conquest were compounded by the loss of trade revenues when the traditional caravan routes were abandoned in favour of sea travel to India and China. Central Asia never recovered from the resulting decline in its culture and prosperity.

The Turks

As Turkic tribal populations from Central Asia moved into the Middle East, they were converted to Islam mainly by Sufi missionaries. Mahmud of Ghazna in Afghanistan (r. 998–1030), and his successors, the Ghaznavids, extended Muslim power in northern India. Mahmud was the first person to be called "sultan," a term that until then had referred to the authority of the state. Another Turkic family, the Seljuqs, prevailed in Iran and farther west a generation after Mahmud. After defeating the Byzantines in eastern Anatolia (modern Turkey) in 1071, the Seljuqs ruled until they were conquered by the Mongols in 1243.

In 1299 Osman I took over the caliphate from the 'Abbasids, establishing a dynasty that endured until 1924. Having absorbed former Seljuq territory in eastern Anatolia and taken western Anatolia from the Byzantines, they reached the height of their power in the sixteenth century, occupying the Balkans as far north as Vienna, the Levant (i.e., the Syro-Palestinian region), and all of northern Africa except Morocco. So vast was their empire that until the nineteenth century Christian Europe thought of Islamic culture as primarily Turkish.

China

The first written references to Islam in China do not appear till the seventeenth century, although the minaret of the mosque in Guangzhou (Canton) and inscriptions in the province of Fujian suggest that maritime trade with the Islamic world may have been under way as early as the eighth century. From the beginning, Persian and Arab merchants were allowed to trade freely so long as they complied with Chinese rules. But it was not until the thirteenth century that Muslim traders began settling in China in numbers large enough to support the establishment of mosques. Muslim communities prospered under the Mongol (1206–1368) and Ming (1368–1644) emperors. With the decline of the overland trade with Central Asia in the 1600s, however, Chinese Muslims were virtually cut off from the rest of Muslim *ummah*.

Unlike Buddhism, centuries earlier, Islam never came to be seen as culturally Chinese. The Uighurs—the Muslim population of Xinjiang (Chinese Turkestan), in the far northwest—are an identifiable minority in Chinese society, distinguished by their Turkic language as well as their religion. Yet even the Chinese-speaking Muslims in the eastern cities of Han China are set apart by their avoidance of pork—a staple of the Chinese diet. The presence of *halal* (ritually acceptable) restaurants and butcher shops is a sure sign of a Muslim neighbourhood.

Chinese Muslims experienced their share of repression under the Communist regime, particularly during the Cultural Revolution of 1966–76. Although the overall situation for Muslims has improved since then, Uighur demands for independence have been severely suppressed, and Uighur nationalists are often called "terrorists." Today there are approximately 50 million Muslims in China. Like other religious communities in contemporary China, they face an uncertain future, but their ethnic base in the country's Central Asian interior is not likely to disappear soon.

South Asia

Islam arrived early in India, carried by traders and Arab settlers. Umayyad armies began moving into the region in the early eighth century, and since then Islam has become an integral part of Indian life and culture.

The Muslim conquest of India was a long process. In the second half of the tenth century the city of Ghazni, in what is today Afghanistan, became the base from which the armies of the sultan Mahmud of Ghazna and his successors advanced over the famous Khyber Pass onto the North Indian Plain. By the fourteenth century all but the far south had come under Muslim rule.

For Muslim rulers, maintaining and expanding their power over a large Hindu population meant continuous warfare. For Hindus, the Muslim regime was undoubtedly repressive; yet Indian Islam developed a unique and rich religious and intellectual culture.

India was something new in the history of Islam's territorial expansion. For the first time, the majority of the conquered population did not convert to the new faith. In ancient Arabia Islam had been able to suppress and supplant polytheism; but in India it had to coexist with a culture that remained largely polytheistic. At the same time Islam was something new to India. In a land where people often had multiple religious allegiances, and community boundaries were fluid, Islam's exclusive devotion to the one God and its clear delineation of community membership represented a dramatically different way of life.

Today, India, Pakistan, and Bangladesh together have the largest Muslim population in the world. The Muslims of India alone number between 100 and 120 million. Even so, they are a minority whose future appears bleak in the face of rising Hindu nationalism, especially following the election of Narendra Modi as prime minister in 2014.

Southeast Asia

Southeast Asia, when Islam arrived there, was home to a wide variety of languages and cultures, and its religious life had been strongly influenced by the Hindu and Buddhist traditions. These influences can still be seen in the ancient Hindu culture on the island of Bali and the great Buddhist stupa complex of Borobudur in Indonesia.

There is no evidence for the presence of Islam in Southeast Asia before the tenth century. But Yemeni traders are reported to have sailed into the islands of the Malay archipelago before the time of the Prophet, and this suggests that the Malay people may have been exposed to Islam at an early date. Scattered evidence from Chinese and Portuguese travellers, as well as passing references by Ibn Battutah, indicate that Islam had spread widely in Southeast Asia by the 1400s. Two centuries later, when British and Dutch trading companies arrived in the region, Islam was the dominant religion and culture of the Malay archipelago.

Muslim communities in small states ruled by sultans are widely reported by the thirteenth century. The earliest of these was Pasai, a small kingdom in northern Sumatra. Some of the states that emerged in the fifteenth century gained considerable prominence both culturally and economically, and Muslim religious scholars from India were attracted to them. In an effort to expand and strengthen his realm, the sultan Iskandar Muda of Acheh (r. 1607–36) became the first Muslim ruler in Southeast Asia to establish alliances with European powers. Acheh also produced noteworthy Islamic legal scholarship, which is still used in the Malay world today.

In Southeast Asia even more than elsewhere, Sufi orders played a crucial part in the process of Islamization. They were also prominent in later political and social struggles for reform and liberation. In the late nineteenth and early twentieth centuries, reform movements in the Middle East inspired similar movements in Indonesia and other countries of the region. Today Islam is the majority religion in Malaysia, Brunei, and Indonesia (the largest Muslim country in the world today, with at least 180 million Muslims), and there are Muslim minorities in all the other countries of Southeast Asia. Today Southeast Asia can claim at least one-third of the world's Muslims.

Cultural Expressions

Islamic Architecture

The functions of the mosque include not only prayer, implied in the Arabic *masjid* ("kneeling place"), but other community activities, implied in the Arabic *jami'* ("gatherer"). Early mosques functioned as treasuries, where financial records were kept, as well as law courts and educational centres. In time these activities moved into their own buildings, but the functions of public assembly and prayer continued to dictate the architectural form of mosques, which is also reflected in two other structures with religious functions: the *madrasah* or religious school, and the tomb or mausoleum.

Every mosque includes four essential features: a fountain for washing upon entering; a large area for kneeling and prostration in prayer; a pulpit from which the leader of Friday noon worship delivers the sermon; and an imageless niche in the wall closest to Mecca, indicating the direction of prayer. Not part of the earliest mosques in Arabia but characteristic of Islam in many places is the minaret, the tower from which the call to prayer is delivered.

Islamic Art

Islamic art is rich, elaborate, and even exuberant. Three elements are particularly distinctive: calligraphy (the decorative use of script and units of text); geometrical decoration (particularly the interlaced motifs called arabesques in the West); and floral designs (especially common in Iran).

Focus

Mohamed Zakariya

Mohamed Zakariya (b. 1942) is the most celebrated Islamic calligrapher in the United States. Born in California, he saw Islamic calligraphy for the first time in the window of an Armenian carpet store. Travelling to Morocco in his late teens, he became fascinated with Islam and Islamic calligraphy. On his return to the United States he converted to Islam.

He made other journeys to North Africa and the Middle East, and spent some time studying manuscripts in the British Museum in London. After studying with the Egyptian calligrapher Abdussalam Ali-Nour, Zakariya in 1984 became a student of the Turkish master calligrapher Hasan Celebi. In 1988 he received his diploma from Celebi at the Research Center for Islamic History, Art and Culture in Istanbul, the first American to achieve this honour. He received his second diploma, in the *ta'lik* script, from the master calligrapher Ali Alparslan in 1997.

Zakariya's work has been displayed in various museums and galleries, and is in a number of private collections. He was the artist commissioned by the United States Postal Service to design its Eid stamp, which made its debut on 1 September 2001.

In addition to teaching calligraphy according to the Ottoman method, Zakariya writes contemporary instructional material and translates classic texts. In 2009, he was commissioned by US President Barack Obama to create a piece of calligraphy that was presented to King Abdulaziz of Saudi Arabia. Mohamed Zakariya's work shows that American Islam has become an integral part of the Muslim world. Now students from that world travel to the United States to study with an American master of an ancient Islamic art.

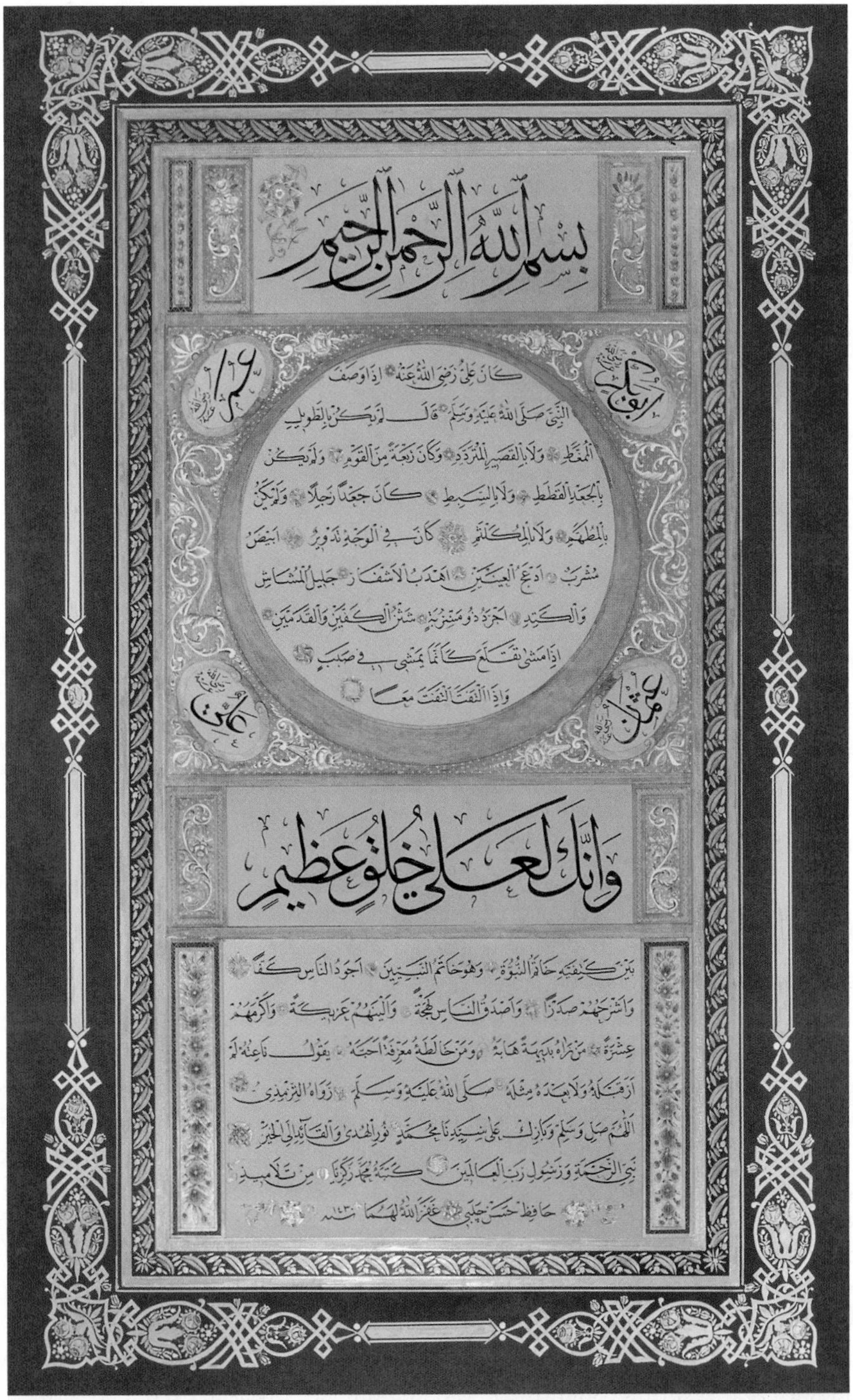

A modern hilye (calligraphic description) of the Prophet by Mohamed Zakariya. The top line reads "In the name of God. Universally Merciful. Specifically Merciful" and the circular section is surrounded by the names of the first four caliphs (courtesy of Mohamed Zakariya).

All three are more abstract than pictorial and therefore point beyond themselves in a way that pictorial images may not. Design using these elements captures the viewer's attention and directs it to the larger structure on which the decoration appears, whether a page of the Qur'an, a prayer rug, or the tiled entrance of a mosque. Religious content is most obvious in the decorative use of calligraphy in mosques, where the texts used are often passages from the Qur'an, but even the craft items sold in bazaars are often adorned with some of the 99 "wonderful names" of God.

Three-dimensional sculpture is prohibited in Islam, but the two-dimensional representation of living creatures is highly developed. Some Persian carpets include animals in their garden scenes. Persian and Indian manuscripts are illustrated with miniature paintings of rulers and legendary heroes. Among Iranian Shi'a, portraits of 'Ali are a focus of popular piety. While representations of the Prophet himself are avoided, his legendary steed Buraq is portrayed in popular art as a winged horse with a human head; this is a common motif on trucks and buses in Afghanistan and Pakistan.

Towards the Modern World

Islam and Modernity

Throughout the history of Islam, many Muslims have sought to reform the rest of the *ummah*. An external impetus has been Muslim interaction with Western Christendom. The first major Western challenges to Muslim power were the crusades. Determined to liberate Jerusalem from Muslim domination, the armies of the first crusade captured the Holy City in 1099 after massacring its Jewish and Muslim inhabitants. For nearly two centuries, Frankish Christian kingdoms existed side by side with Muslim states along the eastern Mediterranean, sometimes peacefully, but most often at war.

In the end most of the crusaders returned home, and those who remained were assimilated. But the spirit of the crusades lived on, as did the distorted images of Islam and Muslims that the crusaders took home with them. The equally distorted images of Christianity and Western Christendom that the crusaders left in Muslim lands have also lived on, and have been reinforced and embellished in response to Western imperialism.

Pre-modern Reform Movements

Common to all reform movements has been the call to return to pristine *islam*, the *islam* of the Prophet's society and the normative period of his "rightly guided" successors. Among those who championed this cause was the religious scholar Ibn Taymiyyah (1263–1328), a jurist of the conservative Hanbali school who waged a relentless campaign against Shi'ism, Sufism, and the blind imitation of established legal traditions, while fighting to revive the practice of *ijtihad*. Perhaps his most famous *fatwa* was one that allowed Muslims in the city of Mardin (in what is now Turkey) to wage war against the occupying Mongols, even though the latter had converted to Islam after their conquest of Baghdad. In so doing, Ibn Taymiyyah contradicted the standard teaching that Muslims should not wage war against Muslim rulers. The "Mardin fatwa" was to exert a powerful influence on subsequent reform movements.

Some four centuries later, Ibn Taymiyyah's ideas became the basis of an uncompromising revivalist movement that, significantly, began in the highlands of Arabia, the birthplace of Islam. The founder of the Wahhabi movement, Muhammad Ibn 'Abd al-Wahhab (1703–92), allied himself with Muhammad 'Al Sa'ud, a local tribal prince, on the understanding that the prince would exercise political power and protect the nascent movement, which would hold religious authority. This arrangement continues today: the kingdom of Saudi Arabia is a Wahhabi state, ruled by the descendants of 'Al Sa'ud.

The Wahhabis preached a strictly egalitarian Islam based on a direct relationship between the worshipper and God. They repudiated the widely cherished hope that the Prophet and other divinely favoured individuals would intercede with God on behalf of the pious. The Wahhabis regarded the veneration of saints, including the Prophet, as a form of idolatry, and even called for the destruction of the sacred black stone of the Ka'ba, on the grounds that it stood as an idol between faithful Muslims and their Lord.

The Wahhabis waged a violent campaign aimed at purging Muslim society of what they considered un-Islamic beliefs and practices. They destroyed the Prophet's tomb in Medina and levelled the graves of his Companions. They attacked the Shi'a's sacred cities of Najaf and Karbala, massacred their inhabitants, and demolished the shrines of 'Ali and his son Husayn. They also went on a rampage in Arab cities, desecrating the tombs of Sufi saints and destroying their shrines.

The basic ideals of Wahhabism have appealed to many revivalists and played an especially significant role in provoking reform efforts within eighteenth- and nineteenth-century Sufism (see below). In recent years, extremist groups influenced by Wahhabi ideology, including Al-Qaeda and the Taliban, have transformed the internal struggle to "purify" Islam into an external war against all perceived enemies, Muslim and non-Muslim alike.

Modern Revivalism and Reform

As the British Empire extended its rule in India and European influence in the Muslim world grew, Muslim thinkers became resentful of the political inertia into which the *ummah* had apparently fallen. Even so, many parts of the Islamic world did experience intellectual, religious, and cultural renewal in the nineteenth century.

In the Middle East, the Arab renaissance was to a large degree stimulated by the developments in the West. Undermined first by the Protestant Reformation and then by the Enlightenment, religious faith and institutions were giving way to secularism and romantic nationalism—ideas that were attractive to many Muslims. As a consequence, nationalistic identities came to compete with Islamic identities and in some cases even supersede them.

Africa

In Africa, meanwhile, a number of Sufi movements arose in the nineteenth century, partly in response to Wahhabi criticisms and partly in reaction against European colonial encroachment on Muslim domains. Several of them succeeded in establishing their own states for some period of time, including the movements led by Usman ('Uthman) dan Fodio (the Sokoto caliphate, 1809–1903) in Nigeria, Muhammad al-Sanusi (the Sanusi movement, 1837–1969) in Libya, and Muhammad Ahmad al-Mahdi (the Mahdi rebellion, 1881–9) in Sudan. Common to all these movements was an activist ideology of ***jihad*** (Arabic for "struggle"), a concept that has two components. Inner *jihad* is the struggle to make oneself more Islamic, while outer *jihad* is the struggle to make one's society more Islamic.

These Sufi movements exerted a lasting influence on most subsequent reformers. In North Africa in particular, Sufi *shaykhs* and religious scholars helped to preserve their countries' religious, linguistic, and cultural identity while in some cases spearheading struggles for independence from French and Italian colonial rule. In the nineteenth century, for example, the Sufi *shaykh* Abdelkader ('Abd al-Qadir) played an important political role in the long campaign for Algeria's independence. King Muhammad V of Morocco, who negotiated his country's independence from France in 1956, was himself a *shaykh* and a "venerable descendant" of the Prophet. And the grandson of al-Sanusi, Idris I, ruled Libya as king from independence in 1951 until he was overthrown in a coup led by Muammar Gaddafi in 1969.

The al-Sanusi movement in Libya promoted reform and Muslim unity across North and West Africa. By contrast, al-Mahdi in Sudan saw himself as God's representative on Earth and set out to establish a social and political order modelled on that of the Prophet. He believed the Ottoman–Egyptian occupation of Sudan to be un-Islamic and waged *jihad* against it. In 1885 he triumphed over the Egyptian forces and established an Islamic state based on strict application of the *shari'ah* law. Although al-Mahdi himself died within a few months, the regime lasted until 1889, when it was overthrown by British and Egyptian forces.

The Indian Subcontinent

The Mughal dynasty founded by Babur in 1526 reached its peak under his grandson Akbar (r. 1556–1605). With its decline in the seventeenth century, demands for reform along traditional lines intensified. One of the strongest voices was that of Ahmad Sirhindi (1564–1624), who called for a return to the *shari'ah*, regarded Sufis as deviants, and condemned Ibn 'Arabi in particular as an infidel.

The most important Islamic reform movement on the subcontinent was begun by Shah Wali Allah of Delhi (1702–62). Although he was a disciple of Ibn 'Abd al-Wahhab, he was a Sufi himself, and instead of rejecting Sufism he sought to reform it. He also sought to reconcile Shi'a–Sunni differences, which had been (and sometimes are still) a source of serious friction. His grandson Ahmad Barelwi transformed that program into a *jihad* against British rule and the Sikhs. In 1826 he established an Islamic state based on the *shari'ah* and adopted the old caliphal title "commander of the faithful." At the opposite end of the spectrum of reaction to British rule was Sayyid Ahmad Khan (1817–98). Like all reformers, Khan called for modern *ijtihad* or rethinking of the Islamic heritage, but unlike most of them he rejected *hadith* tradition as a legitimate basis for modern Islamic living. He founded the Aligarh Muhammadan College (later Aligarh Muslim University), where he attempted to apply his ideas in a modern Western-style program of education.

Ahmadiyah

The career of Mirza Ghulam Ahmad (1835–1908) reflects the social and religious diversity of the Punjab in the 1880s—a time of various movements for renewal of Hindu and Muslim identity, as well as a growing emphasis on self-definition among Sikhs. The author of several volumes of commentary on the Qur'an, in 1889 he accepted from his followers the homage reserved for a prophet. Ahmadis, as they are known, have also revered him as the *mujaddid* (renewer) ushering in the fourteenth century of Islam, the Mahdi of Shi'i expectation, the tenth incarnation of the Hindu deity Vishnu, and the returning Messiah of Christianity (they also maintain that Jesus did not die in Palestine but went to Afghanistan, in search of the ten lost tribes of Israel, and was buried in Srinagar, Kashmir).

The movement has spread widely. Including 4 million in Pakistan, Ahmadis now total at least 10 million, or 1 per cent of the world's Muslims. As early as 1891, orthodox Muslim authorities rejected Ghulam Ahmad's claim to prophethood, and in Pakistan (where the Ahmadis relocated their base in 1947) they have been prohibited from calling themselves Muslims or using Islamic vocabulary in their worship and preaching.

Thus Ahmadiyah's future may lie in its diaspora. Missions have been notably successful in lands not historically Islamic, such as West Africa, the Caribbean, and the overseas English-speaking world. The largest mosque in North America, opened in 1992, is the Ahmadi Baitul Islam mosque in the Toronto suburb of Maple, Ontario.

Muhammad Iqbal

The ideas of Sayyid Ahmad Khan and his fellows culminated in the philosophy of Muhammad Iqbal (1876–1938), the greatest Muslim thinker of modern India. Central to Iqbal's work is the idea of an inner spirit that moves human civilization. Iqbal argued that Western science and philosophy were rightfully part of the Islamic heritage and should be integrated into a fresh *Reconstruction of Religious Thought in Islam* (the title of his only major work in English, published in the 1930s). A poet as well as a philosopher, Iqbal frequently repeated this call for a rethinking of Islamic faith and civilization in his verse.

Recent Developments

Twentieth-Century Secularism

Many of the early Muslim reformers were at once liberal modernists and traditional thinkers. For this reason they are known as *salafis*: reformers who sought to emulate the example of "the pious forebears." But the ideal of equilibrium between tradition and modernity disappeared by the 1920s. Thereafter, Islamic reform meant one of three things: revivalism, reasoned defence (apologetics), or secularism.

Following the Ottoman defeat in the First World War, a young army officer named Mustafa Kemal Atatürk (1881–1938) launched a movement for national liberation. As the first president of the new Republic of Turkey (1923) he abolished the caliphate, transforming what had been a traditional Islamic domain into a modern secular state. Although for centuries the caliphate had been a shadowy office without any power, it had nevertheless embodied the only hope for a viable pan-Islamic state. Its disappearance had far-reaching consequences for Islamic political thought.

Atatürk banned Sufi orders, dissolved Islamic religious institutions, replaced the Arabic alphabet (in which Turkish had traditionally been written) with the Latin, and mounted a nationwide campaign for literacy in the new script. His express aim was to westernize the Turkish republic. He encouraged the adoption of Western-style clothing and even banned the fez—the brimless conical red hat that, like all traditional Muslim headgear, allowed the faithful to touch their foreheads to the ground during prayer. Though Atatürk's ideology has remained the official state policy in Turkey, his program largely failed. Today the country has its own powerful revivalist movements which are often in tension with the government.

Twentieth-Century Islamic Revivalism

Islamic reform movements in general seemed to experience a loss of nerve after the First World War and the break-up of the Ottoman Empire. Despite their differences, the various reform movements of the nineteenth century shared a dynamic spirit of progress. The premature stifling of that spirit may have reflected the lack of a coherent program of reform that post-colonialist Muslim thinkers could build on. In any event, the liberal reform movements of the nineteenth century were transformed into traditional revivalist movements in the twentieth.

On the eve of Atatürk's abolition of the caliphate in 1924, Muhammad Rashid Rida published an important treatise on the Imamate, or Supreme Caliphate, in which he argued for the establishment of an Islamic state that would be ruled by a council of jurists or religious scholars. Such a state would recognize nationalistic sentiments and aspirations, but would subordinate them to the religio-political interests of the larger community. Rida's Islamic revivalism and Arab nationalism came to represent two major trends in twentieth-century Muslim thinking, and his plan for a council of jurists would be implemented in Iran following the revolution of 1978–9.

Contemporary Revivalist Movements

It remains the ideal of Islamic reform to establish a transnational Islamic caliphate. Yet the reality has been a proliferation of local movements reflecting local needs and ideas.

Common to most revivalist movements after 1950 was the ideal of an all-inclusive and self-sufficient Islamic order. This ideal had its roots in the Society of Muslim Brothers (Jam'iyat al-Ikhwan al-Muslimin), founded in 1928 by an Egyptian schoolteacher named Hasan al-Banna. The aim of the Muslim Brothers was to establish a network of Islamic social, economic, and political institutions through which the total Islamization of society might in time be achieved. Working through institutions such as schools, banks, cooperatives, and clinics, they penetrated all levels of Egyptian society.

The political and militaristic aspects of revivalism also had their beginnings in the Muslim Brothers, particularly after the assassination of the generally peaceful al-Banna in 1949. He was succeeded by hardline leaders who advocated active *jihad* against the Egyptian state system, which they regarded as un-Islamic. Among the products of this ideology were the young officers, led by Gamal Abdel Nasser, behind the 1952 socialist revolution that abolished monarchical rule in Egypt.

A charismatic proponent of Arab nationalism in the 1950s and 1960s, Nasser nevertheless clashed with the Muslim Brothers, and in the mid-1960s he imprisoned, exiled, or executed most of their leaders. Among the latter was Sayyid Qutb, who has been claimed as an inspiration by modern Islamist groups. As a theoretician he influenced Islamist ideology; and as an activist he provided younger militants with a model of martyrdom to emulate.

Following the Arab defeat in the six-day Arab–Israeli war of June 1967 and Nasser's death three years later, the Muslim Brothers were suppressed under Anwar Sadat and his successor Hosni Mubarak and superseded by more powerful revivalist movements, some of which advocated the use of violence. Although the Brotherhood spread in other Arab countries, it was more influential on the level of ideology than of social action until the "Arab Spring" of 2011. A similar organization, the Jama'at-i Islami (Islamic Society), was established in 1941 by Mawlana Sayyid Abu al-A'la Mawdudi. Like al-Banna, Mawdudi was committed to pan-Islamic unity, but (also like al-Banna) he concentrated his efforts on his own community—in this case the Muslims of India and (after 1947) Pakistan. The influence of both organizations spread far beyond their original homes.

While most contemporary revivalist movements, including the two noted above, have been open to modern science and technology, they have rejected many Western values and practices—including capitalist democracy, women's liberation, and the free mixing of the sexes—as decadent. Therefore, unlike the nineteenth-century reformers who looked to the West for ideas and models, contemporary revivalists have insisted on finding Islamic alternatives. Mawdudi, for example, wishing to distinguish his Islamic state model from Western democracies, described it as a "theo-democracy" based on the broad Qur'anic principle of consultation and the *shari'ah* law.

State Islam and the Islamic Revolution

Following a coup in 1969, Gaafar Mohamed el-Nimeiri made *shari'ah* the law in Sudan. The result was a bloody conflict between the Muslim north and the generally Christian south that has reduced a formerly rich agricultural country to famine; although South Sudan became an independent republic in 2011, violent clashes continue along the border. Similarly in Pakistan, which for three decades had been a constitutionally Islamic but modern state, the 1977 introduction of *shari'ah* by General Mohammad Zia-ul-Haq led to violent social and political conflict.

In almost every Muslim country there is at least one revivalist movement advocating some form of Islamic state. In Malaysia and Indonesia, the governments themselves espouse Islamic national policies in order to silence extremist demands for radical reform. Nevertheless, in most Muslim countries feelings continue to run high between Islamic movements made up of educated middle-class men and women and despotic regimes determined to hold on to power at any cost.

On 19 December 2010, a Tunisian named Mohamed Bouazizi set himself on fire to protest police and government corruption that made it impossible for him to sell fruits and vegetables from a cart without paying bribes to officials. His self-immolation sparked widespread protests, which led to the overthrow of the Tunisian president. These dramatic events sparked protests in Algeria and Egypt. The largest coordinated protests began in Cairo in late January 2011. On 11 February Egyptian President Hosni Mubarak stepped down, and in 2012 Mohammed Morsi of the Muslim Brotherhood was announced as the new Egyptian president. He served for almost exactly a year before being removed by the Egyptian military on 3 July 2013. Among the other countries swept up in the "Arab Spring" were Syria, Yemen, Bahrain, and Libya. On 18 March 2011 the UN Security Council authorized a resolution to protect civilians under attack in Libya, and the following day the first Western air strike was launched against the military regime of Muammar Gaddafi. He was killed in October 2011, and a new assembly was elected in July 2012. The violence in Syria continues as of late 2014.

In such highly charged social and political conditions, religion serves as a powerful moral, social, and spiritual expression of discontent—not only for Islamic activists, but for a broad spectrum of the community as well. It was on precisely such mass discontent that Imam Ruhollah Khomeini (1901–89) and his fellow Shi'i *mullahs* (religio-legal functionaries) built the Islamic Republic of Iran, in which social, political, economic, and religious life are all controlled by a religious hierarchy under a supreme Ayatollah (*ayat Allah*, "sign of God").

Throughout the long period of secular Shi'i rule in Iran (1501–1979), the authority of the religious *'ulama'* operated in more or less continuous tension with the secular authorities. This tension was greatly increased during the reign of the US-supported Shah Mohammad Reza Pahlavi, who sought to westernize the country and obscure its Islamic identity by emphasizing its pre-Islamic cultural past. In 1963, during the Muharram observances of Husayn's martyrdom, matters came to a head when the Shah's dreaded secret police ruthlessly put down mass demonstrations led by the *'ulama'*. Khomeini, already a prominent religious leader, was sent into exile, where he elaborated his theory according to which the jurist should have all-embracing authority in the community. In 1979 Khomeini returned to Iran at the head of the Islamic revolution. The Islamic republic he founded has had a turbulent history, including an eight-year war with Iraq (1980–8), out of which it emerged greatly weakened but still intact. Pro-democracy protests and challenges to the authority of the *'ulama'* came to international attention with the controversy that surrounded the 2009 election and the protests that erupted in March 2011.

Islam in Western Europe

The Islamic presence in western Europe began with the establishment of Umayyad rule in southern Spain in 711. Commercial, political, and cultural relations were initiated with both Latin and Byzantine states, but medieval Europe would not tolerate a permanent Muslim community on its soil. The campaign to drive the Muslims out of Spain succeeded in 1492 with the conquest of Granada. As a result, the Muslim presence in western Europe today is a relatively recent phenomenon.

In the twentieth century some Muslims migrated to Europe from various colonies as students, visitors, and merchants. Many also went as menial labourers and factory workers, especially after 1945. The majority of these post-war immigrants were men ranging in age from their teens to their forties.

The ethnic makeup of the Muslim communities in Europe was largely determined by colonial ties. Muslims from the French colonies in North Africa, for example, went to France. Indian and, later, Pakistani and Bangladeshi Muslims tended to go to Britain. Those from Turkey and the former Soviet Turkic republics went to Germany and the Netherlands, while Bosnians went to Austria. These patterns, established early in the twentieth century, have continued despite many restrictions.

Muslim communities in Europe tend to reflect ethnic and linguistic rather than sectarian affiliations. In recent years hundreds of mosques and cultural centres have been established in Europe, and Muslim communities have become a dynamic religious and intellectual force in European society. France and Britain no longer confine Muslims to the status of "guest workers," as most other European countries do. Yet even there, the long histories of European racism, ethnocentrism, and colonialism have ensured that many Muslims continue to be treated as second-class citizens. This has created serious problems.

After the Islamic revolution of 1978–9, many Iranians immigrated to Europe, adding yet another layer of ethnic and religious diversity to European Muslim society. The 15-year Lebanese civil war of 1975–90, as well as the disturbances in other Arab countries, including the Gulf War of 1991, also sent many political and economic refugees to the West. Meanwhile, intermarriage and conversion have infused new blood into Western Muslim communities.

Many Muslims born in Europe to foreign-born parents are assimilating. On the other hand, most European countries have taken steps to limit immigration, and since the mid-1980s some of them have repatriated some of their Muslim immigrants. Such actions may have been prompted in part by economic considerations, but also perhaps by nationalistic fear that Muslim immigrants might alter the social and ethnic character of these countries. In 2009, for example, Swiss citizens supported a ban on minarets for new mosques—even though only four of the approximately 150 mosques and Islamic centres in Switzerland have minarets. At the same time, European discrimination against ethnic minorities and the Islamic awakening precipitated by the Iranian revolution have made Muslims more aware of their own religious and cultural identity.

Islam in North America

When the first Muslims arrived on American shores is a matter of conjecture. Suggestions that Muslims from Spain and West Africa may have sailed to America before Columbus should not be discounted, although they have not been proven. Scattered records point to the presence of Muslims in Spanish America before 1550, and it is very likely that the Inquisition drove many to flee to America soon after 1492.

In the sixteenth and seventeenth centuries, hundreds of thousands of Africans were taken as slaves to the Spanish, Portuguese, and British colonies in the Americas. Although the majority were from West Africa, Muslims made up at least 20 per cent of the total. And among the slaves taken from Senegal, Nigeria, and the western Sudan, the majority were Muslims, many of whom were well educated in Arabic and the religious sciences. Some were able to preserve their faith and heritage, and some tried to maintain contact with Muslims in their home areas, but many others were quickly absorbed into American society, adopting their masters' religious affiliations and even their family names.

Islamic customs and ideas can still be traced in the African-American community, and today efforts are underway to reconstruct the story behind them. Beginning in the late 1800s, African-Americans made conscious efforts to recover their Islamic heritage. In the early 1930s, when Elijah Muhammad (born Elijah Poole, 1897–1975) founded the Nation of Islam in America (see Chapter 12), he saw Islam as a religion of black people only, misrepresenting the universalistic and non-racial nature of Islam. But his sons and successors, after travelling in the Muslim world and observing the international and multiracial character of the *hajj* pilgrimage, have moved closer to classical Islam. African-American Muslims often refer to themselves as Bilalians, after Bilal, an African Companion of the Prophet. Islam continues to be the fastest-growing religion in America, particularly among African-Americans.

Before the revival of Islam in the African-American community early in the twentieth century, small numbers of Muslims travelled to Canada and the United States, mainly from Syria and Lebanon. These early immigrants were uneducated men who intended only to work in North America for a few years and then return home, but many married local women and were soon completely assimilated.

The first Muslim missionary in America was Muhammad Alexander Webb, a jeweller, newspaper editor, and diplomat who converted to Islam in 1888, while travelling in India. On his return, Webb created an Islamic propaganda movement, wrote three books on Islam, and founded a periodical entitled *The Muslim World* (not to be confused with the academic journal of the same name). He travelled widely to spread the new faith and established Islamic study circles or Muslim brotherhoods in many northeastern and midwestern American cities. With his death in 1916, however, his movement died as well.

The numbers of Muslim immigrants to North America increased markedly during the twentieth century. Most were of South Asian origin. Many were students who later chose to stay, or well-educated professionals hoping to find better opportunities. But others came to escape persecution in their homelands on account of their religious or political activities. Interestingly, many recent newcomers who arrived as staunch anti-Western revivalists soon forgot their hostility and adapted to North American life.

Although these and other Muslim immigrants may have moderated their political convictions, they retained their religious zeal, which they put to good use in the service both of their own community and of the society at large. They have played a crucial role in preserving the Islamic identity of fellow immigrants and promoting a better understanding of Islam through media activities and academic meetings.

The first mosque in the US was built in 1915 by Albanian Muslims in Maine; another followed in Connecticut in 1919. Other mosques were established in the 1920s and 1930s in South Dakota and Iowa. In 1928, Polish Tatars built a mosque in Brooklyn, New York, which is still in use. The first Canadian mosque was built in Edmonton, Alberta, in 1938, and a number of smaller towns in Alberta also have Muslim communities. In Toronto, the first Muslim organization was the Albanian Muslim Society of Toronto, founded in 1956; in 1968 this organization purchased an unused Presbyterian church and converted it into a mosque. Toronto currently has Canada's largest concentration of Muslims.

The exact numbers of Muslims in North America are unclear. The 2001 Canadian census counted almost 600,000 Muslims, making Islam the second-largest religion in the country, and in 2011, the National Household Survey counted over 1 million Canadian Muslims. The US has not had a religious census since 1936, but its Muslim population today is estimated at between 6 and 7 million. Whatever the numbers may be, Islam is no longer an exotic rarity in North America: it is the faith of many people's co-workers and neighbours.

Issues of gender equality and sexual diversity are rarely discussed in the largest North American Muslim political and religious organizations (such as the Islamic Society of North America), partly because those groups tend to emphasize traditional interpretations of Islam, and partly because they have been preoccupied with matters such as community-building, immigration policy, discrimination, and (to some extent) foreign policy. But as the size of their constituencies has grown, and the range of perspectives within those constituencies has increased, there has been growing pressure to address issues involving gender and sexuality.

Diasporic communities in large urban centres tend to become more open to questions about traditional religious and cultural ideas as they become more deeply rooted (or "assimilated") in their new societies. As contact with the "host" community intensifies, those who question traditional ideas are likely to have much easier access to information and networks of like-minded people than their counterparts in the home country. Some will "exit" their communities of origin and seek full assimilation to the dominant society; but in large communities particularly, some will remain connected and mobilize their challenges to traditionalism from within.

In general, Muslims born and raised in North America are more open to diversity than those born abroad, especially if their communities are not sufficiently homogeneous to support their own separate social institutions (such as schools). The likelihood of dissent is further amplified in North America by relatively high levels of education. In general, higher education increases openness to diversity, as well as to equity claims by women and sexual minorities. The fact that Muslim minorities in North America are less economically marginalized than those in Europe also reduces the likelihood of strict adherence to religious belief.

On the other hand, the great majority of Muslims in Canada and the US are still relatively recent immigrants from places where social norms regarding gender and sexuality are starkly conservative, and the mosques and Islamic centres to which new immigrants become attached are almost invariably conservative on moral questions. Groups seeking to challenge conservative ideas are developing, as we shall see below, but homosexual Muslims in particular continue to face condemnation from mainstream Muslim society.

Marriage and the Family

Marriage under Islam is essentially a contractual relationship negotiated between the prospective husband and the woman's father or guardian. But the Qur'an emphasizes that the true contract is between the husband and the wife, based on mutual consent: the woman's father or guardian is expected to act on her behalf and, ideally, in her interest. Divorce is allowed, but only as a last resort after every effort has been made to save the marriage.

The Qur'an allows polygyny, or simultaneous marriage to more than one wife. But it places two significant restrictions on such marriages. First, it limits to four the number of wives that a man can have at one time (before Islam the number was unlimited). Second, it demands strict justice and equality in a man's material and emotional support for all his wives. If this is not possible, the Qur'an stipulates, "then only one." The Qur'an also warns that "You cannot act equitably among your wives however much you try" (Q. 4: 3 and 129). As a result, the vast majority of Muslim marriages are monogamous.

Even more significantly, the Qur'an changed the nature of polygyny from an entitlement to a social responsibility. The verses dealing with this subject open with a proviso: "If you [men] are afraid that you would not act justly towards the orphans [in your care], then marry what seems good to you of women: two, three, or four" (Q. 4: 3). This statement may be interpreted in two ways. It may mean that a man could marry the widowed mother of orphans in order to provide a family for them. It may also mean that a man could marry two, three, or four orphan girls after they have attained marriageable age, again to provide a home and family for them. In either case, marriage to more than one wife was explicitly allowed as a way of providing for female orphans and widows in a traditional society beset with continuous warfare, where a woman could find love and security only in her own home.

Adultery, Fornication, and "Family Honour"

The Qur'an (17: 32) is explicit in condemning adultery: "And do not come close to adultery—it is truly a shameful deed and an evil way." The punishment provided in the Qur'an (24: 2) for adulterers (married men or women who have sex with someone other than their spouse) or fornicators (unmarried women or men who have sex with anyone) is 100 lashes. Since the illicit act had to be witnessed by four reliable eye-witnesses, such cases were rarely prosecuted.

Yet there have been cases, especially in recent times, where adultery and fornication have been punished by law, and in some places the penalty has been capital punishment by stoning. Among those places is Iran, which according to Amnesty International has carried out six such executions since 2006. The scriptural source used to justify stoning is not the Qur'an but the *hadith* literature. Many activists, both Muslim and non-Muslim, have sought to end this barbaric practice.

Another barbaric practice that has attracted attention in recent years is the murder of family members by their relatives, ostensibly to preserve the family's "honour"; the victims in such cases are almost always young women or girls who are perceived to have brought shame on the family by disobeying male authority. In Canada, the 2009 Shafia case was a horrific example, where a father, his second wife in a polygamous marriage, and their son murdered the family's three teenaged daughters (Zainab, Sahar, and Geeti Shafia), as well as the husband's first wife (Rona Mohammed). The three perpetrators were convicted in 2012 and sentenced to life imprisonment.

There is nothing in the Qur'an that calls for the taking of an innocent life. The thinking behind such killings is rooted not in religion but in honour/shame culture.

Women

Of all the social and political issues that are currently being debated within the Muslim community, perhaps the most important is the question of women's rights. The Qur'an (9: 71) makes it clear that men and women have the same religious duties and obligations:

> The Believers, men and women, are protectors one of another: they enjoin what is just, and forbid what is evil: they observe regular prayers, practise regular charity, and obey God and God's Messenger

Another example can be found in *surah* 33, verse 35:

> For Muslim men and women, for believing men and women, for devout men and women, for true men and women, for men and women who are patient and constant, for men and women who humble themselves, for men and women who give in Charity, for men and women who fast (and deny themselves), for men and women who guard their chastity, and for men and women who engage much in God's praise, for them God has prepared forgiveness and great reward.

The Qur'an allows women to acquire property through bequest, inheritance, or bride dowry and dispose of it as they please. These rights may well be inadequate in the modern world, but they point to a recognition of women's human dignity that until recently was denied in many societies. In general, Islamic law and social custom have tended either to restrict the rights laid out in the Qur'an or to render them virtually inoperative. Although women as well as men are supposed to receive education, some Islamic societies (such as Afghanistan under the Taliban) deny education and employment opportunities for women.

As for the ***hijab*** or veil, the Qur'an does not refer to it at all. It merely demands that women avoid wearing jewellery and dress modestly; and in the next verse it also demands modesty of males. The *hadith* tradition indicates that most Muslim communities adopted the practice of veiling during the time of the caliphate, probably under the influence of Eastern Christian and ancient Greek customs. An extreme extension of the practice, which may also be attributable to non-Arab influences, is the seclusion of women. Under the South Asian system of *purdah*, for instance, women are not only veiled but isolated from men. And seclusion became a hallmark of Turkish life under the *harim* system of the Ottoman aristocracy. In Afghanistan, the *burqa* covers the entire body; even the woman's eyes are obscured by a screen.

In the twenty-first century, the *hijab* has become a powerful—and powerfully ambiguous—symbol, widely condemned as a limitation on women's rights, but often defended by Muslim women themselves as a freely chosen affirmation of their Islamic identity. The question at issue is to what extent women can be excluded from public life. Around the world, social and economic conditions increasingly demand equal participation and rights for women and men alike.

In March 2005 Professor Amina Wadud led a mixed-gender Muslim prayer service in New York City—an event that broke at least three Islamic conventions. Traditionally, women have led prayer

National Hijab Day at the University of Toronto: Sajda Khalil ties a hijab for Mikaela Valenzuela (Lucas Oleniuk / GetStock.com).

only among other women or within their own families; some of the women attending the service had their hair uncovered; and men and women were not separated (the only time such interspersing of genders is accepted by all Muslims is during the pilgrimage to Mecca, when men and women circumambulate the Ka'ba and pray together). Events similar to the New York prayer service have since been held in several North American cities, including Toronto.

Muslim women activists in some mainstream Muslim organizations have challenged male leaders to adopt more inclusive language and develop policies to encourage women's participation. They are also becoming more vocal in their engagement with Western feminism. Although their positions sometimes diverge from those of Western feminists, controversies over issues such as veiling have created significant openings for Muslim women to engage in political debate in their own religious communities.

War, Terrorism, and Violence

Many hoped that the end of the Cold War in 1989 and the moves made in the 1990s towards ending the long and bitter conflict between Israelis and Palestinians might allow for better relations between the Western and Muslim worlds in general. But the Israeli–Palestinian conflict has only deepened, and new conflicts have emerged in recent years.

One major political development was the Iranian revolution of 1979. Almost four decades later, the prospect of an Iran with nuclear weapons has only increased the tensions between the Islamic regime and the West. A second development can also be traced to 1979, when the Soviet Union invaded Afghanistan. Muslims from around the world volunteered to fight with the Afghans, and the US contributed heavily to their training. They were called *mujahidin* (the word is derived from *jihad*), and at the time—before the end of the Cold War—they were seen as "freedom fighters" by much of the world, including US President Ronald Reagan.

Among the other contributors to Afghanistan's "holy war" was Osama bin Laden, the son of a wealthy Saudi Arabian family, who created Al-Qaeda ("the base") to help fund and train *mujahidin*. The Soviet troops were withdrawn in 1988, but Al-Qaeda was not disbanded. In 1996 bin Laden issued a *fatwa* calling for the overthrow of the Saudi government and the removal of US forces in Arabia, and in 1998 he declared war against Americans generally. A series of terrorist actions followed, culminating in the 9/11 attacks of 2001. In response, the US and its allies went to war, first in Afghanistan and then in Iraq.

Muslims around the world have repeatedly condemned terrorist activity. Muslim leaders have pointed out that suicide bombings violate Islam's prohibitions on both suicide and the killing of civilians in war, and in March 2005, on the first anniversary of the 2004 Al-Qaeda train bombing in Madrid, Spanish clerics issued a *fatwa* against bin Laden himself. Even so, it would be another seven years before he was tracked down and killed by US forces.

Anti-US graffiti on the wall of the former US Embassy in the Iranian capital, Tehran, in 2008 (© Roberto Fumagalli / Alamy).

An important reference point in discussions of martyrdom is the Mardin Conference, held in March 2010 in the city that was at issue in Ibn Taymiyyah's famous fourteenth-century *fatwa* legitimizing the use of violence against unjust Muslim rulers. Because many modern terrorists (among them bin Laden) have used this *fatwa* to justify their actions, the Mardin conference brought together 15 senior Islamic scholars from across the Muslim world to discuss the context in which it was issued some 700 years earlier.

In condoning violence against authoritarian rulers in order to re-establish true Islamic rule, Ibn Taymiyyah broke with the teachings of his own conservative Hanbali school. As the scholars who met at Mardin pointed out, however, the *fatwa* was issued in a very particular historical context, in the aftermath of the Mongol conquest and the devastation of Baghdad (the seat of Islamic authority at the time). They concluded that "anyone who seeks support from this *fatwa* for killing Muslims or non-Muslims has erred in his interpretation." They also stated that "It is not for a Muslim individual or a group to announce and declare war or engage in combative *jihad* . . . on their own."

Unfortunately, extremists seem impervious to mainstream Muslim opinion. Muslims can accomplish much in the West if they work with their non-Muslim neighbours to promote justice and moral consciousness. But many non-Muslims see "Islam" and "the West" as mutually exclusive realities, and do not recognize their shared heritage. If future generations are to remain active as Muslims in pluralistic Western societies, it is more important than ever to re-examine old ideas.

Summary

A major development in the history of Islam is now underway in the West. Muslims who, through migration, have moved from majority to minority status are being spurred to define the priorities of their faith. Their decisions about what to pass on to their Western-born children will shape the contours of Islam in the future. At the same time, the Western emphasis on open discussion calls on Muslims from different cultural and regional backgrounds to think clearly about what they do and do not share. Muslims living in the West will use Western technology and democratic institutions to help their brothers and sisters revitalize the Muslim communities in their countries of origin, as well as the rest of the Muslim *ummah*. The potential of modern communications to contribute to this process became clear during the "Arab Spring" of 2011.

Sacred Texts

Variation	Text	Composition/ Compilation	Compilation/ Revision	Use
Sunni and Shi'a	Qur'an	Revelations received by Muhammad between 610 and 632 CE	Authoritative Codex produced between 644 and 656 CE	Doctrinal, ritual, inspirational, educational
Sunni and Shi'a	*Hadith*	Sayings of Muhammad and his early companions collected during their lifetimes	Earliest authoritative collection produced by al-Bukhari (d. 870 CE)	Doctrinal, ritual, inspirational, educational
Shi'a only	Nahj al-Balagha ("the peak of eloquence"; the sayings of 'Ali)	Sayings and sermons of 'Ali, the first Shi'i Imam	Collected by Al-Radi (d. 1015)	Doctrinal, ritual, inspirational, educational
Isma'ili Shi'a only	Ginans (hymns of praise and worship of God)	Collection begun by Pir Nur in the 12th century	Composition and collection continued until the beginning of the 20th century	Doctrinal, ritual, inspirational, educational

Sites

Mecca, Saudi Arabia

The original home of the Prophet Muhammad; also the site of the Ka'ba: the focal point of the annual *hajj* (pilgrimage), when more than 2 million Muslims visit the city over a period of about ten days. Mecca is permanently closed to non-Muslims.

Medina, Saudi Arabia

The home of the first Muslim community and the place where Muhammad was buried. Unlike Mecca, it is open to non-Muslims. The Prophet's Mosque, where he and his first two successors are buried, was originally quite simple, but is now one of the largest mosques in the world.

Al-Azhar University, Cairo

The oldest university in the Western world and an important centre of Sunni learning, Al-Azhar was transformed into a modern institution in 1961, when (under the direction of Egypt's President Nasser) it opened a faculty for women.

Karbala, Iraq

Home of the Shrine of Imam Husayn (the third Imam), who was killed at Karbala in 680. It is of special importance to the Shi'a, who during their daily prayers touch their heads to a small disk of clay from the soil of Karbala. Since 2004, hundreds of innocent worshippers have been killed in suicide bombings near the shrine.

Cordoba, Spain

The city at the heart of the *convivencia* ("shared life") in medieval Spain, described by a tenth-century Benedictine nun as "the ornament of the world."

Istanbul, Turkey

The Byzantine city of Constantinople was renamed Istanbul after its capture by the Turks in 1453. The capital of the Ottoman Turkish Empire and the centre of the sultan's power, it is the site of many imperial buildings, including the Topkapi Palace (the principal residence of the sultans from 1465 to 1856) and its successor, the Western-influenced Dolmabahce Palace.

Haram al-Sharif, Jerusalem

The area of the ancient city Haram al-Sharif (the "Noble Sanctuary"; known to Jews and Christians as the Temple Mount) contains two sacred buildings: the Masjid al-Aqsa—the "farthest mosque," where Muhammad prayed before ascending to heaven, and the Dome of the Rock, a sanctuary built on the spot from which tradition says the ascent began.

Discussion Questions

1. What is the significance of the *hijra* in Muslim history? Why is it so important to Muslims?
2. Write a brief biography of the Prophet highlighting two events in his life that are particularly significant to Muslims. In your answer, explain why those events are so central.
3. What is the Qur'an? What do Muslims understand it to be?
4. Discuss the differences between Sunni and Shi'a Islam. What are the two primary groups within the Shi'a?
5. Outline the development of Sufism, the mystical dimension of Islam.
6. What are the Five Pillars of Islam?
7. What are some of the issues raised by feminist interpretations of the Qur'an and the Muslim tradition?

Glossary

caliph From the Arabic *khalifah* ("one who represents or acts on behalf of another"). The caliph was the Prophet's successor as the head of the Muslim community; the position became institutionalized in the form of the caliphate, which lasted from 632 to 1924.

dhikr "Remembering" God's name; chanted in Sufi devotional exercises, sometimes while devotees dance in a circle.

dhimmis "Protected people": non-Muslim religious minorities (specifically Jews and Christians, as "People of the Book") accorded tolerated status in Islamic society.

Fatihah The short opening *surah* of the Qur'an, recited at least 17 times every day.

fatwa A ruling issued by a traditional religio-legal authority.

fiqh Jurisprudence, or the theoretical principles underpinning the specific regulations contained in the *shari'ah*.

hadith The body of texts reporting Muhammad's words and example, taken by Muslims as a foundation for conduct and doctrine; a *hadith* is an individual unit of the literature.

hajj The annual pilgrimage to Mecca.

halal Ritually acceptable; most often used in the context of the slaughter of animals for meat, but also refers generally to Muslim dietary regulations.

haram "Forbidden," used especially in reference to actions; similar in its connotations to "taboo."

hijab A woman's veil or head covering.

hijrah The Prophet's migration from Mecca to establish a community in Medina in 622 CE. In dates, the abbreviation AH stands for "year of the *hijrah*" (the starting-point of the Islamic dating system).

'Id al-Fitr The holiday celebrating the end of the Ramadan fast; the festival traditionally begins following the sighting of the new moon.

ijma' The consensus of religio-legal scholars; one of the two secondary principles used in jurisprudence; some legal schools give it more weight than others.

ijtihad Personal reasoning applied to the development of legal opinions.

Imamis ("Twelvers") Shi'is who recognize 12 imams as legitimate heirs to the Prophet's authority; the last, in occultation since 874, is expected to return some day as the **Mahdi**.

Isma'ilis ("Seveners") Shi'is who recognize only seven imams; named after the last of them, Isma'il, whose lineage continues to the present in the Agha Khan.

jihad Struggle in defence of the faith; some *jihads* are military, waged in response to threats to the community's security or welfare; others are spiritual, waged to improve moral conduct in society.

kufr Rejecting belief; implies lack of gratitude for God's grace.

Mahdi The Shi'i twelfth Imam, understood in his role as the "rightly guided one" who will emerge from hiding at some unspecified future date to restore righteousness and order to the world.

mi'raj The Prophet's miraculous journey to heaven.

mu'adhdhin The person who calls people to prayer.

qiblah The direction of prayer, marked in mosques by a niche inside the wall nearest Mecca.

Ramadan The month throughout which Muslims fast during daylight hours.

sadaqah Alms given voluntarily, in addition to the required *zakat*.

salat The prescribed daily prayers, said five times during the day.

shahadah The Muslim profession of faith in God as the only god, and in Muhammad as God's prophet.

shari'ah The specific regulations of Islamic law (jurisprudence, or theoretical discussion of the law, is *fiqh*).

shaykh The Arabic term for a senior master, especially in Sufism.

Shi'a From the Arabic meaning "party"; Muslims who trace succession to the Prophet's authority through the line of Imams descended from 'Ali; the smaller of the two main divisions of Islam, accounting for about one-sixth of all Muslims today. "Shi'i" is the adjective form.

sunnah The "life-example" of Muhammad's words and deeds, based mainly on the *hadith* literature; the primary source of guidance for Muslims.

Sunni Muslims who trace succession to the Prophet's authority through the caliphate, which lasted until the twentieth century; the larger of the two main divisions of Islam, accounting for about five-sixths of all Muslims today.

surah A chapter of the Qur'an; there are 114 in all, arranged mainly in decreasing order of length except for the first (the ***Fatihah***).

tafsir Commentary on the Qur'an.

taqlid Following the ***ijtihad*** or legal opinion of a particular jurist.

ummah The Muslim community.

zakat The prescribed welfare tax; 2.5 per cent of each Muslim's accumulated wealth, collected by central treasuries in earlier times but now donated to charities independently of state governments; see also ***sadaqah***.

Further Reading

Ahmed, Leila. 1992. *Women and Gender in Islam: Historical Roots of a Modern Debate*. New Haven: Yale University Press. A frequently cited contribution on this topic.

Alvi, Sajida Sultana, et al., eds. 2003. *The Muslim Veil in North America: Issues and Debates*. Toronto: Women's Press. A good collection of essays about the issues surrounding *hijab*.

Coulson, N.G. 1964. *A History of Islamic Law*. Edinburgh: Edinburgh University Press. Traces the development of Islamic jurisprudence from its inception in the ninth century through to the influence on it of modern Western legal systems.

Jerrilynn D. Dodds, et al., eds. 2008. *The Arts of Intimacy: Christians, Jews, and Muslims in the Making of Castilian Culture*. New Haven: Yale University Press. A beautifully illustrated book that looks at the *convivencia* ("shared life") between Muslims, Christians, and Jews in medieval Spain.

***The Encyclopedia of Islam*, rev. ed. 1963–. Leiden: E.J. Brill.** (First published in 4 vols, 1913–38.) Vast and technical, but authoritative. Entries appear under Arabic head-words, sometimes in unfamiliar transliterations, and so pose a challenge for the beginner.

Esposito, John, ed. 2009. *The Oxford Encyclopedia of the Islamic World*. New York: Oxford University Press. An indispensable reference.

Grabar, Oleg. 1973. *The Formation of Islamic Art*. New Haven: Yale University Press. Concentrates on Islamic art in the Middle East in the early Islamic centuries.

Haddad, Yvonne Y., and Jane I. Smith, eds. 1994. *Muslim Communities in North America*. Albany: State University of New York Press. An examination of Islamic tradition and identity in the modern Western diaspora.

Mottahedeh, Roy. 2002. *The Mantle of the Prophet: Religion and Politics in Iran*. Oxford: Oneworld Publications. One of the best single-volume studies of the events leading up to the Iranian revolution.

Peters, Francis E. 1994. *A Reader on Islam*. Princeton: Princeton University Press. An anthology of historical source readings.

Qureshi, Emran, and Michael A. Sells, eds. 2003. *The New Crusades: Constructing the Muslim Enemy*. New York: Columbia. An excellent collection of essays on Western representations of Islam and Muslim lives.

Safi, Omid, ed. 2003. *Progressive Muslims: On Justice, Gender and Pluralism*. Oxford: Oneworld. A collection of essays by Muslim scholars of Islam on contemporary topics.

Schimmel, Annemarie. 1975. *Mystical Dimensions of Islam*. Chapel Hill: University of North Carolina Press. A survey of Sufism by one of its most respected Western interpreters.

Taylor, Jennifer Maytorena. 2009. *New Muslim Cool*. Documentary film. Educational DVD available from Seventh Art Releasing at <http://www.7thart.com>. The story of Hamza Perez, a Puerto Rican–American hip hop artist who converted to Islam.

Watt, W. Montgomery. 1962. *Islamic Philosophy and Theology*. Edinburgh: Edinburgh University Press. A masterly survey of Muslim religious intellectuals, especially in the first six centuries of Islam.

Recommended Websites

www.uga.edu/islam

The best academic site for the study of Islam, presented by Professor Alan Godlas of the University of Georgia.

www.cie.org/index.aspx

The Council on Islamic Education offers useful resources for teachers.

http://acommonword.com

An interfaith initiative supported by a wide range of Muslim scholars and leaders.

www.msawest.net/islam

An excellent selection of resources on Islam, including searchable translations of both the Qur'an and the *hadith* literature, presented by the Muslim Students Association.

References

Arberry, Arthur J. trans. 1948. *Immortal Rose: An Anthology of Persian Lyrics*. London: Luzac & Co.

———, trans. 1955. *The Koran Interpreted*. London: Allen and Unwin.

Chittick, William C. 2000. *Sufism: A Beginner's Guide*. Oxford: Oneworld.

Menocal, María Rosa. 1998-1999. "Ten Years After: The Virtues of Exile." *Scripta Mediterranea*, vols XIX-XX, 55. Toronto: Canadian Institute for Mediterranean Studies.

Nicholson, Reynold A. 1931. "Mysticism." In *The Legacy of Islam*, ed. T. Arnold and Alfred Guillaume, 210–38. London: Oxford University Press.

———, trans. 1950. *Rumi: Poet and Mystic*. London: G. Allen and Unwin.

———. 2002 [1914]. *The Mystics of Islam*. Bloomington: World Wisdom.

Smith, Margaret. 1928. *Rabi'a the Mystic*. Cambridge: Cambridge University Press.

6 Hindu Traditions

Vasudha Narayanan

Traditions at a Glance

Numbers

Approximately 950 million to 1 billion around the world.

Distribution

Primarily India; large numbers in other regions of South Asia, as well as the United States, Canada, Australia, Western Europe, and many parts of Southeast Asia.

Principal Historical Periods

c. 2500–600 BCE	Indus Valley civilization; composition of the Vedas
c. 500 BCE–1000 CE	Composition of epics and *Puranas*
600–1600	Devotional poetry in local languages, building of major temples in South and Southeast Asia
13th–18th centuries	Northern India under Muslim rule
mid-1700s–1947	British colonial period

Founders and Leaders

Important figures include Shankara, Ramanuja, Madhva, Vallabha, Ramananda, Chaitanya, Swami Narayanan, Ramakrishna, and Vivekananda. Among the hundreds of teachers who have attracted followings in the last century alone are Aurobindo, Ramana Maharishi, Maharishi Mahesh Yogi, Sathya Sai Baba, Anandamayi Ma, and Ma Amritananda Mayi.

Deities

Hindu philosophy recognizes a supreme being (the ineffable Brahman) who is not limited by gender and number and who may take countless forms; classical rhetoric typically refers to 330 million. Some sectarian traditions identify the supreme deity as Vishnu, some as Shiva, and some as a form of the Goddess. The supreme being may be understood as male, female, androgynous, or beyond gender. There are also many local deities.

Authoritative Texts

The Vedas are technically considered the most authoritative texts, though the epics (the *Ramayana* and the *Mahabharata*, including the *Bhagavad Gita*), the *Puranas*, and several works in regional languages have also been very important.

Noteworthy Teachings

Hindus in general recognize a supreme being, variously conceived—personal for some, impersonal for others. Most think of the human soul as immortal and believe that when it reaches liberation it will be freed from the shackles of karma and rebirth. Specific teachings vary depending on sectarian tradition, region, and community.

The earliest compositions in any Hindu tradition are the **Vedas**: four collections of hymns and texts that are said to have been "revealed" to **rishis** (visionaries or seers) through both sight and sound; thus the sacred words are called **shruti** ("that which is heard"). This dual emphasis on seeing and hearing the sacred is characteristic of all Hindu traditions.

When Hindus go on a pilgrimage or visit a temple, they seek an experience known as a ***darshana***: to see and be seen by a particular deity or **guru**. But Hindus also believe in the importance of uttering prayers aloud. Reciting from ancient texts, telling stories of the gods, chanting prayers, singing devotional songs, or meditating on a holy **mantra**—these are just some of the ways in which Hindus actively live their tradition through its sacred words. In short, Hindus experience the divine through both sight and sound. Although sacred texts have been important, for most

← A Hindu wedding in Florida (© Vasudha Narayanan).

Hindus the primary source of knowledge about their traditions has been performance: rituals, recitations, music, dance, and theatre.

It is hard to identify common denominators in Hinduism. While some texts and some deities are widely accepted, there is no single text, deity, or teacher that all Hindus consider supremely authoritative. Similarly, there are many local deities who may or may not be identified with pan-Indian gods. The Hindu tradition is in fact many traditions encompassing hundreds of communities and sectarian movements, each of which has its own hallowed canon, its own sacred place, and its own concept of the supreme deity.

"Hinduism"

The term "Hinduism" is frequently used as a fluid shorthand for diverse philosophies, arts, branches of knowledge, and practices associated with people and communities that have some connection with the Indian sub-continent and do not explicitly self-identify with another religious tradition. Knowledge of the Vedas is not required to qualify as Hindu; there are probably millions of people in India who have never heard of them. Yet all those people would be considered Hindu as long they do not belong to a faith tradition that explicitly denies the exalted status of the Vedas. For many Hindus, plurality of beliefs and practices is a way of life.

The word "Hinduism," like "India" itself, is derived from "Sind": the name of the region—now in Pakistan—of the river Sindhu (Indus). The term was given currency by the British colonizers of India in the eighteenth and nineteenth centuries. To them, "Hinduism" meant the religion of those Indians—the majority—who were not Muslims, although a few smaller groups, including Jainas, Parsis, Christians, Jews, and sometimes Sikhs, were also recognized. As a term for a religious identity, "Hinduism" did not become popular until the nineteenth century.

There are approximately a billion Hindus in the world today. Yet when they are asked about their religious identity, they are more likely to refer to their caste or community than to Hinduism. Under Indian law, the term "Hindu" applies not only to members of a Hindu "denomination" such as Vira Shaiva or Brahmo Samaj, but also to "any other person domiciled in the territories to which [the Hindu Family Act] extends who is *not a Muslim, Christian, Parsi, or Jew* by religion" (italics added). In effect, India's legal system considers anyone who does not profess one of the specified religions to be Hindu. Thus while we can make some generalizations and trace some important lines of historical continuity, we must keep in mind their limitations.

The very concept of religion in the Western, post-Enlightenment sense is only loosely applicable to the Hindu tradition The Sanskrit word **dharma** comes close to "religion" in that it refers to righteousness, justice, faith, duty, and religious and social obligation, but it does not cover everything that that is sacred for Hindus. Many things—from astrology to music and dance, from phonetics to plants—may be essential to an individual Hindu's tradition. Therefore this discussion will include a number of features not usually covered by the term "religion" in the Western world.

Origins

In the early twentieth century Hinduism was believed to have grown from a fusion of the Indigenous religions of the Indus Valley with the faith of an Indo-European people usually thought to have migrated there sometime between 1750 and 1500 BCE. More recently, however, some scholars have argued that the Indo-Europeans ("Aryans") originated in other parts of Asia, while others suggest that the subcontinent itself was their original homeland.

Timeline

c. 3300–1900 BCE	Evidence of Indus Valley civilization (early to mature phases)
c. 1750?–1500	Earliest Vedic compositions
c. 600	Production of *Upanishads*
c. 500	Production of Hindu epics begins
326	Alexander the Great comes to the Northwest border of India
c. 272	Accession of King Ashoka
c. 200	First contacts with Southeast Asia
c. 200 BCE–200 CE	Composition of *Bhagavad Gita*
c. 200 CE	Compilation of *Laws of Manu* and *Natya Sastra* completed
c. 500	Beginnings of tantric tradition
c. 700–900	Alvars and Nayanmars, Tamil *bhakti* poets
c. 700–800	Shankara's Advaita Vedanta
c. 1008–1023	Mahmud of Ghazni raids kingdoms in India several times, strips temples of their wealth; Somnath Temple in Gujarat destroyed
1017	Traditional birth date of Ramanuja, Vaishnava philosopher (d. 1137)
1100–1150	Angkor Wat built in Cambodia
c. 1400	Major endowments at Tirumala–Tirupati temple
1486	Birth of Chaitanya, Bengali Vaishnava *bhakti* leader (d. 1583)
c. 1543	Birth of Tulsidas, North Indian *bhakti* poet (d. 1623)
1757	British rule established in Calcutta
1828	Ram Mohan Roy founds Brahmo Samaj
1836	Birth of Ramakrishna Paramahamsa (d. 1886)
1875	Dayananda Sarasvati founds Arya Samaj
1893	Vivekananda attends World's Parliament of Religions in Chicago
1905–6	Vedanta Temple built in San Francisco
1926	Birth of Sathya Sai Baba
1947	Partition of India and Pakistan on religious lines, resulting in almost a million deaths
1959	Maharishi Mahesh Yogi brings Transcendental Meditation to America and Europe
1965	A.C. Bhaktivedenta Swami Prabhupada, founder of ISKCON, sails to America
1977	Hindu temples consecrated in New York and Pittsburgh

The Harappa Culture

In 1926 excavations revealed the remains of several large towns on the banks of the Indus River in what is now Pakistan. Two of these towns, known today as Mohenjo Daro ("Mound of the Dead") and Harappa, were more than 480 kilometres (300 miles) apart. Yet archaeological evidence suggested a certain uniformity in the culture across the entire northwestern part of the subcontinent. Although that culture is still widely identified with the Indus Valley, some scholars now call it the Harappa culture because it extends well beyond the Indus basin itself.

It is generally believed that the towns were in existence by about 2750 BCE. Inscriptions on carved seals show that there was a written language, although no reading of it is universally accepted. Clearly the Harappans were impressive builders. At Mohenjo Daro there is a huge swimming-pool-like structure, surrounded by porticos and flights of stairs, that scholars believe was designed for religious rituals of some sort. In addition, some houses appear to have included a room with a fire altar, and there are carvings of what looks like a mother goddess that may have been used for offerings of incense. Excavations around the Indus River have uncovered seals showing a man seated in a position that resembles a **yoga** posture, wearing a headdress that suggests he could be a prototype of the god who came to be known as Shiva. Other seals show a horned figure emerging from a *pipal* tree, in front of which stand seven figures with long braids who have been tentatively identified as either holy men or goddesses.

What might have brought the Indus Valley civilization to an end? Some think it was the arrival of the Indo-Europeans around 1750 BCE. Others suggest that flooding, drying of the river, or epidemics might have driven the people farther east. Whatever the answer, the fragmentary evidence found in the Indus Valley suggests that some features of Hinduism may have originated well before 1750 BCE.

We know even less of the early history in other parts of the subcontinent. Nevertheless, scholars have noticed correspondences between sites that were inhabited 4,000 or 5,000 years ago and sites that are of religious significance today. It seems likely that at least some elements of Hinduism as we know it have been present for as long as five millennia.

The Indo-Europeans

The language of the Vedas is an early form of Sanskrit, a member of the language family known as Indo-European. Western scholars in the nineteenth century noted similarities between some Indian and European languages in both grammar and vocabulary. For example, the Sanskrit word ***jnana*** is a cognate of the English word "knowledge"; thus "lack of knowledge" is *ajnana* in Sanskrit and "ignorance" in English. There are hundreds of similar cognates, including the words for "father" and "mother." Based on this evidence, many scholars believe that the Indo-Europeans (also known as "Aryans") originated in Central Asia and that the migration began around 2000 BCE. Others think they originated in the region of modern Turkey and began spreading out as much as 4,000 years earlier.

Yet another school of thought holds that Indo-Europeans originated on the Indian subcontinent. Proponents of this theory base their arguments on astronomical data and evidence concerning a great river that they identify as the legendary Sarasvati. According to the ancient Hindu text known as the *Rig Veda*, the Sarasvati had five Aryan tribes living on its banks; yet geological evidence shows that it was dry by the time the Aryans were supposed to have entered India (c. 1750 BCE). If the Aryans were actually there before the Sarasvati dried up, their dates must be pushed back at least as far as the time of the Harappan civilization.

None of the evidence is conclusive, and some theories on the origins of the Indo-Europeans have been motivated by political, racial, religious, and nationalist agendas. What we do know is that the Indo-Europeans composed many poems and, eventually, manuals on rituals and philosophy. They committed these traditions to memory and passed them from generation to generation orally.

Map 6.1 Hinduism

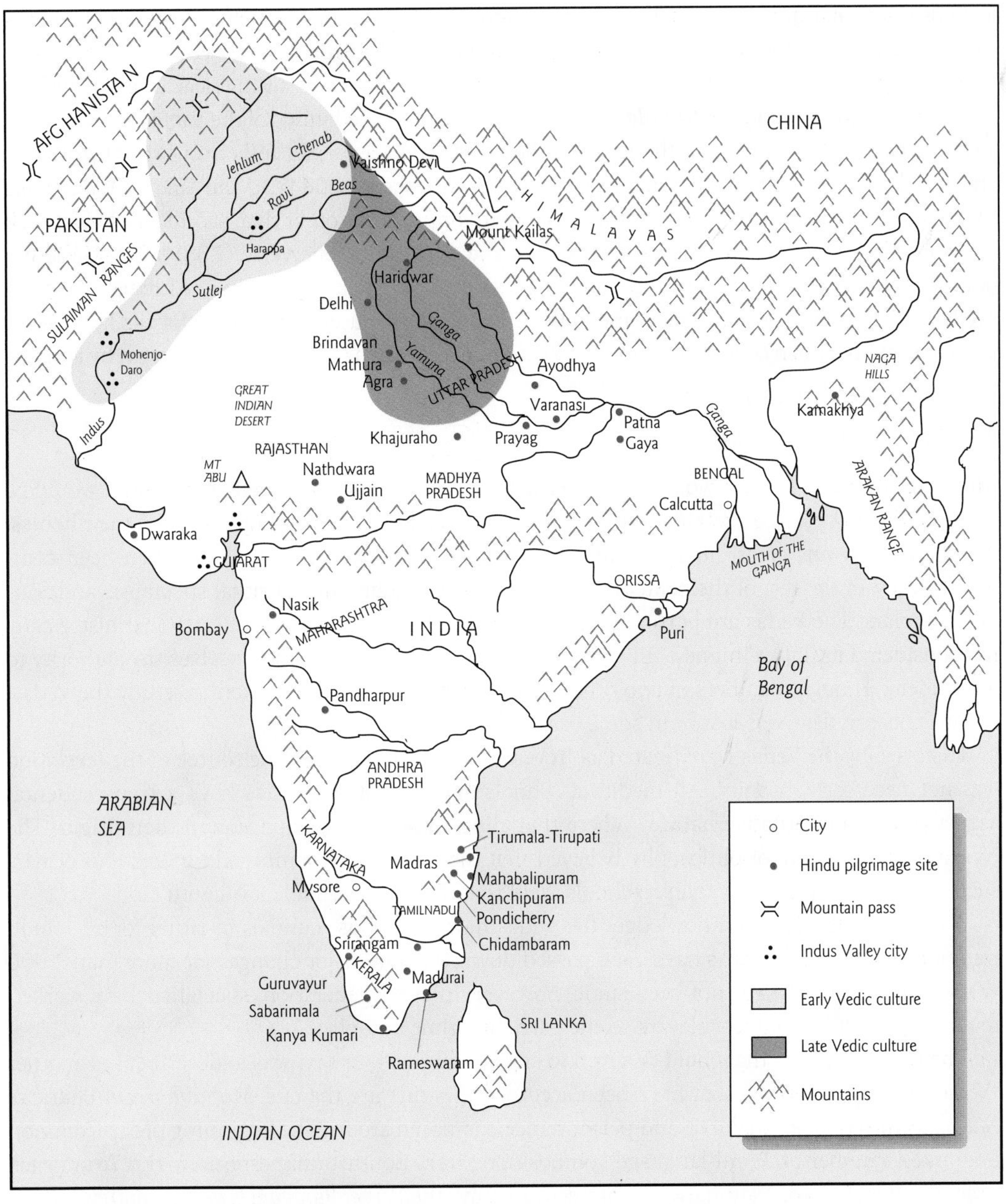

Source: Adapted from Nielsen et al. 1993: 85.

The Vedas

The Vedas (from the Sanskrit for "knowledge") are the works collectively known as *shruti* ("that which was heard"). The Vedic *rishis* "saw" the mantras and transmitted them to their disciples, starting an oral tradition that has continued to the present.

Traditionally regarded as revealed scripture, the Vedas are now generally thought to have been composed between roughly 1500 BCE (possibly 1750 BCE) and 600 BCE. There are four Vedic collections: *Rig*, *Sama*, *Yajur*, and *Atharva*. Each of these consists of four sections: hymns (*Samhitas*; the earliest parts), directions for the performance of sacred rituals (***Brahmanas***), "compositions for the forest" (*Aranyakas*), and philosophical works called the **Upanishads** ("sitting near [the teacher]").

The earliest section of the *Rig Veda* contains 1,028 hymns. The hymns of the *Sama Veda* and *Yajur Veda* are largely borrowed from the *Rig*, and the *Sama Veda* was meant to be sung. The *Upanishads* are the most recent sections of each collection, composed around 600 BCE. The *Atharva Veda* differs from the other three in that it includes material used for purposes other than sacrificial rituals, such as incantations and remedies to ward off illness and evil spirits; one verse (7.38) refers to the use of herbs to make a lover return, and another (7.50) requests luck in gambling. Although the term "Vedas" denotes the whole corpus, some Western scholars have used "Veda" only for the hymns, the *samhita* portion of each collection. This narrower use of the term is generally not accepted by Hindus.

The Status of the Vedas

Almost all educated Hindus would describe the Vedas as their most sacred texts; yet most would be hard pressed to describe their contents. The Vedas are not books that people keep in their homes. A few Vedic hymns are recited regularly, and the philosophical sections have often been commented on, but the rest of the contents are known only to a handful of ritual specialists and Sanskrit scholars. The Vedas are particularly significant to the **brahmins**—the class that historically has considered itself the "highest" in Hindu society—who reserved for themselves the authority to teach them. Though members of two other classes were technically "allowed" to study the Vedas, in time this privilege was lost or in some cases, abandoned.

Historically, the Vedas were treated as "revealed" scripture, though the source of the revelation was not necessarily a deity. All medieval schools agreed that the Vedas have a transcendental aspect and an authoritative nature. Where they differed was on the question of their origin. The Nyaya ("logic") school of philosophy believed that the Vedas were composed by God, but others, such as the Mimamsa and Vedanta schools, held that they are eternal, coeval with God.

The supreme source of knowledge, the Vedas have served as manuals of ritual for all Hindu traditions, and some sections have been passed down without major changes for more than 2,000 years. Interpretations have not been static, however. In every generation, specialists have worked to make the texts' messages relevant to the particular time and place.

The highest honour that could be given to any Hindu religious text was to describe it as another "Veda." Among the works that have been accorded this title are the epic ***Mahabharata***; Bharata's *Natya Sastra*, a treatise on dance and performance composed around the beginning of the Common Era; and a number of Tamil-language compositions from South India, especially the *Tiruvaymoli* ("sacred utterance") of Nammalvar (ninth century) and the *Periya Puranam* (twelfth century), a collection of the life stories of saints who were devotees of Shiva. These texts made no attempt either to imitate the Vedas or to comment on them. They are called "Vedas" only because they reflect the wisdom embodied in the original Vedas, making their eternal truth relevant to a new place and time.

The Vedic Hymns

The figures that were to become the principal Hindu deities—goddesses like Lakshmi and gods like Narayana (Vishnu)—are not mentioned often in the *samhitas*; only the later Vedic hymns address them directly. Rather, the earliest hymns speak of deities who were later superseded, and many of the stories they allude to would not be familiar to most Hindus today.

Indra, for instance, was a warrior god who battled other cosmic powers. Agni was the god of fire who served as a messenger, carrying to the deities the offerings that humans placed in the sacrificial fire. Soma was the name of a god identified with the moon, but also of a plant-based elixir used for ritual purposes.

Sarasvati, as we have seen, was the name of a great river. But Sarasvati was also a goddess described in the *Rig Veda* as beautiful and fortunate, the inspirer of noble thoughts. By the time the *Brahmanas* were composed, Sarasvati had taken over the attributes formerly associated with the goddess Vac ("speech"). Now Sarasvati is speech incarnate, the power of the word, and the mother of the Vedas.

The early hymns typically offer praise to the gods; thus the river Indus is praised for giving cattle, children, horses, and food. But many of them also include petitions—not for salvation or eternal bliss (in fact, the idea of an afterlife is rarely mentioned), but for a good and happy life on this earth. Thus a woman poet named Ghosa asks to be cured of her white-tinted skin, so that she may marry and live happily with her husband.

One of the dominant features of Vedic religious life was the ritual sacrifice, typically performed using fire. From simple domestic affairs to elaborate community events, these sacrifices were conducted by ritual specialists and priests. A delicate connection was understood to exist between the rituals and the maintenance of cosmic and earthly order, or *rta*: truth and justice, the rightness of things that makes harmony and peace possible on earth and in the heavens. A number of hymns composed around 1000 BCE speculate on the origins of life. "The Creation Hymn" (see Document box) expresses wonder at the creation of the universe from nothing and suggests that perhaps no one knows how it all came to be.

Document

The Creation Hymn, *Rig Veda* 10.129

There was neither non-existence nor existence then; there was neither the realm of space nor the sky which is beyond. What stirred? Where? In whose protection? Was there water, bottomlessly deep?

There was neither death nor immortality then. There was no distinguishing sign of night nor of day. That one breathed, windless, by its own impulse. Other than that there was nothing beyond.

Darkness was hidden by darkness in the beginning; with no distinguishing sign, all this was water. The life force that was covered with emptiness, that one arose through the power of heat.

Desire came upon that one in the beginning; that was the first seed of mind. Poets seeking in their heart with wisdom found the bond of existence in non-existence.

Their cord was extended across. Was there below? Was there above? There were seed-placers; there were powers. There was impulse beneath; there was giving-forth above.

Who really knows? Who will here proclaim it? Whence was it produced? Whence is this creation? The gods came afterwards, with the creation of this universe. Who then knows whence it has arisen?

Whence this creation has arisen—perhaps it formed itself, or perhaps it did not—the one who looks down on it, in the highest heaven, only he knows—or perhaps he does not know (Doniger O'Flaherty 1981: 25–6).

Another account, however, describes how the universe itself was created through the cosmic sacrifice of the primeval man (*Purusha*). This account, the "Hymn to the Supreme Person," has figured continuously in the tradition for some 3,000 years. Straining to capture infinity in words, the composer uses the notion of "a thousand" to evoke what cannot be measured or perhaps even imagined:

(1) The cosmic person has a thousand heads
a thousand eyes and feet
It covers the earth on all sides
and extends ten finger-lengths beyond
(2) The cosmic person is everything
all that has been and will be. . . .

Various elements of the universe are said to have arisen from this sacrifice:

(13) From his mind came the moon
from his eye, the sun
Indra and Agni from his mouth
the wind came from his breath.
(14) From his navel came space
from his head, the sky
from his feet, earth;
from his ears, the four directions
thus the worlds were created.

In this context an idea is introduced that will change forever the religious and social countenance of the Hindu tradition:

(12) From his mouth came the priestly class
from his arms, the rulers.
The producers came from his legs;
from his feet came the servant class.

Thus the origins of the four classes (*varnas*) of Hindu society are traced to the initial cosmic sacrifice. Although this verse is the first explicit reference to what came to be called the caste system, it is likely that the stratification of society had taken place long before the *Rig Veda* was composed.

The Upanishads

By the time of the *Aranyakas* and *Upanishads*, in the seventh and sixth centuries BCE, the early Vedic emphasis on placating the gods through ritual sacrifice had given way to critical philosophical inquiry. This period, around the time of Shakyamuni Buddha and the Jaina teacher Mahavira, was one of intellectual ferment, of questioning—and rejecting—authoritarian structures. Yet the *Upanishads* do not totally reject the early hymns and sacrificial rituals. Instead, they rethink and reformulate them. Thus some rituals are interpreted allegorically, and the symbolic structures of the sacrifices are analyzed in some detail.

Most of the *Upanishads* take the form of conversations—between a teacher and a student, between a husband and wife, or between fellow philosophers. In the beginning of one study session a teacher exclaims: "May we work with vigour; may our study illumine us both" (*Taittiriya Upanishad* 11.1.1). After years of Vedic instruction, a departing student receives moving advice from his guru (teacher):

> Speak the truth. Practice virtue. Do not neglect to study every day. Do not neglect truth, virtue, studying or teaching. . . . Be one to whom your mother is a god, your father is a god, your teacher is a god, a guest is like a god. . . . Give with faith . . . give liberally, give with modesty . . . give with sympathy. . . . This is the command. This is the teaching. This is the secret of the Veda. . . . (*Taittiriya Upanishad* 1.11.1–6)

Karma and Samsara

It is in the *Upanishads* that we find the earliest discussions of several concepts central to the later Hindu tradition, among them the concept of **karma**. The literal meaning of "karma" is "action," especially ritual action, but in these texts the word eventually comes to refer the rewards and punishments attached to various actions. This system of cause and effect may require several lifetimes to work out. Thus the concept of karma implies a continuing cycle of death and rebirth or reincarnation called ***samsara***. To achieve liberation (***moksha***) from this cycle, according to the *Upanishads*, requires a transforming experiential wisdom. Those who attain that wisdom become immortal.

A frequent theme of the *Upanishads* is the quest for a unifying truth. This "higher" knowledge is clearly distinguished from the "lower" knowledge that can be conceptualized and expressed in words. Its nature cannot be taught: it can only be evoked, as in this question posed by the seeker in the *Mundaka Upanishad*: "What is it that, being known, all else becomes known?" (1.1.3). The *Brihadaranyaka Upanishad* of the *Yajur Veda* reflects the quest for enlightenment in these lines:

> Lead me from the unreal to reality
> Lead me from darkness to light
> Lead me from death to immortality
> Om, let there be peace, peace, peace.

Significantly, in later centuries the "higher wisdom" is not connected with any Vedic or book learning or conceptual knowledge. It is only through the experience of enlightenment that one is freed from the birth-and-death cycle.

Atman and Brahman

At the heart of that higher wisdom is experiential knowledge of the relationship between the human soul (**Atman**) and the Supreme Being (**Brahman**). Brahman pervades and at the same time transcends not only human thought but the universe itself. To know Brahman is to enter a new state of consciousness. The *Taittiriya Upanishad* associates Brahman with existence or truth, knowledge, infinity, consciousness, and bliss; elsewhere Brahman is described as the hidden, inner controller of the human soul.

Many passages of the Upanishads discuss the relationship between Atman and Brahman, but invariably they suggest rather than specify the connection between the two. In a famous passage of the Chandogya Upanishad, a father has his son dissolve salt in water and tells him that Brahman

Stone shrine (c. 1500 CE), modelled after a wooden processional chariot, in the Vitthala (Vishnu) temple complex in Hampi, northern Karnataka. The two elephants pulling the chariot date from a later time (© Vasudha Narayanan).

and Atman are united in the same way. The father ends this lesson with a famous dictum—tat tvam asi ("you are that")—in which "that" refers to Brahman and "you" to Atman. More than 1,000 years later, philosophers still differed in their interpretations of this passage. For Shankara in the eighth century, "you are that" indicated that Brahman and Atman were identical. Yet for Ramanuja in the eleventh century, it meant that the two were inseparably united but not identical. Some passages of the Upanishads refer to Brahman as the hidden, inner controller of the human soul (Atman); others, as the frame or loom on which the universe is woven.

Women in the Vedas

Three female poets—Ghosa, Apala, and Lopamudra—are named in the early part of the Vedas, and the *Upanishads* mention several women who took part in the quest for ultimate truth. In the *Brihadaranyaka Upanishad*, for instance, Maitreyi, the wife of the sage Yajnavalkya, questions him in depth about the nature of reality, and a woman philosopher named Gargi Vachaknavi challenges a male scholar in a public debate.

Document

How Many Gods Are There?

Vidagdha Shakalyah asked: "Yajnavalkya, how many gods are there?"

He answered . . . in line with the formulaic [mantra], ". . . three hundred and three, and three and three thousand."

"Yes, but Yajnavalkya, how many gods are there, really?"

"Thirty-three."

"Yes, but really, how many gods are there, Yajnavalkya?"

"Six."

"Yes, but really, how many gods are there, Yajnavalkya?"

"Three." . . .

"Yes, but really, how many gods are there, Yajnavalkya?"

"One and a half."

"Yes, but really, how many gods are there, Yajnavalkya?"

"One."

"Yes, but who are those three hundred and three and three thousand and three?"

"They are but the powers of the gods; there are only thirty-three gods" (*Brihadaranyaka Upanishad* 3.9.1–2; trans. Vasudha Narayanan).

These women were probably among the teachers through whom the sacred knowledge was transmitted. While the fathers of the teachers listed in the *Upanishads* are frequently named, in some cases the teachers are identified as the sons of particular women. In the *Brihadaranyaka Upanishad* (VI.5.1) roughly 45 teachers are listed with their mothers' names instead of their fathers'. This suggests that some teachers may have received spiritual instruction from their mothers.

Classical Hinduism

The literature that was composed after the Vedas, starting around 500 BCE, was recognized to be of human origin and was loosely called ***smrti*** ("that which is remembered"). Though theoretically less authoritative than the "revealed" *shruti*, this material was still considered inspired, and it has played a far more important role in the lives of Hindus. Several texts are classified as *smrti*: epics (*itihasas*), ancient stories (***Puranas***), and codes of law and ethics (*dharmashastras*).

For many Hindus the phrase "sacred books" refers specifically to the ***Ramayana*** ("Story of Rama") and the *Mahabharata* ("Great [Epic of] India" or "Great [Sons of] Bharata"). The best-known works in the Hindu tradition, these epic tales invariably constitute children's first and most lasting encounter with Hindu scripture.

The Ramayana

The *Ramayana* has been memorized, recited, sung, and performed on stage, often in dance, for 2,500 years. Its hero is the young prince Rama, whose father, Dasaratha, has decided to abdicate in favour of his son. On the eve of the coronation, however, a heartbroken Dasaratha is forced to exile Rama because of an earlier promise made to one of his wives. Rama accepts cheerfully and leaves for the forest, accompanied by his beautiful wife, Sita, and his half-brother Lakshmana, who both refuse to be separated from him. Bharata, the brother who has now been named king, returns from a trip to discover that Rama has gone into exile and his father has died of grief. He finds Rama and begs him to return, but Rama refuses because he feels he must respect his father's decision to banish him. He asks Bharata to rule as his regent.

While in the forest, Sita is captured by Ravana, the demon king of Lanka. Rama sets out to search for her with the aid of his brother and a group of monkeys led by Hanuman, a monkey with divine ancestry. It is Hanuman who finds Sita and reports her whereabouts to Rama, who, with the monkeys' help, goes to war with Ravana. After a long battle, Rama kills Ravana and is reunited with Sita. They eventually return to the capital and are crowned. Rama is considered the ideal son, husband, and king, and in later centuries he came to be seen as an incarnation of Vishnu. Sita too has been idealized both for her own qualities and for her relationship with her husband. In a sequel to the *Ramayana*, however, Rama's subjects become suspicious about Sita's virtue following her captivity in Ravana's grove. Because there is no way to prove her innocence, and possibly because he does not want to create a legal precedent for excusing a wife who has slept outside her husband's home, Rama banishes his own wife, who by now is pregnant.

The exiled Sita gives birth to twin sons. Some years later, the twins prepare to meet Rama in battle, and it is then that Sita tells them he is their father. There is a brief reunion. Rama asks Sita to prove her innocence in public by undergoing some ordeal, but Sita refuses and asks Mother Earth to take her back. She is then swallowed by the ground.

Many Hindus have considered Sita the ideal wife because she follows her husband to the forest. Others see her as a model of strength and virtue in her own right. She complies with her husband as he does with her; their love is one worthy of emulation. Yet she is also a woman who stands her ground when her husband asks her to prove her virtue. On one occasion, in Lanka, she acquiesces, but the second time she gently but firmly refuses and so rules out any possibility of reunion. The tale has sometimes been retold from Sita's viewpoint under the title *Sitayana*, and even conservative commentators agree with the time-honoured saying "*sitayas charitam mahat*" ("the deeds of Sita are indeed great"). Temples dedicated to Rama and Sita are found in many parts of the world.

The *Mahabharata* and the *Bhagavad Gita*

With approximately 100,000 verses, the *Mahabharata* is said to be the longest poem in the world. It is not found in many homes, but many people own copies of an extract from it called the ***Bhagavad Gita***.

The *Mahabharata* is the story of the great struggle among the descendants of a king named Bharata. The main part of the story concerns a war between two families, the Pandavas and the Kauravas. Though they are cousins, the Kauravas try to cheat the Pandavas out of their share of the kingdom and will not accept peace. A battle ensues in which all the major kingdoms are forced to take sides. Krishna, by this time considered to be an incarnation of the god Vishnu, is on the side of the Pandavas, but refuses to fight but agrees to serve as charioteer for the warrior Arjuna, who would come to be seen as representing the human soul in quest of liberation.

Just as the war is about to begin, Arjuna, who has won several battles, puts down his bow and asks Krishna whether it is correct to take up arms against one's own kin. Krishna replies that it is correct to fight for what is right; peaceful means must be tried, but if they fail one must fight for righteousness ("dharma"). The conversation between Arjuna and Krishna, which unfolds across 18 chapters, constitutes the *Bhagavad Gita*.

The *Gita* teaches both loving devotion to Krishna and the importance of selfless action. It was probably written sometime between 200 BCE and 200 CE, and for centuries people learned it by heart. In verses that are still recited at Hindu funerals, Krishna describes the soul as existing beyond the reach of the mind and the senses, unaffected by physical nature. Just as human beings exchange old clothes for new ones, so the human soul discards one body and puts on another through the ages, until it acquires the knowledge that will free it forever from the cycle of birth and death.

Document

From the *Bhagavad Gita*

On the immortality of the soul:

Our bodies are known to end, but the embodied self is enduring, indestructible, and immeasurable; therefore, Arjuna, fight the battle!

He who thinks this self a killer and he who thinks it killed, both fail to understand it does not kill, nor is it killed.

It is not born, it does not die; having been, it will never not be; unborn, enduring, constant, and primordial, it is not killed when the body is killed. . . .

As a man discards worn-out clothes to put on new and different ones, so the embodied self discards its worn-out bodies to take on other new ones.

Weapons do not cut it, fire does not burn it, waters do not wet it, wind does not wither it. It cannot be cut or burned; it cannot be wet or withered; it is enduring, all-pervasive, fixed, immovable, and timeless. . . .

On the way of action:

Be intent on action, not on the fruits of action; avoid attraction to the fruits and attachment to inaction!

Perform actions, firm in discipline, relinquishing attachment; be impartial to failure and success—this equanimity is called discipline. . . .

When he shows no preference in fortune or misfortune and neither exults nor hates, his insight is sure. . . .

On the mystery and purpose of incarnation:

Whenever sacred duty decays and chaos prevails, then, I create myself, Arjuna.

To protect men of virtue and destroy men who do evil to set the standard of sacred duty, I appear in age after age. . . .

On the nature of God and the way of devotion:

Always glorifying me, striving, firm in their vows, paying me homage with devotion, they worship me, always disciplined. . . .

I am the universal father, mother, granter of all, grandfather, object of knowledge, purifier, holy syllable OM, threefold sacred love.

I am the way, sustainer, lord, witness, shelter, refuge, friend, source, dissolution, stability, treasure, and unchanging seed.

I am heat that withholds and sends down the rains; I am immortality and death; both being and nonbeing am I. . . .

The leaf or flower or fruit or water that he offers with devotion, I take from the man of self-restraint in response to his devotion.

Whatever you do—what you take, what you offer, what you give, what penances you perform—do as an offering to me, Arjuna!

You will be freed from the bonds of action, from the fruit of fortune and misfortune; armed with the discipline of renunciation, yourself liberated, you will join me. . . .

Keep me in your mind and devotion, sacrifice to me, bow to me, discipline your self toward me, and you will reach me!

(Miller 1986: 32–87)

Thus Arjuna is told not to grieve at what is about to take place; but he is also warned that if he does not fight for righteousness, he will be guilty of moral cowardice and will have to face the consequences of quitting at a time when it was his duty (dharma) to protect the people by waging a just war.

Krishna also makes several statements about himself in the *Gita* that mark an important shift in Hindu theology. The *Upanishads* presented the Supreme Being, Brahman, as beyond human conceptualization, but in the *Gita* Krishna speaks of himself as both a personal god, one so filled with love for human beings that he will incarnate himself to protect them, and the ultimate deity, the origin, maintenance, and dissolution of the universe.

The Three Ways to Liberation

In the course of the *Gita*, Krishna describes three ways to liberation from the cycle of birth and death: the way of action, the way of knowledge, and the way of devotion. (Some Hindus would argue that they are three aspects of the same way.) Each way (*marga*) is also a discipline (yoga).

The way of action (*karma yoga*) is the path of unselfish duty, performed neither in fear of punishment nor in hope of reward. To expect a reward leads to bondage and unhappiness, since even if we do receive it, we will not be satisfied for long. Soon that goal will be replaced with another, leading to further action—and further accumulation of karma, which only leads to further rebirth. Other books of the time taught that even the "good" karma acquired by performing good deeds is ultimately bad, because, to enjoy it, we must be reborn. A thirteenth-century Hindu philosopher, Pillai Lokacharya, described good karma as "golden handcuffs." Therefore Krishna urges Arjuna to act without attachment to the consequences.

Krishna also explains the way of knowledge (*jnana yoga*), through which we may achieve a transforming wisdom that also destroys our past karma. True knowledge is insight into the real nature of the universe. Later philosophers say that when we hear scripture, ask questions, clarify doubts, and eventually meditate on this knowledge, we achieve liberation.

The third way—the one emphasized most throughout the *Gita*—is the way of devotion (*bhakti yoga*). If there is a general amnesty offered to those who sin, it is through devotion. Ultimately, Krishna promises that he will forgive all our sins if we surrender and devote ourselves to him (*Gita* 18: 66).

The Deities of Classical Hinduism

The period of the Gupta empire (c. 320–540) was one of great cultural and scholarly activity. In mathematics the concept of zero was introduced, along with the decimal system. Around 499 Aryabhatta established both the value of pi (3.14) and the length of the solar year (365.3586 days); he also proposed that the Earth is spherical and rotates on its axis. Contact with Greek and Roman trade missions from the Mediterranean increased, and coastal towns flourished, particularly in southern India. Meanwhile, Hindus, Jainas, and Buddhists all composed poems and plays that reveal a great deal about the religious life of the time.

Hinduism had not been dormant during the previous seven centuries, but it had been overshadowed to some degree by Buddhism. Now, under the Guptas, Buddhist influences receded and Hindu sectarian traditions became popular. Eventually, some Hindu texts would even assimilate the Buddha as an incarnation of Vishnu.

Precisely when the transition occurred is not clear, but from the Gupta era onward three deities become increasingly prominent: Vishnu, Shiva, and Shiva's consort, variously known as Parvati, Durga, Devi, or simply "the Goddess." Devotees who give primacy to Vishnu are termed Vaishnavas; those who focus on Shiva are termed Shaivas; and some followers of the Goddess are called Shaktas, in reference to her role as the *shakti* ("power") of her divine consort.

Starting around 300 BCE and continuing until roughly 1000 CE, texts called the *Puranas* (from the Sanskrit for "old") retold the "old tales" of the Hindu tradition, shifting the emphasis away from the major Vedic gods and goddesses in favour of other deities. As these gods moved to the forefront, the Hindu tradition as we know it today crystallized.

Vishnu

Vishnu ("the all-pervasive one") is portrayed as coming to Earth in various forms, animal and human, to rid the world of evil and establish dharma or righteousness. In the first of these

The Hindola Torana at Gyaraspur, Madhya Pradesh, dates from the tenth or eleventh century and was probably a gateway to a temple. The ten incarnations of Vishnu are carved on the pillars. Gyaraspur is near the famous Buddhist Sanchi stupa, and Udayagiri, the site of a fifth-century Gupta-era temple complex (© Vasudha Narayanan).

incarnations (***avataras***) he appears as a fish who saves Manu, the primeval man. This story was originally part of the Vedic literature, but is expanded in the *Puranas*.

While bathing in a lake, Manu finds a small fish in his hand. The fish speaks to him and asks him to take it home and put it in a jar. The next day it has expanded to fill the jar. Now Manu is asked to put the fish into a lake, which it outgrows, then into a river, and finally into the ocean. The fish, who is really Vishnu, then tells Manu that a great flood is coming, and that he must build a boat and put his family in it, along with the seven sages or *rishis*, and "the seeds of all the animals." Manu does as he is told, and when the flood sweeps the Earth, those on the ship survive. This story is strongly reminiscent of flood myths in other religious traditions.

Eventually, Vishnu will have ten incarnations in the present cycle of creation. Nine are said to have taken place already, and the tenth is expected at the end of this age. Some of the earliest carvings in India, in the Udayagiri caves of Madhya Pradesh, dated c. 400 CE, depict Vishnu's second and third incarnations, as a tortoise and as a boar who saves the earth goddess Bhu. His seventh incarnation was Rama, the hero of the epic, and according to some narratives the ninth

Vishnu in his boar incarnation, saving the earth goddess Bhu from the demon Hiranyaksha; Udayagiri caves, Madhya Pradesh, India, c. 401 CE (© Vasudha Narayanan).

was Krishna, whom we have already met in the *Bhagavad Gita*. The *Puranas* tell many stories about Krishna: the delightful infant, the mischievous toddler who steals the butter he loves, the youth who steals the hearts of the cowherd girls and dances away the moonlit nights in their company. Some of the later *Puranas* celebrate the love of Krishna and his beloved Radha.

In many other incarnations Vishnu is accompanied by his consort Sri (Lakshmi), the goddess of good fortune, who blesses her worshippers not only with wealth but, eventually, with liberation. All stores display pictures of her, and so do most homes.

Shiva

Like Vishnu, Shiva emerged as a great god in the post-Upanishadic era. Unlike Vishnu, however, he does not reveal himself sequentially, in a series of incarnations. Instead, Shiva expresses the manifold aspects of his power by appearing simultaneously in paradoxical roles: as creator and destroyer, exuberant dancer and austere yogi. The wedding portrait of Shiva and his divine consort, Parvati, is an important part of his tradition, and his creative energy is often represented in the symbolic form of a **linga**: an upright stone shaft placed in a receptacle, *yoni*, that symbolizes the womb. Stories of Shiva and his local manifestations—for instance, as Sundaresvara in the city of Madurai—are popular throughout India.

The Goddess

The great Goddess also appears in multiple forms, although the lines between them are not always clearly defined (Western scholars tend to emphasize the distinctions, while Hindus tend to blur them). Though many goddesses appear in the Vedas, none of them were all-powerful. Likewise, the epics and the early *Puranas* honour many consort goddesses, but no supreme female deity. It is only in the later *Puranas* that we begin to see explicit references to worship of a goddess as the ultimate power, the creator of the universe, and the redeemer of human beings. She was sometimes considered to be the *shakti* or power of Shiva, but often her independence from the male deity was emphasized.

The most familiar manifestation of the Goddess is Parvati, the wife of Shiva. Durga is her warrior aspect, represented iconographically with a smiling countenance and a handful of weapons. As Kali, the Goddess is fierce and wild, a dark, dishevelled figure who wears a garland of skulls; yet even in this manifestation, her devotees call her "mother." In addition there are countless local goddesses with distinctive names and histories. Festivals like the autumn celebration of **Navaratri** ("nine nights") are dedicated to the Goddess, and millions of Hindus offer her devotions every day.

Sarasvati

In the *Puranas* the Vedic goddess Sarasvati becomes the goddess of learning. Although she is the consort of a creator god named **Brahma** (a minor deity, not to be confused with Brahman), portraits usually depict her alone, without any male god. She is a beautiful young woman, radiant with wisdom, sitting gracefully on a rock beside a river. She has four hands; two of them hold a stringed musical instrument called a *vina*, another holds a string of beads, and the last holds a manuscript. The *vina* symbolizes music and the manuscript learning, while the beads signify the counting and recitation of holy names, which leads to transformative knowledge. All these themes would eventually coalesce to form the composite picture of Sarasvati as the patron goddess of arts and education, music and letters.

Other Popular Deities

Ganesha, the elephant-headed son of Shiva and Parvati, is probably the most beloved of all the Hindu gods. He removes obstacles and hindrances, and no new project or venture begins without a prayer to him. Murugan, another son of Shiva, is popular among Tamil-speaking people in India, Sri Lanka, Malaysia, and Canada. And the monkey god Hanuman, a model devotee of Rama and Sita, is everyone's protector.

In South India, Vishnu, Shiva, and Devi are frequently known by local names. Thus Vishnu is known in the Tirupati hills and Srirangam as Venkateshwara ("lord of the Venkata hill") or Ranganatha ("lord of the stage"). Each manifestation has both unique personality and a mythical history that links it with a particular place. Sri or Lakshmi is called the mother of all creation, who bestows

A Ganesha image for the digital age shows the dynamism of the Hindu tradition (© Vasudha Narayanan).

wisdom and salvation and is grace incarnate. Many teachers have composed hymns celebrating her compassion and wisdom. Vedanta Desika (1268–1369) describes her thus:

> She fulfills all [our] desires. She is noble, she gives prosperity, she is filled with good thoughts; she gives righteousness, pleasure, attainment and liberation. She gives the highest state (parinirvana) . . . she helps one cross the ocean of life and death. . . .

The Hindu "Trinity"

In the symbolism of *trimurti* ("three forms"), the gods Brahma, Vishnu, and Shiva either coalesce into one form with three faces or are represented as equal. This has sometimes been interpreted as implying a polytheistic belief in three gods: Brahma the creator, Vishnu the preserver, and Shiva the destroyer. It is true that the *trimurti* concept brings together the three great functions of a supreme god and distributes them among three distinct deities. But this interpretation is misleading in two ways.

First, it suggests that Hindus give equal importance to all three gods, when in practice most focus their devotions on a single supreme deity (whether Shiva, Vishnu, the Goddess, or a local deity who may be unknown in other parts of India) and consider the other deities secondary. Furthermore, Brahma is not worshipped as a supreme deity. Though portrayed in mythology as the creator god, he is only the agent of the supreme deity who created him; that deity, at whose pleasure Brahma creates the universe, may be Vishnu, Shiva, or the Goddess, depending on the worshipper's sect.

Second, the "polytheistic" interpretation of *trimurti* suggests that creation, preservation, and destruction are functions that can be performed separately. But in fact these functions are three parts of an integrated process for which one particular supreme god is responsible. In this context, destruction is not unplanned, nor is it final: it is simply one phase in the ongoing evolution and devolution of the universe. The cycle of creation will continue as long as there are souls caught up in the wheel of life and death. It is in this sense that devotees of Shiva, Vishnu, or the Goddess see their chosen deity as the creator, maintainer, and destroyer of the universe.

Ages of Time

The *Puranas* refer to those cosmic cycles of creation and destruction as the days and nights of Brahma. Each day of Brahma contains approximately 4,320 million earthly years, and the nights of Brahma are equally long. A year of Brahma is made up of 360 such days, and Brahma lives for 100 years. Each cycle therefore amounts to 311,040,000 million earthly years, at the end of which the entire cosmos is drawn into the body of Vishnu or Shiva (depending on which *Purana* one is reading), where it remains until another Brahma is evolved.

Each day of Brahma contains 14 secondary cycles of creation and destruction called *manavantaras*, each of which lasts 306,720,000 years. During the long intervals between *manavantaras*, the world is recreated and a new Manu or primeval man appears and once again begins the human race.

Each *manavantara* in turn contains 71 great eons (*maha yugas*), each of which is divided into four eons (*yugas*). A single eon is the basic cycle. The golden age (*krta yuga*) lasts 1,728,000 earthly years. During this time dharma or righteousness is envisioned as a bull standing firmly on all four legs. The Treta age is shorter, 1,296,000 earthly years; dharma is then on three legs. The Dvapara age lasts half as long as the golden age; thus for 864,000 earthly years dharma hops on two legs. Finally, during the *kali yuga*, the worst of all possible ages, dharma is reduced to one leg. This age lasts for 432,000 earthly years, during which the world becomes progressively worse. It is in this degenerate *kali yuga*—which, according to traditional Hindu reckoning, began around 3102 BCE—that we live today.

There is a steady decline in morality, life span, and human satisfaction through the *yugas*. At the end of the *kali yuga*—still a long time off—there will be no righteousness, no virtue, no trace of justice. When the world ends, seven scorching suns will dry up the oceans, torrential rains will fall, and eventually the cosmos will be absorbed into Vishnu until the next cycle of creation begins. The *Puranas* deal with astronomical units of time; the age of the Earth itself is infinitesimally small in relation to the eons of time that the universe goes through. Individual beings may end their own cycles of birth and death by attaining *moksha*, but this has no effect on the cycles of creation and destruction of the universe.

Temple architecture sometimes reflects the Puranic cycles of time. At the great Vishnu temple of Angkor Wat in Cambodia, for instance, the causeways and passages were designed so that their measurements (when calculated in the units used in the building of the temple) represent the numbers of years in various cycles of time.

Caste and the *Dharmashastras*

"Caste" is a shorthand for the thousands of social and occupational divisions that have developed from the simple fourfold structure laid out in the "Hymn to the Supreme Person": priests, rulers, merchants, and servants. There are more than 1,000 *jatis* ("birth groups") in India, and people routinely identify themselves by their *jati*. Ritual practices, dietary rules, and sometimes dialects differ between castes, and inter-caste marriage is rare.

By the early Common Era, many treatises had been written regarding the nature of righteousness, moral duty, and law. These *dharmashastras* are the foundations of later Hindu laws. The most famous is the *Manava Dharmashastra* ("Laws of Manu"), which probably dates from around the first century.

The *dharmashastras* set out the roles and duties of the four principal castes that make up Hindu society: brahmins (priests), **kshatriyas** (rulers, warriors), **vaishyas** (merchants), and **shudras** (servants). The brahmins were (and are still) the priestly class, the only group in Hindu society supposedly authorized to teach the Vedas. Although not all members of the brahmin community were priests, all enjoyed the power and prestige associated with spiritual learning.

The dharma of the kshatriya class, which was permitted to study the Vedas but not to teach them, was to protect the people and the country. In the Hindu tradition, lines of descent are all-important. Thus many kings sought to confirm their legitimacy by tracing their ancestry to the primeval progenitors of humanity—either the sun or the moon—and even usurpers of thrones invoked divine antecedents. Later Hindu rituals explicitly emphasized kshatriya families' divine connections. The *Laws of Manu* describe in detail the duties of a king. He must strive to conquer his senses, for only those who have conquered their own senses can lead or control others, and must shun not only the vices of pleasure—hunting, gambling, drinking, women—but also the vices of wrath, such as violence, envy, and slander.

The dharma of the vaishya (mercantile) class made them responsible for most commercial transactions, as well as agriculture. The power of wealth and economic decisions lay with the vaishyas, who were likewise permitted only to study the Vedas.

The duty of the last class mentioned formally in the *dharmashastras*, the shudras, is to serve the other classes; they would not be permitted to accumulate wealth even if they had the opportunity to do so. As the *Laws of Manu* put it, "The seniority of brahmins comes from sacred knowledge, that of kshatriyas from valour, vaishyas from wealth, and shudras, only from old age."

In practice, however, the caste system is far more complex and flexible than the *dharmashastras* suggest. For example, the Vellalas of South India wielded considerable economic and political power, even though the brahmins considered them shudras. They were wealthy landowners, and the *dharmashastra* prohibitions do not seem to have had any effect on their fortunes.

Although they emphasize the importance of marrying within one's own class, the *dharmashastras* recognize that mixed marriages do take place, and so they list the kind of sub-castes that emerge from various permutations. A marriage is generally acceptable if the male partner is of a higher caste, but if the woman is higher, their offspring are considered to be of a lower caste than either parent.

Also part of India's social fabric are various "outcastes": groups officially excluded from the caste system either because they originated in mixed marriages in the distant past or, more often, because they are associated with occupations deemed polluting, such as dealing with corpses or working with animal hides (the English word "pariah" comes from the Tamil for "drummer"—an outcaste occupation because drums were made of animal hides). Until the nineteenth century, caste was only one factor among the many considered in the judicial process and in society itself. Legal cases were decided with reference to the immediate circumstances, and local customs were no less important than written texts—sometimes more so. It was India's British colonial rulers who, assuming that the caste laws were binding, attributed a new authority to them.

The caste system is such a strong social force in India that even non-Hindu communities such as the Christians, Jainas, and Sikhs have been influenced by it. Nadar Christians from the south, for instance, will marry only people of the same caste, and similar restrictions are observed all over India. In Southeast Asia, on the other hand, the caste system bears little resemblance to the Indian model: although inscriptions after the eighth century show that brahmins were honoured, the rest of society seems to have been organized in different ways, and the king sometimes awarded specific caste status to various groups. The caste system still functions to a limited extent in some diasporas but has been significantly diluted among Hindus in North America.

The Stages and Goals of Life

The dharma texts of the classical period recognized four stages of life (***ashramas***) for males from the three higher classes in society. First, during studenthood, a boy was to remain celibate and concentrate on learning. Education was to be provided for all those who desired it, and families were to support students. Although the early epics suggest that girls could also become students, it is likely that this right had been withdrawn by the time the *Laws of Manu* were codified.

In the next stage the young man was to repay his debts to society and his forefathers, and his spiritual debt to the gods, by marrying and earning a living to support his family and other students. It was the householder's duty to work and lead a conjugal life with his partner in dharma. Few men went beyond these two stages, and it is likely that most people never had the opportunity to study at all.

Nevertheless, the *Laws of Manu* describes two more stages. When a man's children have grown and become householders themselves, he and his wife may retire to the forest and live a simple life. Finally, in the last stage, an elderly man would renounce the material world altogether and take up the ascetic life of the ***samnyasin***. His former personality was now dead; he owned nothing, relied on food given as alms, and spent the rest of his days seeking enlightenment and cultivating detachment from life. This kind of formal renunciation became rare with the increasing popularity of the *Bhagavad Gita*, which stresses controlled engagement with the world.

The literature of the period just before the beginning of the Common Era also recognized a number of aims that human beings strive for. These are neither good nor bad in themselves, but may become immoral if they are pursued at an inappropriate time of life or with inappropriate intensity. The aims are dharma, the discharging of one's duties; ***artha***, prosperity and power; ***kama***, sensual pleasure of many types, including sexual pleasure and the appreciation of beauty; and finally, *moksha*, or liberation from the cycle of birth and death. The last was sometimes seen as belonging to a different category, but texts like the *Gita* made it clear that we may strive for liberation even in daily work as long as we act without attachment.

Attitudes towards Women

The Hindu scriptures were written by men, and many of their statements about women's position in society may seem contradictory, alternately honouring, respecting, and even venerating women, but also scorning them. The *Laws of Manu* make it only too clear that by the early Common Era women no longer enjoyed the relatively high status suggested in the Vedas. For example: "Though destitute of virtue, or seeking pleasure elsewhere, or devoid of good qualities, a husband must be constantly worshipped as a god by a faithful wife" (*Manu* 5.154). Male commentators through the centuries have quoted such statements approvingly.

The text goes on to say that a wife is the goddess of fortune and auspiciousness (*Manu* 9.26) and that only if women are honoured will the gods be pleased (*Manu* 3.56). On balance, however, the negative statements outweigh the positive ones. Perhaps the most famous of his pronouncements on women is the following:

> By a girl, by a young woman or even by an aged one, nothing must be done independently, even in her own house. In childhood a female must be subject to her father, in youth to her husband, when her lord is dead, to her sons; a woman must never be independent (*Manu* 5.147–8).

Statements like that, and the weight given to them by later commentators, did much to shape Western notions of Hindu women. As influential as *Manu* has been in some communities and at certain times, however, the views it presents cannot be considered prescriptive or normative. In fact, *Manu*'s dictates were not necessarily followed. As we will see, medieval women were more than dutiful wives: they composed poetry, endowed temples, gave religious advice and wrote scholarly works, including commentary on scripture. Far from being ostracized or condemned, those women were respected, honoured, and in some cases even venerated. Despite *Manu* and its proponents, many women of some socio-economic groups enjoyed both religious and financial independence and made substantial contributions to literature and the fine arts.

Some of the contradictions in Hindu thinking about women can be traced to the concept of auspiciousness. "Auspiciousness" refers primarily to prosperity in this life—above all, wealth and progeny. Thus cattle, elephants, kings, and married women with the potential to bear children are all auspicious, as are birth and marriage rituals, because they are associated with the goals of dharma, *artha*, and *kama*. There is also a second level of auspiciousness, however, that is related to the fourth and ultimate human goal: *moksha*. The two levels of auspiciousness have been implicit in Hindu religious literature and rituals. In many contexts, women have auspiciousness in different degrees, which determine the degree of their acceptance in society.

The ideal is the *sumangali*, the married woman who is a full partner in dharma, *artha*, and *kama*, through whom children are born, and wealth and religious merit are accumulated. Only a married woman may be called *Srimati* (the one with *sri* or auspiciousness). Traditionally, a Hindu wife's dharma included not only loyalty to her husband in life but fidelity to his memory after his death. While some of these notions are still adhered to in Hindu life, a woman's position in society depends on a variety of factors, including religious culture.

Schools and Communities of Theology

Vedanta

Six schools of "philosophy" are recognized within the Hindu tradition—Samkhya, Nyaya, Vaisheshika, Mimamsa, Yoga, and Vedanta—and elements of all six can be seen in modern Hinduism. Although popularly called "philosophy," these traditions are closer to theological schools, as they build on many Hindu texts. Yoga has attracted a wide popular following in recent years, but as a philosophical school Vedanta is by far the most important. Although the term "Vedanta" ("end of the Vedas") traditionally denoted the *Upanishads*, in popular usage it more often refers to systems of thought based on a coherent interpretation of the *Upanishads*, *Bhagavad Gita*, and *Brahma Sutras* (roughly 500 aphorisms summarizing the teachings of those texts).

An important early interpreter of Vedanta was Shankara (fl. c. 800). For him, reality is non-dual (***advaita***): the only reality is Brahman, and this reality cannot be described because it is without attributes. Brahman and Atman (the human soul) are identical; Shankara interprets the phrase "you are that" literally and upholds the unity of what most people perceive as two distinct entities. Under the influence of *maya* (often translated as "illusion") we believe we are different from Brahman, but when the illusion is dispelled, the soul is liberated by the realization of its true nature. Liberation, therefore, is the removal of ignorance and the dispelling of illusion through transforming knowledge. We can achieve liberation while still embodied; those who attain that goal act without binding desire and help others to achieve liberation. But *final release* will come only after the death of the body.

Shankara also posits three levels of reality. He recognizes that humans believe life to be real, but points out that when we are asleep we also believe that what happens in our dreams is real. Only on waking do we discover that what we dreamt was not real. So too in this cycle of life and death, we believe that everything we experience is real. And it is—until we are liberated and wake up to the truth. One might argue that the dream seems true only to the individual dreamer, whereas the phenomenal world appears real to millions who seem to share the same reality. But the school of Shankara would say that our limited reality is the result of ignorance and illusion. With the transformative knowledge spoken of in the *Upanishads*, we recognize that we are in reality Brahman and are liberated from the cycle of life and death. But that cycle goes on for the other souls still caught in the snares of *maya*.

Shankara's philosophy was criticized by later philosophers such as Ramanuja and Madhva. One of their principal objections involved the status of *maya*. If *maya* is real, then there are *two* realities, Brahman and *maya*; and if *maya* is unreal, it cannot be the cause of the cosmic delusion attributed to it. Shankara himself circumvents this objection, however, by saying that *maya* is indescribable, neither real nor unreal, and his followers would say that in the ultimate state of liberation, which is totally ineffable, such criticisms are not valid in any case.

The most significant interpreter of theistic Vedanta for the Sri Vaishnava community—devotees of Vishnu and his consorts—in South India was Ramanuja (traditionally 1017–1137), who emphasizes that devotion to Vishnu leads to ultimate liberation. He challenges Shankara's interpretation of scripture, especially regarding *maya*, and his belief that the supreme reality (Brahman) is without attributes. For Ramanuja, Vishnu (whose name means "all-pervasive") is immanent throughout the universe, pervading all souls and material substances, but also transcending them. Thus from one viewpoint there is a single reality, Brahman; but from another viewpoint Brahman is qualified by souls and matter. Since the human soul is the body and the servant of Brahman, who (according to Ramanuja) is also the supreme deity Vishnu, liberation is portrayed not as the realization

The temple tower at Tirukoshtiyur, Tamilnadu. One of the 108 places sung about by the Alvars, this temple was made famous by Ramanuja in the eleventh century CE. Given a secret mantra that would grant salvation, he is said to have climbed the tower and shouted the mantra aloud so that all the devotees in the area could receive the grace of Vishnu (© Vasudha Narayanan).

that the soul and Brahman are the same, but rather as the intuitive, joyful realization of the soul's relationship with the lord.

Sri Vaishnavas differ from other Hindus in that they hold sacred not only Sanskrit texts such as the Vedas and *Gita*, but also the Tamil compositions of the **Alvars**: 12 South Indian poet-saints who lived between the eighth and tenth centuries CE. Specifically, the Sri Vaishnavas call the *Tiruvaymoli* of Nammalvar the "Tamil Veda" and refer to their scriptural heritage as dual Vedic theology. They also revere Ramanuja, whose image is found in many of their temples.

The philosopher Madhva (c. 1199–1278) is unique in classifying some souls as eternally bound. For him there are different grades of enjoyment and bliss even in liberation. He is also explicitly dualistic, holding that the human soul and Brahman are ultimately separate, not identical in any way.

Yoga

Historically, "Yoga" has had many meanings, but in general it is the physical and mental discipline through which practitioners "yoke" their spirit to the divine. Its origins are obscure, though (as we saw) some scholars have suggested that seals from the Harappan culture portray a man sitting in what looks like a yogic position.

For many Hindus the classic yoga text is a collection of short, aphoristic fragments from the early Common Era called the *Yoga Sutras*, attributed to Patanjali, who is said to have lived in the second century BCE. It's likely that yoga had been an important feature of religious life in India for centuries before the text was written.

Patanjali's yoga is a system of moral, mental, and physical discipline and meditation with a particular object, either physical or mental, as the "single point" of focus. It is described as having eight "limbs" or disciplines. The first of these, *yama*, consists of restraints: avoidance of violence, falsehood, stealing, sexual activity, and avarice. (The same prohibitions are part of the "right conduct" taught by the Jaina tradition.) The second, *niyama*, consists of positive practices such as purity (internal and external), equanimity, asceticism, the theoretical study of yoga, and the effort to make God the focus of one's activities. In addition, Patanjali recommends a number of bodily postures and breathing techniques.

A crucial aspect of yoga practice is learning to detach the mind from the domination of external sensory stimuli. Perfection in concentration (*dharana*) and meditation (*dhyana*) lead to *samadhi*: absorption into and union with the divine, culminating in emancipation from the cycle of life and death. This state is variously described as a coming together and transcending of polarities; empty and full, neither life nor death, and yet both. Although Patanjali's yoga is widely considered the classical form, there are numerous variations. "Yoga" is often used to designate any form of meditation or practice with ascetic tendencies, and in broad terms it may refer to any path that leads to final emancipation. Thus in the *Bhagavad Gita* the way of action is called *karma yoga* and the way of devotion is *bhakti yoga*. In some interpretations, the eight "limbs" of classical yoga are not present; *bhakti yoga* simply comes to mean *bhakti marga*, the way of devotion. In this context yoga becomes a way of self-abnegation, in which the worshipper seeks union with the Supreme Being through passionate devotion. Some philosophers, including Ramanuja, have said that *bhakti yoga* includes elements of Patanjali's yoga, but many Hindus use the term "yoga" much more loosely. Few religious teachers have regarded Patanjali's yoga as a separate path to liberation.

Tantra

The term **tantra** refers to a body of ritual practices and the texts interpreting them; it may be derived from a word meaning "to stretch" or "expand." Tantra appears to be independent of the Vedic tradition, having gained importance in both the Hindu and Buddhist traditions around the fifth century. The Shaiva, Shakta, and Vaishnava communities all have their own tantric texts.

Tantra is difficult to define, because of its esoteric nature, its regional and sectarian variations, and its interpenetration with other systems of philosophy and practice. In general, tantric systems have four components: *jnana* (knowledge of the deities and divine powers), *yoga* (praxis); *kriya* (praxis and rituals), and *charya* (conduct and behaviour). Shaivas, Shaktas, and Vaishnavas incorporated elements of tantra in their own practice. For example, when an image of a deity is installed in a temple, a large geometric drawing (*yantra* or *mandala*) representing deities and the cosmos is drawn on the floor and used as an object of meditation and ritual. Worship of the deities in temples is to large extent based on tantric texts and practices. The use of *mantras*—words or short, formulaic phrases that are said to have transformational potency—is also important in the practice of tantra.

Some forms of tantric yoga centre on the *shakti* or power of the Goddess, which is said to lie coiled like a serpent at the base of the spine. When awakened, this power rises through six chakras or "wheels" within the body to reach the final chakra (under the skull) known as the thousand-petalled lotus. The ultimate aim is to allow this power to unite with the divine being in the thousand-petalled lotus. When this union is achieved, the practitioner is granted visions and psychic powers that eventually lead to liberation (*moksha*).

There are many types of tantrism, but the main division is between "left-" and "right-handed" schools. As the left hand is considered inauspicious, the term "left-handed" was applied to tantrism involving the ritual performance of activities forbidden in everyday life, such as drinking liquor, eating fish and meat, and having sexual intercourse with a partner other than one's spouse. "Right-handed" tantrism is more conservative.

Hinduism in Southeast Asia

Hindu culture today is associated almost exclusively with the Indian peninsula, but until the fourteenth century, Hindu influences were strong across Southeast Asia. Extensive trade links were established by the second century CE, and cultural connections were widespread. Many Sanskrit inscriptions and thousands of icons and sculptures portraying Hindu deities indicate that Hinduism was pervasive in Cambodia, Thailand, Laos, Vietnam, Java, Indonesia, and Bali. One of the largest Hindu temples in the world is Angkor Wat, built and dedicated to Vishnu in the twelfth century, and kings and queens of Cambodia had names reminiscent of Indian–Hindu royalty, including Jayavarman, Indravarman, and Indira-lakshmi.

Even so, Hindu traditions in Southeast Asia have distinctive local characteristics. The Khmer people of Cambodia, for instance, emphasized some gods (such as Hari-Hara) and stories that were not so important in India. And although temples in Cambodia, Laos, and Indonesia are often similar to their Indian counterparts in their basic design, they are strikingly different in effect.

Icons of deities such as Shiva, Brahma, Vishnu, and Ganesha have been found all over Southeast Asia. In Cambodia, Shiva is sometimes depicted with two wives, Uma and Ganga. While the *Puranas* say that the river Ganga resides in his hair, other narratives treat the river itself as a deity, a consort of Shiva. For this reason local rivers in Cambodia came to be considered holy, and their identification with the Ganga was emphasized in rock carvings on their banks.

Vishnu reclining on a snake called Ananta, surrounded by Shiva lingas; carved on the rocks in Cambodia's Kbal Spean river (© Vasudha Narayanan).

Knowledge of Indian Vaishnava texts, including the two epics, was widespread among the elite, and carvings of Vishnu in various incarnations can be found in temples across Southeast Asia. The Prambanan temple near Yogyakarta, Indonesia, is one of many in the region whose walls are carved with scenes from the *Ramayana* and the *Puranas*. It also has shrines for Brahma and Vishnu, although the main shrine is dedicated to Shiva. In fact, most of the temples in Southeast Asia were home to more than one deity.

Even though Hinduism was largely displaced by Buddhism by the fifteenth century, and is not widely practised today except in Bali and among descendants of Indian immigrants, cultural traditions associated with it linger. Dances based on stories from the *Ramayana* are part of almost every cultural event, and names of Indian origin are still common in Indonesia, Thailand, and Cambodia.

South Indian Devotion (*Bhakti*)

The standard portrait of Vedic and classical Hinduism is based on the culture of the northern part of the Indian subcontinent. But South India had a flourishing cultural life of its own by 400 BCE and possibly earlier. It was here that an entirely new type of Hindu devotion (***bhakti***) emerged and spread throughout India.

A sophisticated body of literature in the Tamil language existed 2,000 years ago. Its earliest components are a number of poems on secular themes that fall into two groups: one dealing with the outer (*puram*) world of warfare and honour, the other with the inner (*akam*) world of love and romance.

Religious literature apparently flourished after the fifth century, with several poems addressed to Vishnu, Shiva, and Murugan (the son of Shiva and Parvati). The *bhakti* movement began when poet-devotees of Vishnu and Shiva began singing the praises of their deities not in formal Sanskrit but in Tamil—the mother tongue of the people, the language of intimacy and powerful emotion. This represented a major shift in Hindu culture.

By the twelfth century, 75 of these devotees had been recognized as saints: 63 devotees of Shiva known as the Nayanmars ("masters") and 12 devotees of Vishnu known as the Alvars ("those 'immersed deep' in the love of Vishnu"). Composed between the seventh and ninth centuries, the vernacular songs of the Alvars were introduced into the temple liturgy as early as the tenth century, challenging orthodox claims that Sanskrit was the exclusive vehicle for revelation and theological communication. Moreover, brahmin theologians honoured their authors as ideal devotees. This was extraordinarily significant, for some of the Alvars came from lower-caste (perhaps even outcaste) backgrounds, and one of them—Andal—was a woman. Selections from their works, collected in the eleventh century as the *Sacred Collect of Four Thousand Verses*, are recited daily by the Sri Vaishnava community, which considers them the Tamil equivalents of the Sanskrit Vedas.

The poems of the Alvars follow the literary conventions of earlier Tamil poetry, incorporating the symbolism of the *akam* and *puram* poems. Vishnu is seen as a lover and a king, accessible and remote, gracious and grand. In their songs of devotion, the Alvars seek from Vishnu both

Document

From the Songs of Andal

Andal ("she who rules") was an eighth-century Alvar who is worshipped in many South Indian temples dedicated to Vishnu. Every December, her passionate poetry is broadcast over radio stations in Tamilnadu and Karnataka. Tradition says that she refused to marry and longed for union with Vishnu—a wish that her biographers claim was fulfilled. Thus in her life as well as her work Andal represents a radical alternative to Manu's view of women and their role. Icons of Andal can be found in major South Indian Hindu temples across North America as well as in many other parts of the world.

A thousand elephants circle,
as Narana, Lord of virtues,
walks in front of me.
Golden jars brim with water;
Festive flags and pennants fly through this town,
eager to welcome him—
I saw this in a dream, my friend!

Drums beat happy sounds; conches were blown.
Under the canopy strung heavy with pearls,
Madhusudha, my love, filled with virtue,
came and clasped the palm of my hand
I saw this in a dream, my friend!

Those with eloquent mouths recited the good Vedas,
With mantras they placed
the green leaves and the grass in a circle.
The lord, strong as a raging elephant,
softly held my hand as we circled the fire.
I saw this in a dream, my friend!
(*Nachchiyar Tirumoli* 1.1 and 1.6–7; trans. Vasudha Narayanan)

the embrace of the beloved and the protection of the king. Many incidents from the *Ramayana*, *Mahabharata*, and *Puranas* make their way into the Alvars' songs, along with some stories not found in any of these sources. Above all, the poets focus on the supremacy of Vishnu–Narayana, emphasizing how his incarnation as Rama or Krishna and his presence in the temple show his desire to save all beings. In the eighth century, Kulacekara Alvar expressed his longing to see Rama in the temple at Tillai (the modern city of Chidambaram):

> In the beautiful city of Ayodhya, encircled by towers,
> a flame that lit up all the worlds
> appeared in the Solar race
> and gave life to all the heavens.
> This warrior, with dazzling eyes,
> Rama, dark as a cloud,
> the First One, My Lord,
> is in Chitrakuta, city of Tillai.
> When is the day
> when my eyes can behold him
> and rejoice? (*Perumal Tirumoli* 10.1)

Sometimes the Alvars identify themselves with characters from the epics or the *Puranas*, expressing their longing for Vishnu by speaking in the voice of one who is separated from Rama or Krishna. A royal devotee of Rama, Kulacekara Alvar, imagines the grief felt by Rama's father Dasaratha after banishing his son to the forest:

> Without hearing him call me "Father" with pride and with love,
> Without clasping his chest adorned with gems to mine,
> Without embracing him, without smoothing his forehead,
> Without seeing his graceful gait, majestic like the elephant,
> Without seeing his face [glowing] like the lotus,
>   I, wretched one,
>   having lost my son, my lord,
>   Still live (*Perumal Tirumoli* 9.6).

Many of the Tamil saints, both Vaishnava and Shaiva, travelled all over South India and parts of the north, visiting temples in which their chosen deity was enshrined. In this way pilgrimage became an important part of the Hindu tradition. Eventually, 108 sites came to be known as sacred places where Vishnu abides, and the number was even higher for the Shaivas, some of whom split from the mainstream in the twelfth century to form a new sect in what is now the state of Karnataka. Rejecting temple worship as well as the caste system and ritual sacrifice, the Vira ("heroic") Shaivas chose to express their devotion to Shiva symbolically, by carrying a small *linga*.

North Indian Bhakti

North Indian *bhakti* resembled its southern counterpart both in its use of vernacular languages and in the fact that it was open to people of every caste, but it differed in the focus of devotion. Whereas

Document

From the *Tiruvaymoli*

Although philosophical texts say that the soul is beyond gender, devotional poets have often used the language of human love to express their feelings for the divine. In the following extract from the Tiruvaymoli*—the ninth-century masterpiece that is considered to be a "fifth Veda"—the poet Nammalvar speaks in the voice of a young girl who longs for Vishnu as she would for a human lover (the indented lines refer to various incarnations of Vishnu).*

Where do I go from here?
I can't stand the soft bells, the gentle breeze,
the dark water-lily, darkness that conquers day,
dulcet notes, jasmines, the refreshing air.
The Lord, my beguiling one,
    who creates, bores through,
    swallows and spews this earth,
    who measures here and beyond,
does not come.
Why should I live? (*Tiruvaymoli* 9.9.2; trans. Vasudha Narayanan)

South Indian *bhakti* was generally addressed to either Vishnu or Shiva, the object of devotion in the north was often Rama or Krishna (*avataras* of Vishnu), and sometimes the divine being without a form. An early exponent of Krishna devotion was the twelfth-century poet Jayadeva, whose Sanskrit work *Gita Govinda* ("Song of the Cowherd") extols the love of Radha and Krishna; it also contains a reference to the Buddha as an incarnation of Krishna–Vishnu, filled with compassion.

The sometimes synergistic relationship that developed between Hindus and Muslims in northern India (see Focus box, p. 311) was reflected in the delightful, sometimes poignant works composed in the vernacular by poet-singers of the Sant ("holy person" or "truth") tradition. Emphasizing the *nirguna* ("without attributes") Brahman of the *Upanishads*, the Sants held the divinity to be without form. Hence their worship had nothing to do with physical images, and—unlike the Tamil poet-saints, who travelled from temple to temple precisely in order to express their devotion to local manifestations of their chosen deity—they expressed their devotion either in poetry or in silent meditation. They also rejected distinctions between religious communities.

Among the most important Sant poets was Kabir (1440-1518?), who is said to have been both Hindu and Muslim. In his insistence that God is beyond the particularities of any religious community, Kabir had much in common with a Punjabi religious leader named Nanak (1469–1539) and a Sufi Muslim teacher named Dadu (1544–1603). In time, the disciples of Kabir and Dadu were reabsorbed into the general populations of Hindus and Muslims, but Nanak's ultimately formed a separate community: the Sikhs. Kabir was one of several Sant poets whose works became part of the Sikh scripture.

With the spread of the North Indian *bhakti* movement, powerful devotional works in vernacular languages made the classic teachings accessible to everyone. Two important figures in this movement were Surdas and Tulsidas. Surdas (c. 1483–1563) was a blind singer and poet whose Hindi compositions celebrate Radha's devotion to the youthful Krishna as a model of *bhakti*. Tulsidas (1543?–1623) is perhaps best-known for his *Lake of the Deeds of Rama*, a Hindi retelling of the *Ramayana* that many people still quote from, and that formed the basis for a blockbuster TV serial in the 1980s.

Focus

Hindu–Muslim Relations

Islam arrived in India around the middle of the eighth century CE. In southern India the first Muslims were seafaring Arab traders who visited the region's many ports on their way to and from Southeast Asia. Over time, a minority Muslim population became established that was well integrated into the larger society.

Early encounters in northern India took a more hostile form. The invasions led by Mahmud of Ghazni (971–1030) and Muhammad of Ghor (1150-1206) paved the way for the installation of Ghor's general Qutbuddin Aibak as the first Muslim ruler in northern India. The plundering and destruction of sacred Hindu monuments such as the Somnath temple in Gujarat in 1025 have long been a part of the Hindu collective memory. On the other hand, the synergy made possible by the confluence of cultural influences from the Middle East and India gave rise to extraordinary innovations in all the arts.

The period of Mughal rule, from the early sixteenth century to the early eighteenth, was characterized by a growing sense of "Hindu" identity in North India (although "Hindu" was not yet the standard term that it would become under the British). There was also growing antagonism against Muslim rulers, especially Aurangzeb, the last Mughal emperor, who imposed severe hardship on large segments of the population. It was in this political climate that several leaders emerged to fight for Hindus' religious and political freedom. Notable among them was Shivaji (c. 1630–80) from what is now Maharashtra. A hero of national proportions, he is credited with developing the concept of self-rule for Hindus.

A Bengali contemporary of Surdas was Chaitanya (1486–1583), who took the religious name Krishna-Chaitanya, "he whose consciousness is Krishna." Like many theologians who have emphasized *bhakti*, he maintained that humans in the present degenerate age cannot fulfill all the requirements of religious action and duty; therefore the only way to liberation is through trusting devotion to a gracious deity.

For Chaitanya, however, the ultimate goal was not liberation from attachment in the traditional sense but rather the active enjoyment of his intense love of Krishna—a spiritual love equivalent to the passion that the cowherd girls felt for him. Chaitanya is said to have led people through the streets, singing about his lord and urging others to join him in chanting Krishna's names. Chaitanya's movement was revived in the 1800s and eventually led to the formation of the International Society for Krishna Consciousness (ISKCON)—better known as the Hare Krishna movement. Both the Hare Krishnas' theology, locating divine grace in Krishna, and their practice, centred on devotional chanting, can be traced directly to Chaitanya.

Colonialism and Beyond

It was the Portuguese explorer Vasco da Gama who fulfilled Columbus's ambition of finding a sea route from Europe to India. When he landed in the western city of Calicut in 1498, he opened the way for a long line of traders, missionaries, and, eventually, rulers. Before long, the Dutch, English, and French were also travelling to India and establishing settlements there. Early European research

Document

From Kabir

Go naked if you want,
Put on animal skins.
What does it matter till you see the inward Ram?
If the union yogis seek
Came from roaming about in the buff,
Every deer in the forest would be saved. . . .
Pundit, how can you be so dumb?
You're going to drown, along with all your kin
Unless you start speaking of Ram.
Vedas, *Puranas*—why read them?
It's like loading an ass with sandalwood!
Unless you catch on and learn how Ram's name goes,
How will you reach the end of the road?
You slaughter living beings and call it religion:
Hey brother, what would irreligion be?
"Great Saint"—that's how you love to greet each other:
Who then would you call a murderer?
Your mind is blind. You've no knowledge of yourselves.
Tell me, brother, how can you teach anyone else?
Wisdom is a thing you sell for worldly gain,
So there goes your human birth—in vain (Hawley and Juergensmeyer 1988: 50–1).

into Indian languages, especially Sanskrit, led to the historical reconstruction of the movements of the Indo-European people from Central Asia and pioneered the theory of a common Indo-European ancestry. This was the first glimpse that Hindus received of their pre-Vedic history.

In time the foreign powers became involved in local politics. As the Mughal empire disintegrated in the early 1700s, many chieftains enlisted English or French help in their efforts to acquire land. Eventually large parts of the Indian subcontinent were loosely united under British control. In the past, most rulers, Hindu or Muslim, had accepted a large degree of local autonomy, but the British—despite their policy of "religious neutrality"—did not recognize the importance of local

Document

From Mirabai

Mirabai (1450?–1547) was a Rajput princess in Gujarat. A devotee of Krishna, she wrote passionate poetry about her love for him.

Sister, I had a dream that I wed
the Lord of those who live in need:
Five hundred sixty thousand people came
and the Lord of Braj was the groom.
In dream they set up a wedding arch;
in dream he grasped my hand;
in dream he led me around the wedding fire
and I became unshakably his bride.
Mira's been granted her mountain-lifting Lord:
from living past lives, a prize (Caturvedi, no. 27; Hawley and Juergensmeyer 1988: 137).

tradition or practice. At the same time, foreign missionaries were severely critical not only of what they called Hindu "idolatry," but of the caste system and practices such as ***sati*** (self-immolation of widows on their husbands' funeral pyres). The foreigners were not the only ones to call for change, however—some Hindu intellectuals were equally convinced of the need for reform.

The Brahmo Samaj

Ram Mohan Roy (1772–1833) was born into an orthodox brahmin family in western Bengal. He is said to have studied the Qur'an as well as the Vedas, and may also have explored Buddhism. Eventually joining the East India Company, he became familiar with the Christian scriptures and formed close ties with members of the Unitarian movement. He rejected the Christian belief in Jesus as the son of God, but admired him as a compassionate human being, and in 1820 he published a book, *The Precepts of Jesus: The Guide to Peace and Happiness*, that emphasized the compatibility of Jesus' moral teachings with the Hindu tradition.

Roy believed that if Hindus could read their own scriptures they would recognize that practices such as *sati* were not part of the classic tradition. Therefore he translated extracts from Sanskrit texts into Bengali and English and distributed them for free. In 1828 he established a society to hold regular discussions on the nature of Brahman as it is presented in the *Upanishads*. This organization, the Brahmo Samaj ("congregation of Brahman"), emphasized monotheism, rationalism, humanism, and social reform. Although Roy rejected most of the stories from the epics and the *Puranas* as myths that stood in the way of reason and social reform, he drew on the Vedas, particularly the *Upanishads*, to defend Hinduism against the attacks of Christian missionaries. At the same time, with the Unitarians, he accused the missionaries of straying from monotheism in teaching the doctrine of the Trinity (God as father, son, and holy spirit). A pioneer in the area of women's rights, including the right to education, he fought to abolish *sati* and child marriage. He also founded a number of periodicals and educational institutions.

The Brahmo Samaj has never become a "mainstream" movement. Nevertheless, it revitalized Hinduism by calling attention both to inhumane practices and to the need for education and reform, and in so doing played a major part in the modernization of Indian society.

The Arya Samaj

The Arya Samaj was established in 1875 by Dayananda Saraswati (1824–83). Born into a brahmin family in Gujarat, he left home at the age of 21 to take up the life of an ascetic. After 15 years as a wandering yogi, he studied Sanskrit under a charismatic guru named Virajananda, who taught that the only true Hindu scriptures were the early Vedas and rejected what he perceived as later additions to the tradition, including the worship of images. On leaving his teacher, Dayananda promised that he would work to reform Hinduism in accordance with the true teachings of the Vedas.

Dayananda believed that the Vedas were literally revealed by God, and that the vision they presented could be revived by stripping away later human accretions such as votive rituals and social customs, and teaching young people about their true Vedic heritage. To that end, he founded many educational institutions.

Dayananda also believed that the Vedic teachings were not at variance with science or reason. He rejected the notion of a personal saviour god; in fact, he rejected any anthropomorphic vision of the divine, and believed that the human soul is in some way coeval with the deity. In his view, the ideal was not renunciation but a full, active life of service to other humans: working to uplift humanity would promote the welfare of both the body and the soul.

The Ramakrishna Movement

Ramakrishna Paramahamsa (1836–86; born Gadadhar Chatterjee) was a Bengali raised in the Vaishnava *bhakti* tradition, cultivating ecstatic trance experiences. In his early twenties he was employed as a priest at a temple to the goddess Kali, and by his account he experienced the Divine Mother as an ocean of love. From the age of 25 he took instruction in tantra as well as Vedanta. He concluded that all religions lead in the same direction and that all are equally true.

Following his death, his disciples in Calcutta formed the Ramakrishna Mission to spread his eclectic ideas. Among them was Swami Vivekananda (Narendranath Datta, 1862–1902), a former member of the Brahmo Samaj who believed that Western science could help India make material progress, while Indian spirituality could help the West along the path to enlightenment. As a Hindu participant in the 1893 World's Parliament of Religions in Chicago, and later as a lecturer in America and Europe, he presented an interpretation of Shankara's non-dualist (*advaita*) Vedanta in which Brahman is the only reality. As a consequence of the attention he attracted, it was this philosophy that the West generally came to consider the definitive form of Hinduism.

Under Vivekananda's leadership, the movement established a monastic order and a philanthropic mission, both dedicated to humanitarian service. In keeping with Ramakrishna's ecumenical vision, it encouraged non-sectarian worship. It also ignored caste distinctions, founding hundreds of educational and medical institutions that were open to all. The introduction of a Hindu presence in these fields was significant because until then most of India's new schools and hospitals had been run by Christian missionaries.

The monastic wing of the movement maintains that renunciation promotes spiritual growth. Unlike other monastic orders, however, it insists that its members not withdraw from the world but live in and for it, giving humanitarian service to others.

The Struggle for India's Independence

Hindus and Muslims came together to fight for independence from British colonial rule. The earliest eruption was India's First War of Independence, known in Europe as the failed "sepoy mutiny" of 1857. The struggle would continue for another 90 years. Of the many leaders, Hindu and Muslim, who contributed to the achievement of independence in 1947, undoubtedly the best known is the one to whom Rabindranath Tagore, India's famed poet and Nobel laureate, gave the title "Mahatma" ("great soul"): Mohandas Karamchand Gandhi (1869–1948).

Born in Gujarat and trained as a barrister in England, Gandhi practised law in South Africa from 1893 to 1915. It was in response to the racial discrimination faced by the Indian minority there that he began experimenting with civil disobedience and passive resistance as vehicles for protest. After his return to India, where he became the leader of the Indian National Congress in 1921, he combined the techniques he had developed in South Africa with practices drawn from India's Hindu and Jaina religious traditions and applied them to the campaign for India's freedom.

In particular, Gandhi emphasized the principle of non-violence (*ahimsa*) and developed a strategy of non-violent resistance called *satyagraha* ("truth-force"). Also borrowed from religious tradition was his practice of fasting, which he used both for "self-purification" and as a psychological weapon. Gandhi's fasts drew attention to social injustices and the atrocities perpetrated by the British authorities. Faced with brutality, he refused to retaliate, saying that "An eye for an eye makes the world blind." Another major influence was the *Bhagavad Gita*, which he understood as an allegory of the conflict between good and evil within human beings. It remained his guide throughout his life.

In addition to his political work, Gandhi promoted social reform, especially with respect to the people then known as "untouchables." He gave the generic name "Harijan" ("children of God") to outcaste communities such as the Dalits. Although outcastes today reject the name as patronizing, it drew attention to the discrimination built into the traditional structure of Hindu society.

Gandhi's efforts to promote peace between Muslims and Hindus in the context of the struggle for independence were less successful. Many Indians hold that the British followed a "divide and rule" policy that amplified underlying tensions between Hindus and Muslims. Conflict over issues such as leadership and electoral representation eventually led the Muslims to demand their own independent state in the northwest, where they appeared to form the majority of the population. The name of the new country, Pakistan, means "land of the pure," but is also an acronym representing the regions involved: Punjab, Afghania (an old name for the North Western Frontier province), Kashmir, Sindh, and Baluchistan.

The violence that accompanied the partition some 12 million people displaced and 1 million killed—representing a major failure for Gandhi. Within a few months, on 30 January 1948, he was assassinated by a Hindu incensed by what he perceived to be Gandhi's support for the Muslim cause. Since then, Gandhi's influence has been felt in many parts of the world, but perhaps most notably in the US civil rights movement under the leadership of Martin Luther King, Jr.

Independence and the Secular State

Although India is a secular state, personal and/or family law differs depending on the religious tradition that the individual belongs to. In 1771 the colony's first Governor General proclaimed that "in all suits regarding inheritance, marriage, caste and other religious usages or institutions, the laws of the Koran with respect to the Mohamedans and those of the Shaster [*dharmashastra*] with respect to the Gentoos [an archaic term for the inhabitants of India] shall invariably be adhered to." *Dharmashastra* prescriptions were flexible, and Hindus did not consider them "laws" in the Western sense; nevertheless, they became the framework for "Hindu" law under the British. In an effort to accommodate the different religions, the British and later the Indian government upheld the traditional legal structures of Islam, Christianity, and Zoroastrianism (a Persian tradition whose adherents, the "Parsees," had sought refuge in India many centuries earlier). Thus how people marry, divorce, adopt children, inherit property, etc., all depends on their religious affiliation. Legislation was passed in the 1950s to codify the Hindu laws regarding marriage, succession, and so on, but the fact that the new laws did not reflect the diversity of the Hindu traditions led to further tensions between Hindus and Muslims because the laws in the other traditions were not codified. Despite calls for a uniform civil code with the same laws for all citizens, the different legal regimes remain in effect today.

Contemporary Religious Leaders

For more than 2,000 years Hindus have venerated holy men and women. The *Taittiriya Upanishad* exhorts a departing student to think of his ***acharya*** (religious instructor) as a god, and there have been countless other gurus, ascetics, mediums, storytellers, and ***sadhus*** ("holy men") who have commanded anything from obedience to veneration. For many Hindus, religious experience is mediated by someone they believe to be in some way divine.

Followers of Sri Sathya Sai Baba (Sathya Narayan Raju, 1926–2011), a charismatic teacher from Andhra Pradesh in the south, believe him to be an *avatara*. The heads of the monasteries established by Shankara in the eighth century continue to exercise considerable influence in some Hindu communities, as do a number of orator-commentators whose interpretation of the ancient scriptures shows the dynamic and adaptable nature of the Hindu tradition.

All *acharyas* are gurus, but not all gurus are *acharyas*. Gurus, unlike *acharyas*, are not necessarily connected to any sectarian tradition, and they tend to emphasize "universal" and humanist messages, stressing the divinity in all human beings and encouraging their followers to transcend caste and community distinctions. Another difference is that whereas *acharyas* are almost invariably male, many women have been gurus. An example is Ma Amritananda Mayi ("Ammachi"; b. 1953), the leader of a movement that sponsors an international network of charitable, humanitarian, educational, and medical institutions. Known as the "hugging guru," she is one of the most popular religious leaders in the world today.

Many charismatic teachers are called *swami* ("master") by their followers. Others take their titles from the ancient Vedic "seers" known as *rishis*. An example is the founder of the Transcendental Meditation movement: Maharishi ("great seer") Mahesh Yogi (1911?–2008) was one of the most influential teachers in the Western world.

Practices, Rituals, and Arts

Many Hindus are fond of the dictum that "Hinduism is not a religion, it is a way of life." While most know very little about the texts, beliefs, and philosophies of their tradition, they have generally observed the practices all their lives. Performances of various kinds—music and dance, drama and enactments of devotional poetry—are just as important as rituals, since it is through them that most Hindus learn the stories of the epics and *Puranas*.

Temple Worship

It is not clear when temple worship began. The Vedic literature says nothing about temples, although the Harappa civilization does appear to have set some buildings apart for worship. South India has a number of temples that have survived from about the fifth century CE, but in the north many older temples were destroyed by either invaders or Muslim rulers. However, cave carvings depicting incarnations of Vishnu and icons of Shiva suggest that worship at public shrines was established by the early fifth century. Some temples to Shiva and Vishnu in Southeast Asia may date from the same period.

Deities in Hindu temples are treated like kings and queens. The ***murtis***—variously translated as "idols," "icons," "forms," or "objects to be worshipped"—are given ritual baths, adorned, carried in procession, and honoured with all the marks of hospitality offered to royal guests, including music and dance to entertain them. In the Srirangam temple in South India, there are special festivities 250 days a year.

This treatment reflects the fact that for many Hindus *murtis* are not symbols but the deities themselves, fully present and accessible: direct analogues to Vishnu's incarnations as Rama or Krishna. The presence of a deity in the temple does not detract from his or her presence in heaven, immanence in the world, or presence in a human soul. The deity is always complete and whole, no matter how many forms he or she may be manifest in at any given time.

Others, however, believe that the image in a temple is only a symbol of a higher reality. This does not prevent adherents of Shankara's non-dual Vedanta from flocking to shrines to express their devotion—even though they believe it is transforming wisdom, not *bhakti*, that leads to liberation. But some sects—including the Brahmo Samaj and Vira Shaivas—reject images altogether.

A temple has a correlation to the universe itself and to the body of divine beings; for Sri Vaishnavas, the temple is heaven on earth. In South India, even a single glimpse of the temple tower is said to be enough to destroy one's sins.

The strings of flowers sold outside temples may be worn by devotees themselves or presented to the deities inside (© Vasudha Narayanan).

Generally, in Hinduism, there is no congregational prayer. Rather, the priest prays on behalf of the devotees, presents offerings of fruit, flowers, or coconut to the deity, and then gives back some of those blessed objects to the devotees. The food thus presented is now ***prasada*** ("divine favour"), a gift from the deity. In some temples devotees must buy the *prasada*, but in others it is provided at no charge from endowments made in the past. Patrons frequently earmark their donations for particular charitable purposes or functions in the temple, and their donations are inscribed on stones of the temple walls. Such inscriptions are an important source of information about the past. For example, an inscription in Tirumala-Tirupati (Tiruvenkatam) says that in the year 966 a woman called Samavai donated two parcels of land and ordered that the revenues derived from them be used to celebrate festivals and consecrate a silver processional image of Vishnu (known here as Venkateshwara). The fact that she was able to make such donations suggests a certain independence both of lifestyle and of income. Some of the largest Shiva and Vishnu temples are found in the region of the Khmer empire, which stretched from modern Cambodia to parts of Thailand and Laos. Although there are striking similarities to Indian temples, these temples have their own architectural idiom. Shiva temples are shaped like mountains; the large mountain-temples at Bakheng and Bakong in the Siem Reap area of Cambodia, for instance, look more like the Buddhist

Angkor Wat in northern Cambodia was built by King Suryavarman II in honour of Vishnu. Its unusual three-level structure may indicate a connection with South India, which also has a handful of three-storeyed Vishnu temples (© Vasudha Narayanan).

temple of Borubodur in Indonesia, than their counterparts in India. The large Vishnu temple of Angkor Wat in Cambodia, like many temples in India (and Central America as well), is situated and built according to astronomical calculations: the sun rises directly behind the central tower at the time of the spring and autumn equinoxes.

Sculptural and Pictorial Symbolism

The Naga

One of the earliest symbols in the Hindu tradition may be the *naga* (serpent). In many towns and villages there are sacred trees surrounded with small stone images of intertwined snakes. Women worship at these open-air shrines when they want to make a wish regarding a matter such as childbirth. *Nagas* are also important in the iconography of Shiva and Vishnu, and Cambodian narratives trace the origins of the kingdom to the union of a *naga* princess and a Hindu prince from India.

The Dance of Shiva

Shiva is often portrayed as a cosmic dancer known as Nataraja, the king of the dance. In this form Shiva is the archetype of both the dancer and the ascetic, symbolizing mastery over universal energy on the one hand and absolute inner tranquillity on the other.

In the classic Nataraja representation, Shiva has four hands. One of the right hands holds an hourglass-shaped drum, symbolizing sound—both speech and the divine truth heard through revelation. The other right hand is making a gesture that grants fearlessness to devotees. One of the left hands holds a flame, symbolizing the destruction of the world at the end of time. The feet grant salvation and are worshipped to obtain union with Shiva. The left foot, representing the refuge of the devotee, is raised, signifying liberation. The other left hand points to this foot.

Dancing through the creation and destruction of the cosmos, Shiva–Nataraja is the master of both the fierce, violent dance that gives rise to energy, and the gentle, lyric dance representing tenderness and grace. The entire universe shakes when he dances; Krishna sings for him, the snake around his neck sways, and drops of the Ganga River, which he holds in his hair, fall to the earth.

The Linga

In temples, Shiva is usually represented by a *linga*. Although *linga* is generally translated as "phallus," Hindus do not normally think of it as a physical object. Rather, it symbolizes the spiritual potential in all of creation, and specifically the creative energies of Shiva. The union of the *yoni* and *linga* is a reminder that male and female forces are united in generating the universe. Although Shiva is characterized as the "destroyer" in some literature, it is his creative role that is represented in the temple.

Erotic Sculpture

People from other cultures have often been shocked by Hindu temple sculptures celebrating *kama*, sensual love. Probably the most famous examples are found at Khajuraho (c. 1000 CE) in Madhya Pradesh and Konarak (c. 1250), in the eastern coastal state of Orissa. While some art historians have

The dancing Shiva (© Vasudha Narayanan).

suggested that such scenes illustrate passages from various myths and texts such as the *Puranas*, or are symbols of fertility, others have speculated that the sculptures may have been intended to serve an educational purpose for young men who as students were isolated from society, preparing them for adult life in a world where spouses were expected to be partners in *kama* as well as dharma.

Forehead Marks

Perhaps the most common visual sign of Hindu culture is the forehead mark, especially the red dot (*bindi*) traditionally worn by married women. At the simplest level, *bindis* are decorative: unmarried and Christian women wear them as well, and in recent years, the traditional dot of red kumkum powder has been largely replaced by stickers in many shapes and colours. Yet the *bindi*'s value is more than cosmetic: married women see it as a symbol of their role in society. In many parts of India, male ascetics and temple priests also wear forehead marks. As with many elements in Hinduism, the meaning of such marks depends on the gender, marital status, and sect of the person wearing it, the occasion, and, occasionally, his or her caste. Marks denoting affiliation to a particular deity may be made with white clay, sandalwood paste, flower petals, or ash. In general, followers of Vishnu, Krishna, and Lakshmi wear vertical marks; worshippers of Shiva and Parvati wear horizontal or slightly curved crescent marks made of ash or other substances with a red dot in the middle; and a combination of dots and crescents usually indicates allegiance to the Goddess (Devi) in one of her many manifestations.

Domestic Worship

One of the most significant ways in which Hindus express their devotion to a deity or a spiritual teacher is through rituals (**puja**) performed in the home. Many households set aside some space—if only a cabinet shelf—for a shrine to hold pictures or small images of the revered figure. Daily puja typically consists of simple acts in which all family members can take part, such as lighting oil lamps and incense sticks, reciting prayers, or offering food to the deity. More elaborate rituals, however—such as the puja offered to Satyanarayana (a manifestation of Vishnu) on full-moon days—may involve a priest or other specialist.

A number of domestic rituals are specific to the women of the household. In many parts of India, women gather on certain days of the year to celebrate the goddess by fasting and feasting, and then perform "auspiciousness" rituals for the happiness of the entire family. Other women's rituals are found only in certain geographic regions. In the south, for example, women will often gather before a major family celebration (such as a wedding) to ask for the blessing of female ancestors who have had the good fortune to die before their husbands and therefore have preserved their status as *sumangalis* or "auspicious women." And in the north, during some domestic festivals such as Navaratri (see below) prepubescent girls are venerated by older women as temporary manifestations of the Goddess.

In the home as in the temple, speaking a prayer or singing a hymn, worshippers link themselves with the devotional community extending through time. Thus in Sri Vaishnava worship, devotees who recite a verse of Andal's are to some extent participating in her own devotion.

Ayurvedic Medicine

Medicine made great progress in the Hindu world in the first millennium. One of the most important systems was called **Ayurveda**: the *veda* (knowledge) of enhancing life. The physician promotes both longevity and quality of life. The prototype is a deity called Dhanavantari, sometimes identified as an incarnation of Vishnu. The South Indian parallel to Ayurveda is the Tamil system called Siddha.

Ayurveda is considered to be an ancillary to the Vedas. An early compendium on healing, by a physician named Charaka (c. third century BCE), says that every human being should have three desires: the will to live, the drive for prosperity, and an aspiration to reach the world beyond. As with many other subjects, treatises on healing and medicine are often framed as conversations between two sages or between a god and a sage.

Both Charaka and the surgeon Sushruta claimed that their theories had been transmitted to them by the gods. They understood illness as a lack of balance among three elements: air, phlegm, and bile. This analytic approach recalls Greek and Chinese medical theories of roughly the same period. The *Sushruta Samhita* begins by declaring that the physician's aim is "to cure the diseases of the sick, to protect the healthy, to prolong life," while the *Charaka Samhita* includes a detailed statement of the ethics required of a physician. In these respects, the ancient roots of Ayurvedic medicine seem strikingly modern.

Focus

The Significance of Food

The Hindu tradition is preoccupied with food: not just what kind of food is eaten, where and when, but how it is prepared, who prepares it, who has the right to be offered it first, and who may be given the leftovers. Certain dates and lunar phases require either feasting or fasting, and there are different types of fast: some demand abstention from all food, others only from grain or rice. According to some texts, liberation can be attained simply by observing the right kinds of fast.

Contrary to a common Western stereotype, most Hindus are not vegetarians. The strictest vegetarians are generally the Vaishnavas, who are found all over India. In addition, most brahmins are vegetarian—except in Bengal, Orissa, and Kashmir. In the West, members of ISKCON not only abstain from meat, fish, and fowl, but also avoid vegetables such as onions and garlic, which are thought to have negative properties.

These dietary prohibitions and habits are based on the idea that food reflects the general qualities of nature: purity, energy, and inertia. Pure foods such as dairy products and many vegetables are thought to foster spiritual inclinations. By contrast, meat, poultry, and onions are believed to give rise to passion and action, while stale food and liquor are seen as encouraging sloth. Thus a strict vegetarian diet is prescribed for those who seek to cultivate spiritual tranquillity and avoid passion.

Weddings, funerals, ancestral rites, and birthdays require the use of auspicious spices such as turmeric. What one feeds the forefathers is different from what one feeds the gods and human beings; life-promoting rituals call for different foods from rituals associated with death; and the latter must not include non-traditional ingredients such as potatoes and red pepper (both introduced to India by Europeans). Various regional traditions also rely on different foods to rectify imbalances of "cold" and "heat" in the body.

In addition, the nature of a given food is thought to be influenced by the inherent qualities of the person who cooks it. For this reason it was common even in the mid-twentieth century for strictly observant Hindus to eat only food prepared by people of their own caste.

Beyond the practicalities of use or avoidance, food appears in Hindu thought as an important symbol of spiritual experience. The idea of a mystical union between food and the person who eats it is suggested in the *Taittiriya Upanishad* (part of the *Yajur Veda*):

> Oh, wonderful! Oh, wonderful!
> Oh, Wonderful!
> I am food! I am food! I am food!
> I am a food-eater! I am a food-eater! I am a food-eater! (Taittiriya Upanishad III.10.5)

This passage has usually been interpreted as referring to the experience of the Vedic sacrificer, who identifies himself with Brahman both as food and as eater.

The Annual Festival Cycle

In the Hindu tradition there is a festival of some kind almost every month of the year. The most popular are the birthdays of Rama, Krishna, and Ganesha; the precise dates vary from year to year with the lunar calendar, but they always fall within the same periods.

Some festivals have been specific to certain regions. **Holi**, for instance, is a North Indian festival celebrated in March or April with bonfires to enact the destruction of evil, and exuberant throwing of coloured powder to symbolize the vibrant colours of spring. It is now popular all over the world with tens of thousands of people–not all Hindu–joining in the celebrations. It commemorates Vishnu's incarnation as a man-lion in order to save the life of his devotee Prahlada as well as his incarnation as Krishna. Vishnu's fifth incarnation, as a dwarf-brahmin, is celebrated in the state of Kerala in a late-summer festival called Onam. Other festivals, like Navaratri and **Deepavali** (known as Diwali in some areas), are more or less pan-Hindu. A detailed discussion of Navaratri will give us an idea of the variations in observance across different communities.

Celebrating Holi in Jaipur (© Jonathan Irish / National Geographic Society / Corbis).

Navaratri

The festival of Navaratri ("nine nights") begins on the new moon that appears between 15 September and 14 October and is celebrated all over India, but in different ways and for different reasons. In Tamilnadu it is largely a celebration of womanhood. Exquisite dolls representing the goddesses Sarasvati, Lakshmi, and Durga are arranged in elaborate tableaux depicting scenes from the epics and *Puranas*. Every evening, women and children dressed in bright silks visit one another, admire the dolls, play musical instruments, and sing classical songs in praise of one or another of the goddesses. On the last two days—a special countrywide holiday—large pictures of Lakshmi and Sarasvati, draped with garlands of fresh flowers, are placed in front of the display of dolls and worshipped.

In West Bengal, the festival commemorates the goddess Durga's killing of the buffalo-demon Mahisa. Local communities make extravagant statues of Durga for her spirit to inhabit; then, after nine nights, they immerse the statues in water to symbolize her return to the formless state.

In Gujarat, Navaratri is celebrated with two special dances. In the circular dance called *garbha*, a sacred lamp is kept in the centre of the circle as a manifestation of the goddess. The second dance, called *dandiya*, is performed with sticks and recalls the dance that Krishna is said to have performed with the cowherd girls.

According to some traditions, it was during the same nine nights and ten days that Rama battled Ravana. In Ramnagar, Varanasi on the river Ganga, people act out the story of the *Ramayana*, with little boys in the parts of Rama and his brothers, and on the tenth day celebrate Rama's victory.

Some Hindus believe that it was on the ninth day of Navaratri that Arjuna found the weapons he had hidden a year before and paid respect to them before entering battle. Because of this story, the last two days, dedicated to Lakshmi and Sarasvati, celebrate the importance of weapons and machines in life: cars and buses are draped with garlands, while computers and typewriters are blessed with sacred powders. On the ninth day South Indians honour Sarasvati, the patron of learning and music. Musical instruments, writing devices, and textbooks are placed in front of her image, to be blessed by her for the rest of the year.

In many parts of India, the last day of the festival is dedicated to Lakshmi. This is a time for fresh starts—to begin new ventures and acquire new knowledge—and to honour traditional teachers. On the last days of Navaratri, the fortune of learning, the wealth of wisdom, and the joy of music are said to be given by the grace of the goddesses. While most Indians do celebrate Navaratri, then, it is in different ways and for different reasons.

Deepavali

Deepa means "lamp" and *vali* means "necklace" or "row." Thus Deepavali (or Diwali) means "necklace of lights." It is celebrated at the time of the new moon between 15 October and 14 November. Hindu families all over the world decorate their houses with lights, set off firecrackers, and wear new clothes. In some parts of India, Deepavali marks the beginning of a new year, but that is only one of several reasons for the festival. As in the case of Navaratri, the significance of Deepavali varies from region to region.

In South India, for instance, the festival celebrates the dawn when Krishna is said to have killed Narakasura, a demon from the nether world, thus ensuring the victory of light over darkness. In North India, Deepavali marks the return of Rama to Ayodhya and his coronation. And in Gujarat it is the beginning of the new year, when new account books are opened and new clothes are worn. Presents are exchanged in some communities, and it is generally a time of feasting. In Tamilnadu, people say that the river Ganga itself is present in all the waters on Deepavali day. They get up at three or four in the morning for a special purifying bath, and members of some communities greet one another by asking "Have you had a bath in the river Ganga?" Whatever the local customs may be, the celebrations are always family-centred.

Life-Cycle Rites

Every culture has its rites of passage: rituals that mark the transitions from one stage of life to another. In some of the *dharmashastras* the discussion of the life-cycle sacraments begins with the birth of a child. In others the first sacrament is marriage, for it is in this context that each new life is expected to begin.

Two factors are important to note in discussing life-cycle rites. First, not all are pan-Hindu, and even those that are do not necessarily have the same importance in all communities. Some of the rites discussed here are practised only by the "upper" castes and higher economic classes. Second, many important rites, especially those involving girls or women, are not discussed in the classical texts—possibly because those texts were written by men, for whom women were merely partners. It may also be that some of these rites developed after the texts were written. We will discuss the normative *dharmashastra* sacraments first, and then look at a few rites of passage with more localized importance.

Certain kinds of people, animals, rituals, smells, sounds, and foods are considered auspicious in that they are thought to bring about good fortune and a good quality of existence. Auspicious times are chosen for the performance of all sacraments; these times depend on the horoscope of the person concerned, which is cast at birth.

Birth Rituals

The cycle of sacraments (*samskaras*; literally, "perfecting") begins before birth. The time of conception, the rituals administered to a pregnant woman, and her behaviour during pregnancy are all thought to condition the personality of the child. The *Upanishads* describe specific rituals to be followed to produce a learned daughter or a heroic son (though in later times daughters were rarely desired). Although the conception sacrament has been largely discarded, it survives in some communities as one of the rituals observed on the wedding night. Some *dharmashastras* suggest that it is a husband's duty to approach his wife for intercourse at particular times of the month.

At the moment of birth, care is taken to note the exact time, to ensure an accurate horoscope. In the first ceremony performed after the birth, father prays for the intellectual well-being of the child and longevity for himself and the child: "May we see a hundred autumns, may we hear a hundred autumns."

Initiation Rituals

The upper classes were generally called "twice born," in reference to the initiatory rite in which their young males were spiritually reborn as sons of their religious teachers (whether a similar initiation was performed for girls in the early Vedic era is unclear). This rite, the ***upanayana***, marked a boy's initiation into studenthood—the first of the four stages in life. It takes two days to complete. On the first day, the boy is bathed in water into which the essence of all the sacred waters has been invoked through the recitation of verses from the *Vedas*. This ritual is called "peace brought on the waters", and it ends with repeated requests for *shanti* (peace): for the individual, the soul, the body, the divine beings, the family, the community, and the entire Earth. On the second day the boy is given a sacred "thread" or cord to wear over his left shoulder. Some think it represents an upper garment that the student would wear when he was fit to perform a sacrifice; others, that it symbolizes an umbilical cord connecting the boy to his teacher—the spiritual parent through whom he will be reborn. The boy is now taught how to thank the Earth for his food and ask divine beings to bless it. Then comes the actual imparting of the sacred teaching. As the boy sits with his father, a sacred mantra is given to him that he will be expected to chant 108 times in succession, three times each day. Although it is very short—"I meditate on the brilliance of the sun; may it illumine my mind"—this *Gayatri* or sun mantra is considered the most important of all mantras and has become popular among many sections of Hindu society. The boy is then taken outside and shown the sun, the source of light, knowledge, and immortality. He must twine his fingers in a particular way to ward off the harmful rays while looking directly at its heart.

Weddings

According to the *dharmashastras*, a man is born with debts to the sages, the gods, and the ancestors. His wife helps him repay these debts, and without her a man cannot fully perform his religious obligations. For the woman, there is no higher ideal than to be a faithful wife.

Before a wedding can be arranged, the parents of the prospective bride must find a suitable bridegroom; for this they used to rely on the help of friends and extended family, but today the search is often conducted through the internet and social media. Ideally, he will come from the same geographic region, speak the same language, and belong to the same community, though he must belong to a different clan. He should be compatible with the bride in education, looks, age, and outlook, and the two families should be of similar socio-economic status.

When a potential husband is found, the families sometimes compare the young people's horoscopes, not only to assess compatibility and character but also to balance the ups and downs in their future lives. When the horoscopes are compatible, the young people (and their families) meet to decide whether they like each other. At this point both parties may either opt out or request more time to get acquainted.

Obviously, arranged marriages are less common today than in earlier centuries. Now that men and women increasingly study and work together, a couple may meet and decide to get married with or without their families' approval. Such marriages often cross boundaries of caste and community—even language and geography.

To be legally binding, the marriage ceremony must include several basic features: an exchange of flower garlands, the gift of the girl by her parents, the clasping of hands, *sapta padi* (taking seven steps together around fire, the eternal witness), and the giving of "auspiciousness" to the bride. Some weddings include lavish exchanges of presents with friends and extended family members, processions on horseback or in antique cars, and entertainment. At particular moments the couple's close relatives have active roles to play, but the guests are free to come and go as they please. The ceremony itself lasts several hours and for the bride may involve several changes of elaborate clothing and jewels. Often the couple sits on a platform near a fire, to which offerings are made. The bride's father quotes from the *Ramayana*, reciting the words spoken by Sita's father as he gives her in marriage to Rama: "This is Sita, my daughter; she will be your partner in dharma."

In many communities, though not all, the groom's family then presents the bride with a "gift of auspiciousness"—a gold necklace, a string of black beads, or a simple yellow thread carrying the insignia of the particular god that the family worships—that she will wear for the duration of her marriage. There is no equivalent symbol for the groom, although men who have put on the sacred thread will wear a double set of threads after they marry.

In the central rite of the wedding, the bride and groom take seven steps around the fire together as he recites a series of verses from the Vedas, concluding as follows:

> You have taken seven steps with me; be my friend. We who have taken seven steps together have become companions. I have attained your friendship; I shall not forsake that friendship. Do not discard our relationship.

It is worth noting that these passages refer to the wife as the husband's partner in dharma and his companion in love.

Later in the evening the new husband and wife are taken outside for a ritual called "the sighting of Arundhati." In Indian astrology, the seven brightest stars of the Great Bear constellation (the Big Dipper) represent the seven sages, one of whom (Vasistha) is accompanied by a star identified as his wife, Arundhati—a symbol of fidelity throughout India. Just as the stars Vasistha and Arundhati remain close through the years, so the newlyweds are urged to stay together forever.

Funeral Rites

Except for infants and ascetics (who may be buried), cremation by fire is the final sacrament in most communities. No fire is to be lit or tended in the house where the death occurred until the cremation fire has been lit, and the family of the deceased is considered to live in a state of pollution for a period that varies from 12 days to almost a year. Although each religious community (Shaiva, Vaishnava, etc.) has its own list of scriptures to recite from, most funeral rituals will also include portions of the Vedas and the *Bhagavad Gita*.

The rituals are usually performed by the eldest son of the deceased. For the first few days the spirit of the deceased is a *preta* (ghost). To quench the thirst resulting from the body's fiery cremation, the spirit is offered water, as well as balls of rice for sustenance. Some of these rituals go back to the earliest Vedic times, when the dead were thought to need food for the journey to the afterlife on the far side of the moon.

After the designated period of time, the injunctions relating to pollution are lifted in an "adoption of auspiciousness" ceremony. On every new-moon day, the departed soul is offered food in the form of libations with sesame seeds and water. After a year, the anniversary of the death is marked with further ceremonies, and the family is then freed of all constraints.

Women's Rituals

Most women's rituals are domestic, undertaken for the welfare of the family and earthly happiness, but a few are intended solely for personal liberation. Many practices—worship at home shrines or temples, pilgrimages, the singing of devotional songs—are similar to those undertaken by men, but some are unique to married women whose husbands are alive. Underlying many of the rites is the notion that women are powerful and that the rites they perform have potency. Though many women's rituals share certain features, there are considerable differences among communities, castes, and regions.

Early History

Early Sanskrit texts tell of women lighting and tending the sacrificial fire used to make ritual offerings to the gods. They also refer to women ascetics, who would presumably have undergone renunciatory rites similar to those required of men. These privileges appear to have disappeared by the beginning of the Common Era, however.

Calendrical Rituals

Many traditional women's rituals are no longer practised today, but a number of votive rituals are still observed on particular days. These rituals involve the welfare of others—whether the husband

and children, the extended family, or the community. Although Sanskrit manuals say that performing these rites will enable a woman to attain final liberation from the cycle of birth and death, most participants ask only for more worldly rewards, such as marriage, or a long life for their husbands.

After prayers to the family deity, the women may distribute emblems of auspiciousness such as betel leaves, bananas, coconuts, turmeric, and kumkum powder. The rituals may take anywhere between a few minutes and five days to complete, with periods of fasting alternating with communal eating.

In South India married women were traditionally enjoined to stay celibate during the month of Adi (approximately 15 July–14 August). Women of some "lower" castes carry special pots of water and other ritual items to the temples of local goddesses and perform rites in their honour for the benefit of the entire family. Others cook rice and milk dishes in the temples of the local goddesses and distribute the food. In the temple of Draupadi Amman, women and men alike enter a trance state and walk over hot coals in a ceremony called "walking on flowers."

In North India many women's rites focus on the welfare of male relatives. In late summer, for example, girls tie a protective cord around the wrists of their brothers. And in October–November, women undertake two fasts for the well-being of their husbands, as well as one for the health of their sons. These daytime fasts are broken only after the moon rises.

Karva Chauth is a North Indian festival celebrating married women's devotion to their husbands. Participants observe an all-day fast, during which they pray for their husbands' well-being (© shashi sharma / Demotix / Corbis).

Women's Life-Cycle Rituals

In the upper castes the standard life-cycle rituals associated with childhood, marriage, and death are much the same for both sexes. There are many other sacraments associated with women, however, that have not received scriptural ratification. Some of these rites are specific to certain regions and communities.

In the past, for instance, many communities would celebrate a young girl's first menstrual period, since this "blossoming" meant that she was ready for marriage. Today urban communities tend to consider this tradition old-fashioned, but it is still practised in rural areas. The girl is showered with gifts of money or clothing by her family, and the ritual celebration often resembles a mini-wedding.

Special rituals may also attend pregnancy, especially the first. In a popular South Indian ritual, the pregnant woman is dressed in a silk sari, and women of all ages slip bangles onto her arm. In earlier days a bangle-seller was invited and the woman's parents gave all the guests glass bracelets that were supposed to safeguard them from evil spirits.

In another rite the expectant mother's hair is adorned with flowers, to enhance the natural radiance that is often said to accompany pregnancy. In the Hindu tradition women often wear flowers in their hair, but normally only a bride's hair is completely woven with flowers. Rituals such as these acknowledge the importance of a woman's body and celebrate its life-bearing potential.

Women and Pollution

With a few exceptions (among them the Vira Shaiva), most Hindu communities have traditionally regarded menstruation as physically polluting. Menstruating women were excluded from everyday life, and even though strict segregation is no longer widespread, vestiges of the old attitudes remain. Most communities still do not permit menstruating women to attend a place of worship or participate in any religious ritual, and even Vira Shaiva households may prohibit menstruating women from cooking. Virtually all Hindu women take a purifying ritual bath on the fourth day, but many of these observances have been discarded when Hindus migrate to other countries.

The same concept of pollution extends to childbirth. Even though the birth of a child is a happy and auspicious occasion, it is thought to render the entire family ritually impure. For several days after the birth, the family cannot go to a temple or celebrate an auspicious event.

The Performing Arts

The performing arts are central to the practice and transmission of the Hindu traditions. The knowledge related to music and dance was considered to be an ancillary branch of the Vedas. A treatise on theatre and dance called the *Natya Sastra* is attributed to a legendary sage named Bharata, but was said to have originated with the creator god Brahma, who took the reading text from the Rig Veda, the music from the Sama Veda, gestures and make up from the Yajur Veda, and emotional acting from the Atharava Veda and combined them to create the fifth Veda. In oral tradition, the very name "Bharata" is said to incorporate the main elements of music and dance: *Bha-* stands for "*bhava*" or expression; *-ra-* for "raga" or melody; and *-ta* for "tala" or rhythm.

Acting, music, and dance have even been considered ways to liberation. Classical dance requires total control of the body—the same control that is central to the physical discipline of yoga. Theoretically speaking, all dance is divine, but many dances are explicitly devotional in tone. This is particularly true of Bharata Natyam, the classical dance form of South India. While the dancer expresses the human soul's longing for union with the Lord in passionate terms, the audience may also participate in the divine joy of movement, whether that of the dancer, of Krishna with his cowherd friends, or of Shiva Nataraja, the King of the Dance, and through this participation attain the frame of mind that leads to liberation.

Sanskrit texts such as the *Natya Sastra* usually make a distinction between classical and folk dance, but sometimes the boundaries have been fluid, and both forms have derived inspiration from each other. A striking example of public singing and dancing (though originally performed in the home) is the *garbha* dance of Gujarat, in which women and young girls celebrate the Mother Goddess by dancing around a *garbha*: a clay pot holding a lamp. *Garbha* means "womb," the source of all creative energy; it is the Mother Goddess who is present in the lamp inside the clay pot. It seems that when the focus is on *moksha* (liberation), rather than *dharma* (issues of righteousness), women have more freedom to take part in public activities. The androcentric controls imposed on the public activities of women are simply bypassed in contexts where the focus is on the potential for liberation that is inherent in all human beings; thus even though society may disapprove of a woman who has rejected marriage, the women poets who rejected marriage in favour of union with their deity are venerated.

Dancing the *garbha* during Navaratri celebrations in Mumbai (© DIVYAKANT SOLANKI / epa / Corbis).

To study dance forms such as Bharata Natyam, Manipuri, Kathak, Kathakali, or Kuchipudi—classical forms from different regions of India—is not only to learn a fine art. Through them dancers (and audiences) learn not only the stories of the Hindu gods but their physical appearance, their insignia, their demeanour. Whether in India or outside, in Fiji, Trinidad, or South Africa, the classical dances introduce new generations to the affective ethos of the Hindu traditions. To watch them is to know the body languages of Hindu heroes and heroines, and to learn to perform them is to plug into patterns of Indian corporeal knowledge. At the same time the dances offer insight into the allegorical structures of Hindu devotional songs, in which the love between the deity and the human being is often portrayed as the love between a man and a woman. One Hindu text says that dance invites the blessings of the righteous, counsels the fool, cheers the depressed, enhances happiness for women, and gives prosperity in this world and in the next; above all, it pleases Vishnu.

The ostensible reason for the "revelation" of the treatise on dance was to make the Vedas accessible to *all* human beings. However, it is interesting to note that after the fifteenth century (possibly earlier), the only women who sang and danced in public seem to have been courtesans. This was apparently not the case in earlier times; even as late as the twelfth century, sculptures of women dancers, perhaps royalty, adorned the niches of the Belur temple in Karnataka. The apparent prohibition against women from "decent families" dancing in public may have come from a gradual coalescence of the conservative attitudes explicit in many Hindu texts and Islamic mores, as well as the puritanical perspectives of Christian missionaries from Europe.

As for sound, it has been part of Hindu worship since the time of the Vedas. The holy word "**om**," which is chanted at the beginning and end of all Hindu and Jaina prayers and recitations of scripture, and is central to Buddhist practice as well, is perceived to be filled with power. It is understood to have three sounds, *a–u–m*, with the diphthong *au* producing an *o* sound. The sound of *om*, which begins deep in the body and ends at the lips, is considered auspicious. Its history in the Hindu tradition is ancient; the *Mandukya Upanishad* discusses its meaning and power. Hindu philosophers and sectarian communities all agree that *om* is the most sacred sound.

Yet that sound does not have a particular meaning. Almost every Hindu community has speculated about the meaning of *om*. Some say it represents the supreme reality or Brahman. Many philosophers have believed that *om* was present at the beginning of the manifest universe and that it contains the essence of true knowledge. Some say that its three sounds represent the three worlds: earth, atmosphere, and heaven. Others say that they represent the essence of the three Vedas (Rig, Yajur, and Sama). According to followers of the non-dualist philosopher Shankara, the three sounds *a*, *u*, and *m* have the following experiential meanings:

- *A* stands for the world that we see when we are awake, the person who is experiencing it, and the waking experience.
- *U* stands for the dream world, the dreamer, and the dream experience.
- *M* represents the sleep world, the sleeper, and the sleep experience.

These three states we experience on this earth, while a fourth, unspoken syllable represents the state of liberation.

Some Vaishnava devotees, on the other hand, say that *a* represents Vishnu, *u* denotes the human being, and *m* denotes the relationship between the two. Other Vaishnavas say that the sounds represent Vishnu, Sri, and the devotee. In a sense, then, the sound of *om* is a whole greater than the sum of its parts, exceeding in significance the many meanings attributed to it.

Music, too, been perceived as sacred in both origin and function since the time of the Sama Veda. Knowledge of the nature of sound and its proper expression was therefore considered to be religious knowledge. The Vedas specify the different pitches and tones in which the verses were to be recited. The exalted status of the Sama Veda was in part a reflection of the melodious sounds produced when it is sung according to the instructions.

Classical music was largely religious in nature. Treatises on music refer to a divine line of teachers, frequently beginning with the deities Shiva and Parvati, and honour Sarasvati as the patron goddess of the fine arts. Some later Puranas say that Vishnu and Sri are manifested as Nada Brahman or the Supreme Being in the form of sound.

Properly controlled and articulated, sound itself is said to induce a religious experience. Thus the sound of a hymn was considered no less important than the words. *Nadopasana*, meditation through sound, became a popular religious practice. The Alvars composed their poems to be sung and danced, and many devotional poet-composers addressed their songs to the deities.

Recent Developments

Global Hinduism, Interaction, and Adaptation

Ideas, texts, sectarian movements, rituals, and arts connected with the religion that we now call "Hinduism" have been travelling to other parts of the world for more than two millennia. Hinduism is a global religion in at least three ways. There are sizeable numbers of Hindus in almost every part of the world who trace their roots to the Indian subcontinent; people in various countries have accepted Hindu teachers, doctrines, beliefs, or practices; and Hindu ideas and practices have been separated from the name "Hindu" and become part of cultures outside India. An example of the last point can be seen in the United States. Since the New England Transcendentalists of the early nineteenth century, generations of Americans have engaged with ideas, philosophies, and practices rooted in Hindu traditions without identifying them as such: instead, ideas such as reincarnation and practices such as meditation and yoga have been described as "spiritual" or "universal."

One could say that Hinduism comes in both brand name and generic forms. It is rare to find a generic Hindu in India; everyone belongs to a particular caste, community, and sectarian group, all of which are further sub-divided along linguistic and geographic lines. However, Hindu texts and practices have been mined for messages applicable to all human beings. Thus Hindu teachers beginning with Vivekananda and Yogananda, who travelled to North America in the late nineteenth and early twentieth centuries, have stressed the "timeless" and "universal" quality of Hindu concepts and practices.

The Hindu Diaspora

There have been at least three major waves of Hindu migration outside the Indian sub-continent. The first was a gradual process that took place over several centuries in the first millennium and probably involved very small groups of influential elites who carried Hindu ideas and practices to Southeast Asia. The second major migration was the movement of workers (free or indentured) seeking employment in the nineteenth century. The third large wave began in the second half of the twentieth century and has been more varied in its composition The watershed year in the US was 1965, when immigration laws were relaxed to allow skilled, educated professionals such as engineers, physicians, and, later, software professionals to enter the country. Since 1965 diasporic communities in Europe and the Americas have also received political refugees and members of second diasporas (descendants of earlier immigrants from India who are now immigrating themselves).

Temples in the Diaspora

Perhaps the most noticeable feature of global Hindu communities is the tremendous amount of time, money, and energy they devote to the building of temples. Since the 1970s in particular, Hindu immigrants to North America have been transforming their new homes into sacred places.

Places of worship were established as early as 1906 in the San Francisco area, but the first really ambitious attempt to reproduce the traditional architecture and atmosphere of a Vaishnava sacred place came in 1976 with the construction of the Sri Venkateshwara temple in Penn Hills, a suburb of Pittsburgh, Pennsylvania. (Since then, other Venkateshwara temples or shrines have been established in many parts of the United States and Canada.) The Penn Hills temple enshrines a manifestation of Vishnu as Venkateshwara, lord of the hill in the South Indian state of Andhra Pradesh known as Venkata ("that which can burn sins"). The Penn Hills temple was built with the help, backing, and blessing of one of the oldest, richest, and most popular temples in India, the Venkateshwara temple at Tiruvenkatam. Devotees celebrate the significance of having Venkateshwara dwelling on American soil with his consort Sri (known locally as Padmavati, "the lady of the lotus"). In a popular song that was recorded and sold to temple visitors in the 1980s, the following verse is sung in Sanskrit:

> Victory to Govinda [Krishna], who lives in America,
> Victory to Govinda, who is united with Radha who lives on Penn Hills,
> Victory to the Teacher, Victory to Vitthala-Krishna.

Drawing on Puranic lore, the Penn Hills devotees think of their temple's physical location—at the confluence of three rivers, one of them subterranean—as recalling the sacred place in India where the rivers Ganga and Yamuna meet the underground Sarasvati.

The particular place from which Hindu immigrants come has an influence on the kinds of temples they build. In Canada, Australia, and parts of Europe such as France and Switzerland, the numbers of Tamil-speaking immigrants, among them political refugees from Sri Lanka, are reflected in an emphasis on Tamil deities. Temples and shrines dedicated to Murugan, the son of Shiva and Parvati, and an important deity among Tamil-speaking people, are popular in many parts of Canada; both Toronto (Richmond Hill) and Montreal have Murugan temples, but also have shrines to other deities within the main temple to accommodate their devotees. The icon of Murugan in the Richmond Hill temple is said to be the tallest in the world. This temple also claims to have been the first in North America to consecrate images of the Vaishnava philosopher Ramanuja and the 12 Alvars. People from other parts of India as well as second-diaspora Hindus from Guyana, Trinidad, and South Africa have also built temples in the Toronto area, making this one of the most diverse areas for Hindu worship in the world.

North American temples do their best to replicate the traditional pattern of activities: the morning wake-up prayers, the offering of food to the deity, worship, and the recitation of prayers at specific points of the day; however, community participation tends to be limited to weekends, since many devotees must travel significant distances. Although a few seasonal festivals, such as Navaratri and Deepavali are celebrated at the traditional times, for the most part temples try to plan big events around the North American holiday calendar. Thus in the United States most of the major festivals are scheduled to take advantage of the long weekends between Memorial Day (May) and Labor Day (September).

In addition to serving as places of worship, temples in the diaspora serve as community centres, with regular newsletters and website updates to provide "outreach." They also help to educate the diaspora-born in their ancestral traditions through language and religion classes, lectures, study circles, classical music and dance lessons, and summer camps. In addition, perhaps because many of their founding trustees have been physicians, temples in Canada, the US, and Australia

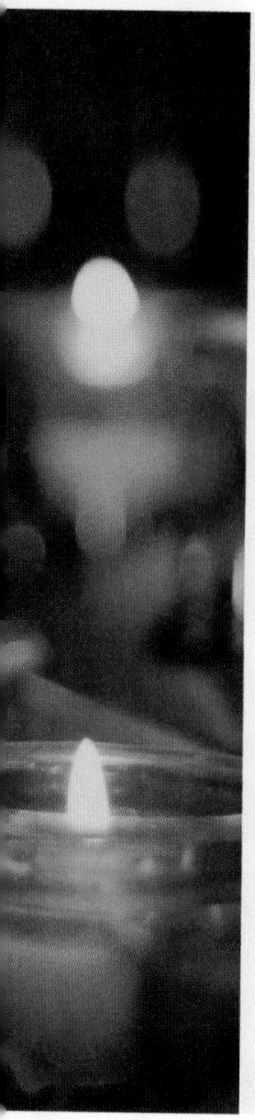

Focus

Yoga in North America

Since it was introduced to the West, in the late nineteenth century, yoga has become one of the most popular activities among middle-class Americans, especially women. Today some 6 to 18 million people in the US report that they either practise or plan to practise yoga. The fact that Americans spend as much as $27 billion a year on yoga-related products suggests that commodification has played an important part in the popularization process.

Is yoga Hindu? Certainly its roots are in traditions that eventually came to be called Hindu. Yet some consider it to be independent of any religious framework: if yoga deepens practitioners' spirituality, it is only in a generic way. Practising yoga outside the religio-spiritual context does not make one Hindu.

To appreciate how different "American yoga" is from "Indian yoga," recall that Patanjali's yoga centred on moral discipline and meditation; although he recommended the kinds of bodily postures and breathing techniques that are at the core of American yoga, for Patanjali these were just two aspects of a much more complex discipline.

Perfection in concentration and meditation lead to *samadhi*, the final state of absorption into and union with the supreme being or higher consciousness. Anyone who reaches this stage is well on the way to emancipation from the cycle of life and death. Obviously, the scope of the yoga taught in North American church basements and fitness centres is much more limited. The kinds of yoga that have become popular since the 1970s focus mainly on physical well-being and stress reduction. The same is true of popular gurus such as Maharishi Mahesh Yogi and Deepak Chopra: they do not connect their teachings with any specific "religion," and they say that the techniques they advocate are compatible with any religious tradition.

frequently organize events such as blood drives and health screenings. In the home country, temples do not serve any of these functions.

Hinduism and the Environment

The history of environmental activism in India is sometimes traced back as far as the late fifteenth century, when a guru named Jambho—inspired by the pastoral life of Krishna the cowherd—taught his followers to minimize harm to the natural world. The community he established took the name Bishnoi, after his 29 ("bish-noi") most important teachings, which included everything from vegetarianism to water conservation and the protection of trees. Based in Rajasthan, the Bishnoi have followed those teachings for more than 500 years.

Today, growing numbers of Hindu leaders and institutions are drawing on the classic texts to encourage eco-activism. Billboards at the Venkateshwara temple in Tirumala-Tirupati, for instance, proclaim that "Trees, when protected, protect us," and temple authorities draw attention to a line from the *Matsya Purana* in which the goddess Parvati declares that "One tree is equal to ten sons."

In a culture where sons are so highly prized, this statement is striking. The Tirumala-Tirupati temple also maintains a large nursery in which tree saplings are grown to be given as *prasada* to pilgrims, who are encouraged to plant them at home. Many environmental activists take inspiration from a section of the Yajur Veda known as the *Song of Peace*:

> May there be peace in the skies, peace in the atmosphere, peace on earth, peace in the waters. May the healing plants and trees bring peace; may there be peace [on and from] the world, the deity. May there be peace in the world, peace on peace. May that peace come to me! (Yajur Veda 36.17)

Modern Reproductive Technology

Of all the technological innovations developed in recent years, those associated with reproduction tend to be among the most controversial. Yet Hindus generally appear to be quite accepting of intervention in this area. In the case of assisted reproduction, this is probably not surprising: the traditional teachings have always emphasized that reproduction is a primary duty. Thus many Hindus today accept artificial insemination, although for most couples the husband is the only acceptable donor.

The ethical considerations become more complex where contraception and gender selection are concerned. For thousands of years, male children have been more welcome than females, largely because of the traditional duty to the ancestors: in a patriarchal, patrilineal society, sons would continue the family line and could be counted on to look after their parents in old age, whereas daughters would need costly dowries and would be of benefit only to their husbands' families. Although Indian law forbids the use of sonograms and amniocentesis for the purpose of sex selection, the ratio of female to male births has dropped significantly in recent years.

The *dharmashastra* texts maintain that the unborn fetus has life; according to popular belief and stories from the *Puranas*, it is even capable of hearing and learning from the conversations that take place around it. Nevertheless, abortions are legal in India and are accepted without any strong dissent from religious leaders or prolonged editorial, legislative, or judicial debate. Thus it appears that some teachings of the dharma texts do not have any compelling authority for Hindus today.

Summary

Through music, dance, stories, rituals, and celebrations, through architecture and literature, the Hindu traditions continue to be practised and transmitted all over the world. The dynamism of these traditions is unmistakable. Scholars continue to interpret Vedanta. People still experience possession by deities, situate their homes in auspicious directions, and choose astrologically correct times for weddings. Ancient manuscripts are still being restored and edited, and new technologies are making the literature accessible to virtually everyone; the tradition confining the sacred word to particular castes is gone forever. In short, Hinduism continues to adapt to the world around it.

Sites

Kamakhya, Assam

One of the most important sites where the power of the Goddess is said to be felt. The temple is dedicated to the goddess Kamakhya, a form of Shakti/Parvati/Durga.

Badrinath, Uttaranchal

One of 108 places sacred to the Sri Vaishnava community, located high in the Himalayas, with a temple of Vishnu in the form of the sages Nara and Narayana.

Srirangam, Tamilnadu

An island temple-town where Vishnu, here called Ranganatha ("Lord of the stage"), reclines on the serpent Ananta ("infinity"); celebrated in the poems of the Alvars.

Madurai, Tamilnadu

A large city that is home to dozens of temples, including a famous complex dedicated to the Meenakshi (a local form of Parvati) and Sundaresvara (Shiva).

Tirumala-Tirupati (also known as Tiruvenkatam), Andhra Pradesh

One of the most important pilgrimage sites in India, dedicated to Venkateshwara (Vishnu).

Puri, Orissa

The site of a famous festival celebrating Lord Jagannath (a form of Vishnu) and his siblings, during which his image is rolled through the streets on a huge chariot. This event is the source of the English word "juggernaut."

Varanasi, Uttar Pradesh

Also known as Banaras; one of the holiest cities in India, located on the river Ganga. After cremation, many Hindus' ashes are brought here to be ritually submerged in the waters.

Mount Kailas, Tibet

A peak in the Himalayan range, said to be the abode of Lord Shiva; sacred to Jainas and Buddhists as well as Hindus.

Sacred Texts

Religion (Sect)	Text(s)	Composition/ Compilation	Compilation/ Revision	Use
Hinduism	Vedas (Sanskrit)	Composed between c. 1500 and 600 BCE		Considered the most authoritative of all texts. Parts of the Vedas were used in both domestic and temple rituals.
	Upanishads: the last section of the Vedas, focusing on philosophy (Sanskrit)	c. 6th century BCE.	Most Vedanta philosophers used these texts in commentaries or wrote commentaries on them. The commentarial tradition continues today.	Philosophical

Sacred Texts (Continued)

Religion (Sect)	Text(s)	Composition/ Compilation	Compilation/ Revision	Use
	Ramayana (Sanskrit)	c. 5th century BCE–1st century CE Very approximate dates	Periodically rendered in local languages. Tulsidas' *Ramcharitmanas* in Hindi is very important.	Doctrinal, ritual, performative, inspirational, devotional, narrative, educational
	Mahabharata (Sanskrit)	c. 5th century BCE–2nd century CE		Doctrinal, ritual, narrative, performative, inspirational, devotional, educational
	Bhagavad Gita (part of the *Mahabharata*; Sanskrit)	c. 2nd century BCE–2nd century CE	Extensive tradition of commentary.	Doctrinal, ritual, performative, devotional, inspirational, narrative, educational
	Puranas (Sanskrit)	1st millennium CE	Often recreated in local languages.	Doctrinal, ritual, devotional, narrative, inspirational, educational
Vaishnava, (specifically Gaudiya and ISKCON)	*Bhagavata Purana* (Sanskrit)	c. 1st millennium CE		Doctrinal, ritual, devotional, narrative, inspirational, educational
	Dharmasutras followed by the *Dharmashastras*. Many texts, of which the *Manava Dharmashastra* ("Laws of Manu") is the most important (Sanskrit).	*Dharmasutras* composed in the 1st millennium BCE; *dharmashastras* in the 1st millennium CE	Extensive tradition of commentary. Medathithi (c. 9th–11th centuries CE?) commented on *Manu*.	Ritual, moral, and legal prescriptions on all aspects of life: personal, domestic, and public; discussions of right behaviour
	Yoga Sutras of Patanjali	c. 200 BCE—300 CE	Commentarial tradition.	Classical philosophical text for yoga
Vaishnava (Tamil)	*Nalayira Divya Prabandham* Sacred Collect of 4,000 verses by the Alvars (Tamil)	c. 8–10th centuries CE; said to have been "revealed" in 11th century.	Extensive commentarial tradition.	Doctrinal, ritual, performative, devotional, inspirational, narrative, educational use
Shaiva (Tamil)	Tirumurai	c. 8th–12th centuries		Devotional and philosophical use
Vaishnava	Poems of Surdas (Hindi/ Braj Bhasha)	16th century		Doctrinal, ritual, performative, devotional, inspirational, narrative, educational use
Vaishnava (Marathi)	*Dnyaneshwari* or *Jnaneswari*	Composed by *Dnyaneshwar*, c. 13th century		Doctrinal, devotional, and educational use

Discussion Questions

1. What is the origin of the word "Hindu"? What elements of the Harappa culture suggest connections with Hindu traditions?
2. Why are the *Ramayana* and *Mahabharata* central to Hinduism?
3. What role do sacred texts play in Hinduism?
4. Identify some of the deities, major and minor, that Hindus worship. How is it that Hindus describe themselves as monotheistic?
5. Who or what is Brahman? What is the relationship between Brahman and deities such as Vishnu, Shiva, and the Goddess?
6. What is *bhakti*? What role does it play in Hinduism?
7. What are the three ways to liberation discussed in the *Bhagavad Gita*?
8. Describe some of the distinctive features of Hinduism as it developed in Southeast Asia.
9. What is the role of the performing arts in Hinduism?
10. What are the primary ways in which women historically contributed to various Hindu traditions?

Glossary

acharya The leading teacher of a sect or the head of a monastery.

advaita Shankara's school of philosophy, which holds that there is only one ultimate reality, the indescribable Brahman, with which the Atman or self is identical.

Alvars Twelve devotional poets whose works are central to the South Indian *bhakti* tradition.

artha Prosperity; one of the three classical aims in life.

ashramas Four stages in the life of an upper-class male: student, householder, forest-dweller, and ascetic.

Atman The individual self, held by Upanishadic and Vedantic thought to be identical with Brahman, the world-soul.

avatara A "descent" or incarnation of a deity in earthly form.

Ayurveda A system of traditional medicine, understood as a teaching transmitted from the sages.

Bhagavad Gita A section of the *Mahabharata* epic recounting a conversation between Krishna and the warrior Arjuna, in which Krishna explains the nature of God and the human soul.

bhakti Loving devotion to a deity seen as a gracious being who enters the world for the benefit of humans.

Brahma The creator god; not to be confused with Brahman

Brahman The world-soul, sometimes understood in impersonal terms; not to be confused with Brahma.

Brahmanas Texts regarding ritual.

brahmin A member of the priestly class.

darshana Seeing and being seen by the deity (in the temple) or by a holy teacher; the experience of beholding with faith.

Deepavali (Diwali) Festival of light in October–November, when lamps are lit.

devanagari The alphabet used to write Sanskrit and northern Indian vernacular languages such as Hindi and Bengali.

dharma Religious and social duty, including both righteousness and faith.

guru A spiritual teacher.

Holi Spring festival celebrated by throwing brightly coloured water or powder.

jnana Knowledge; along with action and devotion, one of the three avenues to liberation explained in the *Bhagavad Gita*.

kama Sensual (not merely sexual) pleasure; one of the three classical aims of life.

karma Action, good and bad, as it is believed to determine the quality of rebirth in future lives.

kshatriya A member of the warrior class in ancient Hindu society.

linga A conical or cylindrical stone column, symbolizing the creative energies of the god Shiva.

Mahabharata A very long epic poem, one section of which is the *Bhagavad Gita*.

mantra An expression of one or more syllables, chanted repeatedly as a focus of concentration in devotion.

moksha Liberation from the cycle of birth and death; one of the three classical aims in life.

murti A form or personification in which divinity is manifested.

Navaratri "Nine nights"; an autumn festival honouring the Goddess.

om A syllable chanted in meditation, interpreted as representing ultimate reality, or the universe, or the relationship of the devotee to the deity.

prasada A gift from the deity, especially food that has been presented to the god's temple image, blessed, and returned to the devotee.

puja Ritual household worship of the deity, commonly involving oil lamps, incense, prayers, and food offerings.

Puranas "Old tales," stories about deities that became important after the Vedic period.

Ramayana An epic recounting the life of Lord Rama, an incarnation of the god Vishnu.

rishi A seer; the composers of the ancient Vedic hymns are considered *rishis*.

sadhu A holy man.

samnyasin A religious ascetic; one who has reached the last of the four stages of life for a Hindu male; see ***ashramas***.

samsara The continuing cycle of re-births.

sati The self-sacrifice of a widow who throws herself onto her deceased husband's funeral pyre.

shruti "What is heard"; the sacred literature of the Vedic and Upanishadic periods, recited orally by the brahmin priests for many centuries before it was written down.

shudra A member of the lowest of the four major classes, usually translated as "servant," though some groups within the *shudra* class could be quite prosperous.

smrti "What is remembered," a body of ancient Hindu literature, including the epics, *Puranas*, and law codes, formed after the *shruti* and passed down in written form.

tantra An esoteric school outside the Vedic and brahminical tradition, which emerged around the fifth century and centred on a number of controversial ritual practices, some of them sexual.

upanayana The initiation of a young brahmin boy into ritual responsibility, in which he is given a cord to wear over his left shoulder and a mantra to recite and is sent to beg for food for the day.

Upanishads Philosophical texts in the form of reported conversations on the theory of the Vedic ritual and the nature of knowledge, composed around the sixth century BCE.

vaishya A member of the third or mercantile class in the ancient fourfold class structure.

Vedas The four collections of hymns and ritual texts that constitute the oldest and most highly respected Hindu sacred literature.

yoga A practice and discipline that may involve a philosophical system and mental concentration as well as physical postures and exercises.

Further Reading

Baird, Robert D. 1993. *Religions and Law in Independent India*. New Delhi: Manohar. Takes up some problems of the status of various groups.

———, ed. 1995. *Religion in Modern India*. 3rd ed. New Delhi: Manohar. Good individual chapters on nineteenth- and twentieth-century sectarian movements.

Basham, Arthur Llewellyn. 1954. *The Wonder That Was India*. London: Sidgwick & Jackson. Arguably still the definitive introduction to the pre-Muslim culture of the subcontinent.

***Brill's Encyclopedia of Hinduism*. 5 vols. 2009–13. Knut Jacobsen (chief editor), Helene Basu, Angelika Malinar, and Vasudha Narayanan, (associate editors). Leiden: Brill.** An excellent and comprehensive resource on the Hindu traditions.

Bryant, Edwin. 2003. *The Quest for the Origins of Vedic Culture: The Indo-Aryan Migration Debate*. New York: Oxford University Press. A balanced and thorough discussion of a controversial topic.

———, ed. *Krishna: A Sourcebook*. 2007. New York: Oxford University Press. A good introduction to one of the most important deities in the Hindu tradition from a variety of sectarian and regional perspectives.

Bryant, Edwin, and Maria Eckstrand. 2004. *The Hare Krishna Movement: The Postcharismatic Fate of a Religious Transplant*. New York: Columbia University Press. An eclectic collection of essays on the International Society for Krishna Consciousness.

Chapple, Christopher, and Mary Evelyn Tucker, eds. 2000. *Hinduism and Ecology: The Intersection of Earth, Sky, and Water*. Cambridge, MA: Center for the Study of World Religions, Harvard Divinity School. Part of an important series in which various traditions address current environmental issues.

Coward, Harold. 2005. *Human Rights and the World's Major Religions*. Vol. 4. *The Hindu Tradition*. Westchester Books. A good introduction to an important topic.

Craven, Roy C. 1976. *A Concise History of Indian Art*. New York: Praeger. Remains one of the best introductions to Indian art.

Dalmia, Vasudha, and Heinrich von Steitencron. 1995. eds. *Representing Hinduism: The Construction of Religious Traditions and National Identity*. New Delhi: Sage. A good set of essays discussing whether Hinduism is one or many traditions.

Dimock, Edward C., Jr, and Denise Levertov, trans. 1967. *In Praise of Krishna: Songs from the Bengali*. Garden City, NY: Doubleday. Lyrical expressions of devotion from eastern India.

Doniger O'Flaherty, Wendy, ed. and trans. 1988. *Textual Sources for the Study of Hinduism*. Manchester: Manchester University Press. A good sourcebook in a rather compressed format, covering the main phases of the Hindu tradition.

Eck, Diana L. 1981. *Darsan: Seeing the Divine Image in India*. Chambersburg, PA: Anima Books. On the significance of coming into the presence of the deity; brief but authoritative.

Embree, Ainslie T., ed. *Sources of Indian Tradition*. 2nd ed. 2 vols. New York: Columbia University Press. 1988. Expands on the de Bary first edition but drops a few items in the process.

Erndl, Kathleen M. 1993. *Victory to the Mother: The Hindu Goddess of Northwest India in Myth, Ritual, and Symbol*. New York: Oxford University Press. Well focused on one region.

Findly, Ellison B. 1985. "Gargi at the King's Court: Women and Philosophic Innovation in Ancient India." In Yvonne Y. Haddad and Ellison B. Findly, eds. *Women, Religion and Social Change*, 37–58. Albany: State University of New York Press. Shows that intellectual activity was not entirely limited to males.

Flood, Gavin. ed. *The Blackwell Companion to Hinduism*. London: Blackwell, 2003. Good essays on a variety of topics in the Hindu tradition.

González-Reimann, Luis. 2009. "Cosmic Cycles, Cosmology and Cosmography." In *Brill's Encyclopedia of Hinduism* vol. 1, 411–28.

Hawley, John S. and Mark Juergensmeyer. 1988. *Songs of the Saints of India*. New York: Oxford University Press. Excellent translations of the works of four medieval saints of North India.

Hawley, John S., and Donna M. Wulff. 1982. *The Divine Consort: Radha and the Goddesses of India*. Berkeley: Berkeley Religious Studies Series. Another useful work on feminine aspects of the Hindu tradition.

———. 1996. *Devi: Goddesses of India*. Berkeley: University of California Press. Expands on the theme of the previous work.

Huntington, Susan L. 1985. *The Art of Ancient India: Buddhist, Hindu, Jain*. New York: Weatherhill. A good introduction to ancient Indian monuments.

Jackson, William J., trans. 1991. *Tyagaraja: Life and Lyrics*. Delhi: Oxford University Press.

Leslie, Julia, ed. 1991. *Roles and Rituals for Hindu Women*. London: Pinter; Rutherford, NJ: Fairleigh Dickinson University Press. A coherent set of essays on the subject.

Lopez, Donald S., Jr., ed. 1995. *Religions of India in Practice*. Princeton: Princeton University Press. A sourcebook containing a fine range of material; strong on ritual.

Manu, Patrick Olivelle, and Suman Olivelle. 2005. *Manu's Code of Law: A Critical Edition and Translation of the Manava-Dharmasastra*. Oxford: Oxford University Press.

Marglin, Frédérique, and John B. Carman, eds. 1985. *Purity and Auspiciousness in Indian Society*. Leiden: E.J. Brill. A useful collection, in an anthropological series.

Miller, Barbara Stoler, trans. 1977. *Love Song of the Dark Lord: Jayadeva's Gitagovinda*. New York: Columbia University Press. An important *bhakti* text.

———, trans. 1986. *The Bhagavad Gita: Krishna's Counsel in time of War*. New York: Columbia University Press. A good translation, accessible to undergraduates.

Mittal, Sushil, and Gene Thursby, eds. 2004. *The Hindu World*. Routledge. Fairly comprehensive coverage, using Sanskrit terms, concepts, and categories.

Narayan, R.K. 1972. *Ramayana: A Shortened Modern Prose Version of the Indian Epic*. New York: Viking. A useful point of access to this classic.

Narayanan, Vasudha. 1994. *The Vernacular Veda: Revelation, Recitation, and Ritual Practice*. Columbia: University of South Carolina Press. The ritual use of the *Tiruvaymoli* among India's scheduled castes as well as brahmins.

———. 1996. "'One Tree Is Equal to Ten Sons': Hindu Responses to the Problems of Ecology, Population, and Consumption." *Journal of the American Academy of Religion* 65: 291–332. Discusses some classic resources for addressing concerns of today.

Nelson, Lance E. ed. 1998. *Purifying the Earthly Body of God: Religion and Ecology in Hindu India*. Albany: State University of New York Press. One of the earliest and best collections of essays on an important topic.

Olivelle, Patrick, trans. 1996. *Upanisads*. New York: Oxford University Press.

———, trans. 1997. *The Pancatantra: The Book of India's Folk Wisdom*. New York: Oxford University Press.

———, trans. 1999. *Dharmasutras: The Law Codes of Atastamba, Gautama, Baudhyayana, and Vasistha*. New York: Oxford University Press. This and the two foregoing items are lucid translations of influential texts.

Orr, Leslie C. 2000. *Donors, Devotees, and Daughters of God: Temple Women in Medieval Tamilnadu*. New York: Oxford University Press. A useful corrective to prescriptive male writings in Sanskrit on Hindu women.

Patton, Laurie L., ed. 2002. *Jewels of Authority: Women and Text in the Hindu Tradition*. New York: Oxford University Press. A wide-ranging collection of essays on Hindu and Buddhist women's relationship to sacred text and mantras.

Pechilis, Karen, ed. 2004. *The Graceful Guru: Hindu Female Gurus in India and the United States*. New York: Oxford University Press. A good set of essays on women gurus, with an excellent introduction by the editor.

Radhakrishnan, Sarvepalli, and Charles A. Moore, eds. 1957. *A Source Book in Indian Philosophy*. Princeton: Princeton University Press. A very good anthology of philosophical texts.

Rajagopalachari, Chakravarti. 1953. *Mahabharata*. Bombay: Bharatiya Vidya Bhavan. A sampling from this vast epic.

Ramanujan, A.K. 1979. *Speaking of Siva*. Harmondsworth: Penguin. Lyrical and moving translations of Kannada poems written by three men and one woman saint from twelfth and thirteenth century south India.

———, trans. 1981. ***Hymns for the Drowning: Poems for Vishnu by Nammawvar*. Princeton: Princeton University Press.** An excellent source for Tamil *bhakti*.

Rangacharya, Adya, trans. 1986. *The Natyasastra: English Translation with Critical Notes*. Bangalore: IBH Prakashana. A text frequently considered India's fifth Veda, important for the role of the performing arts in modern Hindu tradition.

Richman, Paula, ed. 1991. *Many Ramayanas: The Diversity of a Narrative Tradition in South Asia*. Berkeley: University of California Press. Reflects the importance of the *Ramayana* in vernacular South Asian traditions.

———, ed. 2000. *Questioning Ramayanas: A South Asian Tradition*. Delhi: Oxford University Press.

Soneji, Davesh, ed. 2012. *Bharatanatyam: A Reader*. New York: Oxford University Press. A scholarly and multi-disciplinary set of essays on the most popular classical form of dance in India.

Sweetman, Will. 2003. *Mapping Hinduism: "Hinduism" and the Sudy of Indian Religions, 1600–1776*. Halle: Franckesche Stiftungen.

Tharu, Susie, and K. Lalita. 1991. *Women Writing in India: 600 BC to the Present*. New York: Feminist Press. A must-read for all those interested in hearing women's voices from the past. Includes literature not necessarily perceived to be religious or Hindu.

von Stietencron, Heinrich. 1989. "Hinduism: On the Proper Use of a Deceptive Term." In Günther D. Sontheimer and Hermann Kulke, eds. *Hinduism Reconsidered*, 11–27. New Delhi: Manohar. One of the best discussions of the nomenclature of "Hinduism."

Waghorne, Joanne P., Norman Cutler, and Vasudha Narayanan, eds. 1985. *Gods of Flesh, Gods of Stone: The Embodiment of Divinity in India*. New York: Columbia University Press. Explores a range of forms in which Hindus see deity manifested.

Williams, Raymond Brady, ed. 1992. *A Sacred Thread: Modern Transmission of Hindu Traditions in India and Abroad*. Chambersburg, PA: Anima. A good description of the diaspora in the 1970s and 1980s.

Wujastyk, Dominik, intro. and trans. 1998. *The Roots of Ayurveda: Selections from Sanskrit Medical Writings*. Delhi: Penguin. Useful for the relationship between traditional Indian medicine and religion.

Zimmer, Heinrich. 1946. *Myths and Symbols in Indian Art and Civilization*. New York: Pantheon. A classic study, still often cited.

Recommended Websites

www.sacred-texts.com/hin/index.htm

Free online translations (mostly late-nineteenth to early-twentieth century) of the Vedas, epics, *Puranas*, *Yoga Sutras*, *smrti* literature, etc.

www.sscnet.ucla.edu/southasia

Very good links for South Asian culture, religions, and history.

www.harappa.com/har/har0.html

Many links to various aspects of the Indus Civilization.

www.wabashcenter.wabash.edu/resources/result_browse.aspx?topic=569&pid=361

A meta-site with links to many useful resources, including course syllabi.

www.columbia.edu/itc/mealac/pritchett/00 generallinks/index.html

A good site with links to many resources on South Asia.

http://virtualvillage.wesleyan.edu

An on-the-ground look at a "virtual village" in North India.

www.veda.harekrsna.cz/encyclopedia/index.htm

Links to articles on various topics in Hinduism from an ISKCON perspective.

www.sathyasai.org

The official site of Sri Sathya Sai Baba, maintained by his devotees.

http://prapatti.com

Texts and MP3 audios of several Tamil and Sanskrit Vaishnava prayers.

www.hindupedia.com/en/Main_Page

An online encyclopedia offering "a traditional perspective" on the Hindu religion and way of life.

www.hinduismtoday.com

A popular magazine based in Hawaii, rooted in the classical Shaiva tradition, but offering articles of interest to Hindus all over the world.

References

Carman, John B., and Vasudha Narayanan, trans. 1989. *The Tamil Veda: Pillan's Interpretation of the Tiruvaymoli*. Chicago: University of Chicago Press.

Doniger O'Flaherty, Wendy, ed. and trans. 1981. *The Rig Veda: An Anthology, One Hundred and Eight Hymns*. Harmondsworth: Penguin.

Hawley, John S., and Mark Juergensmeyer, trans. 1988. *Songs of the Saints of India*. New York: Oxford University Press.

Miller, Barbara Stoler, trans. 1986. *The Bhagavad-Gita: Krishna's Counsel in Time of War*. New York: Columbia University Press.

Radhakrishnan, Sarvepalli, trans. 1953. *The Principal Upanisads*. London: Allen and Unwin.

7 Jaina Traditions

Anne Vallely

Traditions at a Glance

Numbers

Estimates range from 5 to 8 million worldwide.

Distribution

Primarily India; smaller numbers in East Africa, England, and North America.

Principal Historical Periods

599–527 BCE	Traditional dates of Mahavira
c. 310 BCE	Beginning of the split within the Jaina community
2nd century BCE	Possible composition of *Kalpa Sutra*
5th century CE	Crystallization of the Svetambara and Digambara sects
17th century	Emergence of the Svetambara Sthanakvasi subsect
18th century	Emergence of the Svetambara Terapanthi subsect

Founders and Leaders

The 24 Jinas or Tirthankaras: a series of "ford-builders" who achieved perfect enlightenment and serve as guides for other human beings. The most important are the two most recent, Parsavanath and Mahavira.

Deities

None in philosophy. A few minor deities in popular practice; some Jainas also worship Hindu deities such as Sri Lakshmi. Although the Tirthankaras are not gods, many Jainas revere their images.

Authoritative Texts

The earliest texts were lost long ago. The Svetambara sect reveres a collection called the *Agama*, consisting of various later treatises known as the *Angas*, as well as the *Kalpa Sutra*, which contains the life stories of the Tirthankaras. The Digambara sect believes that the original *Angas* were lost as well and focus instead on a set of texts called *Prakaranas* (treatises).

Noteworthy Teachings

The soul is caught in karmic bondage as a result of violence, both intended and unintended, done to other beings. Non-violence is the most important principle, in thought, word, and deed. Freed from karma, the soul attains crystal purity.

A frail monk sits cross-legged on a bed, leaning against the wall for support as his followers enter the room. Everyone knows this is the last time they will gather for *darshana*—to pay homage to their guru and receive his blessing—for he has taken the vow of **sallekhana** and the process is nearing its end. *Sallekhana* is the ritual death achieved at the end of a long fast. No Jaina is required to undertake such a fast; in fact, Jainas are expressly forbidden to cause harm to any living being, whether in thought, speech, or action. But the Jaina path is one of **renunciation**—of departure from life during life—and *sallekhana* is merely its logical end. Voluntary death is the most radical statement possible of detachment from the body and the world. A dispassionate death is a triumph for the eternal soul on its journey towards perfection.

Overview

Jainism confronts us with a simple yet extraordinary message: the path to happiness, truth, and self-realization is the path of restraint. Happiness is the product not of doing but of not-doing; not of embracing the world but of disengaging from it. It is this emphasis on restraint that gives Jainism

← Jaina pilgrims at a temple in the Jaisalmer Fort, Rajasthan (© Craig Lovell / Eagle Visions Photography / Alamy).

its distinctive ascetic character. But the Jaina tradition cannot be contained within such narrow bounds. For one thing, the Jaina community is well known for its business acumen, worldly success, and strong social identity—in other words, for its effective, dynamic engagement with the world.

Outsiders often perceive a paradoxical disjunction between Jainas' this-worldly achievements and their other-worldly ethos. But this seeming paradox reflects the principle that the path of renunciation is a path of transformative power. The power of renunciation lies not in opposing worldly power, but in transcending and subsuming it. Some of the most interesting dimensions of Jainism can be traced to this interplay between the worldly and the other-worldly. Ultimately, the Jaina path leads away from the world—not just from its sorrows but also from its ephemeral joys, from family and community, from desires and pride, even from one's own body. Conquering our attachment to the world is the most difficult of all battles, but for Jainas it is the only battle worth engaging. Such is the message of the **Jinas** ("victors" or "conquerors"), the 24 ascetic–prophets—the most recent of whom was **Mahavira** (c. 599–527 BCE)—from whom Jainas take their name.

Jainism is a tradition that expresses itself ritually through the veneration and emulation of the Jinas (also known as "**Tirthankaras**"—builders of bridges across the ocean of birth and death, or ***samsara***). The Jina is the highest expression of the Jaina ideal, and the focus of the Jaina devotional apparatus. A commanding figure who could just as easily have been a worldly ***chakravartin***—the

Colossal rock-cut sculptures of the Tirthankaras at the Gwalior Fort in Madhya Pradesh (© Atlantide Phototravel / Corbis).

Timeline

c. 850 BCE	Parsavanath, the 23rd Tirthankara
599–527	Traditional dates of Mahavira
4th century	Possible beginning of split within Jaina community with southward migration of one group
2nd century CE	Umasvati, Digambara author of the *Tattvartha Sutra*
5th century	First Jaina temples
9th century	Jinasena, Svetambara philosopher
10th century	Colossal statue of Bahubali erected in Shravanabelagola, Karnataka
11th century	Dilwara temple complex in Rajasthan
12th century	Hemachandra, Svetambara philosopher
15th century	Lonkashaha initiates reform in the Svetambara tradition
16th century	Banarsidass initiates reform in the Digambara tradition
17th century	Formation of Svetambara Sthanakvasi subsect
18th century	Formation of Svetambara Terapanthi subsect
20th century	Revitalization of the Bhattaraka tradition within the Digambara sect

ideal benevolent ruler—endowed with everything the world has to offer, the Jina "conquers" the world by turning his back on it. Indeed, the Jina is venerated in both his potentialities: as the regal *chakravartin*, magnificently bejewelled and crowned, and as the unadorned ***Arhat*** (perfected being), entirely detached from worldly concerns. World renouncer and world conqueror, though antithetical in their orientations, both trace their beginnings to the good karma accrued through a life of non-violence. Restraint, self-discipline, and commitment not to harm are the starting points for the Jina and the *chakravartin* alike.

To grasp the vigorous character of Jainism, we need to keep in mind that the Jaina path of renunciation is one not of retreat from the harshness of the world, but of triumph over it. The world surrenders its bounty spontaneously to those who conquer it through detachment—though of course the true renouncer is indifferent to such rewards.

Jainas commonly express the essence of their tradition in three words: "*ahimsa paramo dharma*" ("non-violence is the supreme path"). This is not to say that they seek to eradicate the violence of the world. In a universe where every life exists only at the expense of others, such a commitment would be futile; furthermore, all engagement with the world only causes us to sink deeper into its depths, generating ever more karma to fasten to our souls. Rather, the Jaina commitment to non-violence is a commitment to radical non-interference. Jainas equate non-violence with renunciation because it is only through the total cessation of activity—of mind, speech, and body—that one can truly avoid harming others and, consequently, oneself.

There are countless life forms, many of which are invisible to the eye. All possess an eternal soul (***jiva***), and none desires to be harmed. Yet their omnipresence means that we cannot perform any action without causing them harm. And in so doing, we harm ourselves, for every act of violence we

Document

The Imperative of Non-violence

The Acaranga Sutra or "Scripture of Correct Conduct" is the oldest and among the most important texts of the Svetambara tradition. Believed to contain the teachings of Mahavira, it focuses on the requirement of non-violent action.

All living beings love their life. For them happiness is desirable; unhappiness is not desirable. No living being likes to be killed. Every living being is desirous of life (Acaranga Sutra 1:2:3; Jacobi and Muller [2001/1895–1910]).

perpetrate increases the negative karma attached to our souls. Lack of intention to commit harm is an important mitigating factor. But even unintended harm still increases karmic bondage—though the karma in question is less heavy and dark than the kind created when the harm is intended.

Jainism tells us that attachment to the world and to the worldly self comes at the expense of knowing the true Self that has nothing to do with this world—not with its sounds, its colours, or its rhythms, nor with our own talents, aptitudes, or experiences, nor even with the relationships we forge with others. Our worldly, social selves are no more than elaborate sand castles, washed away with each wave of the ocean of *samsara*.

The true Self is fundamentally other. Its deep, silent tranquillity is indifferent to the cacophony of the world. And precisely because it does not lobby for the attention of our consciousness, its presence is easy to ignore amidst the endless distractions created by the demands of the body. Nevertheless, the soul is luminous, radiating peace, and on very rare occasions our conscious minds may catch a glimpse of it. Jainas call this momentary awakening ***samyak darshan*** ("right faith" or "correct intuition" into the workings of the world), and it is the starting point of Jainism.

According to Jainas, there is only one path to emancipation: that of self-discipline and non-harm. Yet this singular path leads to a remarkable variety of Jaina communities. The most fundamental distinction is the one between the two Jaina sects: **Digambara** (naked or "sky-clad") and **Svetambara** (white-clad). The split occurred some 200 years after the death of Mahavira, and was the product of enduring differences regarding ascetic practice, women's spiritual capacity, and the nature of the Jina, among other things.

Other issues that divide Jainas include the worship of images or idols and the use of "living beings" such as flowers, water, and fire in worship. Yet all Jainas share the commitment to renunciation and non-violence. Renunciation is embodied by the "sky-clad" ascetics, but it is also present in the beliefs and practices of lay Jainas, including those who live in a context of plenty. Out of the diversity of Jaina expression emerges the unvarying message that non-violence is the only path to liberation.

The Shramana Revolution

Jainism appeared on the historical scene sometime between the ninth and sixth centuries BCE as part of the same ***shramana*** ("world-renouncing") movement that gave rise to Buddhism. The later date is the more commonly accepted because the historicity of Mahavira (born Vardhamana Jnatrpura) has been widely established. The earlier date is associated with the life of the twenty-third Tirthankara,

Map 7.1 Origin and Dispersion of Jainism

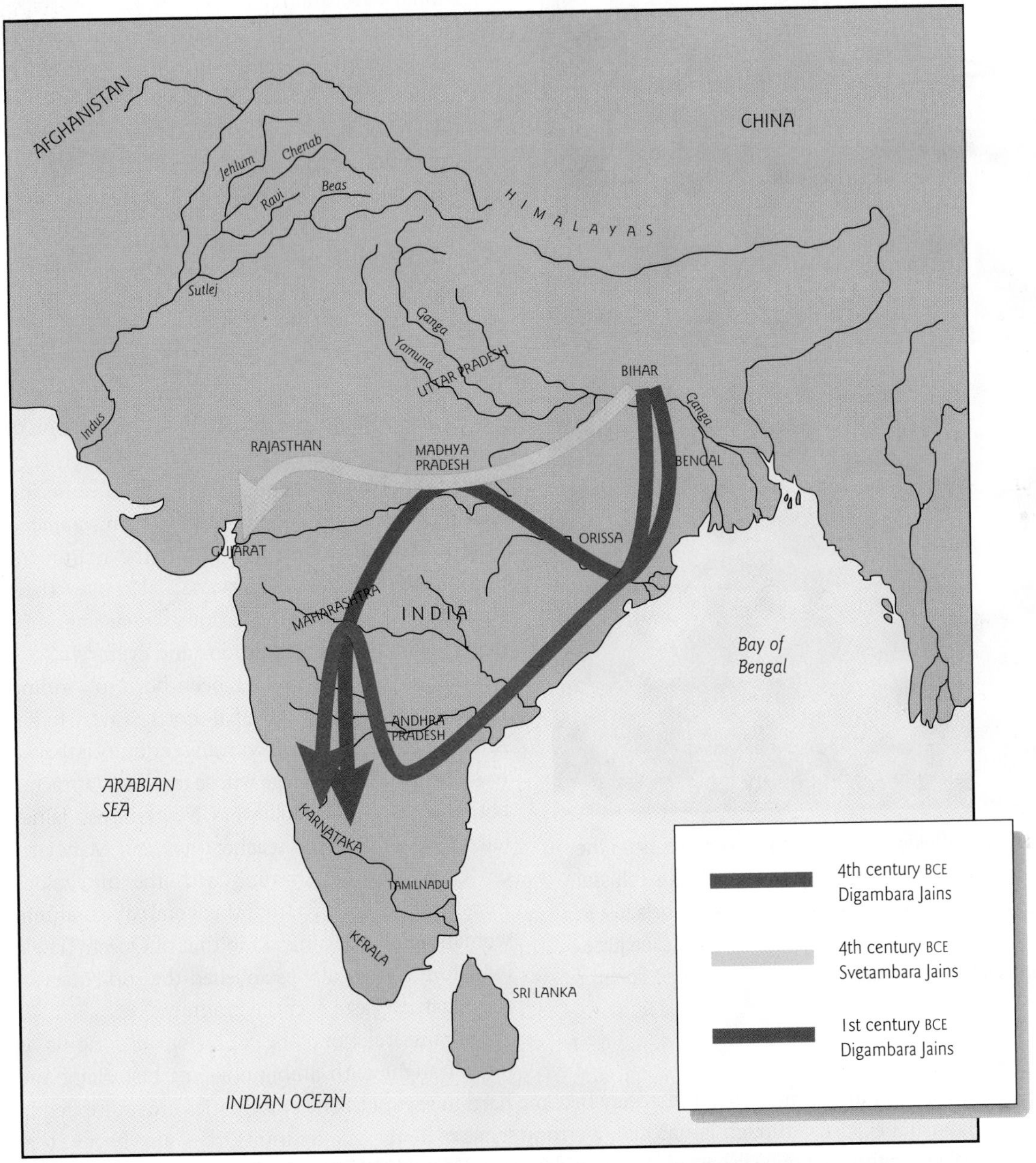

Today most Svetambara Jainas live in central and western India (Gujarat, Rajasthan, Madhya Pradesh, Uttar Pradesh) and most Digambara Jainas in the south, but communities of both sects can be found throughout the country, as well as abroad.

Perched on scaffolding constructed every 12 years for the Great Head Anointing Ceremony, Jainas bathe the colossal 18-metre (57-foot) Bahubali statue at Shravanabelagola in Karnataka with substances such as milk, sugarcane juice, saffron, sandalwood, and vermilion (© Frederic Soltan / Sygma / Corbis).

Parsavanath, for which the only evidence is the occasional scriptural reference.

The followers of Mahavira, like the followers of the Buddha, rejected the brahminical orthodoxy of the day. As their name implies, the "world renouncers" considered the brahmins' preoccupation with cosmic and social order to be fundamentally flawed. All the elements that went into maintaining that order—the hierarchical caste system, the elaborate liturgy, the rituals, and above all the cult of animal sacrifice—were anathema to the renouncers.

The *shramanas* also held similar views regarding the need for salvation from a meaningless cosmos. All regarded the cosmic order not as the creation of a transcendent god—the existence of which they denied—but as a purposeless place of suffering that must be transcended. Finally, each *shramana* group claimed a unique insight into the attainment of ***moksha*** (liberation/nirvana). Despite their similarities, therefore, the various *shramana* groups developed as distinct traditions and even rivals.

Mahavira is said to have been born to a ruling family in the region of Nepal–northeastern India. Almost all that can be said with any certainty is that he was a historical personage whose teachings attracted both disciples and lay followers. Nevertheless, Jainas tell many tales of the teacher they call Mahavira, or "Great Hero," beginning with the miraculous transfer of his embryo from the womb of a brahmin woman named Devananda to that of Queen Trisala (which unequivocally established the supremacy of the kshatriya caste over the brahmins).

In any religion, the question of origins is often fraught with ambiguities, as historicity and mythology are so interwoven that they become hard to separate. The ambiguities are multiplied in Jainism because, although Jainas have a strong sense of historical continuity, they also believe that we are embedded in a system of eternally recurring time, cycles of generation and degeneration so vast that mytho-historical particularities are ultimately meaningless.

Jainas believe that the cycles of generation and degeneration produce predictable patterns in social, moral, and physical life. Thus within each cycle there are periods that favour the emergence of Jinas who teach the path of liberation. Mahavira is merely the final Jina of the current degenerate time period. In the next cycle, which will be one of generation, another 24 Jinas will appear, preaching the same wisdom. And during the cycle of decline that will inevitably follow, yet another 24 will appear, and so on, in an unending cycle of decay and growth.

Focus

The Life of Mahavira in the Kalpa Sutra

Mahavira's Birth

[When] the Venerable Ascetic Mahavira was born, . . . [there] rained down on the palace of King Siddhartha one great shower of silver, gold, diamonds, clothes, ornaments, leaves, flowers, . . . sandal powder, and riches.

. . . [His parents] prepared plenty of food, drink, spices, and sweetmeats, invited their friends, relations, kinsmen. . . . His three names have thus been recorded: by his parents he was called Vardhamana; because he is devoid of love and hate, he is called sramana (i.e., Ascetic); because he stands fast in the midst of dangers and fears, patiently bears hardships and calamities, adheres to the chosen rules of penance, is wise, indifferent to pleasure and pain, rich in control. . . the name Venerable Ascetic Mahavira has been given him by the gods (Jacobi 1884: 251–6).

Enlightenment

When the Venerable Ascetic Mahavira had become a Jina and Arhat, he was a Kevalin [liberated one], omniscient and comprehending all objects; he knew and saw all conditions of the world, of gods, men, and demons: whence they came, whither they go, whether they are born as men or animals or become gods or hell beings, the ideas, the thoughts of their minds, the food, doings, desires, the open and secret deeds of all the living beings in the whole world; he, the Arhat for whom there is no secret, knew and saw all conditions of living beings in the world, what they thought, spoke, or did at any moment (Jacobi 1884: 263–4).

Mahavira's Physical Death

In the fourth month of that rainy season . . . in the town of Papa . . . the Venerable Ascetic Mahavira died, went off, quitted the world, cut asunder the ties of birth, old age, and death; became a Siddha [a liberated being], a Buddha, a Mukta, a maker of the end (to all misery), finally liberated, freed from all pains ... [that night, the kings who had gathered there said]: "since the light of intelligence is gone, let us make an illumination of material matter" (Jacobi 1884: 264–6).

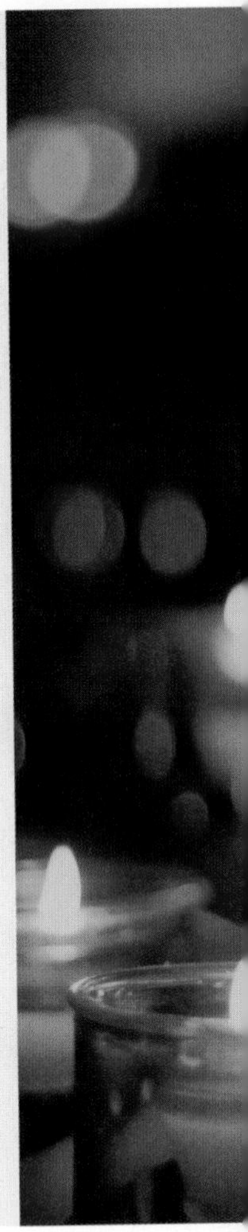

In this context linear time carries very little weight. Jainas move nimbly between the two perspectives. Most crucially, though, they assert that Jainism—like the cosmos itself—has no point of origin. Just as the cosmos has existed from "beginningless time," so too has the struggle for liberation from it—as well as the truth about how to attain salvation. "Jainism" is simply the name we give to this truth. By declaring the cosmos to be eternal, Jainism directs our attention away from the fruitless question of origins to the more pressing existential issue of our bondage in *samsara* (the cycle of birth and death).

Conveying the eternal message of liberation through restraint is an urgent task because it is accessible only to specific incarnations (human beings), residing in specific regions of the cosmos (the *karmabhumi*, or realms of action) and, as noted above, during specific time periods. Under any other conditions the message would not reach us. Thus we who have the good fortune to hear it must not squander our chance to learn from it how to escape.

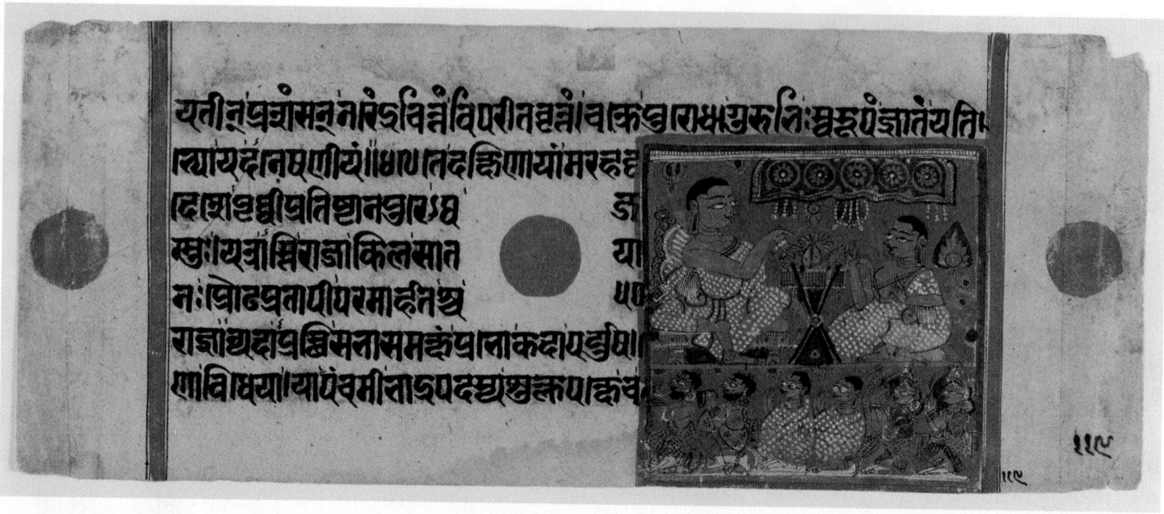

A page from a fifteenth-century copy of the *Kalpa Sutra*, the devotional text narrating the lives of the Jinas (Indian. Mahavira Preaching at the Gunashilaka Shrine, Leaf from a Dispersed Jain Manuscript of the Kalpasutra, 15th century. Opaque watercolor and gold on paper, sheet: 4 1/2 x 11 3/8 in. [11.4 x 28.9 cm]. Brooklyn Museum, Gift of the Ernest Erickson Foundation, Inc., 86.227.48).

The Early *Sangha*

Mahavira established Jainism as a fourfold community (*sangha*) made up of monks, nuns, laymen, and laywomen. His acceptance of women is noteworthy, since the *shramanas* generally regarded women as "objects of desire," to be avoided lest they distract male ascetics from their path. (The Buddha's initial reluctance to include women in his order is well known.) It is said that Mahavira's *sangha* grew to include 36,000 nuns and 14,000 monks, as well as 318,000 laywomen and 159,000 laymen (Jaini 1979: 37). The preponderance of nuns over monks—highly unusual in India—has remained a distinguishing feature of Jainism.

At the age of 72 Mahavira "left his body" and attained *moksha*—a state of complete detachment from the world, from which communication with those still in the cycle of *samsara* is impossible. Thus, unlike followers of traditions in which the central figures are believed to remain accessible through prayer, the Jainas had to sustain their tradition without any hope of ongoing guidance from the Jina.

Mahavira's disciples assumed leadership of the community, but within two centuries the once cohesive community had begun to split into two discrete traditions. The precise causes remain unknown, but many sources suggest that the turning point came in the fourth century BCE, when one group moved south. Thereafter, as the two groups developed in isolation, each came to see the other as deviating from Mahavira's vision.

That the northern group had abandoned the principle of nudity was a particular abomination to the southerners, for whom nudity was among the most elemental expressions of non-attachment and non-violence. The northerners argued that a simple garment had no bearing on spiritual progress. Nevertheless, the difference was so visible that it became the basis for the two groups' self-identification. Eventually, the northerners came to be known as the Svetambara (white-clad) and the southerners as the Digambara (sky-clad, or naked). The lay followers of both groups (including the fully clothed lay followers of the naked monks) likewise took on these names as markers of their religious identity.

This was not the only point of division, however. Another involved women's eligibility for full membership. The Digambaras' insistence on nudity meant that women were automatically disqualified, while the Svetambaras imposed no such condition and therefore did permit women to join them.

Both groups regard women's bodies as inferior to men's because they are weaker, and therefore the ascetic path is more difficult for them. For the Svetambaras, however, that obstacle is not insurmountable; they even maintain that the nineteenth Jina (Mallinath) was female. Digambaras vehemently disagree, arguing that asceticism requires a powerful, "adamantine" body (Jaini 1979: 39). They believe that rebirth in a male body is a prerequisite for full renunciation, but in the interim they permit women to lead a life of semi-renunciation.

Finally, the nature of the Jina's omniscience when embodied (that is, while in life) came to be a point of contention. According to the Digambaras, one who is omniscient must already have transcended bodily appetites and functions. Thus the Jina has no need of sleep or food, and instead of speaking communicates by a divine sound. The Svetambaras, by contrast, believe that all embodied beings are subject to bodily demands; therefore the omniscient Jina eats, sleeps, and communicates as humans do.

Sacred Literature

Scholars of religion today acknowledge that the boundaries separating religions have never been as watertight as their scriptures suggest. The creation of a sacred canon might seem to require the existence of a well-defined community but in practice the development of such a community may depend in part on the creation of such a canon. While a community of some kind must have existed, it would always have been more porous than scriptures suggest.

The sacred literature of the Jainas was transmitted by Mahavira to his followers, but it is not believed to have originated with him. In our time cycle, the eternal teachings were first propounded by the Jina **Rsabha**, and then transmitted anew by each succeeding prophet. Mahavira's teachings were committed to memory by his closest disciples, who then transmitted them orally to other disciples, who in turn passed them along down the generations. Thus the Jaina canon (*Agama*) for many years existed as a purely oral tradition.

The entire *Agama* has three main branches: the *Purva* ("the ancient"), concerned with metaphysics, cosmology, and philosophy; the *Anga* ("the limbs"), which includes discussion of mendicant conduct, doctrine, karma, and religious narratives; and the *Angabahya* ("ancillary limbs"), a subsidiary collection of commentaries on those topics, along with dialogues on matters such as astrology and the cycles of time.

The oral canon was faithfully preserved within the ascetic orders for more than 200 years. In the early fourth century BCE, however, northern India was struck by a devastating famine that is said to have continued for 12 years. The canon was nearly lost altogether as both the ascetics and the householders, whom they depended on for sustenance, struggled to survive.

From this point on, what happened to the *Agama* becomes sketchy and contentious. The *Purvas*—the most ancient section, believed to date from the time of Parsavanath, in the ninth century BCE—disappeared, although it is thought that much of the content was contained in the

Document

From the *Bhaktamara Stotra*

The Bhaktamara Stotra *is one of the most beloved Jaina texts. It is addressed to Adinatha—another name for Rsabha, the first Tirthankara.*

In the fullness of faith
I bow
to the feet of the Jina,
shining as they reflect the gems in the crowns of the gods
who bow down in devotion,
illuminating the darkness
of oppressive sin,
a refuge in the beginning of time
for all souls
lost in the ocean of birth (1)

. . .
Praising you
instantly destroys
the sinful karma that binds
embodied souls
to endless rebirth
just as the sun's rays
instantly shatter
the all-embracing
bee-black
endless dark night (7)
. . .

(*Bhaktamara Stotra*, *Manatunga*, 1, 7, 20–1, 26, 44; Cort 2005: 95–8).

final section of the *Anga*, called the *Drstivada*. According to the Svetambaras, the *Drstivada* was also lost to memory, but its essence was preserved through mnemonic allusions in a text contained within the *Angabahya*.

The Digambaras, however, claim that they managed to retain much of the *Drstivada* and put it in writing around the second century CE. This work, called the *Satkhandagama*, was the first Jaina scripture to be preserved in written form, and it is one of very few canonical works that the Digambaras recognize as authoritative. They reject the scriptures retained by the Svetambaras as inauthentic deviations from the original canon.

In addition to the *Agamas*, vast collections of post-canonical writing were produced by the learned ***acharyas*** (mendicant scholars) of both sects, including Jinasena, Hemachandra, Kundakunda, Haribhadra, and Umasvati. Known collectively as *Anuyogas* ("branches of scripture"), their writings achieved canonical status within their respective traditions and are today among the most celebrated works of ancient and medieval Indian philosophy.

The dispute over the Svetambara and Digambara canons aside, the gulf between the two groups is not as wide as it may appear. Many fundamental ideas—on the nature of the soul, karma, non-violence, the cosmos—are common to both groups, as are many practices. The ***Tattvartha Sutra*** of Umasvati (second century CE) merits special note here. It is an extraordinarily comprehensive treatment of the fundamentals of the tradition, and is cherished by both Svetambara and Digambara communities. Finally, the recent text *Saman Suttam* (1974)[1] is the first cross-sectarian effort to produce a concise summary of Jaina thought. Following are the fundamentals of Jaina cosmology on which the two sects agree.

Document

The Birth of Jain Philosophy

The Tattvartha *("That Which Is")* Sutra *is an authoritative text for both Svetambara and Digambara Jains. Composed in the second century* BCE *by Acharya Umaswati, it seeks to provide a systematic and rational foundation for Jaina teachings.*

Belief in the self and other realities is Right Faith, their comprehension is Right Knowledge, being without attachment is Right Conduct. These together constitute the way to liberation (1: 4; Shah 2004: 88).

Cosmology

Jainas believe that the entire cosmos (*loka*) is made up of six eternal substances called *dravya*, and that knowledge of them is an important step towards self-perfection. These substances are classified in two broad categories: *jiva* (soul) and ***ajiva*** (non-soul). *Jiva* is an eternal substance with consciousness. *Ajiva* is a substance without consciousness and consists of five types: *pudgala* (pure matter), *kala* (time), *dharma* (principle of motion), *adharma* (principle of rest), and *akash* (space). The latter four—all variants of *pudgala*—are "supportive" forms, without which existence would not be possible.

Pudgala is a concrete substance with the attributes of touch, taste, smell, and colour. Although it has no special function, it is the basis of all matter and energy. All activities of the mind and body, including thought and speech, are considered to be *pudgala*. All worldly knowledge is acquired by means of *pudgala*—including the knowledge of how to free ourselves from it! Indeed, it is only through perception, which is also a form of *pudgala*, that we can know the cosmos and its contents.

Thus *pudgala* is not antithetical to *jiva*. It is neutral in this regard, although its natural tendency is to become attached both to other forms of matter and to *jiva*. This is an important point, because renouncers typically speak of matter in highly negative terms (for example, referring to the world as vomit, or the body as a trap). Yet *pudgala* is *jiva*'s friend as well as its foe, for the worldly soul that seeks release from it is nevertheless utterly dependent on it.

The most fundamental existential problem, shared by all beings in the cosmos, is the fact that *jiva* and *ajiva* are thoroughly enmeshed. This is what prevents the soul from achieving bliss, which can be experienced only in a state of purity removed from all that is not-soul. Jainas do not posit an original state of separation from which there was a "fall." Instead they assert that this state of entanglement is eternal, "without beginning," and that we are constantly exacerbating it, since every activity, mental as well as physical, causes vibrations that create ever more particles of binding karma. These karmic particles come in two types—auspicious ("good karma," called ***punya***) and inauspicious ("bad karma," called ***paap***)—but ultimately all forms of karma must be purged. The forces behind those karma-creating activities, and hence the root causes of our bondage, are the passions.

This is the quandary from which the Jaina path of self-restraint offers a coherent way out. By limiting—eventually, eliminating—the inflow of karma and cleansing the soul of the karmic particles that have become encrusted on it through eternity, we can eliminate the cause of the soul's suffering. The process of purging is called *nirjara*, and it is the purpose behind most Jaina practices. Normally, karma dissolves when (after giving its pain or pleasure) it comes to fruition. But karma can be made to "ripen" and vanish prematurely through the practice of ascetic discipline.

Major Developments

As a tiny, heterodox minority within the vast Indian mosaic, Jainas have always been vulnerable to assimilation. How have they managed to differentiate themselves and thrive when other world-renouncing traditions have not? Paradoxically, the success of "other-worldly" Jainism likely owes much to its "this-worldly" understanding. The skills required to forge alliances with ruling elites and make inroads into established economic structures in the medieval period (fifth through seventeenth centuries) were developed in the first two centuries of its existence, when it enjoyed the patronage of the kshatriya rulers.

In the final centuries before the beginning of the Common Era, the fate of all the *shramana* groups depended on their ability to secure royal patronage. The socio-political "alliance" between the kshatriyas and *shramanas* was rooted in a shared ideological opposition to brahminic orthodoxy. The fact that Mahavira (like the Buddha) came from a kshatriya clan was a sign of the kshatriyas' ascent. The alliance was mutually beneficial: the *shramanas* prospered with the economic support of the kshatriyas, while helping to gain them popular support and legitimacy.

In the fourth century BCE, however, Emperor Ashoka converted to Buddhism and the balance of power shifted. The Jainas slowly retreated from their original centres of power in eastern India (Magadha), towards the (then) more peripheral northwestern regions of Rajasthan, Gujarat, and Punjab, as well as into the southern areas of what are now Maharashtra and Karnataka. Nevertheless, the wealth and—more important—the political skills that Jainas had acquired from serving (in legal positions, as advisers, etc.) at the various kshatriya courts gave them a worldly acumen that would serve them well long after their royal support had disappeared.

By the third century BCE, the once unified Jaina community had begun to separate into the two groups that, centuries later, would become the Svetambaras and Digambaras. The split was reinforced by the geographical repositioning of the Svetambaras in the northwest and the Digambaras in the south. Yet Jainas of both sects managed to prosper in their new environments. Although their influence with local elites was always limited, their skills, especially in trade, enabled them to establish secure communities.

Jaina philosophy flourished over the following centuries. Among the *acharyas* who produced important treatises were the Digambaras Umasvati (the second-century author of the *Tattvartha Sutra*), his contemporary Kundakunda, and Haribhadra in the seventh century, and the Svetambaras Jinasena in the ninth century and Hemachandra in the twelfth. Together, the philosophical works of the *acharyas* constitute an enormous and celebrated body of sacred literature.

The preservation of Jaina traditions through the medieval period can probably be attributed to interdependence of Jaina householders and renouncers. Instead of establishing large monasteries, as the Buddhists did, the Jaina ascetics continued to rely for sustenance on householders, who likely served as unofficial enforcers of proper conduct. Although the Buddhist monasteries were supported by lay followers, the relationship between them was never as close as the relationship between Jaina ascetics and householders, who provided **mendicants** with sustenance as often as three times a day. The latter played a central role in the perpetuation of Jaina tradition, and for

Document

The Nature of the Self

Kundakunda was a celebrated second-century acharya *who composed several important texts, including the* Samayasara, *which focuses on the nature of the soul. Though revered by all Jains, he is especially important to the Digambara tradition.*

The defining characteristic of the jiva is that it knows—that is its essence. Jiva and Jnana, self or knower and knowledge are not different, they are identical: the knower is essentially one with knowledge (Kundakunda 1950: 232).

that reason they may have been less vulnerable than their Buddhist counterparts to the rise of the Hindu *bhakti* movement. Furthermore, whereas the concentration of Buddhist monks and scriptures in large, wealthy monasteries made them easy targets for marauding armies, the Jainas were dispersed throughout the society and had no property to plunder. Thus the decentralized nature of Jaina groups may have inadvertently contributed to their survival.

Reform

Idol (*murti*) veneration became an established feature of Jainism very early in its history (third century BCE), but the first Jaina temples did not appear until the early medieval period (c. fifth century CE). With time and growing affluence, the temples became sites not only of devotion but of interaction between householders and the mendicants who gathered there.

The care and management of temples is almost exclusively the responsibility of the laity. The general absence of settled, temple-based communities of mendicants today can be traced to a number of powerful reform movements that arose between the fifteenth and seventeenth centuries and effectively reinvigorated the tradition of ascetic discipline among both Svetambara and Digambara Jainas.

The reformers saw a direct correlation between the proliferation of temples and what they considered to be a growing laxity on the part of many Jaina ascetics, who gradually abandoned itinerancy for the relative comfort of a settled life in and around the temples.

The first in the Svetambara tradition to question the wealth and power of the *caityavasis* (temple-dwelling renouncers) was a fifteenth-century lay reformer named Lonkashaha. He also challenged their deviation from the principle of restraint, and criticized idol-worship and temple-building as contrary not only to the ethos of renunciation but also to the vow of non-violence, given that the construction of idols and temples involved unnecessary violence to living beings. Lonkashaha's critique effectively put an end to the institution of the *caityavasis* and eventually gave rise to two Svetambara sects that remain highly influential: Sthanakvasis (who oppose temple-based Jainism and reside in halls known as *sthanaks* on their peripatetic travels), and Terapanthis (reformers who oppose the use of *sthanaks* as well as temples).

Major changes took place in the Digambara tradition as well, initiated by the lay poet Banarsidass in the sixteenth century. Like Lonkashaha, Banarsidass criticized what he saw as the excessive ritualism and unnecessary violence (the use of flowers, for instance) associated with temple worship.

At the same time he denounced a group of quasi-ascetic clerics called the *bhattarakas*. Analogous to the Svetambara *caityavasis* but with greater political clout, the *bhattarakas* served both as guardians of the temples and as intermediaries between the naked ascetics and the ruling elites—a role that, in addition to gaining them power and wealth, made them vulnerable to corruption.

The Digambaras responded to these critiques with sweeping reforms that led to the decline (though not the disappearance) of the *bhattarakas*. The revitalization sparked by the reformers' critiques put both the Svetambara and Digambara orders in positions of significant strength as they entered the modern period.

Practice

The importance that Jainism attaches to practice is one of its defining features. Correct practice (*samyak caritra*) constitutes one of the "Three Jewels" of Jainism, along with correct intuition (*samyak darshan*) and correct knowledge (*samyak jnana*). Although all three are fundamental, correct practice tends to overshadow the others because it is so conspicuous. Before we look at specific practices, however, it is important to grasp the special significance that the concept of practice has in Jainism, and how it is grounded in Jaina metaphysics.

The Jaina emphasis on practice reflects an understanding of the world and human suffering as *real*—not illusory—and in need of active human intervention. This understanding stands in sharp contrast to that of Vedanta-Hinduism and Buddhism, which essentially see the world and human suffering as products of thought and perception, and therefore focus on changing consciousness as the way to freedom. While Jainas recognize that lack of consciousness plays a key role in the problems of earthly existence, they also believe that the soul is physically (not just mentally) trapped, caught in karmic matter that must be dealt with physically through practices such as penance and fasting.

We have already described the Jaina view of the eternal soul (*jiva*) and matter (*ajiva*) as enmeshed in a labyrinthine web that will never be untangled without concrete action. Because our entrapment is real in a physical sense—not just an illusory state that can be dispelled through clearer thinking—our enlightenment hinges as much on our practice as it does on our worldview. Good intentions can never be enough; action must always be the foremost consideration. It is for this reason that renouncers follow an ascetic discipline designed to heighten their awareness of how they move their bodies in and through space—how they walk, sit, lie down, speak, collect alms, sleep, go to the toilet, etc. It is no exaggeration to say that the focus on practice is a defining feature of the Jaina path.

The elaborate edifice of Jaina practice aims to purify the soul of the *pudgala* that clings to it. By shedding obstructive karma, the soul becomes free to manifest its true nature, radiant and powerful. Practices are of two types: defensive and offensive. In the process known as *samvara*, defensive strategies, such as inculcating detachment and mindfulness, are used to impede the accumulation of new karma, while *nirjara* (purging) uses fasting, meditation, and various forms of physical discipline to "burn off" old karma.

The hallmarks of Jaina practice—ascetic discipline, dietary restrictions, fasting, ***samayika*** (state of equanimity), ***pratikramana*** (prayer of repentance), *sallekhana* (fast to death), even Jina puja (worship of the Jinas)—are undertaken, by both renouncers and householders, with the aim of purification through the dual processes of *samvara* and *nirjara*. The main difference between the paths of the renouncer and the householder lies in the degree of purification they permit; the renouncer's life is structured by a series of vows (***mahavratas***) that make it nearly impossible for new karma to develop.

Because renouncers are largely shielded from the risk of accumulating new karma, they can devote their time to whittling away their existing karmic load. Householders, immersed as they are in worldly activities—working, raising families, preparing food—are awash in karmic influences. Nevertheless, they can limit the influx of negative karma (*paap*) through lay practices (***anuvratas***) such as fasting or limiting possessions, travel, cosmetics, and so on; many women in particular undertake these moderate exercises in restraint. What marks such activities as characteristically Jaina is that they all involve disengagement from the world. Even devotional activities (Jina puja, for example) that outwardly resemble Hindu forms of worship are interpreted by Jainas as practices that foster worldly detachment.

Ideally, the lives of Jainas, whether renouncers or householders, are governed by a series of vows (*mahavratas* and *anuvratas* respectively) that limit worldly engagement, discipline the body, and help the soul develop the tools it will need for its eventual liberation. Thus Jainism is unequivocally a renouncer tradition, even though the vast majority of Jainas at any given time have always been householders involved in worldly pursuits.

Jainism is a renouncer tradition because its defining framework is thoroughly ascetic in character. It creates and moulds religious identity by asking the faithful to accept increasingly restrictive boundaries. The main difference between the *mahavratas* of the mendicants and the *anuvratas* of the householders is the degree to which they restrict worldly engagement.

Ascetic Practice

The *mahavratas* are five "great vows" accepted by everyone who takes up the life of a Jaina ascetic (*muni* or *sadhvi*): *ahimsa* (non-harm), *satya* (truthfulness), *asteya* (non-stealing), *brahmacharya* (celibacy), and *aparigraha* (non-possession/non-attachment). It is said that Mahavira established celibacy as a separate vow, independent of the fourth vow of non-attachment under which it had been incorporated during the time of Parsavanath.

Although the discourse of renunciation often refers to the poetic image of the solitary wanderer, initiation into the renouncer path is very much a collective endeavour. Aspiring ascetics must first seek and receive permission from their families (or spouses), as well as from the leader of a mendicant order.

In addition, the ascetic orders impose certain restrictions themselves. Neither sect accepts individuals who are physically, emotionally, or mentally fragile. The renouncer path was not designed as a refuge for those on the margins of conventional society; it is an arduous path suitable only for the courageous, committed, and stalwart. It is for this reason that the Digambara sect continues to claim that women are not suited for the ascetic life. "Femaleness"—determined as it is by karma—is seen as too great an impediment, making the already challenging life of mendicancy impossible. The renouncer path is to be undertaken only by those who have both the spiritual desire and the physical fortitude for a life of denial.

By drawing the self back from worldly concerns, the vows create the conditions in which its true vitality and force can be unveiled. The first vow (*ahimsa*) is the weightiest of the five; Jainas commonly say that it effectively encompasses all the others. In effect, *ahimsa* forbids all involvement with the world and ensures that no action is undertaken spontaneously, without restraint. Because the vow of *ahimsa* is unconditional in its application, renouncers must be concerned to cause no harm—through speech, action, or thought—even to "one-sensed" beings (invisible air-bodied beings, water, fire, earth) as well as plants, insects, animals, and fellow human beings. Avoiding harm to human beings and animals is easy compared to avoiding harm to water and air and other

A Jaina woman in New Delhi gives food to a nun. Such women are very conscious of the strict dietary rules that govern the renouncers' lives, and take care to ensure that all offerings have been rendered *ajiv* (without life) (© AP Photo / Manish Swarup / CP).

minute forms of life (all of which are equally endowed with an eternal soul); this is a monumental challenge and is the main reason behind the Jaina insistence on correct practice.

Munis and *sadhvis* are not permitted to prepare their own food, since even harvesting plants or boiling water inevitably causes harm to living beings. Thus the ascetics depend entirely on the generosity of householders, and even so they must be vigilant to maintain their vow of *ahimsa*. They are permitted only a small portion of the householder's "leftovers"; they cannot accept food that has been prepared expressly for them, as this would implicate them in whatever violence that preparation entailed; and the food and water they receive in their alms bowls must already have been cooked, boiled, or peeled (in the case of fruits) to ensure that it is *ajiv* (without life).

It is critical to understand the rationale underpinning these practices. The path of renunciation is open to all, irrespective of caste, gender, or social position. But it is extremely demanding, and Jainas know that very few will ever be able to take it. The overwhelming majority who remain householders therefore accept, implicitly or explicitly, that a certain amount of violence will be a regular part of their lives. For these people, to support the renouncers is both a duty and an honour—with the additional benefit of earning them merit or good karma. More important, it sustains a system in which the ideal of living without doing harm remains a genuine possibility for anyone with the requisite strength of character.

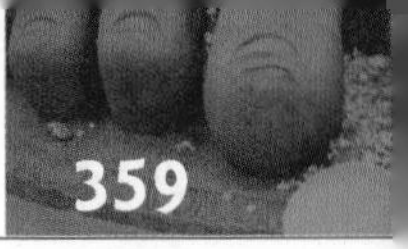

Document

From the Acaranga Sutra on Good Conduct

He who injures these (earth bodies) does not comprehend and renounce the sinful acts; he who does not injure these, comprehends and renounces the sinful acts. Knowing them, a wise man should not act sinfully towards the earth, nor cause others to act so, nor allow others to act so. He who knows these causes of sin relating to earth, is called a reward-knowing sage. Thus I say (Jacobi 1884: 10–11).

. . . the sage who walks the beaten track (to liberation), regards the world in a different way. "Knowing thus (the nature of) acts in all regards, he does not kill," he controls himself, he is not overbearing.

Comprehending that pleasure (and pain) are individual, advising kindness, he will not engage in any work in the whole world: keeping before him the one (great aim, liberation), and not turning aside, "living humbly, unattached to any creature." The rich in (control) who with a mind endowed with all penetration (recognizes) that a bad deed should not be done, will not go after it. What you acknowledge as righteousness, that you acknowledge as sagedom . . . ; what you acknowledge as sagedom, that you acknowledge as righteousness. It is inconsistent with weak, sinning, sensual, ill-conducted house-inhabiting men. "A sage, acquiring sagedom, should subdue his body." "The heroes who look at everything with indifference, use mean and rough (food, &c.)." Such a man is said to have crossed the flood (of life), to be a sage, to have passed over (the samsara) to be liberated, to have ceased (from acts). Thus I say (Jacobi 1884: 46–7).

The *mahavrata* of *ahimsa* prohibits outright many aspects of the renouncers' former householder lives, and no aspect of embodied existence escapes the framework of restraint: eating, talking, sleeping, walking, defecating, urinating, thinking, even dreaming—all must be disciplined in non-harm. Renouncers must not walk on grass, for to do so would cause it harm; they must look carefully wherever they step to be sure they do not harm anything on the ground; they are forbidden from using electricity and flush toilets (which cause harm to fire-bodied and water-bodied beings respectively); and their minds are subject to continuous self-censure as they try to eliminate anger, jealousy, greed, and desire. Negative or aggressive thoughts are believed to accrue bad karma in much the same way that stepping on an insect would. The restrictions on speech, body, and thought contained within the principle vow of *ahimsa* are potentially limitless.

Focus

The Mahavratas

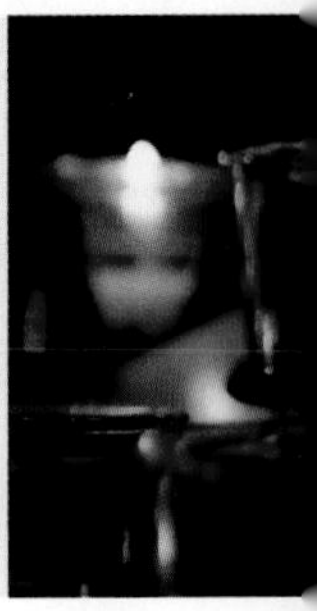

1. Non-violence (*ahimsa*)
2. Truth (*satya*)
3. Non-stealing (*asteya*)
4. Chastity (*brahmacharya*)
5. Non-possession/non-attachment (*aparigraha*)

The subsidiary vows of non-attachment, truthfulness, non-stealing, and celibacy reinforce and enlarge the vow of *ahimsa*. The vows of truthfulness and non-stealing forbid false speech and the use of anything that has not been freely given. *Brahmacharya* is more than a vow of celibacy: it is a vow to renounce all desire. Even dreams of a "carnal" nature have the power to attract karma and therefore require penance. The vow of *aparigraha* entails the renunciation not only of all possessions (home, clothing, money, etc.) but of all attachments, whether to places, people, things—or even dogmatic ideas.

In addition to the actions to be avoided, there are six "obligatory actions" that renouncers are required to perform: equanimity (*samayika*), praise to the Jinas (Jina puja), homage to one's teachers, repentance, body-abandonment, and, finally, the more general pledge to renounce all transgressions.

Together, the *mahavratas* and obligatory actions can appear overwhelming. But the constraints they impose are not seen as barriers to freedom. Rather, they are seen as catalysts to self-realization, the means to the sublime state of unconditional freedom, permanent bliss, and omniscience. Furthermore, each step towards self-realization is believed to bring benefits for the community as well as the individual. For Jainas, the renouncers embody a spiritual power that can work miracles—though of course they are not supposed to use their powers for "worldly" purposes.

The path to the very highest levels of self-realization has 14 stages. Householders rarely rise above the fifth step, and must fully renounce worldly life if they wish to go further. Even so, the householder path offers many opportunities for spiritual progress.

Householder Practice

The "small (or lesser) vows" (*anuvratas*) that govern lay life are normally taken without any formal ceremony. Modelled on the mendicant's *mahavratas*, they reflect the same aspiration to limit worldly engagement. They are identical in name and number to the *mahavratas*, but are interpreted and applied more leniently.

For instance, the *ahimsa anuvrata* is not total. It prohibits the consumption of certain foods, as well as eating after dark (when injury to insects is more likely). But it accepts that harm to one-sensed beings is unavoidable for householders. The subsidiary vows work in a similar manner: truthfulness and non-stealing are emphasized in much the same way as in the *mahavratas*, but celibacy is redefined to mean chastity in marriage. Similarly, the *anuvrata* of *aparigraha* does not require householders to live without possessions. Instead, it demands that they scrutinize their psychological attachment to their possessions.

The *anuvratas* are seen as establishing a compromise between worldly existence and spiritual progress. They do not interfere with the householder's ability to lead a "normal" existence. Quite the contrary: Jainas have long been among the wealthiest, most literate, and most accomplished communities in India. And from the Jaina perspective, there is a direct connection between their socio-economic success and their religious vows.

Reflection–Meditation

Whereas the *mahavratas* and *anuvratas* seek to discipline embodied activities, the practice of *samayika* seeks to halt them altogether. For 48 minutes a day, devotees practise meditation or reflection, cultivating indifference to the concerns of body—attachments and aversions, sufferings

Document

Experiencing the Pure Soul

Jain meditation involves a practice called samayika, *in which the aim is to attain a state of pure awareness, devoid of all attachments and aversions.*

To remain in the state of equanimity without attachment and hatred, and to treat all living beings equal to one's self is called Samayika. Equanimity is the act of remaining calm and tranquil. It implies neutrality of mind and temper. It is essential for the practice of non-violence (Shah, n.d.).

and pleasures—so that they can "dwell in the soul." In the absence of distractions, the Self can experience and enjoy itself. Jainas believe that the practice of *samayika* offers a foretaste of the joy that final release will bring.

Fasting and Dietary Practices

Closely connected in intent is fasting. The Jaina term for the practice, *upvas* (literally, "to be near the soul"), underscores their belief that in order to get close to the soul we must get away from the demands of the body and ego. At the same time fasting is considered a highly effective means of eliminating karma.

Jaina fasts are legendarily long, frequent, and arduous. Lay women, in particular, are celebrated for their heroic fasting, which is believed to benefit their families as well as themselves. The entire household gains social prestige from the women's pious actions, and the auspicious karma created by fasting can bring karmic rewards for the family. The most forceful expression of non-attachment is *sallekhana*, the ritual fast that brings life to an end.

The Fast to Death

Jainas boast that whereas other traditions celebrate birth, they celebrate death. This statement can be traced to the *shramana* tradition, in which the highest goal was to escape embodied existence. A death that is "celebrated" is one that has been accepted voluntarily and with equanimity, indicating total detachment from the body and the world.

Although *sallekhana* is not the universal practice, it is not uncommon even among householders. To be able to "discard the body" without pain or fear, and greet death with calmness and equanimity, is to reap the ultimate reward of a life lived in accordance with Jaina principles.

In addition, *sallekhana* is believed to be highly advantageous for the soul as it journeys forward. A dispassionate death results in a powerful expulsion of bad karma while attracting the good karma required to ensure a good rebirth either in a heavenly realm or in a spiritually advanced human state. Jainas believe that at the moment of physical death, the karma-saturated soul will be instantaneously propelled into a new incarnation, determined by its karma. (A soul free of

A sky-clad monk meditating by the holy footprints of Bhadrabahu, the founder of the Digambara sect (Gamma-Rapho via Getty Images).

all karma, instead of being reborn, would ascend to the realm of liberation, but that is not possible in the current time cycle.)

If the Jaina ideal is a progressive withdrawal from life during life, then *sallekhana* becomes its logical conclusion. The title of an essay on the subject by James Laidlaw captures this idea beautifully: "A Life Worth Leaving" (2005). For Jainas, *sallekhana* is the natural culmination of a life dedicated to detachment from the world; it is the ultimate embodiment of Jaina values, paradoxically achieved through a kind of dis-embodiment. Whether or not they choose *sallekhana*, Jainas endeavour to accept the inevitability of death with self-control and serene detachment.

Jaina Astrology

Jaina astrology has received relatively little scholarly attention, but it is a subject of great interest in the community itself. How Jainas use astrological charts is beyond the scope of this chapter, but it's worth noting that the practice points to an aspect of Jainism that is easily overlooked, namely its recognition of the role that external forces play in the process of self-realization. With no hope of assistance from a creator god, Jainas seeking liberation need to make use of all the assistance that is available. Astrology offers valuable insight into the manipulation of karma for both spiritual and worldly benefit.

Jainas' interest in astrology sheds light on their understanding of karma as something with positive as well as negative aspects. To the extent that astrology seeks to pre-empt misfortune and take advantage of opportunity, it also reminds us that Jaina renunciation is not a matter of flight from the world, but of a resolute fight to overcome it.

Jina Worship

The objects of Jaina worship are the 24 perfected beings known as the Jinas. Temples are constructed to house icons of them, pilgrimages are made to places associated with them, and they are worshipped daily in prayer. Although four of the Jinas are especially revered (Mahavira, Parsavanath, Neminath, Rsabha), all receive regular devotions.

The main Jaina festivals celebrate events in the lives of the Jinas, as do the exquisite Jaina miniature paintings, while Jaina sculpture is devoted almost exclusively to portraits of the Jinas in meditation. Even among the Sthanakvasis and Terapanthis, who reject image worship, the Jinas are ubiquitous in narrative and prayer. Clearly, then, to be a Jaina is to worship the Jinas.

And yet the Jinas are profoundly absent. Having perfected themselves, they are indifferent to their worshippers, whose worldly concerns are literally "beneath them." The existence of a lively devotional cult within a tradition centred on renunciation of all attachments may seem paradoxical, but Jainas insist that the real purpose of devotion is self-transformation through surrender to the ideal that the Jina embodies.

The central prayer in Jainism, the *Namokar Mantra*, suggests how the devotional cult operates. The first part begins by proclaiming homage to the Jinas, then to all liberated beings, to *acharyas*, to religious leaders, and finally to all renouncers everywhere. The second part consists of the statement "This five-fold mantra destroys all sins and is the most powerful of all auspicious mantras." There is no supplication in this prayer—only praise. Those most revered (the Jinas and liberated beings) are incapable of response, as they are beyond the world of give and take. Jains say they recite the mantra to inculcate in themselves the ideals of detachment and non-violence. But they also acknowledge its power to effect transformation through the inflow of good merit. Commonly recited before the start of any undertaking, it is equally revered by Svetambara and Digambara Jainas. Like so many prayers the world over, it is often put to music and collectively chanted. But it can also be recited privately and in silence at any time.

A lay Jaina worshipping at Palitana adopts the attire of an ascetic for the duration of the puja (© Francis Leroy / Hemis / Corbis).

Terapanthis and Sthanakvasis are uncomfortable with the quasi-miraculous language of the latter section of the mantra ("This five-fold mantra . . .") and therefore omit it. But most Jainas consider it an integral part of the prayer.

Puja assists devotees in two ways, helping them along the path of self-realization and at the same time bringing "worldly" benefits. The beneficent power of good karma, earned through devotional practice, makes a reciprocal relationship with a god unnecessary (see Cort 2001). It's important

Table 7.1 The Ṇamōkāra Mantra

Ṇamō arihantāṇaṁ	I bow to the arihants (Jinas).
Ṇamō siddhāṇaṁ	I bow to the siddhas (liberated souls).
Ṇamō āyariyāṇaṁ	I bow to the acharyas (mendicant leaders).
Ṇamō uvajjhāyāṇaṁ	I bow to the mendicant teachers.
Ṇamō lōē savva sāhūṇaṁ	I bow to all mendicants everywhere.
Ēsōpanñcaṇamōkkārō, savvapāvappaṇāsaṇō Maṅgalā ṇaṁ ca savvēsiṁ, paḍamama havaī maṅgalaṁ	This five-fold mantra destroys all sins and obstacles and of all auspicious mantras, is the first and foremost one.

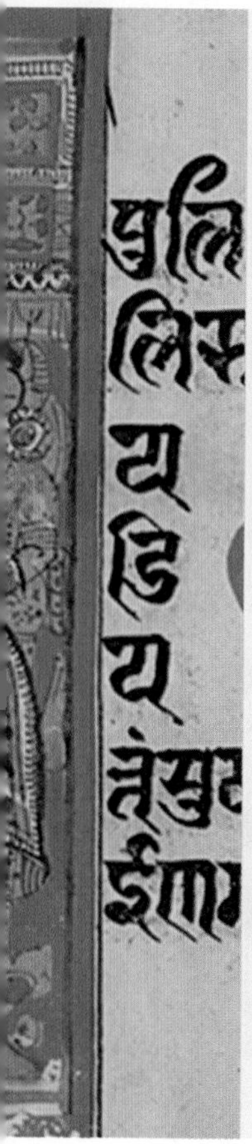

Document

The Sakra Stava (Hymn of Indra)

"Sakra" is an alternative name for the god Indra. In this hymn, the god praises the Jinas.

[Indra, the god of the celestial one, spoke thus]:
"My obeisance to my Lords, the Arhats, the prime ones, the Tirthankaras, the enlightened ones, the best of men, the lions among men, the exalted elephants among men, lotus among men.
Transcending the world they rule the world, think of the well-being of the world.
Illuminating all, they dispel fear, bestow vision, show the path, give shelter, life, enlightenment.
Obeisance to the bestowers of *dharma*, the teachers of *dharma*, the leaders of *dharma*, the charioteers of *dharma*, the monarchs of the four regions of *dharma*,
To them, who have uncovered the veil and have found unerring knowledge and vision, the islands in the ocean, the shelter, the goal, the support.
Obeisance to the Jinas—the victors—who have reached the goal and who help others reach it.
The enlightened ones, the free ones, who bestow freedom, the Jinas victorious over fear, who have known all and can reveal all, who have reached that supreme state which is unimpeded, eternal, cosmic and beatific, which is beyond disease and destruction, where the cycle of birth ceases; the goal, the fulfillment,
My obeisance to the *Sramana Bhagvan Mahavira*
The initiator, the ultimate Tirthankara, who has come to fulfill the promise of earlier Tirthankaras.
I bow to him who is there—in Devananda's womb from here—my place in heaven.
May he take cognizance of me."
With these words, Indra paid his homage to *Sramana Bhagvan Mahavira* and, facing east, resumed his seat on the throne (*Kalpa Sutra* 2; Lath 1984: 29–33).

to add here that even though the devotional cult operates within its own non-theistic framework, Jainas also venerate gods and goddesses who are believed to reside in heavenly realms. These divinities (e.g., Padmavati, the female guardian deity of Parsavanath, or the Hindu god Ganesha) *are* believed capable of interceding on behalf of their followers, and Jainas do pray to them for assistance in worldly matters, but not for assistance along the path of liberation.

Expressive Dimensions

The Jaina community is rich in temples, festivals, art, and literature, as well as active philanthropy. How can a tradition dedicated to renunciation have such a robust culture? Although Jainas maintain that the path to freedom is one of restraint and withdrawal, this is not a forcefully normative message: it simply reflects a sober assessment of the way the world works. To be a "good" Jaina does not require adoption of a mendicant's life, though this is unequivocally the ideal. The tradition accommodates varying degrees of renunciation, and overtly recognizes human shortcomings in this regard.

Each living being is a bundle of karmic proclivities that compel us to engage with the external world. Only humans are capable of taming these proclivities; yet very few of us even recognize their presence, let alone seek to eradicate them. The best that most of us can aim for is to control them by living in a framework of *samyak darshan* ("correct faith"). The life of a disciplined householder is perfectly respectable, as long as it is lived in a mindful manner.

What ignites the spark of spiritual awareness depends on the individual. For some it may be a powerful artistic experience; for others, a philosophical tract, or participation in a public festival. Therefore all cultural expressions that inculcate *samyak darshan* are valued. Building a temple, creating a work of art, taking part in a festival—all help to bring a community together in celebration of shared values. The tenth-century Digambara *acharya* Nemicandra praised "the great monks and *acharyas* who have established the celebration of festivals . . . due to which even the downtrodden and condemned people become religious" (cited in Jain 2008). The ultimate purpose of Jaina music, art, temple architecture, festivals, and rituals, writes Shugan C. Jain, is to "take followers away from worldly pleasures and bring them back to the path of spiritual purification" (2008).

Festivals

The Jaina ritual calendar revolves around three major festivals, with many minor ones in between. The three are Divali, which coincides with the start of the New Year in November–December; **Mahavira Jayanti** in spring; and, most important, the festival known to Svetambaras as Paryushana and to Digambaras as Daslakshana, in August–September.

Although it is common to think of Divali as a Hindu or even pan-Indian festival of light, many Jainas believe it began as a Jaina commemoration of Mahavira's liberation. For Jainas, the "light" that Divali celebrates is the light of omniscience. Yet Jaina celebrations of Divali do not differ much from those of their Hindu neighbours. Because Divali coincides with the new year, the Hindu goddess of wealth, Sri Lakshmi, is enthusiastically worshipped by all. And because the festival marks the start of a new financial year, members of the business community (of which Jainas constitute an important segment) are especially fervent in showing their appreciation of the goddess. Of course, the ascetics are never too far away to remind the Jainas that the greatest wealth is *moksha* itself.

A devotee offers flowers at the Adinath Temple in Ranakpur, Rajasthan (© Boisvieux Christophe / Hemis / Corbis).

Mahavira Jayanti is a joyous festival celebrating the birth of Lord Mahavira. Held in March–April, it is an occasion for great pageantry, with shops, streets, and temples all sumptuously decorated. Jainas enthusiastically undertake pilgrimages, listen to sermons, sing devotional hymns, and take part in pujas as well as ritual re-enactments of the wondrous events associated with Mahavira's birth. Ritual actors in heavenly costume play the roles of the adoring gods and goddesses, who descend from the heavens to pay the baby homage and carry him to the mythical Mount Meru, where he is ceremoniously given his first bath and his name.

The most important of all Jaina festivals, however, is Paryushana/Daslakshana (the Svetambara and Digambara names for the festival, respectively). It is celebrated at the end of the summer rainy season—a four-month period of such lush fecundity that renouncers are forbidden to travel during it, lest they cause unnecessary violence to the innumerable sentient beings that the rains bring to life.

The literal meaning of Paryushana is "abiding together"—a reference to the sustained interaction that takes place between householders and renouncers during the summer. Obliged to stay in one place, the renouncers must seek alms from the same local householders for several months, and the latter take advantage of this daily contact to seek the renouncers' advice on spiritual and worldly issues of all kinds. Paryushana comes at a time of transition in the annual calendar, marking the end of the rains and the resumption of the renouncers' peripatetic rounds. It is the climax of a period of heightened religiosity. The end of the eight-day festival is a day of introspection, confession of sins, and fasting. The penultimate day is celebrated as the Day of Forgiveness, when Jainas seek to wipe the slate clean with one another and with the world itself by asking and offering forgiveness for all, and by reciting the prayer *Micchami Dukkadam*:

> We forgive all living beings
> We seek pardon from all living beings
> We are friendly towards all living beings,
> And we seek enmity with none.

Almost all Jaina cultural expressions (art, ritual, iconography) are tied in one way or another to the Five Auspicious Events in the lives of the Jinas: conception, birth, renunciation, omniscience, and *moksha*. These five events are universally celebrated and powerfully inform the Jaina religious imagination. They are vividly represented in sculptures and miniature paintings, re-enacted in theatre and ritual, and devotedly described in narrative—most famously in the ancient *Kalpa Sutra* text. They are also closely associated with pilgrimages, since every *tirtha* (site of devotion) is linked with one or more of them.

The centrality of the Jinas in the cultural expressions of Jainism—in its rituals and iconography, and as an ethical archetype—is overwhelming. Ultimately, though, Jainism insists that the Jinas are irrelevant: self-realization is not dependent on them, and since the Jinas have by definition passed out of this world into liberation, any connection they might have had with life in this world is radically absent. Clearly, the Jina is not central to Jaina metaphysics in the way that God is central in theistic traditions. Nevertheless, the Jina is the bedrock on which the Jaina imagination has developed and around which Jaina devotional life revolves.

Jainas among Others

Because Jainas have never made up more than a small proportion of the communities they live in, a capacity for effective interaction with non-Jainas has been essential. Jainas themselves credit their adaptive success to their commitment to *ahimsa*: non-violence in thought, speech, and deed makes for easy friendship. Another factor encouraging broad-mindedness and compromise is the doctrine of *anekantavada*: literally meaning "not one-sided," it teaches that all human truth claims are partial and context-bound, and that intolerance is the product of confusing partiality with truth.

Of course Jainism is not a relativist epistemology. It unequivocally affirms the existence of Truth, as well as its ultimate attainability, but argues that those who have not reached enlightenment can never claim more than partial understanding. This perspective may very well foster—as Jainas claim it does—a general attitude of tolerance towards difference.

We have seen how Jainism's ethical principles—the restrictions it places on dietary practices, livelihoods, and so on—serve as "fences" to keep the violence of worldly life at bay. Yet Jainism has never erected social fences to ensure religious purity. To insist on exclusion would likely have doomed a community so small and vulnerable. Instead, Jainas seek the closest possible integration with their neighbours, adopting local languages and customs while safeguarding their fundamental practices and beliefs.

According to Padmanabh Jaini, a prominent scholar of Jainism and Buddhism, the Jaina *acharyas* were prescient when they recommended "cautious integration" with non-Jainas. Well aware of the risk of assimilation into Hindu culture, they also recognized the necessity of forging close social and economic ties with the rest of society.

Perhaps because of its emphasis on the solitary nature of the individual soul, Jainism is not inclined to question the "authenticity" of its followers. Thus Jainas rarely debate who is or is not a "true" Jaina. They do sometimes debate the question of "true" Jaina practices, however. Although the absorption of Hindu influences (e.g., theistic elements, ritual practices) into Jainism has gone on for a long time without causing much anxiety, these issues appear to be taking on increasing significance in the current climate of religious revival, as the symbolic boundaries between traditions are hardening.

Women

Since the time of Mahavira, the majority of those who have responded to Jainism's call have been women. This is highly unusual in the South Asian context, where asceticism is still closely associated with maleness.

Women embraced Jaina asceticism from the beginning, repudiating the "feminine" obligations of wife- and motherhood. Nuns' writings became part of the philosophical tradition, their roles were recognized in the narrative literature, and they were subject to almost all the same rules of ascetic discipline as monks.

Yet women were never considered equal to men. Although women scholar-ascetics are known, they are few in number. Furthermore, religious narratives are often ambivalent, extolling women for their piety and chastity, but also condemning them as capricious and sexually predatory. While Digambara women were permitted to renounce marriage and motherhood for spiritual advancement, they are still not allowed to take the full vows, and their tradition holds that *moksha* is not achievable from within a female body. By contrast, Svetambaras do allow women full entry into mendicancy and do not consider the female body to be an obstacle to liberation. Yet even in the Svetambara sect, nuns are not equal to monks, and senior nuns are expected to demonstrate their ritually subordinate status by showing deference to junior monks.

Nonetheless, the numerical strength of nuns may to some extent have offset the ideological bias in favour of monks. Nuns serve as role models and teachers in Jaina communities, and they are able to operate with considerable autonomy. For instance, although the female leader in the Terapanthi

Nuns descend the steps of the major Jain temple complex and pilgrimage site of Mount Shatrunjaya, Palitana, Gujarat (© Francis Leroy / Hemis / Corbis).

Svetambara order is formally subject to the ultimate authority of the male *acharya*, she has near-absolute control over its nearly 600 nuns.

Still, nuns constitute a tiny portion of the overall Jaina population. The vast majority of Jaina women (and men) live a "worldly" life that includes family, career, and community. Monks and nuns may be the religious heroes of Jainism, but they are utterly dependent on lay women and men for their existence. In defining itself as a fourfold community, Jainism explicitly acknowledges this dependence, and hence the religious importance of the laity. Renouncers could not set themselves apart from the violence of worldly existence if it were not for the householders who shield them from it. Lay Jainas willingly act as buffers between renouncers and the world, enabling the heroic endeavours of the ascetics to bear fruit and in the process creating good karma for themselves. Importantly, it is mainly women who provide the daily necessities of life to mendicants of both sexes. This role is so significant that the entire Jain infrastructure can be said to rest upon it.

It is only through the efforts of lay women that the institution of mendicancy exists: they are the ones who grow or purchase the fruits and vegetables, who perform whatever preparation is necessary to make them acceptable as food (i.e., without life), and who follow the detailed rules that govern the offering. The sustenance they provide is the foundation that makes everything else possible.

Recent Developments

Jainism—like many of the world's religious traditions—has been undergoing a profound revitalization over the last century. This renewal is evident in the growth of Jaina educational institutions, the wide dissemination of Jaina publications (including sacred texts), the emergence of nationwide Jaina organizations, rising numbers of mendicants, a revival of naked mendicancy in the Digambara sect, the birth of a strong and vocal diaspora Jainism, and the development of a more muscular political identity. All these changes have had the effect of creating a Jainism that is both more visible and more self-conscious, and whose followers are increasingly concerned to define what is (and what isn't) "correct" Jaina belief and practice.

Twentieth-Century Reform Movements

The roots of these changes can be traced to India's turbulent colonial period (1857–1947), during which reform movements sought to modernize the Jaina tradition and give it a greater national presence alongside its Hindu, Muslim, and Christian counterparts. Reformers worked to move Jainism away from the conservative, defensive control of insular mendicants whose obsession with purity condemned Jaina teachings to public obscurity. They sought to have Jainism recognized as an essential part of India's national cultural heritage, integrated into its secular educational institutions; and they fought to combat the prejudice against those institutions within their own communities, which feared that secular education would endanger Jaina spiritual goals (Flügel 2005). Their successes were momentous: within a century Jainas would be among the most educated communities in India (their literacy levels second only to those of the tiny Parsi community); their cultural achievements would be recognized as part of India's national heritage (symbolized by the issuance of India's first "Jainism stamp" in 1935); and their scriptures would be widely accessible.

Jaina Identity

The decades since Indian independence (1947) have witnessed simultaneous efforts to define more clearly the boundaries of Jaina identity and to gain recognition of Jainism as a world religion with universal appeal. Although these endeavours might seem contradictory—one constrictive and introverted, the other expansive and extroverted—both are fundamental characteristics of Jainism today. Indeed, the tension between those two poles is characteristic of identity politics in all world religions today.

Relationship with Hinduism

The effort to define Jaina identity took a more political turn after independence, focusing on the community's status as a minority, vulnerable to the overwhelmingly dominant Hindu majority. This development was part of the trend towards pluralistic identity politics that can be seen in all religious and cultural traditions today. In the past, being "a follower of the Jina" was almost certainly not predicated on exclusion of non-Jaina ideas and practices; to the contrary, as we have seen, the Jaina community traditionally followed a strategy of "cautious integration." However, in an environment where Hindu, Muslim, and Sikh nationalisms have found frequent and flamboyant public expression, reform-minded Jainas rejected the treatment of Jainism as a sect of Hinduism under Indian law and began to seek recognition of their community as a discrete minority in India. In particular, they emphasized Jainism's fundamental differences from Hinduism: for example, the fact that Jainas do not believe in any creator God, and do not consider the Vedas to be sacred. Although some Jaina organizations saw no reason to upset the status quo, considering the social, cultural, and ideological commonalities between Jainas and Hindus more important than differences, in January 2014 the reformers' campaign succeeded when the Supreme Court of India granted minority status to the Jaina community.

Jainism around the World

Far less divisive have been contemporary efforts to establish Jainism as a world religion. The co-existence of expansive and constrictive tendencies is characteristic of all contemporary traditions; indeed, to be "modern" is to be simultaneously universal and distinctive; to be

Very few Jain renouncers ever leave India, as most are not permitted to travel by any means other than foot. An exception is the Veerayatan order (established in 1973), which has relaxed many of the traditional rules in order to focus on social work. Here a Veerayatan sadhvi offers religious discourse to lay Jainas in the UK (© Gideon Mendel / Corbis).

globally relevant and utterly singular. Interestingly, one factor that has bolstered both tendencies in Jainism has been the rise of the Jaina diaspora. There are now sizeable Jaina communities in England, the United States, and Canada that are forging their own understanding of what constitutes Jainism. The kind of Jainism that is taking root outside India—removed from the immediate influence of the mendicant tradition—is contributing to significant new developments.

Outside India, for example, the renunciatory ethos becomes harder to sustain, and seemingly less important for Jaina religious identity. Although Jainas everywhere retain their philosophical commitment to the *ahimsa* principle, in diaspora communities it is often expressed in the "worldly" terms of animal rights, ecological health, and societal improvement; aspirations to self-purification and world transcendence seem to be less common. A similar shift is occurring with respect to dietary practices, which are no longer inextricably tied to the ideology of renunciation, although the connection with the *ahimsa* principle remains close. What we seem to be witnessing is a redefinition of *ahimsa* and a de-coupling of the previously inseparable relationship between *ahimsa* and renunciation.

Diaspora Jainas are far less inclined to describe Jainism as an ascetic, renunciatory ideology than as one that is progressive, environmentally responsible, egalitarian, non-sectarian, and scientifically avant-garde. In the same way, the cosmological dimensions of Jainism have been eclipsed by its ethical dimensions. This shift marks Jainism's universalizing aspirations; its message of *ahimsa* as a globally relevant principle establishes its credentials as a world religion.

Finally, Jainism's sectarian differences are less salient in the diaspora than in India, partly because the community's small numbers make them largely irrelevant. To identify oneself as "Jaina" is already to identify with a sub-category within the general category of "Indian," so for many (especially those of the second generation) additional identifiers carry little significance. The markers distinguishing the two Jaina sects may remain meaningful within families, but they carry little currency on the cultural or societal level. As a consequence, Jaina identity is increasingly emphasized, and this development in turn may play a role in the arena of identity politics in India.

Summary

This chapter has explored the historical roots of the Jaina path in ancient India, its flourishing over the past three millennia, and its emergence as a global tradition in the twentieth century. Its beginnings as a world-renouncing tradition have informed its social, cultural, and artistic development, so much so that even its tremendous worldly successes (in business and the professions) and its celebratory festivals have renunciatory dimensions. Jainism communicates a message of restraint, detachment, and non-violence in all its expressions.

The Jaina community has undergone dramatic changes since the time of Mahavira, more than 2,500 years ago, but the centrality of *ahimsa* has remained constant. Though variously understood, it remains the foundation of all expressions of Jainism today, both in India and outside it. The resilience of Jaina teachings must be credited, at least in part, to their effectiveness; that they are now gaining attention well beyond the borders of the Jaina community is testimony to their enduring relevance.

Sites

Gwalior Fort, Madhya Pradesh

According to legend, the city of Gwalior was named for a Jaina saint named Gwalipa after he cured a Rajput chieftain of leprosy. The fort contains architectural treasures from several historic northern Indian kingdoms.

Shravanabelagola, Karnataka

Home of the colossal statue of the renouncer Bahubali (also known as Gomateshwara), a prince who, in the midst of a battle, gained sudden insight into the senselessness of violence and renounced all attachment to worldly existence. Digambaras believe he was the first person in our time cycle to attain *moksha*.

Sammet Shikarji, Jharkand

The "King of the Tirths," this is said to be the place where 20 of the 24 Jinas attained *moksha*. Located in a remote mountain range, the hilltop is covered with temples and shrines.

Rajasthan, India

Although Rajasthan is renowned as the ancient land of the Rajputs, Jainism has had a presence there for more than 2,000 years. The stunningly beautiful Dilwara temple complex near Mount Abu is a major Jain pilgrimage centre.

Palitana, Gujarat

Palitana is famous for the nearly 900 marble temples on Shatrunjaya hill. Constructed over hundreds of years, beginning in the late tenth century, the complex remains a major pilgrimage centre.

Jain Centre, Leicester, England

In 1979, the local Jaina community bought an old church and transformed it into a temple with both Svetambara and Digambara *murtis* imported from India.

Jain Center of Greater Boston

Established in 1973, the Jain Center of Greater Boston was the first such centre in North America. Eight years later the community inaugurated a temple that now serves more than 300 families.

Sacred Texts

Religion (Sect)	Text(s)	Composition/ Compilation	Compilation/ Revision	Use
Jainism (Svetambara and Digambara)	Purva Agama	Ancient and timeless "universal truths" preached by all the Jinas, from the first (Rsabha) to the last (Mahavira). Communicated to disciples by Jina Mahavira and transmitted orally until the 3rd century BCE, when the verbatim recitation of teachings was no longer possible. Both Svetambara and Digambara accept that all the Purvas were eventually lost.	Reconstructed by monks mainly between the 5th and 11th centuries CE. Commentaries and narratives added by scholar-monks.	Object of study for metaphysics, cosmology, and philosophy.
Jainism (Svetambara)	Anga Agama	The 12 Angas were compiled by the principal disciples of Mahavira. Svetambaras believe that the 12th Anga, called the Drstivada, contained the teachings of lost Purvas. All were transmitted orally until the 3rd century BCE (see above).	Reconstructed by monks mainly between the 5th and 11th centuries CE. Commentaries and narratives were added by scholar-monks.	Object of study for rules of mendicant conduct, stories of renouncers, karma.
Jainism (Svetambara)	Angabahya (believed to contain the lost teachings of the Purva and Anga Agamas)	Compiled and orally transmitted by monks who succeeded the principal disciples of Mahavira. Contained the earliest commentaries on the Purva and Anga.	Reconstructed by monks mainly between the 5th and 11th centuries CE. Commentaries and narratives added by scholar-monks.	Object of study for specialized topics, story literature, etc.
Jainism (Digambara)	Satkhandagama (contains parts of Drstivada canon, said to mnemonically contain the lost teachings of the Purva and Anga Agamas)	Orally transmitted until 2nd century CE, when it was put in writing; the first Jaina scripture to be preserved in written form.	No substantial revisions, though commentaries are common.	Object of study for entire canon: metaphysics, cosmology, karma, and philosophy.

Continued

Sacred Texts (Continued)

Religion (Sect)	Text(s)	Composition/ Compilation	Compilation/ Revision	Use
Jainism (Digambara)	Kasayaprabhrta (text based on Drstivada)	Written by Yati Vrasabha based on compilations of Gunadhara, 1st–2nd century CE.	No substantial revisions, though commentaries are common.	Studied for philosophy of detachment.
Jainism (Digambara)	Nataktrayi (Samayasara, Pravanasara and Pancastikaya)	Written by Kundakunda between 1st century BCE and 2nd century CE.	No substantial revisions, though commentaries are common.	Object of study for mysticism, doctrine/ philosophy, and ontology. The most sacred Digambara author and texts.
Jainism (Svetambara and Digambara)	Anuyogas ("Expositions")	From 1st century BCE to 6th century CE.		Object of study for philosophy, etc.
Jainism (Svetambara and Digambara)	Tattvartha Sutra	Written by Umasvati in 2nd century CE.	Many commentaries were written by Svetambaras between the 2nd and 8th centuries CE, but the process of commenting continues.	Object of study for doctrine, cosmology, ethics, philosophy, etc.
Jainism (Svetambara and Digambara)	Bhaktamara Stotra	Written by Acharya Mantunga in 3rd century CE.		Used in devotion.
Jainism (Svetambara)	Kalpa Sutra (lives of the Jinas, especially Parshvanath and Mahavira, and doctrine)	3rd century CE.		Used in devotion and ritually during Paryushana.
Jainism (Digambara)	Adi Purana/ Mahapurana	Written by Acharya Jinasena between 6th and 8th centuries CE.		Object of study for life stories of Tirthankaras and all Digambara rituals.

Discussion Questions

1. Lay (householder) Jainas are integral to the tradition, which has always recognized the centrality of their role. Explain.
2. What are some of the major differences between Svetambara and Digambara Jainism?
3. What are the main reasons believed to be responsible for the split that gave rise to the Svetambara and Digambara sects?
4. How are women understood in Jainism? What are some of the main differences between Svetambaras and Digambaras with regard to women?
5. Although Jainism envisions final liberation (*moksha*) as a purely spiritual state, it does not see the spiritual and the material in oppositional terms. Explain.
6. Non-violence (*ahimsa*) informs every aspect of Jainism, from cosmology to dietary practices and devotional rituals. Elaborate.
7. How do Jainas understand their acts of devotion to beings (the Jinas) they believe to be removed from all worldly matters and unresponsive to their concerns?
8. What is the significance of "right faith" (*samyak darshan*) in Jainism?
9. How do Jainas understand the final state of liberation (*moksha*)?
10. What are some of the main ways in which expressions of Jainism in the diaspora differ from expressions in India today?

Glossary

acharya A mendicant scholar.

ajiva Non-soul, non-consciousness; also referred to as "matter" or "karma."

anuvratas Five vows modelled on the great vows of the renouncers but modified to make them practicable in lay life: non-violence, truthfulness, non-stealing, non-attachment, and chastity.

Arhat A perfected, omniscient being (male or female) who teaches the Jaina dharma while embodied in the world and who upon death will attain *moksha*. All the Jinas were called *Arhats* during their final incarnation on Earth.

chakravartin Universal monarch; one who governs the world ethically.

Digambaras Early Jaina sect with its own sacred scriptures; identified by male mendicants' practice of nudity.

Jina Literally, "conqueror"; an epithet for the 24 ascetic–prophets who conquered the world of desire and suffering, and taught the path to eternal happiness; alternatively called Tirthankara.

jiva Eternal soul/consciousness; all living beings are endowed with *jiva*.

Mahavira Literally, "Great Hero"; epithet of the 24th and final Jina of our time cycle, born Vardhamana Jnatrpura in the sixth century BCE.

Mahavira Jayanti A joyous spring festival celebrating the birth of Mahavira.

mahavratas The five "great vows" adopted by renouncers: absolute non-violence, truthfulness, non-stealing, non-attachment, and celibacy.

mendicants Jaina men and women who renounce all worldly attachments to seek self-realization (and eventually, *moksha*) by pursuing the difficult path of detachment and non-violence. Male mendicants (monks) are called *sadhus* or *munis*, and female mendicants (nuns) are called *sadhvis*.

Namokar Mantra The central prayer in Jainism.

moksha The ultimate goal of the Jaina path: release from the cycle of birth and death; nirvana.

paap Karmic particles of an inauspicious nature ("bad karma").

pratikramana Ritual practice of repentance.

punya Karmic particles of an auspicious nature ("good karma").

renunciation The Jaina ideal: the giving up of all worldly attachments (family, friends, wealth, pride etc.) in order to pursue the path of detachment and non-violence. Though a powerful ideal for all Jains, it is practised fully only by **mendicants**; also referred to as *shramanism*.

Rsabha The first Tirthankara of our current time cycle; also called Adinath.

sallekhana A ritual fast to death undertaken voluntarily, usually in old age or illness.

samayika A desired state of equanimity; ritual practice of meditation.

samsara The endless cycle of rebirth from which Jains seek release.

samyak darshan Right vision, faith, or intuition into the basic truth of the cosmos; spiritual growth depends on the attainment of *samyak darshan*.

shramana A renouncer; one who has given up worldly attachments to pursue spiritual release.

Svetambara One of the two early sectarian nodes within Jainism; mendicants wear simple white robes.

Tattvartha Sutra An important philosophical text accepted by all Jaina sects, composed by Umasvati in the second century CE.

Tirthankara Literally, "ford-maker"; epithet for the 24 Jinas who, through their teachings, created a ford across the ocean of ***samsara***.

Further Reading

Babb, Lawrence A. 1996. *Absent Lord: Ascetics and Kings in a Jain Ritual Culture*. Berkeley: University of California Press. A wonderful exploration of the place of worship in Jaina ritual culture.

Banks, Marcus. 1992. *Organizing Jainism in India and England*. Oxford: Clarendon. An ethnographic study of the historical, sociological, and cultural ties between the Jaina communities of Leicester, England, and Saurashtra, India.

Carrithers, Michael, and Caroline Humphrey, eds. 1991. *The Assembly of Listeners: Jains in Society*. Cambridge: Cambridge University Press. An outstanding edited volume exploring sociological dimensions of the Jaina community by leading scholars in the field.

Cort, John E. 2001. *Jains in the World: Religious Values and Ideology in India*. New York and Delhi: Oxford University Press. A detailed and insightful ethnographic study of the religious lives of contemporary lay Jainas.

Dundas, Paul. 2002. *The Jains*. 2nd edn. London: Routledge. A comprehensive overview of Jainism and an excellent introduction to the subject.

Jaini, Padmanabh S. 1979. *The Jaina Path of Purification*. Berkeley: University of California Press. The standard general study of Jainism.

Laidlaw, James. 1995. *Riches and Renunciation: Religion, Economy, and Society among the Jains*. Oxford: Oxford University Press. Explores the place of renunciation in the life of North India's thriving Jaina business community.

Recommended Websites

www.jaindharmonline.com

A portal dedicated to Jainism and Jaina dharma; it contains information and links to news articles.

www.jainstudies.org

The International Summer School for Jain Studies.

www.jainworld.com

Jainism Global Resource Center, USA.

http://pluralism.org/wrgb/traditions/jainism

Resources from Harvard University's Pluralism Project.

References

Cort, John E. 2001. *Jains in the World: Religious Values and Ideology in India*. New York and Delhi: Oxford University Press.

———. 2005. "Devotional Culture in Jainism: Manatunga and His *Bhaktamara Stotra*." In James Blumenthal, ed. *Incompatible Visions: South Asian Religions in History and Culture*. Madison, WI: Center for South Asia, University of Wisconsin-Madison.

Gelra, M.R. 2007. *Science in Jainism*. Ladnun, Rajasthan: Jain Vishva Bharati Institute.

Jacobi, Hermann, trans. 1884. *Jaina Sutras*, Part I. In F. Max Müller, ed., *Sacred Books of the East*, 22. Oxford: Clarendon Press.

——— and Max Muller. 2001/1895–1910. *Jaina Sutras*. Richmond: Curzon Press.

Jain, S.C. 2008. "Jain Festivals." Unpublished manuscript prepared for the International Summer School of Jain Studies.

Jaini, Padmanabh S. 1979. *The Jaina Path of Purification*. Berkeley: University of California Press.

———. 1990. "Ahimsa." Inaugural Roop Lal Jain Lecture, Centre for South Asian Studies, University of Toronto.

Kundakunda. 1950. *Samayasara*. A. Chakravarti, ed. and trans. Benaras: Bharatiya Jnanapitha, Kashi.

Laidlaw, James. 2005. "A Life Worth Leaving: Fasting to Death as Telos of a Jain Religious Life." *Economy and Society* 34, 2: 178–99.

Lath, M., trans. 1984. *Kalpa Sutra*. V. Sagar, ed. Jaipur: Prakrit Bharati.

Shah, Natubhai. 2004. *Jainism: The World of Conquerors*. Vol. 1.Delhi: Motilal Banarsidass.

Shah, Pravin. n.d. "Pratikraman—Observance of Self-Reflection." Accessed 24 June 2014 at www.jainlibrary.org.

Note

1. This text was compiled by Jinendra Varni and published by Sarva Seva Sangh Prakashan, India. It was translated into English in 1993 by T.K. Tukol and K.K. Dixit.

8 Buddhist Traditions

Roy C. Amore

Traditions at a Glance

Numbers

Most estimates range between 200 and 300 million.

Distribution

South, Southeast, and East Asia, plus minorities on all continents.

Founder

Shakyamuni Buddha, who taught in northern India 2,500 years ago and is believed to be the most recent in a long line of major buddhas.

Principal Historical Periods

5th to 1st century BCE	Early Indian Buddhism; the roots of the Theravada tradition, which eventually spread to Sri Lanka and Southeast Asia
1st century CE	Mahayana emerges and later spreads to Southeast, Central, and East Asia
5th century CE	Vajrayana emerges and begins spreading to the Himalayan region

Deities

The Buddha is not worshipped as a god: he is venerated as a fully enlightened human being. Regional variants of Buddhism have often incorporated local gods and spirits. Mahayana developed a theory of three bodies of the Buddha, linking the historic buddhas to a cosmic force.

Authoritative Texts

Theravada has the *Tripitaka* ("Three Baskets"): *Vinaya* (monastic rules), *Sutras* (discourses), and *Abhidharma* (systematic treatises). Mahayana has many texts in various languages, including Chinese, Japanese, and Tibetan. Vajrayana has the *Kanjur* (tantric texts) and *Tanjur* (commentaries).

Noteworthy Teachings

The Three Characteristics of Existence are suffering, impermanence, and no-self. The Four Noble Truths are suffering, origin of suffering, cessation of suffering, and the Eightfold Path. Other notable teachings include karma, rebirth, and nirvana. In addition, the Mahayana and Vajrayana schools stress the emptiness (non-absoluteness) of all things. All schools emphasize non-violence and compassion for all living beings.

At the heart of Buddhism are the "Three Gems": the Buddha, the **Dharma** (teachings), and the **Sangha** (congregation). Buddhists express their faith in these elements by saying they "take refuge" in them. Many Buddhist ceremonies include a recitation of the "Three Refuges" mantra.

Overview

With his last words to his disciples—"Everything that arises also passes away, so strive for what has not arisen"—the Buddha passed into **nirvana** some 2,500 years ago. After experiencing enlightenment at the age of 35, he had spent the rest of his life teaching that all worldly phenomena are transient, caught up in a cycle of arising and passing away. He set the wheel of dharma (teaching) in motion, established a community (sangha) of disciples, and charged his followers to carry the dharma to all regions of the world. Today there are Buddhists in nearly every country, and Buddhism is the dominant religion in many parts of East, South, and Southeast Asia.

Novice monks at Bagan, Myanmar (Burma) (Martin Puddy / Getty Images).

Buddhism has three main traditions or "vehicles," all of which originated in India. The earliest is **Theravada** (also known as **Hinayana**), which spread to Sri Lanka and Southeast Asia; the second is **Mahayana**, which became the principal school in East Asia; and the third is **Vajrayana**, which developed out of Mahayana and became closely associated with the Himalayan region. All three traditions also have followers in most parts of the world.

The First Gem: The Buddha

Religious Life in Ancient India

By 500 BCE, a tradition that might be called "Ganges Spirituality" was flourishing in northern India. Located halfway between the Bay of Bengal and the Arabian Sea, the region had easy access to a trading route that stretched across the subcontinent. Trade enriched the merchant (vaishya) class and gave rise to a new money-based economy, while agriculture flourished on large estates owned by the two highest classes (brahmins and kshatriyas) and worked by commoners and low castes.

Beneath the prosperity, however, were both social and ideological tensions. The new money economy had created a large merchant class that had financial power but neither the land nor the social status of the traditional landowning classes, who looked down on the new urban rich. At the same time there was tension between the religion of the brahmins and the other religious traditions of the region. While the brahmins considered animal sacrifice essential, the ascetics—among them the Jaina master Mahavira—denounced it.

Another major difference between the brahmin and ascetic traditions had to do with the role of deities. The deities of the Brahmins would respond to devotees' requests for assistance in exchange for regular praise and ritual offerings. Some of the major deities were recognized by the ascetic traditions as well—especially the creator god Brahma and the storm god Indra. But they played quite a small role in the non-brahminic traditions. Minor gods might provide practical help from time to time, but the liberation that the ascetics sought could be achieved only through their own efforts. It was in this environment that Buddhism originated. Some Buddhist concepts were major innovations: the impermanence of the human self or soul, for instance, and social egalitarianism. But others—including the notions of **karma** and successive reincarnations, the ideal of ascetic withdrawal from the world, and the belief that numerous gods, demons, and spirits play active roles in human life—were common to all the Ganges traditions.

The Bodhisattva Vow and Previous Lives

Buddhism, like Hinduism and Jainism, understands the cosmos in terms of an endless succession of universes arising and passing away. Our current universe was already in the declining phase of its life cycle when the Buddha of the present age, Siddhartha Gautama—better known as **Shakyamuni**, the "sage of the Shakya clan"—was born. In every era, when dharma (morality and truth) has declined, a highly developed being is born to become the buddha for that era. (In the same way, Hindu tradition maintains that the lord Krishna comes to save the Earth when dharma has declined.)

No almighty god is needed to send a new buddha: such a highly developed being knows when the time has come. Buddhists tell the story of Shakyamuni with the understanding that there were

Timeline

c. 531 (or 589 or 413) BCE	Shakyamuni's enlightenment
c. 496 (or 544 or 368)	Shakyamuni's *parinirvana* or passing
c. 395	First Buddhist council
c. 273	Accession of King Ashoka
c. 225	Mahendra takes Theravada Buddhism to Sri Lanka
c. 67 CE	Buddhism takes root in China
c. 100	Emergence of Indian Mahayana
c. 200	Nagarjuna, Madhyamika philosopher
c. 350	Asanga and Vasubandhu, Yogacara philosophers
372	Buddhism introduced to Korea from China
c. 500	Emergence of tantra in India
604	"Prince" Shotoku, Japanese regent and patron of Buddhism, issues Seventeen-Article Constitution
c. 750	Padmasambhava takes Vajrayana Buddhism to Tibet
806	Shingon (tantric) Buddhism introduced to Japan
845	Persecution of Buddhism in China
1173	Birth of Shinran, Japanese Pure Land thinker (d. 1262)
1222	Birth of Nichiren, founder of the Japanese sect devoted to the *Lotus Sutra* (d. 1282)
1603	Tokugawa regime takes power in Japan; Buddhism is put under strict state control
c. 1617	Dalai Lamas become rulers of Tibet
c. 1900	Beginnings of Buddhist missionary activity in the West
1956	B.R. Ambedkar (1891–1956) converts to Buddhism, leading to the conversion of 380,000 other Dalits and re-establishing Buddhism in India
1959	China takes over Tibet; the Dalai Lama and many other Tibetans flee to India
1963	Thich Quang Duc immolates himself in protest against the persecution of Buddhists in South Vietnam
2001	Taliban forces destroy colossal Buddhist statues along ancient trade route in Afghanistan
2008	Tibetan protests against Han Chinese domination erupt into violence in the lead-up to the Beijing Summer Olympics. The Dalai Lama denounces the violence while sympathizing with the Tibetans' concerns.
2011	The Dalai Lama renounces his role as the temporal ruler of Tibet

buddhas in previous eras and will be buddhas in subsequent ones. In addition, in every age there are numerous other beings who have achieved some degree of enlightenment. Among them are **Arhats** ("worthy ones" or "saints") and **bodhisattvas** (those who have dedicated themselves to achieving buddhahood).

All Buddhist traditions agree that Shakyamuni lived to the age of 80, but no one is certain when he lived. Some believe he was born in 566 BCE; others argue for 563. In Sri Lanka and Southeast Asia, the standard birth date is 624 BCE, while Japanese scholars, relying on Chinese and Tibetan texts, have adopted a later date of 448 BCE.

Although Shakyamuni achieves enlightenment through his own efforts, he has nearly perfected his "mind of enlightenment" through hundreds of previous lives. Unlike the Hindu *avatara* or the Christian god incarnate, the Buddha is simply a human being who has fulfilled the spiritual potential of all living creatures. What is special about him is the power of his insight to free people from entrapment in suffering. This is what Buddhists have in mind when they say that they "take refuge" in the Buddha.

The story of the Buddha, as Buddhists tell it, begins in an earlier age. During the lifetime of one previous buddha, a young man comes on a crowd of people filling holes in the road in anticipation of that buddha's arrival. But the buddha comes before one hole is filled, and so the young man offers himself as a stepping-stone. Instead of stepping on him, the buddha announces that the young man will become a buddha himself in the distant future.

The young man takes the prophecy to heart and vows to work towards full enlightenment. To solemnly promise to work towards buddhahood is to take a "bodhisattva" vow. *Bodhi* means "enlightenment" and *sattva* means "being," as in "human being." After the young man in our story dies, his karma complex—the matrix of all his past actions—gives rise to a new being. In short, he is reborn, as are all living beings, and over many lives he gradually purifies his inner nature. Stories of more than 500 of those lives are preserved in a collection called *Jataka* ("birth stories").

The best known of the *Jataka* tales is the final one, which tells the story of the bodhisattva's last incarnation before he becomes the Buddha. Here he is reborn as a prince named Vessantara, who as a young boy vows to perfect the virtue of generosity: whenever he is asked for something, he will give it. The consequences of this promise are not serious as long as he is a child, but eventually his father retires and passes the throne to him.

No one complains when Vessantara gives food and clothing from the public treasury to the poor, for his generosity brings rains and prosperity to the kingdom. But when he gives the kingdom's lucky white elephant to citizens of a rival kingdom, the people demand that his father resume the throne. Vessantara is banished. Yet even in exile he continues to give away everything he is asked for, including his wife and children. Finally his father intervenes, Vessantara is reunited with his family, and we learn that the gods have been guiding events to test his resolve. Vessantara's strict adherence to his vow serves as a model for Buddhist self-discipline.

Siddhartha's Birth and Childhood

After Vessantara dies, he is not reborn immediately. Rather, the new being generated by his karma complex waits until a new "wheel turner" is needed to set the wheel of dharma (the *dharmachakra*) in motion once again. Finally, when the world needs him, he chooses to be born into the ruling family of a small kingdom in what is now southern Nepal.

The story of the Buddha's birth and childhood varies somewhat among the Buddhist traditions. What follows is a very brief version, based on the early Pali-language account preserved in the

Theravada tradition. According to this account, the queen of the Shakya people, Mahamaya, is keeping a vow of sexual abstinence in observance of a festival. One afternoon she takes a nap and dreams that the four "world protectors" (minor gods) carry her to a pleasant grove of trees.

There a spiritual being in the form of a sacred white elephant (associated with good fortune) miraculously enters her body and becomes the embryo of the Buddha-to-be. After a pregnancy marked by supernatural signs, Mahamaya sets out for her home city, intending to give birth there. But along the way she stops to rest at a roadside park known as Lumbini, and the baby is born through her side as she holds on to a tree branch for support. In the Theravada tradition, the birth takes place on the full-moon day of the month called **Vaishakha** ("rains"), which usually falls in April or May of the Western calendar (East Asian Buddhists follow a different tradition). That night a bright light illuminates the world to mark the holy event.

The infant bodhisattva is named Siddhartha, "he who achieves success." But Buddhists rarely use that name, preferring titles related to his spiritual role, such as Shakyamuni or (Lord) Buddha.

During the naming ceremony, brahmin sages offer predictions based on his physical features. Later Buddhist texts report that they find 32 major bodily signs and more than 80 minor ones. His unusually long ear lobes are a sign of great spiritual wisdom; his golden complexion shows his inner tranquillity, and the wheel patterns on the soles of his feet point to his role as "wheel-turner." On the basis of these signs, the brahmins predict an extraordinary destiny: the young prince will become either a great emperor or a fully enlightened buddha.

His father orders that no evidence of life's inevitable suffering be allowed near the boy, lest it lead him to renounce the world and become a monk. Evidently the early Buddhists who told this story shared the view of those modern scholars who suggest that, in the absence of adversity, humans would have little reason to pursue the spiritual path.

There are only a few stories of the bodhisattva's childhood. In one of them his first teacher is amazed to find that he already knows the various alphabets. In another he wins a martial arts

Focus

Shakyamuni and Jesus of Nazareth: Life-Story Parallels

Although Shakyamuni and Jesus lived in very different times and places, there are several parallels in their life stories. Whether coincidental, the reflection of common narrative themes, or the result of historical influence, the parallels include the following:

- both infants are conceived without normal intercourse (Mahamaya is a married woman under a temporary vow of celibacy; Mary is a virgin)
- both infants are born in an unusual setting (Shakyamuni in a park, Jesus in a stable)
- the birth is announced by angels (to a meditating sage in the case of Shakyamuni, to shepherds in the case of Jesus)
- birth under a special star or constellation
- adoration by sages or wise men, who foresee spiritual greatness
- departure from home
- temptation by the Lord of Death (Mara, Satan)
- disciples who are sent out as missionaries
- miracle-working

tournament even though he has shown little interest in war. In the most significant story, he is sitting in the shade of a rose-apple tree watching his father perform a spring ground-breaking ritual when he enters a meditational trance, during which the shadow of the tree miraculously stands still even though the sun moves. The memory of this wakeful meditation state will play a role in his achievement of enlightenment.

The Four Sights and the Great Departure

Despite all the king's precautions, Siddhartha learns the bitter truth about life around the time of his thirtieth birthday. By then he is happily married (the earliest sources do not refer to his wife by name, but later texts call her Yashodhara) and the father of a son. During a chariot ride through the royal park, the prince happens to see four sights that will alter the course of his life. The first three—a sick man, a suffering old man, and a dead man—awaken him to life's sorrows. When he asks what is wrong with these men, his chariot driver answers honestly, revealing to him for the first time the harsh realities of life.

The fourth and final sight is an ascetic whose aura of tranquil detachment from the world suggests that there is a way to overcome the suffering of life after all. To this day, Buddhist monks often say that what first attracted them to join the sangha was seeing, as children, the serenity of the older monks and nuns as they passed through the streets on their daily alms-seeking rounds.

On returning home, the bodhisattva ponders the four sights, and that night, with the help of the world protectors, he flees the palace.

He exchanges his princely clothes for those of a poor hunter, obtains an alms bowl, and begins a new life as one of the wandering students seeking spiritual truth along the banks of the Ganges. Determined to learn all eight levels of classical yoga, he soon masters the six levels known to his first guru. He then finds another guru who teaches him the seventh level, but even the deep tranquillity he experiences there is not enough to satisfy him.

Therefore, with five other students, he embarks on an independent program of rigorous ascetic discipline. After six years he is subsisting on nothing more than one palmful of water and one of food per day. He becomes so emaciated that he loses consciousness, but the world protectors preserve him.

Enlightenment

Now convinced that even the most extreme asceticism cannot produce the enlightenment he seeks, the bodhisattva leaves the cave where he has been living and goes to a pleasant town now called Bodh Gaya. There he resumes eating and drinking, but he still needs a method. Then he remembers the wakeful meditational trance he experienced spontaneously as a child:

> I thought of a time when my Sakyan father was working and I was sitting in the cool shade of a rose-apple tree: quite secluded from sensual desires, secluded from unprofitable things I had entered upon and abided in the first meditation, which is accompanied by thinking and exploring with happiness and pleasure born of seclusion. I thought: Might that be the way to enlightenment? Then, following up that memory there came the recognition that this was the way to enlightenment (*Majjhima Nikaya*; Nanamoli 1972: 21).

Document

From the *Dhammapada*

Many sutras include one or more verses that sum up the teaching. These "memory verses" were eventually collected as a separate work called the Dhammapada, *"fundamentals of Dharma." The verses from Chapter One concern the pure mind.*

1. The mind is the source of all mental actions [dharmas],
   mind is the chief of the mental actions, and they are made by the mind.
   If, by an impure mind, one speaks or acts, then suffering follows the mind as a cartwheel follows the footprint of the ox.
2. The mind is the source of all mental states, mind is their leader, and they are made by the mind.
   If, by a pure mind, one speaks or acts, then happiness follows the mind like a shadow.
3. "I was abused." "I was beaten." "I was hurt." "I was robbed."
   Those who dwell excessively on such thoughts never get out of their hating state of mind.
4. "I was abused." "I was beaten." "I was hurt." "I was robbed."
   Those who leave such thoughts behind get out of their hating state of mind.
5. In this world hatreds are never ended by more hating.
   Hatreds are only ended by loving kindness.
   This is an eternal truth [dharma].
6. Some people do not know that we must restrain ourselves.
   But others know this and settle their quarrels.
7. One who dwells on personal gratifications, overindulges the senses, overeats, is indolent and lazy, that person is overthrown by Mara [Death] like an old, weak tree in a windstorm.
8. One who dwells in meditation on the bodily impurities, keeps the senses under control, eats moderately, has faith and disciplined energy, that person stands against Mara like a rocky mountain.
9. Whoever puts on the ochre robe but lacks purity, self-control, and truthfulness,
   that person is not worthy of the robe.
10. Whoever puts on the ochre robe and is pure, self-controlled, and truthful,
    that person is truly worthy of the robe.
11. Mistaking the unessential for the important, and mistaking the essential for the unimportant,
    some persons, dwelling in wrong-mindedness, never realize that which is really essential.
12. Knowing the essential to be important, and knowing the unessential to be unimportant,
    other persons, dwelling in right-mindedness, reach that which is really essential.

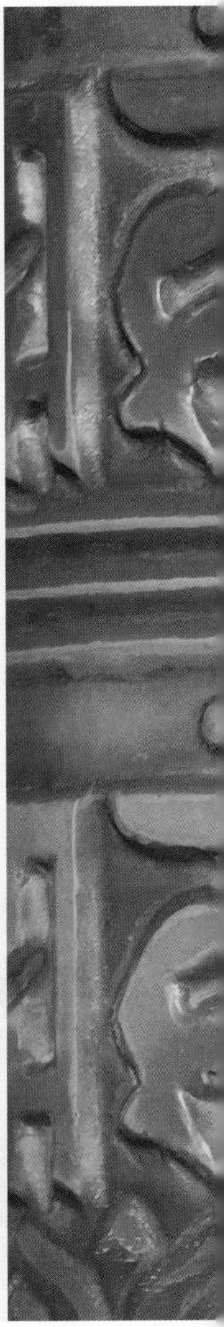

Choosing a pleasant spot beside a cool river, under a *pipal* tree (a large fig tree considered sacred in India at least as far back as the Harappa civilization, known thereafter to Buddhists as the Bodhi tree), he sits to meditate and vows that he will not get up until he has achieved nirvana.

In some versions of the story, it is at this point, just before dusk on the full-moon day in the month of Vaishakha, that Mara, the lord of death, arrives. Mara's main function is to come for people at death and oversee their rebirth in an appropriate place. But he wants to exercise power over events in this world as well. Determined to thwart the bodhisattva's attempt to achieve enlightenment, Mara summons his daughters—whose names suggest greed, boredom, and desire—to tempt him. When that fails, Mara offers him any worldly wish, if only he will return home and live a life of good karma (merit) as a householder. The bodhisattva refuses.

Now Mara becomes violent. He sends in his sons—whose names suggest fear and anger—to assault the bodhisattva. But the bodhisattva's spiritual power surrounds and protects him like a force field.

Having failed in his efforts to tempt and threaten the bodhisattva, Mara challenges him to a debate. Mara himself claims to be the one worthy to sit on the Bodhi Seat—the place of enlightenment—on this auspicious night, and he accuses the bodhisattva of being unworthy. But the bodhisattva has the merit of the generosity, courage, and wisdom he has perfected through countless previous lives, and he calls on the Earth herself to stand witness on his behalf. The resulting earthquake drives Mara away. Buddhists today may understand this story as symbolizing the surfacing of the last remnants of the mind's deep impurities, which the bodhisattva must overcome before he can attain liberation.

Now the bodhisattva begins to meditate in his own way—the reverse of the way taught by the yoga masters. A yogi seeks to move ever deeper into unconsciousness, drawing in the conscious mind as a turtle draws in its head and limbs, shutting out the world. The bodhisattva, by contrast, meditates to become more conscious, more aware, more mindful.

First he remembers his own past lives; the ability to do this is one of the psychic powers that come with spiritual advancement, but it should not be a goal in itself. Then he acquires deeper insight into the working of karma, understanding how the past lives of various people have been reflected in later incarnations. Finally he contemplates how to put an end to suffering, and arrives at what will come to be known as the Four Noble Truths.

Just before dawn, the bodhisattva enters the state of total insight into the nature of reality. After hundreds of lives, he has fulfilled his bodhisattva vow. He is no longer a being striving for

Young Tibetan monks pay their respects to the Buddha by circumambulating the Bodh Gaya Bodhi tree (© Gianni Muratore / Alamy).

enlightenment; now he is a buddha, a "fully enlightened one": "I had direct knowledge. Birth is exhausted, the Holy Life has been lived out, what was to be done is done, there is no more of this to come" (*Majjhima Nikaya*; Nanamoli 1972: 25).

Having completed his journey to enlightenment, he has earned the title Tathagata ("thus-gone one"), and it is by this title that he will most often refer to himself. Another term for the state he has reached is "nirvana" ("*nibbana*" in Pali). This state has two aspects, negative and positive. In its negative aspect nirvana has the sense of "putting out the fires" of greed, hatred, and delusion. In its positive aspect nirvana is the experience of transcendent happiness. A poem by Patacara—one of the first ordained Buddhist women—expresses the way the two meanings come together in the perfect happiness that arrives when evil desires have been extinguished. In the first verse she expresses her longing for nirvana and her frustration at not attaining it; in the second she recalls how the breakthrough finally came as she was turning down the wick on her oil lamp:

> With ploughshares ploughing up the fields, with seed
> Sown in the breast of earth, men win their crops,
> Enjoy their gains and nourish wife and child.
> Why cannot I, whose life is pure, who seek
> To do the Master's will, no sluggard am,
> Nor puffed up, win Nibbana's bliss?
>
> One day, bathing my feet, I sit and watch
> The water as it trickles down the slope.
> Thereby I set my heart in steadfastness,
> As one doth train a horse of noble breed.
> Then going to my cell, I take my lamp,
> And seated on my couch I watch the flame.
> Grasping the pin, I pull the wick right down
> Into the oil . . .
> Lo! the Nibbana of the little lamp!
> Emancipation dawns! My heart is free!
> (*Songs of Sisters*, Rhys Davids 1964: 73)

Reflecting on his experience, the new Buddha believes that the way to enlightenment can be taught, and so begins a teaching career motivated by compassion for all living beings.

Setting the Wheel in Motion

Shakyamuni's first impulse is to seek out and teach his two former yoga teachers, but his heightened psychic powers tell him that both have died. Thus he decides to begin with his five former companions. Perceiving that they can be found at a deer park called Sarnath near Varanasi, he sets out and on the way encounters two merchants who show their respect by offering him food.

In a sense, this act marks the beginning of institutional Buddhism, which depends on the material support (food, medicine, robes, financial donations) given by laypeople in return for the spiritual gifts offered by ordained Buddhists (dharma teaching, chanting, guidance). This pattern of reciprocal giving remains central to all forms of Buddhism. On arriving at the deer park, the Buddha is at first shunned by his friends because he has abandoned their rigorous discipline, but when they see his aura they recognize that he has attained nirvana and ask to know how he did it. He responds with his first *sutra*, often referred to as the "Wheel Turning" discourse because it marks the moment when the wheel of true dharma is once again set in motion.

Another name for it is the "Instruction on the Middle Path." As long as he lived the life of a pampered prince, he did not advance spiritually. Yet the years of ascetic discipline left him too weak to make any real progress. Only after he began to eat, drink, and sleep in moderation was he able to reach enlightenment. In time, this principle of moderation would be developed into a general ethic of the Middle Way. Now the Buddha begins to explain the insight into suffering that he has gained. After a few days of instruction in the Four Noble Truths and the Eightfold Path for overcoming suffering, the Buddha ordains the five as his first disciples and sends them out to teach the dharma to others.

Shakyamuni and his five fellow ascetics in the deer park at Sarnath, the site of his first sermon; from a series of illustrations of the life of Buddha on a temple wall (Roy C. Amore).

Entering Parinirvana

For the next 45 years the Buddha travels, ordaining disciples and teaching thousands of lay followers, including various local kings. He also ordains several members of his own family.

His body is weakening as he nears 80, but he continues to travel until one day, as he and his disciples are dining with the leader of a local tribal group, an odd-smelling dish is brought to the table. He asks his host to serve it only to him, not to his disciples, and on eating it he falls ill. The Compassionate One tells his disciples not to blame the host, who meant well. They ask whom they should follow if he dies, and he tells them to follow the dharma; thus in Buddhism no individual has absolute authority. Finally, in a grove of trees at Kushinagar, at the moment of death, the Buddha experiences *parinirvana*: the final end of the cycle of rebirth, the total cessation of suffering, the perfection of happiness.

Document

A Woman's Compassionate Wisdom

Compassion is a major value in Buddhism. In this story, a woman's compassion for her sick husband not only comforts him but brings him back to health.

Once, while the Lord [Buddha] was staying among the Bhaggis on the Crocodile Hill . . . , the good man Nakulapita lay sick, ailing and grievously ill. And his wife Nakulamata said to him: "I beg you, good man, do not die worried, for the Lord has said that the fate of the worried is not good. Maybe you think: 'Alas, when I am gone, my wife will be unable to support the children or keep the household together.' But do not think like that, for I am skilled in spinning cotton and carding wool, and I will manage to support the children and keep the household together after you are gone.

"Or maybe you think: 'My wife will take another husband after I am gone.' But do not think that, for you and I know that for sixteen years we have lived as householders in the holy life [that is, as celibates, practising strict sexual abstinence].

"Or maybe you think: 'My wife, after I am gone, will have no desire to see the Lord or to see the monks.' But do not think like that, for my desire to see them shall be even greater.

"Or maybe you think: 'After I am gone, my wife will not have a calm mind.' But do not think like that, for as long as the Lord has female disciples dressed in white, living at home, who gain that state, I shall be one. And if any doubt it, let them ask the Lord.

"Or maybe you think: 'My wife will not win a firm foundation, a firm foot-hold in this Dhamma and discipline. She will not win comfort, dissolve doubt, be free from uncertainty, become confident, self-reliant, and live by the Teacher's words.' But do not think like that, either. For as long as the Lord has female disciples dressed in white . . . I shall be one."

Now, while Nakulapita was being counselled thus by his wife, even as he lay there his sickness subsided and he recovered. And not long after, he got up, and leaning on a stick, Nakulapita went to visit the Lord and told him what had happened. And the Lord said: "It has been a gain; you have greatly gained from having Nakulamata as your counsellor and teacher, full of compassion for you, and desiring your welfare" (adapted from Dhammika 1989: 111–13).

The Second Gem: The Dharma

> Avoid doing all evil deeds,
> cultivate doing good deeds,
> and purify the mind—
> this is the teaching of all buddhas.
>
> (*Dhammapada* 183)

The crystallization of the Buddhist tradition began with the transformation of the Buddha's discourses into a set of doctrinal teachings—the dharma—and the movement towards an institutionalized monastic system. "Dharma" (*dhamma* in Pali) is a central concept in Buddhist thought, and the range of its meanings extends well beyond the meaning of "dharma" in the Hindu context.

In classical Indian culture generally, "dharma" carries the sense of social and moral obligation, but Buddhist usage reflects its root meaning: "that which holds." Thus in English we could understand "dharma" to mean eternal truth, which for Buddhists includes the laws of nature, the reality of spiritual forces such as karma, and the rules of moral duty. Believing the Buddha's understanding of those realities to be definitive, generations of thinkers studied and systematized his insights, creating a program of instruction that anyone seeking enlightenment could follow.

The Four Noble Truths and Eightfold Path

At the core of the Buddha's first sermon in the deer park were the Four Noble Truths about suffering and the Eightfold Path to overcoming it. The Truths are:

1. The Noble Truth of Suffering: No living being can escape suffering (**dukkha**). Birth, sickness, senility, and death are all occasions of suffering, whether physical or psychological.
2. The Noble Truth of Origin: Suffering arises from excessive desire.
3. The Noble Truth of Cessation: Suffering will cease when desire ceases.
4. The Noble Truth of the Eightfold Path: It is possible to put an end to desire, and hence to suffering, by following eight principles of self-improvement.

The eight principles that make up the Eightfold Path are not sequential, like the steps on a ladder. All are equally important, and each depends on all the rest. Thus none of them can be properly observed in isolation. They must work in concord, like the petals of a flower unfolding together. They are:

1. right understanding (specifically of the Four Noble Truths),
2. right thought (free of sensuous desire, ill-will, and cruelty),
3. right speech,
4. right conduct,
5. right livelihood,
6. right effort,
7. right mindfulness, and
8. right meditation.

Document

From the *Itivuttaka*

The Itivuttaka *("So I heard") is a collection of the Buddha's teachings said to have been made by Khujjuttara, a woman of the servant class who was held up by the Buddha himself as an exemplary lay disciple. She used the teachings she had heard to teach other women; hence the phrase "So I heard" ("Itivuttaka"), which begins each section of the collection and became its title.*

Even if one should seize the hem of my robe and walk step by step behind me, if he is covetous in his desires, fierce in his longings, malevolent of heart, with corrupt mind, careless and unrestrained, noisy and distracted and with sense uncontrolled, he is far from me. And why? He does not see the Dhamma, and not seeing the Dhamma, he does not see me. Even if one lives a hundred miles away, if he is not covetous in his desires, not fierce in his longings, with a kind heart and pure mind, mindful, composed, calmed, one-pointed and with senses restrained, then indeed, he is near to me and I am near to him. And why? He sees the Dhamma, and seeing the Dhamma, sees me (Dhammika 1989: 49–50).

The Three Characteristics of Existence

Existence has three characteristics, according to the Buddhist dharma: suffering, impermanence, and no-self. "Suffering" refers to all the varieties of pain and deprivation, physical and psychological, that humans are subject to; and "impermanence" is the passing nature of all things; and "no-self" (*anatman* in Sanskrit) refers to the psychological implications of that existential impermanence. *Anatman* means "without Atman": but what is Atman? The Hindu understanding is reflected in the *Upanishads*, where Atman represents the eternal self or soul and is related to Brahman, the underlying energy of the universe. For many Hindus, the innermost self is the most stable and abidingly real feature of the individual, because it participates in the reality of the universe.

The Buddha proposed that no such eternal, unchanging self exists. And in denying the existence of a self, he made the concept of ownership radically unsustainable for his followers: if there is no "I," there can be no "mine." The *anatman* concept does not mean that there is "no person" or "no personality" in the ordinary English sense of those terms. In fact, Buddhist teachings address the components of personality, the *skandhas*, in some detail, suggesting that personality is the product of shifting, arbitrary circumstance. In that respect, Buddhist notions of personality have more in common with modern psychological theory than they do with the religious notion of an eternal soul. Buddhist personality theory implies that wise people, recognizing the impermanence of all things—including themselves—will not become emotionally attached to fixed images of themselves.

Dependent Origination

The principle of causality is a thread that runs throughout the Buddha's dharma. To appreciate its function, think of a pool table where the balls are colliding with one another and the cushions, repeatedly causing one another to change directions: each time you blink, you see a new configuration caused by the previous configuration.

The standard term for this understanding of causality—in which everything that arises does so in response to other factors, and will in turn cause changes in other things—is "dependent origination" or "conditioned coproduction." Buddhist dharma uses the image of a 12-spoked "wheel of becoming" (not to be confused with the eight-spoked Dharma Chakra, the wheel that symbolizes the Eightfold Path) to express the view of life as a cycle of interdependent stages or dimensions.

The 12 links of the chain may be further divided into three stages, reflecting the movement from a past life through the present one and on to the future:

Past	1. Ignorance, leading to
	2. karma formations, leading to
Present	3. a new individual "consciousness," leading to
	4. a new body-mind complex, leading to
	5. the bases of sensing, leading to
	6. sense impressions, leading to
	7. conscious feelings, leading to
	8. craving, leading to
	9. clinging to (grasping for) things, leading to
	10. "becoming" (the drive to be reborn), leading to
Future	11. rebirth, leading to
	12. old age and death

The process does not stop with the twelfth link, of course, since old age and death lead to rebirth, and so the wheel of life turns on and on. Buddhists have analyzed this wheel from many viewpoints and with many similes, but the message is always the same: all living beings are in process and will be reborn over and over again until they realize nirvana.

The *Tripitaka*: Three Baskets of Sacred Texts

Shakyamuni did not write down his teachings, nor did anyone record them. This was in keeping with the Hindu tradition that associated writing with commerce. The sacred teachings of the Hindus were the preserve of the priests, who committed them to memory and transmitted them by sound alone. In fact, the Hindu ritual formulas were understood to have an acoustic effectiveness that would be lost if they were not spoken and heard. Thus for the first four centuries or so, the Buddha's teachings were recited from memory. Different **bhikshus** (monks) memorized different portions, and at the early conferences of sangha members, one of the most important tasks was to recite the teachings in their entirety.

At the first council, held long after Shakyamuni's death, *Bhikshu* Ananda is said to have recited the discourses (*sutras*) on dharma ascribed to Shakyamuni. *Bhikshu* Upali is credited with reciting the section on monastic rules (*vinaya*). The systematic treatises (*abhidharma*) composed after Shakyamuni's *parinirvana* were recited at a later meeting. The oral teachings were finally put into writing by the Theravada monks of Sri Lanka in the first century CE, after a famine had so reduced the monks' numbers as to threaten the survival of the oral tradition. The fact that Theravada Buddhists refer to their scriptures as the *Tripitaka* ("three baskets") suggests that the manuscripts of the three types of texts—written on palm leaves strung together and bundled like Venetian blinds—may have been stored in three baskets. The collection survives in the Pali language and is therefore referred to as the Pali canon.

The *Sutra Pitaka*, or "discourse basket," contains the talks on dharma attributed to Shakyamuni or his early disciples. Many *sutras* are presented as responses to questions from disciples. The opening of the "Discourse on the Lesser Analysis of Deeds" is typical:

> Thus have I heard: At one time . . . the brahmin youth Subha, Todeyya's son, spoke thus to the Lord: "Now, good Gotama, what is the cause, what the reason that lowness and excellence are to be seen among human beings while they are in human form?" (Horner 1967, 3: 248–9)

Subha has asked the timeless question of why bad things happen to apparently good people. Shakyamuni then explains to Subha how the karma accumulated through actions in past lives causes some people to suffer short, unhappy lives and others to enjoy long, blessed lives.

There are five sections (*nikayas*) of the *Sutra Pitaka*, the first "basket." In the ancient world, texts were usually organized not chronologically or alphabetically but by length, from longest to shortest. (The same principle was followed by the early Muslims in organizing the sequence of the *surahs* that make up the Qur'an.) The second basket, the *Vinaya* ("discipline") *Pitaka*, contains both the rules of monastic discipline and stories about how Shakyamuni came to institute each rule. Finally, the *Abhidharma* ("further discourses") *Pitaka* contains seven books by unnamed early Buddhists who systematically analyzed every conceivable aspect of reality in the light of Buddhist principles. For example, the first book of *abhidharma* classifies all mental phenomena according to their karmic consequences, good, bad, or neutral. Other books deal with the various physical elements of nature.

The Wheel of Becoming (Bhava-Chakra) represents the 12 stages of dependent origination. At the centre are three animals representing the three evil root tendencies of human consciousness: greed represented by a rooster with endless desire for more hens; hate represented by a snake spitting venom; and delusion represented by a boar (perhaps because boars were thought to have poor eyesight or bad judgment). The surrounding 12 pictures illustrate the spokes of the wheel of becoming (see list). The wheel is held in the teeth of the demon of death, whose head, hands, and feet are visible behind the wheel.

The Third Gem: The Sangha

The third part of the Triple Gem has two components: the monastic community of ordained men (*bhikshus*) and women (*bhikshunis*), and the broader community, the universal sangha of all those who follow the Buddha's path.

Bhikshus and Bhikshunis

Shakyamuni began accepting disciples in the deer park at Varanasi. Soon an ordination ritual took shape in which the new disciples recited the Triple Refuge, took vows of chastity, poverty, and obedience, and put on the distinctive robes of a monk. In early Indian Buddhism, monks' robes were usually dyed with saffron, which produces a bright orange-yellow. Most Theravada monks still wear saffron robes, but in East Asia other colours were eventually adopted, such as red and brown. There is no special meaning to the colour, although all members of a particular branch of Buddhism wear the same one.

Ordained and Lay Women

Unlike many other religious traditions, Buddhism never defined women as the "property" of men. Nevertheless, the early texts indicate a profound ambiguity about the status of women in Buddhism, and Shakyamuni is said to have resisted the formation of an order for women on the grounds that it would be detrimental to the survival of his teachings. On the other hand, he did permit it, and he encouraged close relatives to join it, maintaining that women were no less capable than men of becoming Arhats (saints), and that the way to nirvana was the same regardless of gender:

> And be it woman, be it man for whom
> Such chariot doth wait, by that same car
> Into Nirvana's presence shall they come (Horner 1930: 104).

Other early Buddhist texts are similarly ambiguous about women. On the positive side, they describe approvingly the support provided to the early sangha by some wealthy women, and one book of the Pali canon, the Therigatha, contains poems by early *bhikshunis*. On the negative side, there was a distinct difference in status between *bhikshus* and *bhikshunis*, who were not allowed to teach their male counterparts.

Ordination

Eventually a preliminary level of ordination was introduced during which novices were required to master the basics of dharma. Each novice was assigned both a rigorous, demanding teacher and a supportive spiritual guide.

The full ordination ritual takes several hours. Friends and relatives pay their respects to the new sangha members, who give presents to their teachers and counsellors in gratitude for their assistance. Because seniority plays a large role in monastic life, careful attention is paid to the exact time and date of every ordination.

The Lay Sangha

Lay Buddhists are considered members of the sangha in its wider sense. The sangha of all disciples includes eight categories of "noble persons," according to the progress they have made towards nirvana. There are four levels: "those who have entered the stream (to nirvana)," those who have advanced enough to return (be reborn) just once more, those who are so advanced that they will never return, and those who have advanced to the state of realizing the Arhat (worthy) path. At each level, those who have just reached the new level are distinguished from those who have matured at that level, making a total of eight classifications.

Controversies, Councils, and Sects

A Theravada *bhikshu* with a palm-leaf umbrella (Roy C. Amore).

Because there was no central authority, the monks had to settle disputes collectively on the basis of their interpretations of the Buddha's discourses—a challenging task in the era before the scriptures were written down. In the fourth century BCE, for instance, a *bhikshu* visiting the city of Vaishali found that his colleagues there were accepting donations of gold and silver. He criticized them publicly, and they demanded that he apologize in front of their lay supporters. As a consequence, a meeting of all the *bhikshus* in the area had to be convened.

The meeting, called the Vaishali Council, decided that monastic discipline did indeed forbid the acceptance of gold and silver. Most of the Vaishali *bhikshus* agreed to abide by the ruling, but a schism developed when one dissident monk raised five points of controversy concerning the status of Arhats. Was an Arhat subject to the same limitations as an ordinary *bhikshu*? Was an Arhat susceptible to sexual misconduct? Was it possible for an Arhat to have doubts about doctrine? Could one become an Arhat merely by instruction, without spiritual practice?

Behind those questions lay an issue that was to fuel serious divisions later on: the level of spiritual attainment possible for Buddhists in this life. Most of the monks held out the prospect of enlightenment for ordinary people, but some of the *sthavira* ("elders") argued that the Arhat level was beyond the reach of all but a few. In this way a division arose between the majority group, who formed the Mahasanghika or "Great Sangha" sect, and the Sthavira group, who formed the Sthaviravada or Theravada sect. This debate foreshadowed the split that would lead to the development of the Mahayana and Theravada schools as distinctly different "vehicles." By the third century BCE there were 18 sects, each with its own oral version of the teachings, although all shared a similar ordination tradition and all followed more or less the same *vinaya* rules. Monks of different sects sometimes lived together in one monastery, especially at the major training centres, and the same was true of the *bhikshunis*, who always lived in their own monasteries, separate from the men.

King Ashoka's Conversion

The spread of Buddhism within India was remarkable. Unlike many reformers, Shakyamuni gained converts across the social spectrum, from the lowest labourers to powerful kings. Among the latter was Ashoka (r. c. 273–232 BCE), who had waged a series of wars to expand his territory and eventually ruled an empire that included most of modern India. Buddhist accounts claim that it was the horrible carnage of his bloody war with the kingdom of Kalinga on the eastern coast that led Ashoka to convert to Buddhism and begin promoting the ethic of non-violence.

Under Ashoka's patronage Buddhism enjoyed its golden age in India. To spread the dharma of non-violence, he ordered that large stones or pillars be erected at the main crossroads throughout his empire, with messages carved on them for the moral instruction of his subjects. Some of these messages are still readable.

A message in the Kalinga region expresses Ashoka's remorse for the death and suffering he caused to its people:

> When the king, Beloved of the Gods and of Gracious Mien, had been consecrated eight years Kalinga was conquered, 150,000 people were deported, 100,000 were killed, and many times that number died. But after the conquest of Kalinga, the Beloved of the Gods began to follow Righteousness (dharma), to love Righteousness, and to give instruction in Righteousness. Now the Beloved of the Gods regrets the conquest of Kalinga, for when an independent country is conquered people are killed, they die, or are deported, and that the Beloved of the Gods finds painful and grievous. . . . (*Thirteenth Rock Edict*; de Bary 1958: 146).

Ashoka then lays out his ideals for governance, saying that he desires security, self-control, impartiality, and cheerfulness for all living creatures in his empire. He spells out his "conquest by dharma" and claims that it is spreading not only within the Indian continent but to the west, to lands whose kings he names.

Although he reminds his subjects that he will not hesitate to deal firmly with rebels and criminals, he promises that his punishments will be just and moderate. Ashoka's promotion of dharma became a model for later Buddhist rulers, who were willing to sentence criminals (and rebels) to punishment or even death, but remained committed to non-violence in other matters.

Buddhism and the State

The King as Wheel-Turner

Indian tradition had long used the term *chakravartin* or "wheel-turner" to refer to kings as world rulers. On one level, the image suggests a ruler whose chariot wheels encounter no opposition. On another, it evokes the wisdom of the ruler who has both the spiritual wisdom to perceive the cosmic order and the political power to impose a similar order in the world.

When the early Buddhists began to refer to Shakyamuni as a *chakravartin*, they were at once according him the honour due to one of his princely birth and redefining the concept of political power, shifting the emphasis away from unchallenged military strength and towards wisdom in the guidance of society.

From the time of Shakyamuni, Buddhism expected rulers not only to provide for the physical welfare of their subjects (for example, by distributing food in times of need) but to promote dharma by setting a good example and sponsoring lectures, translations, and the distribution of literature. The king who promoted dharma would be a true successor to the Buddha, the definitive wheel-turner.

As Buddhism spread throughout Asia, so did its social and moral ideals regarding kingship. A Zen Buddhist story tells of a Chinese king named Wu who has dedicated himself to doing all the good works expected of a Buddhist king, probably with the goal of winning a long and pleasant rebirth in heaven. When Wu learns that a monk named Bodhidharma has arrived from India, he summons the monk to court and proudly shows him the rice kitchens he has established for feeding the poor, the new wing of the palace filled with scribes who are busy translating and copying the sacred texts, and the altar he has set up for daily worship.

After the tour, the emperor asks Bodhidharma how much merit he has made. "None whatsoever!" is the famous response. Bodhidharma explains that true merit comes only from activities that increase one's wisdom and purify one's mind. It seems that the emperor has been doing all the right things for the wrong reason. What this story tells us is that although the rulers were encouraged to support the sangha and promote dharma in their realms, the ultimate goal was the ruler's own spiritual advancement. This helps to explain why Buddhist kings sometimes abdicated to take ordination as *bhikshus*.

Map 8.1 The Spread of Buddhism

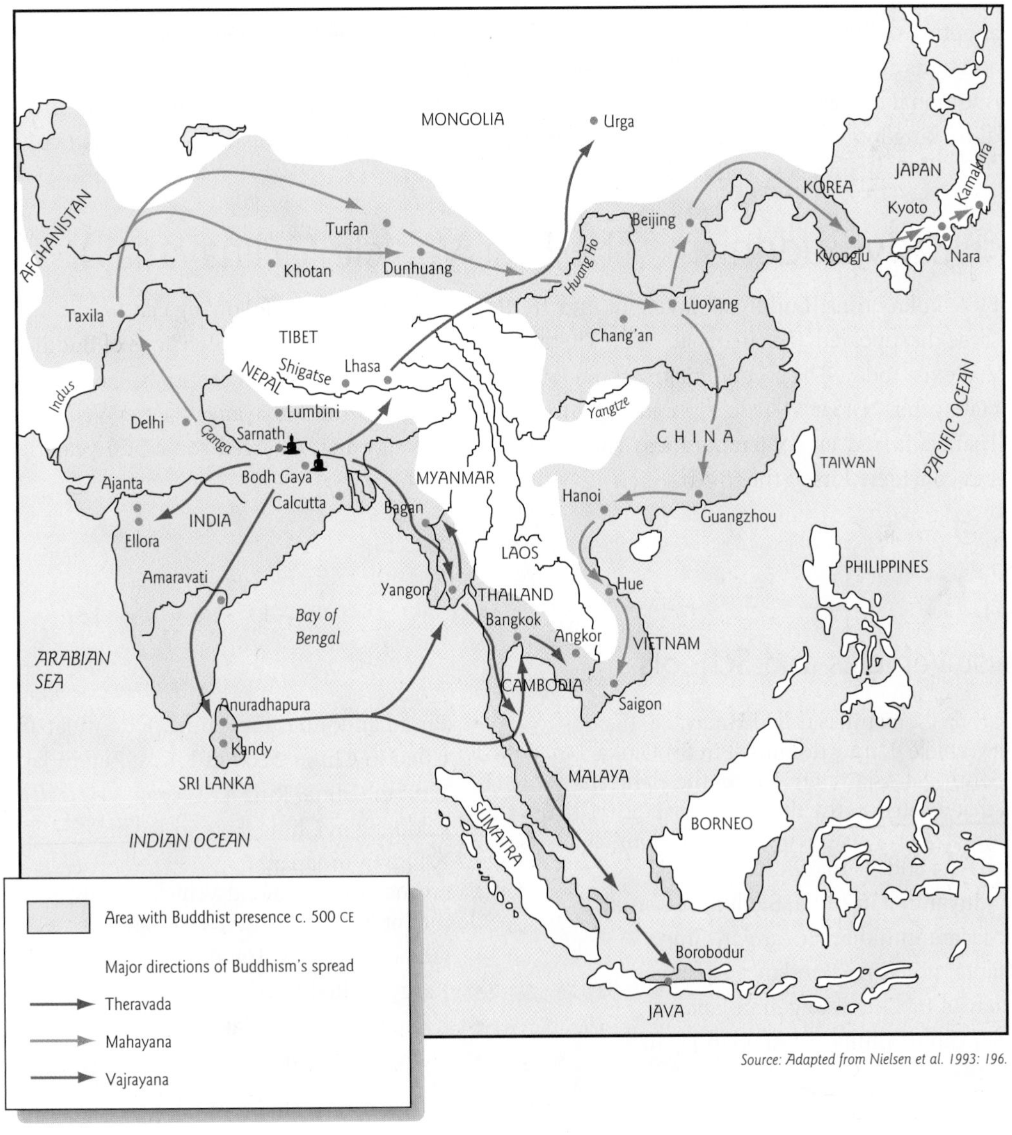

Source: Adapted from Nielsen et al. 1993: 196.

Non-violence as a Public Ethic

One characteristic of Buddhist political rule, at least ideally, was promotion of non-violence. Unnecessarily harsh punishment was forbidden, and kings were expected to release prisoners during Buddhist festivals. (Even today, some Buddhist festivals include the release of caged birds or other animals into the wild.) Justice was to be administered fairly, regardless of the social status of the accused, and quickly. One king of ancient Sri Lanka is remembered for having a rope attached to a bell installed outside the palace walls so that anyone seeking justice could pull it to summon the king, even in the middle of the night.

At the same time, the Buddhist king was expected to maintain an army and a police force, to defend the people. There is no such thing in Buddhist scripture as a "just war" of aggression, but many Buddhists have believed that a defensive war is not against dharma, and that the state may use force to maintain law and order.

With very few exceptions, Buddhism spread by missionary conversion rather than by force. The adoption of Buddhism in new regions was helped by the dedicated, spiritual lifestyle of the monks and nuns and the fact that Buddhist missionaries allowed new converts to continue venerating their traditional deities as well as the spirits of their ancestors. There were territorial wars between Buddhist kingdoms in Southeast Asia, however, and Sri Lanka has a long history of conflict between the Buddhist Sinhalese and Hindu Tamils.

Early Buddhism: The First Vehicle ("Hinayana")

By Ashoka's time, Buddhism had split into 18 distinct sects. Over the following centuries most of these disappeared. The main survivor, Theravada, is one of the three major divisions of Buddhism that exist today. The second major school, which emerged around the first century CE, called itself Mahayana, "Great Vehicle," in contrast to what it considered the Hinayana, "Lesser Vehicle," of Theravada and its contemporaries. The third division, Vajrayana, emerged some 500 years later and considered itself the third vehicle.

Focus

Buddhist Vehicles and Schools

1. Theravada (sometimes called Hinayana, the "Little Vehicle"), now dominant in Sri Lanka and Southeast Asia: a survivor of the eighteen sects that existed in the third century BCE
2. Mahayana (the "Great Vehicle"), now dominant in East Asia and Vietnam:
   - Madhyamika in India, Sanlun in China
   - Yogacara in India, Faxiang in China
   - Tiantai in China, Tendai in Japan
   - Huayan in China, Kegon in Japan
   - Zhenyan in China, Shingon in Japan
   - Pure Land, Jingtu in China, Jodo in Japan
   - Chan in China, Seon in Korea, Zen in Japan
   - Linji in China, Rinzai in Japan
   - Caodong in China, Soto in Japan
   - Nichiren in Japan
3. Vajrayana (the "Diamond Vehicle"), now dominant in Tibet and the Himalayas:
   - Gelugpa ("Yellow Hats")
   - Kargyu ("Red Hats")
   - Karma-pa ("Black Hats")
   - Nyingma ("Ancient" school)

Theravada Buddhism

We know very little about the early history of the "Way of the Elders" (Sthaviravada in Sanskrit and Theravada in Pali), although it appears to have been widespread in India by the time of Ashoka. We do know that the Theravada tradition was conservative, as its name suggests. Rejecting all scriptures composed after the formation of the *Tripitaka*, it considers itself the preserver of Buddhism in its original form.

Theravada in Sri Lanka

A monk named Mahinda (Mahendra in Sanskrit), who was Ashoka's son, is said to have taken Theravada Buddhism to Sri Lanka in the third century BCE. The story is told in the island's *Great Chronicle* (*Mahavamsa*). Mahinda and his assistant monks use psychic powers to travel through the air, and arrive on a large hill near the island's capital, Anuradhapura. There the king of Sri Lanka and his hunting party discover the monks and are soon converted to the Buddha's dharma. (Mahinda's Hill, Mihintale, remains an active centre for monks and lay pilgrims in Sri Lanka today.) The next day, Mahinda enters the capital and teaches dharma to the members of the king's court, who are converted. On the following day the largest space available—the royal elephant stable—is put into service as a hall of dharma instruction, whereupon everyone is converted.

These legends are presumably based on historical events, since one of Ashoka's inscriptions claims that he sent missionaries in groups of five to seek converts far and wide, even in the Hellenistic kingdoms to the west. The king of Sri Lanka could well have been receptive to the idea of an alliance with the great emperor on the mainland, in which case adopting the empire's religion and court rituals would have been an excellent way of signalling willingness to comply with the greater power. The king ordered the building of a proper temple, dharma hall, and **stupa**, and the temple grounds were made complete with the arrival of a Bodhi tree sapling brought from India by Mahinda's sister, herself a *bhikshuni*.

The king underwent a new enthronement ritual, carried out according to Ashoka's instructions, and in this way the island became a cultural extension of Ashoka's empire while maintaining its sovereignty. This uniting of Buddhist leadership and Indian forms of kingship set the pattern for subsequent Buddhist rulers across mainland Southeast Asia. Theravada Buddhism is still the main religion of Sri Lanka, even though the sangha fell on such hard times in the eleventh century that there were not enough monks to continue. Since five senior *bhikshus* are required to officiate at an ordination, *bhikshus* had to be imported from Burma. A similar appeal to Siam in the eighteenth century led to the establishment of a new ordination lineage. The majority of Sri Lankan monks today belong to the Siyam Nikaya ("lineage").

Sri Lanka was populated by various peoples from India, and many aspects of the island's culture reveal close ties to the predominantly Hindu mainland. Among the Hindu transplants to Sri Lanka is a version of the Indian caste system. Shakyamuni taught that people should be judged by their character rather than the hereditary occupational or clan group they were born into. In keeping with this principle, his sangha was open to all social groups. In Sri Lanka, however, the Siyam Nikaya today accepts only members from the Goyigama caste, the equivalent of India's vaishyas.

There are other *nikayas* in Sri Lanka that accept members regardless of caste. The most important of these is the Ramanna Nikaya, which was founded in the nineteenth century as a lineage dedicated to various reforms, including the elimination of caste restrictions.

Theravada in Southeast Asia

The spread of Buddhism into Southeast Asia took place over many centuries. Today Buddhist culture remains dominant in much of the mainland, including Cambodia, Thailand, and Myanmar. It was also influential (as was Hinduism) in the Indonesian islands and the Malay peninsula, although Islamic religion and culture eventually became dominant there.

An account written by a Chinese Buddhist pilgrim in the seventh century suggests that several of the early Buddhist sects were established in Southeast Asia by that time. This diversity follows the pattern in India, where various schools of Buddhism coexisted for centuries before Theravada eventually prevailed. Some early accounts from Southeast Asia emphasize the working of miracles, a feature of Buddhist missionary efforts found later in Tibet and elsewhere. Chanting to invoke blessings and protective powers was also a feature of Buddhism in Southeast Asia, partly because some of the missionaries there came from the Vajrayana school (p. 417).

Until about 1000, various early Buddhist sects as well as Mahayana and Vajrayana schools competed for support, but by the fifteenth century all the region's major rulers had embraced Theravada, perhaps because, in adopting it, they could bring their kingdoms into political alignment with other powerful kingdoms in Sri Lanka and mainland Southeast Asia. Other forms of Buddhism gradually died out, and Theravada training centres and temples of national importance flourished under royal patronage. Today Theravada remains the majority religion of the Thai, Khmer (Cambodian), Burmese, and Lao (Laotian) peoples.

Island Southeast Asia, by contrast, is now predominantly Muslim, but both Buddhist monuments and Buddhist minorities survive. In Indonesia, for example, tourists still flock to the ruins of the majestic temple of Borobudur, which covers a hilltop with a geometrical arrangement of stupas representing the mountains that, according to traditional Buddhist cosmology, anchor the world. Malaysia also has a sizable Buddhist minority, mainly among the Chinese population.

Theravada Practice: Rituals and Mindfulness

The most common Theravada ritual is the Buddha-puja. in which Buddhists chant praise to the Buddha and promise to observe the Five Precepts, vowing to refrain from

- taking life
- taking that which is not given
- sensual misconduct (sexual immorality)
- wrong speech (lying, slander, and the like) and
- intoxicants leading to the loss of mindfulness.

Unlike the "commandments" of the Judeo-Christian tradition, these precepts are moral rules that Buddhists voluntarily undertake to follow.

Merit-Making Rituals

Theravadins also perform a number of more elaborate "merit-making" rituals specifically designed to produce good karma. Of these, two of the most important are almsgiving and the *dana* ritual.

Traditionally, members of the sangha would leave the monastery early each morning carrying bowls to collect their daily food. As they moved silently through the streets, their eyes downcast

Lay Buddhists in Laos lower themselves in respect as they offer food to monks, who silently make their alms rounds early in the morning (© Robert Harding Picture Library Ltd / Alamy).

to maintain a tranquil, composed state of mind, laypeople would come out of their houses, put cooked food into the alms bowls, and then bow low or prostrate themselves as a sign of respect. The practice of going for alms is rare today, but it is still common in Thailand, and efforts have been made to revive it in Sri Lanka.

In time, the practice of giving alms to monks and nuns developed into a ritual called **dana**, from the Sanskrit word for "giving." A *dana* might be held at a temple or a pilgrimage site, but is often held by a family in their home to celebrate some important occasion. The following description of a *dana* ceremony in a Sri Lankan home offers a glimpse of several other Buddhist rituals as well.

As the monks arrive at the door, their feet are washed by the men of the family. (If the guests are *bikshunis*, this hospitality ritual is performed by the women.) On entering, the *bhikshus* first bow before the Buddha altar. A string is run from the Buddha image on the altar to a pot of water, then to the monks, and finally to the laypeople, so that all are holding the string in their right hands. The monks lead a Buddha-puja, then chant from a collection of scriptures called *paritta*, followed by a dharma talk. The water and the string become sacred through the power of the chanting. Then a merit-transfer ritual is performed, in which the merit made by those present through their participation is transferred "to all living beings": "May the merit made by me now or at some other time be shared among all beings here infinite, immeasurable; those dear to me and virtuous as mothers or as fathers are, . . . to others neutral, hostile too. . . ."

In some respects merit transfer resembles the old Roman Catholic traditions of performing penance or purchasing "indulgences" for the benefit of deceased relatives: it is intended to help one's ancestors, and others, in the afterlife. Although the practice might seem to violate the early Buddhist principle that all of us must make our own karma, the scriptures say that Shakyamuni himself advocated it.

Life-Cycle and Death Rituals

Early Indian Buddhists continued to follow the life-cycle rituals of what we now call Hinduism, and as Buddhism spread, converts in other regions also retained their own traditions. Thus there are no specifically Buddhist wedding or childhood rituals. It is in part for this reason that Buddhism has been able exist alongside different traditional belief systems: Sri Lankan Buddhists continue to observe Indian rituals, Thai Buddhists still worship their traditional spirits, and Japanese Buddhists still visit Shinto shrines.

There is a Theravada funeral ritual, however, based on the ancient Indian cremation ceremony. Although the pattern varies from country to country (and where the cost of wood is prohibitive, cremation is replaced by burial), the principal features of the ceremony are similar. The corpse is taken in a procession to the cemetery along a route prepared in advance by filling in potholes, cutting the grass and weeds beside the road, and placing flowers along the way. This tradition has parallels in many parts of the ancient world (similar preparations were made for Jesus' procession into Jerusalem on Palm Sunday).

At the cemetery the body is placed in a wooden structure above a funeral pyre. A brief service is then held that includes chants, prayers, and a ritual in which family members and friends take turns pouring holy water from one container into another while a long prayer is chanted. Then the pyre is lit, ideally by the eldest son of the deceased. In the event that a crematorium is used instead of a funeral pyre, one or more *bhikshus* will still come to recite prayers over the body.

The loss of a loved one is always painful, but Buddhists prepare for it through years of meditation on the inevitability of death. One of Buddhism's strengths is its emphasis on the transience of life, which helps its followers develop a realistic view of the end.

On the sixth night after the death, a dharma-preaching service is held at the home, followed by a *dana* on the morning of the seventh day. Other memorial *dana* rituals are held at the home of the deceased after three months and one year. Family members and friends who were unable to attend the funeral may participate in these memorials. After time has lessened the pain of the loss, the memorial services provide occasions to remember the deceased and enjoy a family reunion.

Vipassana: *Mindfulness Meditation*

Theravada Buddhists practise a simple form of meditation called *vipassana* ("insight" or "mindfulness"). Practitioners concentrate on their breathing, focusing either on the sensation of air passing through the nostrils or on the rising and falling of the abdomen. Although the breaths are usually counted, the point is not to keep count but to focus the mind. Practitioners may also cultivate mindfulness of other parts of the body, personal emotions, or relationships with others. The goal is to live in a totally mindful way.

The Buddha Day Festival

Many Buddhist festivals developed out of earlier seasonal festivals, and there are regional variations. However, Buddhists in most places celebrate the day on which three major events in the life of Shakyamuni are said to have occurred: his birth, his enlightenment, and his *parinirvana*. Known in Theravada countries as Vesak or Wesak (Sanskrit Vaishakha), it is called "Buddha Day" in English.

Mahayana, The Second Vehicle

The Mahayana ("Greater Vehicle") movement appears to have emerged around the first century CE. We know that its members were dismissing older forms of Buddhism as Hinayana ("Lesser Vehicle") by the third or fourth century, and that around the same time it was becoming the dominant form of Buddhism across the region traversed by the Silk Road, from Central Asia to northern China. It remains the main form of Buddhism in China, Korea, and Japan.

Mahayana differed from Theravada in everything from the doctrines and scriptures it emphasized to its rituals and meditation practices. Whereas Theravada saw the discipline of the *bhikshu* as a precondition for enlightenment and liberation, Mahayana offered laypeople the opportunity to strive for those goals as well. Whereas Theravada focused on the historical Shakyamuni, in Mahayana he represented only one manifestation of buddhahood. Furthermore, whereas Theravada insisted that there was no supernatural force on which human beings could call for assistance, Mahayana populated the heavens with bodhisattvas dedicated to helping all those who prayed to them.

How did these differences arise? A possible explanation is that Mahayana Buddhism developed from one or more of the 18 early Indian sects. There is some evidence for a close connection between early Mahayana and two or three of those sects, but it seems more likely that Mahayana emerged in southern India as part of a movement towards more liberal interpretation that spread across several of them.

Despite their differences, Mahayana and the earlier sects share a common core of values and moral teachings, practices (such as meditation, chanting, scripture study, and veneration of relics), and forms of monastic life. In short, Theravada and Mahayana are different vehicles (*yanas*) for travelling the same path to enlightenment.

Mahayana Doctrine

Mahayana Buddhism begins with the same basic teachings as Theravada, but gives more emphasis to some doctrines, such as Emptiness; interprets others, such as the role of the lay sangha and the doctrine of the Buddha Body, in new ways; and includes additional elements, such as the bodhisattva vow.

The Lay Sangha

The practice of venerating Shakyamuni at the stupas enshrining his relics began soon after his death. In time, many laypeople began making pilgrimages to places with major relics, and new stupas were built in all Mahayana countries. (The veneration of sacred relics was an important part of several religions in this period, including Hinduism and Christianity.) Lay Buddhists came to believe that they could earn valuable karmic merit by making a pilgrimage.

This development marked a major shift away from early Buddhism, in which the religious role of laypeople had been restricted to providing material support for the sangha, and the prospects for lay progress along the spiritual path were limited. Anyone who wished to seek enlightenment more seriously was expected to "depart the world" for the monastic life. Mahayana, by contrast, offered laypeople the possibility of attaining enlightenment even while living in the world.

Doctrine of the Three Bodies (Trikaya)

To account for the various ways in which Buddha could be experienced, Mahayana developed a doctrine of "three bodies" (*trikaya*). The earthly manifestation of a buddha is called the Appearance or Transformation Body (*nirmanakaya*). The heavenly body that presides over a buddha-realm and is an object of devotion for Mahayana Buddhists is called the Body of Bliss (*sambhogakaya*). These are supported by the buddha as the absolute essence of the universe, called the Dharma Body (*dharmakaya*).

The Three Bodies doctrine calls attention not only to the oneness of all the buddhas that have appeared on Earth, but also to the unity of the buddha-nature or potential in all its forms. That is, the *trikaya* doctrine envisions one cosmic reality (Dharma Body) that manifests itself in the form both of heavenly beings (Body of Bliss) and of humans such as Shakyamuni (Appearance Body). By connecting the earthly Buddha to the Dharma Body or Absolute, the doctrine of the three bodies also moved Mahayana Buddhism in the direction of theistic religion—in sharp contrast to the Theravada school, which continued to revere the Buddha not as a deity but as an exceptional human being.

Teaching by Expedient Means

The Sanskrit word *upaya* forms part of an expression frequently translated as "skill in means" or "skilful means." The word was used occasionally in Theravada texts with a more general sense, but the roots of the more technical sense were already present. Shakyamuni's teachings were pragmatic, and he tailored his presentation of them to suit each audience's capacity. He urged his followers to use skill in guiding people to spiritual attainment, like the boatman who ferries people to the other side of the river. The analogy implies that once one has reached the other side, there is no further need of the boat for the onward journey.

The Lotus Sutra *and the Parable of the Burning House*

A Mahayana text that emphasizes *upaya* is the *Lotus Sutra*. It treats many Buddhist teachings as steps towards a more complete understanding. As an illustration of this perspective, it tells of a father whose children are inside a burning house. He persuades them to come out by promising them chariots that he does not actually have; this false promise may be a lie, but it serves an important purpose. Similarly, those just starting on the path are taught not the ultimate truth, but temporary formulations that will allow them to advance to a point where they will be able to see the purpose of the earlier stages. From this perspective, even Shakyamuni's teaching is provisional: simply an expedient means of persuading human beings to start along the path. By treating earlier teachings as expedient means, Mahayana thinkers were able to shift the emphasis from Shakyamuni to celestial buddha figures and a notion of cosmic wisdom.

Bodhisattvas and Merit Transfer

Early Buddhism taught that every individual makes his or her own karma, and that there is no supernatural source of grace. By contrast, the Mahayana school proposed that grace is available in the form of merit transferred to humans from bodhisattvas. Mahayana cosmology envisions a multitude of spiritually advanced beings, all of them prepared to share their great merit with anyone who prays for help.

Even though Shakyamuni himself had remained a bodhisattva until the night of his enlightenment, for most Theravadins the highest goal was to reach the status of an Arhat. The Mahayana school criticized this goal as self-centred because it was focused on personal liberation. Thus all Mahayana Buddhists are encouraged to take the bodhisattva vow, pledging not only to attain buddhahood themselves but also to work towards the liberation of all beings.

The corollary of this innovation in Buddhist thought was the Mahayana idea that humans could appeal to merit-filled beings in the heavens for assistance. Early Indian Buddhism had considered Shakyamuni, after his *parinirvana*, to be beyond the realm of direct involvement with human lives, and therefore it had no tradition of appealing to him for assistance. In some Mahayana schools, by contrast, worshippers not only venerate the bodhisattvas but petition them for blessings, much as Roman Catholic and Orthodox Christians ask the saints for help.

Another important characteristic of Mahayana Buddhism is its extension of the concept of merit transfer. As we have seen, early Buddhism taught that merit—that is, karma—is made solely by the individual. The only exception involves the merit transfer ritual. In Mahayana, by contrast, the buddhas and the bodhisattvas are believed to be capable of transferring merit from themselves to human beings.

Some important bodhisattvas have special functions. For example, Bodhisattva Manjusri is the guardian of Buddhist wisdom, and novices entering Buddhist training often call on him to guide and inspire them. The bodhisattva of compassion, Avalokiteshvara ("the Lord who looks down"), is popular in all Mahayana countries. Originally Avalokiteshvara was masculine, but in China he came to be venerated in female form under the name Guanyin. This change of gender is an example of the bodhisattva's power to take any shape necessary to benefit believers. The most venerated of all bodhisattvas, Guanyin has been called the "Virgin Mary of East Asia" by Westerners. Many Mahayana women feel especially close to her because she is believed to bring children to those who lack them and to care for infants who die, as well as aborted fetuses.

Bodhisattva Maitreya (the "Friendly One") is expected to be the next buddha, the one who will turn the dharma wheel once again after the wheel set in motion by Shakyamuni has stopped turning. Some Mahayana Buddhists pray to Maitreya as the "future buddha," requesting that they be reborn when he comes because it will be easier to achieve enlightenment when there is a living buddha to follow.

The heavens in which the buddhas and bodhisattvas reside are known as "fields" or "realms." Those who venerate a certain buddha may be reborn into his heaven. As we shall see, this is a central belief of the **Pure Land** movement, which venerates a celestial buddha of "infinite life" and "infinite light" known in Sanskrit as Amitayus or Amitabha, in Chinese as Amituofo, and in Japanese as Amida (the Japanese spelling is the one most commonly used in English).

The bodhisattvas have had enormous appeal as saviour figures, and in their compassionate self-sacrifice, they have been compared to the Christian Jesus.

Bodhisattva Vows

The practice of taking bodhisattva vows reflects the Mahayana emphasis on giving of oneself to help others. As we have seen, early Indian Buddhists rarely aspired to become buddhas themselves: they were content to hope that in some future life they could achieve the status of Arhat. It was the self-centred nature of this focus on personal liberation that Mahayana philosophers criticized. All Mahayana Buddhists—male or female, lay or monastic—were encouraged to declare their intention to become buddhas someday, but also to remain active in helping to liberate all beings.

In practical terms, taking the bodhisattva vow meant vowing to be reborn in a heaven from which one can transfer merit to others. Although the possibility of helping others by accepting rebirth as a human was not ruled out, the advanced bodhisattvas were thought to live in their own heavenly realms.

Mahayana Schools

The above overview of Mahayana doctrine suggests some substantial differences from Theravada Buddhism. But there are also pronounced differences between the various Mahayana ordination lineages or "schools" that developed first in India and eventually across East Asia. For example, the **Chan** (**Zen** in Japan) school downplays Buddha veneration and has much in common with Theravada, whereas the Pure Land school stresses the necessity of Amida Buddha's help. We will briefly discuss some of the more important schools of Mahayana thought, focusing on their beginnings (usually in India) and noting the names they assumed as they spread across East Asia.

Madhyamaka

Early Buddhism taught that there were six perfections, the last and most important of which was the perfection of a kind of wisdom known as ***prajna***. This wisdom—not to be confused with worldly wisdom or scientific knowledge—is accessible only to those with a highly developed consciousness.

Mahayana thinkers wrote a number of texts on *prajna*, beginning as early as the first century BCE with the *Perfection of Wisdom in Eight Thousand Verses*. The two that were to become the most important were the *Heart* and *Diamond Cutter Sutras*. In all these texts, the key to the highest spiritual wisdom is awareness of the emptiness or nothingness (***shunyata***) of all things.

Sometime in the second century, a brahmin from southern India converted to Buddhism and took the ordination name Nagarjuna. He wrote Buddhist devotional hymns and ethical guides, but his fame is based on philosophical works such as the *Mulamadhyamaka-karika* ("Fundamentals of the Middle Way").

Nagarjuna's philosophical position is called the "Middle Way" (Madhyamaka) because it refuses either to affirm or to deny any statement about reality on the ground that all such statements necessarily fall short of ultimate truth. All realities (dharmas) are equally "empty" of absolute truth or "self-essence." According to Nagarjuna's doctrine of Emptiness, everything in the phenomenal world is ultimately unreal. By a process of paradoxical logic he claims that Emptiness as ultimate reality is itself unreal, although it may be experienced directly in meditation. Nagarjuna summed up this paradox in a famous eightfold negation:

> Nothing comes into being,
> Nor does anything disappear.
> Nothing is eternal,
> Nor has anything an end.
> Nothing is identical,

Or differentiated,
Nothing moves hither,
Nor moves anything thither.
(Chen 1964: 84)

For Madhyamaka and the later Mahayana schools that developed under its influence, including Zen, enlightenment demands recognition of the *shunyata* of all dharmas.

Of course Nagarjuna recognized that his own thinking was no less empty than any other. Thus he made it his philosophical "position" to refrain from taking any dogmatic position. According to his paradoxical logic, *nirvana* is dialectically identical to *samsara*, or the phenomenal world: each is present in the other.

Sanlun: Chinese Madhyamaka

The Sanlun ("Three Treatises") school is the Chinese extension of Nagarjuna's Madhyamika. The monk Kumarajiva (334–414) introduced this teaching into China with his translation of two treatises by Nagarjuna and a third by Nagarjuna's disciple Aryadeva (or Deva, c. 300). These three works became the foundations of the Sanlun school.

The chief Sanlun teaching is essentially a restatement of Nagarjuna's idea that everything is empty (*shunya*), because nothing has any independent reality. An entity can be identified only through its relation to something else. In this unreal phenomenal world we make distinctions between subject and object, *samsara* and *nirvana*, but with the higher wisdom comes understanding of *shunyata* (emptiness).

Yogacara or "Consciousness Only"

In the late fourth century, three Indian *bhikshus* named Maitreyanatha, Asanga, and Vasubandhu founded a new Mahayana school. Though usually called Yogacara ("Practice of Yoga") because it stresses meditation and uses a text by that name, it is also known as "Consciousness Only" (Vijnanavada), because it argues that what most people assume to be realities are merely images taken from a "storehouse consciousness" (*alaya-vijnana*) shaped by past karmic actions and attachments. As a consequence, we can never know if external objects exist.

For Yogacara, both the universe and the perceiver exist only in the process of perceiving. Even our "selves" and our karma are merely reifications of momentary awareness. Sensory impressions are "seeds" that lead to acts or thoughts:

A seed produces a manifestation,
A manifestation perfumes a seed.
The three elements (seed, manifestation, and
perfume) turn on and on,
The cause and effect occur at the same time.
(Chen 1964: 323)

According to this theory, the only way to avoid false substantialization is to so exhaust the consciousness, through yoga and spiritual cultivation, that it becomes identical to the ultimate reality called "thusness" (*tathata*), which corresponds to the "emptiness" of Madhyamaka. Critics from rival schools argued that the storehouse consciousness concept seemed to come close to affirming the Hindu notion of the Atman (eternal soul) that the Buddha had rejected. But the Yogacara writers argued that the storehouse consciousness has no eternal, unchanging substance. Buddhist ideas of the link between one birth and the next as a "karma complex" or "migrating consciousness" were developed by Yogacara into the notion of a storehouse consciousness.

Faxiang: Chinese Yogacara

The Chinese version of Yogacara or "Consciousness Only" also has two names, Weishi ("Consciousness Only") and Faxiang ("Dharma Character"). First introduced into China in the sixth century, the school grew up around a text by Asanga entitled *Compendium of Mahayana*. Perplexity over the meaning of this work spurred a monk named Xuanzang to go to India in search of more scriptures; on his return, the Big Wild Goose Pagoda was built in Xi'an (the Chinese terminus of the silk route) to house the manuscripts he brought back. Although Faxiang did not survive as a vital sect, it had some influence on the development of other schools of thought, including neo-Confucianism.

Pure Land Buddhism

The school dedicated to Amitabha (Amida) most likely began to take shape around the first century. According to an account in the *Larger Sutra on the Pure Land*, attributed to Shakyamuni himself, Amitabha was a buddha of a previous age who in an earlier life, as a young prince named Dharmakara, took 48 bodhisattva vows detailing his intention to strive for enlightenment and help others in specific ways. In the eighteenth vow, Amitabha promised to establish a heavenly region—the "Pure Land" or "Western Paradise"—into which all beings who so desired could be reborn. No extraordinary effort would be required to earn rebirth in that land: admission would be free to all who had faith in Amitabha's compassionate power and made their desire for rebirth in his heaven known by thinking of him.

Suffering, old age, and death will be unknown in the Pure Land—the *sukhavati*, as opposed to the *duhkha-vati*, the land of suffering, that is the world. There will be food, drink, and music for all, and the buddha's followers will be so uplifted by his merit that their progress towards nirvana will be easy. This notion of the "Pure Land" marked a transformation in the Buddhist idea of heaven. In early Buddhism, meritorious individuals could hope to be reborn in a paradise, but they would be unable to "make" new merit or develop their higher wisdom while there. In other words, there was no path leading from heaven to nirvana: once the inhabitants' store of merit was exhausted, they would have to be reborn in human form to make more. But for those in the Pure Land, rebirth on Earth will no longer be necessary.

The *Smaller Sutra on the Pure Land* spells out what is required to benefit from Amitabha's store of merit. Those who have remembered and repeated his name before death will be reborn in his Pure Land. This rebirth cannot be earned by any meritorious works: it is a gift made available through the infinite merits of Amitabha. Theologically, the Christian concept of salvation through faith in divine grace is a parallel.

A third early Pure Land text, the *Meditation on Amitayus Sutra*, offers detailed instruction in vision meditation. But for those unable to undertake the rigorous training required to achieve a vision, it also offers an easier path. Even the meritless or wicked could gain rebirth in the Pure Land through sincere repetition of the sacred formula "Homage to Amitabha Buddha."

The Pure Land school introduced a path to salvation based solely on faith. There is no equivalent in the Theravada tradition. The *Smaller Sutra on the Pure Land* teaches that the only condition for rebirth in the Pure Land is faith in Amitabha's infinite compassion, shown through prayerful repetition of his name. This reliance on an external or "other" power stands in sharp contrast to the self-reliance emphasized in early Buddhism. Over the centuries that followed, Pure Land spread from India to China, Korea, and Japan, becoming the most popular of all Buddhist schools in East Asia.

Jingtu: Chinese Pure Land

In China, Pure Land is known as Jingtu and Amitabha as Amituofo. He is assisted by two bodhisattvas (*pusa*), one of whom is Guanyin, the bodhisattva of compassion.

The recitation of praise to Amituofo is called *nianfo* in Chinese. During the recitation the devotee usually fingers a string of beads. Thus Pure Land Buddhism parallels some forms of Christianity in several ways, with a God-figure (Amida), a mediator (Guanyin), a doctrine of faith and grace, and a devotional practice not unlike the recitation of the rosary. (Some think that the practice of using beads to keep count while reciting a sequence of prayers originated in India.)

In China, Pure Land Buddhism has had a special appeal for the masses of people who seek not only ultimate salvation but also assistance in everyday life. Guanyin is particularly important in this respect, especially for women. She soon came to symbolize the "giver of children"—an adaptation that underlines the more worldly focus of Chinese Buddhism, compared with its Indian counterpart.

Jodo: Japanese Pure Land

In Japan, Pure Land Buddhism is called Jodo, its Buddha is called Amida, and the female bodhisattva is called Kannon. Most Buddhists in Japan today belong to the Jodo school.

Pure Land Buddhism was introduced to Japan by a monk named Honen (1133–1212) who wanted to provide a simpler way to salvation for those unable to undertake the demanding program prescribed in the *Meditation on Amitayus Sutra*. The devotional practice he taught relies entirely on faith in Amida's power of salvation, and consists in chanting the "Homage to Amida Buddha" mantra. Repetition of this phrase, called the *nembutsu* in Japanese, leads to a heightened

Document

Pure Land Buddhism: Honen's Testament

The method of final salvation that I have propounded is neither a sort of meditation, such as has been practised by many scholars in China or Japan, nor is it a repetition of the Buddha's name by those who have studied and understood the deep meaning of it. It is nothing but the mere repetition of the "Namu Amida Butsu," without a doubt of his mercy, whereby one may be born into the Land of Perfect Bliss. The mere repetition with firm faith includes all the practical details, such as the three-fold preparation of mind and the four primordial truths. If I as an individual had any doctrine more profound than this, I should . . . be left out of the Vow of the Amida Buddha (Tsunoda 1958: 208).

state of consciousness, especially during services as the chanting quickens, building to a feverish pace. (For a detailed discussion of Pure Land in Japan, see Chapter 7.)

Honen's disciple Shinran (1173–1262) underlined the need for the "other-power" of Amida's grace in a "degenerate" age when Buddhist dharma was thought to be in decline. Condemning the magical and syncretic tendencies that he saw in other schools, Shinran taught the *nembutsu* as an act of faith and thanksgiving. In a moving passage about the salvation of the wicked, Shinran says:

> People generally think . . . that if even a wicked man can be reborn in the Pure Land, how much more so a good man! This latter view may at first sight seem reasonable, but it is not in accord with the purpose of the Original Vow, with faith in the Power of Another. The reason for this is that he who, relying on his own power, undertakes to perform meritorious deeds, has no intention of relying on the Power of Another and is not the object of the Original Vow of Amida. Should he, however, abandon his reliance on his own power and put his trust in the Power of Another, he can be born in the True Land of Recompense. . . . Amida made his Vow with the intention of bringing wicked men to Buddhahood. Therefore the wicked man who depends on the Power of Another is the prime object of salvation (Tannisho; Tsunoda 1958: 217).

Both Honen and Shinran faced opposition from rival schools and were exiled by the authorities, but they found wide support among the people. Shinran founded a new sect called "True Pure Land" (Jodo Shinsu) or Shin Buddhism. He also did something revolutionary: like Martin Luther, the sixteenth-century German priest who launched the Protestant Reformation in Europe, he chose to marry, maintaining that husband and wife are to each other as the bodhisattva Kannon is to the believer. In so doing he laicized Buddhism. Although this break with the tradition of monastic celibacy was widely opposed, today most Buddhist priests in Japan are married, and temples are usually passed down through their families; the oldest son is typically expected to train for the priesthood so that he can continue the family tradition.

Chan–Zen Buddhism

The founder of Chan Buddhism (better known in the West by its Japanese name, Zen) was Bodhidharma—the same sixth-century Indian monk who told King Wu that all his good works had earned him no merit at all. In sharp contrast to the Pure Land sect's emphasis on "other power," Chan emphasized "self-power" and the attainment of personal enlightenment through rigorous practice of meditation. Although there is no surviving evidence that a similar school existed in India, Chan tradition traces Bodhidharma's lineage to the Buddha's disciple Kashyapa, whose intuitive insight is celebrated in the story of the "flower sermon" (see Focus box).

The Chinese pronunciation of the word *dhyana* (*jhana* in Pali) was "*chan*": hence the name of the school that Bodhidharma founded in China, centred what he called a "mind to mind, direct transmission" of enlightenment, with "no dependence on words." Just as the Buddha relied on a single enigmatic gesture to deliver his "flower sermon," so Bodhidharma and later Chan masters used surprising, shocking, paradoxical, or even violent actions to bring about the state of mind best known in the West by the Japanese term *satori*. One master twisted a disciple's nose so hard that the pain and indignity led to a breakthrough. Another shoved his disciple into a thorn bush, with the same result. Another would simply hold up a finger. Many made impossible demands on

Focus

The Flower Sermon

This story begins with the disciples asking Shakyamuni for a dharma talk. He agrees, and as he takes his seat on the teaching throne, all grow silent, eagerly waiting to hear his words. Instead of speaking, however, Shakyamuni simply holds up a white lotus flower.

All are dumbfounded except for Kashyapa, who in that moment experiences an intuitive flash of enlightenment. The Buddha acknowledges his understanding with a smile, and Kashyapa becomes the first patriarch in a lineage that stresses the achievement of the state of mind called *dhyana* in Sanskrit: the state reached by the young Shakyamuni while meditating under the rose-apple tree.

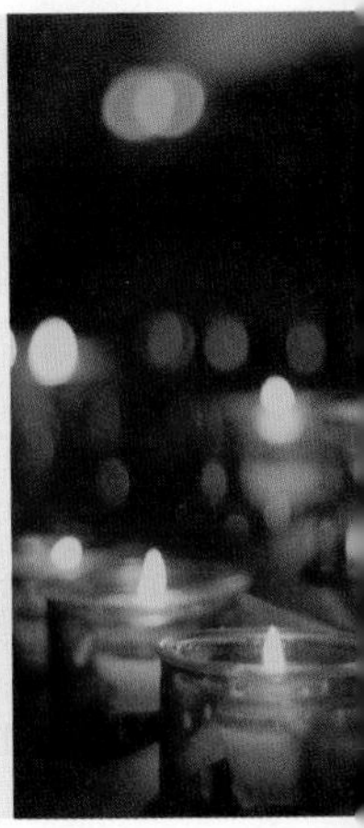

their students, including the master who held up one hand and demanded to be told what sound it made: this was the origin of the familiar Zen **koan** "What is the sound of one hand clapping?" One master would instruct his disciples to imagine hanging by their teeth from a branch suspended over some danger, then being asked a question that demands a response—for example, "Do all persons have Buddha-nature?" If the disciple correctly answers "Yes," he will fall and die. But if he refuses to answer, he will seem to communicate an untruth. The master demands to know: "What would you do?" Since there is no logical way out of this dilemma, the correct answer must be found in some place other than the rational mind.

In the early sixth century, Bodhidharma took this school of thought to China and settled into a cave in the mountains above the village of Shaolin. He was known especially for meditating while facing the wall of his cave. One legend has it that after nine years of "wall-gazing meditation," his legs atrophied. Another says that he began teaching his students self-defence as an antidote to their long hours of sitting meditation. His teaching is summed up in these four lines attributed to him:

> A special transmission outside of doctrines. Not setting up the written word as an authority. Pointing directly at the human heart. Seeing one's nature and becoming a buddha (Robinson 1959: 332).

These lines put into words Kashyapa's "flower sermon" experience of the transmission of enlightened consciousness by direct contact between master and disciple, without textual or doctrinal study.

Because of its distaste for book learning, Chan became known for its transmission of enlightenment "outside the scriptures," independent of "words or letters." The special Chan state of consciousness is transmitted only "from mind to mind"—from master to disciple—without the intervention of rational argumentation. It advocates the "absence of thoughts" to free the mind from external influences.

The Lineage of Chan Patriarchs

One winter day a Chinese man is said to have arrived at Bodhidharma's cave, hoping to study under the master. But he was not invited in. Hours passed and darkness fell but the man waited throughout the night, shivering in the ever deepening snow. In the morning Bodhidharma finally asked him what he wanted. He explained that he wanted a teacher who would open his mind to

Dozens of elementary and high schools in the town of Shaolin combine academic studies in the mornings with martial arts training in the afternoons. Although most of the schools are Buddhist in orientation, two are Muslim; there are also some schools for girls, although the majority are male-only. The best students from each age group perform hourly for tourists, as in this photo (© VISUM Foto GmbH / Alamy).

enlightenment. Bodhidharma refused, telling him it was hopeless for someone like him, with little wisdom and only feeble resolve, to expect any serious breakthrough. After several more hours, the man cut off his left arm and presented it to Bodhidharma as proof of his resolve. Bodhidharma accepted him as a disciple.

The story continues with the new disciple, now named Huike, asking Bodhidharma for help in pacifying his anxious mind. The master replied, "Bring me your mind so that I can pacify it." Huike explained that he had long sought his mind, but he could not find it. "So there," says Bodhidharma, "I have pacified your mind!" The one-armed Huike went on to become the first Han Chinese patriarch. Most Chan monasteries in China, Korea, and Japan are located part-way up a mountain, where the cool, dry atmosphere optimizes the chances of a spiritual breakthrough. For this reason Chan has been called the "mountain school."

Huineng and the Poetry Contest

During the era of the fifth Chan patriarch, in the late seventh century, a young boy from southern China named Huineng arrived at the Shaolin monastery seeking admission as a novice. He was not accepted, perhaps because he spoke a different dialect, but he stayed to work in the kitchen.

Huineng had made the journey because he had learned that the monastery taught a radical new form of Buddhism that offered the possibility of a direct breakthrough to a higher level of consciousness, without undue dependence on knowledge of scriptures or the performance of rituals. He understood the essence of Buddhism to involve an intuitive, mystical experience, the "direct pointing of the mind" that Bodhidharma had taught.

When it came time for the aging fifth patriarch to choose his successor, candidates were asked to compose a poem expressing their state of enlightenment. The most senior disciple produced this verse:

This body is the Bodhi-tree;
The soul is like the mirror bright;
Take heed to keep it always clean,
And let no dust collect upon it.
(Suzuki 1991)

This poem nicely captures the Chan point of view. Instead of practising ritual veneration of the Buddha who was enlightened under a Bodhi tree long ago in a distant land, one is to think of one's own body, here and now, as the Bodhi tree, the place of enlightenment. A bright, shiny mirror perfectly reflects reality, and a pure mind should do the same. Thus the senior disciple's poem encourages regular meditation to keep the mind clear and pure. That night, however, Huineng produced a counter-poem:

The Bodhi (True Wisdom) is not like the tree;
The mirror bright is nowhere shining:
As there is nothing from the first,
Where does the dust itself collect?
(Suzuki 1991)

This poem deepens the understanding of Chan enlightenment. It goes beyond merely bringing the enlightenment experience, symbolized by the Bodhi tree, to the "here and now." In denying the imagery of the Bodhi tree and the mirror, it implies that the pure mind corresponds to the state of emptiness central to the Mahayana tradition.

The fifth patriarch acknowledged Huineng's deep understanding and awarded him the robe and staff of the patriarch—but with the advice that he should go back to the South. This he did, and even though he was still a layman, he began teaching the deep state of intuitive wisdom that became known in the West as *satori*. Eventually he was ordained and recognized as the true sixth patriarch. It was Huineng who spread Chan into southern China, from which it was eventually taken to Korea, where it is known as Seon, and Japan, where it is called Zen.

Zen Sects: Linji (Rinzai) and Caodong (Soto)

There are two main Zen sects, Linji (Rinzai in Japan) and Caodong (Soto in Japan). The first is named after Linji, a ninth-century Chan monk who is said to have entered training as a shy young boy. After training diligently for more than a year, he was permitted to meet with the master, Huangbo. When the master asked why he had come, Linji humbly requested instruction in enlightenment, whereupon the master hit him hard with his stick.

Document

Chan Buddhism

The Platform Sutra *is attributed to Huineng and was compiled by one of his disciples in the early 700s.*

Meditation and Wisdom

Good friends, how then are meditation and wisdom alike? They are like the lamp and the light it gives forth. If there is a lamp there is light; if there is no lamp there is no light. The lamp is the substance of light; the light is the function of the lamp. Thus, although they have two names, in substance they are not two. Meditation and wisdom are like this (*The Platform Sutra of the Sixth Patriarch*, sec. 15; Yampolsky 1976: 137).

On Saving Oneself

Good friends, when I say "I vow to save all sentient beings everywhere," it is not that I will save you, but that sentient beings, each with their own natures, must save themselves. What is meant by "saving yourselves with your own natures"? Despite heterodox views, passions, ignorance, and delusions, in your own physical bodies you have in yourselves the attributes of inherent enlightenment, so that with correct views you can be saved (*The Platform Sutra of the Sixth Patriarch*, sec. 21; Yampolsky 1976: 143).

When Linji told his teacher what had happened, he was advised to try again, which led to a second beating. After three such beatings Linji concluded that he was not worthy. The master granted his request to leave, but asked that he first visit an old hermit monk who lived farther up the mountain. After hearing Linji describe what had happened, the hermit exclaimed, "Poor old Huangbo, he must have nearly exhausted himself hitting you!" This lack of sympathy so shocked and angered Linji that he experienced a breakthrough and burst out laughing. "Why the sudden change?" demanded the hermit. "There's not so much to old Huangbo's Zen after all" was the reply. On returning to Huangbo, Linji threatened to hit the master with his own stick. "Just get back to your training," said the master.

When Huangbo died, Linji succeeded him as master and gave his name to a new ordination lineage that emphasizes exactly the kind of "sudden enlightenment," or *satori*, that he experienced in response to Huangbo's apparently irrational behaviour. Later Linji/Rinzai masters continued to find that they could stimulate a breakthrough to Chan (Zen) consciousness by delivering unexpected blows and shouts, or otherwise confounding their pupils.

At the centre of this approach is the koan (from Chinese **gongan**): a paradoxical anecdote that is specifically designed to defy rational understanding and force the student out of the reason- or word-centred state of mind into a more intuitive, body-centred mode. The typical koan retells an incident in which, by doing something unexpected, a master sparked an enlightenment experience in his student. The point of the retelling is to evoke the same experience in successive generations of disciples. We will return to koan training in the Practice section below.

The second Zen sect, Caodong/Soto, seeks "gradual enlightenment" through long hours of *zazen* (sitting meditation). Both sects use koans and *zazen*, so the differences lie mainly in emphasis, Linji/Rinzai relying more on koans and Caodong/Soto on *zazen*.

Mahayana Practice

Meditation

Meditation is central to all forms of Buddhism. The goals include quieting the mind and heightening mental alertness, with the ultimate goal of breaking through into a state of pure mind known as the buddha-mind or emptiness (*shunyata*). In some Mahayana schools, terms such as "buddha-nature" and "buddha-mind" became virtual synonyms for "enlightenment."

The practice of meditation is particularly intense in the Soto Zen school. Typically, after half an hour of seated meditation (*zazen*), during which attention is focused on breathing, a bell is rung to signal that it is time to rise and practise walking meditation—focused on the slow lifting of the feet high off the ground—for a similar length of time. Then another bell signals a return to *zazen*.

In the Pure Land tradition, as we have seen, rebirth is granted through the grace of Amida (Amitabha). The *Meditation on Amitayus Sutra* promises that whoever achieves a vision of Amida will be reborn in his Pure Land, and explains 16 forms of "vision meditation" designed to help the devotee achieve that goal and develop a special rapport with him. Such visualization would eventually become a central element in Vajrayana Buddhism.

Koan Training

The first koan presented to Zen disciples is known as "Joshu's *Mu*." It tells of a time when the ancient master Joshu and a disciple were walking through the monastery grounds and saw one of the stray dogs that lived there. The disciple asks Joshu, "Does a dog have buddha-nature?" Joshu replies "*mu*" ("no"; *wu* in the Chinese original). There are many layers to this reply. We might think that the standard Buddhist answer to this question would be "yes," since all living beings have buddha-nature. Yet Joshu answers with a word that seems to deny that fundamental doctrine. The key to this paradox lies in the fact that *mu*, "no," is the very word used in Buddhism to express emptiness, the "nothingness" state of mind that characterizes the buddha mind. Thus Joshu's negation is in reality an affirmation.

The correct response to the koan lies not in a rational answer to the master's question but in the experience of breaking through the confines of the rational mind to a new level of consciousness. It is the master's task to reject all false responses to the koan until the breakthrough is achieved.

Focus

Roshi Robert Aitkin

Roshi Robert Aitkin of the Zen Center in Hawaii tells a story from his time as one of a group of students who were assigned "Joshu's *Mu*" in Japan. One of the other students, frustrated at working on the koan in silence, began to shout: "mu! muU! muUU! muuuuuuuUU!." Day after day he continued to shout, and finally the master acknowledged his breakthrough, demonstrating that there is no single correct approach. Whatever the route taken, once a student has broken through to the first level of spiritual enlightenment, a second koan is assigned.

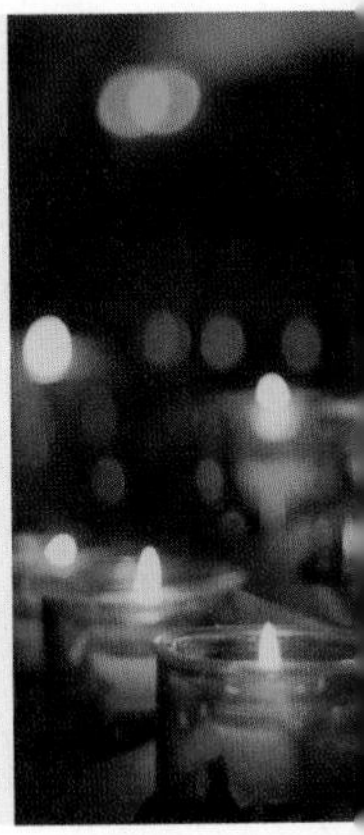

Mount Putuo, off the southern coast of China, is one of the four mountains that Chinese Buddhists hold most sacred, each of which is associated with a particular bodhisattva. Putuo is dedicated to Guanyin, and it includes a temple and a huge Guanyin statue (Sanguis1973 / Dreamstime.com / GetStock).

Disciples must report to the master regularly to respond to the assigned koan, and may be hit or shouted at if their "answers" are inadequate. Mastering one's first koan can take years.

Mahayana Holidays

In Mahayana countries, the Buddha's birth, enlightenment, and *parinirvana* are remembered on separate days, determined by the lunar calendar. Festivals honouring other buddhas and bodhisattvas are also observed, especially Guanyin's birthday. Different sects also celebrate the anniversaries of their patriarchs (for example, Nichiren in Japan).

Under the influence of the ancestor cults of China and Japan, the dead are honoured by an "all souls' day." In China this day is celebrated by burning paper boats to free the *preta* ("hungry ghosts") who have perished in violence. At the Japanese feast called Obon, two altars are built, one for offerings to the dead ancestors and the other for the "ghosts." Traditionally, Chinese Buddhists avoided non-essential outside activity during the "ghosts" month, to lessen the risk of a ghostly encounter. Buddhism has also adopted local customs surrounding occasions such as the beginning of the new year. In China pilgrimages are made to four sacred mountains, each dedicated to a different bodhisattva. In Japan the temple gong is struck 108 times on New Year's Eve, symbolizing forgiveness of the 108 kinds of bad deeds.

Vajrayana, The Third Vehicle

"Vajrayana"—from *vajra*, meaning both "diamond" and "thunderbolt"—is just one of several names for the third vehicle of Buddhism. The diamond image suggests something so hard that it cannot be broken or split, while the thunderbolt suggests a very particular kind of power. Long before the emergence of Buddhism, the thunderbolt was the sceptre of the Hindu storm god Indra, and it came to be represented by a wand, used regularly in Vajrayana rituals, that is shaped somewhat like an hourglass, or a three-dimensional version of the familiar infinity symbol. Despite the thunderbolt connection, the symbolism is not physical or astronomical: rather, the curved prongs represent various buddhas, and the power that the wand symbolizes is the power of the enlightened awareness. It remains a central symbol in the principal Vajrayana school today, Tibetan Buddhism.

Followers of Vajrayana refer to it as the "third turning of the wheel of dharma," the culmination of the two earlier vehicles, Theravada and Mahayana. This is exemplified in a system of Vajrayana training that takes place in three stages named after the three vehicles. In the "Hinayana" phase (corresponding to Theravada), beginners concentrate on basic moral discipline. In the "Mahayana" stage, they receive instruction in basic Mahayana doctrines. And in the third and highest stage, the Vajrayana, they learn the doctrines and practices that Vajrayana itself considers the most advanced.

The view of Vajrayana as the third turning of the wheel also makes sense in historical terms, for it is the most recent vehicle. Emerging in India during or after the third century, it spread to virtually all parts of the Buddhist world, although it disappeared from Southeast Asia centuries ago, and in East Asia had to settle for a minor role in relation to the more popular Mahayana schools. Where Vajrayana became the majority religion was in the region of Nepal and Bhutan, and across the Himalayas in Tibet and Mongolia. Hence some refer to Vajrayana as "northern" Buddhism—northern from the point of view of the Ganges region where Buddhism first developed (from that perspective, Theravada is "southern" and Mahayana "eastern").

Vajrayana Practice

Mantras

Vajrayana incorporates numerous elements that originated in India, in both Hindu and Buddhist practice, but in many cases gives them its own emphasis. An example is its use of mantras: sacred syllables or phrases thought to evoke great spiritual blessings when properly spoken or chanted. Although mantras are also central to the Pure Land ("Homage to Amida Buddha") and Nichiren ("Homage to the Lotus Sutra") schools, the Vajrayana (also known as Mantrayana) tradition puts an emphasis on sound that recalls the ancient brahminic idea that the priests' chanting of the ritual formulas in itself had a particular acoustic efficacy.

The best-known Vajrayana mantra is the Sanskrit phrase *Om mani padme hum*. *Mani* means "jewel" and *padme* "lotus," while *om* and *hum* are not words but sacred syllables. In English we might say "O the jewel in the lotus," or simply "Om jewel lotus hum." But the phrase can be interpreted in several ways. Some Vajrayana practitioners see the jewel and lotus as symbolic of the male and female principles, and understand their union to represent the harmony of the cosmic forces. Others believe that the phrase refers to the bodhisattva Avalokiteshvara in feminine form as the "jewelled-lotus lady." Some think that its six syllables refer to six realms of rebirth, or six spiritual perfections. Whatever the interpretation, the mantra evokes a cosmic harmony.

The eyes of the Swayambhunath Buddha survey the Kathmandu Valley in all four directions. The Nepali script for the number one, symbolizing unity, forms the "nose" (© Tuul / Hemis / Corbis).

Mantras need not be spoken to be effective: they can also be written on banners or slips of paper and hung on trees or lines, or rotated in cylindrical containers called prayer wheels. The repetition achieved through rotation is thought to provide additional benefit.

Tantras

Another Indian tradition that Vajrayana incorporated is tantrism. "Tantric" Buddhism, like Hindu tantrism, envisions cosmic reality as the interplay of male and female forces and teaches a set of practical techniques for tapping into the spiritual energy produced by that interplay. The image of a male figure in sexual embrace with his female consort is common in Vajrayana art. Known in Tibetan as the *yab–yum* (father–mother), this union of male and female symbolizes the coming together of the complementary elements essential to enlightenment, such as compassion and wisdom.

Thus a central component of tantric Buddhism is the concept of sexual union. Some tantric texts suggest that since the world is bound by lust, it must be released by lust as well. While the "right-hand" school understood this principle symbolically, the "left-hand" school interpreted it more literally, practising ritual unions in which the man and woman visualized themselves as divine beings. Such practices, properly undertaken, would defeat lust and transcend it. The texts that lay out such techniques are called tantras. The Tibetan canon includes a vast library of tantras under the heading *Kanjur* and various commentaries under the heading *Tanjur.*

The Vajrayana tantras classify the many buddhas and bodhisattvas in various families, which are often depicted in a sacred geometric design called a **mandala**. The "head" of the family occupies the centre of the design, surrounded by the other members, each of whom occupies a specific position.

Practitioners meditate on their chosen buddhas or bodhisattvas in order to achieve visions that will help them along the path to enlightenment. The Vajrayana guru initiates the disciple into the symbolic meanings of the various members of the family and their relationships, as well as the rituals required to develop inner wisdom.

Having built up a visualization, practitioners begin to identify with their chosen figures and tap into their energies. Visualizing themselves as identical with them, practitioners become aware of the centres of power ("chakras") in their own bodies and may perceive themselves to be at the centre of a sacred space defined by a mandala. At the culmination of this process of gradual enlightenment, initiates aspire to dissolve slowly into emptiness (*shunyata*), liberated from ego attachment.

A classic mandala pattern reflects tantric Buddhism's emphasis on the *Mahavairocana* ("Great Sun") *Sutra*. For example, a mandala might centre on Mahavairocana, surrounded by the buddhas of the four directions: Aksobhya in the east, Amida in the west, Amoghasiddhi in the north, and Ratnasambhava in the south, all of whom together represent the various emanations of buddhahood itself. It is also characteristic of tantric Buddhism to give female counterparts not only to the buddhas but to the bodhisattvas who accompany them; thus mandalas often include numerous figures.

These deities have dual aspects, pacific and angry, depending on their functions (e.g., to assist in beneficial activities or to repel evil forces). The union of wisdom and compassion, considered the key to enlightenment, is represented by the father–mother image evoked by the embrace of deities and their consorts.

Vajrayana in East Asia

Introduced to China in the eighth century under the name Zhenyan ("true word" or "mantra"), tantric Buddhism enjoyed only a brief period of popularity there, but in 806, a Japanese monk who had been studying in China introduced it to his homeland, where it flourished under the name Shingon. Shingon Buddhists practise a "right-handed" tantrism and believe that enlightenment comes with the realization that one's own Buddha-nature is identical with the Great Sun Buddha, Mahavairocana, and can be achieved in this life.

Zhenyan was transmitted to Korea in the same period. Known there as Milgyo, it maintained a distinctive identity until the fourteenth century, when it was amalgamated with Mahayana schools.

Vajrayana in Tibet

Shakyamuni was born in the foothills of the Himalayas and converted his home region (now part of Nepal) a few years after his enlightenment. But the high Himalayan plateau was so difficult to reach that Buddhism made little headway there for the first 1,200 years of its history. It was not until the late eighth century that a few Buddhist missionaries found their way there at the invitation of Tibetan kings.

Vajrayana is said to have been established in Tibet by a *bhikshu* named Padmasambhava, who combined instruction in dharma with magic involving the world of the spirits. Revered as Guru Rinpoche ("precious teacher"), Padmasambhava is particularly identified with a school of Tibetan Buddhism known as the Nyingma ("ancient"), which traces its origins to his time.

Tibetan Buddhism is divided among three main ordination lineages or orders. The best-known, the Gelugpa, was founded by the reformer Tsongkhapa (1357–1419). On ceremonial occasions, members of this order wear large yellow hats, whereas the Kargyu and Karma-pa orders wear red and black hats, respectively.

The Tibetan Book of the Dead

A unique feature of Tibetan Buddhism is the text called the Bardo Thodol ("Liberation by Hearing on the After-Death Plane"), better known as The Tibetan Book of the Dead. A set of written instructions concerning the afterlife, the Bardo Thodol was to be read aloud to the dying, to help them achieve liberation during the three stages of the *bardo* state between death and rebirth.

During the first stage the dying person loses consciousness, experiences a transitional time of darkness, and then emerges into a world filled with objects unknown on the earthly plane. A brilliant light then appears. If the person recognizes the light as the Dharma Body of Buddha, he or she will

Buddhist nuns during morning chanting service in Lhasa, Tibet (© Tom Salyer / Alamy).

attain liberation and experience nirvana rather than rebirth. More often, however, bad karma prevents people from recognizing the true nature of the light, and instead they turn away in fear. Thus most people then pass on to a second *bardo* stage, in which some consciousness is regained. One may be aware of one's own funeral, for example. Peaceful deities appear for seven days, then wrathful deities appear for seven more days. These are all the Buddha in the Body of Bliss form, and those who meditate on them as such will experience liberation. Those who do not recognize them will gradually assume a new bodily form within a few weeks of death. Liberation is possible right up to the moment of rebirth, but karma keeps most people in the grip of *samsara*, the wheel of death and rebirth. In the third stage the individual's karma is judged and the appropriate rebirth is determined.

The Office of the Dalai Lama

To understand the office of Dalai **Lama** and the controversial Chinese claim that Tibet is a part of China, we need to understand the historic relationship between Tibet and the Mongols. As the rulers of China from 1222 to 1368, the Mongols did not invade Tibet, but they appointed the head of

Focus

The Fourteenth Dalai Lama

Born: 6 July 1935, in a peasant farming village northeast of Lhasa. His name was Lhamo Thondup.

Signs: After the death of the thirteenth Dalai Lama, in 1933, the head of his corpse turned to the northeast, and a senior monk had a vision that included a monastery and a house with a distinctive guttering. When the search party found the house, in 1938, the three-year-old boy who lived there called one member of the party by name, and picked out the toys and other objects loved by the thirteenth Dalai Lama. He was then taken from his family to the monastery to begin training.

Instruction: After 18 months the boy was reunited with his family, who moved with him to Lhasa. In 1940 he was ordained as a novice and installed as the spiritual leader of Tibet. A long course of Buddhist studies followed.

High Office: An earthquake and threats of invasion from China prompted his installation as the political leader of Tibet in 1950, at age 15.

Exile: By 1959 the Chinese had taken over Tibet. To avoid arrest or worse, the Dalai Lama crossed the Himalayas to Dharamsala in northern India. From there he led the Tibetan government in exile until 2011, when he officially turned over the leadership to Lobsang Sangay, a Harvard-trained legal scholar. This brought to an end the tradition of joint religious and political leadership that began in the seventeenth century.

Writings: The Dalai Lama has written numerous books on Tibetan Buddhism, meditation, and philosophy, as well as an autobiography, *Freedom in Exile*.

Politics: The Dalai Lama continues to use non-violent means to advocate for the well-being of the Tibetan people. Negotiations with the Chinese government have so far not been fruitful. It remains to be seen whether his formal renunciation of political power will ease the tensions with China.

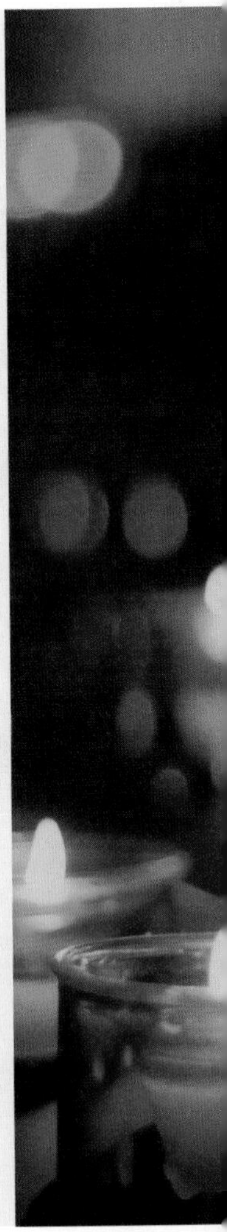

the Shakya monastery to serve as their viceroy for the region. Some two centuries later, a Gelugpa missionary named Sonam Gyatso (1543–88) went to Mongolia and converted its ruler, Altan Khan, who created the title Dalai Lama ("Ocean of Wisdom") and bestowed it posthumously on Gyatso's two predecessors, designating Gyatso the third in the succession. With the sponsorship of the Mongol princes, the Gelugpas soon became the dominant sect in both Mongolia and Tibet.

The first Dalai Lama to become the temporal as well as the spiritual leader of Tibet was the fifth, Ngawang Lobsang Gyatso (1617–82). With Mongol aid he subdued the challenge of the rival Karma-pa lineage and constructed the famous Potala palace in Lhasa. He recognized his teacher, Lobsang Chogye Gyaltsen (1569–1662), as an incarnation of Amida Buddha and gave him the title Panchen Lama. The position still exists, but has become controversial because the Dalai Lama and the Chinese government disagree on the identity of the legitimate Panchen Lama.

The fifth Dalai Lama also established diplomatic relations with the Manchu (Qing) dynasty, which came to power in China in 1644. As a result, Tibet became embroiled in the eighteenth-century rivalry between the Manchus in Beijing and the Oirots of Mongolia, and became a Manchu protectorate. Those old Tibetan ties with Mongolia and China are the basis of modern China's claim to Tibet. The former Tibet is now divided into three Chinese provinces known collectively as the Tibetan Autonomous Region, or TAR.

Choosing a New Dalai Lama

Considered to be a manifestation of the bodhisattva Avalokiteshvara, each Dalai Lama is said to be the reincarnation of the previous one. When a Dalai Lama dies, a search is undertaken to find a boy who shows intellectual qualities and personality characteristics similar to those of the deceased; then various objects are presented to him to see if he chooses those that were the Lama's favourites. Finally, the State Oracle enters a trance state to contact the spirits who must confirm the selection. The fourteenth and current Dalai Lama, Tenzin Gyatso, was chosen in this way from a family of Tibetan descent living in China. A senior monk's vision played a key role in locating the boy.

Interaction and Adaptation in East Asia

China

Chinese converts interpreted a number of Buddhist ideas in ways that served to harmonize them with Indigenous traditions; (see Chapter 6). The Buddhist concept of rebirth on a higher or lower level of life was combined with the Chinese concepts of retribution for good and evil and a home with the ancestors to produce a system of many-layered heavens and hells, with a variety of saviour figures, including Guanyin and the bodhisattva Dizang ("earth-store"; Jizo in Japanese), to relieve the suffering of those reborn in hell. The scripture *Yulanpenjing* tells of a monk named Mulian, who after his enlightenment sought to rescue his mother from hell. This Buddhist expression of filial piety was the basis for the "all souls' day" celebrated on the fifteenth day of the seventh month in China, Korea, and Japan, where it is known as Obon.

Nevertheless, Buddhist monasticism was deeply alien to a social system based on kinship and veneration of ancestors. The practice of celibacy put the family lineage in jeopardy, and Chinese society looked down on those who did not work to support themselves. Thus Chinese monks eventually started to grow their own food. As a Chinese Zen master proclaimed, "A day without work is a day without eating."

At the same time, imperial officials saw Buddhism as a direct threat to the state's authority, as this seventh—century memorial to the first Tang emperor shows:

> Thus people were made disloyal and unfilial, . . . discarding their sovereign and parents, becoming men without occupation and without means of subsistence, by which means they avoided the payment of rents and taxes. . . . I maintain that poverty and wealth, high station and low, are the products of a man's own efforts, but these ignorant Buddhist monks deceive people, saying with one voice that these things come from the Buddha. Thus they defraud the sovereign of his authority and usurp his power of reforming the people (Hughes and Hughes 1950: 77).

Two centuries later, in 845, the Chinese state launched a campaign of persecution against Buddhism that, according to a report prepared for the emperor, led to the destruction of more than 40,000 temples and the laicization of 260,500 monks and nuns.

Folk Buddhism and the Milo Cult

The image of the "friendly" bodhisattva Maitreya underwent a transformation in China not unlike that of the Indian Avalokiteshvara into the Chinese Guanyin. Before the seventh century, Maitreya was a heroic figure, and he has more than once been the focus of political rebellions in China, including the one that led to the founding of the Ming dynasty (1368). In the fifteenth century, however, he began to appear as Milo, a laughing monk with a pot-belly who would travel from village to village, putting interesting objects into his hemp bag and then giving them out to children, like Santa Claus. With his happy-go-lucky nature (*maitri* means "friendly" in Sanskrit), his large belly, and his affinity for children, the "Happy Buddha" reflects the importance that Chinese culture attached both to children and to worldly prosperity.

Korea

Physical proximity created close links between China and Korea. The Han dynasty conquered the northern part of the peninsula in the late second century BCE and Buddhism was introduced roughly two centuries later, spreading from the northern kingdom of Goguryeo first to Baekche in the southwest and then to Silla in the southeast. It became most influential after Silla conquered the two other kingdoms and united the country (668–935).

The new religion expanded on an unprecedented scale during the Silla period. Among the major schools of Buddhism introduced from China were the Theravada tradition of the *vinaya* (monastic discipline) and the Faxiang (Yogacara) school, which eventually developed into a syncretic tradition. The most influential school, however, was Chan ("Seon" in Korea), introduced in the early seventh century. Nine Seon monasteries, known as the Nine Mountains, were eventually established.

In a commentary on the *Flower Garland Sutra*, the monk Wonhyo (617–86) argued that the different teachings complement one another, and together make up one whole truth:

> The world itself is, essentially speaking, in everlasting Enlightenment. In other words, the essential base upon which the whole complex of relationships among the different living beings is standing, is the ultimate eternal reality which is . . . the source of life and light, . . . which make it possible for our life . . . to be truly human, to be enlightened (Rhi 1977: 202).

In the late twelfth century, a charismatic monk named Chinul united the various schools to create the Jogye sect, which became the orthodox form of Buddhism in Korea. Nevertheless, Buddhist influence withered for several centuries after Confucianism was adopted as Korea's state ideology in the 1400s. Confucian scholars petitioned the court to restrict the number of Buddhist temples, supervise the selection of monks, and reorganize the ecclesiastical system while reducing the number of sects to facilitate state control. Temple properties were confiscated, the serfs attached to monasteries were drafted into the army, and Buddhist monks were banned from Seoul, the capital.

Japan

Buddhism reached Japan from Korea in the sixth century—almost 900 years after Shakyamuni's time—and it had been transformed along the way. A turning-point was the warm reception it received from the regent, "Prince" Shotoku, who welcomed it (and Confucianism) for its civilizing effects and in 604 issued the "Seventeen-Article Constitution," a set of moral guidelines for the ruling class that urged reverence for the Three Gems. How Buddhism developed in Japan will be explored in detail in Chapter 11.

Cultural Expressions

Stupas and Pagodas

After the Buddha's *parinirvana*, several kings requested the honour of enshrining his cremated remains in their kingdoms. Accordingly, the remains were divided into seven portions. The urn that had held them and the cloth that had covered it were also given the status of primary relics, and so nine memorials were built. Then, as Buddhism spread additional memorials were built over other sacred objects, including the remains of major disciples and portions of scriptures.

When asked before his death how he ought to be buried, the Buddha had said that a Tathagata's remains should be enshrined in a memorial stupa like that of a great ruler. Thus each portion of his remains was placed in a small casket, richly decorated with jewels, and interred in an above-ground crypt, which was covered with earth to form a large mound and then bricks, which were plastered and whitewashed. Finally, a pole was erected over the mound to represent Mount Meru, a cosmic mountain that in Indian mythology reaches from earth towards the pole star, and around whose axis the world is thought to turn. There are several terms for these memorial mounds. The Sanskrit *stupa* and its Pali equivalent, *thupa*, are cognate with the English word "tomb." The term used throughout East Asia is "pagoda," which derives from the Sanskrit *dagoba* and connotes "womb" in the sense that burial is the forerunner of a rebirth. Whatever the local term, there are stupas on the grounds of nearly every Buddhist temple in the world, and it is the custom for devotees to circumambulate them (always in a clockwise direction, with the right side of the body facing the holy structure).

In addition to the main stupa, a temple complex may have smaller ones built as memorial crypts for important local Buddhists. Lay Buddhists sometimes strew flower petals at these stupas and vow that they too will overcome death and achieve nirvana someday.

Building small stupas has been a popular merit-making ritual. In Myanmar, thousands of small devotional stupas have been built through the centuries, often of sand at the shore. Since the merit comes from the builder's devotional state of mind, there is no need for the structure itself to endure.

The shape of the stupa or pagoda underwent changes through the centuries. In East Asia, the pagoda developed into elegant stone or wooden towers with either five or seven storeys representing the levels of the heavens symbolized by the wooden disks of the original Indian stupas; thus pagoda architecture made the "heavenly section" of the original stupa the dominant part of the structure.

Temples

Buddhist monasteries grew out of the simple refuges—usually a collection of thatched huts—in which early monks lived during the rainy season, when they settled down for a period of intense study and meditation. Wealthy devotees would earn merit by paying for the construction of permanent buildings, and over time a temple complex would take shape consisting of living quarters, a small shrine, and a meeting hall. Eventually, to accommodate lay worshippers, the shrine developed into a large temple housing images of the Buddha. Today, besides the stupa and temple, the grounds usually contain a Bodhi tree, dharma hall, monastery, library, and refectory.

Early cave temples carved in stone were clearly modelled after the simple huts of the early sangha. By the Gupta period (c. 320–540), Buddhist temples had taken on the rectangular shape and other architectural features of Hindu temples at the time. In some regions cliff-side cave complexes were developed that included all the essentials of a temple complex, including separate caves for shrines, living areas, and even large dharma halls. In China, the rectangular wooden buddha hall reflected the influence of the tile-roofed imperial hall of state, with the buddha statue enshrined in the posture of an emperor. This style was the one that made its way to Japan, where the best-known example, the Todaiji temple in Nara, houses a bronze image of the cosmic buddha Vairocana more than 16 metres (52 feet) high.

Images of the Buddha

The first images of the Buddha date from the first century CE, a time when the devotional aspects of Mahayana Buddhism were becoming increasingly popular. Until then, it was apparently assumed that no physical form could or should depict him. Instead, the Buddha and his teaching were symbolized by the stupa and symbols such as his footprint, the Wheel of the Law, the Bodhi tree, or an empty seat. Early statues and reliefs show the Buddha standing, seated either with dangling legs or in the lotus position of yogic meditation, or reclining at the moment of the *parinirvana*.

Hand gestures or **mudras**, similar to those found in Hindu portrayals of deities, became an important feature of Buddhist art. In one, the Buddha touches the earth with the fingers of his right hand, "calling the earth to witness" as he did in his encounter with Mara on the eve of his enlightenment. "Teaching the Dharma" is symbolized by a pose in which both hands are held over the chest, with the tips of the left thumb and forefinger touching to form a wheel. Another *mudra* shows the Buddha with his right hand raised, palm outward, indicating the "Granting of Protection." This is usually combined with the "Fulfilling a Wish" *mudra*, in which the left hand is extended down with the palm outward and fingers pointed down. Disciples are typically shown with their two palms together in the gesture called "Paying Respect," Namaste.

Buddhist iconography also includes the 32 major signs of Shakyamuni's status, the most obvious of which are the *usnisa* (the protuberance on the top of his head that was supposed to be the locus of his supernatural wisdom) and elongated ear lobes. Some art historians think that these features were associated with royalty (elaborate hair styles, earlobes stretched by heavy earrings), but Buddhists see them as signs of Shakyamuni's supernatural nature. Other signs include wheel images on the soles of his feet, and fingers that are all the same length.

In China the Buddha is often depicted like an emperor surrounded by his court, seated in a serene posture and flanked by his disciples Kashyapa and Ananda. Nearby stand the bodhisattvas and stern-looking Arhats (*lohans* in Chinese), while the four World Protectors stand guard.

Story Illustrations

Buddhist paintings and relief carvings often illustrate scenes from the life of the Buddha or the *Jataka* collections recounting Shakyamuni's previous lives. The walls of temples are often lined with such images, so that circumambulating visitors can see the story of the Buddha's life unfold.

As Buddhism spread, other cultures developed their own distinctive iconography. In China, images of Shakyamuni gradually took on a more Chinese appearance, and the figure of Guanyin developed into the graceful, standing feminine form now found throughout East Asia. There is a distinctive Korean representation of Maitreya as a pensive prince with one leg crossed over the other knee. This pose spread to Japan and can be seen in the famous wooden statue of Maitreya in Kyoto's Koryuji temple, which was founded in 622 for the repose of "Prince" Shotoku.

Zen Art and the Tea Ceremony

The highly ritualized tea ceremony was introduced by Zen monks and spread from monasteries to become one of the most familiar symbols of Japanese culture. The Zen influence is also reflected in the minimalism of Japanese painting, in which empty space plays a central role, and the raked-sand gardens (the space accented only by the occasional boulder) typically found in the courtyards of Zen temples. Another cultural expression of Zen values is the Japanese art of flower arranging, which originated in the practice of creating floral offerings for altars and special ceremonies.

Buddhism in the Modern World

India

Buddhism's intellectual and institutional influence within India lasted until the seventh century, but its royal support disappeared as Buddhist kings were replaced by Muslim rulers. A related factor may have been the loss of lay support as Hinduism absorbed a number of elements from Buddhism, including its ascetic dimension. Hindus understood the Buddha as an *avatara* of Vishnu: while some saw him in a positive light as a champion of non-violence, others thought it was his role to attract insufficiently committed Hindus away from the "true" religion. Monasteries throughout India were abandoned or repurposed by other traditions, and some of the most famous Buddhist scholar-monks left for Tibet beginning in the eleventh century. As a result of this migration and the loss of lay adherents, Buddhism largely disappeared from India until the mid-twentieth century, although it did survive in a few eastern regions, as well as Tibet, Nepal, Bhutan, Sikkim, and Assam.

B.R. Ambedkar and the Mass Conversion of Dalits

One catalyst for the revival of Buddhism in India was Dr Bhimrao R. Ambedkar (1891–1956), the lead author of the Indian constitution. Although he was born into the "untouchable" Dalit class, his intelligence led a brahmin teacher named Ambedkar to formally adopt him. With the help of that teacher and the local Muslim ruler, the young Ambedkar earned an undergraduate degree in India and eventually a doctorate from the London School of Economics. On his return to India he became an advocate for Dalit rights at a time when his older contemporary M.K. Gandhi was pursuing the same goal. The two disagreed, however, on the best way to that goal.

Ambedkar blamed Hinduism for the discrimination that Dalits faced. Hindu leaders such as Gandhi hoped that Hinduism could be reformed to eliminate, or at least greatly reduce, that discrimination, but Ambedkar foresaw that entrenched social and economic interests would make substantial reform impossible. Setting out to find a religion that would not discriminate against his people, he recognized in Buddhism a form of spirituality that was compatible with Indian cultural values, but that from its origins had taught the equality of all humans, regardless of birth status.

The history of Buddhism supports Ambedkar's view. The Buddha accepted followers without any regard for their caste. Seniority in the sangha was based solely on date of ordination, and the names of early Buddhist leaders suggest that they came from all social classes.

In 1956, at a large rally in city of Nagpur, in the heart of Hindu India, Ambedkar and his wife took the Three Refuges and Five Precepts from a Buddhist monk, and thousands of Dalits followed their example. Since then, many more Dalits have converted to Buddhism.

A mass conversion ceremony held in Mumbai in 2007 recalled the original mass conversion of Dalits to Buddhism under Ambedkar's leadership in 1956. The people in red robes are Tibetan monks and nuns, many of whom now reside in India (© AP Photo / Rajesh Nirgude, File).

Document

Ambedkar on Religion and Democracy

Here Dr Ambedkar argues the necessity of fraternity for democracy.

What sustains equality and liberty is fellow-feeling. What the French Revolutionists called fraternity . . . [and] the Buddha called, Maitree [friendship or love]. Without Fraternity Liberty would destroy equality and equality would destroy liberty. If in Democracy liberty does not destroy equality and equality does not destroy liberty, it is because at the basis of both there is fraternity. . . .

In examining the possibilities of [democracy's] functioning successfully one must go to the Religion of the people and ask—does it teach fraternity or does it not? . . . If it does not, the chances are poor. . . . Why did Democracy not grow in India? . . . The answer is quite simple. The Hindu Religion does not teach fraternity. Instead it teaches division of society into classes or varnas and the maintenance of separate class consciousness. In such a system where is the room for democracy? (Ambedkar 2008: 270).

Shakyamuni's critique of social inequity has also contributed to a growing appreciation of his place in Indian history. As we noted above, there was a time during the period of Buddhist–Hindu competition when Hindus thought of the Buddha as an *avatara* of Vishnu. That some modern Hindu scholars recognize the Buddha as an important and admirable figure in his own right marks a significant change.

Theravada in Modern Sri Lanka

After the fifteenth century, Sri Lanka was colonized by the Portuguese, Dutch, and British in turn, all of whom promoted some form of Christianity. Buddhism declined in prestige but hung on, and in the late 1800s it received an important boost from the founders of the Theosophical Society, Helena P. Blavatsky and Henry S. Olcott. Sinhalese Buddhists have been active ever since in publishing English-language materials on Buddhism, and they remain loyal to the Theravada tradition despite the presence of largely Hindu India to the north and 500 years of Christian missionary efforts under colonial rulers.

Since independence in 1948, Buddhism has had considerable influence on the policies of Sri Lanka's ruling parties, which draw support from the Sinhalese majority. This has led to feelings of oppression in the Hindu minority, most of whom are descendants of South Indian Tamils who migrated to the island over the past two millennia. (The Sinhalese are thought to have come from North India.) Conflict between the government and Tamil separatists led to more than two decades of bloodshed, even though both Hinduism and Buddhism teach non-violence. Although the civil war finally came to an end in 2009, relations between the two religious communities remain severely strained.

Nevertheless, Sri Lankan Buddhism continues its rich intellectual and ritual life. The symbolic centre of that life is the Temple of the Tooth in Kandy, where an eye tooth said to be a relic of

The Kandy Perahera features torchlit processions in which more than 100 elaborately costumed elephants are paraded through the streets. Musicians and dancers come from surrounding villages, each with its own distinctive attire and dance style. (© M.A. PUSHPA KUMARA / epa / Corbis).

Shakyamuni himself is enshrined. At the time of the Perahera festival, one of the miniature gold stupas that house the tooth is placed in a howdah on the back of an elephant and paraded through the streets of Kandy for several nights.

Theravada in Modern Southeast Asia

Theravada remains the most important vehicle across most of mainland Southeast Asia, though East Asian Mahayana traditions are dominant in Vietnam, Malaysia, and Singapore.

The end of Burmese kingship in the late nineteenth century, the years of British colonialism, and long periods of military rule since independence have severely weakened the Burmese sangha's traditional political influence. Its members have been cut off from significant contact with other Buddhist countries, and its temples have fallen into disrepair. Yet the *bhikshus* are still important in the traditional village-centred society, and the recent easing of military control offers some hope for renewal of Buddhist values.

Similarly in modern Cambodia, the overthrow of Prince Norodom Sihanouk (r. 1941–55) meant the end of the Buddhist kingship ideal of a government that provides for the basic human needs of all citizens. Since then, the political influence of the Cambodian sangha has been limited. Under the communist regime of Pol Pot (r. 1975–9) and the Khmer Rouge, many *bhikshus* were among the innocents slaughtered in the "killing fields." Yet by the late 1980s Khmer Rouge soldiers and *bhikshus* were working together on village projects. Today Buddhism continues to play its traditional role at the village level, most laypeople of all political stripes remain Buddhists, and all political factions appeal to Buddhist values to legitimate their claims to power.

In Thailand the tradition of monastic training for the king continues, and members of the royal family take part in rituals that symbolize the close ties between Buddhism and the monarchy. At the beginning of each season, the king changes the clothing on the Buddha image in the Temple of the Emerald Buddha and gives the image a ceremonial bath.

In Laos—under communist rule since the 1960s—Buddhism has lost the governmental support that it traditionally enjoyed. The traditional relationship of *bhikshus* and laity continues in the villages, however.

Finally, although Theravada has never gained a foothold in Vietnam, Theravada missionaries have recently had some success in Singapore and Malaysia, especially among English-speaking Chinese. Apparently some Mahayana Buddhists in Singapore have been attracted to Theravada as a purer form of the tradition than the Chinese schools that incorporated elements of Chinese folk religion. The Young Buddhist Association of Malaysia has been very active in encouraging dharma study.

Several reform movements are having an impact on Theravada Buddhism today. Retreat centres have been established in Thailand in an effort to reintroduce the lay practice of meditation among laypeople, and the Thai intellectual Sulak Sivaraksa (b. 1932) has argued for a Buddhist vision of society in which the means of development are harnessed for the good of everyone rather than the profit of a few capitalists. He has founded several organizations dedicated to that goal, including the Asian Cultural Forum on Development and the International Network of Engaged Buddhists.

Mahayana in Vietnam

Theravada images and monastery foundations dating from before the ninth century have been found in Vietnam, but Chinese Mahayana traditions—notably Thien (from Chan) and Tinh-do (from Chinese Jingtu, "Pure Land")—have been dominant ever since then. Although Thien is largely a monastic tradition and Tinh-do mainly a lay movement, the two have influenced each other, and all Thien monasteries also teach Pure Land practices.

Twentieth-century efforts to reform Vietnamese Buddhism were interrupted by the Second World War. Then in 1954 the country was divided into a communist North and an anti-communist South, where the Roman Catholic president Ngo Dinh Diem (r. 1954–63) imposed restrictions on Buddhists. It was in protest against these restrictions that, in May 1963, an elderly monk named Thich Quang Duc assumed the lotus position on a busy street in Saigon, had gasoline poured over him, then calmly struck a match and became a human torch. A number of monks and nuns followed his example, attracting worldwide attention and contributing to the fall of the Diem government.

Self-sacrifice is an important theme in the thought of Thich Nhat Hanh (b. 1926), a Vietnamese monk who became not only a Thien (Chan–Zen) master but a poet and peace activist. In response to the atrocities of the Vietnam war, he developed what he called an "engaged Buddhism" to bring the resources of Buddhist wisdom to bear on contemporary conflicts. For him, the self-immolations of 1963 must be understood in the context of the Buddhist belief in the continuity of life beyond one human life span. He believes that changing the world requires that we first change our awareness, especially through meditation and the "art of mindful living." Commenting on the *Heart Sutra*, he says:

> If you are a poet, you will see clearly that there is a cloud floating in this sheet of paper. Without a cloud, there will be no rain; without rain, the trees cannot grow; and without trees, we cannot make paper. If we look even more deeply, we can see the sunshine, the logger who cut the tree, the wheat that became his bread, and the logger's father and mother. Without all of these things, this sheet of paper cannot exist. . . . Everything co-exists with this sheet of paper. So we can say that the cloud and the paper "inter-are." We cannot just be by ourselves alone; we have to inter-be with every other thing (Nhat Hanh 1988: 3).

Buddhism in Modern China, Korea, and Japan

In the 1920s, while Chinese intellectuals were advocating greater openness to Western ideas, a Chan monk named Taixu ("Great Emptiness") called for both political and monastic reform, as well as a restatement of dharma in such a way as to speak to modern Chinese society. Like other Buddhist modernists, he believed that Buddhism should aspire to establish the heavenly Pure Land on Earth.

Government policy regarding Buddhist communities varies with their ethnicity. Temples of the majority Han Chinese population are mostly self-governing, but minority Buddhist communities, especially Tibetans, are strictly regulated because they are perceived to constitute a potentially threatening separatist movement. For that reason, any display of support for the Dalai Lama is prohibited. Even so, many Tibetan Buddhists took part in anti-government protests during the run-up to the Beijing Olympics in 2008, and in recent years dozens (most of them monks and nuns) have sacrificed themselves in what may be the ultimate form of non-violent protest: self-immolation.

In Korea, the overthrow of the pro-Confucian Joseon dynasty by Japan in 1910 freed Buddhism from the restrictions that had been imposed on it for centuries. Throughout the occupation (1910–45), however, religion was controlled and manipulated by the Japanese, and the influence of Japanese Buddhism led some Korean monks to abandon their vows of celibacy. The renewal of Korean Buddhism had to await the country's liberation from Japan, and the process was further delayed by the devastating civil war of 1950–3. The more conservative Jogye struggled to restore the traditions of Korean Buddhism, and in 1954 regained control of virtually all the major Korean monasteries.

Today in Japan Buddhism is often described as the religion of the dead, whereas Shinto is called the religion of the living because of its association with the joys of life. So closely is Buddhism associated with the memorialization of the dead that the family shrine dedicated to the ancestors is called the *butsudan*—literally, the Buddhist altar. (For more on the complex interactions of Buddhism and other Japanese traditions, see Chapter 11.)

An interesting development in modern Japan is the Kyoto school of Buddhist philosophy. Its founder was Nishida Kitaro (1875–1945), who came of age in the period when Japan was looking to the West for ideas to help it modernize and sought to fuse Japanese Zen ideas with continental European philosophy. In keeping with Zen's emphasis on direct experience, he wrote of what he called "pure experience"—"experience just as it is without the addition of the slightest thought or reflection." For example:

> the moment of seeing a colour or hearing a sound that takes place . . . before one has added the judgment that this seeing or hearing is related to something external. . . . When one has experienced one's conscious state directly, there is not as yet any subject or object; knowing and its object are completely at one. This is the purest form of experience (Nishida, *Zen no kenkyu*; Takeuchi 1987: 456).

This approach is consistent with Zen founder Bodhidharma's call for a "direct pointing of the mind." Among Nishida's successors was Nishitani Keiji (1900–90), played a role in the emergence of an international Buddhist–Christian dialogue movement in the 1970s.

Buddhism in the West

Alfred North Whitehead (1861–1947), the Anglo-American philosopher, once said that Christianity was "a religion seeking a metaphysic," whereas Buddhism was "a metaphysic generating a religion." For a long time, Western scholars were not certain whether Buddhism fitted their definition of "religion" at all, since—despite its rituals, scriptures, and monastic traditions—it did not centre on a personal deity.

Knowledge of Buddhism in the West was almost non-existent before the mid-nineteenth century, but in 1879 a book entitled *The Light of Asia*—a moving poetic account of the Buddha's life by Edwin Arnold—attracted wide public attention. Even so, it was not until the beginning of the twentieth century that a few Western seekers began to publish first-hand accounts of Buddhist meditational practice. By the 1930s, Buddhist societies had been established in Great Britain, France, and Germany.

Buddhist influences in North America have tended to come more from the Mahayana and Vajrayana traditions than the Theravada. This has been the case ever since the World's Parliament of Religions conference in Chicago in 1893. Among the delegates was a Zen monk named Shaku Soyen (1856–1919), who later returned to America to spread Buddhism. His young translator, Daisetsu T. Suzuki (1870–1966), became the most influential Buddhist writer in North America. Suzuki made two extended visits to the United States, and wrote many popular books sprinkled with stories of Zen masters and koans. Popularized by Alan Watts, these writings caught the attention of Westerners looking for alternatives to Christianity.

Some Westerners have considered Zen a form of mysticism. Though others have argued that there is no experience of union with a personal god in Zen, if "mysticism" is understood in the broader sense of spiritual experience as a transformation of human consciousness, then Zen practitioners may well share something in common with Christian mystics. Catholic missionaries and theologians, coming from a long contemplative tradition, have sought to learn from Zen insights and techniques. Zen meditation has also attracted the attention of experts in depth psychology.

Zen was the first form of Buddhism to make significant inroads in North America, but it was not the only one. Immigrants from Japan also brought with them Nichiren Shoshu and various Pure Land sects. In addition, two lineages of Vajrayana or Tibetan Buddhism have gained converts in North America since the 1960s. The Kargyu lineage is represented both by the Naropa Institute in Boulder, Colorado, and by a community of Tibetans and converts based in Halifax, Nova Scotia, while the Dalai Lama's Gelugpa lineage has centres in New York and elsewhere.

Ethnic Congregations

Existing alongside the Western converts are Chinese and Japanese Buddhists who, beginning in the late 1880s, settled along the west coast of North America, especially in California and British Columbia, and gradually found the financial resources to build their own temples. These ethnic congregations represented many branches of Buddhism, although the popularity of Pure Land in East Asia is reflected among ethnic Buddhists in North America.

There are also organizations such as the Buddhist Association of America and the Buddhist Association of Canada, which serve mainly immigrants of Chinese origin, and the Buddhist Churches of America (and of Canada), which serve True Pure Land followers, who are mainly ethnic Japanese. Similar, if smaller, groups with roots in Vietnam and Laos also have their own networks. Over time, some congregations have adopted Christian styles of worship, with pews, hymnals, and group leaders who take on all the responsibilities of North American clergy. There are now Buddhist Sunday schools, cemeteries, and wedding rituals conducted by *bhikshus* who are referred to as "priests."

In North America, ethnic Buddhist temples serve as community centres. Visitors are welcome, but the emphasis on community affairs tends to limit congregation membership to people from the same ethnic community. Buddhist meditation centres, on the other hand, have attracted many Western converts. Umbrella organizations such as the Buddhist Council of Canada are helping to bring Western "meditation Buddhists" into closer contact with ethnic congregations.

The influence of Buddhist thought in the West has been greater than the relatively small number of Western Buddhists might suggest. Without necessarily becoming Buddhists, many people in the West use modified versions of Buddhist meditational practices to calm their minds or improve their concentration before athletic or artistic performances. At the same time, Buddhist (and Hindu and Jaina) values such as non-violence and concepts such as rebirth and karma have spread well beyond the traditional religious context.

Recent Developments

Buddhism continues to spread far beyond the land of its origin, but it has also faced setbacks in recent decades. In Sri Lanka and Southeast Asia it was weakened and challenged by the Christian missions and Western values introduced during the colonial era. And the loss of kingship in most of the Buddhist countries of southern Asia has undermined the political support system that existed for many centuries. Like other religions, Buddhism has also been challenged by modern, secular ways of life. Buddhists generally do not see the scientific worldview as a serious challenge, since the Buddha himself emphasized rational thought. Still, the concepts of karma and rebirth do not fit comfortably into the standard scientific worldview.

It is also true that *bhikshus* are no longer the main educators, social workers, dispute settlers, and advisers in Buddhist countries, especially in the major cities; their roles are mainly limited to those of ritual leaders and directors of religious education. Yet Buddhists are not converting in any significant numbers to other religions, and most do make some effort to live according to Buddhist values.

The Female Sangha

Over time the *bhikshuni* sangha died out in many Buddhist countries. The specific reasons may have varied, but in general the female order was vulnerable simply because it was smaller and less well connected to political power than the male order. In Sri Lanka, for instance, when both sanghas were devastated by famine, the king imported monks from Siam to revive the male order, but there is no evidence of similar action on behalf of the female sangha.

Recently, though, some effort has been made to revive the practice of *bhikshuni* ordination in Theravada countries. Some Theravada women take the same ten precept vows as male novices, consisting of the five precepts that lay persons take, plus five more. In Sri Lanka a female order observing ten precepts was started 1905 with the help of women from Burma, and in 1996 a new order of *bhikshunis*, adhering to all 235 precepts (the 227 that monks take plus 8 specific to women) was established in 1996 with the help of *bhikshus* from Sri Lanka and Korea.

Even without ordination, many Theravada women pursue a very active religious life both at home and in the temples. In Thailand laywomen can take vows of poverty and service similar to those taken by Roman Catholic nuns. Some of these women say they would not seek ordination if it were available, because they would have less freedom to serve others if they were bound by the *vinaya* rules. In modern times, Theravada has also moved towards greater acceptance of

Document

Jewel Brocade

In The Sutra of Sagara, the Naga King, *which was translated into Chinese in the third century, a princess named Jewel Brocade cleverly uses the Mahayana doctrine of the emptiness of all things to refute a male disciple who represents the stereotypical patriarchal position. No distinction between male and female spiritual abilities is valid, she argues, because all distinctions are ultimately invalid.*

You have said: "One cannot attain Buddhahood within a woman's body." Then, one cannot attain it within a man's body either. What is the reason? Because only the virtuous have eyes of Emptiness. The one who perceives through Emptiness is neither male nor female. The ears, nose, mouth, body, and mind are also Empty (Paul 1979: 236).

women's capacity for high religious achievement. A Thai laywoman named Upasika Kee Nanayon (1901–79), for instance, was revered by Buddhists of both sexes for her mastery of meditation and her instructional talks.

The status of women in the Mahayana tradition tended to be higher from the beginning. Certainly Mahayana took a more sympathetic view of laypeople in general than earlier forms of Buddhism did. The fact that Mahayana encouraged women as well as men to take the bodhisattva vow indicates that it considered women capable of enlightenment in a way that Theravada did not.

An order of Mahayana nuns following a *vinaya* of the Dharmagupta sect has continued as an unbroken lineage in China and Taiwan, and some of their *bhikshunis* may now be found in many countries. The founder of the Soto Zen school, Dogen, taught females as well as males, and although the Soto convents died out, the Rinzai school today has both nuns and female masters. and outside Japan, Zen masters give equal status to practitioners of both sexes.

Tibetan Buddhism has a long tradition of ordained women, several of whom have been in the forefront of Tibet's struggle against Chinese domination. Ani Pachen ("Great Courage") was known as Tibet's Joan of Arc after she led her clan in rebellion against the Chinese takeover in 1949. She was imprisoned and tortured, but refused to renounce Buddhism or her loyalty to the Dalai Lama. On her release from prison in 1981, she again played a leading role in Tibetan demonstrations against Hanification before escaping to join the exile community in Dharamsala, India.

A Renewed Sense of Mission

According to the Buddhist understanding of long-term historical cycles, the dharma will continue to decline until the next buddha restarts the wheel. This somewhat pessimistic view of the future stands in sharp contrast to the views of many other religions, including Christianity. Yet it does not in any way diminish Buddhists' zeal or sense of mission.

In a sense, the many volunteer associations promoting Buddhist solutions to modern problems are performing the same functions as the Buddhist kings of the past who provided leadership in education, economic development, and social values. Meditation centres offer help with modern problems such as stress and overdependence on material possessions, and most of them emphasize the importance of breaking through the normal bonds of ego, self-centredness, and the assumption of permanence. *Bhikshu* Buddhadasa (1906–93), a Thai reformer, identified the fundamental problem as the attitude of "me and mine." This attitude may be part of the human condition, but Buddhists believe it is made worse by the materialistic and individualistic emphasis of contemporary values.

Buddhist Economics

Another problem that Buddhists are addressing is the need for alternatives to modern patterns of economic development. The term "Buddhist economics" was first used by the economist E.F. Schumacher, who had exposure both to Gandhi's advocacy of small-scale, people-oriented development and to the efforts of U Nu to implement "Buddhist Socialism" in Burma as a middle path between communism and capitalism. (U Nu was a devout Buddhist who in 1947 became the country's first prime minister.) Not surprisingly, Buddhist economics proposes a middle path between the environmental and social disasters of over- and underdevelopment. It advocates local-level, low-tech, people-oriented projects that will help everyone, and criticizes all projects that serve to make the rich richer and the poor poorer. Other advocates of Buddhist economics include the Thai monks Ven. Prayudh Payutto, who sees the Middle Path as the best way to sustainable development, and Ven. Prabhavanaviriyakhun, whose book *Buddhist*

Sites

Lumbini Park, Nepal

The site of the Buddha's birth, with the pond where Mahamaya is said to have bathed, a Bodhi tree, and a park surrounded by monasteries for visiting monks.

Bodh Gaya, Bihar, India

The site of the Buddha's enlightenment. In addition to a huge Bodhi tree (said to be descended from the one under which he sat) there is a temple, and the park is surrounded by temples and monasteries representing different schools of Buddhism.

Sarnath, Uttar Pradesh, India

The deer park near Varanasi where the newly enlightened Buddha preached his first sermon and ordained his former companions.

Bangkok, Thailand

On the grounds of the Grand Palace in Bangkok is the temple housing a jade sculpture known as the Emerald Buddha. The nearby Wat Pho temple complex is filled with interesting temples, and across the river is the picturesque Wat Arun, "Temple of the Dawn," where a tall **pagoda** sparkles at dawn and sunset.

Angkor, Cambodia

Angkor (from a Sanskrit word meaning "city") was the heart of the Khmer Empire. Of the hundreds of religious temples and shrines it is home to, the most famous is the (originally Hindu) Angkor Wat.

Shaolin, China

The Shaolin monastery is the home of Chan (Zen) Buddhism as well as many East Asian martial arts traditions. A two-hour hike up a mountain path leads to Bodhidharma's cave.

Kathmandu, Nepal

There are two great Buddhist temples in Kathmandu. Swayambhunath sits high on a hill, its Nepali-style "eyes" overlooking the countryside. The other, Bodhanath, is a Tibetan-style stupa surrounded by shops and cafés.

Lhasa, Tibet

The home of the Potala Palace (the home of the Dalai Lamas before the Chinese occupation) and the Jokhang temple.

Ajanta Caves, Maharashtra, India

A complex of stone temples carved into a cliffside, filled with Buddhist sculptures and paintings.

Kandy, Sri Lanka

The Temple of the Tooth in Kandy, northeast of Colombo, is the most important Buddhist site in Sri Lanka. The Perahera festival is a spectacular 10-day event in which some Hindus also participate.

Economics argues that achieving sustainable development will require (as he puts it in the title of another book) "reforming human nature." This theme is also central to the social critic Sivaraksa, who laments the spread of consumer greed throughout the world. In a variation on Descartes's "I think, therefore I am," Sivaraksa says that the slogan of consumerism is "I shop therefore I am."

Cooperation among Buddhists

Buddhists in various countries are now forming networks across national borders; one example is the International Network of Engaged Buddhists, based in Bangkok. Many Buddhists now identify themselves first as Buddhists and only secondarily as Zen or Theravada Buddhists. This trend is strengthened by the growing tendency of Buddhist periodicals and Internet sites to feature articles by writers from a variety of traditions.

The sense of common purpose has been strengthened by the international exposure of the Dalai Lama, who has travelled to most Buddhist countries and in every case has been very well received. Strictly speaking, he is the spiritual head of just one Tibetan order, but Buddhists everywhere recognize Tenzin Gyatso as their spokesperson in some sense. His forced exile is seen as a loss for Tibet, but in the long run it may provide the impetus that Buddhism needs to regain its traditional role as one of the world's most vigorous and successful religions.

Summary

Buddhists understand Shakyamuni, the Sage of the Shakya clan, to be the latest in a long line of spiritual masters who have become fully enlightened, teaching Buddhas. In the 2,500 years since his birth, his followers have preserved the teachings of the Buddha and others as sacred texts, selections from which are chanted to bring understanding and blessing to all. Buddhist thought makes no sharp distinction between animals and humans, and holds that all living beings are reborn according to their karma and progress along the path to enlightenment. Buddhism is organized by ordination lineages as subdivisions among three Vehicles: Theravada, Mahayana, and Vajrayana. No one individual holds authority over all Buddhists, but the current Dalai Lama is world-renowned as the face of Buddhism today. Although Buddhism is a missionary religion, its approach today is generally low-key, centred on activities such as meditation training and informal "dharma talks."

What gives Buddhism its energy? What makes it work for so many people in so many different times and cultures? The answer may lie in the continuing power of the Triple Gem to shape people's spiritual lives. Buddhists feel confident "taking refuge" in the Buddha not as a god but as a great human being; in the Dharma as a set of living teachings that go to the heart of reality; and in the Sangha as a community of people committed to following the Buddha's path as closely as possible. They also feel confident that, in the distant future, when the wheel of dharma set in motion by Shakyamuni ceases to turn, the future buddha Maitreya will appear on Earth and turn the wheel yet again for the benefit of all beings.

Sacred Texts

Religion	Texts	Composition/ Compilation	Compilation/ Revision	Use
Buddhism: Theravada	*Tripitaka: Vinaya* (discipline), *Sutras* (sermons), and *Abhidharma* (further dharma)	Each of the various early sects had its own collection of texts, which were transmitted orally for several centuries before they were first written down in the 1st century BCE, in Sri Lanka.	Only the Theravada versions of the texts survive in full; commentaries include Buddhaghosa's *The Path of Purification* (5th century).	Study and discussion; selections called *Parittas* are chanted as blessings in various rituals; and verses from the *Dhammapada* (part of the *Sutra* collection) often used for guidance in everyday life.
Buddhism: Mahayana	*Lotus* and *Heart Sutras*, as well as hundreds of other sutras and commentaries	Some written in early 1st century CE; others said to have been recovered from hiding.	Commentaries written on many major sutras.	Chanted for study or blessing rituals; different Mahayana schools had their own favourite texts.
Buddhism: Mahayana, Pure Land	*Sukhavati* (Pure Land) *Sutras*, of various lengths	Composed during early centuries of CE.	Commentaries written by major thinkers.	Studied and chanted; the source of the Bodhisattva vows that Pure Land practitioners take.
Buddhism: Mahayana, Chan	*Platform* and *Lankavatara Sutras*, among others; *Mumonkan* (koan collection)	Favourite Mahayana scriptures, plus stories of masters unique to Chan tradition.	Numerous translations of teachings, updated frequently over time.	Doctrinal, ritual, inspirational, educational; it can take years for students to work their way through the 48 koans of the *Mumonkan*.
Buddhism: Vajrayana	*Kanjur* (sutras and tantras)	Includes many Tibetan translations of Mahayana sutras.	Commentaries called *Tanjur* expanded on the *Kanjur* texts.	Study, chanting, rituals.

Discussion Questions

1. How does the life of the Buddha compare with that of Christ (or the leader of some other spiritual tradition)?
2. What were the main elements of the brahmin tradition that Buddhism rejected?
3. What role, if any, do deities play in Buddhism?
4. What does Buddhism mean by the goal of purifying the mind?
5. What is the status of Tibetan Buddhist culture in contemporary China?
6. Why does the Chinese government object when the leaders of other countries meet with the Dalai Lama?
7. Why has the *Bhikshuni sangha* been lost in several Buddhist countries? What efforts are being made to restore it?
8. What is "Engaged Buddhism"?
9. Why did Dr Amdedkar and many other Dalits convert from Hinduism to Buddhism?
10. Is it fair to call Buddhism a system of self-development rather than a religion?

Glossary

anatman "No-soul," the doctrine that the human person is impermanent, a changing combination of components.

Arhat/*lohan* A worthy one or saint, someone who has realized the ideal of spiritual perfection.

bhikshu, bhikshuni An ordained Buddhist monk and nun, respectively.

bodhisattva In Theravada, a being who is on the way to enlightenment or buddhahood but has not yet achieved it; in Mahayana, a celestial being who forgoes nirvana in order to save others.

Chan/Seon/Zen A tradition centred on the practice of meditation and the teaching that ultimate reality is not expressible in words or logic, but must be grasped through direct intuition; see also **koan** and ***zazen***.

dana A "giving" ritual, in which Theravada families present gifts of food, at their homes or a temple, to *bhikshus* who conduct rituals including chanting and merit-transfer.

dharma In Buddhist usage, teaching or truth concerning the ultimate nature of things.

dukkha The suffering, psychological as well as physical, that characterizes human life.

Hinayana "Lesser Vehicle"; the pejorative name given by the Mahayana ("Greater Vehicle") school to earlier Indian Buddhist sects, of which Theravada became the most important.

karma The energy of the individual's past thoughts and actions, good or bad; it determines rebirth within the "wheel" of samsara or cycle of rebirth that ends only when *parinirvana* is achieved. Good karma is also called "merit."

koan/*gongan* A paradoxical thought exercise used in the Chan–Zen tradition to provoke a breakthrough in understanding by forcing students past the limitations of verbal formulations and logic.

lama "Wise teacher"; a title given to advanced teachers as well as the heads of various Tibetan ordination lineages.

Mahayana "Greater Vehicle"; the form of Buddhism that emerged around the first century in India and spread first to China and then to Korea and Japan.

mandala A chart-like representation of cosmic Buddha figures that often serves as a focus of meditation and devotion in the Mahayana and Vajrayana traditions.

mudra A pose or gesture in artistic representations of Buddha figures; by convention, each *mudra* has a specific symbolic meaning.

nirvana The state of bliss associated with final enlightenment; nirvana "with remainder" is the highest level possible in this life, and nirvana "without remainder" is the ultimate state. See also ***parinirvana***.

pagoda A multi-storey tower, characteristic of Southeast and East Asian Buddhism, that developed out of the South Asian mound or stupa.

parinirvana The ultimate perfection of bliss, achievable only on departing this life, as distinct from the nirvana with

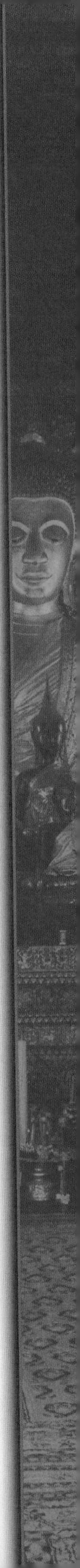

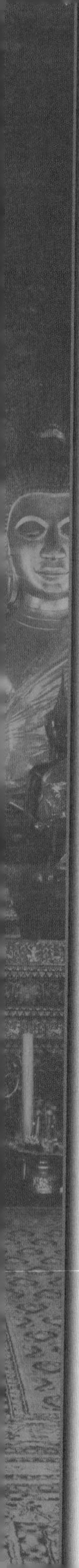

the "remainder" achievable while one is still in the present existence.

prajna The spiritual wisdom or insight necessary for enlightenment.

Pure Land The comfortable realm in the western region of the heavens reserved for those who trust in the merit and grace of its lord, the celestial buddha Amitabha (Amida).

sangha The "congregation" or community of Buddhist monks and nuns. Some schools also refer to the congregation of laypersons as a sangha.

Shakyamuni "Sage of the Shakya clan," a title used to refer to the historical Siddhartha Gautama, the Buddha.

shunyata The Emptiness that is held to be ultimately characteristic of all things, stressed especially by Madhyamaka doctrine.

stupa Originally a hemispherical mound built to contain cremation ashes or a sacred relic; in East Asia the stupa developed into the tower-like pagoda.

sutra A discourse attributed either to Shakyamuni himself or to an important disciple.

Theravada "Teaching of the Elders," the dominant form of Buddhism in Sri Lanka and Southeast Asia.

Tripitaka "Three baskets"; the collection of early sacred writings whose three sections consist of discourses attributed to the Buddha, rules of monastic discipline, and treatises on doctrine.

Vaishakha/Vesak A Theravada festival held at the full moon around early May, marking Shakyamuni's birth, enlightenment, and *parinirvana*.

Vajrayana The tantric branch of Buddhism that became established in Tibet and the Himalayan region, and later spread to Mongolia and eventually India.

vinaya The rules of practice and conduct for monks; a section of the Pali canon.

vipassana "Insight" or "mindfulness" meditation practised by Theravada Buddhists.

zazen Sitting meditation in the Chan–Zen tradition.

Zen See **Chan**.

Further Reading

Amore, Roy C. 1978. *Two Masters, One Message*. Nashville: Abingdon. Compares and contrasts the figures of Buddha and Jesus.

Batchelor, Martine. 2006. *Women in Korean Zen: Lives and Practices*. Syracuse: Syracuse University Press. A good account based on ten years of Zen practice in Korea.

Dalai Lama. 1990. *Freedom in Exile: The Autobiography of the Dalai Lama*. New York: HarperCollins.

Dalai Lama, His Holiness The. 2002. *How to Practice: The Way to a Meaningful Life*. Trans. and ed. by Jeffrey Hopkins. New York: Pocket Books.

Fisher, Robert E. 1993. *Buddhist Art and Architecture*. London: Thames & Hudson. An overview of South and East Asian developments.

Gross, Rita M. 1993. *Buddhism after Patriarchy: A Feminist History, Analysis, and Reconstruction of Buddhism*. Albany: State University of New York Press. Material for provocative debate.

Lopez, Donald S., Jr. 2002. *The Story of Buddhism: A Concise Guide to Its History and Teachings*. New York: HarperCollins.

Queen, Christopher S., and Sallie B. King, eds. 1996. *Engaged Buddhism: Liberation Movements in Asia*. Albany: State University of New York Press. Twentieth-century activism from India and Thailand to Tibet and Japan.

Seager, Richard Hughes. 2000. *Buddhism in America*. New York: Columbia University Press.

Shaw, Ronald D.M., trans. 1961. *The Blue Cliff Records: The Hekigan Roku [Pi yen lu] Containing One Hundred Stories of Zen Masters of Ancient China*. London: M. Joseph. Koans especially prized by the Japanese.

Sivaraksa, Sulak. 2005. *Conflict, Culture, Change: Engaged Buddhism in a Globalizing World*. Somerville, MA: Wisdom Publications. A recent book by an important Thai Buddhist social critic.

Recommended Websites

http://lhamo.tripod.com

A site focusing on women in Buddhism.

www.americanbuddhist.net

Offers a broad overview of Buddhism, including Buddhist activism.

www.buddhamind.info

A comprehensive site, including an ezine with cartoons, pictures, and much more.

www.dharmanet.org

A useful overview of the history and varieties of Buddhism in China, but does not address current issues.

www.dhamma.org

A good source on Theravada-style *vipassana* meditation.

www.freetibet.org

Site of the Free Tibet Campaign, a movement started by Tibetans in exile and their supporters.

www.sakyadhita.org

Site of The International Association of Buddhist Women, with links to various country sites including USA and Canada.

References

Ambedkar, Dr Bhimrao Ramji. 2008. *Riddles in Hinduism*. Scotts Valley, CA: CreateSpace Independent Publishing Platform.

Bloom, Alfred. 1965. *Shinran's Gospel of Pure Grace*. Tucson: University of Arizona Press.

Chen, Kenneth. 1964. *Buddhism in China: A Historical Survey*. Princeton: Princeton University Press.

de Bary, William Theodore, ed. 1958. *Sources of Indian Tradition*. New York: Columbia University Press.

Dhammika, Sravasti, ed. 1989. *Buddha Vacana*. Singapore: Buddha Dhamma Mandala Society.

Horner, I.B. 1930. *Women under Primitive Buddhism: Laywomen and Almswomen*. New York: Dutton.

———, trans. 1967. The *Collection of the Middle Length Sayings (Majjhimanikaya)*. vol. 3. London: Luzac.

Hughes, Ernest R., and K. Hughes. 1950. *Religion in China*. London: Hutchinson.

Hurvitz, Leon. 1976. *Scripture of the Lotus Blossom of the Fine Dharma*. New York: Columbia University Press.

Nanamoli [formerly Osborne Moore], trans. 1972. *The Life of the Buddha as It Appears in the Pali Canon, the Oldest Authentic Record*. Kandy: Buddhist Publication Society Inc.

Nhat Hanh, Thich. 1988. *The Heart of Understanding: Commentaries on the Prajnaparamita Heart Sutra*. Berkeley: Parallax Press.

Nielsen, N.C., et al., eds. 1993. *Religions of the World*. 3rd ed. New York: St Martin's Press.

Paul, Diana Y., ed. 1979. *Women in Buddhism: Images of the Feminine in Mahayana Tradition*. Berkeley: Asian Humanities Press.

Rhi, Ki-Yong. 1977. "Wonhyo and His Thought." In Chai-Shin Yu, ed., *Korean and Asian Religious Tradition*, 197–207. Toronto: Korean and Related Studies Press.

Rhys Davids, Caroline A. 1964. *Psalms of the Early Buddhists*. vol. 1 (Psalms of Sisters). London: Luzac, for the Pali Text Society.

Rhys Davids, Thomas W., trans. 1881. *Buddhist Sutras*. In F. Max Müller, ed., *Sacred Books of the East*, 11. Oxford: Clarendon Press.

Robinson, Richard H. 1959. "Buddhism: In China and Japan." In R.C. Zaehner, ed., *The Concise Encyclopedia of Living Faiths*, 321–47. London: Joseph.

Sivaraksa, Sulak, *Challenges to Governance in Southeast Asia*, http://www.sulak-sivaraksa.org/en/index.php?option=com_content&task=view&id=75&Itemid=103 accessed 1 February 2013.

Suzuki, D.T. 1991. *An Introduction to Zen Buddhism*. New York: Grove Press.

Takeuchi, Yoshinori. 1987. "Nishida Kitaro." In Mircea Eliade, ed., *The Encyclopedia of Religion* 10: 456–7. New York: Macmillan.

Tsunoda, Ryusaku. 1958. *Sources of Japanese Tradition*. New York: Columbia University Press.

Yampolsky, Philip, trans. 1976. *The Platform Sutra of the Sixth Patriarch*. New York: Columbia University Press.

9 Sikh Traditions

Pashaura Singh

Traditions at a Glance

Numbers
25 million around the world.

Distribution
Primarily northern India, especially Punjab, Haryana, and Delhi, with minorities in other provinces of India and many other countries, including Canada, the United States (especially California), and Britain.

Founders and Leaders
Founded by Guru Nanak c. 1500 CE, and developed by a succession of nine other inspired teachers, the last of whom, Guru Gobind Singh, died in 1708.

Deity
The Supreme Being is considered to be One and without form. Guru Nanak refers to the deity as Akal Purakh ("Timeless Person"), Kartar ("Creator"), and Nirankar ("Formless"), among many other names.

Authoritative Texts
The Adi Granth (also known as Guru Granth Sahib) is a compilation of divinely inspired hymns by six Gurus, 15 poet-saints, and 15 Sikh bards; the Dasam Granth, a collection of hymns made in the time of the tenth Guru, is also revered as a secondary scripture.

Noteworthy Teachings
There is One Supreme Reality, never incarnated. In addition to reverence for the Gurus and the sacred scriptures, Sikhs emphasize egalitarianism, tolerance, service to others, and righteous life in this world as the way to ultimate liberation from the cycle of rebirth.

"Sikh" is a Punjabi word meaning "disciple." People who identify themselves as Sikhs are disciples of **Akal Purakh** ("Timeless Being," God), the 10 Sikh **Gurus**, and the sacred scripture called the **Adi Granth** ("Original Book"). The youngest of India's Indigenous religions, Sikhism emerged in the Punjab approximately five centuries ago and quickly distinguished itself from the region's other religious traditions by its preference for active engagement with the world rather than ascetic renunciation.

Today the global Sikh population numbers approximately 25 million, of whom more than 20 million live in India, mainly in Punjab. Sikhs make up only about 2 per cent of the country's 1 billion people, but their contributions to its political and economic life are significant. The rest of the world's Sikhs are part of a global diaspora that includes substantial communities in Southeast Asia, Australia, New Zealand, East Africa, Britain, and North America.

Overview

The religious environment of the fifteenth-century Punjab was suffused with the thought of the North Indian **Sants**. The founder of Sikhism, Guru Nanak (1469–1539), shared both the mystic and the iconoclastic tendencies of "poet-saints" such as Kabir, Ravidas, and Namdev. Nevertheless, he declared his independence from the prevailing thought forms and sought to kindle the fire of independence in his disciples.

The foundation of the Sikh tradition was Nanak's belief in the possibility of achieving spiritual liberation in a single lifetime through meditation on the divine Name (***nam***), the constant presence

← Entering the Darbar Sahib (Golden Temple) in Amritsar (Ashok Sinha / Getty Images).

of Akal Purakh in the heart, and the living of an ethical life in the world. The interaction of this belief with two environmental factors—the rural base of Punjabi society and the historical circumstances of the period during which Nanak's successors built on the foundations he laid—determined the historical development of Sikhism.

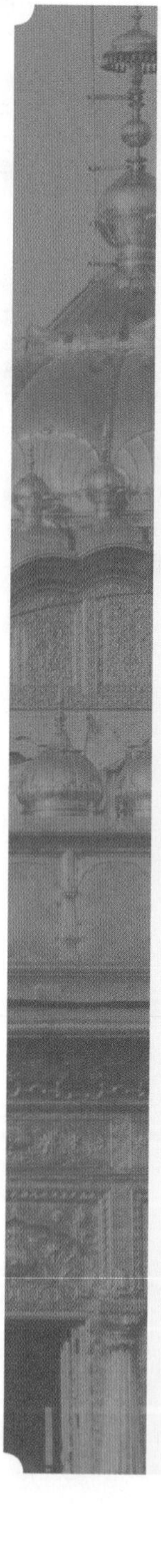

Timeline

1469	Birth of Guru Nanak, the founder of the Sikh tradition
1499	Guru Nanak's mystical experience
1519	Establishment of the first Sikh community at Kartarpur
1539	Guru Nanak is succeeded by Guru Angad
1577	Guru Ram Das establishes the town of Ramdaspur (Amritsar)
1604	The Adi Granth is compiled under Guru Arjan's supervision
1606	Guru Arjan's martyrdom on the orders of Emperor Jahangir
1675	Guru Tegh Bahadur's martyrdom on the orders of Emperor Aurangzeb
1699	Guru Gobind Singh organizes the Khalsa
1708	The succession of human Gurus ends with the death of Guru Gobind Singh; from now on the Guru is the scripture, known as Guru Granth Sahib
1765	Sikhs capture Lahore
1799	Punjab united under Maharaja Ranjit Singh
1849	Annexation of the Punjab by the British
1865	Publication of the first printed edition of the Guru Granth Sahib
1873	Singh Sabha movement is established
1892	Singh Sabha establishes Khalsa College in Amritsar
1920	Shiromani Gurdwara Prabandhak Committee (SGPC) is established
1925	Sikh Gurdwara Act gives the SGPC legal authority over all gurdwaras
1947	Punjab is partitioned between India and Pakistan
1973	The Sikh political party, the Akali Dal, passes the Anandpur Sahib Resolution, demanding greater autonomy for all Indian states; relations with the central government become increasingly strained
1984	Indian army attacks the Golden Temple and other gurdwaras in the Punjab
1999	Sikhs celebrate the tri-centenary of the Khalsa
2004	Manmohan Singh is elected the first Sikh prime minister of India
2008	Tri-centenary celebration of the installation as Guru of the Guru Granth Sahib
2010	Tri-centenary celebration of Sikh rule established by Banda Singh Bahadur in 1710
2012	Indian Parliament passes the Anand Marriage (Amendment) Act, 2012 to register Sikh marriages

The name "Punjab" ("five waters") refers to the five tributaries of the Indus river that define the region. Historically, it was a geographical crossroads where the cultures of the Middle East, Central Asia, and India met and through which a series of Muslim invaders made forays into the subcontinent.

Sufi Islam had become established in the Punjab by the eleventh century. By the fifteenth century the Buddhists had disappeared from the region, although a few Jaina ascetics remained. There were also three distinct Hindu communities, devoted to Shiva, Vishnu, and the Goddess, along with a cluster of tantra-influenced yogic sects known collectively as the Nath tradition. This diverse religious universe required the Sikhs to define themselves in an ongoing process of interaction and debate.

Guru Nanak

Guru Nanak was born in 1469 to an upper-caste professional family at Talwandi (Nanakana Sahib), not far from what is now Lahore, Pakistan. By then the Punjab had been under Muslim control for more than 200 years. When the Mughal Emperor Babur (1483–1530) came to power, in 1526, Nanak had already established a community of his followers in the village of Kartarpur. For the next two centuries the Sikh tradition evolved in the historical context of the Mughal regime.

Guru Nanak's Mystical Experience

Much of what we know about Guru Nanak comes from hagiographical ***janam-sakhis*** ("birth narratives") that began circulating orally during his lifetime. His life may be divided into three distinct phases: an early contemplative period; a mystic enlightenment followed by years of pilgrimage; and a conclusion in which he established the first Sikh community.

Employed as a steward by a Muslim nobleman, the young Nanak spent the beginning and end of each day absorbed in meditation and devotional singing (***kirtan***). Early one morning, while he was bathing in the Vein River, he disappeared without a trace. Three days later he stepped out of the water and proclaimed: "There is no Hindu, there is no Muslim."

The significance of this statement becomes clear in the context of a religious culture divided between the Islamic and Hindu traditions. Nanak emphasized the common humanity underlying the external divisions. After his immersion in the waters—a metaphor of dissolution, transformation, and spiritual perfection—Nanak was ready to proclaim a new vision. One of his own hymns describes his experience:

> I was a minstrel out of work; the Lord assigned me the task of singing the Divine Word day and night. He summoned me to his Court and bestowed on me the robe of honour for singing his praises. On me he bestowed the Divine Nectar (***amrit***) in a cup, the nectar of his true and holy Name (M1, *Var Majh* 27, Adi Granth / AG 150).[1]

This hymn marks the beginning of Nanak's ministry to preach the message of the divine Name. He was then 30 years of age, had been married for more than a decade, and was the father of two young sons. Yet he left his family to travel to both Hindu and Muslim places of pilgrimage where he tested his ideas in debate with the leaders of different religious persuasions.

Map 9.1 The Punjab

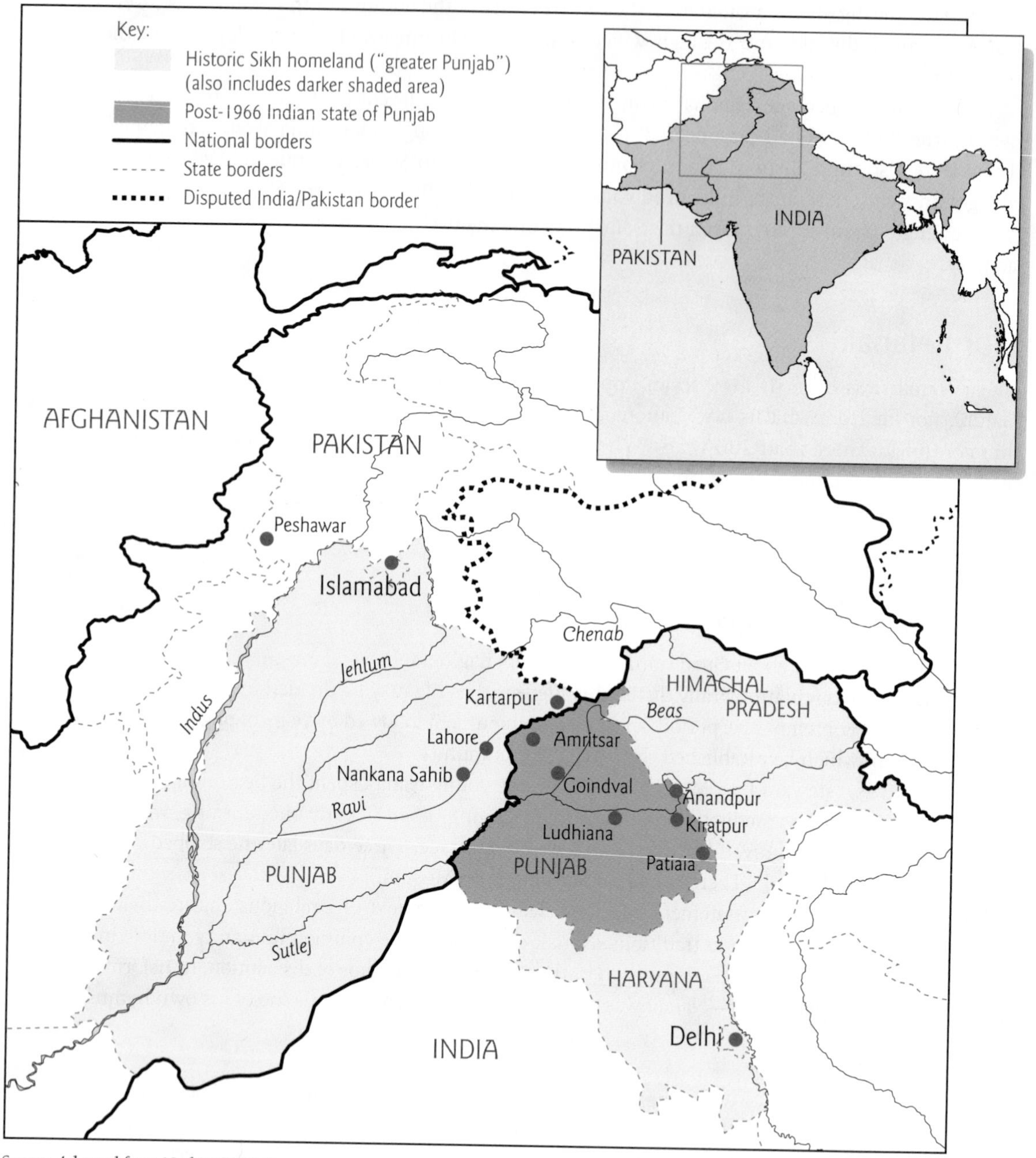

Source: Adapted from Nesbitt 2005: 9.

Foundation of the Sikh Panth

At the end of his travels, Guru Nanak purchased a parcel of land in central Punjab, where he founded the village of Kartarpur in 1519. There he lived for the rest of his life as the "spiritual guide" of a new religious community. His charismatic personality won him many disciples, who received the message of liberation through hymns of unique genius and notable beauty, which became central to Sikh congregational worship. The Kartarpur community formed the nucleus of the Nanak-**Panth** (Path of Nanak). In his role as what the sociologist Max Weber called an "ethical prophet," Nanak called for a decisive break with existing religions and laid the groundwork for a new, rational model of human behaviour based on divine authority.

The authenticity and power of Guru Nanak's message derived from his personal experience of Divine Reality, which gave him a perspective from which to interpret and assess existing traditions. He understood his work to be divinely commissioned, and he demanded obedience of his followers as an ethical duty.

Some of the 974 hymns of Guru Nanak that are preserved in the Adi Granth contrast the beliefs and practices of other traditions with his own. At the same time he recognized "true Hindus" and "true Muslims" and invited them to follow his path of inner spirituality based on ethical values. Understanding that they would grasp his message more easily if it was expressed in the language of their own religious heritage, he reached out to them using concepts from their respective traditions (see Document box).

Dhadhis are traditional singers and musicians who specialize in martial ballads. This *dhadhi* is playing a *sarangi* outside the Golden Temple in Amritsar (© Andrea Maguglianí / Alamy).

Document

Guru Nanak Speaks to Muslims and Hindus

To Muslims:
Make mercy your mosque and devotion your prayer mat,
Righteousness your Qur'an;
Meekness your circumcising, goodness your fasting;
For thus the true Muslim expresses his faith.
Make good works your Ka'bah, take truth your Pir
Compassion your creed and your prayer.
Let service to God be the beads which you tell
And God will exalt you to glory
(M1, *Var Majh*, AG 140–1).

To Hindus:
Make compassion the cotton, contentment the thread,
Continence the knot, and truth the twist.
This is the sacred thread of the soul,
If you possess it, O Brahmin, then place it on me.
It does not break or become soiled with filth.
This can neither be burnt, nor lost.
Blessed are the mortals, O Nanak,
Who wear such a thread round their neck
(M1, *Var Asa*, AG 471).

Guru Nanak's belief that "one should live on what one has earned through hard work and share with others the fruit of one's exertion" (AG 1245) was reflected in the Kartarpur community. Members supported themselves through agricultural work and shared what they earned through the institution of the **langar**, the communal meal that is offered to everyone attending the **gurdwara** (the Sikh place of worship) and is prepared as a community service by members of the congregation (**sangat**). As established by Guru Nanak, the *langar* tradition requires people of all castes and conditions to sit side-by-side in status-free rows—female next to male, socially high next to socially low, ritually pure next to ritually impure—and share the same food. This was the first practical expression of his mission to reform society. Promoting community service, egalitarianism, and belonging, the *langar* marked a major step in the definition of a distinctive Sikh identity.

Finally, before his death in 1539, Guru Nanak created the institution of the Guru. Bypassing his own son Sri Chand, an ascetic who had renounced the life in the world that Sikhism embraced, he chose his disciple Lehna as his successor, renamed him Angad ("my own limb"), and bowed before him, becoming a disciple himself. In this act of humility, Guru Nanak clearly asserted the primacy of the message over the messenger, gave the office of Guru charismatic authority, and established that the Guru is "one," whatever form the occupant of the office might take.

The Ten Gurus

The 62 "couplets" or "stanzas" composed by Guru Angad throw light on the historical situation of the Panth during his period and mark the doctrinal boundaries of the Sikh faith in strict conformity with Guru Nanak's message. He also refined the **Gurmukhi** ("from the Guru's mouth") script in which the Guru's hymns were recorded (the original script was a version of the business shorthand that Guru Nanak had used as a young man). The use of this script signalled the early Sikhs' rejection of the hegemonic authority attributed to Sanskrit, Arabic, and Persian by scholars of the period while reinforcing the Sikhs' distinct identity. In fact, language has been the single

Document

Guru Nanak on Women

Guru Nanak spoke out against the inferior position assigned to women in Punjabi society, as the following verse from his Asa Ki Var *("Ballad in the Asa mode") shows:*

From women born, shaped in the womb,
To woman betrothed and wed;
We are bound to women by ties of affection,
On women man's future depends.
If one woman dies he seeks another;
With a woman he orders his life.
Why then should one speak evil of women,
They who give birth to kings?
Women also are born from women;
None takes birth except from a woman.
Only the True One [Akal Purakh/God], Nanak [Guru Nanak often addresses himself],
needs no help from a woman.
Blessed are they, both men and women,
Who endlessly praise their Lord.
Blessed are they in the True One's court,
There shall their faces shine
(M1, Var Asa, AG 473; McLeod 1997: 241–2).

Langar at a gurdwara in Siliguri, India (© RUPAK DE CHOWDHURI / Reuters / Corbis).

most important factor in the preservation of the Sikh cultural heritage. The idea that spiritual truth could be inscribed in their own language was empowering for Punjabis.

The third Guru, Amar Das (1479–1574), introduced a variety of institutional innovations that strengthened the unity of the Panth. In addition to founding the town of Goindval, he established two annual festivals (Divali and Baisakhi) that provided regular opportunities for the growing community to get together; introduced a system of 22 *manjis* (seats of authority) as bases for missionaries seeking converts, and oversaw the preparation of the Goindval **pothis** ("volumes"): the initial collection of the compositions of the first three Gurus and some of the medieval poet-saints. As the geographical base of the Panth expanded, missionaries needed copies of the **bani** ("divine Word") that they could carry with them, and growing numbers of Sikhs needed a common frame of reference for communal worship. Thus Guru Amar Das had scribes make copies of the hymns for distribution.

The reforms that Guru Amar Das instituted regarding women were perhaps even more significant. He abolished both the wearing of the veil and the practice of **sati**, permitted widows to remarry, appointed women as missionaries (roughly half of the original 22 *manjis* were held by women) and gave all Sikh women equal rights with men to conduct prayers and other congregational ceremonies.

These early steps speak of the practical wisdom of the second- and third-generation Sikhs, who had to find ways to convey Guru Nanak's message without the benefit of direct emotional experience. In every religious tradition, translation into a standard written form and objectification in rituals and ceremonies become imperative as the gap separating new converts from the founder and original disciples widens.

The fourth Guru, Ram Das (1534–81), established the town that would come to be known as Amritsar ("nectar of immortality") and ordered the construction of a large pool there. The fact that the Panth was equal to such complex projects points to the support that Guru Nanak's message had attracted in just a few decades. In addition, Guru Ram Das contributed 679 new hymns to Sikh scripture, and expanded the number of melodies (**ragas**) specified for their singing from 19 to 30. The musicality and emotional appeal of his hymns had a tremendous impact, and the liturgical requirement to sing as well as recite the sacred Word contributed significantly to Sikhs' self-image as a distinct community. Indeed, the process of distinguishing between "us" and "them" was effectively completed under Guru Ram Das, who proclaimed the "loyal Sikhs of the Gurus (**gursikhs**)" to be spiritually greater than the "**Bhagats**, Sants, and Sadhs" (AG 649).

It was the fifth Guru, Arjan (1563–1606), who built the Darbar Sahib ("Divine Court," also known as Harimandir Sahib and, later, the Golden Temple) in Amritsar: surrounded by the sacred pool, it remains the central symbol of the Sikh faith to this day. He also organized the scriptural corpus he had inherited into the Adi Granth, the definitive statement of Sikhism.

By the mid-seventeenth century, a Persian author was able to comment that "there were not many cities in the inhabited countries where some Sikhs were not to be found." So significant was the growth of Sikhism that it attracted the attention of the Mughal authorities. The fact that, ethnically, the majority of Sikhs were Jats—agriculturalists with distinctly martial cultural traditions—would play a significant role in the community's relationship with those authorities.

Rise of Sikh–Mughal Conflict

To a large extent, the peaceful growth of the Panth through the sixteenth century can be attributed to the liberal policy of Emperor Akbar (r. 1556–1605). Within eight months of Akbar's death, however, Guru Arjan himself was dead, executed by order of the new emperor, Jahangir (r. 1605–28).

Document

Bhai Gurdas on the Gursikh

Arising at the ambrosial hour the Gursikh bathes in the sacred pool.
Having chanted the Guru's divine Words his thoughts then turn to the *dharamsala*.
Proceeding there he joins the fellowship and hears with love the Guru's sacred words (*gurbani*).
All doubts are driven far away as devotedly he serves his fellow Gursikhs.
By honest labour he performs duty's calling, and from what it yields distributes food.
Giving it first to other Gursikhs and then feeding himself upon what remains.
Light has shown in the dark age of the Kaliyug, the Guru a disciple and the disciple a Guru.
This is the highway which the *Gurmukh* (one oriented toward the Guru) treads!

(*Varan Bhai Gurdas* 40: 11; McLeod 2003: 33).

Document

Guru Arjan's *Mundavani*: The Epilogue of the Guru Granth Sahib

In this dish (sacred scripture) three things are mingled—truth, contentment, deep reflection.
With them mixed the blessed Name, its nectar sweet sustaining all.
They who eat with lingering joy shall know the truth, their souls set free.
They who taste will make this food their constant fare for evermore.
Darkness reigns yet they who trust the all-fulfilling grace divine;
Find beyond this sunless world your all-pervading light.
(AG 1428; McLeod 1997: 295).

This "first martyrdom" became the decisive factor in the crystallization of the Sikh Panth, pushing the community in the direction of separatism and militancy.

The sixth Guru, Hargobind (1595–1644), signalled this new direction when, at his investiture, he donned two swords, one symbolizing temporal (*miri*) and the other spiritual (*piri*) authority. Another symbol of temporal authority was Hargobind's construction, facing the Darbar Sahib, of

Bathing in the Pool of Nectar (© Raghu Rai / Magnum Photos).

the Akal Takhat ("Throne of the Timeless Being"), the first of an eventual five "thrones" of religious authority. Under his leadership the Panth took up arms to defend itself against Mughal hostility. But this new martial orientation did not mean that the Sikhs had abandoned their spiritual base. As Bhai Gurdas explained, the Guru was simply "hedging the orchard of the Sikh faith with the hardy and thorny *kikar* tree." Relations with the Mughal authorities eased under the seventh and eighth Gurus, Har Rai (1630–61) and Harkrishan (1655–64), although the Gurus kept a regular force of horsemen. But the increasing strength of Sikhism under the ninth Guru once again attracted Mughal attention in the 1670s. Guru Tegh Bahadur (1621–75) encouraged the Sikhs to be fearless in their pursuit of a just society: "He who holds none in fear, nor is afraid of anyone, is acknowledged as a man of true wisdom" (AG 1427). In so doing, he posed a direct challenge to Aurangzeb, who had imposed Islamic laws and taxes, and ordered the replacement of Hindu temples with mosques. Guru Tegh Bahadur was summoned to Delhi, and when he refused to embrace Islam he was publicly executed on 11 November 1675. If the martyrdom of Guru Arjan had helped to bring the Panth together, this second martyrdom helped to make human rights and freedom of conscience central to its identity.

The Khalsa

Tradition holds that the Sikhs who were present at Guru Tegh Bahadur's execution concealed their identity for fear of meeting a similar fate. For this reason the tenth Guru, Gobind Singh, resolved to impose on Sikhs an outward form that would make them instantly recognizable. On **Baisakhi** Day 1699 he created the **Khalsa** ("pure"), an order of loyal Sikhs bound by a common identity and discipline (***rahit***). The nucleus of the new order were the "Cherished Five" (***Panj Piare***) who were the first to respond to his call for volunteers. To this day, the Khalsa initiation ceremony follows the same pattern: initiates drink sweet "nectar" (***amrit***) that has been stirred with a two-edged sword and sanctified by the recitation of five prayers.

The Khalsa

Three aspects of the Khalsa are particularly significant. First, in undergoing the *amrit* ceremony, the Khalsa initiates were "reborn" as spiritual children of Guru Gobind Singh and his wife, Sahib Kaur, and given new surnames: *Singh* ("lion") for men and *Kaur* ("princess") for women. This collective identity gave Khalsa members a powerful sense of belonging. Second, the Guru himself received the nectar of the double-edged sword from the hands of the Cherished Five. In so doing, he symbolically transferred his spiritual authority to them, paving the way for the termination of the office he occupied as a human Guru.

Finally, it was at the inauguration of the Khalsa that Guru Gobind Singh delivered the nucleus of what would become the order's *Rahit* ("Code of Conduct"). To ensure that Khalsa members would never seek to conceal their identity as Sikhs, he made five physical symbols mandatory:

1. *Kes*, unshorn hair, symbolizing spirituality and saintliness;
2. *Kangha*, a wooden comb, signifying order and discipline in life;
3. *Kirpan*, a miniature sword, symbolizing divine grace, dignity, and courage;
4. *Kara*, a steel "wrist-ring," signifying responsibility and allegiance to the Guru; and
5. *Kachh*, a pair of short breeches, symbolizing moral restraint.

Document

On Martyrdom

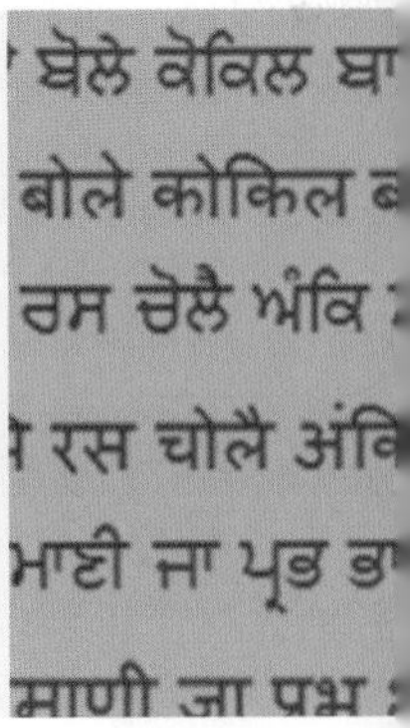

These loyal members of the Khalsa who gave their heads for their faith; who were hacked limb from limb, scalped, broken on the wheel, or sawn asunder, who sacrificed their lives for the protection of hallowed gurdwaras never forsaking their faith; and who were steadfast in their loyalty to the uncut hair of the true Sikh: reflect on their merits, O Khalsa, and call on God, saying, *Vahiguru!* (*Ardas*; McLeod 1984: 104).

Known (from their Punjabi names) as the **Five Ks** (*Panj Kakke*), these outward symbols of the divine Word imply a direct correlation between *bani* ("divine utterance") and *bana* ("Khalsa dress"). Every morning, in putting on those symbols (as well as the turban, in the case of male Sikhs) while reciting prayers, Khalsa Sikhs dress themselves in the word of God; their minds are purified and inspired, and their bodies are girded to do battle with the day's temptations. Four sins are specifically prohibited: cutting the hair, using tobacco (this injunction was later expanded to include all intoxicants), committing adultery, and eating meat that has not come from an animal killed with a single blow.

The launch of the Khalsa was the culmination of Sikhism's formative period, but it was only one of the major reforms instituted by Guru Gobind Singh. After adding a collection of the works of Guru Tegh Bahadur to the Adi Granth, he closed the Sikh canon, and before his death in 1708 he brought to an end the succession of human Gurus. Thereafter, the authority of the Guru would be invested not in an individual but in the scripture (Guru-Granth) and the corporate community (Guru-Panth).

Crystallization

The term "crystallization" comes from Wilfred Cantwell Smith, who identified several stages in the development of a religious tradition. The process begins with the vision of a mystic whose preaching attracts followers and continues with the organization of a community, the positing of an intellectual ideal of that community, and the development of its institutions. Smith maintains that in the case of Sikhism the last two stages were reached under the fifth Guru, Arjan, and the tenth, Gobind Singh. Of course the crystallization process continues as the community responds to changing conditions.

The Sacred Scriptures

The Adi Granth is the primary scripture of the Sikhs, comprising the hymns of the first five Gurus and the ninth, plus material by four bards, 11 Bhatts ("court poets"), and 15 Bhagats ("devotees" of the Sant, Sufi, and Bhakti traditions, including the poets Kabir, Namdev, Ravidas, and Shaikh Farid): a total of 36 contributors ranging historically from the twelfth century to the seventeenth. The standard text contains 1,430 pages, and every copy has exactly the same material on each page.

Document

From the Sacred Writings of the Sikhs

Guru Nanak exalts the divine Name:

If in this life I should live to eternity, nourished by nothing save air;
If I should dwell in the darkest of dungeons, sense never resting in sleep;
Yet must your glory transcend all my striving; no words can encompass the Name.

(*Refrain*) He who is truly the Spirit Eternal, immanent, blissful serene;
Only by grace can we learn of our Master, only by grace can we tell.

If I were slain and my body dismembered, pressed in a hand-mill and ground;
If I were burnt in a fire all-consuming, mingled with ashes and dust;
Yet must your glory transcend all my striving, no words can encompass the Name.
If as a bird I could soar to the heavens, a hundred such realms in my reach;
If I could change so that none might perceive me and live without food, without drink;
Yet must your glory transcend all my striving; no words can encompass the Name.
If I could read with the eye of intelligence paper of infinite weight;
If I could with the winds everlasting, pens dipped in oceans of ink;
Yet must your glory transcend all my striving; no words can encompass the Name
(M1, *Siri Ragu* 2, AG 14–15; McLeod 1984: 41).

The tenth Guru, Gobind Singh, praises the sword. This passage, often repeated at Sikh functions, now serves as the anthem of the Khalsa:

Reverently I salute the Sword with affection and devotion.
Grant, I pray, your divine assistance that this book may be brought to completion.
Thee I invoke, All-conquering Sword, Destroyer of evil, Ornament of the brave.
Powerful your arm and radiant your glory, your splendour as dazzling as the brightness of the sun.
Joy of the devout and Scourge of the wicked, Vanquisher of sin, I seek your protection.
Hail to the world's Creator and Sustainer, my invincible Protector of the Sword!
(*Bachitar Natak*, Dasam Granth, 39; McLeod 1984: 58).

The second sacred collection, the **Dasam Granth**, dates from the 1690s and is attributed to the tenth (*dasam*) Guru, Gobind Singh. Eighteenth-century revisions added his *Zafarnama* ("Letter of Victory"; see p. 458) and fixed the sequence of its contents, which include devotional texts, autobiographical works, miscellaneous writings, mythical narratives, and popular anecdotes.

The third category of sacred literature consists of works by Bhai ("Brother") Gurdas (c. 1558–1637) and Bhai Nand Lal Goya (1633–1715), which are officially approved for singing in the gurdwara. The last category of Sikh literature is made up of three distinct genres. The *janam-sakhis* ("birth narratives") date from the late sixteenth century but are based on earlier oral traditions. The *rahit-namas* ("manuals of code of conduct") provide rare insight into the evolution of the Khalsa code in the eighteenth and nineteenth centuries. And the *gur-bilas* ("splendour of the Guru") literature praises the mighty deeds of the two great warrior Gurus, Hargobind and Gobind Singh, in particular.

Document

Bhai Gurdas on External Religious Observance

If bathing at *tiraths* ["pilgrimage centres"] procures liberation, frogs, for sure, must be saved;
And likewise the banyan, with dangling tresses, if growing hair long sets one free.
If the need can be served by roaming unclad the deer of the forest must surely be pious;
So too the ass which rolls in the dust if limbs smeared with ashes can purchase salvation.
Saved are the cattle, mute in the fields, if silence produces deliverance.
Only the Guru can bring us salvation; only the Guru can set a man free (*Varan Bhai Gurdas*, 36:14; McLeod 1984: 67).

Finally, it is important to emphasize that the Adi Granth is inextricably embedded in Sikh daily life. It is not merely to be read and understood, but to be interiorized, to be practised and lived.

Sikh Doctrine

The primary source of Sikh doctrine is the Adi Granth. Its first words are Guru Nanak's invocation of One God (*1-Oankar*) in the **Mul Mantar** ("Seed Formula"). This succinct expression of the nature of the Ultimate Reality is the fundamental statement of Sikh belief:

> There is One ("1") Supreme Being, the Eternal Reality, the Creator, without fear and devoid of enmity, immortal, never incarnated, self-existent, known by grace through the Guru. The Eternal One, from the beginning, through all time, present now, the Everlasting Reality (AG 1).

By beginning with "One" (the original Punjabi text uses the numeral rather than the word), Guru Nanak emphasizes the singularity of the divine; as he put it in a later hymn, the Supreme Being has "no relatives, no mother, no father, no wife, no son, no rival who may become a potential contender" (AG 597). At the same time he draws attention to the unity of Akal Purakh, the Eternal One, the source and the goal of all that exists. The Mul Mantar illuminates the Sikh understanding of a Divine Reality that is at once transcendent and immanent, a personal God of grace for his humblest devotee. The vital expression of the One is through the many, through the infinite plurality of creation. This understanding of the One distinguishes the Sikh interpretation of monotheism from its Abrahamic counterparts. The Gurus fiercely opposed any anthropomorphic conception of the divine. Nevertheless, Akal Purakh watches over the universe as lovingly as any parent. Simultaneously "Father, Mother, Friend, and Brother" (AG 268), God is without gender.

In general, then, Sikhs worship a transcendent, non-incarnate, universal God who is nevertheless partly embodied in the divine Name (*nam*) as well as the collective Words (*bani*) and persons of the Gurus. Only through personal experience can he be truly known.

Creation

According to Guru Nanak's cosmology hymn, the universe was brought into being by the divine order, will, or command (**hukam**). This *hukam* is an all-embracing principle, a revelation of the nature of God:

> For endless eons, there was only darkness.
> Nothing except the divine order existed.
> No day or night, no moon or sun.
> The Creator alone was absorbed in a primal
> state of contemplation . . .
> When the Creator so willed, creation came
> into being . . .
> The Un-manifest One revealed itself in the
> Creation.
> (AG 1035–6).

In Sikh cosmology, the world is divinely inspired, the place that gives human beings the opportunity to perform their duty and achieve union with Akal Purakh.

The Value of Human Life

For Guru Nanak, human life is worth a "diamond," but its value drops to a "farthing" if we do not realize our true spiritual nature (AG 156):

> One is blessed with the rarest opportunity of the human birth through the grace of the Guru. One's mind and body become dyed deep red (with the love of the divine Name) if one is able to win the approval of the True Guru (AG 751).

For Guru Arjan, the human being is the epitome of Creation: "All other creation is subject to you, O man/woman! You reign supreme on this earth" (AG 374). Like Guru Nanak, he emphasizes the opportunity that human life offers: "Precious this life you receive as a human, with it the chance to find the Lord" (AG 15). But those who seek the divine beloved while participating in the delights of the world are rare.

Karam, Sansar, and Divine Grace

The notions of **karam** (karma, "action," the principle of moral cause and effect) and ***sansar*** (*samsara*, "reincarnation") are fundamental to all religious traditions originating in India. In Sikh doctrine, however, karam is not an inexorable, impersonal law. Rather, it is subject to the "divine order" (hukam), an all-embracing higher principle that is the sum total of all divinely instituted laws. Thus karam can be overridden in the name of justice by Akal Purakh's omnipotent grace.

Divine Revelation

Guru Nanak used three key terms to describe the nature of divine revelation: *nam* ("divine Name"), **shabad** ("divine Word"), and *guru* ("divine Preceptor"). *Nam* refers to the divine presence that is manifest everywhere, though most people fail to perceive it because of the self-centred desire for personal gratification. Because this self-centredness (**haumai**, meaning "I, I" or "me, mine") separates us from Akal Purakh, we continue to suffer within the cycle of rebirth. Yet Akal Purakh takes pity on human suffering, and therefore he reveals himself through the Guru in the form of the *shabad* ("divine Word"): the utterance that awakens those capable of hearing it to the reality of the divine Name that is immanent in everything.

Remembering the Divine Name

Under the influence of *haumai*, humans become so attached to worldly pleasures that they forget the divine Name and waste their lives in evil and suffering. To achieve spiritual liberation, we must transcend that influence by adopting the strictly interior discipline of **nam-simaran**, "remembering the divine Name." There are three levels to this discipline: repetition of a sacred word (usually *Vahiguru*, "Praise to the Eternal Guru"), devotional singing, and sophisticated meditation on the nature of Akal Purakh. The first and the third levels are undertaken in private, while the second is a public, communal activity. As *nam-simaran* gradually brings practitioners into harmony with the divine order (*hukam*), blissful equanimity grows until the spirit reaches the "realm of Truth" and attains mystical union with Akal Purakh.

The primacy of divine grace over personal effort is fundamental to Guru Nanak's theology. Yet personal effort is imperative: "With your own hands carve out your own destiny" (AG 474). By teaching his followers to see their own "free" will as part of Akal Purakh's will, Guru Nanak encouraged them to create their own destinies. The necessity of balance between meditative worship and righteous life in the world is summed up in the triple commandment to earn one's living through honest labour, adore the divine Name, and share the fruits of one's labour with others.

Four Notions of Guruship

In Indic traditions the guru is a human teacher who communicates divine knowledge and guides disciples along the path to liberation. In Sikhism, however, the term encompasses four types of spiritual authority: the eternal Guru, the personal Guru, Guru-Granth, and Guru-Panth.

God as Guru

Guru Nanak uses the term "Guru" to refer to Akal Purakh himself, to the voice of Akal Purakh, and to the Word, the Truth of Akal Purakh. To experience the eternal Guru is to experience divine guidance. Guru Nanak himself acknowledges Akal Purakh as his Guru: "He who is the infinite, supreme God is the Guru whom Nanak has met" (AG 599). In Sikh usage, therefore, the Guru is the voice of Akal Purakh, mystically uttered within the human heart, mind, and soul (*man*). Akal Purakh is often characterized as *Nirankar*, "the One without Form," and Guru Arjan explicitly states that he is not to be anthropomorphized: "Do not believe that he is in the form of a human being" (AG 895).

Sikhs evoke the absolute knowledge and power of the divine Name by chanting "*Vahiguru! Vahiguru!*" ("Hail the Guru"). The sound vibrations of this phrase are believed to be supremely powerful. In addition, the Sikh scripture often uses Hindu and Muslim names for God. Hindu (particularly Vaishnava) names such as Ram, Hari, and Govind, and Muslim names such as Allah,

Karim, and Sahib, express different aspects of Akal Purakh, as Guru Nanak recognized (AG 1168). And Guru Arjan provided a comprehensive list of the names from various contemporary religious traditions associated with different attributes of God (AG 1083). In the Sikh context, however, these names acquire meaning only when they are viewed through the lens of the Mul Mantar. Most important, the "truth of the Name" is a reality that lies beyond any name.

The Teacher as Guru

The personal Guru is the channel through which the voice of Akal Purakh becomes audible. Nanak became the embodiment of the eternal Guru only when he received the divine Word and conveyed it to his disciples. The same voice spoke through each of his successors. In keeping with the theory of spiritual succession known as "the unity of the office of the Guru," there was no difference between the founder and his successors: all represented the same fire, passed from one torch to the next. Similarly in the Adi Granth, the compositions of six individual Gurus are all signed "Nanak." The actual composers are identified by the code word *Mahala*, "King" with an appropriate number. Thus the hymns labelled "Mahala 1" (M 1) are by Guru Nanak, while those labelled M 2, 3, 4, 5, and 9 are by Gurus Angad, Amar Das, Ram Das, Arjan, and Tegh Bahadur, respectively.

The Scripture as Guru

Sikhs normally refer to the Adi Granth as the Guru Granth Sahib ("Honourable Scripture Guru"). In so doing, they acknowledge their faith in it as the successor to Guru Gobind Singh, with the same status, authority, and functions as any of the 10 human Gurus. The perennial source of divine guidance for Sikhs, it is treated with the most profound respect.

The Community as Guru

The phrase "Guru-Panth" is used in two senses: as "the Panth of the Guru" it means the Sikh community; as "the Panth as the Guru," it refers to the idea that the Guru is mystically present in the congregation. Although the Khalsa has always claimed to speak authoritatively on behalf of the whole Panth, at times non-Khalsa Sikhs have interpreted the Guru-Panth doctrine as conferring authority on the broader community. In practice, consensus is achieved by following democratic traditions.

Sikh Ethics

The Adi Granth opens with a composition of Guru Nanak's known as the *Japji*. In it the Guru asks how Truth is to be attained, and answers thus: "Submit to the divine Order (*hukam*), walk in its way" (AG 1). In other words, Truth is attained not by intellectual effort, but by personal commitment. To know Truth, one must live it. Indeed, truthful conduct is at the heart of Guru Nanak's message. Cultivating wisdom, contentment, justice, humility, truthfulness, temperance, love, forgiveness, charity, purity, and reverence of Akal Purakh promotes socially responsible living, hard work, and sharing.

The *Panj Piare* (Cherished Five) take part in a procession to celebrate the 347th birth anniversary of Guru Gobind Singh, in Bhopal, India, 16 January 2013 (© SANJEEV GUPTA / epa / Corbis).

Service

The key to a righteous life is to render service to others. Such service must be voluntary and undertaken without any desire for self-glorification. Nor should those who give aid sit in judgment on those who receive it. The Sikh Prayer (*Ardas*, "Petition") emphasizes the importance of "seeing but not judging." The ideals are social equality and human brotherhood. Therefore discrimination based on caste or gender is expressly rejected. The Gurus also emphasized the importance of optimism in the face of adversity.

Justice

Guru Nanak regarded the violation of human rights as a serious moral offence: "To deprive others of their rights must be avoided as scrupulously as Muslims avoid the pork and the Hindus consider beef as a taboo" (AG 141). The use of force is permitted, but only in defence of justice and then only as a last resort. Guru Gobind Singh taught that peaceful negotiation must be tried first. A famous verse from the *Zafarnama* ("Letter of Victory")—a poem addressed to Emperor Aurangzeb after the latter, instead of negotiating, sent his forces against the Sikhs—makes this point explicitly: "When all other methods have been explored and all other means have been tried, . . . then may the sword be used." For the Khalsa, the quest for justice is the primary ethical duty.

Oneness of Humankind and Religion

Sikhism is committed to the ideal of universal brotherhood. In a celebrated passage from his *Akal Ustat* ("Praise of the Immortal One"), Guru Gobind Singh declares that "humankind is one, and all people belong to a single humanity":

> The temple and the mosque are the same, so are the Hindu worship and Muslim prayer. All people are one; it is through error that they appear different. . . . Allah and Abhekh are the same, the Purana and the Qur'an are the same. They are all alike, all the creation of the One (verse 86).

To this day, Sikhs conclude their morning and evening prayers with the words "In thy will, O Lord, may peace and prosperity come to one and all."

Practice

Prayer

Devout Sikhs rise during the "ambrosial hours" (between 3 and 6 a.m.) and begin their daily routine with approximately an hour of devotions, beginning with meditation on the divine Name and continuing with recitation of five prayers, including Guru Nanak's *Japji* ("Honoured Recitation") and Guru Gobind Singh's *Jap Sahib* ("Master Recitation"). Evening prayers are selected from a collection of hymns entitled *Sodar Rahiras* ("Supplication at That Door"), and the *Kirtan Sohila* ("Song of Praise") is recited before retiring for the night. Learnt by heart in childhood and recited from memory every day, these prayers are always available to provide guidance.

Focus

Daily Liturgical Prayers

The Early Morning Order (3–6 a.m.)

1. ***Japji*** ("Honoured Recitation")
2. ***Jap Sahib*** ("Master Recitation")
3. The Ten ***Savayyas*** ("Ten Panegyrics")
4. ***Benati Chaupai*** ("Verses of Petition")
5. ***Anand Sahib*** ("Song of Bliss")

The Evening Prayer

Sodar Rahiras ("Supplication at That Door")

The Bedtime Prayer

Kirtan Sohila ("Song of Praise")

Congregational Worship

In every gurdwara a copy of the Guru Granth Sahib is ceremoniously installed each morning on a cushioned, canopied stand. All who enter the gurdwara are expected to cover their heads, remove their shoes, and bow before the sacred volume by touching their foreheads to the floor. Worshippers sit on the floor, and it is the Punjabi custom for men to sit on the right side of the hall and women on the left, but this is not mandatory.

Sikhism has no ordained priesthood. Instead, every gurdwara has a **granthi** ("reader") who, in addition to reading from the Guru Granth Sahib, takes care of the book and serves as custodian of the gurdwara. Although the office is also open to women, in practice most *granthis* are men.

Worship consists mainly of *kirtan*, led and accompanied by musicians (*ragis*) playing harmoniums and *tabla* drums. Through *kirtan* the devotees attune themselves to the divine Word and vibrate in harmony with it. Many today believe that *kirtan* helps them cope with the obstacles that modern society puts in the way of spiritual life.

At some time during the service, either the *granthi* or a traditional Sikh scholar may deliver a homily based on a particular hymn or scriptural passage. Then all present will join in reciting the *Ardas* prayer. The Sikh understanding of the Adi Granth as living Guru is most evident in the practice known as "taking the Guru's Word" or "seeking a divine command," in which the Guru Granth Sahib is opened at random and the first hymn on the left-hand page is read aloud in its entirety (beginning on the previous page if necessary). In this way the congregation hears the Guru's **Vak**

The *granthi* reads from the Guru Granth Sahib in Yuba City, California (AP Photo / Appeal-Democrat, David Bitton).

("Saying") for that particular moment or occasion. Taken in the morning, the Vak serves as the inspiration for personal meditation throughout the day; taken in the evening, it brings the day to a close with a new perspective on its joys and sorrows. The reading of the Vak is followed by the distribution of **karah prashad**—a sweet, rich paste of flour, sugar, and butter that is "sanctified" by the recitation of prayers during its preparation and by resting next to the scripture during the service and represent the bestowal of divine blessings on those who receive it. At the end of congregational worship everyone shares in the *langar* meal prepared and served by volunteers as part of the community service expected of all Sikhs. This custom is a powerful reminder of the egalitarianism that is so central to Sikhism.

The Annual Festival Cycle

The most important festival is Baisakhi (Vaisakhi) Day, which usually falls on 13 April. Celebrated throughout India as New Year's Day, it has been considered the birthday of the Sikh community ever since the institution of the Khalsa on Baisakhi Day in 1699. Sikhs also celebrate the autumn festival of lights, Divali, as the day when Guru Hargobind was released from prison. These two seasonal festivals were introduced by the third Guru, Amar Das, and Guru Gobind Singh added a third: Hola Mahalla, the day after the Hindu festival of Holi (March/April), is celebrated with military exercises and various athletic and literary contests.

The anniversaries of the births and deaths of the Gurus are marked by the "unbroken reading" of the entire Sikh scripture by a team of readers over a period of roughly 48 hours. The birthdays of

The Golden Temple is illuminated to mark Divali (© MUNISH SHARMA / Reuters / Corbis).

Guru Nanak (usually in November) and Guru Gobind Singh (December–January) and the martyrdom days of Guru Arjan (May–June) and Guru Tegh Bahadur (November–December) in particular are celebrated around the world.

Life-Cycle Rituals

At the centre of every important life-cycle ritual is the Guru Granth Sahib.

Naming a Child

When a child is to be named, family members take the baby to the gurdwara and present *karah prashad* to the Guru Granth Sahib. After various prayers of thanks and a recitation of *Ardas*, the Guru Granth Sahib is opened at random and the first letter of the first composition on the left-hand page is noted; then a name beginning with the same letter is chosen. In this way the child takes his or her identity from the Guru's word. Then a boy is given the second name *Singh* and a girl the second name *Kaur*. *Amrit* is applied to the eyes and head; the infant is given a sip of the sweetened water to drink; and the first five stanzas of Guru Nanak's *Japji* are recited.

Marriage

"They are not said to be husband and wife, who merely sit together. Rather, they alone are called husband and wife who have one soul in two bodies" (AG 788). This proclamation of Guru Amar Das has become the basis of the Sikh view of marriage, which emphasizes the necessity of spiritual compatibility between the spouses. In a traditional society where the family is more important than the individual, the fact that Sikh marriages have traditionally been arranged is not inconsistent with that principle.

To be legal, a Sikh wedding must take place in the presence of the Guru Granth Sahib. The bride and groom circumambulate the sacred scripture four times, once for each of their four vows:

1. to lead an action-oriented life based on righteousness and never to shun obligations of family and society;
2. to maintain reverence and dignity between one another;
3. to keep enthusiasm for life alive in the face of adverse circumstances and to remain detached from worldly attachments; and
4. to cultivate a balanced approach in life, avoiding all extremes.

The circular movement around the scripture symbolizes the cycle of life in which there is no beginning and no end.

Khalsa Initiation

The Khalsa initiation ceremony (***amrit sanskar***) must also take place in the presence of the Guru Granth Sahib. There is no fixed age for initiation: candidates need only be willing and able to accept the Khalsa discipline. Five Khalsa Sikhs, representing the original Cherished Five, conduct the ceremony. Each recites from memory one of the five liturgical prayers while stirring the *amrit* with a double-edged sword.

Document

On Religious Differences

Despite his militancy, Guru Gobind Singh shared Guru Nanak's conviction that religious boundaries are irrelevant to God:

There is no difference between a temple and a mosque, nor between the prayers of a Hindu and a Muslim. Though differences seem to mark and distinguish, all men/women are in reality the same. Gods and demons, celestial beings, men called Muslims and others called Hindus—such differences are trivial, inconsequential, the outward results of locality and dress. With eyes the same, the ears and body, all possessing a common form—all are in fact a single creation, the elements of nature in a uniform blend.

Allah is the same as the God of the Hindus, Puran and Qur'an are the same. All are the same, none is separate; a single form, a single creation (*Akal Ustat*, *Dasam Granth*, 19–20; McLeod 1984: 57).

The novices then drink the *amrit* five times so that their bodies are purified of five vices (lust, anger, greed, attachment, and pride), and five times the *amrit* is sprinkled on their eyes to transform their outlook on life. Finally, the *amrit* is poured on their heads five times, sanctifying their hair so that they will preserve its natural form and listen to the voice of conscience. At each stage of the ceremony, the initiates repeat the words *Vahiguru Ji Ka Khalsa! Vahiguru Ji Ki Fateh!* ("Khalsa belongs to the Wonderful Lord! Victory belongs to the Wonderful Lord!").

Death

A dedicated Sikh welcomes death, for it means the perfecting of his or her union with Akal Purakh and final release from the cycle of rebirth. In India, the body of the deceased is bathed, dressed in new clothes, and placed on a pyre for cremation, after which the ashes are scattered in a nearby stream or river. In the diaspora, family and friends gather at a funeral home with the facilities for cremation. Following devotional singing and eulogy, *Ardas* is offered by the *granthi*. Then the casket is taken to the cremation furnace, usually accompanied by family and friends. While the casket is burning, the congregation recites the late-evening prayer, *Kirtan Sohila*.

In addition, a reading of the entire scripture takes place either at home or in a gurdwara. At the conclusion of the reading, which may take up to ten days to complete, the final prayers are offered in the memory of the deceased.

Differentiation

Encounter with Modernity

The Khalsa spent most of its first century fighting the Mughals and Afghan invaders. Immediately after the death of Guru Gobind Singh, Khalsa Sikhs led by Banda Singh Bahadur took part in a civil war that ended in 1710 with the defeat of the Mughals and the establishment of Sikh rule in Punjab. Although the Mughals returned to power in 1716, in 1799 Ranjit Singh (1780–1839) succeeded in unifying the Punjab and declared himself Maharaja. For the next four decades Sikhs enjoyed more settled political conditions, and with territorial expansion, people of different cultural and religious backgrounds were attracted into the faith.

Although the Maharaja himself was a Khalsa Sikh, his rule was marked by religious diversity within the Panth. Khalsa members realized that they needed the support of those Sikhs who lived as members of the Nanak Panth but did not accept the Khalsa code of conduct. The Khalsa conceded the religious culture of these **Sehaj-dharis** ("gradualists") to be legitimate even though the latter revered Hindu as well as Sikh scriptures and in some cases even worshipped Hindu images.

Sikh Reform Movements

The successors of Maharaja Ranjit Singh could not withstand the advancing British forces. After two Anglo–Sikh wars, in 1846 and 1849, the Sikh kingdom was annexed to the British empire. It was in this context that three reform movements tried to restore a distinct spiritual identity to a people whose religious tradition was just one among a vast array of traditions encompassed within colonial India.

The Nirankari movement sought to purge Sikhism of Hindu influences (especially image worship) and recall Sikhs to the worship of the "formless and invisible God" (*Nirankar*), while the Namdharis emphasized chanting of the divine Name. As the number of his followers grew, the Namdharis' leader, Baba Ram Singh, promoted boycotts as a form of non-violent resistance to the British occupation of the Punjab. After more than 60 of them were executed without trial, the Namdharis came to be seen as political martyrs and forerunners of the twentieth-century Gandhian movement for the independence of India.

The third reform movement, the **Singh Sabha** ("Society of the Singhs"), was established in 1873 and sought to reaffirm Sikh identity in the face of two threats: the casual reversion to Hindu practices under Maharaja Ranjit Singh and the proselytizing efforts not only of the Hindu Arya Samaj, but of Christian missionaries. By the end of the nineteenth century the dominant wing of the Singh Sabha, the Tat ("Pure" or "True") Khalsa, had made the Khalsa tradition the standard of orthodoxy for all Sikhs.

In the twentieth century, the Tat Khalsa reformers contributed to two important legal changes. In 1909 they obtained legal recognition of the distinctive Sikh wedding ritual in the Anand Marriage Act (1909). Then in the 1920s they helped to re-establish direct Khalsa control of the major historical gurdwaras, many of which had fallen into the hands of corrupt "custodians" supported by the British. Inspired by the Tat Khalsa, the Akali movement of the 1920s secured British assent to the Sikh Gurdwara Act (1925), under which control of all gurdwaras passed to the Shiromani Gurdwara Prabandhak Committee (SGPC; "Chief Management Committee of Sikh Shrines"). The Akalis were the forerunners of the modern political party known as the Akali Dal ("army of the immortal").

The SGPC Rahit Manual

Control of the gurdwaras gave the SGPC enormous influence. By 1950 it was the central authority on all questions of religious discipline, and in that year it published the code of conduct called the *Sikh Rahit Maryada*.

Based on the teachings of the Guru Granth Sahib, supplemented with teachings from revered Sikh leaders, the *Sikh Rahit Maryada* enjoins Sikhs to cultivate a pure and pious inner spirituality (*bani*), to adopt the Five Ks as external signs of virtue, and to abstain from the four cardinal sins (hair-cutting, adultery, intoxicants, and the consumption of improperly slaughtered animals). The manual encourages the worship of God and meditation on his name, Khalsa initiation, and attendance at divine services. It also calls on Sikhs to earn an honest living, to share selflessly with the less fortunate, to nurture virtues such as compassion, honesty, generosity, patience, perseverance, and humility, and to avoid superstition, idols, and images.

Not punitive in intent or effect, the *Sikh Rahit Maryada* calls for tolerance of those who stray as well as the *Sehaj-dharis*, assuming that in time they will accept the full Khalsa discipline. The only code of conduct sanctioned by the Akal Takhat, the *Sikh Rahit Maryada* is distributed free of charge by the SGPC, and is now available in Hindi and English for Sikhs living outside their historical homeland.

Variations in Modern Sikhism

The Sikh Panth has never been monolithic or homogeneous, and it continues to encompass a number of variations. The Khalsa itself includes a rigorously observant order called the Nihangs, who are ready to die for their faith at any time. Another group within the Khalsa, the Akhand Kirtani Jatha ("continuous singing of the Sikh scriptures"), follows a special discipline that includes a strictly vegetarian diet and requires that female members wear a small turban.

In recent years the Internet has allowed many groups to claim that they represent the "true" Panth. Of the 25 million Sikhs in the world today, only about 20 per cent are orthodox **Amrit-dharis** ("initiates"). But many other Sikhs follow most of the Khalsa code even though they have not been initiated.

Many Sikhs (the majority in the diaspora) who cut their hair but still use the Khalsa names "Singh" and "Kaur" and do not consider themselves to be "lesser Sikhs" in any way. Finally, there are Khalsa Sikhs—especially in the diaspora—who have committed one or more of the four sins after initiation. Although they are known as "Apostates," that designation is not necessarily permanent: Sikhism recognizes that people may change as they move through different stages in life, and their status within the Panth changes accordingly. In short, there is no single way of being a Sikh.

Cultural Expressions

Social Norms

Guru Nanak's successors shared his belief that the key to liberation lay not in ascetic renunciation but in the life of the householder. To understand family relationships, we must look at the Sikh perspectives on caste and gender. Rejection of caste-based discrimination was a fundamental feature of Sikhism from the beginning, and the *Sikh Rahit Maryada* explicitly states that "No account should be taken of caste" in the selection of a marriage partner. In practice, however, most Sikhs still marry within their own group, though inter-caste marriage is increasing among urban professionals.

In Punjabi society, marriage connects not just two individuals but, more important, two groups of kin. It is in this context that the concept of honour continues to play a significant role in family relationships.

The Role of Women

Despite their egalitarian principles, the Sikh Gurus lived in a traditional patriarchal society, and its values were reflected in their ideas about women. Thus the ideal woman was defined by her conduct in the context of the family as a good daughter, sister, wife, and mother. However, they also expected men to live up to the cultural norms of modesty and honour. There was no tolerance for premarital or extramarital sexual activity, and rape was regarded as a particularly serious violation, for the dishonour and loss of social standing it brought to the families of both the perpetrator and the victim. Furthermore, the rules governing the Khalsa are clearly egalitarian in principle. Candidates for initiation cannot be accepted without their spouses; hence the proportions of male and female initiates are roughly equal. And Khalsa women wear all of the Five Ks.

A number of women are remembered for their contributions to the Panth, some but not all of them sisters, wives, or daughters of the Gurus. Guru Nanak's older sister Nanaki supported his travels, while his wife Sulakhani raised their children during his long absences. Mata Khivi, the wife of the second Guru, made important her contributions to the development of the *langar* tradition. In 1705, when the forces of Guru Gobind Singh had abandoned him in battle Mai Bhago persuaded them to return and fight. And after the Guru's death in 1708, his wife Sundri organized the compilation of the Dasam Granth and issued a number of edicts to Sikh congregations.

In modern times, Bibi Jagir Kaur was twice elected president of the SGPC, in 1999 and 2004. Other exceptional women include the mystic Bibi Nihal Kaur; Bibi Balwant Kaur, who established a gurdwara and a women's group in honour of Bebe Nanaki in Birmingham, England; and Bibi Jasbir Kaur Khalsa, who devoted her life to the promotion of Sikh music and established a Chair for its study at the Punjabi University in Patiala, India. Female musicians often perform in the gurdwaras. Women have also played important roles in the Akhand Kirtani Jatha and the Healthy, Happy, Holy Organization (3HO; now known as Sikh Dharma).

It is true that most Sikh institutions are still dominated by men, and many Sikh women are still subject to patriarchal cultural assumptions. In this they differ little from their counterparts in India's other major religious communities. Even so, Sikh women have been asserting themselves with growing success in recent years.

Music

Sikhism is the only world religion in which the primary medium for the founder's message is song. In specifying the *ragas* to which the hymns were to be sung, Guru Nanak and his successors sought to promote harmony and balance in devotees' minds. Thus *ragas* likely to arouse passions were adapted to produce a gentler effect.

Art

The earliest known paintings of Guru Nanak appear in a *janam-sakhi* from the mid-1600s.The first examples of Sikh graphic art are illuminated scriptures from the late sixteenth century. Sikh scribes followed the Qur'anic tradition of decorating the margins and the opening pages of the text with abstract designs and floral motifs. Both fine and applied arts flourished under the patronage of Maharaja Ranjit

Nineteen Eighty-Four, by The Singh Twins, 1998 (© The Singh Twins: www.singhtwins.co.uk).

Singh. In addition, a distinctive architecture developed at his court. Murals and frescoes depicting major events from Sikh history can still be seen at historic gurdwaras, including the Darbar Sahib.

Two great Sikh artists emerged in the twentieth century. Sobha Singh (1901–86) was skilled in Western oil painting, but he drew his themes from the romantic lore of the Punjab, the Indian epics, and the Sikh tradition; he is particularly well known for his portraits of the Gurus. Kirpal Singh (1923–90) specialized in realistic depictions of episodes from Sikh history, including appalling scenes of battle and martyrdom. A number of Sikh women have also made names as artists. Amrita Shergill (1911–41) has been described as the Frida Kahlo of India. Raised largely in Europe, she studied art in Paris but returned to India in 1934 and explored village life in paintings that have been declared National Art Treasures. Arpana Caur (b. 1954) is a bold modern painter who addresses current issues and events directly. The Singh Twins (b. 1966), born in England, apply styles and techniques of the classic Indian miniature tradition to contemporary themes. Their painting *Nineteen Eighty-Four*, inspired by the storming of the Darbar Sahib, is a powerful reflection not only on the event itself but on the responses it evoked in the Sikh diaspora.[2]

Literature

A rich literary tradition began with the introduction of the Gurmukhi script. The *janam-sakhi* remained the dominant literary genre before the emergence of the twentieth-century novel. The impact of Sikh devotional literature is clear in celebrated early modern authors such as Kahn Singh Nabha (1861–1938), the poet Bhai Vir Singh (1872–1957), and Mohan Singh Vaid (1881–1936), who wrote stories, novels, and plays as well as non-fiction. All three emphasized optimism, determination, faith, and love towards fellow human beings. Writers played a leadership role in the Singh Sabha reform movement. Although much contemporary Punjabi literature reflects Western influences, Sikh devotional literature has continued to inspire more recent writers such as Harinder Singh Mehboob (1937–2010).

Interaction and Adaptation

Twentieth-Century India

Doctrinal Authority

By 1950, as we have seen, the SGPC had become the principal authority in both religious and political affairs for the worldwide Sikh community. Although it has often been challenged by Sikhs outside the Punjab, the SGPC claims to speak on behalf of the majority of Sikhs, and hence to represent the authority of the Guru-Panth.

Still, the ultimate authority is the Akal Takhat in Amritsar, which, in addition to issuing edicts on doctrine or practice, punishes violations of religious discipline and activities "prejudicial" to Sikh interests; it also recognizes individuals who have performed outstanding services for Sikhism.

The Partition of India

In 1947 the British withdrew from India and the independent republics of India and Pakistan came into being. Most of the 2.5 million Sikhs living on the Pakistani side of the divided Punjab became refugees; though many settled in the new Indian state of Punjab, some moved on to major cities elsewhere in India.

Since 1976 India has defined itself as a secular state, and Article 25 of the Constitution guarantees freedom of religion. However, a sub-clause of the same Article states that "persons professing the Sikh, Jaina, or Buddhist religion" fall within the general category of Hinduism. When the Constitution was drafted, the Sikh members of the Constituent Assembly refused to sign on because it did not recognize the Sikhs as a group with an independent identity. Since that time, both Sikh and Hindu politicians have deliberately stirred up popular resentment for political purposes.

In 2002 the National Commission to Review the Constitution recommended amending Article 25 to remove Sikhs, Jainas, and Buddhists from the "Hindu" category, but to date this has not been done.

"Operation Blue Star"

In 1973 the Akali Dal passed the Anandpur Sahib Resolution, demanding greater autonomy for all the states of India. As a result, relations with the Indian government became strained, and in an apparent attempt to sow dissension in the Akali ranks, the Congress government encouraged the rise of a charismatic young militant named Jarnail Singh Bhindranvale (1947–84). But this strategy backfired in the spring of 1984, when a group of armed radicals led by Bhindranvale decided to provoke a confrontation with the government by occupying the Akal Takhat building inside the Darbar Sahib complex. The government responded by sending in the army. The assault that followed—code-named "Operation Blue Star"—resulted in the deaths of many Sikhs, including Bhindranvale, as well as the destruction of the Akal Takhat and severe damage to the Darbar Sahib itself.

A few months later, on 31 October, Prime Minister Indira Gandhi was assassinated by her own Sikh bodyguards. For several days Hindu mobs in Delhi and elsewhere killed thousands of Sikhs. These events divided Sikhs around the world into two camps, liberal and fundamentalist.

In 2006, four years after Gurbaj Singh Multani was forbidden to wear a kirpan to his Montreal school, the Supreme Court of Canada ruled that the ban violated his Charter right to freedom of religion (CP PHOTO / Fred Chartrand).

The Sikh Diaspora

Over the last century about two million Sikhs have left India. Wherever they have settled—in Singapore, Malaysia, Thailand, Hong Kong, Australia, New Zealand, East Africa, and the United Kingdom, as well as Canada and the US—they have established their own places of worship. Today there are more than 500 gurdwaras in North America and the United Kingdom alone.

New cultural environments have required some adaptation. For example, congregational services are usually held on Sunday, not because it is the holy day—in India there is no specific day for worship—but because it is the only day when most Sikhs are free to attend.

Western societies have also presented Sikhs with serious challenges. Men who wear turbans have often faced discrimination from prospective employers, and Khalsa Sikhs have had to negotiate with various institutions for permission to wear the *kirpan*. At the same time, loss of fluency in the Punjabi language means that younger Sikhs are at risk of theological illiteracy. Members of the diaspora have made concerted efforts to revive interest in Sikh traditions by supporting "Sunday school" classes and youth camps. In addition, many Sikh families now worship at home as well as at the gurdwara.

White Sikhs

Around 1970, a number of yoga students in Toronto and Los Angeles were inspired by their teacher, a Sikh named Harbhajan Singh Puri (Yogi Bhajan), to convert to the Sikh faith and join his Healthy, Happy, Holy Organization ("3HO"). Eventually renamed Sikh Dharma, the organization has since established itself in various North American cities. All members—male and female—wear the same white turbans, tunics, and tight trousers, and for this reason they have come to be known as "White Sikhs." They live in communal houses, spending long hours in meditation and chanting as well as yoga practice.

Although Punjabi Sikhs in general praise their strict Khalsa-style discipline, other aspects of the White Sikh culture are quite alien to them. In India, for instance, white clothing is normally a sign of mourning; only the Namdharis dress entirely in white. And the only Sikh women who wear turbans are members of the Akhand Kirtani Jatha. Finally, the concept of honour, which plays such an important part in Punjabi society, is irrelevant to the White Sikhs. Even in North America, therefore, the two groups have little to do with one another.

Recent Developments

Religious Pluralism

The fact that the Adi Granth includes works by 15 non-Sikh poet-saints suggests that interfaith dialogue has always been integral to Sikhism. The co-existence of multiple religious worldviews, some of which may be incompatible, has always been a fact of life. But awareness of that fact has increased sharply with increasing urbanization, mass education, international migration, and advances in communications. Especially in democratic states that do not attempt to impose a single religion, people of different faiths must learn how to live together in harmony.

Interfaith dialogue and interaction provide opportunities for spiritual reflection and growth. It is in this context that Sikhism emphasizes the importance of keeping an open mind while preserving the integrity of one's own tradition. The Gurus strongly opposed any claim, by any tradition, to possession of the sole religious truth. Thus participants in interfaith dialogue must recognize that the religious commitments of others are no less absolute than their own, and allow for disagreement on crucial points of doctrine. At the same time we must be willing to let the "other" become in some sense ourselves.

Political Militancy

Another issue confronting Sikhs around the world is the tendency to associate their tradition with violence. The use of warrior imagery to evoke the valour of the Sikhs has been standard since colonial times. Relatively little attention has been directed to the other, perhaps more demanding, dimensions of Sikhism. What is expected of Sikh warriors is not violence but militancy in the sense that they are prepared to take an active and passionate stand on behalf of their faith.

In Canada the association with violence was underlined by the 1985 bombing of Air India Flight 182, in which 329 people—most of them Canadian citizens—were killed. This happened in the highly volatile context of the 1984 assault on the Darbar Sahib. Nearly two decades passed before the two Vancouver men suspected of masterminding the attack were brought to trial, and in the end they were acquitted. It took more than 20 years and several government inquiries for Canadians in general to recognize that the bombing was a Canadian tragedy, the result of a Canadian plot and the failure of Canadian security officials—a conclusion that former Supreme Court Justice John Major made clear in his 2010 report on the investigation into the attack.

In India, separatist violence was contained within a decade and the Akali Dal reasserted its right to work within the democratic system. In the long run, peaceful demonstrations and political engagement have proved more effective than violent struggle. In response to longstanding Sikh demands, the Indian Parliament in 2012 lifted the requirement that Sikh marriages be registered under the Hindu Marriage Act.

Sexuality and Bioethical Issues

The Adi Granth and the Sikh Rahit Maryada are silent on homosexuality. However, the official response to same-sex marriage has been negative, and the Akal Takhat has forbidden the performance of such marriages in the gurdwara. Since the Sikh ideal is the life of the householder, any sexual relationship that is not procreative and within the bounds of a marriage is opposed. Thus only heterosexual unions are officially accepted.

For centuries in Punjab, as elsewhere throughout the subcontinent, sons have tended to be preferred to daughters. The Gurus explicitly prohibited female infanticide, and the *rahit-namas* include specific injunctions against it. Yet in recent years the proportion of females to males in the Punjabi population has declined, apparently because, contrary to the Sikh principle of gender equality, female fetuses are being aborted. Thus although Sikhism does permit medical abortion when the mother's life is in danger, or in cases of incest or rape, it does not condone abortion for the purpose of sex selection.

Diaspora Sikhs are beginning to debate issues such as genetic engineering and the use of embryos in medical research. Advocates of organ donation often point to the example of Guru Tegh Bahadur, who sacrificed himself to defend the rights of Hindus. Many Sikhs believe that life begins at conception, and therefore object to the use of embryos in research. On the other hand, some defend such research on the grounds that it will benefit humanity.

Environmental Issues

Guru Nanak himself spoke of the natural world with great tenderness: "Air is the Guru, water the Father and earth the mighty Mother of all. Day and night are the caring guardians, fondly nurturing all creation" (AG 8). Today environmental issues are coming into prominence both in the Punjab and in the diaspora. The celebration of Guru Har Rai's birthday in March has been fixed as "Sikh Environment Day." And in recent years the environmentalist Balbir Singh Seechewal has made it his mission to spread ecological awareness. He singlehandedly organized the restoration of the river associated with Guru Nanak's mystical experience, and he encourages congregations across the Punjab to plant trees in every available space.

Internet Technology

It is astounding to see how quickly Sikh websites are multiplying. The ability to locate a reference from the Guru Granth Sahib in seconds, or listen to *kirtan* and the daily Vak from the Golden Temple, is inspiring for Sikhs around the world. Online courses offer instruction in everything from the Gurmukhi script to playing the instruments associated with Sikh worship. Webmasters have become the new authorities speaking on behalf of Sikhism, eroding the power of institutional structures. Websites such as Gurmat Learning Zone (GLZ), Sikh-Diaspora, Sikhchic, and SikhNet are among many forums that now host discussions of contemporary Sikh issues. Of course, Sikhism is not the only tradition in which institutional authority is eroding; in an increasingly secular, globalized world, all religions are facing similar challenges.

Sikh Visibility

On 15 September 2001, an American Sikh became the first victim of the racial backlash that followed the 9/11 terrorist attacks. Balbir Singh Sodhi was shot dead in Phoenix, Arizona, by a self-described "patriot" who mistook him for a Muslim. More recently, on 5 August 2012, a gunman burst into the gurdwara in Oak Creek, Wisconsin, and opened fire, killing five men and one woman, and injuring three police officers before turning his gun on himself. It has been widely assumed that the killer, a white supremacist, thought the Sikhs were Muslims. Clearly, even today, too many people in the West simply do not know who Sikhs are.

Organizations such as the Canadian Sikh Coalition are working to raise awareness of Sikhism in Canada and elsewhere. In the US, civil rights organizations such as the Sikh Coalition, SALDEF

A prayer vigil in memory of the six people who died when a gunman opened fire in a Sikh temple in Oak Creek, Wisconsin, in 2012 (© AP Photo / Appeal-Democrat, Nate Chute).

(Sikh American Legal Defense and Education Fund), and Sikhs For Justice (SFJ) are providing legal aid and have dynamic information systems and extensive data bases.

The situation is somewhat better in academic circles. Participants at the first North American conference on Sikh studies, held in 1976 at the University of California, Berkeley, generally felt that Sikhism was "the forgotten tradition" in North America. This is no longer the case. In the last two decades the scholarly literature on Sikhism has grown steadily, and the mistaken notion that Sikhism represents a synthesis of Hindu and Muslim ideals has been almost entirely abandoned. Today there are eight endowed chairs in Sikh studies in North America, and Sikhism is increasingly recognized in undergraduate academic programs.

Summary

The Sikh tradition has evolved in response to three fundamental factors: the ongoing tensions of the period in which the Panth evolved, when Punjab was governed by Mughal rulers and under constant threat of invasion from Afghanistan; the martial character of Punjabi society's rural base, which helped to bring the Panth into conflict with Mughal authorities and thus to shape its future direction; and, above all, the religious and cultural innovations of Guru Nanak and his successors.

The Sikh community has been engaged in renewal and redefinition throughout its history, and that engagement has only intensified in recent years. Today the question "Who is a Sikh?" is the subject of often acrimonious online debate. Each generation of Sikhs has had to respond to that question in the light of new historical circumstances. Not surprisingly, diaspora Sikhs approach these issues from different perspectives, depending on the cultural and political contexts they come from. In many cases they rediscover their identity through their interaction with other religious and ethnic communities. New challenges demand new responses, especially in a postmodern world where notions of self, gender, and authority are subject to constant questioning. Thus the process of Sikh identity-formation is an ongoing phenomenon.

Sites

Patna, Bihar

The birthplace of Guru Gobind Singh and the site of the Takhat Sri Patna Sahib. one of the five seats of authority in the Sikh world.

Amritsar, Punjab

The holiest of all places for Sikhs, Amritsar was named for the "pool of nectar" that surrounds the Darbar Sahib. Facing the latter and connected to it by a causeway is the Akal Takhat, the most important of the five *takhats*.

Anandpur, Punjab

The birthplace of the Khalsa; the Takhat Sri Kesgarh Sahib stands on the spot where Guru Gobind Singh is said to have created the "Cherished Five" in 1699.

Talwandi Sabo, Punjab

Guru Gobind Singh stayed at Talwandi Sabo for several months c. 1705, and it was there that he prepared the final version of the Adi Granth. This is also the site of the Takhat Sri Damdama Sahib.

Nanded, Maharashtra

The site of the Takhat Sri Hazur Sahib, where Guru Gobind Singh installed the Adi Granth as the "Eternal Guru" shortly before his death in 1708.

Sacred Texts

Religion	Texts	Composition/Compilation	Compilation/Revision	Use
Sikhism	The Adi Granth / Guru Granth Sahib; the primary scripture	The first collection of Guru Nanak's hymns was compiled in the 1530s. This *pothi* ("sacred volume") was expanded by the succeeding Gurus. A four-volume collection produced in 1570, under Guru Amar Das, came to be known as the Goindval Pothis.	The fifth Guru, Arjan, produced a prototype of the Adi Granth in 1604. The tenth Guru, Gobind Singh, added the works of his father and closed the canon in the 1680s. Before he passed away in 1708, he installed the Adi Granth as Guru Granth Sahib.	In worship, the hymns of the Guru Granth Sahib are sung in melodic measures (*ragas*), while prayers are recited. The sacred text also plays a pivotal role in all Sikh ceremonies, including life-cycle rituals, and is the central authority regarding both personal piety and the corporate identity of the Sikh community.
	The Dasam Granth; the secondary scripture	The first collection of works attributed to the tenth Guru, Gobind Singh, dates to the 1690s.	18th–19th centuries: subsequent collections added the *Zafarnama* of Guru Gobind Singh and fixed the sequence of compositions.	Portions of the Dasam Granth are used as liturgical texts in the daily routine of the Sikhs and the Khalsa initiation ceremony.

Discussion Questions

1. Do you think that Guru Nanak intended to establish a new religion, independent of Hindu and Muslim traditions? What is the evidence in his works?
2. How did Sikhism evolve in response to changing historical circumstances during the time of the 10 Gurus?
3. How did the martyrdoms of Guru Arjan and Guru Tegh Bahadur contribute to the emergence of militancy as a core tradition within the Panth?
4. How did modern Sikhism come into being? What role did the Singh Sabha play in defining Sikh doctrine and practice?
5. What is the role of the Guru Granth Sahib in Sikh life?
6. Why is the practice of *kirtan* central to Sikh congregational worship?
7. What role has the institution of the gurdwara played in the Sikh diaspora?

Glossary

Adi Granth Literally, "original book"; first compiled by Guru Arjan in 1604 and invested with supreme authority as the Guru Granth Sahib after the death of Guru Gobind Singh.

Akal Purakh "The One Beyond Time," God.

Amrit "Divine Nectar"; the Khalsa initiation nectar.

Amrit-dhari "Nectar-bearer"; an initiated member of the Khalsa.

Amrit sanskar The formal ceremony initiating Sikhs into the Khalsa.

Bhagat "Devotee"; one of the poets of traditions other than Sikhism whose work is included in the Adi Granth (e.g., Kabir).

Bani "Divine Utterance"; the works of the **Gurus** and the **Bhagats** recorded in the Adi Granth.

Baisakhi An Indian new year's holiday in mid-April, when Sikhs celebrate the birthday of the Khalsa.

Dasam Granth "The Book of the Tenth Guru"; the secondary Sikh scripture, attributed to Guru Gobind Singh.

Five Ks The Panj Kakke, or five marks of Khalsa identity: ***kes*** (uncut hair), ***kangha*** (wooden comb), ***kirpan*** (sword), ***kara*** (wrist ring), and ***kachh*** (short breeches).

Granthi "Reader"; the reader and custodian of the Guru Granth Sahib who performs traditional rituals in the gurdwara.

gurdwara Literally, "Guru's door"; the Sikh place of worship.

Gurmukhi Literally, "from the Guru's mouth"; the vernacular script in which the compositions of the Gurus were first written down. It has since become the script of Punjabi language.

gursikhs Literally, "Disciples of the Guru."

Guru "Teacher"; either a spiritual person or the divine inner voice.

haumai "I-ness, my-ness"; self-centred pride.

hukam "Divine order, will, or command"; an all-embracing principle, the sum total of all divinely instituted laws; a revelation of the nature of God.

janam-sakhis "Birth testimonies"; traditional accounts of the life of Guru Nanak.

karah prashad A sweet pudding or paste of flour, sugar, and butter that is prepared in an iron (***karah***) bowl with prayers, placed in the presence of the Sikh scripture during worship, and then distributed in the congregation.

karam "Actions" or karma; the destiny or fate of an individual, generated in accordance with deeds performed in one's present and past existences.

Khalsa Literally, "pure"; an order of Sikhs bound by common identity and discipline.

kirtan The singing of hymns from the scriptures in worship.

langar The term for both the community kitchen and the meal that is prepared there and served to all present following services at the gurdwara.

miri-piri The doctrine that the Guru possesses both temporal (***miri***) and spiritual (***piri***) authority.

Mul Mantar Literally, "Basic Formula"; the opening creedal statement of the Adi Granth, declaring the eternity and transcendence of God, the creator.

nam "The divine Name."

nam-simaran "Remembrance of the divine Name," especially the devotional practice of meditating on the divine Name.

Panj Kakke See **Five Ks**.

Panj Piare The "Cherished Five"; the first five Sikhs to be initiated as members of the Khalsa in 1699; five Sikhs in good standing chosen to represent a *sangat*.

Panth Literally, "path"; hence the Sikh community.

pothi Volume or book.

raga A series of five or six notes on which a melody is based.

Rahit The code of conduct for the Khalsa.

sangat Congregation; group of devotees in Sikhism.

Sants Ascetic poets who believed divinity to exist beyond all forms or description.

Sansar "Cycle of birth and death"; Transmigration in Sikh terminology.

sati The immolation of a widow on her husband's funeral pyre.

Sehaj-dhari Literally, a "gradualist"; a Sikh who follows the teachings of the Gurus but has not accepted the Khalsa discipline.

shabad Literally, "divine Word," a hymn of the Adi Granth.

Singh Sabha Literally, "Society of Singhs"; a revival movement established in 1873 that redefined the norms of Sikh doctrine and practice.

Vak "Saying"; a passage from the Guru Granth Sahib that is chosen at random and read aloud to the congregation as the lesson of the day.

Further Reading

Dusenbery, Verne A. 2008. *Sikhs at Large: Religion, Culture, and Politics*. New Delhi: Oxford University Press. A collection of essays bringing together different perspectives on the cultural and political dimensions of the Sikh diaspora and of Sikhism as a global religion.

Fenech, Louis E. 2008. *The Darbar of the Sikh Gurus: The Court of God in the World of Men*. New Delhi: Oxford University Press. Traces the evolving nature of the court of the Sikh Gurus in the broader historical context of Indo-Persian courtly tradition.

Grewal, J.S. 1991. *The New Cambridge History of India: The Sikhs of the Punjab*. Cambridge: Cambridge University Press. A classic chronological study of Sikh history from the beginnings to the present day.

Jakobsh, Doris R. 2012. *Sikhism*. Honolulu: University of Hawai'i Press. A comprehensive overview of Sikhism in its Indian context and as an increasingly global tradition.

Mandair, Arvind-pal S. 2010. *Religion and the Spectre of the West: Sikhism, India, Postcolonialism, and the Politics of Translation*. New York: Columbia University. A recent study of the Sikh tradition from a postcolonial perspective.

McLeod, W.H. 1984. *Textual Sources for the Study of Sikhism*. Manchester: Manchester University Press. An anthology of selections covering all aspects of Sikh belief, worship, and practice.

———. 1999. *Sikhs and Sikhism*. New Delhi: Oxford University Press. An omnibus edition of four classic studies on the history and evolution of Sikhs and Sikhism by one of the world's leading scholars in the field.

———. 2003. *The Sikhs of the Khalsa*. New Delhi: Oxford University Press. A study of how the *Rahit* or "Code of Conduct" came into being, how it developed in response to historical circumstances, and why it still retains an unchallenged hold over all who consider themselves Khalsa Sikhs.

Nesbitt, Eleanor. 2005. *Sikhism: A Very Short Introduction*. Oxford: Oxford University Press. An ethnographic introduction to Sikhism, its teachings, practices, rituals, and festivals.

Oberoi, Harjot. 1994. *Construction of Religious Boundaries*. New Delhi: Oxford University Press. A major reinterpretation of Sikh religion and society during the colonial period.

Singh, Harbans, ed. 1992–8. *The Encyclopaedia of Sikhism*, 4 vols. Patiala: Punjabi University. A four-volume reference work covering Sikh life and letters, history and philosophy, customs and rituals, social and religious movements, art and architecture, and locales and shrines.

Singh, Nikky-Guninder Kaur. 2011. *Sikhism: An Introduction*. London and New York: I.B. Tauris. An introduction to Sikh religion and culture, highlighting various issues related to doctrine, worship, ethics, art, architecture, and diaspora.

Singh, Pashaura. 2006. *Life and Work of Guru Arjan: History, Memory and Biography in the Sikh Tradition*. New Delhi: Oxford University Press. A reconstruction of the life and work of the fifth Guru, based on history, collective memory, tradition, and mythic representation.

Recommended Websites

www.columbia.edu/itc/mealac/pritchett/00generallinks/index.html
A good site with links to many resources on South Asia.

www.sikhs.org
The Sikhism Home Page, Brampton, ON.

www.sikhnet.com
SikhNet, Espanola, New Mexico.

www.sgpc.net
Shiromani Gurdwara Parbandhak Committee, Amritsar.

www.sikhchic.com
Online magazine: journey through the Sikh universe.

www.sikhcoalition.org
Sikh advocacy group in the United States of America.

www.saldef.org
Sikh American Legal Defense and Education Fund.

www.sikhsforjustice.org
Sikhs for Justice (SFJ) is a human rights organization.

References

McLeod, W.H. 1984. *Textual Sources for the Study of Sikhism*. Manchester: Manchester University Press.

———. 1989. *Who Is a Sikh? Problem of Sikh Identity*. Oxford: Clarendon Press.

———. 1997. *Sikhism*. London: Penguin Books.

Singh, Pashaura. 2006. *Life and Work of Guru Arjan: History, Memory and Biography in the Sikh Tradition*. New Delhi: Oxford University Press.

Notes

This chapter is dedicated to the memory of my teacher, Professor Willard G. Oxtoby.

1. This reference means that the passage quoted comes from the 27th stanza of the ballad (*Var*) in the musical measure *Majh*, by Guru Nanak (M1), on page 150 of the Adi Granth (AG).
2. For a discussion of this work by the artists themselves, see http://www.sikhchic.com/article-detail.php?cat=21&id=747. *Nineteen Eighty-Four and the Via Dolorosa Project* (2009) is a semi-autobiographical documentary film in which the artists draw parallels with the Christian faith.

10 Chinese and Korean Traditions

Terry Tak-ling Woo

Traditions at a Glance

Numbers

Indigenous traditions such as shamanism, Confucianism, and Daoism do not require exclusive membership: they also tend to be less institutionalized than monotheistic religions. Their membership is therefore very difficult to count.

Confucianism: Most estimates are in the range of 6 million, but because East Asians generally do not consider Confucianism to be a religion, the true number is impossible to gauge.

Daoism: As with Confucianism, exact numbers are impossible to determine because of issues around definition; estimates range from 20 million to as many as 400 million.

Chinese folk or popular religion: Daoism is sometimes counted as a folk religion. This category also includes numerous new religious movements and traditional sects whose devotees may consider their practices and beliefs to be more cultural than religious. Estimates range from 225 to 445 million.

Korean shamanism and popular religion: Estimates range from 1 to 7 million.

Distribution

Confucians and Daoists live mainly in East and Southeast Asia, Australia and New Zealand, Western Europe, and North America. Adherents of popular religions remain primarily in East Asia, with small pockets in diasporic communities in Australia, New Zealand, North America, and Europe.

Founders and Teachers

Mythical founders and heroes include Yao, Shun, and Yu in China, and Dangun in Korea. Famous first teachers—some mythical, some historic—include the Yellow Emperor, Confucius, and Laozi in China, and Choe Chung in Korea.

Deities

For Confucians, the place of a deity is filled either by Heaven or by Heaven and Earth together. Some Daoists see the Way as personified by Laozi as a deity. Popular religions, both Korean and Chinese, include hundreds of deities.

Authoritative Texts

Popular and shamanistic religions are not textually oriented. For Confucians, the classics from the Zhou and Han dynasties are the foundational texts. For Daoists Laozi and, to a lesser degree, Zhuangzi are fundamental, but otherwise different groups focus on different texts, including the *Unity of the Three* and the Classics of *Great Peace* and *Purity and Tranquility*.

For Buddhists, Mahayana texts such as the *Lotus*, *Vimalakirti*, *Heart*, *Diamond*, *Pure Land*, and *Flower Garland Sutras* are central. The only Chinese text considered "canonical" in the monotheistic sense is the *Platform Sutra* of the Chan school.

Noteworthy Teachings

No East Asian tradition is exclusive; many believers attend temples and shrines of various kinds. The three elite traditions—Daoism, Confucianism, and Buddhism—differ fundamentally in doctrine and vary greatly in practice, but they share a utopian view of a peaceful and harmonious society whose members are devoted to self-cultivation and discipline. In addition, some schools of Buddhism look to an afterlife in the Pure Land of a celestial buddha such as Amituofo (Amitabha). Popular religions syncretize teachings from all three traditions, as well as from more recently introduced religions such as Christianity and Islam.

← The Dragon and Tiger pagodas, Lotus Lake, Kaohsiung, Taiwan (© Pat Behnke / Alamy).

From the beginning, religion in East Asia was inextricably linked to politics. Social harmony and stability in governance have always been central concerns, along with physical sustenance and security.

Overview

The foundational layers of animism and shamanism remain visible today in traces of tribal practices focused on dealing with the insecurities of life. Philosophers, shamans, and "masters of the methods" such as prognosticians and geomancers all sought to bring peace. Early Confucian and Daoist writings thus included political teachings along with metaphysical ruminations, advice on cultivating good health and moral character, and instructions for achieving mystical union with the divine. It was into this religious landscape that Buddhism (*Fojiao*, "teaching of the Buddha")

The three tiers of the Temple of Heaven (Tiantan) in Beijing symbolize the relationship between Heaven, Earth, and human beings; and the circular shape reflects the belief that Heaven is round whereas the Earth is square. It was here that the emperor made offerings to Heaven and prayed for bountiful harvests (© Imagemore Co., Ltd. / Corbis).

was later introduced from India and central Asia. The central focus on peace and harmony led the various religions to embrace a generally tolerant, inclusive, and syncretic ethos.

This ancient syncretism is still visible in the practice of folk religion today. Next time you go to a Chinese restaurant, take a look around and see if there is a shrine at the door, or perhaps the back of the sitting area. Chances are good that you will see a red shrine with three incense sticks in a censer, a plate of fruit at the front, a candle on each side, and at least one figure standing in the centre. If the figure is holding a halberd or lance, it will represent Guan Gong, who symbolizes the Confucian virtues of integrity or loyalty and the sense of what is right (*yi*). A traditional cap and a flowing beard signify the Daoist lineage ancestor Lu Dongbin, while a female figure usually represents Guanyin, the Buddhist bodhisattva of compassion. If there is no figure, the back panel of the shrine will often carry a verse of thanksgiving addressed to the local earth god.

When the Chinese speak of *sanjiao*, they are talking about the three (*san*) teachings, philosophies, or religions (*jiao*) of Confucianism, Daoism, and Buddhism. Collectively, these are sometimes described as the elite tradition. A much more diffuse fourth tradition, often described as folk or popular religion, honours an assortment of spirits that varies from place to place. For the most part the four traditions have coexisted in peace, and many people consult specialists from across the spectrum—Confucian teachers, Daoist priests, Buddhist monks, spirit mediums, astrologers, *feng-shui* practitioners. In general, Chinese religions are more interested in right action than right belief.

The Classical Period to the Qin (c. 2300 BCE–206 BCE)

Confucian Beginnings

Origins

Not all of the philosophy that the West calls Confucianism originated with Kongzi or **Confucius** (c. 551–479 BCE).[1] Some of its seminal ideas can be found in the Five Classics: the *Classic* or *Book of Changes*, the *Classic of Documents* or *Book of History*, the *Classic of Odes* or *Book of Poetry*, the *Records* or *Book of Rites*, and the *Spring and Autumn Annals*. (A sixth work, the *Classic of Music*, is now lost.) Some parts of these works may predate Confucius himself, and others were likely written after his time. Nevertheless, Confucius is revered as the first of three foremost classical philosophers in the Confucian tradition; the other two are Mengzi (**Mencius**; c. 343–289 BCE) and **Xunzi** (c. 310–219 BCE).

Originating during the Zhou dynasty (c. 1046–256 BCE), the Classics were first standardized during the Han (202 BCE–220 CE) and they have been central to the state examination curriculum since the establishment of the first state-supported Confucian college in 124 BCE. Historically, they provided the ideology behind government policy for some 2,000 years in addition to serving as blueprints for family relations and guides to individual moral and spiritual transformation.

The Classics record a society in transition. During the Shang era (c. 1750–1040 BCE) the world was understood to be under the control of anthropomorphic deities, ghosts, and spirits. In the Zhou era this "supernatural" worldview was gradually replaced by the understanding that the world operated according to impersonal natural principles. The content of the Classics therefore ranges from descriptions of deities, ghosts, and spirits, and the rites (**li**) performed for them, to philosophical explanations of the natural principles underlying those rites. The ultimate goal was the creation of a harmonious society through careful self-cultivation. Over time, the Classics were reinterpreted with this goal in mind.

Timeline

2357 BCE	Time of China's Sage kings Yao, Shun, and Yu; some accounts place Dangun, the mythical founder of Old Joseon (Korea), in the same period
c. 2200–1750	Xia dynasty (China)
c. 1750–1046	Shang (Yin) dynasty (China)
c. 1046–256	Zhou dynasty (China)
722–479	Spring and Autumn period
551	Birth of Confucius (d. 479); some accounts place Laozi around the same time, some place him earlier, and others say that he never existed
479–221	Warring States period
c. 400–100	Huang–Lao school
c. 343	Birth of Mengzi (Mencius) (d. 289); Zhuangzi (369?–286?) was a slightly older contemporary
c. 310	Birth of Xunzi (d. 219), who witnessed the carnage of the late Zhou period
c. 300	Old Joseon suffers major losses (Korea)
221–206	Qin dynasty (China); destruction of Confucian texts by the First Qin Emperor
202 BCE–9 CE	Early (also Former or Western) Han dynasty; Confucian texts recovered and edited based on copies that had been preserved and the recitations of scholars who had memorized them
108	Old Joseon is defeated by the Han
25–220	Latter or Eastern Han
124	Emperor Wu establishes the Confucian state college and state examination system
c. 50 BCE–668 CE	Three Kingdoms of Goguryeo, Baekje, and Silla (Korea)
c. 48 CE	Birth of Ban Zhao (d. 112), who advocated education for women
142	Zhang Daoling founds the Daoist Celestial Masters (later Orthodox Unity)
220–589	Period of North–South disunion or Six Dynasties (China)
317	Northern China falls to invaders from North and Central Asia
c. 370–380	Buddhism introduced to Goguryeo and Baekje, and (later) Silla (Korea)
527	Buddhism is made state religion of Silla
c. 530	Baekje monks introduce Buddhism to Japan
618–907	Tang dynasty (China)
600s	Tang rulers send Daoist priests, texts, and images to Goguryeo
629–630	Chinese monk Xuanzang makes pilgrimage to India
647	Second Tang emperor orders the construction of Confucian temples with tablets commemorating 22 orthodox Confucians

661	Korean monks Wonhyo and Uisang start out for China
668–936	Kingdom of United Silla (Korea)
682	United Silla establishes the National Confucian College
824	Death of Han Yu, defender of Confucianism
890–936	Later Three Kingdoms (Korea)
918–1392	Goryeo period (Korea); Buddhism is the state religion
960–1279	Song dynasty (China)
1158–1250	Jinul synthesizes the practice-focused Seon (Chan) school and doctrinal schools like Hwaeom (Flower Garland)
1368–1644	Ming dynasty (China)
1392–1897	Joseon persecution of Buddhism (Korea)
1400s	Both China's Empress Xu and Joseon's Queen Sohye write texts entitled *Instructions for the Inner Quarters*
1500s	Joseon neo-Confucianism
1529	Death of Confucian Wang Yangming
1644–1911	Qing (Manchu) dynasty (China)
1900s	East Asia is reconfigured in response to Western challenges; new religions are established and traditional ones renewed
1910–45	Japanese occupation of Korea
1911	Qing dynasty falls and China becomes a republic
1945	Korea divided between Democratic People's Republic (North) and Republic (South)
1949	People's Republic of China (PRC) established
1950s	New Confucian movement finds a home in Hong Kong
1966–76	Communist government promotes "Great Proletarian Cultural Revolution" in attempt to eradicate traditional Chinese values and practices
1980s	Revival of Daoism in PRC after more than a century of persecution
1989	Confucius' birthday officially celebrated in PRC for the first time since 1949
2004	First Confucius Institute opens in Seoul
2006	First World Buddhist Forum—the first government-sponsored religious conference held in China since 1949—opens in Hangzhou
2007	A privately funded International Forum on the *Daodejing* is approved by the PRC government
2011	First International Daoism Forum held at the foot of Hengshan, one of the five sacred Daoist mountains

Confucian Concerns

The concerns addressed in the Classics can be categorized in four broad areas: individual, familial, political, and cosmic. The first duty of the exemplary Confucian (***junzi***) is to promote a peaceful, prosperous, and harmonious society. The Classics make it clear that such a society cannot be achieved by men alone, for there can be no harmony in the public world without harmony in the private world of the family—the domain of the Confucian woman. They also explain how sacrifices and rituals give symbolic expression to the relationship between the outer and inner worlds. The essential function of ancestor rituals in particular was to encourage right relationships, especially between men and women.

Confucians believe that correctness in human relationships is crucial to a stable society. There are five types of relationship—ruler and minister (state official), parent and child (traditionally, father and son), husband and wife, elder and younger siblings (often translated as "brothers"), and friends—all of which must be guided by ***ren*** (goodness, humaneness, benevolence, and compassion). Except in the case of "friends," the first member of each pair is deemed "senior" and is expected to take into account the effect of his or her actions on others in general; the second person is "junior" and is expected be upright and loyal.

Confucian Exemplars and Sages

The prototypes of the Confucian sage are three mythical "sage kings" named Yao, Shun, and Yu, whose stories are told in the *Classic of Documents*. The virtues they embody are civil, familial, and filial rather than military, and their stories are understood as implicit critiques of rule by force.

Yao is admired for bringing harmony to his domain and making sure that the common people were well fed and prosperous. In the simple agrarian society of his day, Yao's virtue was said to have radiated throughout the land. The *Classic of Documents* recounts how, when Yao recognized that his own son was not virtuous enough to be a good ruler, he asked his ministers to find a more appropriate successor. They recommended a man of humble status named Shun because he had managed to live in harmony with his family and fulfill his filial duties even though his father was blind (literally and figuratively) and stupid, his stepmother deceitful, and his half-brother arrogant. In other words, Shun had triumphed over adversity. Accordingly, Yao married his two daughters to Shun, observed his conduct for three years, and then offered him the throne.

The last sage king, Yu, is associated with the largely legendary Xia dynasty—the predecessors of the Shang. Yu's father was said to have thrown the natural cycle into chaos by building dams to contain floodwaters, but Yu worked with nature by digging deep canals to channel the water away. According the *Documents*, this story was told to Wu, the first king of Zhou, as a lesson in governance.

Divination and the Pantheon of Spirits

At least two related elements from the stories of the sage kings survived into the Shang dynasty: an intense interest in "right" governance and a belief in divine intervention through revelation to the king. The Shang kings served as shamans, practising divination and communicating directly with the spirits that were believed to hold the real power over the empire. Religious ritual was thus an indispensable part of governance.

At the apex of the Shang pantheon of spirits sat the Lord-on-High or Shangdi. Thought to be the ancestor of the Shang clan, he was the sky god who commanded rain, thunder, and wind. Below

Table 10.1 Major Chinese (C) and Korean (K) Historical Periods at a Glance

C	c. 2300 BCE–206 BCE: Classical Period through Qin Dynasty
K	?–108 BCE: Old Joseon
C	202 BCE–220 CE: Han Dynasty
K	c. 50 BCE–668 CE: Three Kingdoms
C	220–589: Six Dynasties Period
C	589–907: Sui and Tang Dynasties
K	668–1392: United Silla, Later Three Kingdoms, and Goryeo
C	960–1644: Song, Yuan, and Ming Dynasties
K	1392–1910: Joseon and the Korean Empire
C	1644–present: Qing Dynasty and Republican Period
K	1910–45: Japanese occupation
K	1945–present: Korea partitioned between North and South

him were the nature spirits believed to animate natural phenomena, followed by celestial spirits such as the sun and moon; then "Former Lords" who were associated with the Shang but were not royal clan members; and, finally, direct human ancestors, both male and female.

The Mandate of Heaven

After more than 700 years in power, the Shang dynasty fell to the Zhou in 1046 BCE. It was in the context of this power shift that the concept of the Mandate of Heaven was developed. When the first Zhou ruler, King Wu, died, leaving a young son, his brother the Duke of Zhou served as

Document

On the Mandate of Heaven

The Mandate of Heaven appears in the Classic of Documents *in the form of a public announcement legitimating the Zhou overthrow of the Yin (an alternative name for the Shang).*

Heaven has rejected and ended the Mandate of this great state of Yin. Thus, although Yin has many former wise kings in Heaven, when their successor kings and successor people undertook their Mandate, in the end wise and good men lived in misery. Knowing that they must care for and sustain their wives and children, they then called out in anguish to Heaven and fled to places where they could not be caught. Ah! Heaven too grieved for the people of all the lands, wanting, with affection, in giving its Mandate to employ those who are deeply committed. The king should have reverent care for his virtue (D. Nivison in de Bary and Bloom 1999: 36).

regent, but he returned the throne to the boy once he was old enough to rule. Such loyalty was revered by the early Confucians, and the Duke's popularity rivalled that of Confucius himself. The personification of restraint, humility, and willingness to listen to advice, the Duke declared that Heaven had withdrawn the Mandate of Heaven from the later Shang kings because they had failed to provide for the people.

In this way moral character became the primary determinant of the right to rule. The idea that good governance was a duty to Heaven reflected the Zhou belief in a moral force or supreme deity that took an interest in human affairs. How to encourage kings to rule ethically became a central concern for Confucians. In the *Classic of Odes*, King Wen (the father of Wu) is imagined addressing the last Shang king:

> King Wen said, Woe!
> Woe upon you, Yin and Shang!
> You have been the harsh oppressor,
> you have been grasping and crushing.
> You have been in the places of power,
> you have held the functions.
> Heaven sent recklessness down in you,
> and you rise by acts of force
> (Owen 1996: 20).

Thus the mandate to rule was taken away from the cruel Shang and passed to the virtuous Zhou. In this political transition, the term "god" (*di*) became associated with the earthly political ruler, while Heaven came to be portrayed as an impartial universal power, a cosmic moral force that cares for human welfare and so gives the people a wise and good king.

Humanization: The Transition from Shang to Zhou

With the establishment of the Zhou dynasty, the concept of Heaven displaced the more personal "Lord on High" of the Shang. Although divination continued, the methods and materials changed, reflecting a change in the understanding of the universe. The bones and tortoise shells used for Shang divination were replaced by plant stalks—a change that reflected a conceptual shift away from an enchanted universe towards a more rational, impersonal one.

This shift did not mean that ancient beliefs and practices disappeared. The understanding that the world is controlled by ghosts, nature spirits, and celestial beings remains an integral part of Chinese religion, especially in folk traditions. Nevertheless, new schools of thought developed. Legalists stressed the power of law in the advancement of human well-being; Naturalists concentrated on natural elements and processes (see Focus box); and Confucians focused on human relationships. Philosophers came to see the world as regulated by impersonal processes, which they sought to understand in order to use them as models for human society.

The quest to understand natural processes was driven in part by the desire to find a natural—hence "correct"—foundation on which to structure human society. The 64 hexagrams that are the basis of the *Classic of Changes* (also known as the *Yijing*), a divination text originating around 1000 BCE, were said to capture the metaphysical structure, transformations, and "Way" of the universe, providing both a general blueprint and a specific guide for humans facing a cosmos in continual flux.

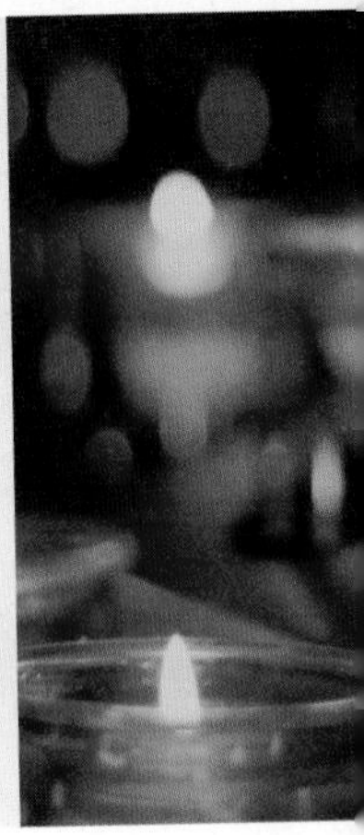

Focus

The Yin–Yang School

The Naturalists, also known as the yin-yang school, believed that those who followed the laws of nature would thrive while those who did not would perish. Yin–yang theory was later combined with the theory of the five "agents" or "elements" or "processes" (*wuxing*)—metal, wood, earth, water, and fire—to form a theory of cycles that are generated and overcome. Thus metal generates water, water generates wood, wood generates fire, fire generates earth, and earth generates metal; then the cycle begins again. This cosmology suggests there is nothing in the world that cannot be defeated; and, at the same time, that there is no destruction from which growth cannot come.

Rites: Performance and Principles

The section on "Principles of Sacrifice" in the *Rites* explains that a ruler must have a wife as a helpmate. The principle of complementarity is reflected in the division of labour between the king in the public world and the queen in the private realm. The necessary balance of yin and yang is reflected in the first two trigrams of the *Changes* or *Yijing*. *Qian* (Heaven and the creative) is represented by three solid lines ☰, while *kun* (Earth and the receptive) is represented by three broken lines ☷.

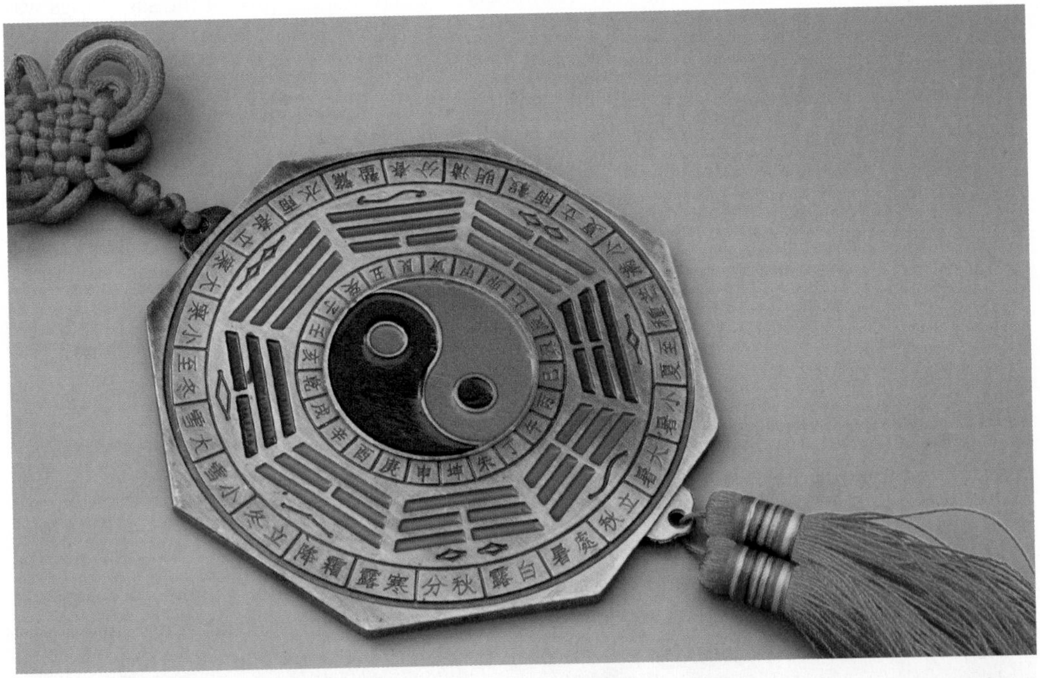

A *bagua* (eight trigrams) mirror is said to ward off evil spirits. This one contains the yin-yang symbol at its centre, surrounded by the eight trigrams and two circles (iStockphoto / Thinkstock).

The rituals described in the *Rites* evolved over time, as did the understanding of their role in the lives of the individual, the state, and the society. Belief in their magico-religious efficacy was gradually replaced by a sense of their value in terms of discipline, education, and moral development. The deeply religious culture of the Shang was humanized by Zhou-era philosophers such as Confucius. In *Master Tso's Commentary* on the Spring and Autumn Annals, for example, when a duke remarks that the spirits will protect him because his sacrificial offerings are "bountiful and pure, " he is corrected: "It is not simply that ghosts and spirits are attracted to human beings: it is virtue that attracts them" (adapted from J. Legge in Sommer 1995: 25).

Confucius

Confucius spoke of himself as a transmitter of tradition rather than an innovator. On the connection between goodness and ritual, he famously said:

> Respect without ritual becomes tiresome, circumspection without ritual becomes timidity, bold fortitude without ritual becomes unruly, and directness without ritual becomes twisted (Sommer 1995: 46).

Confucius used the word *li* ("rites" or "ritual") to mean not only religious ritual but also the rules of social etiquette and everyday courtesy. He encouraged his students to practise *li* in all five fundamental relationships, and urged them to seek the spirit and principles behind the rites. Central to the Confucian understanding of history was the perfection that the sage kings achieved by governing in accordance with the Way. Confucius believed that the time of the sage kings was preceded by a utopian age:

> When the Great Way was practised, the world was shared by all alike. The worthy and the able were promoted to office and men practised good faith and lived in affection. Therefore they did not regard as parents only their own parents, or as sons only their own sons. The aged found a fitting close to their lives, the robust their proper employment; the young were provided with an upbringing, and the widow and widower, the orphaned and the sick, with proper care. Men had their tasks and women their hearths. . . . all evil plotting was prevented and thieves and rebels did not arise, so that the people could leave their outer gates unbolted. This was the age of Grand Commonality [*Datong*] ("Evolution of Rites," trans. B. Watson, in de Bary and Bloom 1999: 342–3).

In time, greed and selfishness ended the Grand Commonality and ushered in the period of Lesser Prosperity, during which the sage kings emerged as exemplars of correct, ethical governance. The primary source of Confucius' teachings on how to govern in such a potentially chaotic era is the collection known as the *Analects*.

The Confucian ideal was the *junzi* (translated variously as "gentleman," "noble," or "superior person"). Although the standard meaning of *junzi* was "son of a lord," indicating inherited social nobility, in the *Analects* the *junzi* is a person of noble character, committed to the development of ***de***—another word that underwent a shift in meaning with Confucius. Originally referring to a kind of magical charismatic power, in the *Analects* it signifies a moral power rooted in ethical behaviour. The fact that Confucius used these words in non-traditional ways did not mean that the meanings he gave them were new; the socio-political ideals he promoted were already present in the classic texts (*Odes*, *Documents*, *Spring and Autumn Annals*, and *Changes*). Confucius used the single word *ren* to capture virtues such as respect, liberality, trustworthiness, earnestness, and kindness. He believed that the most effective way to cultivate *ren* was through careful observance of *li*.

Above all, Confucius emphasized filial piety or devotion, explained in the *Rites* as "caring for" one's parents according to the Way: that is, to the greatest extent possible without neglecting one's responsibilities in other relationships (8.2.1). For Confucius, ritual observance was essential to the maintenance of harmony, for he believed that those who treat their parents with the proper respect will be equally loyal to a government ruling with the Mandate of Heaven. Above all, humaneness is reflected in loyalty and empathetic understanding or reciprocity (4: 15). Confucius sums up his teachings in the "silver rule": "What you would not want for yourself, do not do to others" (15: 23).

Since all human beings are by nature similar, all have the potential to be noble; however, individuals set themselves apart through their habits and actions (17: 2). Thus even as he democratizes the idea of nobility, Confucius creates a hierarchy of character based on moral cultivation. This hierarchy is all about the mastery of the "heart-mind" (***xin***):

> Through mastering oneself and returning to ritual one becomes humane. If for a single day one can master oneself and return to ritual, the whole world will return to humaneness. . . . Look at nothing contrary to ritual; listen to nothing contrary to ritual; say nothing contrary to ritual; do nothing contrary to ritual (12: 1).

Confucius believed that if the ruler wants goodness, the people will be good: "The virtue (*de*) of the exemplary person is like the wind, and the virtue of small people is like grass: When the wind blows over the grass, the grass must bend" (12: 19). To recreate the Grand Commonalty, therefore, the good, wise, and humane must rule over the small-minded and morally inferior.

The Confucian mandate is to limit the negative consequences of ignoble behaviour. When a recluse describes Confucius as "a scholar who withdraws from particular men" and suggests that instead he should withdraw from society, Confucius sighs and responds: "If the Way prevailed in the world, [I] would not be trying to change it" (18: 6). Personal goodness is not enough: ethical nobility must be expressed through action in the public realm.

Mengzi

The second most prominent classical thinker after Confucius is Meng Ke, whose name was latinized as Mencius. He lived more than a century after Confucius, by which time large conscript armies had been formed and the human cost of war had increased accordingly. Mengzi travelled from state to state, trying to persuade their rulers to stop the carnage for the sake of the people. At the same time he emphasized the practical value of humaneness (*ren*) and the importance of the moral sense of what is right (*yi*).

The book *Mencius* is a collection of conversations between Mencius and his disciples, his opponents, and feudal rulers. Among the issues discussed are human nature and government. Mencius traced many of the problems of his day to the human heart-mind (*xin*), of which he identified four types. The heart-mind of compassion yields benevolence; that of shame leads to observance of rites; that of respect moves people to duty or right behaviour; and that of right and wrong brings wisdom (6.A.6 ibid., 163).

Mencius taught that sensitivity to others' suffering is innate, but must be consciously developed if a ruler is to govern as the sage kings did. In later times, a great man was needed to encourage the ruler to cultivate the heart-mind; then, once the prince had become benevolent and dutiful, everyone would emulate him. Mencius did not believe that the effect of the prince's character on the people was automatic or magical, however. Even though human nature was essentially good, the common people needed supervision: otherwise they would be driven only by material needs and desires, with no higher consciousness. The best way of nurturing the heart-mind of the people, Mencius taught, was to teach them to reduce their desires.

Mencius's belief in the potential of the mature heart-mind allowed him to take some unconventional positions. When someone suggested that Shun, the son-in-law of King Yao, had failed in filial piety because he did not inform his parents of his marriage to Yao's daughters, Mencius argued that the parents' heart-minds were not sufficiently developed for them to consent to his marriage, while Shun's own heart-mind was so well developed that he could act according to his own conscience.

Similarly, Mencius once remarked that it would be better if the *Documents* had never been written if its contents had to be accepted without critical thought. Most famously, he argued that rebellion is justified when the ruler has lost the Mandate of Heaven. For Mencius it was not enough simply to follow the classical teachings: we must use our heart-minds to determine the morally correct course of action.

Mencius was not only a political thinker. He has also been described as a mystic because of his emphasis on ***qi*** (or *ch'i*): the "flood-like vital force, energy or ether" that appears simultaneously to give substance to virtue and to be nourished by it:

> This is a *ch'i* which is . . . vast and unyielding . . . which unites rightness and the Way. Deprive it of these and it will collapse. It is born of accumulated rightness and cannot be appropriated by anyone through a sporadic show of rightness. Whenever one acts in a way that falls below the standard set in one's heart, it will collapse (2.A.2; ibid., 77–8).

Xunzi

Xun Kuang or Xun Qing (c. 310–219 BCE), better known as Master Xun or Xunzi, was a generation younger than Mencius. Living at the end of the Warring States period, he likely witnessed the bloody conflict that ended in the conquest of the last feudal states by the first Qin emperor (Qin Shi Huang). So perhaps it is not surprising that he did not agree with Mencius on the innate goodness of human beings: he believed that human nature was evil, and goodness required conscious effort. Nevertheless, he did share the core Confucian beliefs in the possibility of sagehood and the value of culture and learning.

Xunzi believed that education and ritual were essential to the maintenance of the hierarchy required for an orderly society. But he was not blind to the misuse and corruption of Confucian values. Like Confucius, who says in the *Analects* that the "village paragon is the thief of virtue" (17: 13), and Mencius, who describes such a paragon as an honest man who "might be confused with the virtuous" but in fact "cringingly (tries to please) the world" (Lau 1970: 203), Xunzi spoke out against contemporary officials and scholars who "have all become confused" (Watson 1963: 141).

The collection known as the *Xunzi* was compiled more than a century after Xunzi's time, during the Han dynasty. Its form marks a major departure from the recorded conversations of the *Analects* and *Mencius*: it consists mainly of essays on topics such as the original nature of human beings, learning, self-cultivation, government, and military affairs. The first chapter, "Encouraging Learning," underlines the necessity of effort to achieve moral progress:

> Learning should never cease. . . . A piece of wood as straight as a plumb line may be bent into a circle as true as any drawn with a compass and, even after the wood has dried, it will not straighten out again (Watson 1963: 15).

Why do human beings need to be "straightened out"? Because they are "warped" with innate desires that must be curbed through education and ritual. In his chapter "A Discussion of Heaven," Xunzi continues Confucius' effort to humanize the Zhou tradition, rejecting the supernatural in favour of the rational and natural. He sees Heaven, Earth, and humanity as forming a trinity in which each component has its own function. As human beings, even sages do not seek to understand Heaven, let alone to take over its "godlike" role. Rather, humans should simply focus on living well.

Even though Xunzi believed the world to operate without supernatural intervention, he supported the performance of traditional rituals because he believed they had been perfected by the ancient kings. Only a sage can fully understand the rites, he said; but the noble person finds comfort in performing them, while the common person accepts them as a reflection of the reality of the spirit world. Xunzi took ritual and music out of the realm of magic, interpreting their functions in practical terms. Thus the purpose of teaching the rites is to cultivate the virtues that promote harmony, such as courtesy and humility.

Daoism

Origins

Not everyone believed in the Confucian way. Daoists developed a counterpoint to the Confucian focus on social hierarchy, political involvement, emotional and moral discipline, and ritual regimentation, a counterpoint based on the concept of the **Dao** ("way"; also spelled **Tao**). Although they did not seek to overturn Confucianism, they pointed out its limitations.

Historically, Daoism was understood to have two branches, philosophical and religious. Daoist philosophy traced its origins to the third and fourth centuries BCE, but Daoist religion was thought to have emerged only in the second century CE, with the formation of two millenarian groups (the Celestial Masters and Yellow Kerchiefs). Recent research, however, shows that philosophers in the northeastern state of Qi (present-day Shandong) were discussing ideas related to both philosophical and religious Daoism as early as the fourth century BCE.

Although the literature of that time does not use the term "Daoist," it does refer to a Huang–Lao school, named for the mythical "Yellow Emperor" (Huangdi), and the legendary philosopher **Laozi**. Huang–Lao teachings correspond roughly to what we now consider philosophical Daoism; its teachings took shape around the early fourth century, when King Xuan of Qi (r. 319–301 BCE) offered appointments at the Jixia Academy to scholars from various states, north and south, in the hope that they would find solutions to the problems of the day. Among those scholars were Mencius, Xunzi, the Naturalist Zou Yan of the **Yin-yang Five Phases** (*Wuxing* or five elements) school, and a student of the Huang–Lao teachings named Huan Yuan.

Daoist nuns from the Quanzhen (Complete Truth) sect perform daily rituals on Wudang Mountain. The three head officiates wear the lotus crown and robes embroidered with trigrams. The yellow banners in the background mark the space as sacred and contain writing that resembles Chinese characters but is "heavenly," not of the human realm (© Michael Saso).

Philosophical Daoism

The term "philosophical Daoism" refers to an early prototypical Daoism concerned with ideas such as the nature of virtue, cultivation of the heart-mind, and good governance. Its early history has conventionally been associated with two main sources: the ***Daodejing*** (*Classic of the Way and Power*), a multi-layered, multi-authored verse text traditionally attributed to the "old master" Laozi; and the ***Zhuangzi***, named for the thinker whose ideas it purports to represent (in fact, both works are collections of texts written at different times by different authors).

Focus

The *Guanzi*

The *Guanzi* originated in the fourth century and took its current form in the first century BCE. It was categorized as Daoist during the Han but later reclassified as Legalist, and therefore neglected by students of Daoism. Yet recent research has found that two of its sections, both dealing with mental discipline, are directly relevant to the ideas in the two classical Daoist texts. The first, *Techniques of the Mind I*, addresses the broader concerns of government as well as methods of self-cultivation. The second, *Inward Training*, focuses exclusively on spiritual cultivation and bridges the streams of philosophical and religious Daoism.

At least three new sources have proved helpful in reconstructing the early development of philosophical Daoism. Two of them are found in the *Guanzi*, a collection of writings traditionally attributed to a very early (seventh century BCE) figure named Guan Zhong; and the third, the Huang-Lao manuscripts, is a recently discovered bundle of silk manuscripts, dating from the second century BCE, that include illustrations of "guiding and stretching" exercises similar to modern-day ***taiji*** (the sequence of slow-motion movements known in the West as Tai Chi).

Development towards Religious Expression

Religious Daoism is widely associated with colourful rituals, belief in deities, ghosts, and spirits, meditation in search of union with the Dao, and the use of drugs in pursuit of immortality or transcendence. Thus it may appear to be diametrically opposed to philosophical Daoism. Yet the two streams do share several fundamental elements: self-discipline, the quest for transcendence of the ordinary self, the ideal of non-action (***wuwei***), and the assumption that religion and politics are inseparable.

What makes it difficult to recognize these common elements is the fact that religious Daoism also incorporates two traditions that are clearly not philosophical: a southern tradition of shamanism and a northern tradition known as the "way of recipes, methods, and immortality." Unlike the (northern) divinatory shamanism of the Shang and Zhou eras, this southern shamanism was distinctly religious and non-philosophical. Its character can be seen in a collection called *Songs of the South*, which features lavish descriptions of gods and goddesses, "soaring phoenixes," and fabulous unions between humans and gods. The northern tradition of "recipes, methods, and immortality," for its part, centred on a quest for an elixir of everlasting life conducted by "masters of technical methods" such as magicians, doctors, diviners, and astrologists. The integration of these very different traditions only adds to the difficulty of understanding the early history of "religious" Daoism.

Different Streams of Daoism

The conjunction of these diverse traditions produced several distinctive streams in early Daoism. Three elements recur in the classical texts: the concept of the Dao as "the One," the primary force in the universe; the need for inner discipline to reach the deep tranquillity necessary to experience unity with that force; and, finally, the use of the first two elements to achieve benevolent government.

It has been suggested that the concerns of the classical texts can be classified in three streams: Individualist, Primitivist, and Syncretist. The Individualist stream is mystical; concerned mainly with inner cultivation and union with the cosmos, it is basic to all six of the classical texts. To this the Primitivist stream, which can be seen in the *Laozi* as well as parts of the *Zhuangzi* (ch. 8–10 and the first part of 11), adds an appeal for a simple agrarian way of life. Finally, the Syncretist stream, found in the later chapters of the *Zhuangzi*, *Techniques of the Mind I*, and the *Huang–Lao* manuscripts, combines teachings of Laozi and Zhuangzi with those of other schools. The exact chronology of the various writings is not known, but the *Daodejing* and *Inward Training* are generally considered to be the earliest. Anecdotes in the *Zhuangzi* that describe encounters between Confucius and Laozi would make the two men contemporaries, but their historical authenticity is questionable. The first seven chapters of the *Zhuangzi*, if they were in fact composed by Zhuang Zhou (Zhuangzi, 369?–286? BCE) are also of some antiquity.

Finally, the *Songs of the South* are traditionally attributed in part to Qu Yuan, a famously righteous minister who is remembered in the Dragon Boat festival, though most of them were probably written about a century after his death in 278 BCE. Brief descriptions of the six sources follow.

The Dragon Boat Festival (*Duanwujie*), held on the fifth day of the fifth month of the lunar calendar, commemorates the loyal Chu minister Qu Yuan (c. 340–278 BCE), who drowned himself after he was unjustly banished. The boat races recall the efforts made to keep fish from eating Qu's body (© Imaginechina / Corbis).

Inward Training *in Daoist and Confucian Contexts*

Inward Training, a short text on cultivation of the heart-mind embedded in the *Guanzi*, serves as a bridge between philosophical and religious Daoism and provides examples of the cultural beliefs and practices from the Zhou era that Confucians and Daoists shared.

Like the *Daodejing*, *Zhuangzi*, *Techniques of the Mind I*, and *Huang–Lao* sources, *Inward Training* recommends a type of meditation known as "holding fast to the One." But it also refers to concepts uncommon in those philosophical texts—the vital essence (*jing*), vital energy or breath (*qi*), and the numinous or the spirit (*shen*)—that became core features of religious Daoism, in which the integration of these three elements (through meditation and dietary practices) was believed to confer longevity and even physical immortality or spiritual transcendence.

Inward Training recalls early Confucianism when it suggests that the virtue of an exemplary person has a kind of mystical efficacy. The emperor in particular was believed to be capable of "righting" conditions in the empire by virtue of the harmony he embodies. Section 9 uses the same terms that Confucians do to describe the exemplary person (*junzi*) who cultivates this power-virtue (*de*). Like the ideal Confucian ruler, his Daoist counterpart possesses a virtue-power that influences lesser persons.

Whereas Laozi and Zhuangzi suggest some antipathy towards Confucians, *Inward Training* hints at a shared desire for tranquillity and recovery of our original or Heavenly nature. Later forms of Daoism, however, did include practices that some Confucians found abhorrent, including the use of esoteric sexual practices, the ingestion of poisonous cinnabar (mercuric sulphide) to attain immortality, and its emphasis on escaping or transcending the world rather than serving it.

Laozi and the Daodejing

If the apparent incongruity of such practices seems puzzling, it may be helpful to remember the famous first line of the *Daodejing*: "The way that can be spoken of / Is not the constant way" (Lau 1963: 57). The fluidity implied by this holy ineffability is characteristic of Daoism.

Unlike the authors (or editors) of *Inward Training*, Laozi takes a dim view of Confucian rites: "The rites are the wearing thin of loyalty and good faith / And the beginning of disorder" (Lau 1963: 99). Yet, like the Confucians, he wants to ensure that "the offering of sacrifice by descendants will never come to an end" (ibid., 115). The sage of the *Daodejing* shares with Confucius the ideal of discipline: the only difference is that he seeks to achieve it not through human-created rites but through the all-embracing cosmic Way.

The term *de* in the *Daodejing* refers to a "virtue-power" that embodies the mystic inner power attained through alignment with the unseen world, the power that allows a sage ruler to infuse his realm with the harmony he has achieved by "doing nothing," *wuwei*. (It's important not to take this phrase literally: in this context, "doing nothing" refers to a state of mind or being in which one is so permeated by the Way that one acts in concert with it, free of self or intention.)

The Daoist sage invites the Dao to dwell in him by making himself as empty as the hollow of a cup or the space in a room. Soft as the water that flows over rocks yet in time wears them down, he is spare in his desires. Overturning convention, he knows the honoured male but keeps to the traditionally subservient and humble female. He knows the symbolic goodness of white but keeps to the unenlightened black (ibid., 127). He embraces the One and remains an uncarved block, transcending dichotomies. He refuses to be sculpted with conventional virtues—though Laozi makes it clear that he also teaches conventional values:

> What others teach I also teach.
> "The violent will not come to a natural end."
> I shall take this as my precept
> (Lau 1963: 103).

Yet even as the *Daodejing* counsels against violence—just as the Confucian sages do—it criticizes as "false adornments" the Confucian concepts of the wise sage and righteous benevolence. It also finds fault with profit, ingenuity, and learning. Simplicity should replace false values: "Exhibit the unadorned and embrace the uncarved block, / Have little thought of self and as few desires as possible" (Lau 1963: 75).

Unlike the Confucian who concentrates on the virtuous, the Daoist sage "abandons no one" (ibid., 84). "He is "drowsy," "muddled," and "foolish" (ibid., 77), and does not claim to be right (ibid., 79); he is self-effacing and "avoids . . . arrogance" (ibid., 87). Such a sage is capable of surviving even the tumult of the Warring States.

Zhuangzi

Unlike the sage of the *Laozi*, the sage of the *Zhuangzi* shuns politics. Even more strikingly, in the *Zhuangzi* great sages are not the only ones with wisdom: a humble cook may also be wise. The fanciful and the historical exist side by side, like black and white, or female and male. The aspiration to transcend dichotomies is at the core of Zhuangzi's teachings: he "recognizes . . . a 'this' which is also 'that', a 'that' which is also 'this'" (Watson 1968: 39).

The sage allows his mind to wander, blending with the vastness that is the Way. He follows things as they are. In contrast to Laozi's *wuwei* or "non-action," Zhuangzi describes a state of "self-so-ness" or spontaneity (***ziran***). Although the principle is not inconsistent with the Confucian ideal of following nature, it is expressed in remarkably different terms. The story of Cook Ding illustrates the Daoist position. When the prince asks the cook for advice, Ding counsels the same approach to governance that a cook would take to carving an ox: instead of hacking at the carcass, he would look for the hollows in the joints. In the same way, the ruler should not rely on preconceived rules and principles, but should examine the situation at hand to understand its natural structure. The condition in which it is possible to assess a situation clearly is that of Oneness through emptiness.

The Huang–Lao Silk Manuscripts, Techniques of the Mind I, *and* Songs of the South

The last three textual sources of early Daoism were likely compiled through the late Zhou, Qin, and early Han periods. The ideas recorded in the *Huang–Lao Silk Manuscripts* are drawn from a variety of schools, but their underlying theme is Laozi's ideal of the tranquil sage king who governs through non-action. The prototypical Daoist Huang–Lao scholars were active at court during the early Han, although they disappeared after Emperor Wu (r. 140–87 BCE) made Confucianism the state religion. Sealed in a tomb in 168 BCE, the manuscripts were unknown until 1973.

Like the Huang–Lao teachings, *Techniques of the Mind I* reflects the Daoist concerns outlined in *Inward Training*, the *Daodejing*, and the *Zhuangzi*. It explains how self-cultivation—specifically, restraining desire and emptying the mind—can help a ruler attain the tranquillity necessary to respond harmoniously to any situation in its "self-so-ness."

Women and the Feminine in the Classical Texts

Neither *Inward Training* nor the *Daodejing* discussed women. The latter talks abstractly about the "mother" and the "spirit of the valley," which is both the "root of heaven and earth" and the "mysterious female" that never dies (Lau 1963: 62). Nor does Zhuangzi concern himself much with women: wives are mentioned only as companions in life who are grieved in death, and conventional gender roles are accepted. The Daoist Liezi is described as taking over the domestic realm of the feminine after he has attained mature spiritual understanding:

> He went home and for three years did not go out. He replaced his wife at the stove, fed the pigs as though he were feeding people, and showed no preferences in the things he did. He got rid of the carving and polishing and returned to plainness, letting his body stand alone like a clod. In the midst of entanglement he remained sealed, and in this oneness he ended his life (Watson 1968: 97).

This association of sacred oneness with animals and the feminine is not surprising. Nor is Zhuangzi's implied criticism of Confucian-style "carving and polishing," given the Daoist preference for non-action and the natural. Images of female power in itself—without reference to men—are limited to a teacher called the Woman Crookback and the Queen Mother of the West, who heads the pantheon of goddesses. These are mythical characters, however: unlike the Confucian classics, the *Zhuangzi* does not celebrate any historical woman. In the *Songs of the South*, the theme of men seeking union with the feminine, and women with the masculine, becomes prominent.

Mohism

Mohism was the third most influential religious system before the introduction of Buddhism. Master Mo (Mozi, 470–391 BCE) coexisted with Confucians and Daoists, and his teachings reflect similar concerns, but were also markedly different. Mozi taught an undifferentiated love, a love of all without distinction. He believed that Heaven willed people to love one another, and that those who failed to do so would be punished; that the ultimate purpose of government was to provide food, shelter, and security for all; and that members of a society should help one another avoid harm and deprivation.

The Han Dynasty (202 BCE–220 CE)

State Confucianism, Huang-Lao and Religious Daoism, and the Introduction of Buddhism

Early Chinese religious beliefs and practices faded or were recontextualized in new ideas, rituals, and structures. Ancient shamanic traditions endured, and interest in divination using the *Yijing* persisted. Although eclipsed by Confucianism at court, Daoism re-emerged in the form of religious anti-Han rebel groups like the Yellow Kerchiefs and Celestial Masters. It was into this varied religious landscape that Buddhism was introduced.

Popular Beliefs and Practices Assimilated

The worship of deities continued into the Han. During a drought, ordinary folk appealed to the Queen Mother of the West for help. By the Latter Han, she was the head deity of a paradise in the far west that was believed to connect Heaven and Earth; she also became the goddess who bestowed immortality and a protector-deity who granted wealth and children—a precursor to the Buddhist ***pusa*** (*bodhisattva* or enlightened being) Guanyin (Avalokitesvara).

Political Daoism

The influence of the Huang–Lao thinkers during the early Han can be seen in the fact that the King of Huainan, Liu An, sponsored a collection of Huang–Lao writings called the *Masters of Huainan* (*Huainanzi*), a copy of which he presented to Emperor Wu (his nephew) in 139 BCE.

A mural from the Mogao Caves (or Grottoes) at Dunhuang, in western China, shows the celestial buddha Amituofo (Amitabha) seated on his lotus throne and surrounded by bodhisattvas (© dbimages / Alamy). Mogao is one of three extraordinary Buddhist cave-temple systems in north central and western China (the others are Yungang and Longmen). Beginning in 366 CE, more than 400 grottoes were carved out of the rock at Mogao alone and filled with Buddhist paintings, sculptures, and manuscripts.

A comprehensive guide to just governance, it emphasizes the ruler's need to still his passions and rid himself of prejudice so that he can respond appropriately to all situations.

The court historian Sima Tan (d. 110 BCE) was also a follower of the Huang–Lao school. In his discourse "On the Six Lineages of Thought" he describes the Daoists approvingly as "mov[ing] in unison with the Formless and provid[ing] adequately for all living things' (H. Roth 1999; S. Queen in de Bary and Bloom 1999: 279). By contrast, he writes that the New Text Confucians (who by that time were in the ascendant) "labour much yet achieve little" (ibid.). Distancing himself from purposeful "right" action, Sima Tan made clear his preference for the Daoists.

Nevertheless, underlying both traditions is a fundamental emphasis on self-cultivation for the sake of harmony in the universe. Both Confucians and Daoists seek to control the heart-mind in order to attain the tranquillity necessary to achieve union with the Way. Both believe that oneness with the Dao, hence with Heaven and Earth, allows us to transcend our selves and serve others.

The Introduction of Buddhism

Buddhism, like Daoism, emphasizes meditation, breath control, and abstinence from certain foods. Like both Indigenous religions, it focuses on purity of the heart-mind and mastery of the passions. But its trajectory and methods tend to be more extreme. For example, the *Sutra in Forty-Two Sections* stresses the hindrance that lust poses for a man seeking enlightenment, and the Buddha instructs his monks not to look at women, let alone talk to them. During the Han dynasty, the features that Buddhism appeared to share with Confucianism and Daoism helped to mask its more fundamental differences. Sometimes Daoist terms and ideas were used to convey Buddhism to potential converts.

Document

From the *Sutra in Forty-Two Sections*

The Sutra in Forty-Two Sections *is a defence of Buddhism purportedly written by a Chinese convert at the end of the second century. But it was most likely composed in the fifth or sixth century, when Buddhism was at the height of its influence. The following excerpts address the deleterious effects of passion, especially lust.*

Those who are addicted to the passions are like the torchbearers running against the wind; their hands are sure to be burned.

From the passions arises worry and from worry arises fear. Away with the passions, and no fear, no worry.

People cleave to their worldly possessions and selfish passions so blindly as to sacrifice their own lives for them. They are like a child who tries to eat a little honey smeared on the edge of a knife.

The Lord of Heaven offered a beautiful maiden to the Buddha, desiring to test the Buddha's intentions and teachings. The Buddha replied, "You are but a leather bag filled with filth, why do you come?" (quoted in Chen 1964: 34–5).

Confucianism

The Birth of Political State Confucianism

The victory of the Qin unified the Warring States. To minimize dissent, however, the first emperor ordered the destruction of almost all the scholarly books that might encourage deep reflection on social and political values, among them the Confucian classics. Although one copy of each work was preserved in the imperial library, those copies were destroyed in a fire when the capital was sacked. Thus when the Han dynasty (202 BCE–220 CE) replaced the short-lived Qin, a great many works had to be reconstructed.

The political and intellectual changes that took place during the Han would continue to shape imperial ideology as well as religious beliefs and practices for the next 2,000 years. To the four virtues identified by Mencius—humaneness, right action, ritual appropriateness, and wisdom—was added a fifth: trustworthiness. Also central to Han ideology were the notions that Heaven, Earth, and humankind form a trinity; and that the celestial and terrestrial powers respond to human entreaty. Confucian thinkers reflected the influence both of Xunzi and of a chapter in the *Rites* called "Centrality and Equilibrium": they believed that humans who were sincere in their efforts to bring about peace and harmony could share in the creative, transformative powers of Heaven and Earth.

Echoing Mencius and Xunzi, Han Confucians identified economic welfare as the basis of morality. The government, in particular the emperor, was obliged to provide both the physical sustenance and the moral education necessary for people to lead secure and happy lives. Following Xunzi, Han Confucians also promoted moral education through ritual, music, and literature.

Both a Confucian canon (in the form of the Five Classics) and political or state Confucianism were established during the Han. Philosophers seeking a holistic account of the universe and humankind's place in it tried to syncretize the Confucian tradition with other philosophies. The result was a Confucianism that blended ideas from traditional texts with those of thinkers such as the masters of technical methods, who sought to manipulate the cosmos; and the Naturalists, who developed the notions of *qi* and yin-yang–five phases. It was also during the Han that a number of influential non-canonical texts were written or compiled and edited, among them the *Biographies of Exemplary* (or *Virtuous*) *Women*, *Admonitions* (or *Lessons*) *for Women*, and the *Classic of Filiality*. The first two in particular defined what was expected of women and formed the foundation of a specifically female Confucian tradition.

The Compilation of the Five Classics

Han Confucians believed that Confucius himself had transmitted the Zhou tradition through the canonical texts, and that he had had a hand in the selection, compilation, and editing of all five Classics. However, later scholars have shown that a good portion of their content originated after Confucius' time.

The first classic, the *Changes* or *Yijing*, assumed particular importance during the Han. It is divided into two parts: a series of short passages interpreting the 64 hexagrams, and 10 appendices or "wings" (traditionally attributed to Confucius) that elaborate on those interpretations. Confucius is also said to have edited or written a short introduction to each section of the second classic, the *Documents*. Although some of the content is now thought to date from as late as the fourth century

CE, this volume was historically considered an accurate account of China's ancient rulers, from the sage kings to the early Zhou.

The third classic, the *Odes*, consists of roughly 300 poems, mostly from the early Zhou, that Confucius is believed to have chosen and edited. They include songs from both ordinary people and the aristocracy and were often interpreted politically as expressions of popular sentiment—praising virtuous rulers and criticizing bad ones.

The fourth classic, the *Rites*, consists of three separate texts, some of which Confucius is credited with compiling and editing: *Rites of Etiquette and Ceremonials* for minor officials, *Rites* (or *Institutions*) *of Zhou*, and the *Records* or *Book of Rites*, which explores the principles behind particular rites. The contents, which likely date from the mid- to late Zhou and the early Han and took their current form over time, range from minutely detailed advice on how to live daily life to broad philosophical discussions of the meaning of state rituals.

Map 10.1 Indigenous Chinese Religions

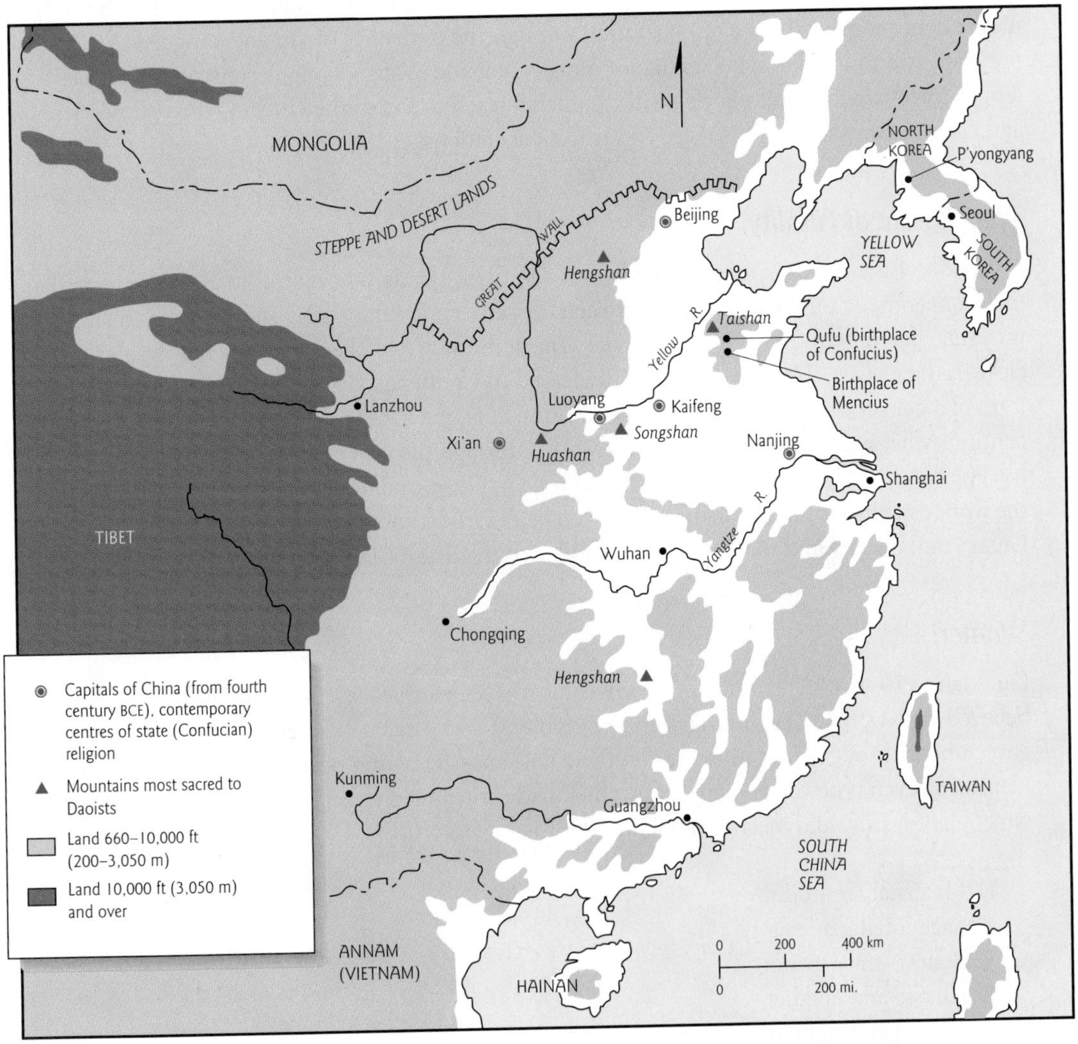

Source: Adapted from al Faruqi and Sopher 1974: 111.

The fifth and last classic, the *Spring and Autumn Annals*, is a terse chronicle of events in Confucius' native state of Lu from 722 to 481 BCE that Confucius is said to have compiled to express his judgment of them. It was therefore used as a guide to moral laws and principles.

The text-focused Confucians were the hardest hit by the Qin emperor's book burning. And it was the Confucians of the third and second centuries BCE who took up the task of retrieving and reassembling the lost texts, including those of other schools.

Dong Zhongshu

The most influential Confucian at the court of Emperor Wu was **Dong Zhongshu** (195?–105? BCE). He promoted a "natural model" of the way the world works, based on the idea of correlation between the macrocosm of Heaven and Earth and the microcosm of the human body.

Dong set out to integrate Confucian thought with the supernatural thinking of court diviners, the correlative thinking of the Huang–Lao movement (see p. 496), and the yin-yang thinking of the Naturalist school. Dong took ideas from Mencius and Xunzi and combined them with the Naturalist concept of vital force (*qi*) operating through the dynamics of yin and yang. At the close of the Han, two rationalist scholars named Yang Xiong and Wang Chong deconstructed Dong's system of correlation, separating classical Confucian teachings from the yin-yang–five phases school, and cleared away some of his more extravagant accretions.

The Classic of Filiality

A version of the five relationships known as the three bonds was central to Han Confucianism; they concentrated on the distinction between the senior and junior roles encapsulated in emperor–minister, parent–child and husband–wife. The importance of the minister's role was especially clear in the *Classic of Filiality* (traditionally traced to Confucius' disciple Zengzi). Presented in the form of a conversation between Zengzi and Confucius, the *Classic of Filiality* extends the notion of continuity between the human and spirit worlds through the veneration of ancestors and connects filial piety to the idea of the triad formed by Heaven, Earth, and human beings. Following the *Rites*, the work establishes filiality as the foundation of all virtues and the basis of public morality. By the Latter Han, *Filiality* and the *Analects* were added to the list of Classics.

Women

Liu Xiang (79–8 BCE) is said to have written the *Biographies of Exemplary Women* because he believed that women (beginning with the empress) had a critical, albeit indirect, role to play in government through their influence on their husbands. Drawing on the *Odes* and *Documents*, he identified seven types of women, six of which had contributed to peace and prosperity, and one of which had destroyed dynasties (Raphals 1998: 19):

1. Maternal rectitude
2. Sage intelligence
3. Benevolent wisdom
4. Chaste and obedient
5. Chaste and righteous

6. Skill in argument
7. Vicious and depraved.

Under "Maternal Rectitude" he tells the famous story of Mengmu, the widowed mother of Mencius. She is said to have moved three times to facilitate her son's education. On one occasion, when Mengmu asked how his day at school had gone and Mencius answered nonchalantly "As usual," she took a knife and destroyed the cloth she had been weaving to teach him that a man who does not take learning seriously is like a woman who neglects her responsibility to her family.

Ban Zhao

Like a man's moral development, a woman's cultivation began at home, in the family. Self-cultivation was especially important for women because of the influence a mother was thought to have on her fetus. According to the *Rites*, boys and girls should be separated after the age of seven. At ten, boys were sent out to study the six arts (rites, music, archery, chariot racing, calligraphy and mathematics) while girls were kept home to learn domestic skills and develop the mental discipline they would need to care for their future families. In addition to learning how to weave, sew, and prepare food, girls were taught etiquette—the social conventions required for harmonious relations—and how to perform the rituals, including the sacrifices required to keep peace with the ancestors.

Born into a family of scholars, **Ban Zhao** (c. 48–112 CE) said that she wrote *Admonitions for Women* for her daughters, who had not had the benefit of systematic training in their roles either as wives or as daughters- and sisters-in-law in their husbands' families. Well-educated, socially prominent, and politically influential, Ban Zhao was typical of aristocratic women in Han society. According to one later history, she worked in the imperial libraries and supervised the writing of treatises on astronomy and the chronological tables of nobles. Recognizing Ban's erudition, the emperor appointed her as tutor to the women at court, and she later served as an advisor to Empress Deng. *Admonitions* is divided into seven chapters:

1. Humility
2. Husband and wife
3. Respect and caution
4. Womanly qualifications
5. Whole-hearted devotion
6. Implicit obedience
7. Harmony with younger brothers- and sisters-in-law.

Ban describes three rituals performed at the birth of a girl and explains the principles behind them. First, whereas a baby boy was placed on the bed, a girl was placed below it, to signify her lowliness; second, she was given broken pieces of pottery to play with to signify that she must work hard; and third, her birth was announced to the ancestors to draw attention to her future role in their veneration.

Ban belongs firmly in the Confucian lineage. She believed that relationships are founded on the cosmic principles of yin and yang: because yang is rigid, a man was honoured for his strength; and because yin is yielding, a woman was considered beautiful for her gentleness. Over time, the name Ban Zhao became synonymous with womanly erudition. Some 400 years after her death, she was included in a list of exemplary women venerated in state sacrifices.

Daoism

Differentiation during the Han

Although the Huang–Lao school disappeared from the Han court after Confucianism was made the state religion, Daoist practice continued to develop outside the palace, among the common people.

Inner and Outer Alchemy

The first text on inner alchemy was published in the mid-second century. Traditionally ascribed to Wei Boyang, an alchemist from the south, *The Seal of the Unity of the Three* took its name from its three main subjects: cosmology from the *Changes*, *wuwei* from Daoism, and alchemy. Wei fused the three elements into a single doctrine. Like Dong Zhongshu, Wei used correlative cosmology, drawing on yin-yang and five phases to describe the cosmos in relation to the Dao, the relative to the Absolute, multiplicity to Oneness, and time to timelessness.

The classical texts taught that the three vital elements of essence, energy, and numinous spirit must be returned to their original wholeness (broken by worldly activity and the disruptive awareness of things as separate from one another) by meditation: "holding fast to the One," "sitting and forgetting," visualizing the cosmos within one's body, and following the internal circulation of vital energy. According to Wei, practitioners of inner alchemy sought to return to the Dao by reversing the processes of disunion—as though they were sculptures "unsculpting" themselves to recover their original unity as uncarved blocks. In practice, through meditative visualization, devotees sought to move from form to essence, from essence to vital energy, from vital energy to spirit, and from spirit to emptiness or the Void, which, though formless, can be visualized as the highest deity: the Great One, Supreme Unity, or Supreme Oneness (Taiyi).

Belief in physical immortality was strong. It was thought that, after a long period of inward concentration, when the spirit had been purified, a "spirit embryo" containing or representing the True Self would be born. There were also some who believed that immortality could be achieved through the ingestion of cinnabar.

The Celestial Masters and Yellow Kerchiefs

Over time, the Confucian underpinnings of the Han regime were challenged by political corruption, natural disaster, and military turbulence. The resulting economic and social turmoil provoked uprisings, some of which reflected Daoist influences. At the same time, the *Classic of the Great Peace* (*Taipingjing*) was circulating, prophesying the coming of a celestial master who would bring peace to a time of surging chaos.

The Great Peace likely influenced both the Celestial Masters and the Yellow Kerchiefs (*Taiping Dao* or "Way of Taiping"). Founded in 142 CE, the Celestial Masters (*Tianshi*; later renamed Orthodox Unity) traced its origins to a deified Laozi who revealed to **Zhang Daoling** the teachings of Orthodox Unity and gave him a covenant establishing a new relationship between the gods and humans. A central feature of this covenant was the abolition of traditional blood sacrifices: no longer would the gods be influenced by animal offerings. Instead, they would operate as a kind of celestial bureaucracy, modelled after the governmental bureaucracy, to whom believers could present their appeals. The priests were expected to provide their services in return for an annual donation of five bushels of rice from devotees.

Initiates of the Celestial Masters gained access to esoteric sacred texts. The *Daodejing* was used in liturgy; practices included chanting and meditation; and purity chambers were provided for the cultivation of the spirit embryo. The sect established a theocracy in the state of Shu (Sichuan) and was the state religion of the Wei kingdom until it was dispersed across northern China, unintentionally aiding the spread of Daoism.

The Yellow Kerchiefs movement, based in Shandong, was established with the express purpose of challenging the Han regime in the name of the Yellow Emperor. Like the Celestial Masters, the Yellow Kerchiefs practised confession, repentance of sins, meditation, and chanting; they also believed in inherited guilt, passed on from ancestors to descendants. They attracted a massive following, but when they rose in rebellion in 184 they were crushed and the movement disappeared.

Buddhism

When Buddhism was first introduced to China, Confucianism was soon to become the official religion, and the various prototypical Daoist elements had yet to be synthesized. At first the Chinese had difficulty understanding the relationship between rebirth and the idea of no-self (***wuwo***, or *anatman*; see Chapter 5). If there was no enduring soul, what was reborn? Misunderstanding of this concept led Han Buddhists to erroneously teach the indestructibility of a soul that is bound to the cycle of rebirth through cause and effect (***yinguo*** or karma). The idea of an enduring soul was familiar to China, but the idea of karma was something new. Contrary to the Indigenous idea that descendants would inherit the sins of their ancestors, Buddhism suggested that reward and punishment would be bound to the individual alone.

One unexpected development during the Han encounter between Buddhism and Daoism was the idea that when (according to Daoist lore) Laozi left China and travelled to the west, he became the Buddha and converted the western "barbarians" to Buddhism. Thus both traditions were considered members of one religious family, and altars were set up for Huang–Lao and the Buddha in the imperial palace. Even so, the *Taipingjing* attacked Buddhism on four counts that reflected core Chinese concerns: it encouraged the abandonment of parents; to become a monk it was necessary to abandon wife and children; the requirement of celibacy defied the duty to continue the family lineage; and the monks' dependence on alms promoted begging.

In time, Buddhism disentangled itself from Daoism and established its own communities of monks, nuns, and lay practitioners, which became more popular than their Daoist counterparts. Reciprocal relationships and mutual influence developed as the traditions matured: Confucianism and Daoism influenced the evolution of Buddhism, and Buddhism in turn had a profound influence on the development of the two Indigenous traditions.

The Six Dynasties Period (220–589)

The Six Dynasties period, covering the Three Kingdoms (220–280), Jin Dynasty (265–420), and Southern and Northern Dynasties (420–589), was politically fractured, marked by struggle against both "barbarian" invaders from North and Central Asia and a foreign religion, Buddhism. Religious teachings in this period were shaped by the tension between China's desire to preserve its traditional values and political independence and its sometimes-grudging admiration and acceptance of an increasingly sinicized Buddhism.

Tensions notwithstanding, Buddhist ideas were attractive, and as they began to permeate Chinese society, different spheres were allocated to each religion. Buddhism was seen as medicine for spiritual disorders, and Confucianism continued to play an important role in family life despite its loss of official status. It survived not only through individual study of the classic texts, but also in handbooks offering practical advice on everyday matters.

The development of large-scale religious organizations like the Celestial Masters was greatly strengthened by the new model of Buddhist monastic discipline. The nascent Daoist and Buddhist movements went far beyond the traditional state- and family-centred cults such as those dedicated to Heaven, the ancestors, or the gods of soil and grain. Although they respected the foundational values of filial piety and socio-political harmony, they did not show the traditional respect for hierarchies: thus monks and nuns refused to bow before kings.

Confucianism

Interaction with Daoism and Buddhism

The fall of the Han dynasty, in 220, marked the beginning of almost four centuries of instability. During this period (the Six Dynasties), China experienced repeated invasions, Confucianism lost state support, and those seeking religious guidance increasingly looked to Daoism and Buddhism.

Wang Bi

Among the Confucian literati was one who has also been described as a neo-Daoist. In his short life (226–249), Wang Bi wrote extensive commentaries not only on the *Analects* and *Changes* (a text revered by Daoists as well as Confucians) but also on *Laozi*. Like the Seven Sages of the Bamboo Grove—famous neo-Daoist eccentrics who were near-contemporaries of his (see p. 513)—Wang was interested in ***xuanxue*** (study of the "dark" or mysterious and profound). Above all, he emphasized the concept of principle (***li***, written differently in Chinese from the *li* meaning "rites"), which would become the linchpin for the neo-Confucians of the Song period (960–1279), nearly 1,000 years later.

Criticism of Buddhism

As Daoism and Confucianism drew closer together, both criticized Buddhism on the same grounds that the *Taipingjing* had. There were also questions about Buddhist practices. To shave one's head, for instance, was construed as an act of gross disrespect, since it amounted to harming the body given by one's ancestors. Industrious Confucians interpreted Buddhist monks' ascetic withdrawal from productive work as a shirking of responsibility, and the monastic tradition of begging for food as parasitism. In addition, Confucians and Daoists argued that Buddhism lacked authority because it was not mentioned in the Five Classics. Furthermore, the Buddhist renunciation of worldly pleasures went far beyond the Confucian ideal of moderation, effectively denying the value that Confucianism attributed to life in the world (de Bary and Hurvitz in de Bary 1972: 125–38). Finally, there was the seemingly irrational nature of some Buddhist teachings. According to Mouzi, Confucians were baffled by the Buddhist practice of reflecting on the impurities of the body:

> The ascetic engages in contemplation of himself and observes that all the noxious seepage of his internal body is impure. Hair, skin, skull and flesh; tears from the blinking of the eyes and spittle; veins, arteries, sinew and marrow; liver, lungs, intestines and stomach; feces, urine, mucus and blood: such a mass of filth when combined produces a man. . . . awakened to the detestability of the body, concentrating his mind, he gains *dhyana* (ibid., 129).

This emphasis on the impurity of the body was especially harsh for women, given the additional defilements of menstruation and childbirth. Although it contradicted the Indigenous Chinese idea that the body is a gift from the ancestors, fundamentally good, the negativity of other Buddhist ideas about women was not inconsistent with Chinese ideas. The depictions of "Vicious and Depraved" females in Liu Xiang's *Biographies of Exemplary Women* are quite in line with Buddhist notions of women's physical and spiritual impurity.

Buddhism

Amid the chaos of the Six Dynasties, Chinese Buddhism developed in two distinctive streams. In the north, where many states were under non-Han rule, Buddhism political dissenters were attracted by monks' claims of mysterious powers such as clairvoyance and the ability to make themselves invisible. In the south, where many Han scholars and officials had taken refuge and society was steeped in an apolitical neo-Daoism, Buddhism was only occasionally drawn into politics.

Hinayana (*Xiaocheng* or "Small Vehicle") as well as Mahayana (*Dacheng* or "Great Vehicle") traditions were practised in China. In this early period, meditation was more closely associated with the Hinayana school, while Mahayana Buddhists were more interested in exploring what constitutes wisdom (*zhi* or *prajna*). Several texts on the Perfection of Transcendental Wisdom (*prajnaparamita*), such as the *Heart* and *Diamond* sutras, had been translated into Chinese by the end of the 300s, and many Mahayana texts were translated after the famous scholar-monk Kumarajiva arrived in 401, including the *Lotus* and *Vimalakirti Sutras*.

Buddhism and Daoism

Nevertheless, the Chinese continued to think of Buddhism as a variant of Daoism. The Perfection of Transcendental Wisdom writings teach a notion of emptiness or the void that recalls the Daoist belief in non-being. The monk Zhi Dun's idea that there is a transcendental absolute (*li*), an essence and ultimate truth that is expressed in the relative mundane world, found echoes in Wang Bi's *li* or principle. Moreover, just as a buddha is free of all attachments, a sage is free from all desires; and in both, all dualities and distinctions disappear. As one Fan Ye (398–445) said:

> If we examine closely its teachings about purifying the mind and gaining release from the ties of life, and its emphasis upon casting aside both "emptiness" and "being," we see that it belongs to the same current as do the Taoist writings (Chen 1964: 64).

In addition, Buddhism's dual focus on wisdom and compassion echoed the traditional Chinese concern with security, stability, and harmony, while the Buddhist notion of impermanence was in tune with Chinese assumption of continual change. At the same time, Buddhist teachings on suffering and the path to liberation resonated with people in a time of instability.

The first five storeys of the Big Wild Goose Pagoda in Xian were built in 652 as a part of a temple complex designed to house Buddhist artifacts brought from India (© GRANT ROONEY PREMIUM / Alamy).

Reasons for the Popularity of Buddhism

People were attracted to Buddhism for many reasons, including its art (paintings and sculptures) and architecture (pagodas modelled after stupas); the promise of enlightenment, or at least a better chance at happiness in this life; a well-tested, progressive program of precept-taking, chanting, meditation, and study to help the faithful achieve that goal; and the sophisticated philosophy, literature, and erudition of its proponents. Even though some found the monastic life unfilial, others were positively attracted to the idea of a religious community (*sangha* or *sengjia*) that was separate from the family and clan.

New ideas added to the fascination with Buddhism. Concepts such as ***lunhui*** (the cycle of rebirth, or *samsara*), *niepan* (extinction/release or *nirvana*), *yinguo* (cause and effect or karma), and narratives of heavens and hells offered the Chinese a novel understanding of the cosmos. As Buddhism became more popular, it also offered new possibilities to women. Baochang's *Lives of Nuns* is a testament to the devotion and accomplishments of the first Chinese nuns, many of whom were ordained in the fifth century by a quorum of nuns from Sri Lanka. Of course, their male counterparts were remembered as well, in parallel biographies like the *Lives of Famous Monks*, also by Baochang, and Huijiao's *Lives of Eminent Monks*.

Power Struggle between Sengjia *and State*

It was not long before the *sengjia* attracted charges of extravagant spending on its monasteries and monks were accused of moral laxity, graft, and corruption. According to a memorial submitted to Emperor An of the Eastern Jin dynasty in 389,

> Monks [and] nuns . . . are vying with each other to enter into cliques and parties. . . . I have heard that the Buddha is a spirit of purity, far-reaching intelligence, and mysterious emptiness. . . . But nowadays the devotees are vile, rude, servile, and addicted to wine and women (quoted in Chen 1964: 74–5).

Document

From the *Lives of Nuns*

The Lives of Nuns, *by a sixth-century monk named Baochang, tells the stories of 65 Buddhist nuns who lived between 316 and 516. Two earlier efforts to capture the religious lives of women are the anonymous Buddhist* Song of the Sisters *and Liu Xiang's Confucian* Biographies of Exemplary Women. *The following excerpt tells of a young devotee who rejected a marriage arranged by her family.*

Sengduan had vowed that she would leave the household life rather than be married off. Nevertheless, her beauty of face and figure were well known in the region, and a wealthy family had already received her mother and elder brother's agreement to a betrothal. Three days before the marriage ceremony Sengduan fled in the middle of the night to a Buddhist convent whose abbess hid her . . . and supplied her with everything she needed. Sengduan also had a copy of the Bodhisattva Guanshiyin [another name for Guanyin] Sutra that she was able to chant from memory after only two days of study. She rained tears and made prostrations day and night without ceasing. Three days later, during her worship, she saw an image of the Buddha, who announced to her, "Your bridegroom's lifespan is coming to an end. You need only continue your ardent practice without harboring sorrowful thoughts." The next day her bridegroom was gored to death by an ox (Tsai: 49–50).

Where government was entrusted to monks and nuns, as in the Eastern Jin (317–420), they were accused of meddling in politics. In 403 Huan Xuan, who usurped power from the Eastern Jin, demanded that monks and nuns bow to him, as laypeople were obliged to, but the famous monk Hui Yuan (344–416) successfully argued against this command. The leader of a well-organized and strictly disciplined community that worshipped the celestial Amituofo of the Pure Land, he contended that Buddhists can be divided into two groups: the laity who, because they remain in the world, should obey all rules; and the monastics who, having left home, have abandoned the secular realm and therefore should not be required to adhere to its rules.

Success and Subsequent Inter-religious Conflict

The popularity of Buddhism proved to be its undoing. While in the south hostility towards it was channelled into written form, in the north it resulted in full-blown persecution, once under Emperor Taiwu of Northern Wei in 446, and twice under Emperor Wu of Northern Zhou, in 574 and then again in 577.

Scholars suggest that Taiwu, who was likely of Turkish background, was predisposed against Buddhism because he wanted to prove his acculturation to Chinese values. His antipathy was aggravated when he discovered that weapons had been hidden in a monastery; that men were becoming monks to avoid corvee labour and conscription; and, worse yet, that monks were secretly living with women in subterranean apartments. He was further outraged when he learned that some monks had sold off grain intended for the poor in times of famine.

To make things worse, the monastic system was a powerful organization operating alongside the state, and even its architecture rivalled that of the imperial buildings. Taiwu's Daoist–Confucian prime minister Cui Hao, whose brother and wife were both Buddhists, encouraged him to take such harsh measures against Buddhists, monastics and lay, that even the Daoist Kou Qianzhi counselled against them. The other northern ruler to torment the Buddhists was Emperor Wu of the Northern Zhou. Unlike Taiwu, however, he included Daoists in his persecutions.

A different Emperor Wu, this one in the south, was a devout Buddhist himself. Liang Wudi (502–549) ceded the responsibilities of governance to the monks and nuns, abolished all Daoist temples, and returned all Daoist priests, men and women, to lay life. Many Daoists fled north.

Ideas Central to Chinese Buddhism

Non-duality and Emptiness

As more Buddhist teachings made their way into China, it became clear that the Hinayana and Mahayana doctrines sometimes contradicted one another (see Chapter 5). The *Heart Sutra*, for example, presents the Madhyamaka (*zhonglun* or *sanlun*) teaching of non-duality, which negates Hinayana teachings such as the five components of personality (*skandhas* or *yun*). The second stanza of this short but essential sutra, often chanted in liturgy, begins with the bodhisattva of compassion, Avalokiteshvara or Guanyin, in a deep trance, recognizing that the five components are "in their own-being . . . empty," and that the same is true of "feelings, perceptions, impulses, and consciousness."

Doctrinal Categorization and Skillful Means

The *Lotus Sutra* offered a way of understanding these divergent teachings. Two ideas developed to account for the theoretical differences: doctrinal categorization or classification and skillful means or *upaya*. The first term refers to the notion that the Buddha's talks can be classified into varying doctrines based on different periods and audiences. The second idea explains why: the Buddha's lectures reflected both his own development and his skillful shaping of his ideas to suit the capacities of his audience. The famous story of the burning house (see Chapter 5) is reinforced by the following passage, also in the *Lotus Sutra*, according to which there is only one Buddha vehicle:

> [T]he Buddhas of the past used countless numbers of expedient means, various causes and conditions, and words of simile and parable in order to expound the doctrines for the sake of living beings. These doctrines are all for the sake of the one Buddha vehicle (Watson 2001: 9).

Guanyin

Over time, the Chinese accepted the three baskets of the Hinayana, but gave priority to Mahayana teachings. In the *Lotus Sutra*, the Buddha himself says nothing about the classic Hinayana themes, but he does advise the faithful to call on Guanyin:

> If a woman wishes to give birth to a male child, she should offer obeisance and alms to Bodhisattva Perceiver of the World's Sounds [Guanyin] and then she will bear a son blessed with merit, virtue, and wisdom. And if she wishes to bear a daughter, she will bear one with all the marks of comeliness, one who in the past planted the roots of virtue and is loved and respected by many persons (Watson 2001: 121).

The idea of a selfless being who defers enlightenment, is capable of taking on an infinite number of forms, and disregards socio-cultural and religious boundaries in order to aid the suffering had the effect of expanding and deepening Chinese religiosity. The *Lotus Sutra* continues:

> If they [the people] need a monk, a nun, a layman believer, or a laywoman believer to be saved, immediately [Guanyin] becomes a monk, a nun, a layman believer, or a laywoman believer and preaches the Law for them. . . (ibid., 123).

The innumerable guises of Guanyin recall the first two lines of the *Daodejing*: "The way that can be spoken of / Is not the constant way; / The name that can be named / Is not the constant name" (Lau 1963: 57). And the *pusa's* compassion resonates with the ideal of the sage, central to both Confucianism and Daoism. But the Buddhist Guanyin introduced a stronger version of the Indigenous ideas of transformation implicit in the *Changes*: he/she can take any form necessary to rescue those in need.

This early image of Guanyin (550–560) clearly represents the bodhisattva as male: the robe lies on a flat chest. But later devotees often understood "him" to be female. While Guanyin can take any form, she/he is usually sumptuously dressed and recognizable by Amituofo's face in her/his crown (© Peter Horree / Alamy).

Lay Practice

As part of its accommodation to local ideals, Buddhism shifted its focus from monasticism to lay practice. One of the most popular sutras, the *Vimalakirti*, teaches that there is no need to abandon home and family in order to become enlightened: in it the Buddha's students tell him that Vimalakirti—a wise, pure, celibate layman—understands the teachings better than they do. This lay orientation no doubt helped in the sinicization of Buddhism.

The Mind in Both Aspects: Pure and Impure

The mind that is "upright" and "deeply searching," that "aspires to *bodhi*," illustrates two core Mahayana ideas: that Mind or Consciousness is crucial in the alleviation of suffering, and that it has two aspects—which means that those three positive characteristics can never be separated from their opposites: non-uprightness, not deeply searching, and not aspiring to *bodhi*. The first idea belongs to the Yogacara or Consciousness Only school (see Chapter 5), known as Faxiang in China. The second is an expression of the concept of the non-dual One Mind found in the teachings on the Matrix of the Tathagata (*Tathagatagarbha*) and discussed at length in the

Lankavatara Sutra and a treatise entitled *The Awakening of Faith* (*Dacheng qixin lun*), which has no Sanskrit original.

The two aspects of the One Mind may take several forms: the universal and the particular, the transcendental and the phenomenal, the pure and the impure. The Matrix (*garbha*) also has two aspects, symbolizing both the seed of the Tathagata (the Buddha) and the womb in which it may grow. It represents Buddha-nature and the capacity for enlightenment that are inherent in all human beings (a concept that parallels Confucian and Daoist ideas about sagehood). But it is important to understand that (in line with the concept of no-self) Buddha-nature has no substance: it is not a thing, even in the sense that a soul would be a thing. When the One Mind is unhindered by defilements, the luminosity of Buddha-nature will be clear. Thus Buddha-nature is not something we possess, but something we are. The key to uncovering or cultivating the One Mind is meditation.

Mofa *or End Time*

From the beginning, Buddhism taught that the universe was in a phase of decline when Shakyamuni was born to set the wheel of dharma in motion again. The Three Stages School (*Sanjiejiao*), founded in the late sixth century, developed that idea, teaching that time was divided into three periods—those of the Correct Law, the Counterfeit Law, and the Decadent or Final Law—and that the Chinese were living during the last of the three, the end times (*mofa*). During the time of the Buddha, people were able to attain enlightenment through practice, but during the time of false teachings Buddhism becomes increasingly formalized, so that fewer and fewer people are able to benefit from it. During the end time, humans lose their aspiration for enlightenment and Buddhism is incapable of leading them to buddhahood.

Help from the Celestial Buddhas

So what if one is a layperson living in the end time and cannot reach enlightenment? One group of practitioners offered a solution: When you cannot do it on your own, ask to be reborn in the Pure Land of a celestial buddha such as Amituofo.

The *Larger Pure Land Sutra*, or *Sutra on the Buddha of Infinite Life*, is one of three **Pure Land** (**Jingtu**) sutras; the other two are the *Smaller Pure Land* or *Amitayus Sutra* and the *Contemplation* (*Amitayurdhyana*) *Sutra*. According to the *Larger Sutra*, Amituofo, in a previous incarnation, vowed to bring into his Western Paradise all who "sincerely and joyfully entrust themselves to me, and call my Name even ten times" (Inagaki 1994: 244–5). And according to the *Contemplation Sutra*, one may simply repeat the mantra for rebirth into the Pure Land ten times: "Homage to Amitayus Buddha" (*Namo Amituofo*). The mantra can be used as a focus in silent meditation or chanted aloud.

Flower Garland

Another important idea that shaped Chinese Buddhism is found in the *Flower Garland Sutra* (*Avatamsaka* or **Huayan**): that is, the belief that all things are interconnected.

Some Chinese schools, such as Tiantai and Huayan, were organized around a particular teaching or doctrine (those of the *Lotus* and *Flower Garland Sutras* respectively), while others, such as **Chan** and Pure Land, were centred on a core practice (meditation and chanting, respectively). We will look at the most influential schools in the next section. But first we will return to Daoism and see how it was faring during this period.

Daoism

Buddhist Influences

Daoism assimilated beliefs and practices from Buddhism, blending them into the various streams of Daoist thought and developed them while remaining faithful to its own beliefs and practices. Thus Daoist teachings were reinterpreted in terms of *yinguo* (karma) and *lunhui* (rebirth), and Daoist rituals were adapted to reflect the new ideas about death that Buddhism had introduced. Both monastic and lay institutions were established, culminating in the construction of the first Daoist temple in the fifth century. Some Daoist leaders stayed active politically, but others turned inward and focused on individual cultivation.

The quest for transcendence took two forms: the pursuit of spiritual transcendence through meditation, and the pursuit of physical immortality through methods that included a sexual ritual known as the joining of energy or the union of breaths and the ingestion of poisonous substances such as cinnabar.

Mysterious Learning and Outer Alchemy

The Seven Sages of the Bamboo Grove concentrated on private individual cultivation, and (like the Confucian Wang Bi), they were interested in *xuanxue*. Discouraged from participating in public life after the fall of the Han, and inspired by Zhuangzi's notions of spontaneity and spiritual freedom, they gained a reputation for eccentric behaviour (one of them was said to have roamed around naked in his hermitage). Having fled the turmoil of northern China for the south, the Seven Sages engaged in "pure conversation" on metaphysical rather than political topics, and reflected Confucian and Buddhist as well as Daoist influences.

It was likely sometime in the 300s that the *Liezi*—the third most important Daoist "philosophical" text, after the *Daodejing* and *Zhuangzi*—was compiled, bringing together stories about one of the Daoist thinkers mentioned in the *Zhuangzi*. A less important but still informative text, probably written in the 320s, was Ge Hong's *Baopuzi* ("The master who embraces spontaneous nature"): a collection of essays on classic Daoist themes, including methods of driving away harmful spirits, reaching the gods, and alchemical recipes for achieving longevity and immortality.

The Highest Clarity and Numinous Treasure Schools

Two new religious Daoist schools emerged in the latter part of the same century. Yang Xi, a medium and shaman, formed the Highest Clarity (Shangqing) school when he received scriptures from the immortal Lady Wei of the Heaven of Highest Clarity. Yang and his followers sought to become "true beings" or "perfected persons" (*zhenren*) through practices that included the use of outer alchemy to facilitate flights to the star deities who controlled human destiny. Devotees ate very little, believing that fasting would make their bodies light and radiant for their ascent to the heavens.

The second new school, Numinous Treasure (Lingbao), was founded a few decades later by Ge Chaofu, a grandnephew of Ge Hong who received from his clan ancestors a series of revelations involving the Buddhist concepts of karma, rebirth, and cycles of time (*kalpas*). Whereas Highest Clarity focused on the individual, Numinous Treasure looked outward to the local community and beyond to all of humanity, suggesting a synthesis of Daoist and Buddhist ideas. The *Scripture for the Salvation of Humanity* (*Durenjing*) illustrates this synthesis, describing a cosmic deity who sends an emissary to Earth to reveal the *Durenjing* and ferries suffering humans to liberation and peace—paralleling the service performed by Amituofo and the historical Buddha Gautama himself.

Numinous Treasure focused especially on purification and communal renewal rituals. The goals of the former were typical of the era: prevention of disease, warding off natural calamities, and salvation of ancestors. Performed around a temporary altar, they began with cleansing of the body and purification of the heart-mind through confession of sins; a communal feast was then held to celebrate the reinstatement of harmony between the gods and human beings. In community renewal rituals (still practised today), deities were invited down into the altar, incense was offered, and the sponsors of the rituals were granted audiences with the gods, during which they would request favours for their communities.

The Sui and Tang Dynasties (589–907)

China Reunited

In 589 China was reunited for the first time since the fall of the Han, and in 618 the Tang came to power. Daoism and Buddhism both reached new heights of popularity over the next three centuries of relative peace and prosperity, and Confucianism experienced a renewal.

Confucianism

The second Tang emperor, Taizhong, established an academy for scholar-officials where the curriculum was based on the classical texts of Confucianism and—for the first time in Chinese history—it became possible for a commoner to work his way into officialdom. Taizhong also ordered all districts to build Confucian temples, and in 647 installed in each temple 22 tablets commemorating orthodox Confucians of the Han era. A century later, the title "King of Manifest Culture" was bestowed on Confucius, who now displaced the Duke of Zhou as the "uncrowned king" of Chinese civilization.

In time, the Confucian curriculum was expanded to include 12 works, among them the *Analects* and the *Classic of Filiality*. The revival of interest in Confucian thought was reflected in three writers: Madame Zheng, author of the late seventh-century *Classic of Filiality for Women*; **Han Yu** (768–824), a prominent scholar-official intent on reintroducing Confucianism to the people; and Han's contemporary Song Ruozhao, who wrote the *Analects for Women*.

Madame Zheng's Classic of Filiality for Women

The wife of a government official, Madame Zheng set out to create a female Confucian tradition starting from Ban Zhao. Her *Classic of Filiality for Women* emphasizes the importance of chastity, filial piety, intelligence, and wisdom. Zheng imagines Ban Zhao teaching a group of women that a wife should encourage her husband in good behaviour and guide him with "modesty and deference" (T. Kelleher in de Bary and Bloom 1999: 826). When the women ask if they must obey their husbands' every command, Ban cites numerous historical examples of wives who corrected or criticized their husbands and explains:

> If a husband has a remonstrating wife, then he won't fall into evil ways. Therefore, if a husband transgresses against the Way, you must correct him. How could it be that to obey your husband in everything would make you a virtuous person? (ibid., 827)

Han Yu's Defence of Confucianism

Han Yu marks an important point of Confucian renewal. Although Confucian principles had been reintroduced into government, they had little popular currency. In an effort to bring Confucian teaching back to the people, Han Yu wrote *Essentials of the Moral Way*. In it he answers the question "What is the teaching of the former kings?" as follows:

> To love largely is called a sense of humaneness; to act according to what should be done is called rightness. To proceed from these principles is called the moral Way; to be sufficient unto oneself without relying on externals is called inner power. . . . Its methods are the rites, music, chastisement, and government. Its classes of people are scholars, peasants, craftsmen, and merchants. . . . (C. Hartman in de Bary and Bloom 1999: 569)

Song Ruozhao's Analects for Women

The *Analects for Women* is usually attributed to Song Ruozhao, though some say that the actual author was her sister Ruohua. From a scholarly family, Ruozhao was appointed to the court as a scholar, and taught the imperial princesses. The *Analects* focuses on emotional restraint and self-cultivation, beginning with a chapter entitled "Establishing oneself as a person."

Daoism

The founder of the Tang dynasty, Li Yuan, claimed descent from Laozi, and under his family's rule Daoism once again became the state religion. Some patriarchs from the Highest Clarity School held government posts. The "Brilliant Emperor" Xuanzhong wrote a commentary on the *Daodejing* and invited the Highest Clarity patriarch Sima Chengzen to court; princesses were ordained as Daoist priestesses and performed state rituals; colleges of Daoism were established; and the *Daodejing* was briefly included in state examinations. By 739 there were 1,137 abbeys for Daoshi and 550 for Nuguan (male and female Daoist priests respectively). Classical Daoism reached the height of its power and popularity during the Tang.

Buddhism

The first two centuries of the Tang dynasty are often seen as the apex of Buddhism in China. Monks visited the imperial court often, and several Chinese Buddhist schools developed around individual sutras. In addition, one sutra was used to legitimate the rise to power of China's first and only female emperor. The *Great Cloud Sutra* prophesied the imminent arrival of a female Maitreya

The only female emperor in Chinese history, Wu Zetian (625–705) ruled from behind the throne for a time after her husband's death; then, encouraged by Buddhist monks and prophecies, she took the throne herself (The Art Archive / British Library).

(Milo), a salvational figure who would bring peace and prosperity to the land. After the death of her husband, the Emperor Gaozong, Wu Zetian claimed to be that figure and took the throne as Empress Wu of the Zhou dynasty.

The two types of Buddhist schools, doctrinal and practical, were often described as two wings of a single bird. Among the doctrinal schools that were influential during the Tang were Tiantai, based on the *Lotus Sutra*; Huayan, based on the *Flower Garland Sutra*; and Faxiang (Yogacara, or Consciousness Only). Vajrayana Buddhism, known in China as Zhenyan (True Word or Mantra), was introduced in the 700s, but was soon absorbed into other schools.

Towards the end of the dynasty, the scholar-monk Zongmi (780–841) integrated Confucianism and Daoism into a Buddhist framework in his *Treatise on the Original Nature of Man*—a classic example of the Chinese tendency towards syncretism.

Late Tang Persecution of Buddhism

Zongmi's efforts notwithstanding, Daoist priests eventually persuaded Emperor Wuzong to put an end to the spread of Buddhism in China. In 845 Wuzong issued an edict that summarized the charges against the foreign religion that had "poisoned the customs of our nation":

> . . . At present there are an inestimable number of monks and nuns in the empire, each of them waiting for the farmers to feed him and the silkworms to clothe him, while the public temples and private chapels have reached boundless number, all with soaring towers and elegant ornamentation sufficient to outshine the imperial palace itself . . . (B. Watson in de Bary and Bloom 1999: 585–6).

The Song, Yuan, and Ming Dynasties (960–1644)

In the aftermath of the late Tang persecution, the monastic community was decimated, and the only schools that retained strong followings among ordinary people were the two that focused on practice rather than study: Chan (Meditation) and Jingtu (Pure Land). After the fall of the Tang, however, Daoism itself was stripped of its status as the state religion. The Song (960–1279) would prove to be a period of renewal for Confucianism, which synthesized ideas from both Daoism and Buddhism and reasserted itself at the state level as neo-Confucianism.

Document

From the *Platform Sutra*, fourth chapter, "*Samadhi* and *Prajna*"

The Platform Sutra is the only "canonical" non-Indian Buddhist text. It records the teachings of Huineng, the sixth patriarch of the Chan school. In the following passages, he explains that practising meditation and non-attachment does not mean having no thoughts, and that there is no "right" way to become enlightened.

Learned Audience, some teachers of meditation instruct their disciples to keep a watch on their mind for tranquillity, so that it will cease from activity. Henceforth the disciples give up all exertion of mind. Ignorant persons become insane from having too much confidence in such instruction. Such cases are not rare, and it is a great mistake to teach others to do this. . . .

In orthodox Buddhism the distinction between the Sudden school and the Gradual school does not really exist; the only difference is that by nature some men are quick-witted, while others are dull in understanding. Those who are enlightened realize the truth in a sudden, while those who are under delusion have to train themselves gradually. But such a difference will disappear when we know own mind and realize our own nature. Therefore these terms *gradual* and *sudden* are more apparent than real (Price and Wong 1990: 95).

Daoism

The Complete Truth School

The Daoist school of Complete Truth (*Quanzhen*; also translated as Perfect Realization, Perfect Truth, or Complete Perfection) was founded in the twelfth century and is still active today. Associated with the White Cloud Abbey in Beijing, it is distinctive in its monasticism—a feature that its founder, Wang Chongyang, modelled on Buddhism. Wang also argued against the superstitions and supernatural elements that had accrued to Daoism over time, and taught a more down-to-earth understanding of transcendence or immortality:

> Leaving the world does not mean that the body departs. . . . When you realize the Tao, your body will be in the sphere of the ordinary, but your mind will be in the realm of the sages. Nowadays, people want to avoid death forever and at the same time leave the ordinary world. They are very foolish, indeed, and have not even glimpsed the true principle of the Tao (Kirkland 2004: 188).

Wang urged his disciples to read across all three major traditions, especially the Confucian *Classic of Filiality*, the Buddhist *Heart Sutra*, and the *Daodejing*. His "Fifteen Precepts for Establishing the Teaching" includes practical recommendations alongside more elevated principles. For example, he advises that to achieve harmony in spirit and vital energy, the body must be well rested. He also recommends using herbs for healing, living a simple life, and maintaining good Daoist friends. The "basic motif of the art of self-cultivation," he wrote, is the "search for the hidden meaning of Nature and mind" (Sommer 1995: 202).

Sun Buer

Where Confucians have Ban Zhao, the Daoists have Sun Buer (1119–83), the wife of Wang Chongyang's disciple Ma Danyang. The following story is likely apocryphal, but it highlights the difficulties that women of her time faced in their search for enlightenment.

One day Sun heard Wang say that an immortal was expected to emerge in the city of Luoyang, far from her home in Shandong. She asked Wang for permission to go there, but he refused, predicting that she would be molested and the shame would kill her.

Undeterred, Sun went to her kitchen, heated some oil in a wok, poured cold water into it, and stood over the boiling oil as it spattered her face. When Wang saw her scars, he recognized her sincerity and agreed to teach her the methods of inner alchemy, but he advised her to hide her knowledge even from her husband. To ensure that she would be left alone, Sun pretended to be insane. Eventually, she slipped out of the house and travelled to Loyang. There—as Wang had anticipated—two men accosted her. When a rain of enormous hailstones helped her escape, the men recognized her special nature and spread the story. Left in peace for 12 years, Sun became the only female among the famed seven masters of the Complete Truth School.

Revival of Orthodox Unity

Daoism continued to thrive until the twelfth century, when the Mongolian Kublai Khan extended his rule to the south. There he gave exclusive authority to the Orthodox Unity sect, renamed for the revelations given to the Celestial Masters. After the Mongols were overthrown, Orthodox Unity was entrusted with the compilation of the Daoist canon (*Daozang*), which was printed in 1445.

Confucianism

The Emergence of Neo-Confucianism

Meanwhile, the ongoing development of Confucianism culminated in the emergence of what the West calls neo-Confucianism. This development reached its apex with **Zhu Xi** (1130–1200), but much of Zhu's work drew on thinkers from the preceding century, among them Zhou Dunyi, Zhang Zai, and the brothers Cheng Yi and Hao. Although neo-Confucianism traced its roots to the ancient writings, much of its philosophy reflected Buddhist and Daoist influences. Thus Zhou Dunyi (1017–73) advocated what he called "quiet-sitting"—a practice clearly modelled on Daoist and Buddhist meditation—and his most important work, "An Explanation of the Diagram of the Great Ultimate," was based on a Daoist representation of the creation of the material world.

For Zhou, the Great Ultimate and the Ultimate Non-being are identical. Through movement, yang is generated from the Ultimate Non-being/Great Ultimate. When its limit is reached, it becomes quiet and yin is generated. When yin reaches its limit, then activity, or yang, begins again. Thus the alternation between stillness and movement produces yin and yang, which in turn give rise to the five vital elements: fire, water, earth, metal, and wood. When Ultimate Non-being interacts with the essences of yin-yang and the five elements, a mysterious union occurs, from which Heaven and Earth come into being.

Document

From Zhang Zai's *Western Inscription*

Zhang Zai (1020–77) took Zhou Dunyi's universal cosmology and expressed it in terms of a human family. The following excerpt shows how he correlated the essential Confucian elements of self, family, humanity, and virtue to the broader elements of nature and the cosmos.

Heaven is my father and Earth is my mother, and even such a small creature as I finds an intimate place in their midst.

Therefore that which fills the universe I regard as my body and that which directs the universe I consider as my nature.

All people are my brothers and sisters, and all things are my companions. The great ruler (the emperor) is the eldest son of my parents (Heaven and Earth), and the great ministers are his stewards. . . .

He who disobeys [the Principle of Nature] violates virtue. He who destroys humanity is a robber. He who promotes evil lacks [moral] capacity. But he who puts his moral nature into practice and brings his physical existence into complete fulfillment can match [Heaven and Earth]. . . . (W.T. Chan in Sommer 1995: 188).

Zhu Xi and the School of Principle

Working from Zhou's cosmology, the School of Principle (*Lixue*) explicitly linked *li*, the principles or patterns of nature, to human relationships and theories about education and government. Zhu Xi, considered the founder of this new school, synthesized the ideas of the earlier Song thinkers and gave Confucianism a metaphysical bent.

Zhu focused on the nature, place, and function of self in the Great Ultimate. Like most Chinese philosophers, he understood human beings to be part of the fabric of the universe. Although he was interested in Buddhist-style "quiet sitting," Zhu was quintessentially Confucian in his focus on self-cultivation.

Zhu commented on "Centrality and Equilibrium" and "The Great Learning" (*Daxue*), another chapter from the *Rites*, in which self-discipline or self-cultivation is the first link in a chain that extends from the individual through the family to the state and recalls the ideal of the Grand Commonality. A famous passage from "The Great Learning" argues that proper self-cultivation begins with the acquisition of knowledge:

> In antiquity, those who wanted to clarify their bright virtue throughout the entire realm first had to govern their states well. Those who wanted to govern their states well first had to manage their own families, and those who wanted to manage their families first had to develop their own selves. Those who wanted to develop themselves first rectified their own minds, and those who wanted to rectify their minds first made their thoughts sincere. Those who wanted to make their thoughts sincere first extended their knowledge. Those who wanted to extend their knowledge first had to investigate things (Sommer 1995: 39).

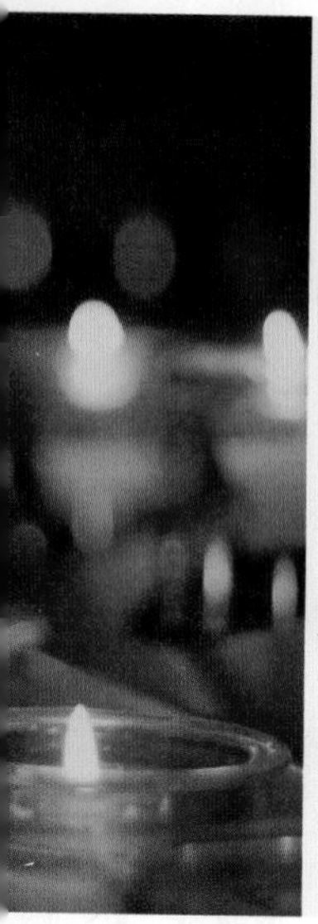

Focus

Zhu Xi on Human Nature

Following Zhou Dunyi and Zhang Zai, Zhu Xi believed human beings—like everything else in the universe—to be the product of the interaction between heavenly "principle" and the material forces of yin-yang and the five elements. Thus humans possessed both principle and material force. Like Mencius, Zhu Xi believed human nature to be intrinsically good; yet human action was not necessarily good. Zhu Xi attributed this apparent contradiction to the effects (or lack thereof) of material force on the three aspects of human personality: heavenly nature (i.e., principle), human feelings, and mind. Reflecting Zhou's cosmology, Zhu wrote that "Nature is the state before activity begins and feelings are the state when activity has started, and the mind includes both of these states" (W.T. Chan in Sommer 1995: 192). Nature, being Heaven-given, is always good; but feelings can be good or bad, while the mind brings nature and feelings together but remains a separate entity.

Women in Neo-Confucianism

Neo-Confucianism continued to thrive into the Ming dynasty (1368–1644). After the Ming regained control from the Mongols, the education of women—esteemed as the transmitters of culture to the young—received renewed attention. Empress Xu, the wife of the third Ming emperor, wrote *Instructions for the Inner Quarters* (*Neixun*) under the inspiration of her mother-in-law Empress Ma, who had believed it her duty, as Mother of the people, to challenge her cruel, hot-tempered husband. Empress Xu's book reflects the same sense of a woman's broader responsibility. When a set of "Four Books for Women" was compiled during the Ming, Empress Xu's *Instructions* was one of them, along with Ban Zhao's *Admonitions*, Song Ruozhao's *Analects*, and Madame Zheng's *Filiality*.

Wang Yangming

Approximately three centuries after Zhu Xi's death, **Wang Yangming** (1472–1529) challenged his view that the process of self-cultivation must begin with studying the classics and learning about the outside world. He argued that our moral sense is innate in our heart-minds, and takes precedence over any external learning; this teaching became known as *Xinxue*, the School of the Heart-Mind.

Buddhism

Critics of Wang Yangming charged that his focus on the heart-mind reflected the influence of Buddhism. It is true that his emphasis on intuitive, innate knowing resonated with both the Chan view of enlightenment and the general Mahayana belief in the universality of Buddha-nature. The Chan of the early Tang period had developed broadly into two schools with different notions on how to achieve enlightenment: a Northern "gradual" school and a Southern "sudden" school associated with the sixth patriarch, Huineng (see Chapter 5). By the end of the Tang, the two schools were represented by two distinct lineages—Linji and Caodong—both of which survive today.

New literary genres also developed: discourse records (*yulu*) of individual masters, and "lamp" or "flame" records of lineages, which were later edited into collections of *gongan* (public documents or case records). A record of a Chan master's exchange with a student became a *gongan* when a living master wrote a commentary on it that "proved" him to be a part of the lineage of enlightened masters. Eventually, the cases became pedagogical tools used to bypass the student's intellect and spark sudden enlightenment. Famous collections of these stories and their commentaries include the *Book of Serenity, Blue Cliff Record*, and the *Gateless Gate*, collected and edited in the twelfth and thirteenth centuries. (See the document box for a comparison of Chan and Daoist dialogue on the Buddha and the Dao respectively.)

Popular Buddhism

The second school of Buddhism to survive the Tang persecution relatively well, Jingtu, offered comfort with the promise of an afterlife in the "pure land" of Amituofo. In time, other forms of popular Buddhism developed, but they tended to be more prosaic in their promises. The monk Zhuhong (1535–1615), for example, classified actions in terms of merit and demerit: to "help a person recover from a slight illness" was worth five points, while to "rescue one person from the death penalty" was worth 100. Conversely, failure to help a sick person meant two demerit points;

Document

Excerpts from the *Gateless Gate* and *Zhuangzi*

Scholars have noted a general eccentricity in Chan dialogues that is shared by the Daoist Zhuangzi. The two excerpts that follow, the first from the Chan Gateless Gate *and the second from the* Zhuangzi, *point to an earthy irreverence in both traditions.*

A Chan gongan:
A monk asked [Yunmen Wenyan, c. 863–949]: "What is Buddha?" [Yunmen] answered him: "Dried dung."

[Wumen's] comment: It seems to me [Yunmen] is so poor he cannot distinguish the taste of one food from another, or else he is too busy to write readable letters. Well, he tried to hold his school with dried dung. And his teaching was just as useless.

Lightning flashes,
Sparks shower.
In one blink of your eyes
You have missed seeing (Reps 1989 [1960]: 106–7).

A dialogue from *Zhuangzi:*
Master Tung-kuo asked Chuang Tzu, "This thing called the Way—where does it exist?"

Chuang Tzu said, "There's no place it doesn't exist."

"Come," said Master Tung-kuo, "you must be more specific."

"It is in the ant."

"As low a thing as that?"

"It is in the panic grass."

"But that's lower still!"

"It is in the tiles and shards."

"How can it be so low?"

"It is in the piss and shit!"

Master Tung-kuo made no reply (Watson 1968: 240–1).

and the penalty for murder was 100 points. According to this scheme, those who earned 10,000 points would see their wishes granted; but if one died with more demerit than merit points, one's descendants would suffer for it (Chen 1964: 437–8). This system was adapted from a monk who had learnt it when he was a Daoist, which may explain the non-Buddhist idea of transference of ancestral demerit points

Popular Religion

The White Lotus Society is thought to have originated in the eleventh century as a lay movement dedicated to Amituofo that over time incorporated other elements, including Daoist longevity practices and millenarian expectations surrounding a messianic Milo. White Lotus members played a substantial role in overthrowing the Mongols, who had established Tibetan Buddhism as the state religion, and establishing the native Ming. But the first Ming emperor feared the Society's power and sought to suppress it. In time, "White Lotus" became a pejorative term, used by officials to refer to any religious group they considered suspect.

The Qing Dynasty and Republican Period (1644–present)

The Challenges of Modernity

The Qing Manchus retained Tibetan Buddhism as the state religion, but they continued to use Confucianism for government until 1911, when dynastic rule was replaced by republicanism. The end of the Qing was marked by hostility against traditional beliefs and practices. By mid-century "China" had splintered into the People's Republic of China (PRC) on the mainland, the Republic of China on the island of Taiwan, and the British Crown Colony of Hong Kong, existing alongside sizable Chinese communities in the city-state of Singapore and elsewhere in Southeast Asia, as well as a global diaspora.

Yet despite the persecution that traditional institutions and folk spiritualties have suffered over the last 120 years, popular annual celebrations, folk religious practices, Confucianism, Daoism, and Buddhism continue to thrive outside the mainland. Moreover, many religious beliefs and practices have experienced a renaissance in the PRC itself since the 1980s.

Confucianism

Encounter with the West and Modernization

In 1838 the Qing emperor appointed Lin Zexu to put an end to the opium trade initiated by the British in hopes of balancing their trade deficit with China. In addition to confiscating and destroying vast quantities of the drug, Lin composed an open letter of protest to Queen Victoria in which, as a Confucian, he framed his argument in moral terms:

> The wealth of China is used to profit the barbarians [the British]. . . . By what right do they then in return use the poisonous drug [opium] to injure the Chinese people? Let us

> ask, where is your conscience? I have heard that the smoking of opium is very strictly forbidden by your country; that is because the harm caused by opium is clearly understood. Since it is not permitted to do harm to your own country, then even less should you let it be passed on to the harm of other countries—how much less to China! (S.Y. Teng and J. Fairbank in deBary and Lufrano 2000: 203).

The British responded to this high-minded appeal with the first Opium War (1839–42; a second war would follow in 1856–60). The defeat of the hopelessly outgunned Chinese was a watershed in East Asian history, presaging the end of the dynastic system and leading to a profound reassessment of the Confucian way of thinking. The final military nail in the coffin was Japan's victory in the Sino-Japanese War of 1894–5. That Japan—a former vassal state—had not only succeeded in modernizing along Western lines but had defeated China meant that radical reform was necessary. Some reformers urged the abandonment of all traditions; others argued that certain aspects of China's cultural heritage should be preserved. Among the latter was Kang Youwei (1858–1927), who believed that the adoption of Shinto as the state religion had saved Japan from the stultifying influence of Buddhism, giving it a strong national identity, and helped it to focus on modernization. Although he argued that Confucianism could play a similar role for China, the ancient teaching continued to lose ground.

"New Confucians" in Post-dynastic China

Soon after Kang, Sun Yatsen, the father of modern republican China, found precedents for democracy in the Confucian Mencius and the neo-Confucian Cheng Yi. He identified three principles as fundamental to democracy—nationalism, citizen rights, and human welfare—and argued that they represented "a completion of the development of . . . three thousand years of Chinese ideas about how to govern and maintain a peaceful world" (Bell and Hahm 2003: 9).

Sun Yatsen's insights notwithstanding, state Confucianism was disestablished following the formation of the Chinese Republic in 1911. But scholars such as Fang Dongmei—who settled in Taiwan after the communist takeover of the mainland—encouraged the ongoing development of Confucianism in the diaspora.

Diaspora Attempts to Reconstruct Chinese Culture

In 1958 a group of "New Confucians" based in Hong Kong responded to Western critics of China with an English-language "Manifesto for a Reappraisal of Sinology and the Reconstruction of Chinese Culture." Following a discussion of "what the West can learn from Eastern thought," the authors concluded with a few remarks on the future "intellectual development of China and of the world." Noting the friction caused by the expansion of Western civilization, they called for "respect and sympathy toward other cultures" and "genuine compassion and commiseration." Second, since "scientific learning is inadequate," they called for "a different kind of learning, one that treats [Man] as a conscious, existential being [and] applies understanding to conduct, by which one may transcend existence to attain spiritual enlightenment." Finally, they suggested that the end product of that new learning would be "a moral being that . . . can truly embrace God" (quoted by J. Berthrong in de Bary and Lufrano 2000: 559).

Even though they clearly identified themselves with the Confucian tradition, the authors included Daoism and Buddhism in their discussion; and their use of the Christian term "God" shows their willingness to adopt foreign concepts. Their efforts are reflected in the work of scholars such as Du Weiming of Harvard and John Berthrong of Boston University; the controversial Daniel A. Bell, a Canadian who describes himself as a Confucian philosopher and scholar, who teaches at the Center for International and Comparative Political Philosophy in Beijing; and Lee Kuan Yew, the first president of Singapore, who tried (unsuccessfully) to introduce both Confucian and religious studies into the new republic's high schools.

This Ming dynasty bottle shows Zhongli Quan, one of the eight Daoist "Immortals" who serve as patrons of various groups and trades. Recognizable by his two topknots, exposed belly, and fan, Zhongli is believed to have been a successful Han general who discovered the Dao only after he had experienced defeat for the first time; he is also said to have had an impressive knowledge of alchemy (© The Metropolitan Museum of Art, Image source: Art Resource, NY).

Winds of Change in the People's Republic of China

Since the 1980s, the PRC has reintroduced state celebrations of the sage's birthday (the Republic of China, Taiwan, has always celebrated it). Some elementary schools have integrated classical literature into their curricula, along with a focus on rites and ethics, and introduced traditional garb such as the scholar's robe into their classrooms.

Scholars also note that the Chinese government's emphasis on a "harmonious society," non-interference in foreign policy, soft diplomacy, the establishment of Confucius Institutes outside China, and the development of online sites for Chinese language and culture all reflect the Confucian concern to promote social security and stability through the disciplined self-cultivation of individual persons.

Daoism and Popular Religion

Even as neo-Confucianism became entrenched as state ideology during the Qing dynasty (1644–1911), Daoism continued to inspire popular morality books and a variety of practices from meditation to *taiji* and ***qigong*** (breath exercises that help the movement of vital energy through the body). However, it suffered enormous setbacks after the Opium Wars, when Western-inspired reformers began to attack traditional beliefs and practices.

Daoism, with its Eight Immortals (legendary figures who play a role not unlike that of human saints) and its elaborate liturgies inviting the deities into this realm, can be difficult to distinguish from folk religion. Modernizers perceived both

Daoism and folk religion as superstitious and hostile to progress, especially after the failure of the anti-Western uprising (1899–1901) known in the West as the "Boxer Rebellion." The Boxers had believed they could drive out the foreigners on the strength of their martial arts skills alone, which they thought would make them impervious to Western guns and cannon.

Buddhism

Reform and Modernization

Of the three elite religions, Buddhism has been the most successful in modernizing itself. A leader in that effort was a layman named Yang Wenhui (1837–1911). He published Buddhist texts, started a school for monastics in Nanjing, and inspired Tan Sitong (1865–98) to propose a process through which millennia-old institutional and cultural barriers in Chinese society might be cleared away. In his book *Renxue* ("On Benevolence") Tan argued that the Confucian notion of *ren* was the same as Mohism's love without distinction, Buddhism's compassion, and Christianity's love. Appealing to Huayan ideas of interconnectedness, he described a state of oneness or non-differentiation in which communication between people is always possible. Tragically, he was beheaded for plotting against the Qing government, but his wife, Li Run, remained true to his ideal of non-differentiation and established a school for girls in rural Hunan—a feat unheard of in the early twentieth century.

Elsewhere, several monks also worked to revive and reform Buddhism. Yinguang (1861–1940) was a conservative monk credited with reviving the Pure Land school, while Taixu (1890–1947) argued that of all religions, Buddhism was the one most compatible with modern science; he also advocated a modern education for monastics. He made his reputation as an activist in 1912 when he and another monk, Renshan, announced that they had petitioned the government for permission to open a new school for monastics and planned to use the monastery's resources to run it.

The monk-officers of the temple successfully prevented the construction of the school. But the seeds of Humanistic Buddhism had been sown. Instead of retreating into meditation or scriptural study, monastics and laypeople alike were encouraged to become "engaged" in the world: in education, social work, medicine, and politics. In 1929 the Chinese Buddhist Association was established in Shanghai and charged with reforming and reviving Buddhism in China.

Government Treatment of Religion

In 1949 the PRC guaranteed freedom of religion. The official policy, in line with Marxist historical materialism, stated that to coerce religious people without material improvement of society was "useless and positively harmful." Nevertheless, in 1950 the Chinese Buddhist Association decamped to Taiwan with the Nationalist government and was replaced by a state-administered Buddhist Association. And in 1966 the government launched the Cultural Revolution. Fuelled by the Marxist notion of religion as an opiate that blunts the masses' instinct for justice and hinders advancement, the "revolutionaries" systematically targeted all religious traditions. By the mid-1970s the social and economic foundations of traditional Chinese society had been destroyed, and the government acknowledged that a new approach was necessary. Today the Chinese government recognizes five religions as "legitimate": Buddhism, Daoism, Roman Catholicism, Protestantism, and Islam (Confucianism is considered a philosophy rather than a religion.) At the same time, although it is not officially recognized, popular religion is experiencing a revival in the PRC.

Popular Religion

A loose collection of beliefs and practices centred on the power of deities, ghosts, and spirits, popular religion may draw elements from any of the more established traditions, including Christianity and Islam. Spirits of all kinds are seen as compassionate helpers, regardless of tradition.

The goals of practitioners have remained stable through the ages: children (especially sons), happiness, academic success, prosperity, safety at work (especially in potentially dangerous occupations such as fishing and policing), and even political change. They can be divided into two streams: personal religiosity and political activism.

One important element in personal religiosity is the belief that the spirits of the deceased continue to intervene in the world, and that their power can be harnessed for the benefit of the living. This belief finds expression not only in ancestral tablets in temples, or family altars dedicated to ancestors, but also in shrines in commercial establishments. Local folk heroes and heroines, buddhas, bodhisattvas, Daoist perfected beings: all can be called on for help. But popular religion can also be externalized in a less individual, more dogmatic and partisan way. When an idea such as the Mandate of Heaven or a messianic figure such as Milo (Maitreya) is incorporated into popular religion, it can give rise to politically charged movements like the White Lotus Society, the Boxers, or the Heavenly Kingdom of Great Peace.

Daoism and folk religion are re-establishing themselves in the PRC, and Daoism is especially popular in Europe and the Americas, where its dual focus on living a simple, balanced life and promoting health, longevity, and transcendence are increasingly valued. The *Daodejing* ranks only second to the Bible as the most translated book in the world.

Recent Developments

Study after study tells us that the Chinese, Koreans, Japanese, and Vietnamese are the least religious of all ethnic groups. This calls into question the term "religion." Clearly, Chinese traditions fit badly into the monotheistic frame of reference.

Revival of Confucianism

The first two generations of the twentieth-century New Confucians wrote from the cultural margins—Hong Kong, Taiwan, Singapore, Boston—while China lagged far behind the West developmentally. Yet by the late 1970s it was clear that communism had failed to improve life for the people. Thus in 1978 a process of economic and political reform began. Rapid industrial and economic growth lifted half a billion people out of poverty by 2004, and by 2012 China had achieved exceptional economic stability, despite a global financial disaster. Despite (or because of) this remarkable material success, some long-standing problems remained and some new ones surfaced: social alienation, radical individualism, ecological degradation, and infractions of human rights. As antidotes, both political and academic leaders recommended the revival and integration of traditional Confucian values such as integrity, loving respect, and belief in the unity of human beings with the cosmos.

The New Confucianism that had developed in the diaspora was harnessed to neutralize international fears that economic success would turn China into an imperialistic superpower. In 1984, just six years after the reform process began, the state-supported China Confucius Foundation was created with the explicit mandate to expand the influence of Confucianism both internally and internationally. By 2007 there were close to 200 Institutes around the globe, all supported by the Chinese government. None of this activity is "religious" in the Western sense. Yet the Chinese government's strategy of persuasion through education, both in and outside China, clearly recalls the traditional Confucian belief that moral development is fundamental to a peaceful society.

Daoism under Reconstruction

Daoism has been more popular than Confucianism in the West: Daoist teachings were integral to the counterculture movement of the 1960s, and some Westerners continue to cherish the Daoist ideals of *wuwei* and *ziran*. Daoism has also been used to encourage "green" thinking in Taiwan, and as the PRC becomes prosperous enough to turn its attention to the natural environment, the value of the Daoist emphasis on achieving harmony with the cosmos is being recognized there as well.

Folk Religiosity

Many popular religious groups focus on cultivating inner calm and peace. Others, such as the Taiwan-based Yiguandao (Unity, Pervasive Truth, or Consistent Way) movement, are millenarian, believing that these are the end times and urging repentance of sins and reunion with the Eternal Mother. Still other movements are syncretic, combining elements from Confucianism, Daoism, Buddhism, Christianity, and Islam; one of these movements, Tien De or Tiande (Heavenly Virtue), professes to use cosmic energy and spiritual healing to cure disease.

Humanistic Buddhism: A Religion for This World

Buddhism is the most successful "Chinese" religion in the West. Three "Humanistic" groups influenced by the reformer Taixu have been particularly active in growing global Buddhism, and all three have attracted strong lay participation. Foguangshan (Buddha's Light Mountain), which accepts all the teachings of eight traditional schools (Tiantai, Huayan, Sanlun, Faxiang, Lu, Zhenyan, Chan, and Jingtu) focuses on education and has three universities, one of which is the University of the West in Rosemead, California. The founder of Fagushan (Dharma Drum Mountain), Sheng Yen (1930–2009), was a modern scholar-monk who instituted an ongoing campaign for "Six Ethics of the Mind": Family Ethics, Living Ethics, School Ethics, Environmental Ethics, Workplace Ethics, and Ethics between Ethnic Groups.

The third group, Cizi or Tzu Chi (Compassionate Relief), is a charitable foundation based in Taiwan that is active in disaster relief around the world. It was founded by a Buddhist nun named Cheng Yen (1937–) after three Catholic nuns observed to her that Buddhism was not well organized to help the sick and the poor in her town. With the help of housewife-disciples, Cheng established Cizi in 1966.

Korean Religions

Theoretically, traditional Korean religiosity can be classified as non-theistic at the elite level and polytheistic at the popular level, but in practice (like its Chinese counterpart) it tends to be syncretic. Thus neither of these categories necessarily excludes the other. It is even possible to identify a quasi-monotheistic belief in a purposeful and creative Way (or Heaven, or Heaven-and-Earth) co-existing with both the polytheistic belief in ancestral spirits and nature deities and the non-theistic belief in an impersonal natural Way.

Korea and China: A Shared History

Ancient Korean culture shows traces of influences from both continental East Asia and Central Asia. Migration from China to the Korean peninsula was underway as early as the Zhou dynasty (1046–256 BCE), and political relations between the two populations have always reflected a mixture of kinship and antipathy, relatedness and differentiation.

This early twentieth-century painting shows the Mountain God with three symbols of longevity: a crane (left), a deer (right), and pine trees (foreground). An example of Korean syncretism, the Mountain God is variously portrayed as the legendary founder Dangun, a Confucian sage, a Daoist immortal, and a Buddhist bodhisattva (© The Trustees of the British Museum).

The earliest written records of Korea are Chinese. Sima Qian's *Records of the Grand Historian* describes Wiman, one of the later kings of the proto-state of Old Joseon, as a refugee from northern China who ruled over Chinese refugees and Indigenous inhabitants at Wanggeom (present-day Pyongyang) in the sixth and fifth centuries BCE. Another Chinese source, the sixth-century *History of the Wei Dynasty*, tells how the mythical king Dangun founded Old Joseon during the time of China's legendary sage king Yao.

Old Joseon

An early Korean source, now lost, told of Dangun's divine grandfather Hwanin and father Hwanung. Hwanin knew that his son wanted to descend from heaven and live in the world of human beings, so he settled Hwanung in a cave on Mount Taebaek.

But Hwanung was not alone in the cave: a bear and a tiger were also living there, and they asked him to transform them into human beings. So Hwanung gave them a bundle of sacred mugworts and 20 cloves of garlic, with instructions to eat these foods and avoid the sunlight. After 21 days the bear became a woman, but the tiger had failed to avoid the light and therefore was not transformed. The woman remained alone, unable to find a husband, so she prayed for a child. In response to her prayers, Hwanung transformed himself, lay with her, and gave her a son, Dangun Wanggeom.

This foundation myth became a marker of national identity when Korea faced a series of Mongol invasions (1231–70). According to the thirteenth-century *Memorabilia of the Three Kingdoms*, the god Hwanung descended into the human world and married a she-bear who gave birth to Dangun (a bear cult still exists among the Ainu people of Japan). Yi Suenghyu in his *Songs of Emperors and Kings* (1287) gives a variant account in which the great king Hwanung gave medicine to his granddaughter to change her into a human being; she then married a tree god and bore Dangun (a tree cult was prevalent in the southern portion of the Korean peninsula). Interestingly, there is no reference to Dangun in the official *History of the Three Kingdoms*, compiled a century earlier, under Confucian inspiration, by Gim Busik.

The Three Kingdoms (c. 50 BCE–668 CE)

The proto-state of Old Joseon was followed by the Three Kingdoms of Goguryeo, Baekje, and Silla. Goguryeo's foundation myth (found in a collection from the thirteenth century) recalls the *Songs of the South* in both form and content, telling how the founder Jumong, who eventually took the title King Dongmyeong, was born from an egg after the sun—Haemosu, the Son of Heaven—shone on the breast of his mother, the eldest daughter of the River Earl. After ruling for 19 years, Dongmyeong forsook his throne and rose to heaven. Goguryeo was closely linked to Baekje, whose founder, King Onjo, is said to have been Dongmyeong's son.

Silla's foundation myth, like Old Joseon's, was recorded in Iryeon's *Memorabilia*. Like King Dongmyeong, King Hyeokgeose ("Bright") was born from an egg. His birth was announced by an eerie lightning-like emanation from a well. When the people cracked open the egg, they found a beautiful boy inside. When they bathed him he emitted light; the "birds and beasts danced for joy, heaven and earth shook, and the sun and the moon became bright" (Lee et al. 1993: 33). Soon after, a dragon appeared and brought an infant girl from under her left rib. When the two reached the age of 13, they married and became king and queen.

Document

The Lay of King Dongmyeong

From the Collected Works of Minister I of Korea

In early summer, when the Great Bear stood in the Snake,
Haemosu came to Korea,
A true Son of Heaven.
He came down through the air
In a five-dragon chariot,
With a retinue of hundreds,
Robes streaming, riding on swans,
The atmosphere echoed with chiming music.
Banners floated on the tinted clouds.
. . .
North of the capital was the Green River,
Where the River Earl's three beautiful daughters
Rose from the drake-neck's green waves
To play in the Bear's Heart Pool.
Their jade ornaments tinkled.
Their flowerlike beauty was modest—
They might have been fairies of the Han River banks,
Or goddesses of the Lo River islets.
The king, out hunting, espied them,
Was fascinated and lost his heart.
Not from lust for girls,
But from eager desire for an heir
(Lee et al. 1993: 24).

Daoism

Korea's foundation myths contain several elements reminiscent of the shamanist stream in Daoism, including nature deities (the River Earl), marriage between gods and human beings (Hwanung and the bear-woman), and ascension into heaven (King Dongmyeong). In Silla, the people believed in the Holy Mother of Mount Fairy Peach: a goddess, the guardian of the country, who was said to live on a mountain to the west of the capital, recalling the Queen Mother of the West in the *Zhuangzi*. These apparently Daoist elements have led some scholars to suggest that her cult was a composite of an Indigenous mountain deity cult and a Daoist immortality cult. Her tale (see Document box) underlines the syncretic nature of Korean religion, linking the Holy Mother with a Buddhist nun as well as a Chinese emperor and King Hyeokgeose (Hyokkose) of Silla.

This mythological syncretism is reinforced in Silla's history. In the 700s Gim Jiseong, a vice-minister of state, kept one image each of Amitabha, the buddha of the West, and Maitreya, the buddha of the Future. He read Mahayana literature but also enjoyed Laozi and the *Zhuangzi*. Echoes of Daoist scripture continued into the 1400s, during the staunchly neo-Confucian Joseon or I dynasty, when literati (much like the Seven Sages of the Bamboo Grove) retired from official life to engage in metaphysical conversation.

Murals in Goguryeo tombs suggest that the Daoist cult of immortality merged with local beliefs in prognostication. The early Tang court sent a Daoist adept and a copy of the *Daodejing* to Korea. In the same period, a Buddhist monastery near the border with China was converted into a Daoist temple; and in 643, at the request of the Goguryeo king, eight Daoist priests were sent there from China. By 650, the Daoist influence at the Goguryeo court was so strong that a monk who opposed the state's adoption of Daoism fled and sought refuge in Baekje.

Document

The Holy Mother of Mount Fairy Peach

The phrases "art of the immortals" and "art of longevity" suggest that the Holy Mother embraced Daoism as well as Buddhism.

During the reign of King Chinpyong [579–632], a nun . . . wished to repair a hall for the Buddha . . . but could not carry out her desire. A beautiful immortal fairy, her hair adorned with ornaments, appeared in the nun's dreams and consoled her: "I'm the holy goddess mother of Mount Fairy Peach [Mount West], and I am pleased that you would repair the Buddha Hall. I offer you ten *kun* of gold. . . ." The holy mother, originally the daughter of a Chinese emperor, was named Saso. Early in her life she learned the art of the immortals. . . . When Saso first came to Chinhan, she gave birth to a holy man who became the first ruler of Silla—perhaps he was Hyokkose. . . . Saso donated gold to make a Buddha image, lighted incense for the living beings, and initiated a religion. How could she be merely one who learned the art of longevity and became a prisoner in the boundless mist? (Lee et al. 1993: 94)

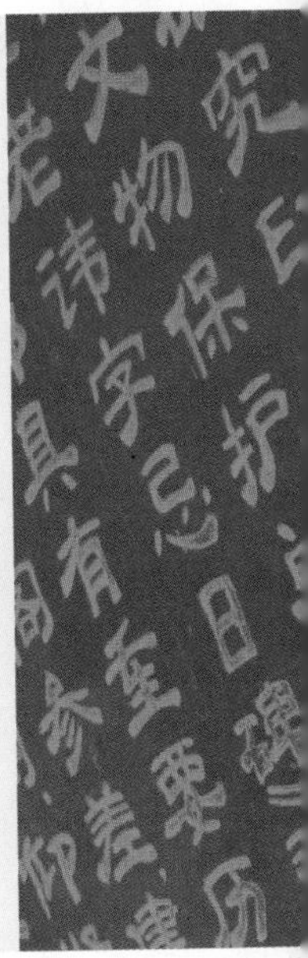

Shamanism

With its focus on deities, ghosts, and spirits, Daoism found deep resonance in Korean shamanism (*mugyo*). Each village had its own deity: a local mountain god or goddess in inland regions and a dragon king by the sea. Traditional household deities included the gods of the hearth, the roof beam, and the outhouse. Shamans (*mudang*) regularly performed rituals at community celebrations and ceremonies.

Buddhism

A Buddhism that was focused on karma and the search for happiness was introduced to Goguryeo by a Chinese monk in 372 and to Baekje by an Indian monk in 384; both received imperial support. In Silla King Pophung and his minister Yi Chadon made Buddhism the state religion in the sixth century. In 540, when King Chinhung established a youth group, he made the Buddhist five precepts (p. 400) part of its ethical foundation. And in 661 two monks named Wonhyo and Uisang set out for China in search of new teachers.

In the end they did not travel far. One night, while waiting out a rainstorm, they unknowingly slept in an ancient tomb and drank water that had collected in a human skull. The next morning Wonhyo was horrified to see what he had used as a drinking vessel; then he realized that his response had been determined solely by his mind. Having achieved enlightenment, Wonhyo returned home, left the monastery, and developed what came to be known as "interpenetrated Buddhism" (*tongbulgyo*), harmonizing the teachings of the Samron (Sanlun or Madhyamaka) and Yusik or Yugagyo (Weishi or Yogacara) schools. Wonhyo's *tongbulgyo* reflected the teachings of his friend Uisang, who had completed the trip to China and returned to found the Hwaeom school—the Korean version of the Huayan (Flower Garland) tradition.

United Silla, Later Three Kingdoms, and Goryeo (668–1392)

Confucianism

Today Korea has the largest network of Confucian shrines in the world. The process of Confucianization started around 600, but it was not until the Goryeo period (918–1392), when Buddhism was at its height, that Confucianism became firmly rooted. King Taejo ("Ultimate Ancestor"), who united the Three Kingdoms that splintered from Silla and founded Goryeo in 918, was an ardent Buddhist, but he also encouraged Confucian learning.

Taejo replaced Silla's tradition of governance by a hereditary aristocracy with the examination-based bureaucratic system of Tang China. He is also said to have left for his successors a list of "Ten Injunctions" that brought together Buddhist, Confucian, and Indigenous perspectives. The first injunction, for example, clearly honours the Buddhist tradition:

> The success of the great enterprise of founding our dynasty is entirely owing to the protective powers of the many Buddhas. We therefore must build temples for both Son [Meditation] and Kyo (Textual) Schools and appoint abbots, that they may perform the proper ceremonies and themselves cultivate the way (Lee 1985: 132).

But the third injunction pays tribute to the Confucian tradition:

> . . . if the eldest son is not worthy of the crown, let the second eldest succeed to the throne. If the second eldest, too, is unworthy, choose the brother the people consider the best qualified for the throne.

And the fourth injunction emphasizes the primacy of Indigenous traditions:

> In the past we have always had a deep attachment for the ways of China and all of our institutions have been modelled upon those of Tang. But our country occupies a different geographical location and our people's character is different from that of the Chinese. Hence, there is no reason to strain ourselves unreasonably to copy the Chinese way . . . (H. Kang in Lee 1993: 263).

Soon after this, the influence of Confucianism was further reinforced when Choe Chung (948–1068) established a private Confucian Academy.

Buddhism

A new era began around 800 CE with the establishment of the Seon (Chan) school. Although the established Gyo (doctrinal) schools resisted its innovations, two monks, Uicheon (1055–1101) and Jinul (1158–1210), effectively synthesized the Seon and Gyo.

Jinul brought together the two views on enlightenment, sudden and gradual, with the dictum "sudden enlightenment followed by gradual practice." He integrated *gwanhwa* (meditating on the word) or *gongan* practice into Seon, turned his back on the excesses of other Buddhist schools, and established the Jogye Order as a new community of pure-minded and disciplined Seon practitioners on Mount Jogye.

The *Tripitaka Koreana* is the most complete collection of Buddhist texts in the world. Engraved in Chinese characters on 80,000 woodblocks, it was completed between 1237 and 1248. This immense government-sponsored project was undertaken in an effort to win the Buddha's protection against invasion by the Mongols (© John Van Hasselt / Sygma / Corbis).

Joseon (1392–1910)

Confucian Antipathy to Buddhism

In Korea as in China, Buddhism's success eventually led to corruption and backlash. The founder of the Joseon dynasty, another Taejo, banned the building of new Buddhist temples; then his son Taejong disestablished temples and confiscated their estates and workers, including slaves. Buddhist activities were confined to specific areas—in particular, outside the cities and on the mountains.

Around the same time, families began installing shrines for ancestral tablets in their homes, in accordance with Confucian custom. Eventually, the responsibility for performing the rites of ancestor veneration was entrusted to the first son, who became the only one with the right of inheritance. This system of primogeniture put an end to the Goryeo system under which daughters were also entitled to inherit and couples could hold property jointly.

Neo-Confucianism

In the early 1500s, the philosopher Jo Gwangjo continued to root out superstitions deemed incompatible with Confucianism. He encouraged government by moral suasion and instituted a system of local self-government based on the idea of a village code or "Family Compact," outlined by the

Chinese neo-Confucian Zhu Xi. At the heart of this system was a notion of reciprocity expressed in mutual encouragement of morality, supervision of conduct, decorum in social relations, and aid in times of hardship or disaster.

Zhu Xi's influence extended into the metaphysical realm. He believed that human beings have in them both a principle or pattern of nature that is wholly good and a vital or material force that can be good or bad. The latter is good when desires and emotions are expressed in appropriate balance and bad when a lack or an excess is expressed. This inspired a famous exchange of letters between the Korean philosophers I Hwang (Toegye) and I I (or Yulgok) in the mid-1500s.

At the centre of this exchange, known as the "Four–Seven Debate," was the relationship between the four heart-minds—which, according to Mencius, reflect the fundamental goodness of human nature—and the seven emotions (happiness, anger, sorrow, fear, love, hate, and desire)—which, according to "Centrality and Equilibrium," cause some human actions to be less than good when they are not expressed in correct proportion.

Both taking Zhu Xi as their starting-point, I Hwang and I I arrived at different conclusions. I Hwang argued that principle or pattern in nature (*i*) rises and material force (*ki*) follows, implying that human nature is mixed from the beginning. I I, on the other hand, argued that if principle pervades everything, is uniform and undifferentiated, then it must be material force that initiates action, implying that human nature is originally wholly good. Behind the philosophers' quest for a deeper understanding of human nature was the commitment to psychological–moral transformation of the self—the neo-Confucian equivalent of classic Confucian self-cultivation.

The quest for self-improvement was not limited to men. Three prominent documents written by or for women were Queen Sohye's *Instructions for the Inner Quarters* (1475); a letter written by the seventeenth-century Confucian Song Siyol on the occasion of his daughter's marriage, emphasizing a mother's influence on her children; and a letter from Lady Hyegyeong (1735–1815) to her brother's son in which she sought to impress on him the Confucian virtues of filiality and respect for elders, as well as compassion for paternal aunts.

As neo-Confucianism became increasingly entrenched at the state level and Daoism was gradually assimilated into Joseon culture, Buddhist monastics argued for reconciliation of the various religions—in effect, syncretism. As the sixteenth-century monk Hyujeong wrote in his *Mirror of Three Religions*: "An ancient man said: 'Confucianists plant the root, Taoists grow the root, and Buddhists harvest the root'" (Lee et al. 1993: 662). Nevertheless, Confucianism retained its dominant position.

Recent Developments: 1897 to the Present

From the late-nineteenth century to the mid-twentieth, Korea was forced to contend with both Japanese imperialism and the increasing presence of the West. Korean responses to the West varied. One of the few English-speaking politicians of the time, Yun Chiho (1864–1945), favoured wholesale Westernization and an end to the relationship with China, which was then known as the "sick man of East Asia." Like his contemporaries in China, Yun argued that if Koreans were poor and oppressed, Confucianism was to blame.

Yun's antipathy towards Confucianism was not unreasonable, for in addition to being seen as regressive, it was associated with Japanese imperialism. During Japan's occupation of Korea (1910–45), the old Royal Confucian Academy was renovated and institutions like the Society for the Promotion of the Confucian Way were established to aid the imposition of Japanese culture on the Koreans.

Contemporary Confucianism

Other Korean scholars agreed that Korea's adherence to the conservative teachings of Zhu Xi, which focused on maintaining the status quo through mastery of classical literature, had held it back. However, like the Chinese New Confucians, they also believed that a renewed transnational Confucianism based on traditional values could help to bring peace and stability to the whole world. Among those scholars was Bak Eunsik (1859–1925), who preferred the Confucianism of Wang Yangming even though Wang had been overshadowed by Zhu Xi in Korea. Bak saw hope in Wang's emphasis on the "manifesting" of the naturally "clear character" through cultivation of the heart-mind and uncovering of the innate goodness in human beings. He was not alone in his choice of Wang's Confucianism as a response to modernity.

Gim Chungnyol, who studied with the New Confucian Fang Dongmei in the 1950s and 1960s, was an activist in the Korean democracy movement in the 1970s and 1980s. He believed that Confucianism could serve as an antidote to the excesses of capitalist industrialization. But the movement for the revival of Confucianism in Korea is not monolithic. So Chonggi, for one, was critical of authoritarian rule even if it was Confucian, but he believed that a Confucianism of the people could be good for Korea. The recent establishment of an Institute of Confucian Philosophy and Culture at Sungkyunkwan University suggests a revival of scholarly interest in the Confucian tradition. Even so, popular support for Confucianism as a religion is not strong.

Buddhism

The Japanese occupation was particularly difficult for Korean Buddhists. The traditional temple system was replaced with the Japanese system. Temple abbots were given the right to private ownership and inheritance, and some monks adopted the Japanese customs of marrying and having children. In 1920 the 31 main temples were put under the oversight of the Japanese government. After the defeat of Japan in 1945, deep rifts developed between the "Japanized" monks and those who had remained celibate. In time the Jogye Order became the dominant school and took over the management of the temples from the married priests. Beginning in the 1960s, Korean Buddhism adopted a Protestant model of active missionizing, encouraging lay associations and focusing on youth, and the South Korean government devoted many resources to restoring and reconstructing historic temples.

Won Buddhism

Won or Circle Buddhism (Wonbulgyo) is a twentieth-century school that can be placed in the Seon tradition because of its practice of meditation and its emphasis on harnessing the mind. Its symbol, the circle, stands for ultimate reality and the belief that, in the words of its founder, Sotaesan (1891–1943), "All beings are of one Reality and all things and principles originate from one source, where the truth of no birth and no death and the principle of cause and effect operate on an interrelated basis as a single, perfect organ." Today Won Buddhism has a global presence.

North Korea

In 1953 the Korean peninsula was divided into two parts. North Korea, like the PRC, is communist, and although its laws support religious freedom, in practice religion is barely tolerated. There are reports that Buddhism fares a little better than Christianity, but it still has a very limited presence in the country.

South Korea

In the early 2000s nearly half of South Korea's population professed to have no religion—a similar pattern to the Chinese. Those who did claim an institutional affiliation were almost equally divided between Buddhism and Christianity (mainly Protestant, especially Pentecostal). Confucianism claimed only 0.3 per cent and the Indigenous shamanic tradition was statistically invisible, even though both traditions still seem pervasive in Korean life.

There are more than 200 new religions in South Korea. Because their beliefs and practices are syncretic, often more "cultural" than "religious," they may not be captured in census statistics. But they demonstrate the pervasiveness of Korean religiosity and its multiple influences. Some modern progressives urge the revival of folk traditions as a way of reclaiming Korean culture; yet others call for shamanism to be rooted out as mere superstition. A sampling of new religious movements shows that Korean religious responses to modernity are diverse.

The oldest of the new movements, the Religion of the Heavenly Way or Cheondogyo, was founded in 1860 in response to Catholicism. It syncretizes Korean, Chinese, and Christian values, and combines monotheism and belief in the equality of all human beings with the broad East Asian vision of religious practice as enabling humans to live in harmony with the universe.

Another response to Western culture and globalization is the Religion of the Great Ancestors (Daejonggyo), which sees itself as a revival of ancient Korean shamanism. Founded in 1910,

Students wearing traditional costumes perform during one of the regular celebrations of Confucius held at Sungkyunkwan University in Seoul (© Seoul Shinmun / epa / Corbis).

it depicts God as Korean and presents the heavenly triad of Indigenous ancestors—Hwanin, Hwanung, and Dangun—as an alternative to the Christian Trinity. Other new religions, such as Dahn Yoga, have been influenced by the Daoist practice of internal alchemy aimed at both physical longevity and spiritual transcendence.

Summary

The ancient popular beliefs and practices at the root of the elite religions of China and Korea do not claim exclusive truth. They come from many different places and cultures. Yet most of them share a single aspiration to harmony—individual and communal, earthly and cosmic. Further-

Sites

Beijing, People's Republic of China

The Imperial Palace complex (the "Forbidden City") includes the Altar or Temple of Heaven, where the Ming and Qing emperors performed the grandest sacrifices. Beijing is also home to the ancestral temple of both dynasties (the Taimiao), a Confucian temple dedicated to scholar-officials, and the tombs of the later Ming emperors.

Qufu, Shandong province, People's Republic of China

Among the monuments in the birthplace of Confucius are a temple, a family mansion, and a cemetery containing Confucius' tomb and the remains of more than 100,000 of his descendants.

Xian, Shaanxi province, PRC

Xian (formerly Chang'an) was China's capital through many dynasties. The famous terracotta warrior guardians were discovered nearby.

Wudangshan, Hubei province, PRC

Mount Wudang is home to many Daoist monasteries, as well as a complex of palaces and temples that contain some of the finest examples of Chinese art and architecture; most were built during the Ming dynasty (1368–1644), but some Daoist buildings date from as early as the seventh century.

Guangzhou, Guangdong province, PRC

It was in Guangzhou that Huineng (638–713), the sixth Chan patriarch, was enlightened. His remains are enshrined in the Nanhua Temple, north of Guangzhou.

Cheongju City, South Korea

The first book in the world to be produced using movable metal type was printed in 1377 at the Heungdeok Temple in Cheongju. *The Monk Baegun's Anthology of the Great Buddhist Patriarchs' Seon Teachings*, better known as *Jikji* (*Straight Pointing*) is now housed in the National Library of France.

Seoul, South Korea

The Changdeokgung (Palace of Prospering Virtue) complex was established by Taejong, the third Joseon king. It includes Jongmyo, the oldest of the surviving Confucian shrines dedicated to the ancestors of Joseon.

more, many see the achievement of harmony as dependent on the disciplined transcendence of self. Although individual groups vary in their specific goals and methods, they have all tended to believe that basic human desires—for material well-being, health, familial joy, personal security, social stability, spiritual maturity, and, ultimately, release from the cycle of rebirth—should be harnessed and directed towards the care of others: family and friends, the community, the state, and the natural world.

Like Korea's, China's religious culture has undergone significant transformations over the last 1,500 years, incorporating new influences—from Confucianism, Daoism, and Buddhism to Christianity—without abandoning its Indigenous shamanistic traditions. Today both societies remain pluralistic and syncretic. None of the traditional religions have disappeared. Buddhism has thrived in Taiwan while Christianity has flourished in Hong Kong and South Korea. New religious movements have developed in Taiwan and Hong Kong; and there are now more than 200 active new ones in South Korea. But religious freedom remains elusive in the People's Republic and North Korea. How the various religions will develop and interact with one another remains to be seen.

Sacred/Foundational Texts

Religion	Classical and Sacred Texts	Composition/ Compilation Process	Compilation/ Revision Process	Use (Oral, Legal, Ritual)
Confucianism (Texts are understood to come from sages and are not considered "sacred")	*Book of Music, Poetry, History, Changes, Rites* and the *Spring* and *Autumn Annals*	5th–3rd centuries BCE	175 CE stone engraving of the Classics after the burning of the books in 213 BCE; the *Book of Music* is lost	Used for home education; curriculum assigned for state examination and official learning
Confucianism	*Classic of Filial Piety, The Analects, Er Ya* (the earliest Chinese dictionary), three commentaries on the *Spring and Autumn Annals* and *Rites* in three sections (*The Rites of Zhou, The Book of Rites*, and *Ceremonial Rites*	7th–10th centuries	The Five Classics increased to Nine and then Twelve Books and inscribed on stone	As above
Confucianism	Zhu Xi formulates standard texts into the *Four Books* (*Great Learning Centrality and Equilibrium* both from the *Book of Rites, Mencius, The Analects*) and *Five Classics* from ancient times	10th–13th centuries	With *Mencius*, the Twelve Classics become Thirteen	As above
Confucianism	Four Books for women include *Admonitions for Women, Filial Piety for Women, Analects for Women*, and *Instructions for the Inner Quarters*	1st–2nd centuries	7th–9th centuries see two new additions; *Instructions* is added in the 15th century; *Filial Piety* replaced by a *Handy Record of Rules for Women*	Education for women

Sacred/Foundational Texts (Continued)

Religion	Classical and Sacred Texts	Composition/ Compilation Process	Compilation/ Revision Process	Use (Oral, Legal, Ritual)
Daoism (early texts seen primarily as words of wisdom from sages)	Daodejing	Contested but early 3rd century BCE generally accepted	3rd century CE Wang Bi commentary	Liturgical use and acts as basis for movements seeking legitimacy from Laozi
Daoism	Zhuangzi	First seven chapters attributed to namesake; 4th to 3rd centuries BCE	Guo Xiang believed to be the compiler of the current text	Known as the Classic of South China (*Nanhuajing*) and used in education
Daoism	*Techniques of the Mind* and *Inward Training*	4th century BCE	Both were lost to the main tradition and "found" recently in the Legalist *Guanzi*	Likely used as meditation manual
Daoism	*Classic of the Great Peace*	1st century CE	Reassembled in 6th century after its destruction in 3rd century	Ritual use and instructional manual
Daoism	*Master Who Embraces Spontaneous Nature or Simplicity*	320s	14th century saw the combination of the "inner" and "outer" sections of the current text	Used as manual for external alchemy
Daoism	High Clarity scriptures	Revealed 364 to 379	Edited into *Pronouncements of the Perfected* by Tao Hongjing	Doctrinal and ritual use
Daoism	*Scripture for the Salvation of Humanity* of the Lingbao school	Revealed 4th century	12th century 61-chapter version presented to Song emperor	Used in recitation
Daoism	*Fifteen Precepts for the Establishing of the Teaching*	12th century	Collected as part of Wang Chongyang's writings	Doctrinal for Complete Truth school
Buddhism	Three Baskets of the Theravada/Hinayana	Originals from India; see chapter on Buddhism	Most translated during the 3rd to 6th centuries	Used in study and as reference for monastic law
Buddhism	Many; core to Chinese and Korean practice are treatises like *The Awakening of Faith*; sutras such as the *Pure Land* (in three volumes), *Lotus*, *Flower Garland*, *Platform of Hui-neng*, *Vimalakirti*, and others (see Chapter 8); and Recorded Sayings by Chan masters like Baegan's *jikji*, Wumen's *Gateless Gate*, and the *Blue Cliff Records*	Most from South Asia except for *The Platform Sutra* and records of sayings from masters of the Chan school; and *The Awakening of Faith* which has no Sanskrit original	Most translated during the 4th to 6th centuries	See Chapter 5
Popular tradition	Innumerable tracts of religious rituals and devotion	Throughout history	New writings appear based on new movements	Instructional and ritual

Discussion Questions

1. How does the popular shrine described at the beginning of this chapter illustrate the syncretic quality of Chinese religion?
2. What assumptions and values do Confucianism and Daoism share? What sets them apart?
3. Would you consider Confucianism to be patriarchal, misogynist, and oppressive for women? Explain your position, using evidence from China and Korea.
4. What are some of the core spiritual concerns in the early prototypical Daoist texts? How did they influence the goals, methods of cultivation, and institutional development of religious Daoism?
5. Compare and contrast classical and neo-Confucianism. What accounts for their differences?
6. What qualities would make an ideal Buddhist woman?
7. Explore points of tension and convergence between Confucianism, Daoism, and Buddhism.
8. What allows for such disparate groups as the Seven Sages of the Bamboo Grove and Complete Truth to coexist under the umbrella of Daoism? What makes them both Daoist?
9. Who are the "New Confucians"? What issues are they tackling? What are their goals?
10. How does Engaged or Humanistic Buddhism differ from traditional Buddhism?
11. What do the Korean foundation myths suggest about the nature of Korean culture and religiosity?
12. What are some of the challenges facing modern Korean Buddhism?
13. In this book, the religious traditions of East Asia have been organized geographically in two groups: "China and Korea" and "Japan." Would a different organization, based on the traditions—Indigenous shamanism (as in Shinto and *mugyo*), Daoism, Confucianism, and East Asian Buddhism—be more appropriate or less so? Why?

Glossary

Ban Zhao (c. 48–112 CE) The influential female Confucian scholar who wrote *Admonitions* (or *Lessons*) *for Women*.

Chan From Sanskrit *dhyana* (meditation); the Buddhist school known as Seon in Korea and Zen in Japan.

Confucius (551–479 BCE) The first teacher of Confucianism, known in Chinese as Kongzi or Kongfuzi.

Dao/dao (also ***Tao/tao***) Either the "Way" in the sense of the Ultimate or the "way" in the sense of the path taken by followers of a particular tradition.

Daodejing The *Classic of the Way and Power or Virtue* is the multi-authored foundational Daoist text purportedly written by Laozi.

de Power or virtue.

Dong Zhongshu (195?–105? BCE) The most prominent Confucian of the New Text school, who helped establish Confucianism as the state religion.

five phases The generative and destructive cycles between metal, wood, water, fire, and earth represent a dynamic view of the cosmos. The concept is also translated as five agents or elements depending on the meaning. See *wuxing*.

Han Yu (768–824) Played a pivotal role in the revival of Confucianism in a period when it was overshadowed by Daoism and Buddhism.

Huayan Flower Garland Buddhism; Hwaeom in Korea.

Jingtu **Pure Land** Buddhism.

junzi A person of exemplary or authoritative behaviour, especially in Confucianism; traditionally translated in English as "gentleman," implying the virtues of the upper class; a superior person, or one of virtue and exceptional character.

Laozi The "Old Master"; the putative patriarch of Daoism and author of the *Daodejing*; may or may not have been an actual historical figure.

li The single English transliteration used for two different Chinese words. *Li* in the first sense refers to ritual practice and decorum and is usually translated as "rites." *Li* in the second sense refers to the pattern in a natural material such as wood or stone; it was used by the neo-Confucians to designate the force that pervades the cosmos and is translated as "principle."

lunhui Rebirth or *samsara*.

Mencius (c. 343–289 BCE) The second most prominent Confucian thinker, known in Chinese as Meng Ke, Master Meng, or Mengzi; he believed that human nature is inherently good.

pusa Bodhisattva; an enlightened being who foregoes release/liberation to stay in the world and help others.

qi material force or vital energy

qigong A "breath" discipline or set of exercises used to enhance health and spiritual well-being; also the vital or material energy or force that animates everything in the universe.

ren The central Confucian virtue, usually translated as "humaneness," "benevolence," "goodness," or "compassion."

taiji The "Great Ultimate," understood to coexist with the Ultimate of Non-being; also the term for the slow-motion exercise sequence widely known in English as Tai Chi.

Wang Yangming (1472–1529) The Ming Confucian who challenged Zhu Xi's understanding of self-cultivation and established the neo-Confucian School of Mind.

wuwei "Not-doing" as a way of being in the world: a state not of "doing nothing" but of acting without intention or self-interest; an ideal for both Daoists and Confucians, though most prominently associated with the former.

wuxing Five agents, elements, or phases. See also **five phases** and **yin-yang**.

xin The single English transliteration used for two different Chinese characters: the first is translated throughout this chapter as "heart-mind" when discussing Daoism and Confucianism and is associated with both the thinking and feeling capacities; the same character also refers to Mind or Consciousness in Buddhism. The second character means trustworthiness, a quality valued by Daoists and Confucians alike.

Xunzi (c. 310–219 BCE) The third most important classical Confucian thinker; he believed that human nature is evil and that conscious effort is required to develop goodness.

yi A moral sense of what is right, what is required and appropriate for a situation; most often used in conjunction with *ren*.

yinguo Cause and effect or karma.

yin-yang wuxing "Yin" and "yang" originally referred to the shady and sunny sides of a mountain, but in time they came to be associated with female and male qualities and, more broadly, complementary forces in the universe. *Wu* means "five" and *xing* can be translated as "element," "agent," "force," or "phase." Together, these terms specify the dynamic nature of the universe—a concept integral to the Naturalist school of thought, which was popular during the Han dynasty.

Zhang Daoling According to tradition, he established the oldest surviving Daoist school, the Way of the Celestial Masters, after Laozi appeared to him in a vision in 142 CE.

Zhuangzi (369?–286?) The second most important early Daoist thinker, after Laozi; also the title of the book attributed to him.

Zhu Xi (1130–1200) The most important member of the neo-Confucian School of Principle. He synthesized early Song Confucian writings, focused on book learning, and sought to find the principle/pattern common to Nature.

ziran Spontaneity or "self-so-ness."

Further Reading

Bell, Daniel A., and Chaibong Hahm, eds. 2003. *Confucianism for the Modern World*. Cambridge: Cambridge University Press. Draws from Chinese, Korean, and Japanese texts and histories to argue that Confucianism is relevant to our world.

Buswell, Robert E., ed. 2007. *Religions of Korea in Practice*. Princeton: Princeton University Press. Presents primary-source selections regarding ordinary devotional beliefs and practices as well as critical analysis; also includes a helpful introductory essay by Don Baker.

Elman, Benjamin A., ed. 2002. *Rethinking Confucianism: Past and Present in China, Japan, Korea, and Vietnam*. Los Angeles: UCLA Asian Pacific Monograph Series. Explores issues of gender and national variations, and asks who represents Confucianism.

Kirkland, Russell. 2004. *Taoism: The Enduring Tradition*. London: Routledge. An introductory text by an author who believes Daoism has been misrepresented and seeks to offer a new perspective.

Kohn, Livia, ed. 1993. *The Taoist Experience: An Anthology*. Albany: SUNY Press. Primary sources (with brief notes) for a range of philosophical, liturgical, and alchemical texts, mostly from medieval Daoism.

Lopez, Donald S., ed. 1996. *Religions of China in Practice*. Princeton: Princeton University Press. Includes essays on the religious practices of ethnic minorities such as the Manchus and Yi; Stephen Teiser's introductory essay provides a helpful overview.

Miller, James. 2003. *Daoism: A Short Introduction*. Oxford: Oneworld. Covers the historical development, political involvement, and physical practices of Daoism as well as its understanding of nature.

Rainey, Lee Dian. 2010. *Confucius and Confucianism: The Essentials*. London: Wiley-Blackwell. A delightfully accessible introduction to the origins and development of Confucianism, with an account of its contemporary relevance.

Robinet, Isabelle. 1993. *Taoist Meditation: The Mao-Shan Tradition of Great Purity*. Julian F. Pas and Norman J. Giradot, trans. Albany: SUNY Press. A detailed study of the Shangqing (Highest Clarity) tradition.

Wu, Ch'eng-en. 1970 [1943]. *Monkey*. Arthur Waley, trans. New York: Grove Press. A fictional look at popular religious beliefs and practices in medieval China.

Yao, Xinzhong. 2000. *An Introduction to Confucianism*. Cambridge: Cambridge University Press. Focuses on China; Korea and Japan are dealt with very briefly.

Yu, Anthony. 2005. *State and Religion in China*. Chicago and La Salle, IL: Open Court. Argues persuasively that religions in China have always been closely involved with worldly politics.

Recommended Websites

www.orientalarchitecture.com

Asian Historical Architecture offers photographs of numerous religious sites in China, Korea, and other countries in Asia, with brief historical notes and descriptions of how the buildings are used.

www.clickkorea.org/

A general-interest site, sponsored by the Korea Foundation; to access essays on Korean religions, select the main category "Thought & Religion" and then choose from six subcategories.

www.stanford.edu/~pregadio/index.html

"The Golden Elixir: Taoism and Chinese Alchemy" is hosted by Fabrizio Pregadio of Stanford University, who gives a concise introduction to Daoism and includes an impressive list of sources on alchemical beliefs and practices in Daoism.

eng.taoism.org.hk

The Taoist Culture and Information Centre offers an insider's view of Daoism's history and place in the world today. The site is sponsored by a Daoist temple in Hong Kong and maintained with the help of scholars from North America, Europe, and China.

www.chinakongzi.org

The Chinese-language site of the China Confucius Foundation (CCF). Established in 1984, the CCF is dedicated to promoting the teachings of Confucius.

www.ica.org.cn

The mandate of the International Confucian Association is to advance the study of Confucianism in order to promote peace and prosperity around the world. Its site is also available in Chinese.

english.hanban.org/node_10971.htm

The English-language site of the Confucius Institute/Classroom offers information on teaching materials, tests, teachers, and scholarships.

college.chinese.cn/en

The Confucius Institute Online; the contents of this site are available in many languages, including Chinese, French, German, Russian, Korean, Spanish, Japanese, and Arabic.

www.fgs.org.tw/english/index.html

Foguangshan (Buddha's Light Mountain) is an ecumenical group that favours Pure Land teachings; it is based in Gaoxiong in southern Taiwan.

www.dharmadrum.org/

Fagushan (Dharma Drum Mountain) is a Chan group headquartered in New Taipei City in Taiwan.

tw.tzuchi.org/en/

Tzu Chi (Compassionate Relief), also transliterated as Cizi, is a Taiwanese group, led by the nun Zhengyan, involved primarily in healthcare.

References

al-Faruqi, I., and D.E. Sopher, eds. 1974. *Historical Atlas of the Religions of the World*. New York: Macmillan.

Bell, Daniel A., and Chaibong Hahm, eds. 2003. *Confucianism for the Modern World*. Cambridge: Cambridge University Press.

Chen, Kenneth. 1964. *Buddhism in China. A Historical Survey*. Princeton, New Jersey: Princeton University Press.

Ch'oe, Yongcho, Peter Lee, and W. Theodore de Bary, eds. 2000. *Sources of Korean Tradition*. Vol. II. New York: Columbia University Press.

Cleary, Thomas. 1989. *Immortal Sisters: Secret Teachings of Taoist Women*. Berkeley: North Atlantic Books.

de Bary, Theodore, ed. 1972. *The Buddhist Tradition in India, China and Japan*. New York: Vintage Books.

———, and Irene Bloom, comp. 1999. *Sources of Chinese Tradition*, 2nd edn. Vol. 1. New York: Columbia University Press.

———, and Richard Lufrano, comp. 2000. *Sources of Chinese Tradition*, 2nd edn. Vol. 2. New York: Columbia University Press.

Fung, Yu-lan. 1934/1953. *A History of Chinese Philosophy*. Vol. 2. Derk Bodde, trans. Princeton: Princeton University Press.

Inagaki, Hisao, trans. 1994. *The Three Pure Land Sutras*. Kyoto: Nagata Bunshodo.

Jochim, Christian. 1986. *Chinese Religions: A Cultural Perspective*. Englewood Cliffs, NJ: Prentice-Hall.

Kirkland, Russell. 2004. *Taoism: The Enduring Tradition*. New York and London: Routledge.

Lau, D.C., trans. 1970. *Mencius*. Middlesex and New York: Penguin.

———, trans. 1963. *Lao Tzu: Tao Te Ching*. Middlesex and New York: Penguin.

Lee, Ki-Baik. 1985. *A New History of Korea*. Edward Wagner, trans. Cambridge, MA: Harvard University Press.

Lewis, Mark Edward. 2009. *China Between Empires. The Northern and Southern Dynasties*. Cambridge, MA, and London: The Belknap Press of Harvard University Press.

Little, Reg. 1995. "Confucius in Beijing: The Conference of the International Confucian Foundation." *Culture Mandala: The Bulletin of the Centre for East-West Cultural and Economic Studies*. Vol. 1, issue 2, article 4. Available at http://epublications.bond.edu.au/cm/vol1/iss2/4.

Lee, Peter H., et al., eds. 1993. *Sourcebook of Korean Civilization*. Vol. I. New York: Columbia University Press.

Owen, Stephen, ed. and trans. 1996. *An Anthology of Chinese Literature*. New York, London: W.W. Norton.

Pregadio, Fabrizio. 2006. *Great Clarity: Daoism and Alchemy in Medieval China*. Stanford: Stanford University Press.

Price, A. F. and Wong Mou-lam. 1990 (1969). *The Diamond Sutra & The Sutra of Hui-neng*. Boston: Shambhala.

Raphals, Lisa. 1998. *Sharing the Light: Representations of Women and Virtue in Early China*. Albany: SUNY Press.

Reps, Paul, comp. 1989 (1960). *Zen Flesh, Zen Bones: A Collection of Zen and Pre-Zen Writings*. New York, London, Toronto, Sydney, Auckland: Anchor Books, Doubleday.

Roetz, Heiner. 2008. "Confucianism between Tradition and Modernity, Religion, and Secularization: Questions to Tu Weiming." *Dao* 7: 367-380.

Roth, Harold D. 1999. *Original Tao: Inward Training and the Foundations of Taoist Mysticism*. New York: Columbia University Press.

Sommer, Deborah, ed. 1995. *Chinese Religion: An Anthology of Sources*. New York, Oxford: Oxford University Press.

Watson, Burton, trans. 2001. *The Essential Lotus: Selections from the Lotus Sutra*. New York: Columbia University Press.

———. 1997. *The Vimalakirti Sutra*. New York: Columbia University Press.

———. 1968. *The Complete Works of Chuang Tzu*. New York: Columbia University Press.

———. 1963. *Xunzi: Basic Writings*. New York: Columbia University Press.

Note

1. Some scholars prefer 552, based on scientific dating of an eclipse mentioned in the records of the time.

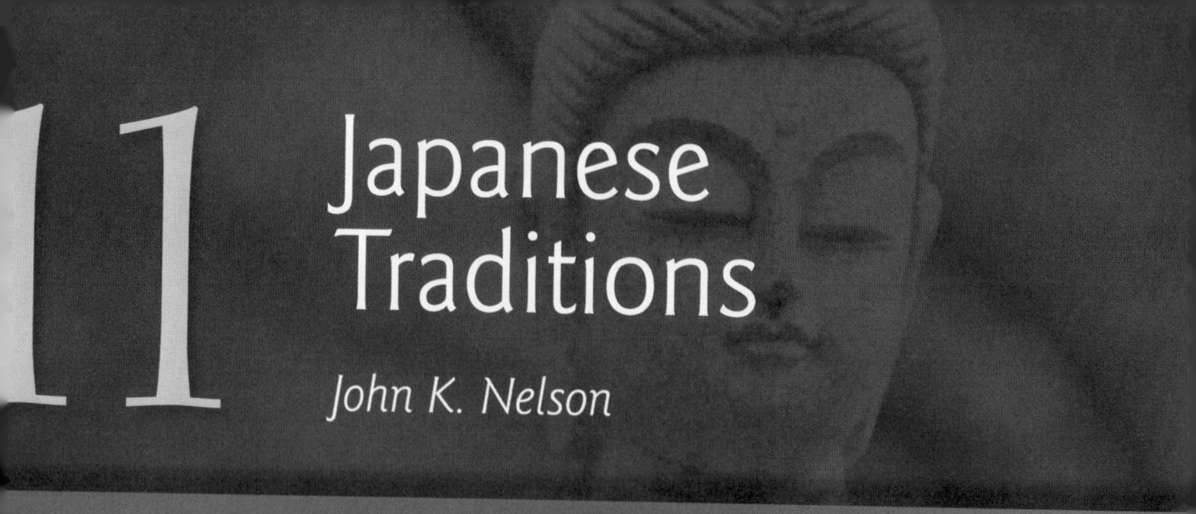

11 Japanese Traditions

John K. Nelson

Traditions at a Glance

Numbers

All numbers are based on self-assessment by the groups concerned. Because most Japanese religions are complementary rather than exclusive, the numbers reported by various sects may reflect occasional participation rather than membership.

Shinto: Estimates range from 3.5 million self-described adherents to more than 100 million if New Year's visits to shrines are counted as indicating "Shinto" affiliation.

Buddhism: Estimates range from 84.8 million, based on a 2009 government assessment of membership in the major denominations, to more than 100 million.

"New" religions: Estimates range from 10 to 30 million worldwide.

Christianity: Generally estimated at a little under 1 million nationwide.

Distribution

Buddhism, Shinto, and "new" religions are practised in every part of Japan, as well as in overseas communities. Japan itself counts approximately 75,000 Buddhist temples and more than 80,000 Shinto shrines, although many of the latter do not have resident clergy.

Founders

Shinto is an ethnic religion with no founder. Important founders of new Buddhist schools include Saicho (Tendai), Kukai (Shingon), Eisai (Rinzai Zen), Dogen (Soto Zen), Honen (Pure Land), Shinran (True Pure Land), and Nichiren (Nichiren).

Deities

Shinto has a vast number of deities, many of which are specific to local communities. The Sun Goddess, Amaterasu, has been promoted as the supreme deity since the late 1800s because of her affiliation with the imperial household. However, one of the most widely distributed deities is Hachiman, associated with military valour.

The primary Buddhist deities include the Medicine Buddha, the Cosmic Buddha, and Amida, the Buddha of the Pure Land, along with various bodhisattvas associated with compassion, healing, and deliverance from hell.

Authoritative Texts

Since the nineteenth century, the primary texts for Shinto have been the *Kojiki: Record of Ancient Matters* and the *Nihon Shoki*. The various Buddhist denominations and "new" religions all have their own primary texts.

Noteworthy Teachings

Shinto emphasizes harmony with nature, sincerity, and ritual purity. Each Buddhist denomination and "new" religion (Tenrikyo, Rissho Koseikai, etc.) likewise emphasizes its own distinctive teachings: secrets about the nature of reality, how universal salvation can be achieved through the Buddha of the Pure Land, the perfection of the *Lotus Sutra*, the necessity of performing memorial rites for ancestral spirits, and so on.

Long before the establishment of shrines to local deities and Buddhist temples, in the third and sixth centuries respectively, local clans had developed close relationships with both deities of the natural world and the spirits of their ancestors. Reciprocity was a key dynamic of these relationships, in which humans sent their petitions to the deities, accompanied by ritual offerings, and the

← The great "floating" torii gate at the Itsukushima Shinto shrine. Each of the main posts is a giant camphor tree, said to be some 500 years old (GARDEL Bertrand / hemis.fr / Getty Images).

deities were expected to respond by providing bountiful harvests, plentiful children, and stable political and social conditions. There was brand-name loyalty to the ancestral spirits of one's own household and clan; yet there was also acknowledgement of the powers of the many other deities (***kami***) associated with natural phenomena such as fire, water, mountains, and the spirits of animals and plants. When the harmonious balance of the relationship between humans and spirits was disturbed—by plague, famine, earthquake, typhoons, war, death—efforts to restore it via ritual were renewed. This pattern is common to all Japanese religions.

To discuss Japan's religious traditions with any degree of accuracy, it is necessary to juggle and juxtapose perspectives from cultural studies, history, politics, and anthropology, as well as religious studies. Even then, to encompass all the traditions that inform Japanese society today is a challenge. Shinto, the "way of the *kami*," is often said to be more than 2,000 years old. Yet it has gone through several transformations, some as recently as 150 years ago. Buddhism likewise defies easy assumptions; for example, only a few denominations have anything to do with meditation. Layered on an even older tradition of venerating ancestral spirits, the seven major Buddhist denominations today have their roots in the medieval period and yet must continually reinvent themselves to retain the financial support of the Japanese people. Nearly every temple has a homepage, and many monks use social media to stay in touch with their flocks, but there is no guarantee that a younger generation highly skeptical of religion in general will develop affiliations with local temples. It is no exaggeration to say that Japanese religious traditions force us to rethink the social, cultural, and individual dimensions of religion in a rapidly changing world.

Overview

The Rousing Drum

In a small city in central Japan, tens of thousands of people fill the evening streets for the festival of the "rousing drum." At 9:30 an enormous drum, a metre and a half (five feet) in height, will emerge from the city's main Shinto shrine, having been blessed by priests in solemn rituals. It will then be hoisted and affixed to a platform that will be carried through the streets by as many as 170 men. Adding to the weight of the platform will be two male strikers, one on each side of the drum, and eight "guardians" representing local officials. But the weight is only part of the challenge that the bearers face, for as the drum makes its way through the streets it will be "attacked" by neighbourhood teams with their own (smaller) drums mounted on platforms, who will fight for a position of honour immediately behind the main drum.

Fuelled by generous amounts of sake, the ensuing clashes seem anything but conducive to community solidarity. The festival is like a steam vent designed to release the pressure created by class and economic differences. In fact, injuries are common; parked vehicles are frequently damaged, and houses belonging to greedy landlords or stingy merchants may be vandalized. Old-timers remember with pride the year when the local police station was trashed. Yet the event is promoted as representing "the spirit of Furukawa."

Mr Sato's Funeral

After nearly a week of preparation, the funeral for Mr Sato Hideo (in Japan, the surname precedes the given name) is unfolding with the precision of a military operation. In a building constructed specifically for funerals, on the grounds of a large temple, the casket sits at the front of a hall

The *okoshidaiko* or "rousing drum" festival takes place every spring in the city of Furukawa, Nagano prefecture. Smaller drums from neighbourhood associations try to topple a large drum representing the city government and main Shinto shrine as it is carried through the streets (City of Hida).

Timeline

c. 8000 BCE	Hunter-gatherers produce sophisticated cord-pattern pottery, arrowheads, and human figures with possible religious significance
c. 450–250 CE	Immigration from north Asia introduces new technology, cultural forms, language, religious rituals, etc.
c. 250–600	Kofun period; rulers interred in massive burial mounds (*kofun*), with grave goods and clay models of attendants that indicate complex local hierarchies in this life and the next
538	Introduction of Buddhism; Yamato clan establishes its dominance
594	"Prince" Shotoku (*Shotoku taishi*) promotes Confucian principles alongside Buddhism; later acknowledged as patron saint of Buddhism in Japan
600s	Early temple-building; ruler referred to as "heavenly sovereign" (*tenno*)
710–794	Nara period; capital city, Heijokyo, located on site of present-day Nara

Continued

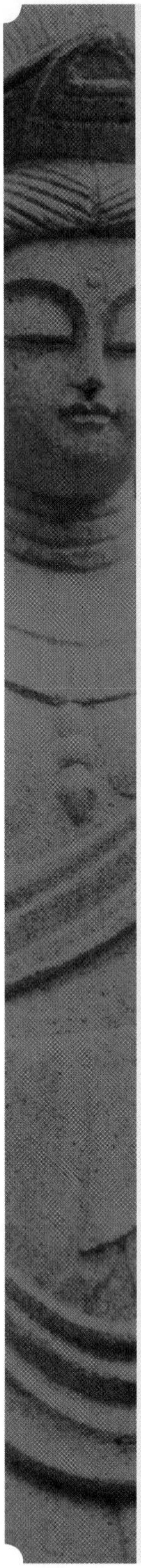

712, 720	Compilation of two key texts (*Kojiki*, *Nihon Shoki*) used to legitimate imperial rule and aristocratic privileges; more than 1,000 years later, these texts would be used in the campaign to revitalize "Shinto"
752	Dedication of Todaiji temple and completion of its Great Buddha image
785	Saicho, founder of Tendai sect, establishes a temple on Mount Hiei near Kyoto
794–1184	Heian period; capital city, Heiankyo, moved to what is now Kyoto
834	Kukai, founder of Shingon sect, establishes a monastery on Mount Koya
1039	Tendai monks attack monasteries of rival Buddhist sects
1052	Beginning of the "Final Decline of the Buddhist Dharma" (age of *mappo*) marked by fires, famines, earthquakes, wars, pestilence, etc.
1175	Honen begins propagating "Pure Land" Buddhism
1185–1333	Kamakura period, characterized by dominance of the samurai class; capital moved to Kamakura
1200	Eisai establishes Rinzai Zen school with support of the samurai
1233	Dogen establishes Soto Zen school
1253	Nichiren forms a sect centred on recitation of the *Lotus Sutra*
1254	Honen's disciple Shinran introduces "True Pure Land" Buddhism
1274, 1281	Attempted invasions by Mongol armies are thwarted when violent storms, called "divine winds" (*kamikaze*), sink many of their ships
1430–1500	Major fires, famine, epidemics, social disorder; Onin War (1467) devastates Kyoto and marks start of regional power struggles
1474–1550	True Pure Land peasant protest movement spreads throughout the country
1542	Systematization of Shinto shrines, priestly certification via Yoshida clan
1549	Christianity enters Japan with the Jesuit Francis Xavier
1573–1602	Gradual centralization of political power; Oda Nobunaga, Toyotomi Hideyoshi, and Tokugawa Ieyasu establish military regimes that subdue regional lords
1603–1867	Edo Period; Tokugawa clan dominates all political, military, and bureaucratic activity; country closed to outside trade in 1633
1638	Shimabara rebellion; Christianity banned
1644–1860	Rise of neo-Confucian teachings as challenge to Buddhist dominance
1705	First major pilgrimage of commoners to Ise Grand Shrines
1812	Beginning of movement to revitalize Shinto
1853–1867	Commodore Matthew Perry arrives in Japan and demands open ports; Christian missionaries return; regional wars between feudal and imperial forces end with defeat of Tokugawa shogunate
1868	New Meiji government orders separation of *kami* and buddhas, resulting in destruction of temples and religious art throughout the country
1879	Establishment of Yasukuni Shrine, where the spirits of military dead are venerated

1890–1944	State campaign to establish ideology centred on notions of imperial divinity, sacred nature of Japan, and military conquest
1936–1945	War in the Pacific, ending in the systematic destruction of most major and many minor Japanese cities
1945–1953	Allies occupy Japan; emperor renounces divinity; Shinto's status as state religion revoked
1995	Aum Shinrikyo attack on Tokyo subway; government passes new laws regulating religion organizations and activity
2011	Great Eastern Japan Earthquake of 11 March kills more than 19,000 people and causes a meltdown of three nuclear reactors, as well as tremendous property damage. In the aftermath, Japan's religious organizations provide substantial material and spiritual relief.

decorated with hundreds of white chrysanthemums. In the centre of the display, a portrait of Mr Sato is surrounded by candles and food offerings that recall a Buddhist altar.

Professional funeral directors, men and women wearing black suits, black armbands, and white gloves, direct the proceedings. Hired by the family and subcontracted by the temple, they have orchestrated every part of the ceremony: the syrupy background music, the guest books, the arrangements for donations, the refreshments, transportation to the crematorium for relatives.

As the mourners file in, three at a time, each takes a pinch of sand-like incense and sprinkles it on glowing charcoal before bowing to the portrait. Smoke soon fills the room—but no one leaves for fresh air. In three hours, after the body has been cremated at a high-tech facility nearby, family members and close relatives will use special chopsticks to select bone fragments for the urn.

All the identities Mr Sato assumed in his 83 years—son, brother, soldier, father, businessman, civil servant, poetry aficionado, grandfather, gardener, world traveller—are now consigned to the past as he takes on his final role as "ancestor." This will remain Mr Sato's identity for the next 33 years—the time it will take before his spirit fully leaves this world and joins the undifferentiated collectivity of the family's "distant" ancestors. Until then, his spirit must be venerated regularly with rituals, offerings, and grave visitations, lest it take offence and seek retribution.

Performing Belief

A young woman dressed all in black except for red shoes and screaming red hair, walks towards a large public park with an electric guitar slung over her shoulder. It's Sunday afternoon and her band, the Killers, is about to put on a concert of very loud atonal music known as "Visual Kei"—similar to punk, but less structured and rhythmic. She hopes that a talent agent she's invited will offer them a contract. How could he resist, after he's seen the drummer (a cute girl with a green mohawk, yellow bikini top, and numerous piercings) launch an exploding canister above the crowd, releasing a giant paper spider web, while the "music" becomes a car-crash of metal and sirens, with sparks flying from a spinning metal wheel?

As is her custom before such a performance, she veers off the main path and enters a small temple. Using a ladle from a stone basin filled with clean water, she purifies her hands and mouth.

Then, in the main hall, she joins her hands together and bows to the **bodhisattva** of compassion, Kannon, who bestows her mercy on all who ask. Before leaving, she stops at a small shrine to Benten, deity of music and performance, where she bows, claps her hands twice, throws a coin into the coffer, and asks that today's concert be the best ever, that the talent agent actually show up, and that he give them the break they need. Were you to stop her and ask if she is "religious," she would likely say "no way!" before telling you to get lost.

Persistent Themes

The preceding vignettes present a challenge to Western cultural assumptions about the nature of "religious" belief and practice in general. In Japan, religious belief generally takes a back seat to religious activity. Taking action—if only to purchase an amulet—may significantly reduce anxiety about an upcoming examination, a relationship problem, or a health condition. Which particular shrine or temple one visits depends on the situation that one wants a blessing for.

A conventional survey of Japanese religions would emphasize the doctrines, institutions, and leaders associated with the three major traditions: Buddhism, Confucianism, and Shinto. Although this chapter will certainly touch on these, many scholars now question the validity of this approach. One of those major traditions did not exist as such before the late 1800s, and the Japanese word for "religion" was not coined until the 1880s, when, as part of a government modernization campaign, the characters meaning "teachings" (*kyo*) and "sect" (*shu*) were combined to form *shukyo*. Yet lack of specific "religion" does not mean that religious belief, feeling, or orientation were lacking (Pye 2004). Japan has no fewer than seven major and 16 minor schools of Buddhism, countless "new religions," and more than 80,000 different *kami*. So it's not surprising that Japanese people might feel confused when asked which particular sect they belong to. Most have no trouble tolerating doctrinal diversity at the popular level. Nor do most of their religious traditions require adherence to one set of beliefs. In fact, those traditions have been subordinate to the themes outlined below for more than 1,000 years.

Seeking Benefits

Central to most Japanese religious traditions is the pragmatic desire to secure benefits, either in this world or in the next. It matters little whether a given place of worship is devoted to the Buddha or to a particular local *kami*: the important thing is that the prayers offered there help the individual resolve a conflict, start a new business, find a marriage partner, or conceive a child. A person may visit both temples and shrines, engage priests to perform rituals, and make regular offerings until the desired outcome is obtained—or until it seems clear that all those efforts have failed. Then he or she may have little to do with any organized religion until the next problem arises. "Turning to the gods in a time of trouble" is a well-known expression that summarizes Japan's pragmatic attitude towards religion.

To Christians, Jews, or Muslims, this attitude may smack more of self-interest than of religion. Where are the moral codes, the commandments, the sacred texts? Where is the congregation of fellow believers with whom the faithful can share their sorrows and joys? How is it possible to draw from multiple religious traditions without violating at least some basic principles?

One way to understand the diversity of religion in Japan is to imagine religious life as a marketplace in which consumers decide which shops to patronize on the basis of cost and product availability. Variables of time, place, and occasion also enter into consumers' calculations: thus a religious "product" appropriate for the end of summer—for example, the ritual prescribed to protect the ripening rice crop from insects, typhoons, or fire—is not the same ritual required to protect one's business from financial trouble or one's soul from the flames of hell. Just as consumers go to different stores, depending on the kinds of goods they need to buy, so Japan's religious consumers know which traditions offer the appropriate assistance for the situation at hand.

Once the right religious "product" or service has been determined, a reciprocal relationship is created that entails certain obligations and expectations. In exchange for tangible assistance from a *kami*, bodhisattva, or buddha, one must show one's gratitude, not only by performing formal rituals but by treating that spiritual agent with special respect. Japanese literature is full of stories in which an ungrateful or arrogant person who has offended a deity ends up chastened and contrite.

Religious and Spiritual Agents

One of the most fundamental themes of Japanese culture and civilization has been the idea that there is a kind of life-energy that circulates throughout the phenomenal world, and that humans can align themselves with it through worship of the *kami*. Capable of entering any object to exercise their

Tendai and Shingon Buddhists perform a purification and blessing ritual that has its roots in ancient India. Participants in the "consecrated fire" ritual (*homa* in Sanskrit, *gomadaki* in Japanese) inscribe wooden slats with their names and a prayer or petition; their requests are then transported into the spirit realm via the fire and the chanting of the priests (John K. Nelson).

Document

The Gomadaki Ritual

The gomadaki *ritual (see photo, p. 551) combines external, physical action and internal meditation. As participants place their offerings in the fire, they are instructed to perform a series of visualizations.*

First, visualize one's own body: form Amitabha's meditation hand gesture (*mudra*), and visualize the syllable KIRIKU . . . above the heart-moon energy centre (*chakra*). It becomes a fully open red lotus blossom . . . that emits a great clear light in the midst of which is the "form body" . . . of Amitabha. Next, form Amitabha's meditation *mudra* and imagine these ritual offerings entering the mouth of the chief deity, going to the lotus blossom of his heart, becoming vast numbers of brightly shining *chakras*; then from each and every one of his pores these brightly shining *chakras* flow out through the entirety of empty space. Next, the various buddhas and bodhisattvas of the world, having received the offerings, cause these brightly shining *chakras* to enter one's own and the donor's heads. As a result, the evil consequences of greed, hatred and ignorance are completely erased from our bodies, the calamities and unhappiness caused by evil people and evil destinies are destroyed, vitality and lifespan increase, and peace and tranquility are attained (Payne 2006: 213–19).

power, *kami* can be found in flowing water, rain, mountains, clouds, fire, earth, and wind, as well as in certain animals that serve as their agents, messengers, and avatars. Their peaceful side helps humans prosper, while their destructive side can only be endured and appeased through rituals.

Mythology

We can see examples of these dynamics in the myths explaining the origins of Japan. The basic contours of the Japanese creation myth first took shape in the ***Kojiki***, a collection of regional stories compiled in 712 CE to legitimate the dominance of the Yamato clan by associating it with the divine origins of the land. Yet these stories were not widely known until the late nineteenth century, when they were circulated as part of a state campaign to create a cultural heritage for the new nation.

The positive and peaceful side of the primordial *kami* couple, Izanagi and his "wife" Izanami, can be seen in their creation of the islands that make up Japan and the primary elements of the natural world: seas, straits, winds, trees, mountains, plains. After a false start produces a "leech baby" that must be cast aside, Izanami dies giving birth to the deity of fire As her grieving partner consigns her to the land of the dead, he laments: "Alas, I have given my beloved spouse in exchange for a mere child!" (Philipi 1985: 57).

The destructive side of the *kami* is then revealed. First, the enraged Izanagi kills the fire deity and journeys to the netherworld to beseech his wife to return. She agrees to negotiate with the gods of the underworld on the condition that Izanagi does not look at her. But he cannot resist, and is horrified to see her corpse full of "squirming and roaring maggots" (ibid., 62). As he flees, she cries out, "He has shamed me!" and sends her "hags" to stop him. After several narrow escapes, Izanagi reaches the land of the living and uses a huge boulder to block the opening to the netherworld, but not before Izanami vows that she will cause 1,000 of his subjects to die each day; he counters that he will cause 1,500 to be born.

Map 11.1 Japan: Major Cities and Religious Sites

Source: Adapted from Young 1995: 211.

To purify himself after this ghastly encounter with death, Izanagi bathes in a river. As he does so, the female *kami* of the sun, **Amaterasu**, is born from his left eye; she will become the primary deity associated with the imperial family. Then the male moon *kami* springs from his right eye, and the last imperial *kami*, associated with the land, issues from his nose. Izanagi rejoices: "I have borne child after child, and finally . . . have obtained three noble children" (ibid., p. 71).

What this myth tells us is that the *kami* are responsible for both the world's blessings and its destructive powers. Whenever human well-being is threatened, the *kami* will be petitioned for help.

Foundations

Japanese history has no written records from the first four centuries of the Common Era. However, Chinese accounts from the fourth century describe "the land of Wa" (Japan) as ruled by a female queen who used "black magic and witchcraft" to control the *kami* and maintain power. The belief that early rulers (second to fifth century CE) embodied the *kami* legitimized their rule as a function of divine will.

When these rulers died, earthen mounds were built to house their tombs, in which were placed items that they would need in the netherworld. The Miyazaki region of southeast Kyushu is particularly rich in the number of earthen burial mounds. Unlike their counterparts in Egypt and China, however, the Japanese did not sacrifice human beings to accompany their masters into the afterlife. Instead, they relied on clay models to provide the servants, musicians, shamans, and soldiers that the ruler would need in the next world. These early rulers became guardian spirits of the clans, communities, and regions they once ruled.

These traditions changed dramatically after 538 CE, when the ruler of what is today western Korea wrote to the Japanese king praising Buddhism as a religion "superior to all others" (see Document box). Buddhism offered a whole new set of deities that could be petitioned to protect the ruler and maintain the status quo.

For its first 150 years in Japan, Buddhism was sustained mainly by clans with ties to Korea. But in time its promises of "salvation" attracted state patronage. Meanwhile, a steady stream of immigrants fleeing wars in southern China and the Korean peninsula were arriving with cultural knowledge—in astrology, philosophy, and divination, architecture, and courtly protocol—that contributed significantly to the development of the fledgling state. Among the concepts and practices brought from the mainland were several that we now associate with religious Daoism. Attention was paid to the movement of the stars, for example: the constellations painted on the ceilings of imperial tombs links the Japanese court to its counterparts in Korea and China, where the same constellations can be found. Stories about magical peaches ("Momotaro") and time-travel ("Urashima Taro") also recall Daoist ideas about immortality and alchemy. Even elements of the material culture associated with the imperial household—the mirror, sword, and jewel, as well as the colour purple—have roots in continental Daoism, which itself was influenced by the older traditions of shamanism (Senda 1988: 133–8).

Document

From the *Nihon Shoki* ("Chronicles of Japan")

Japan's second oldest book after the Kojiki *(712), the* Nihon Shoki *(720) combines origin myths with more factual accounts. The following extract purports to be from the Korean document recommending Buddhism to the Japanese king.*

This Dharma is superior to all others. It is difficult to grasp and difficult to attain. Neither the Duke of Zhou nor Confucius was able to comprehend it. It can give rise to immeasurable, limitless merit and fruits of action, leading to the attainment of supreme enlightenment. The treasure of this marvelous Dharma is such that it is as if one owned a wish-fulfilling gem that granted every desire. Every prayer is granted and nothing is wanting. Moreover, from distant India to the three kingdoms of Korea, all receive these teachings and there is none who does not revere and honour them (*Nihon Shoki* account in Bowring 2006: 15).

Japan's first Buddhist temple was constructed in 596 CE, with the assistance of Korean builders, and the first Buddhist rituals were conducted there by specialists (women as well as men) from the Korean kingdom of Baekje. Incredibly, temples established in those early years can still be seen in places like Osaka (Shitennoji) and Nara (Horyuji and Todaiji).

Todaiji

The founding of the Todaiji temple brings together many of the themes we've been discussing. Designed to house a monumental bronze statue of the Cosmic Buddha (Vairocana), the temple was planned by the emperor Shomu in the early 740s in response to a series of earthquakes and poor harvests. Before starting construction, however, he sent a high-ranking monk to the distant island of Kyushu to ask a powerful *kami* there for his approval. Not only did the *kami* approve: he demanded to be transported to the site so as to keep the local deities from interfering. His shrine still stands on a hillside overlooking the temple.

Aspects of this story remain relevant today. Temples and shrines still conduct rituals for the health of the emperor and the stability of the nation. And though Westerners tend to see the two dominant religious traditions in Japan as discrete entities, most Japanese do not distinguish between them.

Other Spiritual Agents

The concept of the bodhisattva was discussed at some length in Chapter 8. In Mahayana Buddhist thought, a bodhisattva is an enlightened being who delays entry into nirvana in order to help all living beings who have not yet been released from worldly suffering.

The bodhisattva with the greatest reputation for intervening in human affairs is undoubtedly Kannon, who arrived in Japan from China under the name Guanyin. Countless "miracle" tales testify to Kannon's commitment to alleviating the suffering she perceives (*kan*) and hears (*on*). The economic golden years of the 1980s saw a revival of interest in Kannon: her cult was promoted at pilgrimage sites and in temples, and giant statues of her, some reaching 108 metres (354 feet), were erected in various places; 108 is the number of the human frailties that Kannon is said to help overcome (Reader 1991: 191, 157, 36).[1] While all the traditional attributes of Kannon are still present, her all-embracing motherly qualities in particular have attracted a new generation of devotees.

Another bodhisattva who has provided comfort to millions of Japanese is Jizo (Ksitigarbha in Sanskrit) or (more respectfully and affectionately) Ojizo-sama. Known for his ability to free tormented souls from hell, he also protects children and travellers, and since the 1970s he has taken on the job of conducting the souls of deceased children and aborted fetuses to salvation. Anyone visiting a temple in Japan today is likely to see rows of Jizo statues, many with little berets on their shaved heads (he is a monk, after all), and offerings of coins or pebbles at their feet. A woman who has aborted a pregnancy or suffered a miscarriage may pay a monthly fee for a temple to care for the fetus's soul, performing periodic rituals and offerings to appease its unhappy and potentially dangerous spirit.

Unsettled Spirits

How can the spirit of an unborn child be dangerous? The roots of this tradition lie in a combination of native Japanese, Korean, and Chinese folk beliefs with Daoist dynamics and Buddhist-inspired demonology. In ancient times, the spirits of people who had lost their lives to powers beyond their

The Jizo statues at this temple in Osaka were purchased by women who had aborted their fetuses and entrusted the care of their spirits to the temple. The faded red cloths symbolize a child's bib (John K. Nelson).

control were expected to become angry and vengeful, and rituals of pacification were required to calm them. One of Japan's most respected scholars of death and dying, Gorai Shigeru, believes that all Japanese funeral and memorial rites are rooted in the idea that the spirits of the dead must be placated before they can become benevolent ancestral influences (Gorai 1994: 105).

At the level of the state, to neglect or ignore the vengeance-seeking spirits of assassinated rivals or powerful enemies killed in battle was to invite retribution in the form of earthquakes, droughts, or storms, sickness or infertility. Thus spirit appeasement was high on the list of state-sponsored ritual activities. When Buddhism arrived in the early sixth century, it took up its share of that responsibility, which until then had been the exclusive domain of shamans.

Pivotal Developments in Japanese Religious History

During the formative Nara period (710–794), the government set up a ministry to manage the shrines of the *kami*. At the same time, a council of senior Buddhist monks formed the Sangha Office to oversee monastic conduct and training. The same basic administrative structure would remain in place for nearly 350 years, reasserting itself whenever a strong centralized government took charge. Knowing all too well from Chinese history how religious organizations and ideas could undermine the state, the early Japanese rulers carefully monitored all religious appointments and construction projects.

Tendai and Shingon

For three centuries Buddhism remained the preserve of the Nara elite, who commissioned temples dedicated to their ancestors, consigned their second or third sons to Buddhist monasteries, and sponsored Buddhist art as a way to earn merit. In 804, however, two monks named Saicho and Kukai travelled to China for further study, and there they encountered some important new perspectives, one of which emphasized the written word. The *Lotus Sutra*, which had originated in north India and been translated into Chinese, taught that there is only one vehicle to salvation—the body we live in, here and now—and that we all have the potential to become buddhas ourselves. The monks who had mastered the teachings of the *Lotus Sutra* saw themselves as instrumental to the welfare of the state.

When Saicho and Kukai returned to Japan, they took with them volumes of teachings and commentaries, paintings, mandalas, and ritual implements. It might sound like little more than a wholesale borrowing of religious "software" from another culture, but the traditions they founded helped to domesticate Buddhist teachings and rituals in very pragmatic ways.

For one thing, both Saicho's Tendai and Kukai's Shingon taught a kind of short-cut approach that put the possibility of enlightenment and salvation within the reach of common people (not just monks and nuns) in their own lifetime. Through incantation, ritual gestures, meditation, visualization, and austerities, individuals could connect with and obtain benefits from deities in other spheres of existence. Whereas earlier Buddhist schools considered the human body problematic because of its fragility, desires, and impermanence, the new doctrines, which we now identify as "tantric" or "esoteric," attributed a spiritual value to it: much as geothermal steam and seismic activity can be transformed into electricity, bodily desires could be harnessed through ritual and directed towards the quest for salvation and enlightenment.

A young *bugaku* dancer performs on the grounds of Osaka's Shitennoji temple. Established in 593 CE, the temple has been in continuous operation ever since (John K. Nelson).

The fact that both sects established their headquarters on sacred mountains near Kyoto—Tendai on Mount Hiei and Shingon on Mount Koya—suggests that they continued to respect the local *kami*. The Japanese phrase ***honji suijaku*** (which comes from the *Lotus Sutra* and means "manifestation from the original state") helps to explain the implications of the relationship between the two traditions. *Honji*, meaning "original ground," refers to the fundamental reality and power of a particular buddha or bodhisattva, while *suijaku* refers to the "trace" or particular form in which that entity chooses to manifest him- or herself in Japan. Thus the *kami* of a particular mountain or powerful clan came to be seen as the "provisional manifestation" (*gongen*) of a particular buddha or bodhisattva. For many centuries, the *honji suijaku* principle made Buddhist and Shinto deities interdependent, although the Buddhist deities were usually superior.

Focus

Taboo Terms at Shinto Shrines

In an effort to resist total assimilation into the new tradition, the priests and priestesses of major shrines developed a kind of code for referring to Buddhism without adopting its vocabulary. Thus Shakyamuni Buddha became the "Central One," a temple a "tiled roof," and sutras "dyed paper." Buddhist monks, with their shaved heads, were called "long hairs," death became "getting well," and illness was "slumber" (Felicia Bock, cited in Bowring 2005: 191).[2] Using these terms, the participants in a *kami* ritual could acknowledge the importance of Buddhist concepts while keeping a certain distance from them.

From the ninth century onward, Buddhism increasingly overshadowed the traditional ritual practices centred on *kami*. The *honji suijaku* principle was applied to local shrines as a way both to incorporate their deities and to allow them to achieve salvation along more obviously Buddhist lines. A number of rituals could be performed by officiants of either tradition. For example, the early eleventh-century noblewoman who served for nearly four decades as the chief spiritual medium at the Kamo Shrine in Kyoto was a devout Pure Land Buddhist.

New Emphases in Japanese Religious Practice

New Sects in the Kamakura and Muromachi Periods

Around the world, people deeply affected by changing political, economic, and cultural conditions have often been open to innovations in religious belief or practice that promise to help them cope with challenging new circumstances. In Japan, three new types of Buddhist practice emerged during the Kamakura period (1185–1333): Pure Land, Nichiren, and Zen (the three principal forms of Buddhism still practised in Japan today). At the same time, innovations in *kami* worship laid the foundations for what would eventually be known as "Shinto."

The relative stability of the Heian period ended in 1185, when the courtly families in power since the early days of Japanese civilization were overthrown. Once the imperial capital of Kyoto was under the control of the new regime, which drew its power from the warrior elite that we call ***samurai***, the centre of political power shifted north to Kamakura, near what is today Tokyo.

For the elites of the Kyoto region, the move was a disaster. Yet they were predisposed to expect conflict, corruption, and vice because a popular Buddhist teaching had predicted that the year 1052 would mark the beginning of the degenerate age known as ***mappo***, during which the Buddhist dharma would decline. Social chaos and bloody political disorder were accompanied by earthquakes, typhoons, pestilence, and famine. Living at a time before the science behind such disasters was understood, people believed they were trapped in a kind of hell on Earth.

Pure Land Salvation

It is no wonder, then, that a new interpretation of Buddhism promising salvation gained wide acceptance. For centuries, Buddhism had been almost exclusively the faith of the elite, but it began to

Document

From Genshin's "Essentials of Salvation" (985 CE)

The first division, the corrupt land that one must shun [in order to reach the Pure Land] comprises the three realms in which there is no peace. . . . The first of these, hell, is . . . divided into eight parts: the hell of repeated misery, the hell of black chains, the hell of mass suffering, the hell of wailing, the hell of great wailing, the hell of searing heat, the hell of great searing heat, the hell of incessant suffering.

The rewards of the Pure Land are of endless merit. . . . First is the pleasure of being welcomed by many saints. Second is the pleasure of the first opening of the lotus. Third is the pleasure of obtaining in one's own body the ubiquitous supernatural powers of a Buddha. Fourth is the pleasure of the realm of the five wonders. Fifth is the pleasure of everlasting enjoyment. Sixth is the pleasure of influencing others and introducing them to Buddhism. Seventh is the pleasure of assembling with the holy family. Eighth is the pleasure of beholding the Buddha and hearing the Law. Ninth is the pleasure of serving the Buddha according to the dictates of one's own heart. Tenth is the pleasure of progressing in the way of Buddhahood (Yampolsky, trans., 2008: 217–22).

attract the common people after Genshin (942–1017) organized Pure Land beliefs into a coherent system. His *Essentials of Salvation* (completed in 985) describes in graphic detail the six realms of existence (hell, hungry ghosts, demonic beings, animals, human beings, and heavenly beings) through which all must pass, in multiple incarnations, before reaching the perfection of the Pure Land.

For the first time in Japan, Buddhist monks began to concern themselves with the salvation of ordinary people, although it would take another two centuries before a new institutional form gave practical expression to that concern. It was a Tendai monk, frustrated by his sect's preoccupation with politics, who developed Pure Land Buddhism as we know it today. Honen (1133–1212) believed that, in an age of *mappo*, it was impossible to attain salvation by the traditional means (following the precepts, chanting, meditating). The only hope lay in the saving grace of Amida, who did not discriminate according to social rank, past karma, or present activity: sincere faith and repeated recitation of the ***nembutsu***, "*Namu Amida Butsu*," alone were enough. In this way Honen opened the door to the notion of universal salvation.

This concept might sound pleasingly democratic today, but at the time it was seen as radical because it meant there was no fundamental difference between a layperson and a learned monk. Honen was banished from the Kyoto region in 1207, along with his disciple Shinran (1173–1262), who had just caused a scandal by marrying—a "degenerate" practice that was fairly common among monks (as was keeping a concubine) but had never been made public. Shinran reasoned that if the power of Amida Buddha was great enough to save even those of the lowest social status, then marriage would not be an obstacle to salvation.

Honen's exile lasted only four years, but Shinran was banished for seven, during which he is said to have preached among farmers and fishermen, refining his "True Pure Land" doctrine to the point of maintaining that a *single* sincere repetition of the *nembutsu* would secure salvation. Shinran believed humans were incapable of the disciplined "self-power" (***jiriki***) necessary for attaining salvation: therefore we must rely on "other-power" (***tariki***) for deliverance from suffering.

In the tumult of the Kamakura period (and beyond), Pure Land spread via small groups called *ko*, where emphasis was on *nembutsu* practice. Around 1450, the sect's eighth hereditary leader, Rennyo, began to systematize the teachings and organize the scattered Pure Land communities to create a kind of militant security force dedicated to protecting the Honganji temple in what is today Osaka.

They were not the first Buddhists to take aggressive action: as early as 1039, Tendai "monk warriors" had attacked rival sects and temples, and even challenged the legitimacy of the imperial court. Four centuries later, however, the True Pure Land insurrection was led not by monks but by common people and masterless samurai. With nothing to lose and salvation guaranteed through their faith, they held their own against experienced armies. By 1500 they controlled several provinces, although they were finally defeated and brought partially under control by the warlord Oda Nobunaga (1534–82).

Rinzai Zen and Kamakura Culture

The word "Zen" is the Japanese version of the Chinese *chan*, which in turn translates the Sanskrit term for meditation, *dhyana*. Whereas the Pure Land traditions prescribed recitation of the name of Amida Buddha, the Chan/Zen tradition emphasized seated meditation (***zazen***) as the path to enlightenment and, eventually, salvation.

Zen became established in much the same way as Pure Land, but with an important difference: it was imported directly from China, and its development was led by Chinese masters who settled in Japan in the thirteenth century. Although the seeds of Zen meditation can be found in Tendai as early as the ninth century (when the practice of "constantly sitting" was introduced), it was not until the later twelfth century that the tradition took root in Japan.

In 1168 a Tendai monk named Eisai (1141–1215) travelled to China expecting to find the traditions in which Tendai and Shingon had originated, only to discover that they had been superseded by Chan Buddhism. Chan had survived a nationwide campaign of persecution, launched in 845, that had targeted other Buddhist traditions because of their lavish wealth, landholdings, political meddling, and "parasitic" monks and nuns who did nothing for society. By contrast, Chan monks worked with their hands and displayed none of the elaborate trappings that characterized other traditions.

Eisai studied Chan for the next 20 years while continuing to serve as a Tendai monk. Then he made a second trip to China (1187–91), during which he studied with a Linji (Rinzai in Japanese) Chan master who certified his enlightenment. In addition to Chan, Eisai imported other Buddhist and Confucian teachings to Japan—as well as a hot drink that helped to keep sleepy monks awake during meditation. His work "Drink Tea and Prolong Life" is credited with promoting tea in Japan; and the tea ceremony (developed a century later) was deeply influenced by Zen aesthetics and symbolism.

In an effort to attract the patronage of the military rulers in Kamakura, Eisai wrote a treatise, "The Propagation of Zen for the Protection of the Country," that led to his temporary exile from all Tendai temples in the Kyoto region. After a short time in Kamakura, where he secured patrons and established a small temple, he returned to Kyoto and in 1202 built Japan's first Zen temple, Kenninji. Its many rebuildings have preserved a number of cultural treasures as well as beautiful examples of classic Zen landscape gardens and architecture.

It's worth asking why a samurai warrior would be attracted to an austere Chinese tradition focused on the achievement of "sudden enlightenment" through the practice of *zazen* and the mental exercise of the koan. One reason was that those practices were conducive to a particularly rich and refined type of artistic expression. Zen-inspired poetry, stories, paintings, and sculpture were valued for their subtle and elegant evocation of concepts such as emptiness, the cycle of rebirth (*samsara*), impermanence, and enlightenment (*satori* in Japanese). At the same time, in a society that accorded the highest status to the warrior, Zen-style discipline was valued as a way of training oneself to endure hardship, pain, and even the finality of death.

The Rinzai tradition was assisted in its institutional development by its ongoing relationship with the ruling samurai, but another factor in its success was the "Five Mountain" monastery system, which made leading Rinzai temples into administrative outposts that helped to monitor local conditions and implement new laws on behalf of the military rulers. Although the temples managed their own affairs without interference, they were expected to further the state's agenda in return for its patronage.

The Kenninji temple in Kyoto marked its 800th anniversary by commissioning this powerful painting by Koizumi Junkasu for its ceiling (John K. Nelson).

Soto Zen: The Gradual Path

The other major Zen school, Soto, promotes "gradual enlightenment" through the practice of "just sitting" without the mental stimulation of the koan. According to the standard accounts (which may or may not be true), the Tendai monk Dogen (1200–53) was troubled by a persistent question: if humans are born with an innate Buddha-nature, as Tendai taught, why should they need to make any effort to achieve enlightenment? After studying at Kenninji with Eisai's successor, in 1223 Dogen travelled with an official mission to China, where encounters with the Caodong tradition and a monastery cook (see Focus box) led to his own spiritual awakening.

On his return to Japan in 1227, Dogen recognized that his Soto Zen could not compete with either Tendai or the increasingly influential Rinzai Zen school. Leaving Kyoto for the countryside, he found rural elites to be more receptive than urban samurai to his new way to liberation. The Eiheiji monastery, which he founded in 1244 near present-day Fukui city, is still the headquarters of the Soto school, and it continues to train young monks in *zazen* coupled with rigorous study and physical labour.

The popularity of Soto Zen grew rapidly after the early fifteenth century, when its monks began performing funerals for laypeople. At a time when only members of the clergy were entitled to funeral services, Soto monks would posthumously ordain deceased laypeople as monks or nuns and thereby assist them on the way to salvation (Bodiford 1992). This brilliant innovation helped to gain Soto a wide following.

Nichiren

The last new Buddhist sect of the Kamakura period was founded by a charismatic monk who drew on the Tendai practice of reciting mantras but embraced the teachings of the *Lotus Sutra* as the path to

Focus

Dogen and the Cook

As a young monk travelling in China, Dogen met an elderly monk who was working as a *tenzo* (head cook). Surprised, Dogen asked him, "Reverend sir, why don't you do *zazen* or read the ancient texts? What is the use of working so hard as a cook?" The *tenzo* laughed and replied, "My foreign friend, it seems you don't really understand Zen practice or the words of the ancients."

Ashamed and surprised, Dogen asked, "What is practice? What are words?" The *tenzo* said, "One, two, three, four, five." Dogen asked again, "What is practice?" and the *tenzo* replied, "Everywhere, nothing is hidden" (adapted from Dogen 1996).

salvation for both the nation and the individual. Believing that it provided an all-encompassing guide to both secular and spiritual affairs, Nichiren (1222–82) instructed his followers to study its teachings and chant the mantra "*namu myoho renge kyo*" ("Hail the marvellous teaching of the *Lotus Sutra*!"). To Nichiren, all other Buddhist teachings were merely provisional, no longer relevant in the age of *mappo*.

Expelled from his monastery in Kyoto, he travelled to Kamakura, where he preached on street corners the radical message that "the *nembutsu* is hell, Zen is a devil, and Shingon is the nation's ruin." He was exiled twice for subversive teaching and claimed to have avoided execution only because of a divine intervention that shattered the executioner's sword as it was about to fall on his neck. His 1260 work "On Establishing the True Dharma to Bring Peace to the Nation" established him as a pioneer in the politicization of religion. If the nation suffered invasions, plagues, and social disorder, he argued, it was because the ruler had not adopted the *Lotus Sutra* as his guide to sound governance.

When the Mongol dynasty actually invaded Japan in 1274, Nichiren's warnings were seen as a kind of prophecy, and he was pardoned. Retiring to Mount Minobu (not far from Mount Fuji), he established a temple there that became a training facility for the next generation. In time, disciples such as Niko, Nissho, and Nichiko established their own sects, and centuries of factionalism followed. Several of Japan's most prominent "new religions"—Soka Gakkai, Rissho Koseikai, Nichiren Shoshu—trace their roots to one or another of these denominations.

Confucianism and the Beginnings of Shinto

Another development that influenced the modern Japanese state was the introduction of Confucianism. Although Confucian ideas (dating from the fifth century BCE) had been present at the very beginning of Japanese civilization in the sixth century CE, they had not developed into a distinct body of knowledge or ritual practices. During the political and social disruptions of the Kamakura and Muromachi periods, however, Japan's ruling classes took a new interest in ideas that promoted order in society.

Confucianism laid out the "Way" that every member of society should follow, as determined by his or her position in that society. Awareness of the responsibilities in each relationship would promote reciprocity between superiors and subordinates, which in turn would foster a stable and harmonious society. Zen monks found these teachings to resonate with their own traditions, and so recommended them to rulers for nearly four centuries.

The Emergence of "Shinto"

And what of the older religion based on the ritual veneration of *kami*? Recent scholarship has demonstrated that it was only in the medieval period that "Shinto" began to take form as a distinct and self-conscious entity. Since the seventh century, the Grand Shrines at Ise (pronounced *ee-say*), dedicated to the sun goddess Amaterasu, had been the preserve of the imperial family. With the triumph of the samurai, however, the shrines lost their main source of financial support, and by the early 1400s they were in obvious decline. Therefore the priests opened up Ise to visits from samurai and lower-ranking officials and developed new rituals for them. Purification was of primary importance, but in the fifteenth century, in recognition of the institutional power of Tendai and Shingon and the *honji suijaku* doctrine, Ise ritual practices were coupled with Buddhist notions of enlightenment so that, instead of competing, the two traditions complemented one another. At one time there were more than 300 Buddhist temples on the Ise grounds.

With its emphasis on rituals rather than texts, the "way of the *kami*" lacked the kind of conceptual structure that was so central to Buddhism. Still, the Ise priests reversed the *honji suijaku* principle and argued that, although the indigenous *kami* could have Buddhist counterparts, they were not subordinate to them. With new doctrines in place, pilgrimage at an all-time high, and

The Itsukushima shrine complex on the island of Miyajima is about 90 minutes by train and ferry from Hiroshima (John K. Nelson).

increasing interest in the power of Ise's deities to provide benefits even for common people, the *kami* tradition assumed a new importance in the life of the nation. An organized system began to emerge in 1542, when the central government granted the powerful Yoshida clan the authority to appoint and demote shrine priests outside Ise.

Continuities of Religious Practice

The variety of benefits that worshippers may seek is almost endless: from health and prosperity to fertility and good weather to enlightened governance and salvation in the afterlife. Equally diverse are the religious practices believed to produce these benefits. Here are just a few examples:

- Individuals, families, businesses, or entire communities can contract religious specialists to conduct rituals at a temple or shrine. Petitioners typically address their requests to a particular spiritual agent (buddha, bodhisattva, or *kami*) believed capable of exerting a beneficial influence on the situation in question. However, rituals may also be conducted at home, and until very recently, many families had both a Buddhist altar (where ancestral spirits were venerated alongside Buddhist deities) and a Shinto altar (honouring the local and regional *kami* thought to protect the family). The religious observances conducted at such altars have usually been the responsibility of the family's female members.
- By purchasing amulets or talismans, individuals can establish an informal relationship with the deity of a particular temple or shrine. Since the spiritual energy invested in these objects fades over time, purchasers must return regularly for replacements.
- Undertaking a pilgrimage is another way of accessing benefits in this world and beyond. Even today, the 88 sacred temples of the island of Shikoku are visited by more than 100,000 pilgrims a year. Some walk the entire route of 1,400 km (870 miles) at once, but most take buses or private transportation and complete the route in segments, as time permits. Smaller, less demanding pilgrimage routes exist all over Japan.
- Monetary donations and the performance of good deeds for a temple/shrine or its priests are thought to generate merit beneficial to one's spiritual condition.
- Grand festivals (*matsuri*) involving the entire community are believed to benefit even those who do not take part in them. Although many Buddhist temples have also adopted this practice, Shinto shrines in particular regularly parade their central object of worship through the community in a portable shrine. In large communities, the annual *matsuri* commands a staggering degree of financial, personal, and administrative commitment. Furukawa's "rousing drum" festival (p. 546) involves an entire city of 74,000, while Osaka's Tenjin Matsuri attracts crowds of nearly 2 million.

Another important practice is the veneration of spirits. East Asian religious traditions maintain that the spirits of the dead continue to play an active part in the world. Whoever a deceased person might have been in life—a religious leader, a soldier killed in war, a sweet-tempered grandmother—his or her spirit may become angry or vengeful in death; to prevent this, additional rituals must be performed long after the funeral. Only if the spirits are satisfied with the respect they receive will they become beneficial allies.

One of Japan's great holidays is the Obon festival, held in mid-August in most places, when the spirits of the dead are said to return to this world to receive ritual offerings of food and drink made by their loved ones. In addition, individuals and families regularly memorialize departed family members at household altars (*butsudan*).

The household altar is just one example of the material impact that religious traditions have had on Japanese culture. From paintings and sculpture, architecture and landscape design, to ritual attire and habits of personal hygiene derived from purification rituals, the list of cultural influences is almost endless. Let's consider just a few of the things that a visitor to Japan would likely encounter in the course of a week.

Even before leaving the airport, a visitor might see an example of *ikebana*, the Japanese art of flower arranging. Developed in Buddhist temples, where the deceptively simple arrangements were used in memorial services, the practice eventually filtered through all social classes. Today there are many different styles of *ikebana*, but most still share a few basic features, including organic materials (stems and leaves are at least as important as flowers), sensitivity to the season, balanced composition, and poetic or religious symbolism (a classic three-part arrangement, for instance, is likely to symbolize heaven, earth, and humanity).

A similar combination of natural materials, restrained composition, and religious symbolism is found in the Japanese garden. The art of garden design also originated at temples, where a few artfully placed rocks in a bed of gravel might symbolize islands in the sea of eternity. Gardens

The *kami* at Kanda Shinto Shrine are known for helping in business ventures and the search for a spouse. Aspiring artists create self-portraits on wooden plaques as a way to personalize their petitions to the deities—and to advertise their talents (© Alex Hunter / Alamy).

were later constructed at imperial palaces and on the estates of the wealthy, and today even the most humble residence will often have a garden that evokes ancient cultural values. The temple, with its sweeping roof lines, overhanging eaves, and verandas, has also been a major influence on architecture. Inside the house, one room would typically be modelled on the abbot's quarters in a temple, with a hanging scroll painting in an alcove, an *ikebana* arrangement, and open space conveying a sense of space in harmony with form. Even ultramodern condominiums today often include alcoves.

The influence of religious traditions can also be seen in literature and popular culture. The minimalism of the *haiku*, for example, is said to derive from Zen's emphasis on penetrating to the essence of reality. In its 17 syllables, the *haiku* typically gives us both sharply defined detail and a connection to a wider universe, as in this example by Matsuo Basho (1644–94):

> The sea darkens;
> the plaintive calls of the wild ducks
> are faintly white.

Another art form that uses minimalism to evoke reflection on the nature of reality is Noh theatre. The slow, mesmerizing cadences—reminiscent of Buddhist chanting—of the masked actors usually convey a lesson of some kind, whether about karma, the consequences of desire, or the spiritual power of monks. Even *anime* and *manga* stories refer to religious practices, spiritual powers gained through ascetic training (*shugyo*), and divinities who use their powers for both good and evil ends. The early comics of Osamu Tezuka (1928–89) and the feature films of the animator Miyazaki Hayao (b. 1941; *Totoro, Princess Mononoke, Spirited Away*) are full of allusions to Japan's spiritual history.

Global and Domestic Trends

We often talk about "globalization" as a recent phenomenon, but the worldwide exchange of people, ideas, and goods actually began in the fifteenth century, when European powers began navigating the globe in search of new territory for their kings and the Christian church. The first Europeans to reach Japan were some shipwrecked Portuguese sailors who arrived there in 1543, but in 1549 they were followed by Jesuit missionaries, led by Francis Xavier.

Christianity's Rise and Fall

In the fifteenth century Japan was embroiled in ongoing internal conflict; had this not been the case, it is doubtful that the Jesuits would have been permitted to enter at all. Yet a unique convergence of social and political factors enabled them to broker agreements with a number of local warlords. It was also a stroke of luck that they arrived during the rise to power of Japan's first military unifier, Oda Nobunaga, who hoped that Christianity would weaken Buddhism in Japan.

In 1571 Nobunaga attacked Mount Hiei, killing more than 3,000 Tendai monks and attendants. The lesson was not lost on the Pure Land militants: only one more major battle was required to bring them under control. Although Nobunaga died in 1582, his chief aide quickly established himself as a visionary leader and patron of religion. Toyotomi Hideyoshi (1537–98) continued the unification effort that Nobunaga had begun, and financed the construction of many temples and

Document

"Tidings from the West"

In 1709, a scholar named Arai Hakuseki interviewed Giovanni Battista Sidotti (1668–1714), a Jesuit missionary who had entered Japan illegally and been imprisoned to await execution. Respecting Sidotti's learning, Arai recorded the interviews, with his comments, in Seiyō kibun *("Tidings from the West"), and sought to persuade the authorities that such foreigners should be deported rather than put to death.*

Sidotti: As a rule, in each section of the world, there is a doctrine that is held with esteem. There are only three different types of this doctrine. One of these is called Christian. The second type is called heathen or gentile. The third type is called Mohammedan.

Hakuseki: This is probably what is referred to in China as Huihuijia [Islam].

Sidotti: In the region known as Europe everyone is a Christian. However, each region has a different sect of Christianity. I belong to the Catholic sect. When that Christianity first came about, it was the original law and from it came various heresies.

Hakuseki: This is probably a reference to that teaching's various heterodoxies [*itan*].

Sidotti: Luther, Arius, Calvin, and Manichaeus, these are all heresies. In Holland they are followers of the heresy of Luther.

Hakuseki: Luther is a person's name. In Portuguese he is called Lutero. Originally, he was a Christian, but he established his own lineage. From what I understand . . . it is like how from the founder of the Zen School sprung up various esoteric lineages . . .

(adapted from Josephson 2012: 263–4).

shrines. For a time, he even tolerated Christianity, which by 1590 may have acquired as many as 100,000 converts, though some conversions were forced by local warlords seeking to facilitate trade with Europeans. However, the situation changed dramatically in 1596, when the cargo of a Spanish ship was seized and its captain threatened military reprisals via an armada stationed in the Philippines. The Japanese authorities responded by expelling a number of European missionaries and putting some Japanese converts to death.

The third of Japan's unifiers, Tokugawa Ieyasu (1548–1616), at first tolerated the Catholic presence, largely because it facilitated trade, but in time he came to see the priests as disruptive of the social order he was trying to build. His successors cracked down hard in the 1620s, requiring all adults to register at the local Buddhist temple; those who resisted or refused to step on an image of Jesus or Mary were threatened with torture if they did not recant their Christian faith.

In 1637 an estimated 25,000 oppressed peasants and rogue samurai mounted an armed insurrection from Shimabara on the island of Kyushu. Using Christian symbols on their flags, these rag-tag rebels held off the government's forces for nearly seven months until they ran out of food and gunpowder. With the defeat of the Shimabara rebels, the Tokugawa regime closed the door on both Christianity and Europe. From 1641 to 1853, the only port open to the outside world was Dejima, a small artificial island near Nagasaki, and it was rigidly controlled. Christianity went into hiding in remote valleys and on far-flung islands. Believers adopted Buddhist practices but continued reciting mass and worshipping images of the Virgin Mary disguised as Kannon.

Unification and Stability

As part of its effort to impose stability, the Tokugawa regime introduced laws designed to create four distinct classes: samurai, farmers, artisans, and merchants. This structure (like the temple registration law) was inspired by the Confucian doctrines introduced to Japan by Chinese Zen monks some four centuries earlier. In addition, a number of newer Confucian texts were reinterpreted to promote the stratification and regulation of society. Each social class was given specific guidelines regarding occupation, travel, and civic duties, and both Buddhist and Shinto institutions were required to adopt a hierarchical organizational model. The Tokugawa **shoguns** had Zen monks as some of their closest advisers in the early years, but as the regime tightened its control over the nation, it also sought advice from scholars influenced by Confucian texts and subsequent commentary.

The overall mood of society was changing as well. During the medieval period, Buddhism had flourished because its doctrines of salvation in the next life offered hope to people whose prospects in this life were bleak. Now, with growing economic prosperity in the cities and order imposed by a police state, neo-Confucian scholars began to criticize Buddhism.

We have already seen how Buddhism benefited from state patronage but also suffered because of its involvement in political affairs. Temple-building increased dramatically with the imposition of the temple registration requirement; Soto Zen temples alone multiplied from several thousand to 17,500 in the early Tokugawa period. But the growing emphasis on political rather than spiritual matters was reflected in a breakdown of morality among many monks (Williams 2005). One seventeenth-century Confucian scholar commented that "the freedom with which they [Buddhist monks] eat meat and engage in romantic affairs surpasses that of even secular men" (Jansen 2000: 217). Although Buddhism remained central to ritual life, it was losing its vitality as a force in society. It is not surprising, therefore, that alternative perspectives began to emerge.

Religion Meets Modernity

Scholars in particular were eager for new philosophies that would explain the meaning of life and the individual's purpose in society. Some embraced Confucian principles; among them was Yamaga Soko (1622–85), who codified samurai ethics and combined them with Confucian values to create the "way of the warrior" known as ***bushido***.

In the next century, however, the ***Kokugaku*** ("Native Learning") movement rejected Confucianism as well as Buddhism in favour of "true" Japanese spiritual traditions. Scholars like Motoori Norinaga (1730–1801) tried to use ancient texts such as the *Kojiki* (the source of the foundation myth of Izanagi and Izanami) to discover the will of the *kami* regarding the roles of a ruler and his subjects. The logical implication was that the solution to Japan's political problems and the threats it faced from abroad lay in direct imperial rule—although to voice this opinion publicly would surely have been considered treason.

Meanwhile, at the popular level, "new religions" began to appear. In 1838, for example, Nakayama Miki, the wife of a wealthy farmer, said that "God the Parent" had chosen her to transmit divine truths about how to live happily and honourably. She was imprisoned more than once, but as the Tokugawa regime was ending she succeeded in establishing the new religion known as Tenrikyo.

Another new religion, Kurozumikyo, traced its origins to a revelation received by a Shinto priest who claimed to have experienced "divine union" with Amaterasu. And Konko-kyo (1859) was based on a privileged communication between a farmer and a *kami* he discovered to be the saviour of mankind.

In 1825, the scholar and samurai Aizawa Seishisai (1781–1863) had advocated unification of religion and the state, as in the European colonial powers that were encroaching on Japan's sovereignty. He urged the adoption of Shinto as the national faith and the sun deity Amaterasu as the primary *kami*. Although these ideas were controversial at the time, they would become central to the leaders of samurai clans in the far west and south.

In 1868, following a brief civil war, those clans overthrew the Tokugawa regime. Well aware of how far behind Japan had fallen during its period of isolation, and fearing colonization by the West, the new government embarked on an unprecedented program of industrialization, militarization, and nation-building. This agenda, legitimized by a new emphasis on the emperor's status as a direct descendant of the *kami* (exactly as Aizawa had recommended four decades earlier), would dramatically alter Japan and the Asian region in both positive and negative ways.

Recent Developments

Nationalism and Shinto

How does a government create a nation of citizens where only feudal loyalties existed before? This was the challenge that faced the Meiji government (1868–1911). The term *meiji* means "enlightened rule," and its adoption signified a shift away from clan rule to a parliamentary system. In its effort to emulate those Western nations where religion served to legitimate policy, the Meiji government promoted a kind of national cult based on the emperor and his associations with various *kami*.

The Meiji state subjected Buddhism to a brief but dramatic period of persecution, in part because it had served the Tokugawa feudal regime so well. Institutions that had been fully syncretic, combining worship of buddhas and *kami*, were now divided. Their ritual specialists were either forced into lay life or re-educated as government-certified Shinto priests. Even more extreme was the brief period (1868–72) when many Buddhist temples, icons, and artifacts were destroyed by over-zealous officials. The remains of Buddhist statues decapitated during this period can still be seen at temples all over Japan.

Document

The Great Way

The "father" of modern Shinto studies was Tanaka Yoshito (1872–1946). This excerpt comes from his 1936 book Shinto Gairon.

The Japanese people, being endowed with a true Japanese spirit, sincerely hold an absolute faith in shrines. . . . Buddhism and Christianity are merely religions and nothing more; but Shinto and shrines are politics, as well as morality, as well as a great religion. A combination of these three aspects, that is the Way of the Gods. It is the Great Way of the subjects of Japan (Breen and Teeuwen 2000: 328).

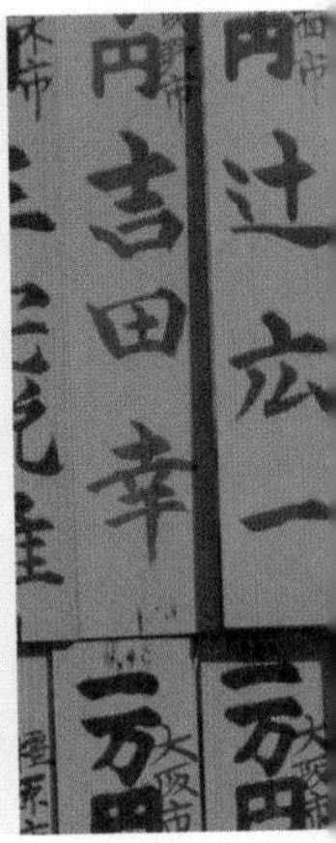

Shinto was designated the official religion, although adherence to it was described as a matter of "civic duty" rather than religious conviction. Not everyone supported these policies, of course, but it became increasingly difficult to resist the state's agenda. A series of wars with China (1894–95), Russia (1904–5), and Korea (1910)—which cost some 80,000 lives while gaining Japan overseas resources that it would use to expand its manufacturing and military base—inspired a general patriotic fervour that drowned out all but the most courageous voices of opposition.

It was during this period that the government sponsored the establishment of a shrine to the soldiers who had died for the nation. Although Shinto shrines had traditionally avoided association with the impurity of death, the Yasukuni Shrine in Tokyo combined Shinto-style rituals with Buddhist ancestor worship and shamanic traditions of spirit appeasement and control. The imperial household, high-ranking government officials, and leading businessmen, intellectuals, and even Buddhist monks all visited the shrine regularly to pay their respects. According to the government, there was no greater glory than to die for the nation and be enshrined at Yasukuni. An imperial edict on education informed the youth of Japan that, "should emergency arise," they were expected to "offer [themselves] courageously to the State; and thus guard and maintain the prosperity of Our Imperial Throne coeval with heaven and earth" (Hardacre 1989: 122). The "divine wind" (*kamikaze*) attacks on American naval vessels in the Pacific, undertaken in desperation at the end of the Second World War, were extreme expressions of this ideology.

Several of Japan's postwar prime ministers have visited Yasukuni Shrine despite constitutional guidelines that prohibit the state from favouring a particular religion. Each visit has set off anti-Japanese demonstrations in China and Korea, both of which were occupied by Japan during the war and whose leaders object to the honouring of 14 officers identified as "class-A" war criminals.[3] Debates over how to honour Japan's war dead continue.

Postwar Restructuring and Religious Adaptation

After Japan's defeat in 1945, eight years of occupation by Allied forces laid the groundwork for its transformation into a stable democracy. The emperor was obliged to renounce his divinity and Shinto was stripped of its status as the *de facto* state religion. In the spiritual void that followed the war, constitutional guarantees of religious freedom encouraged a proliferation of new religious movements. Among them were Soka Gakkai and Rissho Koseikai (both based on the *Lotus Sutra*), Shinnyo-en (derived from Shingon), Mahikari (True Light), and Perfect Liberty Kyodan (Obaku Zen), each of which claims to have more a million followers today.

Much of the success of these movements can be attributed to their focus on dealing with life's problems, but they also offered a sense of community to people uprooted by postwar urbanization and industrialization. Some smaller groups have seen it as their role to serve as agents of radical personal and social transformation. The most extreme example was the Aum Shinrikyo ("Supreme Truth of Aum") cult, established in 1987. Aum was responsible for a number of crimes and murders, including a sarin gas attack on the Tokyo subway system in 1995 that killed 12 people and injured 5,000. According to the group's leader, Asahara Shoko, Japanese society was so thoroughly corrupt that it needed to be "cleansed" by an apocalypse. As a result of these attacks, the Japanese government passed more rigorous laws to monitor all religious organizations.

Japan's 74,000 Buddhist temples benefited greatly from the rising tide of the Japanese economy. A number of Zen temples began offering retreats designed to foster a spiritual discipline that could help those competing for success in their careers or higher education. A growing desire to venerate

A Japanese Buddhist temple can be compared to a franchise business in that it is affiliated with a particular brand yet operates independently. Each temple is required by law to have a board of trustees who work with the resident priest to ensure stability and continuity. Here, temple trustees relax after a ritual commemorating ancestral spirits (John K. Nelson).

the ancestors in style created a market for services ranging from elaborate funerals to rituals memorializing aborted fetuses or deceased household pets.

"Funeral Buddhism" has become a common derogatory term, applied to temples that have benefited from the income generated by funerals, memorials, and the sale of grave plots on their property. Many people have been turned off by this trend, seeing it as hypocritical for Buddhism—a tradition dedicated to the alleviation of suffering—to profit from situations of grief and loss. Younger people in particular object to paying membership fees to local temples just so that they will be in good standing when they have to arrange a funeral. In urban areas especially, increasing numbers of people are holding non-religious memorial services.

Summary

Today Japan's religious traditions appear to be entering an experimental phase. Ancient shrines and temples still attract many people, but most visitors are more interested in history and sacred art than in "religious experience." In response to negative perceptions of Buddhism, a number of progressive temples have been engaging more directly with social problems, offering community services, providing sanctuary for victims of domestic violence, and working for environmental

Buddhist clergy provided material, psychological, and spiritual relief after the earthquake and tsunami of 2011. "Café de Monk" volunteers travelled between temporary housing settlements to offer victims a chance to speak with a monk (photo courtesy of the Rev. Kaneta Taiō).

causes. Following the earthquake and tsunami of 11 March 2011 (in which more than 19,000 people died), and subsequent nuclear meltdown at Fukushima, clergy of all faiths provided both material and spiritual care for the survivors. Many temples became shelters, and monks helped survivors cope with the emotional and psychological after-effects. The nuclear disaster led to much soul-searching among Japan's religious leaders, and many have urged their denominations and parishioners to address the dangers of nuclear power.

The current period is one of great challenges for the Shinto tradition as well. In urban areas, Shinto festivals continue to attract broad-based participation, especially among women, who for generations were barred because of their gender. In rural areas, however, it can be difficult to find enough people to carry a village's portable shrine in a procession. Although new religions continue to develop, there is an increasing tendency among many to reject traditional religious affiliations, especially when they impose financial demands. It is predicted that, as Japan's baby-boom generation passes away, funeral rituals will become less identifiably Buddhist and more like the eclectic services typical of North America and Europe. Although young people appear to distrust organized religion in general, partly because of financial scandals and partly because of the Aum terror attack, many still seem interested in more individualistic expressions of spirituality. Books related to the occult, fortune-telling, and the spirit world always seem to sell well. This suggests that the ancient tradition of "turning to the gods in times of trouble" will likely remain a guiding paradigm.

Document

The Japan Buddhist Federation's Appeal for a Lifestyle without Dependence on Nuclear Power

Issued in 2011, the declaration from which the following statement is taken represented a rare moment of cooperation between the various schools of Japanese Buddhism.

We, the Japan Buddhist Federation, will strive to reduce our dependence on such nuclear power that threatens life, and to realize a society based on sustainable energy. We must choose a path in which personal happiness is harmonized with human welfare, instead of wishing for prosperity at the expense of others. We would like to make an appeal for building societies that protect each and every life, [and for] letting go of excessive materialistic greed, finding contentment in the feeling of moderation, and living in humility with nature (translated by Sakai and Watts 2012).

Sites

Izumo Shrine, Shimane Prefecture

Mentioned in several ancient accounts of the nation's founding, Izumo is a registered "National Treasure." A visit is recommended to those seeking marriage partners.

Nara

Nara was Japan's capital from 710 to 784. Its Todaiji and Horyuji temples are said to be the world's largest and oldest wooden buildings respectively.

Kamakura

This former fishing village near Tokyo was the capital of the samurai from 1185 to 1333 and has one of the world's most famous large Buddha statues.

Kyoto

Japan's capital for more than 1,000 years (794–1869), Kyoto is home to Japan's first Zen temple (Kenninji) and its second most important Shinto shrine (Kamigamo), as well as the picturesque Golden Pavilion, which was built as a shogun's palace and is now part of a Zen temple.

Ise Shrines

The most important of all Shinto sites. The main sanctuaries are rebuilt every 20 years; in this way, ancient wood-joinery techniques are passed on to the next generation of builders.

Nikko

The same eighth-century Buddhist monk who founded the Rinnoji Temple in Nikko also established the nearby Futarasan Shrine, dedicated to the *kami* of the surrounding mountains.

Sacred Texts

Religion	Text	Composition/ Compilation	Compilation/ Revision	Use
Shinto	*Kojiki*	8th century; compiled by O no Yasumaro at emperor's request	13th-, 15th-, 19th-, 20th-century versions	Legitimates imperial rule; provides myth for founding of Japan; select parts used in ritual purification; ideological use
Shinto	*Nihon Shoki*	8th century; Prince Toneri; O no Yasumaro	13th-, 15th-, 19th-, 20th-century versions	More historical than the *Kojiki*, it has been more useful to scholars researching the origins of Japanese civilization
Tendai Buddhism	*Lotus Sutra*; writings of founder, Saicho; other esoteric Buddhist texts	3rd-century China, brought to Japan in early 9th century	Translations are updated; commentaries added periodically	Ritual, doctrinal, and ideological
Shingon Buddhism	Mahavairocana and Vajrasekhara *sutras*	7th century (India)	Periodic updates, new translations, and commentaries	Doctrinal, ritual, inspirational, educational
Rinzai Zen Buddhism	Various *sutras*, including the *Lankavatara*; apocryphal stories of enlightened masters; koans	12th century (and earlier)	Numerous translations of teachings, updated frequently over time	Doctrinal, ritual, inspirational, educational
Soto Zen Buddhism	*Heart*, *Diamond*, and *Lankavatara Sutras*; writings of Dogen	13th-, 16th-, 18th-century texts and commentaries	Periodic updates, new translations, and commentaries	Doctrinal, ritual, inspirational, educational
Pure Land Buddhism	*"Infinite Life" Sutra*	3rd century (China)	Periodic updates, new translations, and commentaries	Doctrinal, ritual, inspirational, educational
True Pure Land Buddhism	*Tannisho*, sayings of Shinran the founder	13th-century version	Periodic updates and commentaries	Doctrinal, ritual, inspirational, educational
Nichiren Buddhism	*Lotus Sutra*; writings of founder, Nichiren	13th-century version	Translations are updated; commentaries added periodically	Doctrinal, ritual, inspirational, educational

Discussion Questions

1. Why is it common among contemporary Japanese to visit a Buddhist temple and on the same trip stop at a Shinto shrine to purchase an amulet, yet say one is "not religious?"
2. What are several of the principal spiritual agents in Japan that interact with human beings and the natural world?
3. Identify two of Japan's most popular bodhisattvas and how they are said to help humans in moments of crisis.
4. How did the monks Saicho and Kukai help to establish what can be called "Japanese Buddhism" in the eighth century?
5. Identify and differentiate the three types of Buddhism that emerged in the medieval period.
6. What are some of the contributions of Zen Buddhism to Japanese culture? Be sure to reference both aesthetic and political aspects.
7. Explain why accessing spiritual benefits has more meaning for Japanese people than the teachings of particular religious denominations.
8. What role did religion play in the creation of a "modern Japan" between the late nineteenth century and the Second World War?

Glossary

Amaterasu Female deity of the sun, born from the eye of the primordial deity Izanagi following his purification; enshrined at Ise as the patron deity of the imperial family.

bodhisattva A Buddhist "saint" who has achieved spiritual liberation but chooses to remain in this world to help alleviate the suffering of individuals.

bushido Literally, the "way of the warrior"; an ethical code that combined a Confucian-style emphasis on loyalty with the discipline of Zen.

honji suijaku Literally, "manifestation from the original state"; the concept that *kami* are manifestations of buddhas or bodhisattvas.

jiriki Literally, "self-power"; the principle that individuals can attain liberation through their own abilities and devotional activities.

kami The spirits that animate all living things, natural phenomena, and natural forces. Shrines were built to accommodate their presence during rituals.

Kojiki A collection of stories commissioned to legitimate the imperial regime by linking it with Japan's mythical origins. It was published in 712 CE but was soon replaced by the *Nihongi* and remained largely forgotten until the eighteenth century.

Kokugaku Literally, "learning about one's country"; the intellectual movement of the eighteenth and nineteenth centuries that privileged Japanese culture and ideas over those from abroad.

mappo The period of "decline of the (Buddhist) dharma," thought to have begun in 1052; a time of social disorder, during which individuals could not achieve liberation without the aid of buddhas and bodhisattvas.

nembutsu The key prayer of the Pure Land traditions: *Namu Amida Butsu* ("praise to the Amida Buddha").

samurai A popular term for the *bushi* ("warrior"), who served regional warlords in various capacities; samurai made up the top 5 per cent of society during the Edo period (1603–1867).

shogun The supreme military commander of Japan, appointed by the emperor and effectively ruling in his name.

tariki The "outside power," offered by buddhas and bodhisattvas, without which individuals living in the age of the Buddhist dharma's decline (*mappo*) would be unable to achieve liberation.

zazen Seated meditation.

Further Reading

Ambros, Barbara. 2012. *Bones of Contention: Animals and Religion in Contemporary Japan*. Honolulu: University of Hawaii Press. A thorough exploration of the newly popular practice of memorializing pets and what it implies for both Japanese society and its Buddhist traditions.

Bowring, Richard. 2006. *The Religious Traditions of Japan, 500–1600*. Cambridge: Cambridge University Press. A comprehensive and highly readable account of Japanese religious history covering more than 1,000 years.

Covell, Stephen. 2005. ***Japanese Temple Buddhism: Worldliness in a Religion of Renunciation.*** **Honolulu: University of Hawaii Press.** A pioneering examination of contemporary temple Buddhism, with an emphasis on the Tendai denomination.

Jaffe, Richard. 2002. ***Neither Monk nor Layman: Clerical Marriage in Modern Japanese Buddhism.*** **Princeton: Princeton University Press.** An engaging analysis of the tension between the historical image of Buddhist clergy as celibate and the modern expectations that they will have families and run their temples like businesses.

Nelson, John. 1996. ***A Year in the Life of a Shinto Shrine.*** **Honolulu: University of Hawaii Press.** A study of what goes on behind the scenes at a major Shinto shrine in the city of Nagasaki.

———. **2005.** ***Spirits of the State: Japan's Yasukuni Shrine.*** **28 min. Documentary film, distributed by Films for the Humanities (www.films.com).** A documentary, made for university audiences, about the controversy surrounding Yasukuni Shrine, where the spirits of the military dead are enshrined and venerated by the state.

———. **2013.** ***Experimental Buddhism: Innovation and Activism in Contemporary Japan.*** **Honolulu: University of Hawaii Press.** A study of priests from all of Japan's Buddhist denominations, evaluating the crisis facing temples in Japan today, and documenting some of their creative responses to their loss of patronage and declining social significance.

Prohl, Inken, and John Nelson, eds. 2012. ***Handbook of Contemporary Japanese Religions.*** **Leiden: Brill.** More than 20 scholars contributed chapters surveying postwar and contemporary developments in Japanese religions and religious practices.

Reader, Ian. 2005. ***Making Pilgrimages: Meaning and Practice in Shikoku.*** **Honolulu: University of Hawaii Press.** A detailed study of the Shikoku pilgrimage, including the religious significance of the 88 sacred temples that make up the route.

Rowe, Mark. 2011. ***Bonds of the Dead: Temples, Burial, and the Transformation of Contemporary Japanese Buddhism.*** **Chicago: University of Chicago Press.** A groundbreaking book that explores Japanese Buddhism's reliance on mortuary rituals in the postwar period.

Schnell, Scott. 1999. ***The Rousing Drum: Ritual Practice in a Japanese Community.*** **Honolulu: University of Hawaii Press.** An ethnographic look at a major festival in a small mountain city and what it means to the cultural identity of the local people.

Swanson, Paul, and Clark Chilson, eds. 2006. ***The Nanzan Guide to Japanese Religions.*** **Honolulu: University of Hawaii Press.** A very useful compilation of scholarly articles on many topics related to Japanese religions.

Thal, Sarah. 2006. ***Rearranging the Landscape of the Gods: The Politics of a Pilgrimage Site in Japan, 1573–1912.*** **Chicago: University of Chicago Press.** A comprehensive history of the wrenching changes forced on a former Buddhist temple, now converted to a major Shinto shrine.

Watsky, Andrew. 2004. ***Chikubushima: Deploying the Sacred Arts in Momoyama Japan.*** **Honolulu: University of Hawaii Press.** One of the best studies of the artistic, architectural, and aesthetic contributions of the sixteenth-century Toyotomi regime to the religious landscape of Japan.

Williams, Duncan. 2005. ***The Other Side of Zen: A Social History of Soto Zen in Tokugawa Japan.*** **Princeton: Princeton University Press.** Surprising and often shocking in its account of corruption and exploitation among monks from the sixteenth to the nineteenth centuries, this study reveals the "dark" side of institutional Zen, which dominated Japanese society for more than 250 years.

Recommended Websites

http://nirc.nanzan-u.ac.jp/en/publications/jjrs/

A semi-annual journal dedicated to the academic study of Japanese religions.

www2.kokugakuin.ac.jp/ijcc

The English-language website for the Institute of Japanese Culture and Classics at Kokugakuin University, specializing in Shinto studies. Many online publications.

global.sotozen-net.or.jp/eng/index.html

The English-language website of the Soto Zen school introduces key teachings and practices. (Each Buddhist denomination has a similar site; many temples also have their own sites.)

www.jodo.org

An English-language website offering a variety of resources on Pure Land Buddhism.

www.onmarkproductions.com/html/buddhism.shtml

A photo library devoted to artwork, especially sculpture, depicting Buddhist and Shinto deities in Japan.

http://zen.rinnou.net

A brief overview of history, temples, and teachings from the Joint Council of Rinzai-Obaku Zen

References

Bodiford, William M. 1992. "Zen in the Art of Funerals: Ritual Salvation in Japanese Buddhism." *History of Religions* 32.

Bowring, Richard. 2005. *The Religious Traditions of Japan: 500–1600*. Cambridge: Cambridge University Press.

Breen, John, and Mark Teeuwen. 2000. *Shinto in History: Ways of the Kami*. Honolulu: University of Hawaii.

Dogen, Eihei. 1996. "*Tenzo kyokun*: Instructions for the *Tenzo*." Yasuda Hoshu and Anzan Hoshin, trans. White Wind Zen Community. Retrieved online at http://www.wwzc.org/translations/tenzokyokun.htm.

Gorai, Shigeru. 1994. *Nihonjin no shiseikan* ("Japanese views of death"). Tokyo: Kadokawa Shoten.

Hardacre, Helen. 1989. *Shinto and the State: 1868–1945*. Princeton: Princeton University Press.

Jansen, Marius. 2000. *The Making of Modern Japan*. Boston: Harvard University Press.

Josephson, Jason. 2012. *The Invention of Religion in Japan*. Chicago: University of Chicago Press.

Kamens, Edward. 1990. *The Buddhist Poetry of the Great Kamo Priestess: Daisaiin Senshi and Hosshin wakash*. Michigan monograph series in Japanese studies no. 5. Ann Arbor.

MacWilliams, Mark. 2012. "Religion and Manga." In *Handbook of Contemporary Japanese Religions*, ed. Inken Prohl and John Nelson. Leiden: Brill.

Payne, Richard K. 2006. "The Shingon Subordinating Fire Offering for Amitābha, 'Amida Kei Ai Goma.'" *Pacific World: Journal of the Institute of Buddhist Studies* 8 (Fall): 191–236.

Philipi, Donald L. 1985. *The Kojiki*. Tokyo: Tokyo University Press.

Pye, Michael. 2004. "The Structure of Religious Systems in Contemporary Japan: Shinto Variations on Buddhist Pilgrimage." Occasional Paper No. 30, Centre for Japanese Studies. University of Marburg.

Reader, Ian. 1991. *Religion in Contemporary Japan*. Honolulu: University of Hawaii Press.

Sakai, Jin, and Jonathan Watts. 2012. *This Precious Life: Buddhist Tsunami Relief and Anti-Nuclear Activism in Post 3/11 Japan*. Yokohama: International Buddhist Exchange Center.

Senda, Minoru. 1988. "Taoist Roots in Japanese Culture." *Japan Quarterly* 35, 2.

Williams, Duncan. 2005. *The Other Side of Zen: A Social History of Soto Zen in Tokugawa Japan*. Princeton: Princeton University Press.

Yampolsky, Philip, trans. 2008. "The Essentials of Salvation." In Haruo Shirane, ed., *Traditional Japanese Literature: An Anthology, Beginnings to 1600*. New York: Columbia University Press.

Young, W.A. 1995. *The World's Religions*. Englewood Cliffs: Prentice-Hall.

Notes

1. One of these colossal statues of Kannon appears at the end of the 2006 film *Kamikaze Girls* as the backdrop for a battle between an all-girl motorcycle gang and one of the protagonists.
2. For more on the *saiin* tradition, see Kamens (1990).
3. For a treatment of this topic suitable for classroom use, see my documentary film *Spirits of the State: Japan's Yasukuni Shrine* (2005).

12 New Religions and Movements

Roy C. Amore

Timelines

1830 CE	Church of Jesus Christ of Latter-day Saints (United States)
1844	Baha'i Faith (Iran)
1929	Nation of Islam (United States)
1930	Soka Gakkai (Japan)
1940s	Wicca (England)
1954	The Church of Scientology (United States)
1965	International Society for Krishna Consciousness (ISKCON) (United States)
1965	The Kabbalah Centre (United States)
1974	Raëlian Movement (France)
1990	Falun Dafa (China)

The youngest of the Abrahamic religions covered in this volume is well over 1,000 years old, but innovations in religion did not end with Islam. The early nineteenth century saw the emergence of many new faiths, and more have developed since then. This chapter explores a selection of religions either newly coming to or arising in the West. First, though, we need to consider what distinguishes a "religion" from a "sect" or a "cult."

Defining New Religions, Sects, and Cults

What is a "new religion"? The question might be easier to answer if scholars could agree on what constitutes a religion. But there are hundreds, if not thousands, of ideas on that subject. Even a definition as seemingly basic as "belief in a god or goddess" would not take into account non-theistic traditions such as Buddhism and Jainism. Fortunately, our task here is not to define religion, but to understand what is meant by the terms "sect" and "cult," and how those terms are applied to new religious movements.

Sociologists of religion such as Max Weber, writing in the early 1900s, used the word "**sect**" to refer to Christian splinter groups, new institutionalized movements that had broken away from mainstream denominations, usually to practise what they considered to be a purer form of the faith. Often the breakaway group would denounce its parent and set itself apart by adopting stricter rules, new modes of worship, or distinctive clothing. With the passage of time, however, most sectarian movements either faded away or moved back towards the mainstream. In other words, new movements would begin as sects (or sectarian movements) and evolve into churches (new denominations). A similar process can be seen in the histories of many other religions.

As for "**cult**," it was originally a neutral term, used as a synonym for "worship" or even "religion." Today, though, its connotations—at least in the popular media—are almost always negative: a cult is generally assumed to be a small group under the control of a charismatic leader who is suspected of brainwashing followers and promoting self-destructive, illegal, or immoral behaviour.

← Baha'i "Lotus" temple, New Delhi (© Prisma Bildagentur AG / Alamy).

A movement that is accepted by outsiders as a "new religion" will enjoy all the constitutional protections and tax exemptions afforded to established religions. But a movement that gets labelled as a "cult" is likely to attract scrutiny, if not harassment, from legal authorities and government officials. In divorce cases where custody of the children is in dispute, it is not unusual for one parent to use association with a "cult" to argue that the other parent is unfit. And in the 1994 race for the California Senate, one candidate received damaging media attention because his wife was thought to be associated with a cult (Lewis 2003: 208).

Yet the definitional lines between a cult and a sect (or new religion) are quite vague. By the usual definitions, for example, the **Hare Krishna** movement was a sect of Hinduism in India, but in the West its members' unusual practice and dress soon led to their branding as a cult. This suggests that the "cult" label has less to do with the nature of the movement itself than with how sharply it differs from the mainstream religious culture—in other words, that one person's religion is another person's cult.

Yet there are several traits that many cults seem to share. Cults typically claim to have some special knowledge or insight, perhaps based on a new interpretation of an old scripture or revealed through contact with spirits (or even aliens). Their practice often includes rituals that promote ecstatic experiences, and they tend to emphasize individual spiritual experience more than institutional organization (see Dawson 2006: 28–9).

Perhaps the most widely shared characteristic, however, is a charismatic leader who demands extreme loyalty. Adherents may be required to work long hours for little or no pay, cut ties with family and friends from the past, denounce former religious beliefs, or even submit sexually to the leader. In extreme cases, leaders may go so far as to demand that followers be willing to die for the cause. The mass suicide (forced or voluntary) of more than 900 members of the Peoples Temple at Jonestown, Guyana, in 1978 is one famous example. In most mass suicides, whether coerced or voluntary, the underlying belief was that the current world order was about to be replaced by a new order in which the cult's members would be rewarded for their loyalty. That is, the movements had a **millenarian** belief in an imminent "end of time" or "apocalypse" leading to the dawning of a "new age."

What gives rise to new religious movements? It has often been noted that they tend to appear at times of serious cultural disruption or change. The Indigenous prophetic movements discussed in Chapter 2 are classic examples, emerging in societies whose traditional cultures were breaking down under the pressure of European colonization. Similarly, the massive cultural changes of the 1960s gave rise to several new religions in North America.

Hundreds of new religious movements have established themselves over the past two centuries. This chapter focuses on a small selection of those that have been most successful or have attracted the most attention. We will discuss them in three groups, organized according to their spiritual roots: traditional Asian religions, Abrahamic traditions, and other forms of spirituality.

New Religions from the East

Soka Gakkai

Soka Gakkai was founded in Japan before the Second World War and emerged as an important force only after 1945—a period that saw a flowering of new Japanese religions. But its roots lie deep in Buddhist history, in the tradition of the controversial thirteenth-century monk Nichiren.

The dominant tradition of Nichiren's day was the Pure Land school of Mahayana Buddhism, which taught the saving power of Amida Buddha. Nichiren, however, believed that a Mahayana scripture called the *Lotus Sutra* represented the culmination of all Buddhist truths, and warned that Japan would be doomed if the people ignored its teachings. At the same time he became so critical of the Pure Land sects that their leaders persuaded the emperor to exile him to a remote island, where he continued to write tracts criticizing other Buddhist sects and promoting his own.

Nichiren's prophecies of impending doom seemed to come true when the Mongols attempted to invade Japan in 1274. Thus he was allowed to return from exile and, with his followers, establish a sect based on his teachings, together with the *Lotus Sutra*. It is to this sect, eventually known as Nichiren Shoshu ("True Nichiren"), that Soka Gakkai traces its roots.

Soka Gakkai ("Association for Creating Values") was established in 1930 as a lay organization within Nichiren Shoshu. Its founder was a reform-minded schoolteacher named Makiguchi Tsunesaburo, who wanted to promote moral values among young people. Many of its leading figures were imprisoned during the Second World War because they refused to recognize the divinity of the Emperor as required by the officially Shinto Japanese state, and Makiguchi himself died in prison before the war ended.

His successor, Toda Josei, adopted an aggressive recruitment strategy based on an ancient Buddhist missionary principle. To break down resistance to their message, Soka Gakkai members might gather outside the home of a potential convert and chant all day and all night, or point out to shop-owners that Soka Gakkai members would shop at their stores if they converted. Although critics complained that this approach amounted to harassment and coercion, it was effective, and Soka Gakkai grew exponentially under Toda's leadership. Meanwhile, small groups of practitioners began to establish themselves throughout much of Asia, Europe, and the Americas. Often the leaders of these local groups were ethnic Japanese, but the majority of the members were not. As usual with new religious movements, young people made up the majority of the converts.

Document

Nichiren "On Attaining Buddhahood in This Lifetime"

Soka Gakkai follows the Nichiren practice of chanting the mantra "myoho-renge-kyo," *"Homage to the Lotus Sutra." Here Nichiren explains the thinking behind that practice.*

If you wish to free yourself from the sufferings of birth and death you have endured since time without beginning and to attain without fail unsurpassed enlightenment in this lifetime, you must perceive the mystic truth that is originally inherent in all living beings. This truth is *Myoho-renge-kyo*. Chanting *Myoho-renge-kyo* will therefore enable you to grasp the mystic truth innate in all life.

The Lotus Sutra is the king of sutras, true and correct in both word and principle. Its words are the ultimate reality, and this reality is the Mystic Law (*myōhō*). It is called the Mystic Law because it reveals the principle of the mutually inclusive relationship of a single moment of life and all phenomena. That is why this sutra is the wisdom of all Buddhas (Nichiren 1999: 3).

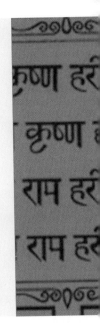

Today Soka Gakkai International (SGI)—founded in 1975 as a worldwide organization under the umbrella of Soka Gakkai in Japan—claims 12 million members. Most "new religions" in Japan promise this-worldly happiness, and Soka Gakkai is no exception. In particular, it stresses the here-and-now benefits of chanting the sacred mantra *namu myoho renge kyo* (translated on the Sokka Gakkai website as "I devote myself to the Lotus Sutra of the Wonderful Law"): passing a test, getting a promotion, improving one's outlook on life. Soka Gakkai is also active in youth activities, and sponsors events that give urban youth a taste of life in a more traditional setting.

At the core of Soka Gakkai is the belief that the practice of Nichiren Buddhism can bring about a personal transformation that will empower the individual to take effective action towards the goals of peace, justice, social harmony, and economic prosperity. An example of the organization's economic perspective can be seen in a 2008 speech by SGI President Daisaku Ikeda, in which he called for "humanitarian competition" in a new economic order that would avoid both the excessive greed of capitalism and the lack of competition historically associated with socialism (Ikeda 2008).

The profile of Soka Gakkai in Japan has been somewhat diminished since 1991, when Nichiren Shoshu officially severed its links with Soka Gakkai. It was the climax of a long dispute between the conservative clergy and the reform-minded lay organization. But the international organization has continued to grow, even establishing a university in California in 1995, and the split has not affected Soka Gakkai's practice. Members continue to follow the religious teachings of Nichiren Shoshu, studying the *Lotus Sutra* and chanting the sacred mantra.

Falun Dafa (Falun Gong)

Falun Dafa (Law Wheel of the Great Law), popularly known as Falun Gong, developed out of a Chinese Buddhist qigong tradition. The term ***qi*** (pronounced "chi" and often spelled *chi* in the older transliteration system) refers to unseen energy flowing through the body, while ***qigong*** refers to various techniques of breathing and movement that are said to permit energy to flow properly through the body, promoting healing, health, and long life. Although Western science has been reluctant to incorporate the flow of energy into its worldview, the belief in *qi* and the various ways to strengthen it have been part of East Asian cultures for centuries.

Li Hongzhi, who brought Falun Dafa to prominence in China in 1992, explains it as a system of Buddhist cultivation passed down through the centuries, and considers himself only the most recent in a long line of teachers. The system's Buddhist roots are reflected in its name: the *falun* or Dharma Wheel is an auspicious symbol in Buddhism. Li's teachings of compassion and self-development are based on Buddhist principles and he uses Buddhist symbols and terms, but Falun Dafa is not officially recognized as a traditional school of Chinese Buddhism. Thus the Chinese government has been able to outlaw Falun Dafa without contravening its policy on the five religions it does recognize.

Although Falun Dafa has traditional roots, Li Hongzhi adapted the practice to everyday life. It spread quickly in China and was openly accepted by the government as one of many recognized qigong practices. But Li's refusal to accept governmental control and the organization's rapid growth began to attract attention within the Communist Party, which was particularly concerned by Falun Dafa's popularity among younger party members and their children. When some senior party officials began expressing alarm in early 1999, the leaders of Falun Dafa organized a demonstration in the section of Beijing where the top government officials live and work. Sitting silently in orderly rows, without banners or placards, they intended only to call attention to their right to practice and to show that Falun Dafa was not a political threat, but the government was alarmed by the sudden presence of so large a gathering in the heart of Beijing.

Government officials persuaded the Falun Dafa leadership to send the demonstrators home. Then, three months later, the organization was banned on the grounds that it was an unregistered religion and discouraged people from seeking proper medical attention. Falun Dafa members throughout China were arrested, fired, imprisoned, sent to prison camps, tortured, or killed.

Li Hongzhi had left China two years before the ban was imposed. He now lives in New York City, which has become the base of a worldwide organization claiming more than 100 million followers in over 100 countries.

The Falun Dafa symbol (Courtesy of Falun Dafa Association, http://en.falundafa.org/introduction.html). Note the Daoist yin-yang (*taiji*) symbols and Buddhist rotating swastikas. The outer symbols rotate individually, and together they rotate around the central swastika, first in one direction and then in the other. The colours are said to vary depending on the level of visions experienced by the practitioner.

Practice

Whereas some people practise *qigong* purely for its physiological benefits, Falun Dafa practitioners seek both physical and spiritual purification. The organization describes Falun Dafa as "a high-level cultivation practice guided by the characteristics of the universe—Truthfulness, Benevolence, and Forbearance" (Li 2000: "Introduction").

Practitioners are said to develop a *falun* or "law wheel" in the abdomen. This is not the same as the *qi*, which is naturally present in everyone. Once acquired, the *falun* spins in synchrony with the rotation of the planets, the milky way, and other objects in the universe. When rotating clockwise, the *falun* absorbs and transforms energy from the universe, and when rotating counter-clockwise, it dispenses salvation to oneself, to others, and to the universe. According to Li, healing comes not from the *qi* but from the *falun* when it is rotating counter-clockwise. The *falun* changes its rotational direction according to its own dynamics, and it continues to rotate even when one is not actually practising the Dafa exercises. The energy cluster emitted by the *falun* is called *gong*—hence the alternative name Falun Gong. The *gong* is said to glow like light.

Li divides Falun Dafa exercises into five sets, with names such as "Buddha showing a thousand hands," which is the foundational set of exercises, meant to open the body's energy channels. When the exercises are done properly, it is said that the body will feel warm, indicating that the energies have been unblocked and energy is being absorbed from the universe. The study of Li's writings, especially the *Zhuan Falun* (Turning the Law Wheel) is another central practice, intended to cultivate morality in everyday life.

Although Falun Dafa teaches non-violence, practitioners have faced serious persecution in China, and it is regularly denounced as an evil cult working against the good of the people. Although it has not been banned in Hong Kong, which has been a part of China since 1997, when the organization wanted to hold a major international rally there in 2007, Beijing blocked the event by refusing to grant visas to Falun Dafa members from abroad. Outside mainland China, Falun Dafa is severely critical of the Chinese government. It maintains protest booths near the mainland government's Liaison Office in Hong Kong, showing pictures of torture in China, and a Falun Dafa band provided the music for a mass pro-democracy protest march by Hong Kong residents in 2014. Supporters say that many practitioners are imprisoned in long-term work camps, where they are used to produce goods that are sold in the West. The organization also claims that organs are involuntarily removed from prisoners to be used for transplants. Amnesty International has lent some credence to these accusations.

International Society for Krishna Consciousness (ISKCON)

In September 1965 a 70-year-old Hindu holy man arrived by freighter in New York City with virtually nothing but a short list of contacts. A few weeks later, he sat under a now famous tree in Tompkins Square Park and began to chant:

> Hare Krishna Hare Krishna,
> Krishna Krishna Hare Hare,
> Hare Rama Hare Rama,
> Rama Rama Hare Hare.

He had learned this "great mantra" from his guru in India, who had learned it from his guru, and so on—it was said—all the way back to a sixteenth-century Hindu mystic named Chaitanya, who was reputed to enter a state of mystical ecstasy while chanting the three names of his god: Krishna, Hare, Rama. Within a year of his arrival, A.C. Bhaktivedanta Swami Prabhupada had established the International Society for Krishna Consciousness (**ISKCON**) and the "Hare Krishna" movement had begun to take root in America.

The Hare Krishna movement was new to the West, but it was not a new religion. Rather, it was a Western mission of **Vaishnava** Hinduism, the school devoted to Vishnu. Traditional Vaishnavas worship Vishnu both as the Supreme Godhead and in the forms of his 10 major avatars—the animal or human forms he has assumed at different times to "come down" (*avatara*) to Earth to save humanity. In this system, Krishna, "the dark-complexioned one," is the eighth avatar. However, Prabhupada belonged to a Bengali variant in which the Cowherd (Gopala) Krishna himself is the Supreme Godhead—the source of everything, including other divine forces. As such, Krishna is understood to encourage a very personal relationship between the devotee and himself. Like other forms of Hinduism, ISKCON teaches that the soul is eternal and subject to reincarnation according to the individual's karma; however, those who practise loving devotion to Krishna will go to his heaven when they die and thus escape the cycle of rebirth. The foundational texts for ISKCON are the *Bhagavad Gita* and a collection of stories about Krishna's life called the *Srimad Bhagavatam*.

Between the founding of ISKCON in 1966 and his death 11 years later, Srila Prabhupada travelled throughout North America and around the world spreading his version of Hinduism. His recorded addresses and voluminous writings laid down the fundamental beliefs and practices of the movement. Soon the Hare Krishna movement was establishing centres across North America and abroad. Each centre included a temple with an altar area featuring images of Krishna and his consort Radha, as the male and female aspects of the divine, as well as pictures of the guru, Prabhupada. In addition, schools were started to educate the children of devotees in Vedic (ancient Hindu) culture, and farms were established that undertook to work the land in traditional ways consistent with Vedic norms.

Document

From Swami Prabhupada

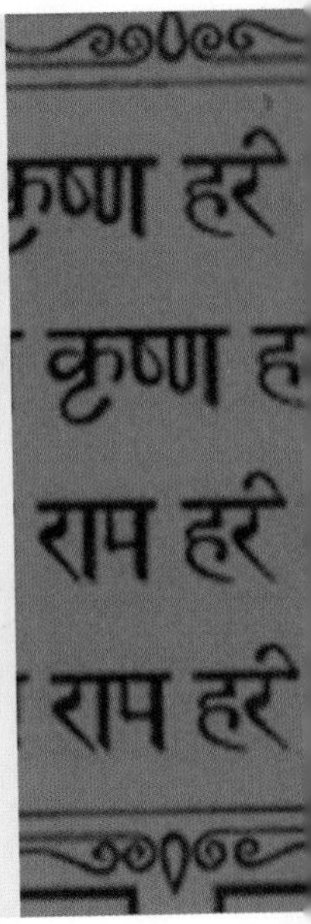

On the ethical ideals of Krishna Consciousness:

A person in Krishna Consciousness, fully devoted in the transcendental loving service of the Lord, develops many good qualities. . . . Lord Chaitanya described only some of them to Sanatan Goswami: A devotee of the Lord is always kind to everyone. He does not pick a quarrel with anyone. He takes the essence of life, spiritual life. He is equal to everyone. Nobody can find fault in a devotee. His magnanimous mind is always fresh and clean and without any material obsessions. He is a benefactor to all living entities. He is peaceful and always surrendered to Krishna. He has no material desire. He is very humble and is fixed in his directions. He is victorious over the six material qualities such as lust and anger. He does not eat more than what he needs. He is always sane. He is respectful to others; but for himself he does not require any respect. He is grave. He is merciful. He is friendly. He is a poet. He is an expert. And he is silent. (Prabhupada 1968:104).

It is not uncommon for new religions to undergo a difficult period of adjustment after the death of the charismatic founder/leader. Following Prabhupada's death, ISKCON vested authority not in a single guru, but in a Governing Body Commission (GBC), which recognized 11 devotees who had risen to high positions under Prabhupada's leadership as gurus and authorized them to ordain recruits and oversee operations in 11 regional zones. Some of the gurus got into trouble with the law over matters including illegal guns, drugs, child abuse, and murder, and by the 1980s six of the original group had quit or been removed from office by the GBC.

Practice

As we saw in Chapter 6, the *Bhagavad Gita* depicts Krishna telling Arjuna that he, Krishna, is the highest of all gods, and that although the yoga (spiritual practice) of good karma actions and the yoga of spiritual wisdom are both valid paths, the best path is **bhakti** yoga: loving devotion to Krishna.

These ideas, combined with Chaitanya's mystical practice of chanting the praises of Krishna while dancing in ecstasy, are at the heart of the tradition that Prabhupada introduced to the West. Devotional services, *pujas*, to Krishna are held several times a day. One male or female devotee, acting as the *puja* leader, stands near the altar and makes offerings of fire and vegetarian food to the images on the altar, which include, in addition to Krishna himself, his consort Radha and his brother Balarama. While the *pujari* performs these rituals, the other devotees chant and dance to the accompaniment of hand-held cymbals and drums and a small organ called a harmonium. As the pace builds, the chanting becomes louder and the dancing more feverish, and when it reaches a climax, many devotees jump high into the air.

Devotees are given a Sanskrit name, wear saffron-coloured robes, and show their devotion to Krishna by adorning their bodies with painted marks called *tilaka*, made of cream-coloured

Hare Krishna devotees try to recruit new members by chanting their mantra in public places; here, in front of a mural by R. Cronk at southern California's popular Venice Beach (© LHB Photo / Alamy).

clay from the banks of a holy lake in India. Two vertical marks represent Krishna's feet, or the walls of a temple, and below them is a leaf representing the sacred *tulasi* (basil) plant. The diet is strictly vegetarian, and recreational drugs of all kinds, including alcohol and caffeine, are avoided.

Great effort is put into keeping the temple clean, and every activity is to be done "for Krishna," as an act of devotional service. In this way the mental state known as Krishna consciousness is developed. Some devotees attend the temple only for major activities, but others live in or near it. Single male and female devotees have separate living quarters, while married couples and families often live in nearby houses or apartments. Sexual activity is allowed only within marriage and only for the purpose of procreation. Some devotees have outside employment and turn their wages over to the temple. Others work full-time for the movement.

Most temple-based male devotees shave their heads except for a pigtail at the back of the head. Women are required to dress very modestly. Devotees carry a small bag containing a string of 108 chanting beads (the number 108 is sacred in India partly because it represents the multiple of the 12 zodiac houses and 9 planetary bodies as understood in Indian astrology). Using the beads if their hands are free, devotees chant the Hare Krishna mantra hundreds of times each day as they go about their duties at the temple.

The Hare Krishnas provoked strong reactions, both positive and negative. On the positive side was the enthusiasm shown by celebrities like George Harrison of the Beatles; his song "My Sweet Lord" (1970) contributed greatly to the acceptance of the movement. But there were many negative reactions as well. Some were provoked by the movement's efforts to raise money by chanting in public places. Others centred on the fact that in the early years ISKCON discouraged contact between devotees and their former friends and family. As a consequence, the media quickly branded the movement a "cult," and a new profession known as "deprogrammer" came into existence. Hired by concerned parents, deprogrammers would kidnap the young people and confine them in a motel room for days while trying to break the "cult program" that had been "brainwashed" into them. Sometimes these efforts succeeded, but many young people returned to the Hare Krishnas as soon as they were free to do so.

The schools operated by ISKCON for children of devotees became controversial. In 2000 a class action suit was filed in Dallas by 44 former students who claimed to have been victims of physical, emotional, and sexual abuse in ISKCON-operated schools in the US and India. By the time the final settlement was reached, hundreds of others had joined the list of plaintiffs and ISKCON had been forced to seek bankruptcy protection. The claims, totalling $20 million, were settled by 2008, and ISKCON emerged from bankruptcy protection.

ISKCON now runs approximately 350 temples and centres worldwide. It has been especially successful in the former states of the Soviet Union, including Russia, and in South America. The spread of ISKCON back to India has been a remarkable development. After starting his mission in America, Prabphupada established a number of temples in India, where ISKCON has been welcomed as a movement reviving Gaudiya Vaishnava devotion. Today Indian devotees may outnumber Western ones.

Religions Arising from the Abrahamic Lineage

We now turn our attention to some new religions arising from the three Abrahamic religions. The Church of Latter-day Saints can be classed either as a branch of Protestant Christianity or as a new religion developing out of Christianity. The Baha'i Faith originated in Iran in the context of Shi'i Islam. The Kabbalah Centre draws on a Jewish mystical tradition that is centuries old, while the Nation of Islam was established in the US by leaders raised in the Christian tradition.

Church of Jesus Christ of Latter-day Saints (Mormons)

The founder of the **Church of Jesus Christ of Latter-day Saints**, Joseph Smith, Jr (1805–44), claimed that in 1820, as a boy in upstate New York, he had experienced a vision of God and Jesus in which he was told not to join any of the existing denominations. In subsequent visions, he said, an angel named Moroni had persuaded him that he had been divinely chosen to restore the true Church of Christ. He founded his new Church in 1830.

As a textual basis for the enterprise, Smith published the *Book of Mormon*, which he said he had translated from gold plates inscribed in "reformed Egyptian" that had been entrusted to him by Moroni during a hilltop meeting near Palmyra, New York. Though subsequent editions referred to Smith as the "translator," the title page of the 1830 first edition declared him "author and proprietor." The *Book of Mormon* uses the language of the 1611 King James Bible to tell the otherwise undocumented story of two groups, both descended from one of the lost tribes of Israel

Document

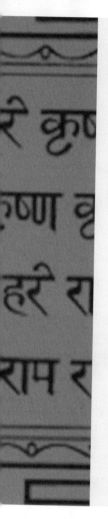

From *The Book of Mormon*, Chapter I

Here the prophet-historian named Mormon explains how he was instructed to recover the texts hidden by Ammaron, a record-keeper among the Nephites—one of four groups said to have migrated from Jerusalem to the Western hemisphere more than five centuries before the time of Jesus.

1. And now I, Mormon, make a record of the things which I have both seen and heard, and call it the Book of Mormon.

2. And about the time that Ammaron hid up the records unto the Lord, he came unto me, (I being about ten years of age, and I began to be learned somewhat after the manner of the learning of my people) and Ammaron said unto me: I perceive that thou art a sober child, and art quick to observe;

3. Therefore, when ye are about twenty and four years old I would that ye should remember the things that ye have observed concerning this people; and when ye are of that age go to the land Antum, unto a hill which shall be called Shim; and there have I deposited unto the Lord all the sacred engravings concerning this people.

4. And behold, ye shall take the plates of Nephi unto yourself, and the remainder shall ye leave in the place where they are; and ye shall engrave on the plates of Nephi all the things that ye have observed concerning this people.

5. And I, Mormon, being a descendent of Nephi, (and my father's name was Mormon) I remembered the things which Ammaron commanded me.

6. And I, being fifteen years of age and being somewhat of a sober mind, therefore I was visited of the Lord, and tasted and knew of the goodness of Jesus. (*Book of Mormon*, 1961: 460–7).

that supposedly migrated from the Near East to the New World around 600 BCE and became the ancestors of the Indigenous peoples of the Americas. Including accounts of visitations by Christ sometime after his crucifixion, the book is understood by **Mormons** to be a scriptural account of God's activity in the western hemisphere, parallel with the Bible and its account of divine events in the eastern hemisphere.

Also scriptural for Mormons are Smith's *The Pearl of Great Price*, a book of revelations and translations, and *Doctrine and Covenants*, a collection of his revelatory declarations. General reflection is interspersed with guidance for particular circumstances in a manner reminiscent of the letters of Paul or certain *surahs* of the Qur'an.

Facing ridicule and persecution in New York, Smith led his followers westward. They established settlements in Ohio and Missouri, and, when driven out of Missouri in 1839, moved on to Nauvoo, Illinois. By now the Mormons were calling themselves the Church of Jesus Christ of Latter-day Saints. It was in Nauvoo that Smith secretly introduced "plural marriage" (polygamy), rumours of which added to the suspicions of outsiders. He also declared himself a candidate for the US presidency in the 1844 elections, advocating a blend of democracy and religious authority that he called "theodemocracy." Some of these innovations caused strife between factions of the Latter-day Saints, and in 1844 Smith and his brother were killed by an anti-Mormon mob.

A number of the traditionalist, anti-polygamy Mormons stayed in the Midwest as the Reorganized Church of Latter-day Saints, with headquarters in Independence, Missouri. In 2001 they renamed themselves the Community of Christ. Although they continue to regard the *Book of Mormon* and the *Doctrine and Covenants* as scripture, they emphasize the Bible and see their faith not as a "new religion" but as a branch of Christianity in the line running from the Hebrew prophets through Jesus to Joseph Smith.

The larger branch of the Mormons, the Church of Jesus Christ of Latter-day Saints, has a separate history. In 1847 many Mormons moved to Utah under the leadership of Brigham Young, who had been president of an inner council of 12 that Smith had organized on the pattern of the apostolic Church. Although they were unsuccessful in their bid to make Utah a Mormon state, they dominated the Utah Territory and the US government chose Young to serve as its governor.

Practice

The Mormon code of behaviour included not only a rigid sexual morality but strict abstinence from tea and coffee as well as alcohol and tobacco. Young adults are expected to serve as volunteer missionaries for two years—a practice that has helped spread awareness of the faith and attract new members around the world. Distinctive Mormon doctrines include the notion that God is increasing in perfection as human beings improve. Distinctive practices include the baptism (by proxy) of the deceased; because of this practice, Utah has become a world centre for genealogical research. Mormons have also taken a keen interest in archaeology, in the hope that physical evidence of the events described by the *Book of Mormon* will be found in the western hemisphere.

The controversial practice of plural marriage was officially dropped in 1890, after the federal government threatened to abolish it, and soon faded among mainstream LDS members. But a few congregations broke away to form independent sects known collectively as "Fundamentalist Mormons." The largest of these sects, the Fundamentalist Church of Jesus Christ of Latter-day Saints (FLDS), in particular is known for allowing its male leaders to have multiple wives. Because the women involved are often quite young, FLDS congregations have come under intense scrutiny. In 2007, FLDS leader Warren Jeffs was sentenced to 10 years in prison for being an accomplice to rape.

Whether the Mormons constitute a new religion or merely a new Christian denomination is open to question. Joseph Smith saw himself as reforming the Christian Church, and the fact that Mormons keep the Bible as scripture argues for inclusion under the umbrella of Christianity. On the other hand, the Mormons' new, post-scriptural revelations, new scriptures, and new modes of worship (e.g., using water rather than wine for the Eucharist) suggest a new religion. The issue came into focus during the lead-up to the 2000 federal election, when Massachusetts governor Mitt Romney was seeking nomination as the Republican candidate for president. Some conservative Christians who admired his strong family values were reluctant to support his candidacy because of his Mormon faith. However, in the 2012 presidential campaign, the Billy Graham Evangelistic Association removed Mormonism from its list of cults following a visit between Romney and Graham.

The Baha'i Faith

Baha'i developed out of Islam in the mid-nineteenth century, when Islam was already more than 1,200 years old. Although it has many elements in common with Islam, it gives those elements a new and more nearly universal configuration. The main point of divergence is that Baha'is believe that their leader, Baha'u'llah, was a new prophet, whereas Muslims believe there can never be another prophet after Muhammad.

The roots of Baha'i lie in the eschatology of Iranian Shi'ism. Ever since the last imam disappeared in 874, Twelver Shi'a had been waiting for a figure known as the **Bab** ("gateway") to appear and reopen communication with the hidden imam. After 10 centuries, most people no longer expected this to happen anytime soon. But seeds of messianic expectation germinated in the soil of political unrest.

Thus in 1844 Sayyid 'Ali Muhammad declared himself to be the Bab, the gateway to a new prophetic revelation. Although he was imprisoned in 1845, his followers, the Babis, repudiated the Islamic *shari'ah* law, and in 1848 the Bab proclaimed himself the hidden Imam. He was executed by a firing squad in 1850, but he left behind a number of writings that have been considered scriptural.

Baha'is have a major temple in every major region of the world. Architects are instructed to take their inspiration from the traditional culture and building styles of the region, while incorporating the number 9 (sacred to Baha'is) and formal gardens in the Iranian style. The temple above, in Haifa, Israel, is Middle Eastern in design. By contrast, the "Lotus temple" in New Delhi (featured in the chapter-opening photo) evokes the sacred flower that is a symbol of Indian culture (© E Simanor / Robert Harding World Imagery / Corbis).

The leadership momentum passed to Mirza Husayn 'Ali Nuri (1817–92), whose religious name was Baha'u'llah, "Glory of God." Although he had not met the Bab, he had experienced a profound feeling of divine support while imprisoned in Tehran in 1852. On his release the following year, he was banished, first to Baghdad in Turkish-controlled Iraq, where he became a spiritual leader of Babis in exile, and then, in 1863, to Istanbul. Before going, he declared himself to be "the one whom God shall manifest" as foretold by the Bab. He also claimed to have had a "transforming" 12-day mystical experience in 1862.

The transfer to the Mediterranean world expanded the sphere of Baha'u'llah's spiritual activity well beyond the horizons of Iranian Shi'ism. Now he was in a position to address the entire Ottoman Empire. Although he was banished to Acre in Palestine a few years later, his following continued to grow. Nearby Haifa (today in Israel) remains the world headquarters of the Baha'i faith today.

Baha'u'llah wrote prolifically in Acre, producing more than 100 texts that Baha'is believe to be God's revelation for this age. Among the most important are *Kitab-i Aqdas* ("The Most Holy Book," 1873), containing Baha'i laws; *Kitab-i Iqan* ("The Book of Certitude," 1861), the principal doctrinal work; and *Hidden Words* (1858), a discourse on ethics. *The Seven Valleys* (1856), a mystical treatise, enumerates seven spiritual stages: search, love, knowledge, unity, contentment, wonderment, and true poverty and absolute nothingness.

For 65 years after Baha'u'llah's death in 1892, authority was passed on to family heirs. His son 'Abbas Effendi was considered an infallible interpreter of his father's writings, and on his death the mantle of infallibility was bequeathed to his grandson, Shoghi Effendi Rabbani. Shoghi Effendi appointed an International Baha'i Council, and from 1963 leadership was vested in an elected body of representatives called the Universal House of Justice.

Baha'i teachings are based on Baha'u'llah's writings. The soul is believed to be eternal, a mystery that is independent both of the body and of space and time; it can never decay. Yet it becomes individuated at the moment of the human being's conception.

The Baha'i notion of prophethood is in line with the Abrahamic religions. Prophets are sent by God to diagnose spiritual and moral disorder and to prescribe the appropriate remedy. Baha'is, like Muslims, believe that the world has known a sequence of prophets. However, they do not believe the prophets' messages to have been community-specific: instead, they understand the prophets to speak to the entire world. They also believe that, in accordance with their doctrine of "progressive revelation," more prophets will come in future ages.

It may well be their ideal of world community that has done the most to make the Baha'i tradition attractive to serious searchers. Baha'u'llah himself wrote that he came to "unify the world," and Baha'is have asserted the unity of religions. Over a doorway to one Baha'i house of worship is the inscription, "All the Prophets of God proclaim the same Faith."

Baha'is actively advocate economic, sexual, and racial equality. Extremes of poverty and wealth are to be eliminated, and slavery rooted out—along with priesthood and monasticism. Women are to enjoy rights and opportunities equal to men's, marriage is to be strictly monogamous, and divorce is frowned on. Baha'is have consultative status with the United Nations as an official non-governmental organization. World peace is to be achieved through disarmament, democracy, and the rule of law, along with the promotion of international education and human rights. Although these goals are clearly compatible with modern secular values, they have a spiritual quality for Baha'is, who cite Baha'u'llah as saying that human well-being is unattainable until unity is firmly established.

Unity of the races is actively proclaimed, and interracial marriage welcomed. In recent decades this emphasis has been a major factor in the appeal of the Baha'i Faith to African-Americans. Once the US eliminates racism at home, some Baha'is claim, it will be the spiritual leader of the world.

Practice

Baha'is strive to live a peaceful and ethical life. Personal spiritual cultivation is encouraged, and recreational drugs and alcohol are forbidden. Since the Baha'i Faith sees itself as the fulfillment of other religions, Baha'is are unusually open to dialogue with other faiths.

Baha'is follow a distinctive calendar in which the number 19 (which figured in the tradition's early mystical thinking) plays an important role. Beginning with the spring equinox (the time of the Iranian new year), there are 19 months of 19 days each, with four additional days (five in leap years) to keep up with the solar year. Local Baha'is gather for a community feast on the first day of each month, and the final month, in early March, is devoted to dawn-to-dusk fasting, as in the Muslim observance of Ramadan.

Although the 19-day calendar does not recognize the seven-day week, many Baha'is in the West meet on Sundays for study and reflection. Important days in the annual cycle are essentially historical: several days in April and May are associated with Baha'u'llah's mission, for instance. In addition, the Bab's birth, mission, and martyrdom are commemorated, as are the birth and passing (or ascension) of Baha'u'llah.

Document

Baha'i Prayer

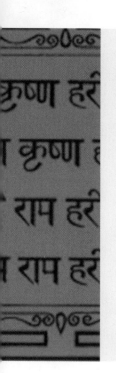

A prayer by 'Abdu'l-Bahá, reflecting the Baha'i belief that the oneness of humankind overrides any religious, racial, or national divisions.

Oh kind Lord! Thou Who art generous and merciful! We are the servants of Thy threshold and we are under the protection of Thy mercy. The Sun of Thy providence is shining upon all and the clouds of Thy mercy shower upon all. Thy gifts encompass all, Thy providence sustains all, Thy protection overshadows all and the glances of Thy favour illumine all. O Lord! Grant unto us Thine infinite bestowals and let Thy light of guidance shine. Illumine the eyes, make joyous the souls and confer a new spirit upon the hearts. Give them eternal life. Open the doors of Thy knowledge; let the light of faith shine. Unite and bring mankind into one shelter beneath the banner of Thy protection, so that they may become as waves of one sea, as leaves and branches of one tree, and may assemble beneath the shadow of the same tent. May they drink from the same fountain. May they be refreshed by the same breezes. May they obtain illumination from the same source of light and life. Thou art the Giver, the Merciful! (*Baha'i Prayers*, 1969: 43–4).

Baha'i devotions at the monthly feasts feature a cappella singing but no instrumental music. Prayers are spoken in Farsi (Persian), Arabic, or other languages. Readings are mainly from Baha'i scriptural writings by Baha'u'llah or the Bab, but they may be supplemented with devotional readings from other traditions. Those who grow up as Baha'is may make a personal profession of faith at the age of 15. Converts simply sign a declaration card. Baha'i weddings vary depending on the tastes of the couple, but always include the declaration "We will all, truly, abide by the will of God." At funerals there is a standard prayer for the departed, which is virtually the only prayer said in unison by Baha'is.

Personal devotions are similar to Islamic practice: the faithful wash their hands and face before praying, and set prayers are said at five times of the day. Also reminiscent of Islam is the practice of repeating the phrase *Allahu-'l Abha* ("God is the most glorious"). These similarities notwithstanding, the Baha'i faith has gone its own way. Its revelation does not conclude with the Qur'an, and its ideals for society depart from those reflected in the *shari'ah*. There have also been political tensions with Islam. Muslims have tended to see the Baha'is as Israeli sympathizers, and in Iran the Baha'i community suffered serious losses in lives and property after the Islamic revolution of 1979.

Since the late 1800s the Baha'i Faith has spread around the world. It now claims some 5 million adherents in 235 countries. These include 750,000 in North America and several times that number in India. More than one-quarter of local councils are in Africa and a similar number in Asia. There are nearly as many councils in the southwestern Pacific as in Europe.

The Nation of Islam

It is estimated that at least 20 per cent of the Africans taken as slaves to the Americas were Muslims. One early promoter of Islam (or a version of it) among African-Americans was Noble Drew Ali, who in 1913 founded the Moorish Science Temple of America in Newark, New Jersey. By the time of his death in 1929, major congregations had been established in cities including Chicago, Detroit, and Philadelphia.

Whether Wallace D. Fard (1893–1934?) was ever associated with the Temple is unclear; his followers say he wasn't. But the idea that Islam was the appropriate religion for African-Americans was in the air when he established the **Nation of Islam** (NOI) in Detroit in 1930. Fard's version of Islam bore little resemblance to either the Sunni or the Shi'i tradition. For Muslims, who understand Allah to be a purely spiritual entity, the most fundamental difference lay in the NOI's claim that Allah took human form in the person of Fard himself. These claims may have originated in Fard's first encounter with Elijah Poole (1897–1975), a young man who had felt called to a religious mission of some kind, but had stopped attending church before his fateful 1923 meeting with Fard. He later described the meeting:

> when I got to him I . . . told him that I recognized who he is and he held his head down close to my face and he said to me, "Yes, Brother." I said to him: "You are that one we read in the Bible that he would come in the last day under the name Jesus." . . . finally he said; "Yes, I am the one that you have been looking for in the last two thousand years" (quoted in Sahib 1951: 91–2).

Fard was so impressed with the young man—who later changed his name to Elijah Muhammad—that he authorized him to teach Islam with his blessing. Elijah quickly became Fard's favourite disciple.

The men who developed the theology of the Nation of Islam were more familiar with the Bible than the Qur'an, but the story they told was no more familiar to mainstream Christians than it was to Muslims. They maintained that all humans were originally black and lived in harmony as one tribe called Shabazz for millions of years, until an evil man named Yakub rebelled and left for an island where he created a white race by killing all dark babies. Eventually, the evil white race subjugated the blacks, bringing oppression and disunity to humankind. God sent Moses to try to redeem them, but that effort failed. Now the blacks needed to undergo a "resurrection" and recognize themselves as proud members of the great and peaceful Shabazz people.

Martha Lee has argued that the Nation of Islam is a millenarian movement (1996: 3). In the NOI version of history, white rule has lasted more than 6,000 years and is approaching the "end time," when the Mother of Planes—a huge aircraft base in the sky—will destroy the "white devils." The "Fall of America" is to be expected soon. (In fact, Elijah Muhammad originally prophesied that it would occur in the mid-1960s, but when that prediction failed to come true, NOI thinking about the "end time" became less literal.)

The NOI came to the attention of the authorities in Detroit when it was rumoured that Fard had promised life in heaven for anyone who killed four whites. This was probably not true, although he had preached that anyone who killed four devils would go to heaven. In any event, Fard disappeared after he was expelled from Detroit in 1933. Elijah Muhammad took over the leadership, but the movement fragmented, and some factions were quite hostile to him. In 1935, he moved to Washington, DC, where he preached under the name Elijah Rasool (Lee 1996: 26).

In 1942, however, he was convicted of sedition for counselling his followers not to register for the draft. His wife, Clara, directed the organization during the four years he spent in prison, and after his release in 1946 the NOI's numbers soon began to grow. Much of the credit for the movement's expansion in the 1950s has been given to a convert named Malcolm X.

Document

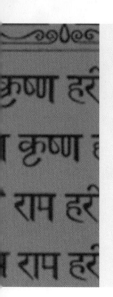

Elijah Muhammad on the True God and the Tribe of Shabazz

After criticizing the Christian concept of God as a "mystery," Elijah Muhammad writes that the true God is now "making Himself manifest":

He is not anymore a mystery . . . , but is known and can be seen and heard the earth over. This teaching of a mystery God enslaves the minds of the ignorant. My poor people are victims of every robbery. They are so pitifully blind, deaf and dumb that it hurts, but I am going to prove to them that Allah is with me. . . .

Allah (God) loves us, the so-called Negroes (Tribe of Shabazz), so that He will give lives for our sake today. Fear not, you are no more forsaken. God is in person, and stop looking for a dead Jesus for help, but pray to Him who Jesus prophesied would come after Him. He who is alive and not a spook (Muhammad 1997 [1965]: 3).

Malcolm X

Malcolm Little (1925–65) was born in Nebraska but spent much of his childhood in Lansing, Michigan. When he was six, his father was run over by a streetcar; the coroner ruled it a suicide, but the Little family believed he had been killed by a white supremacist group. After his father's death, the family was impoverished and his mother suffered a nervous breakdown, so the children were put in foster care. Eventually Malcolm moved to Boston and became involved with criminals. It was while he was serving time for theft that he was encouraged by his brother to join the NOI. He read widely, and after his release in 1952 became a key disciple of Elijah Muhammad. Like other converts at that time, he took the surname X to protest the absence of an African name and to recall the X branded on some slaves. Before long he had become the leader of the Harlem temple. His eloquence brought him national attention as an advocate for Black Power, and he came to symbolize black defiance of white racism in America.

Despite his success, however, Malcolm X became alienated from the movement. In 1964 he broke away from it and founded Muslim Mosque, Inc. Increasingly aware of the differences between NOI theology and that of traditional Islam, he converted to Sunni Islam and made the pilgrimage to Mecca, where he learned that Islam was not an exclusively black religion, as the NOI had taught. It was a life-changing experience. Changing his name to El Hajj Malik El-Shabazz, he began to teach an understanding of Islam as a religion for all races. Less than a year later, in February 1965, he was assassinated while giving a speech in New York. Three members of the NOI were convicted of the murder, although some people suspected that the FBI's Counter Intelligence Program had instigated it (Lee 1996: 44).

Wallace Muhammad

The early 1970s also saw a softening of the NOI's attitude towards whites and an increasing willingness to work with other black organizations. When Elijah Muhammad died in 1975, the leadership passed to his son Wallace, who moved the NOI closer to the mainstream and helped put the NOI on a more solid financial basis. He also renamed the temples, adopting the Arabic word for mosque, "masjid." This, together with a new emphasis on studying the Qur'an, brought the NOI into Sunni Islam. In 1975 Wallace renamed the organization the World Community of al-Islam in the West (WCIW), and in 1981 it became the American Muslim Mission. In 1985 the name was changed again to the American Society of Muslims. He also renamed himself, and as Warith Deen Muhammad (the inheritor of the religion of Muhammad) became a mainstream American Sunni leader until his death in 2008.

Louis Farrakhan

Not all members of the former NOI agreed with these reforms, however. Among the dissenters was Minister Louis Farrakhan. In 1978 he broke with WCIW and formed a new organization modelled on the NOI. He restored the original name, reinstituted the Saviour's Day festival—formerly the most important holiday—and attracted many members.

In 2001 a former member of the revived NOI published an account of his experience that was particularly critical of Farrakhan's financial dealings. According to Vibert L. White, Jr, members were pressured to donate large sums, and many struggling black-owned businesses were left with unpaid bills for their services to the organization, even as substantial amounts of money were finding their way to various members of the Farrakhan family (White 2001).

Farrakhan also appears to have courted African Muslim leaders, including Libya's Muammar Gadaffi, for support. Perhaps this helps to explain why he has moved the NOI towards the Islamic mainstream by encouraging Islamic-style daily prayers and study of the Qur'an. The most difficult change he made was to drop the doctrine that identified Fard as Allah and Elijah Muhammad as his Messenger. In a 1997 conference, Farrakhan publicly affirmed that Muhammad was the last and greatest prophet of Allah (Walker 2005: 495).

In 1995 Farrakhan organized a "Million Man March" on Washington, DC, to draw attention to the role of the black male and to unite for social and economic improvement. The March was a joint effort sponsored by many black organizations, and most of the participants had a Christian background. As the main organizer, however, Farrakhan set the agenda. Dennis Walker writes:

> The March was an Islamizing event. A range of Muslim sects were allowed to appear before the multitude and recite the Qur'an in Arabic on a basis of equality with the Christian and black Jewish clerics whom Farrakhan had inducted. It was a recognition in public space of Islam as part of the being of blacks that had had no precedent (Walker 2005: 508).

Although the March was criticized for excluding black women and promoting a Muslim agenda, as well as its lack of transparency in accounting, it did bring several African-American organizations into fuller cooperation and helped draw public attention to the challenges faced by African-Americans.

The Kabbalah Centre

The Kabbalah Centre in Los Angeles teaches a new form of spirituality based on traditional Jewish mysticism. As an organization, it traces its roots to a centre for **Kabbalah** studies founded in

Jerusalem in 1922 by Rabbi (or Rav) Yehuda Ashlag. But the tradition stretches back through the sixteenth-century master Isaac Luria to the (probably) thirteenth-century text called the *Zohar* and beyond. The Centre itself claims that its teachings go back some 4,000 years.

The National Institute for the Research of Kabbalah (later renamed the Kabbalah Centre) was founded in 1965 by Rabbi Philip S. Berg. Raised in New York City, he had trained as a rabbi but was not practising when, during a trip to Israel in 1962, he met Rabbi Yehuda Brandwein, the Kabbalist dean of a *yeshiva* in Jerusalem's Old City, and a descendant of many famous Hasidic scholars. With Brandwein as his mentor, Berg became an active Kabbalist.

Berg's followers claim that he succeeded Rabbi Brandwein as leader of the entire Kabbalah movement, including leadership of the Jerusalem yeshiva. At the yeshiva itself, however, Brandwein's son Rabbi Avraham Brandwein is considered the leader, and the version of Kabbalah taught there is in no way new.

In itself, Berg's Kabbalah is not new either, but his approach to it is radically different. Traditionally, the study of Kabbalah was restricted to mature male Jews, aged 40 or older, who had already completed years of Talmudic studies. Yet Berg taught Kabbalah to his secretary, who would later become his wife and a leading figure in the movement herself. Within a few years, the Bergs set out to make Kabbalah available to the world at large: young and old, male and female, Jews and Goyim alike. This was the new dimension of Berg's Kabbalah, and it sparked a great deal of controversy in traditional Jewish circles.

On its website the Centre defines Kabbalah as "ancient wisdom and practical tools for creating joy and lasting fulfillment now." The emphasis on "practical tools" is significant, for the purpose of Kabbalah study, as the Centre presents it, is to unlock the human potential for greatness. It is a fundamental tenet of Kabbalah (as it is of Eastern traditions such as Hinduism and Buddhism) that humans will be reincarnated over and over again, returning to this world as many times as necessary "until the task of transformation is done" (Kabbalah Centre).

Document

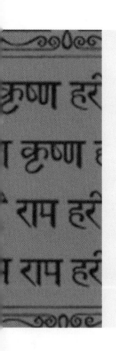

Kabbalah: Thoughts on God

God's only desire is to reveal unity through diversity. That is, to reveal that all reality is unique in all its levels and all its details, and nevertheless united in a fundamental oneness (Kabbalist Aharon Ha-Levi Horowitz, 1766–1828; in Levi 2009: 929).

The essence of divinity is found in every single thing—nothing but It exists. Since It causes everything to be, no thing can live by anything else. It enlivens them. *Ein Sof* exists in each existent. Do not say, 'This is a stone and not God.' God forbid! Rather all existence is God, and the stone is a thing pervaded by divinity (Moses Cordovero, 1522–70; in Levi 2009: 937).

Shards of Light are drawn out of the destructive entities that reside within my being. Their life force is cut off and I am then replenished with Divine energy. Life grows brighter each and every day as billions of sacred sparks return to my soul! ("Focus in Front").

Another fundamental principle is that the reality perceived by our five senses is only a tiny portion of the totality, and that events occurring in the knowable 1 per cent of reality are the product of events in the unknown 99 per cent. Berg's followers maintain that Kabbalah teachings give access to the larger reality that normally remains unknown.

Practice

Kabbalists experience God as the energy that underlies and permeates all things. To illustrate how God and the material world interrelate, Kabbalah uses a diagram usually referred to as the Tree of Life. The space above the tree represents God as *Ein Sof*, "The Endless." The tree itself pictures the ten ***spherot***, shining circles of fire, representing the ten attributes of God in the world. The topmost circle represents the Crown (*Keter* or *Kether*). Below it the other nine circles are arranged in three sets, each with a circle in the left, centre, and right columns. Read from the top down, these three sets represent the spiritual, intellectual, and material (earth-level) qualities of creation. The *spherot* in the right-hand column represent masculine attributes of God and those on the left feminine attributes. The *spherah* in the centre of the nine *spherot* is "Glory," which brings harmony and interconnectedness among the lower nine *spherot*. The 10 *spherot* are numbered from top to bottom, and are connected by 22 lines (corresponding to the 22 letters of the Hebrew alphabet) that show how they interact. In an interesting twist on most theological systems, Kabbalists believe that their practice facilitates the flow of divine energy into the world. Whereas mainstream Judaism, Christianity, and Islam stress the absolute power of God, in Kabbalah God needs human effort to work in the world.

Kabbalists do not attempt to interpret the Bible literally; instead, they use a complex kind of numerology. The ancient Hebrews used letters as numbers, assigning their numerical value according to their position in the 22-letter Hebrew alphabet. Totalling the numbers in certain words could reveal hidden connections between them and lead to new interpretations. For example the numerical values of YHWH, the name for God revealed to Moses, and *aleph*, the first letter of the alphabet, are both 26. For Kabbalists, this is significant because one of the words for Lord or Master in Hebrew, *aluph*, is based on the word *aleph*. Inspired by the numerological practices of ancient Kabbalah, modern Kabbalists maintain that determining the numerical value of one's name can lead to new insights.

One of those practices involves meditating on the 72 names for God, based on combinations of Hebrew letters that Kabbalah finds hidden in *Exodus* 14: 19–21, the biblical account in which Moses calls to God for help before leading the people into the sea as the Egyptian army pursues them. Kabbalists took these three verses, each having 72 letters in Hebrew, and developed 72 names of God by combining them into triads of three letters each. To get the first name, they took the first letter of verse 19,

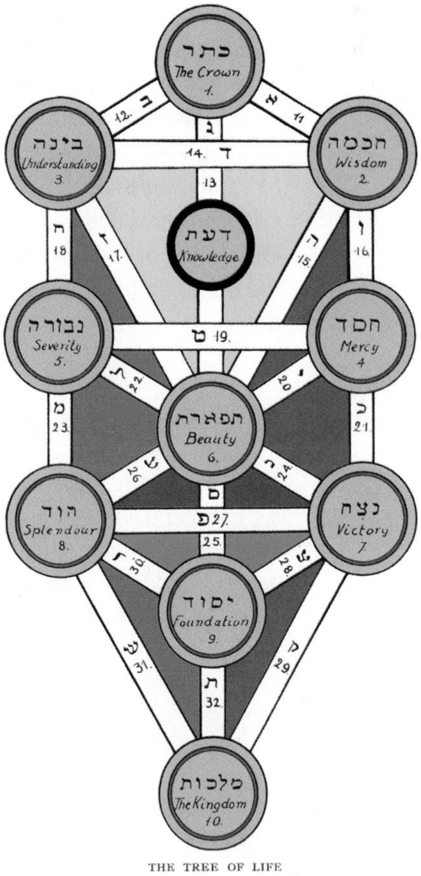

The Tree of Life (Mary Evans Picture Library / Alamy).

the last of verse 20, and the first of verse 21. The next name is composed of the second letter of verse 19, the second from last of verse 20, and the second of verse 21, and so on for a total of 72. These 72 names are then arranged in a grid with 8 columns and 9 rows. According to the Kabbalah Centre, the 72 Names of God "work as tuning forks to repair you on the soul level"; each three-letter sequence "act[s] like an index to specific, spiritual frequencies. By simply looking at the letters, as well as closing your eyes and visualizing them, you can connect with these frequencies" ("72 Names").

Traditional Kabbalah employs a dualistic symbolism of light and darkness, and many of the Centre's teachings focus on moving from darkness to light. For example, it stresses that instead of running away from adversaries, one should confront and learn from them, just as the biblical Jacob wrestled with the angel and gained light from the experience. Kabbalists see Jacob's angel as a personification of the personal darkness with which every individual must struggle in order to reach the light. Kabbalah practice helps to remove the darkness that covers the ego so as to reveal the light, the spark.

Like many other religious institutions, the Kabbalah Centre claims that its spiritual understanding fulfills other religions. In sharp contrast to most, however, it does not require its members to give up their former religious identities.

Like **Scientology** (see below), the Kabbalah Centre has benefitted from the media attention attracted by adherents such as Madonna, who has sometimes included references to Kabbalah in her lyrics (Huss 2005). At the same time, the large sums of money donated by celebrities have raised questions about the Centre's finances and accounting. Some Jews have accused the Centre of exploiting Kabbalah for worldly gain, which the Kabbalist tradition explicitly forbids. Other criticisms have focused on the Centre's claims linking worldly happiness with Kabbalah practice. One leader of the Centre in London, England, was heavily criticized for seeming to suggest that the 6 million Jews killed in the Holocaust died because they did not follow Kabbalah practices to unblock the light.

Religions Inspired by Other Forms of Spirituality

Not all new religions are offshoots of established mainstream religious traditions. We turn now to a selection of new religions deriving from unconventional sources. **Wicca** is a modern phenomenon inspired by pre-Christian European traditions, with a significant feminist component. Scientology and the **Raëlian Movement** draw on more secular sources, including science fiction and new forms of depth psychology. Finally, we will look at some spiritual manifestations of the **New Age** movement.

Wicca: The Witchcraft Revival

In the late Middle Ages, after centuries of condemning the remnants of "pagan" tradition in northern Europe as "witchcraft," the Roman Catholic Church mounted a systematic campaign to eradicate those remnants once and for all. Although accusations of witchcraft were frequent well into the 1700s, by the early twentieth century witchcraft was widely considered a thing of the past in industrialized societies.

Around the time of the Second World War, however, a movement emerged in England that claimed witchcraft to be the original religion of Britain and sought to revive it. The leading figures in this movement were two men, Gerald B. Gardner and Aleister Crowley, but women's interest increased after 1948, when Robert Graves published *The White Goddess*, a work on myth that posited a mother goddess in European prehistory. In 1953 Doreen Valiente wrote *The Book of Shadows*, a kind of a liturgical handbook for witchcraft.

The first modern use of the Old English word "Wicca" is attributed to Gardner in 1959. Within a few years, an Englishman named Alex Sanders, who claimed descent from witches in Wales, was attracting media attention to the movement; a 1969 film entitled *Legends of the Witches* was based on his writing. Sanders also initiated many witches who in turn founded covens (assemblies) in Great Britain and continental Europe, but it is a Gardner initiate named Ray Buckland who is credited with introducing Wicca to the United States. Soon people with no connection to the Gardner lineage were establishing covens, and the name Wicca was becoming known outside the "Craft" itself.

It is difficult to estimate the number of Wicca adherents. Canadian census data suggest that approximately 10,000 Canadians identified as Wicca in 2011. Assuming a similar ratio of Wicca to the whole population of the US would lead to an estimate of around 100,000 in 2011. The corresponding figures for those who identified as Pagan are around 15,000 in Canada and 150,000 in the US.

The Covenant of the Goddess, which was organized in California in 1975, is an umbrella organization representing many but not all covens. It is open to any Wicca coven that worships the goddess or ancient gods. It recognizes two levels of leadership (priestesses/priests and high priestesses/priests), and reports that approximately two-thirds of coven leaders are women.

The feminist movement had a major impact on Wicca in North America. Zsuzsanna Budapest established a female-only coven in 1971; her book *The Holy Book of Women's Mysteries* (1980) focuses on goddesses and rituals for women. Journalist Margot Adler became interested in the movement after listening to a tape sent by a witchcraft circle in Wales. Investigating other women's involvement in the Craft, she found that the visionary or aesthetic element played an important part, along with the mysteries of birth and growth, a concern for the natural environment, and particularly a sense of feminist empowerment. Feminism is also central to Starhawk (Miriam Simos), for whom the religion of the Goddess is the pulsating rhythm of life, and human sexuality a reflection of the fundamentally sexual nature of the Earth itself. At a lake high in the Sierra Nevada Mountains of California, she writes,

> it seems clear that earth is truly Her flesh and was formed by a sexual process: Her shakes and shudders and moans of pleasure, the orgasmic release of molten rock spewing forth in fiery eruptions, the slow caress of glaciers, like white hands gently smoothing all that has been left jagged (Starhawk 1982: 136).

In general, this kind of neopagan witchcraft seeks a return to primal nature and repudiates the classical Western religions that it holds responsible for repressing human sexuality. At the same time, its feminist emphasis challenges the patriarchal traditions of Judaism and Christianity. Although men can take an active part in it, Wicca is particularly empowering for women, and this has surely been part of its appeal.

Wiccans celebrate the winter solstice at Stonehenge (AP Photo / Matt Dunham / CP).

Practice

Wiccans celebrate as many as eight *sabbats* (festivals) during the annual cycle or "wheel of the year." Four have fixed dates: Candlemas (1 February), May Day (1 May), Lammas (1 August), and Hallowe'en (31 October). The other four mark the important days of the solar cycle: the Spring and Autumn equinoxes and the Fall and Winter solstices.

Although practices vary in their details, standard activities include healing rituals and celebration of important life-cycle events: birth, coming of age, marriage, death. Among the most important symbols are the circle, the four directions, and the four elements (earth, water, fire, air). Some of the rituals are symbolically sacrificial, paralleling (or parodying) the Christian Eucharist. Some covens announce upcoming services only by word of mouth and require that strangers be introduced by a trusted friend.

In 1993 members of the Covenant of the Goddess took part in the centennial World's Parliament of Religions in Chicago. In an age of interfaith acceptance, Wiccan priestesses and priests sought public and governmental recognition of their work as chaplains in hospitals, prisons, universities, and military units, but they could not provide any formal documentation of clerical training. To obtain the necessary credentials, some Wiccan leaders enrolled in Unitarian theological seminaries. Since then, the term "witch" has begun to be used to distinguish credentialled clergy (group leaders) from lay adherents.

Scientology

The Church of Scientology was founded in 1954 by L. Ron Hubbard (1911–86). Official biographies emphasize the breadth of his experience and learning. As a boy in Montana, for instance, he was exposed to the traditional teachings of the Blackfoot nation. In his youth he was introduced to Freudian psychology by a mentor who had trained with Freud and, travelling to Asia with his family, learned about a variety of ancient spiritual traditions. As an adult he not only became a prolific author in various genres, including science fiction, but served as a naval officer in the Second World War and, after being severely wounded, assisted his return to health by discovering how to remove deep-seated blocks in his mind. Following his recovery he began to advocate a new theory of what the soul does to the body. He called this theory **dianetics**, from the Greek *dia* (through) and *nous* (mind or soul).

Hubbard's 1950 book *Dianetics: The Modern Science of Mental Health* sold millions of copies. Soon followers were forming groups across the US, and in 1954 they became the first members of the Church of Scientology. The Church's official website defines Scientology—a word derived from the Latin *scio* (knowing) and the Greek *logos* (study)— as "knowing about knowing" and describes it as an "applied religious philosophy."

The Creed of Scientology begins with several generic statements about human rights, including freedom of expression, association, and religion. Reflecting Hubbard's belief that the underlying principle of all life forms is the drive to survive, it asserts that all humans have the right to defend themselves, and the duty to protect others. It also affirms that "the laws of God forbid" humans to destroy or enslave the souls of others, that the spirit alone can heal the body, and that the spirit can be saved.

Scientologists understand the universe to consist of eight intersecting planes or "dynamics," beginning with the self, the family, and so on at the bottom and moving up to the spiritual universe (the seventh dynamic) and the Supreme Being or Infinity (the eighth). The nature of the Infinity or God dynamic is not clearly defined, but it seems to have less in common with the "personal God" of Christianity, who knows, wills, and acts like a (super-) human person, than with "impersonal" principles or divinities such as the Dao of Daoism, the Brahman of the Hindu *Upanishads*, and the transcendent cosmic Buddha of some forms of Mahayana Buddhism.

Scientology uses the term "**thetan**" (pronounced "thay-tan") for the soul. Each thetan is thought to be billions of years old. Like the Atman of Hindu belief, the thetan is reincarnated, passing from one body to another at death.

Scientologists prefer to think of the movement as originating with its practitioners rather than with Hubbard himself. But he was its inspiration, he gave it direction from the first, and his writings and lectures constitute its religious literature. In a sense, the spread of Scientology began with the publication of *Dianetics* and its translation into numerous languages, even before the official founding of the Church in 1954. Various publications helped to spread Scientology to Britain and Europe. Today Scientologists have an organized presence in most countries.

As a strategy for spreading Scientology's influence, Hubbard decided to focus on high-profile celebrities. "Celebrity Centres" offering posh facilities for practice and training have attracted several celebrities, whose names have given the organization credibility.

Credibility was important because the movement was haunted by controversy. Several Scientologists, including Hubbard's wife, Mary Sue, were convicted of criminal activity involving the infiltration of various government agencies and theft in an effort to remove documents thought to reflect badly on the operation. L. Ron Hubbard was named as an unindicted co-conspirator (*United States vs Mary Sue Hubbard et al.*, 1979).

After Hubbard's death in 1986, the leadership passed to David Miscavige. As a boy, Miscavige had suffered from allergies and asthma, but was apparently cured following a dianetics training session. He joined Scientology in 1976, and within three years rose from a cameraman filming Hubbard to an executive role, restructuring the various divisions to comply with various laws and protect Hubbard from personal liability. After the trial, Mary Sue Hubbard resigned from her leadership role and a new division was created under the leadership of Miscavige, who was charged with protecting the integrity of Hubbard's teachings. He has served as the organization's paramount leader since 1986, although his role is that of an administrator rather than a spiritual leader.

As early as 1982, some dissenting followers of Hubbard were beginning to form alternative organizations outside the Church of Scientology. These "heretical" organizations are known collectively as the "Free Zone." The name comes from Hubbard himself, who claimed that planet Earth, under the galactic name Teegeeack, had been declared a "free zone" millions of years ago. In that context, "free" meant free of political or economic interference from other planets in the galaxy, but in the organizational context it meant free to follow the teachings of Hubbard without either payment to or interference from the Church of Scientology. The Church of Scientology tries to maintain exclusive rights to Hubbard's practices and refers to **Free Zoners** as "squirrels"—the equivalent of heretics. But the International Free Zone Association claims that it is the Free Zoners who are faithful to Hubbard's original teachings and practices.

Practice

In the 1960s Hubbard developed a step-by-step method for clearing the mind, or thetan, of mental blocks (called **engrams**) and restoring it to the ideal "Clear" state. Engrams are the result of traumatic experiences, and they remain with the thetan until they are cleared, even carrying over from one life to the next. In some ways they are comparable to bad karma in the religions of India. Hubbard's process for clearing engrams, called "auditing," involves the use of a device called an "**E-meter**," which is supposed to indicate when an engram blockage has been discovered in the mind. The E-meter (electro-psychometer) was originally developed by a polygraph expert named Volney Mathison, who had noticed that subjects tended to give readable responses to words that triggered unconscious as well as conscious thoughts. Mathison and Hubbard knew each other because they both wrote science fiction, and Hubbard began to use the "Mathison E-meter" in his dianetics practice. Although Mathison later distanced himself from Hubbard, the latter obtained a patent on a modified version of the device. The Hubbard E-meter is manufactured at the movement's California headquarters and sold to members for use in auditing.

Another important practice—the equivalent of scriptural study—is the study of Hubbard's thought and writings. Students are encouraged to continue this "training," striving to reach ever-higher levels. Progress can take years of expensive auditing. After sufficient progress has been made to "go Clear," advanced training begins. This phase introduces some of Hubbard's imaginative science-fiction concepts, among them the idea that an extraterrestrial named Xenu, the ruler of a galactic confederation, came to Teegeeack (Earth) 75 million years ago, bringing with him thousands of aliens who had tried to revolt against his leadership. He put these political prisoners around volcanoes in which he detonated H-bombs. Then he captured the souls of the dead, now known as Thetans, and implanted in them various ideas that we now associate with other religions.

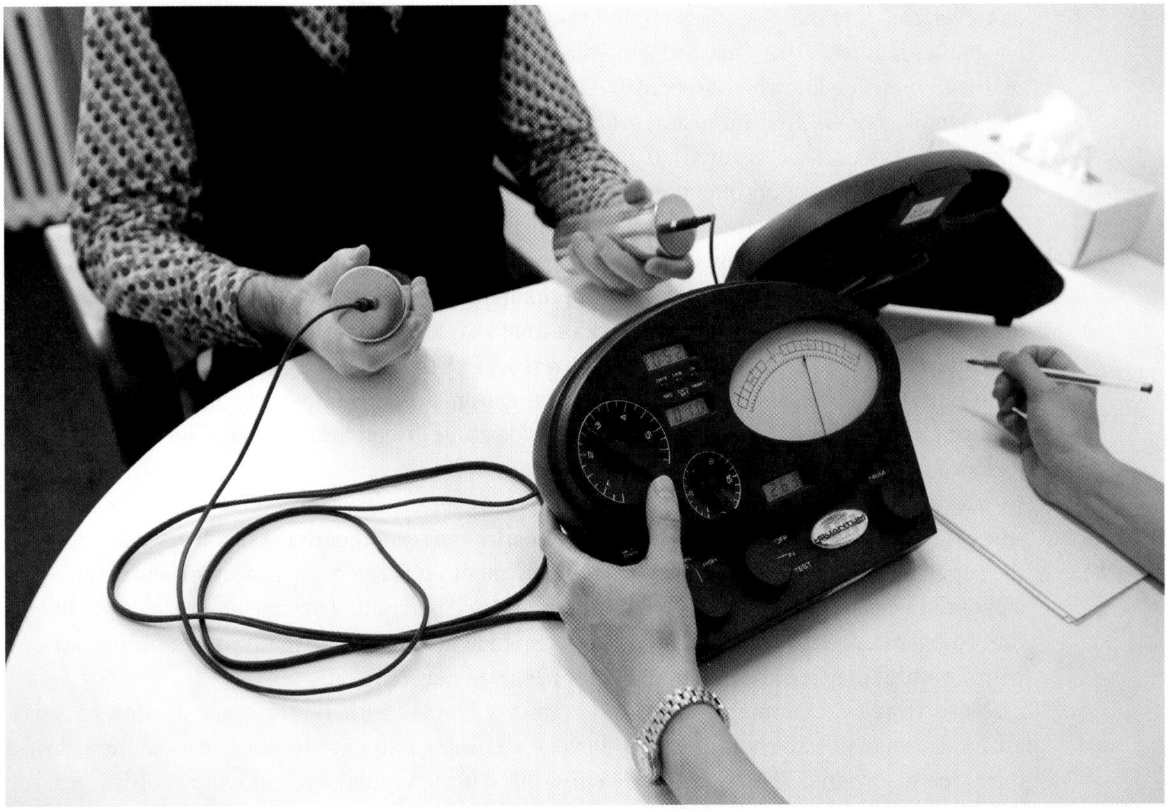

An E-meter auditing session at the Scientology Church in Zurich (© ALESSANDRO DELLA BELLA / Keystone / Corbis).

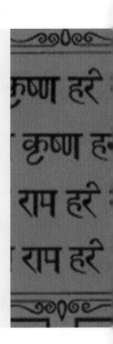

Document

L. Ron Hubbard on the Benefits of "Clearing"

A Clear can be tested for any and all psychoses, neuroses, compulsions and repressions (all aberrations) and can be examined for any autogenic (self-generated) diseases referred to as psychosomatic ills. These tests confirm the Clear to be entirely without such ills or aberrations. (Hubbard 1968: 13).

One of the incidental things which happen to a Clear is that his eyesight, if it had been bad . . ., generally improves markedly . . . (16).

Migraine headaches are psychosomatic and, with the others [arthritis, dermatitis, allergies, asthma, some coronary difficulties, eye trouble, bursitis, ulcers, sinusitis, etc.] are uniformly cured by Dianetic therapy. . . . Clears do not get colds (113).

A Clear . . . has complete recall of everything which has ever happened to him or anything he has ever studied (208).

However, traces of their essences remain to this day, and some of their souls accumulated on the few bodies that were left. They are known as "body thetans." Those who complete all seven levels of this training are known as Operating Thetans (OTs).

Scientologists try to minimize the formation of new engrams. Thus Scientologist women are encouraged (though not required) to give birth in silence, in order to minimize the trauma of birth and therefore the creation of engrams in the baby thetan. Gestures are used for communication between the mother and attendants, and the mother is urged to minimize her cries of pain. Since Scientology prohibits drugs, mothers are also encouraged to give birth without the aid of painkillers.

Scientology does not anticipate any form of divine judgment after death. Thus funeral services focus on celebrating the life of the deceased and wishing his or her thetan well in the next incarnation. After the funeral, friends and relatives of the deceased are encouraged to undergo auditing to rid themselves of the engrams resulting from grief. Scientologists may opt for cremation or burial. Hubbard was cremated, and before his death he discouraged the building of any elaborate memorials to him.

Scientology has come under intense public scrutiny and criticism for several reasons. Professional psychologists and other scientists are not sympathetic to the underlying claims of dianetics, and the fact that each level of training costs additional money has given rise to accusations that it is just a pyramid scheme designed to bilk money from the rich and gullible. Some observers have claimed that Hubbard once suggested to a meeting of science-fiction writers that, instead of writing for a penny a word, they could make millions by starting a new religion.

Marc Headley, a former Scientology employee, broke with the movement after 15 years, escaping on a motorcycle with security personnel chasing him until he crashed. Later he returned to rescue his Scientologist wife as well. In 2009 Headley published an exposé of his years in Scientology. In *Blown for Good: Behind the Iron Curtain of Scientology* he describes his early years as a child of Scientologists who sent him to Scientology schools whenever they could afford it. Eventually he took a job with the organization. Promoted to the headquarters where the tapes, E-meters, and other equipment were manufactured, he happened to be chosen as the subject on whom Tom Cruise would practise auditing. In an interview with *The Village Voice*, Headley explained that, as Cruise's trainee, he was instructed to tell inanimate objects such as bottles or ashtrays to move in a certain way; when they did not move, Headley was instructed to move the objects himself and then thank them for moving. The purpose of this exercise, according to Headley, was to rehabilitate the mind's ability to control things and be controlled (Ortega 2009). He also claimed that employees lived and worked in sub-standard conditions for little or no pay, and were not allowed to leave the premises. In Scientology circles, critics such as Headley are known as Suppressive Persons, or SPs.

Despite the controversies that surround it, Scientology has been recognized as a valid new religion in several countries, including South Africa, Spain, Portugal, and Sweden, and in the US it was granted tax-free status as a religious organization in 1993. The movement has had problems elsewhere, however, especially in France, where a number of Scientology leaders, including Hubbard himself in 1978, have been convicted of fraud, and the 2009 fraud conviction of the organization as a whole was upheld in 2013. Scientology now claims more than 12 million followers in over 100 countries. Critics who believe that number to be grossly exaggerated suggest that it is based on the numbers of people who have ever bought a Scientology book or taken a Scientology course since the movement's inception. Based on the quantities of E-meters and other supplies shipped during his time with the organization, Headley estimates that there were roughly 10,000 to 15,000 active Scientologists in the 1990s.

The Raëlian Movement

The Raëlian Movement traces its origins to a winter day in 1973 when a French journalist and racing enthusiast named Claude Vorilhon impulsively decided to drive to the site of an old volcano where he had enjoyed family picnics in the past. There he saw a small flying saucer hovering near the ground. An extraterrestrial creature—approximately 1.2 metres (4 feet) tall and resembling a bearded human with a greenish skin tone—walked over and spoke to Vorilhon in French. In the course of this and subsequent encounters, the alien, whom Vorilhon came to know as Yahweh, recounted details of Vorilhon's own life and explained that he used telepathy to draw the Frenchman to this spot. Yahweh invited him inside the spaceship and told him that all life on Earth was originally created in a laboratory by aliens called Elohim—the plural form of the word for a god in biblical Hebrew (*eloh*), frequently used in the Torah to refer to the one God. The International Raëlian Movement translates "Elohim" as "those who came from the sky," replacing the traditional idea of creation by a deity with creation by sky people.

Yahweh explained that a few weeks earlier he had used telepathy to urge Vorilhon to refresh his memory of the book of Genesis because he wanted to talk to him about it; now Vorilhon understood why he had recently, for no apparent reason, purchased a Bible and started to read it. The alien interpreted the reference to God's creation of heaven and earth (in Genesis 1: 1) as a reference to the aliens "from the sky," and the verse saying that the spirit of God moved over the face of the earth (Genesis 1: 2) as a reference to the alien spacecraft. Yahweh said that a "day" in the context of the six days of creation was equal to 2,000 Earth years, and that the aliens had used advanced scientific techniques to create the first plants and animals in such a way that they would be able to reproduce themselves thereafter.

Despite minor differences in physical appearance (the result of differences in the methods used by the various teams that created each group), the humans were formed "in the image of" the Elohim themselves. But this alarmed the Elohim on the home planet, who feared that humans might someday travel there and cause trouble. Therefore it was decided to keep humans' scientific knowledge at a primitive level. However, the team of scientists working in what is now Israel had created an unusually intelligent group of humans, and wanted to give them greater scientific knowledge. That team, Yahweh explained, was the "serpent" that tempted Eve, and the "Garden" from which Adam and Eve were expelled was in fact the laboratory of the Elohim. The story of Noah and the flood in Genesis 7 is also given a novel twist. In the Raëlian interpretation, the flood is the result of nuclear explosions set off by the Elohim on the home planet who fear that humans have been given too much knowledge, and Noah thwarts their plan by taking cells of each creature aboard an orbiting satellite. Then, after the flood, Noah waits for the nuclear fallout to settle before returning to Earth with a cargo that includes a pair of humans from each of the races created by the Elohim scientists.

The biblical story of the Tower of Babel gets a new interpretation as well. Traditionally, the great Tower was a symbol of arrogance, which God punished by making humans (who until then had all spoken the same language) unable to understand one another. In the alien's account, the "Tower of Babel" is the name of a spaceship built by the Hebrews in partnership with the Elohim scientists who had been banished to Earth for making humans too intelligent. This project so alarms the Elohim on the home planet that they thwart the progress of human science by scattering the Hebrews throughout the world. The cities of Sodom and Gomorrah are destroyed not by fire, in punishment for sexual sin, but by nuclear explosion, in response to the threat posed to the home planet by scientific progress on Earth. And God's order that Abraham sacrifice his son is translated into a test by the Elohim to see if the leader of the Hebrew scientists was still loyal to them. The New Testament gets some novel interpretations as well: for example, the resurrection of Jesus is attributed to cloning.

Yahweh told Vorilhon that he had been chosen to receive the truth because he had a Jewish father and a Catholic mother, and was a free-thinking opponent of traditional religion. As a result of his UFO encounter, Vorilhon was told to change his name to Raël, "messenger of the Elohim." Feeling called to prophecy, he was told to write down the message in book form, and to spread the word in anticipation of the Elohim's return.

Two years after his initial encounter, Raël says, he was transported to the planet of the Elohim, where he received further instruction and met with past religious leaders. He wrote an account of the visit in his book *They Took Me to Their Planet*.

In 1974 Raël called a press conference in Paris, at which he introduced his movement to the media. By 1980 the International Raëlian Movement had taken on most of the features of an organized religion: scripture, rituals, festival days, a communal building. It is organized hierarchically on the model of the Roman Catholic Church, with Raël himself at the pinnacle, like a pope, and lesser officials with titles such as Bishop Guide and Priest Guide. Susan Jean Palmer (1995) notes that although the movement advocates gender equality and is libertarian about sexuality and gender roles, women are not well represented in the leadership hierarchy, especially at the upper levels.

The leadership hierarchy may reflect Roman Catholicism, but the Raëlian cosmology is nothing like that of traditional Christianity. Not only does it reject belief in gods of any kind, but it teaches that the whole of the observable universe is just a small atom of a larger structure, which is itself part of a larger one, and so on infinitely. At the same time every atom is itself a universe on the next smaller scale, with structures descending in size infinitely. Time and space are infinite in this cosmos, which runs on scientific principles without any need for divine command or intervention.

The Elohim are expected to return by 2035, but only on condition that humans are ready to welcome them, have tolerance for one another, and respect the environment. The Movement hopes one day to create an "embassy" (ideally in Israel) where the Elohim can interact with humans.

Raëlians reject the theory of evolution. Instead, they believe that the Elohim brought all life to Earth from another planet 25,000 years ago, and that we earthlings in turn may someday take life to another planet. The term "Intelligent Design," which some conservative Christians have promoted as an alternative to Darwinian evolution, has been adopted by Raëlians. But whereas for conservative Christians Intelligent Design is a way to get God and creationism back into the post-Darwinian picture, for Raëlians the term represents a third option for those who, like themselves, reject both evolution and creation by a god. In a postscript to his book *Intelligent Design: Message from the Designers*, Raël calls his approach a Third Way, between Darwin and Genesis. The Raëlian symbol is a swastika inside a six-pointed star that is said to be based on a design of interlocking triangles that Raël saw on the UFO. In fact, though, it seems identical to the Jewish Star of David. Raëlians claim that their swastika has nothing to do with Nazism, and point out that for thousands of years it was a symbol of good luck and prosperity used in religious traditions such as Buddhism and Jainism. They say that the symbol as a whole reflects the Raëlian belief that the universe is cyclical, without beginning or end.

Practice

Becoming a Raëlian involves two ceremonies. First, initiates must renounce all ties to theistic religions. This "Act of Apostasy" is followed by a baptismal ceremony in which information about the initiate's DNA is supposedly transmitted to the Elohim.

Raëlians practise a spiritual technique that Raël learned from the Elohim. "Sensual meditation" or "meditation of all senses," involves turning inward to experience the lesser universes within the atoms of one's own body, and then turning outward to experience the greater universes beyond our own; eventually, the most adept will be able to visualize the planet of the Elohim. The goal is to awaken spiritual potential by first awakening the physical sensibilities.

There are four Raëlian holidays: the first Sunday in April, celebrated as the day the Elohim created Adam and Eve; 6 August, the day of the Hiroshima bombing, which for Raëlians is the

Raël with a full-scale model of the spaceship he encountered in 1973 (© Clonaid / epa / Corbis).

beginning of the Apocalypse; 7 October, the date that Raël met with Jesus, Buddha, and other past prophets aboard a spaceship during the second encounter; and 13 December, the day when Raël first encountered the Elohim.

Raëlians are expected to avoid mind-altering drugs, coffee, and tobacco, and to use alcohol either in moderation or not at all. They celebrate sensuality, advocate free love, and discourage traditional marriage contracts. The movement's liberal policy regarding marriage and sexual partners has made it an attractive religious home for gays and lesbians.

As part of his effort to free humans from traditional religions, Raël has called for a massive "de-baptism" campaign across Africa or (as he calls it) the United Kingdom of Kama. He argues that "spiritual decolonization" is a prerequisite for future development. Raelians also denounce the practice of clitorectomy, which is common in some parts of Africa, and have raised funds to pay for restorative surgery.

Although Raëlians reject the concept of the soul, they believe that a kind of everlasting life can be attained through cloning. Clonaid, a Raëlian cloning enterprise founded in France in 1997, has announced the births of several cloned babies; however, none of these claims have been substantiated.

Because Raëlians do not believe in gods, their movement is not classified as a religion. But it does recognize religious leaders such as Jesus and Buddha as prophets inspired by the Elohim to communicate as much of the truth as humans were able to absorb in their time. Raël himself is identified with Maitreya, the future Buddha, although Buddhists themselves reject this idea.

Just as Christianity sees itself as completing Judaism, and Islam sees Muhammad as the "seal of the prophets," Raëlians see their movement as the culmination of earlier religions, which incorrectly understood the role of the Elohim. According to Raël, the Elohim say that only 4 per cent of humans are advanced enough to understand the truth about them, so it is not surprising that his movement has not made converts by the millions. Nevertheless, it claims more than 65,000 members in 84 countries.

The New Age Movement

The expression "New Age" has had many connotations. For nineteenth-century millenarian Christian movements (among them the Jehovah's Witnesses), which looked forward to the literal fulfillment of the apocalyptic prophecies in the biblical books of Daniel and Revelation, the term referred to the end time when the Kingdom of God would be established on Earth. For the Nation of Islam, by contrast, the "new age" was the time when African-Americans would emerge strong and triumphant.

The term "New Age" was in use as early as 1907 as the title of a progressive British political and literary journal that introduced its readers to topics such as Freudian psychoanalysis. But the "consciousness revolution" of the 1960s brought expectations of a different sort of "new age." The transpersonal psychology movement, for instance, emphasized spiritual insights and therapeutic techniques that were diametrically opposed to the mechanistic approach of orthodox Freudianism. One centre of transpersonal psychology was the Esalen Institute in Big Sur, California, founded in 1962, which offered seminars, workshops, and encounter groups.

To some, the idea of the Age of Aquarius popularized in the 1967 musical *Hair!* meant the advent of a universal religion to replace the Christianity of the Piscean age. To others, it meant little more than freely available music or drugs. Those varied expectations came together in 1969, when as many as half a million young people congregated in a farmer's field near Woodstock, New York. By the late 1980s, "New Age" had become a kind of shorthand for a variety of self-help practices promising spiritual insight, worldly success, physical healing, and psychological peace.

Scholars looking for the historical roots of New Age spirituality often point to Emanuel Swedenborg, an eighteenth-century Swedish mystic who wrote about the evolution of the human soul; the nineteenth-century American Transcendentalist Ralph Waldo Emerson; or the Russian founder of the Theosophical movement, Helena P. Blavatsky, who claimed to have discovered the wisdom of the ages in Asian teachings such as Hindu Vedanta. Those looking for antecedents of New Age therapeutic techniques often point to the Swiss physician Paracelsus (1493–1541), who claimed that humans were subject to the magnetism of the universe. Two centuries later, the German physician Franz Anton Mesmer postulated that healing takes place through a kind of magnetism in bodily fluids, analogous to ocean tides, which he sought to manipulate with magnets or the wave of a wand or a finger. The effort to direct their flow, called mesmerism, was reflected in the development of hypnosis. As for what New Agers call "channelling," it can be traced back at least as far as the nineteenth-century séance, in which the bereaved sought to make contact with their deceased loved ones through a "spirit medium." Together these practices opened the way for subjects that had been left on the sidelines of a scientific and technological age—astrology, hypnosis, alternative healing—to enter the mainstream. All these could be seen as alternatives to orthodox religion, medicine, and society generally, and perhaps also to the exclusivist claims made by mainstream orthodoxies.

If any of the metaphysical and therapeutic resources sketched so far had connections with the major Western religious traditions, they were marginal at best. So how did the New Age movement come to be so closely associated with religion? At least part of the answer can be found in its connections with Eastern religious traditions.

A prominent feature of the 1960s was a fascination with the depths of awareness that Hindu yoga and Japanese Zen Buddhism in particular were believed to offer. The *Yijing* (or *I Ching*), an ancient Chinese divination manual, became a bestseller, and many people were introduced to Eastern religious symbolism through the writings of the Swiss psychologist Carl G. Jung and the Jungian comparative-religion scholar Joseph Campbell. "Exotic" religions seemed to offer something that the familiar Western traditions did not.

Across North America and Europe, people explored Chinese *qigong* and acupuncture, Indian yoga and ayurvedic medicine, and Buddhist meditation techniques. In India, Maharishi Mahesh Yogi's Transcendental Meditation movement attracted high-profile devotees, including the Beatles, Mia Farrow, and Clint Eastwood. Deepak Chopra, an endocrinologist practising in the West, returned to his native India to explore traditional ayurvedic medicine and found it compatible with modern Western medicine. The Thailand-born and Western-educated Chinese master Mantak Chia, working in New York, has written extensively on the potential of Daoist techniques for healing and sexual energy. And the list goes on.

The New Age movement is open to many possibilities, including female leadership. In this respect it stands in sharp contrast to the male-dominated structures of the established religions and professions. This may constitute one of its lasting contributions.

Is there any single word that sums up the spirit of the New Age? One candidate would be "holistic." Implying a quest for wholeness, sometimes with an overtone of holiness, it was coined in the context of evolutionary biology to refer to the whole as something more than the sum of its parts. Thus holistic diets and therapies seek to treat the whole person, body and mind, and holistic principles are fundamental to the ecological movement; the Gaia hypothesis, for instance, sees the Earth as a single organism whose survival depends on the interaction of all its components (a perspective central to James Cameron's film *Avatar*). New ages yet to come are bound to view ecological holism as an increasingly urgent goal.

Summary

The new religions we have discussed cover the spiritual landscape, from East to West to outer space. None of them is seriously challenging the traditional religions for influence. Some seem to have already peaked in numbers, at least in North America. Since new religious movements typically need strong, charismatic leaders, most have trouble sustaining themselves after their founders have left or died. But others are still making significant gains in numbers, wealth, and influence.

The few new religions that survive and prosper will eventually become established as normal parts of the religious landscape, as "religions" without the "new." Judaism, Christianity, and Islam made this transition long ago. The Baha'i Faith and the Mormons have made it more recently. Which, if any, of the new religions that emerged in the late twentieth century will survive into the twenty-second is impossible to tell from this vantage point, but is surely an interesting topic for debate.

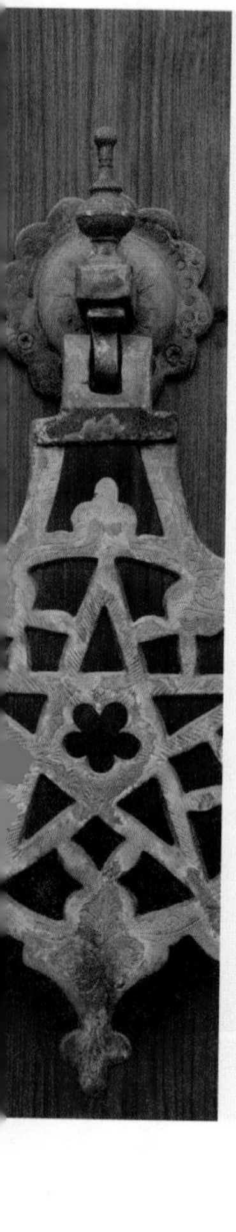

Sites

Baha'i Temple, Wilmette, Illinois

The Baha'i Temple for North America, located just north of Chicago, is a nine-sided building—nine being a sacred number to Baha'is—set in a beautiful park. It is open to the public.

Kabbalah Centre, Los Angeles

The Kabbalah Centre of Los Angeles offers classes, a bookstore and related activities, as well as an online university. There are affiliated Centres in many other large US cities, as well as Toronto and worldwide.

New Vrindaban, West Virginia

Located in a rural area near Moundsville, New Vrindaban is an ISKCON community named after Vrindaban, India—a place associated with Krishna. Its temple was constructed using traditional Indian tools and techniques and (like most Hare Krishna temples) includes a vegetarian restaurant that is open to the public. The community grows its own organic food.

Soka University of America, Orange County, California

Founded by Soka Gakkai International, Soka University of America is located atop a hill with a beautiful view overlooking mountains and the Pacific Ocean in Orange County, California. Although affiliated with Soka Gakkai, the university welcomes students from all backgrounds.

Temple Square, Salt Lake City, Utah

The Tabernacle. Family History Library, Salt Lake Temple, and other Mormon-related museums are open to the public. The Tabernacle, renowned for its acoustics and architecture, is home to the famous Mormon Tabernacle Choir.

Sacred Texts

Religion	Texts	Composition/ Compilation	Compilation/ Revision	Use
Soka Gakkai	The *Lotus Sutra*	Probably composed in the early 1st century CE; considered the highest expression of Mahayana thought	Supplemented by writings of Nichiren and modern leaders	Read and chanted; the phrase "Homage to the Lotus Sutra" is chanted as a mantra
Falun Dafa (Falun Gong)	*Falun Gong* by Li Hongzhi	First published in 1993. Li's works have been translated into most major languages	The English translation has been revised several times	Li's books and videos are used as guides to practice
ISKCON ("Hare Krishnas")	*Srimad Bhagavatam*, *Bhagavad Gita*, and other Krishna-centred devotional texts	Ancient Hindu texts of debatable date, now available in English and other major languages	Commentaries by Swami Prabhupada	Studied and chanted during puja
LDS (Mormons)	The Bible, plus Smith's *The Book of Mormon*, *Doctrine and Covenants*, and *The Pearl of Great Price*	*The Book of Mormon* was published in 1830. *Doctrine and Covenants* (selected writings) in 1835; *The Pearl of Great Price* was compiled by F.D. Richards and published in England in 1851	All three texts have been revised at various times	Used in worship and for life guidance
Baha'i	*The Most Holy Book*, *The Book of Certitude*, *Hidden Words*, and *The Seven Valleys*	Written by Baha'u'llah between 1856 and 1873	Edited by 20th-century Baha'i leaders	The *Most Holy Book* is used as a source of legal guidance, The *Book of Certitude* for doctrine, *Hidden Words* for ethical guidance, and *Seven Valleys* for mystical guidance
Nation of Islam	The Qur'an, plus Elijah Muhammad's *Fall of America* and *Message to the Blackman*	Elijah Muhammad's works date from the 1950s and '60s	Louis Farrakhan's *A Torchlight for America* (1993)	The Qur'an is studied, recited and used in Sunni services, along with *Muslim Daily Prayers*
Kabbalah Centre	Hebrew Bible, The Zohar	The Kabbalah Centre attributes the Zohar to Rav Shimon Bar Yochai rather than Moses de Léon	The Bible is interpreted through numerology and the 72 names of God	Spiritual practices of Zohar and related approaches are used to guide daily life
Wicca	Important early works include Graves' *The White Goddess* (1948) and *The Book of Shadows* (c. 1950)	Other publications added a feminist emphasis, such as *The Holy Book of Women's Mysteries*	Newer writers such as Starhawk have popularized the movement	Used in rituals and sabbats

Continued

Sacred Texts (Continued)

Religion	Texts	Composition/ Compilation	Compilation/ Revision	Use
Scientology	Hubbard's *Dianetics: The Modern Science of Mental Health* and *Scientology: The Fundamentals of Thought*	1950s		Used in "auditing" process
Raëlian Movement	*Intelligent Design: Message from the Designers*	Published in 2005: a compilation of Raël's publications from the 1970s–80s	Other texts include *The Maitreyya* and *Sensual Meditation*	Teachings are studied and used as guidance for sensual meditation practice

Discussion Questions

1. What kinds of social and economic factors may contribute to the rise of new religious movements?
2. Why is the line between a "cult" and a "religion" so difficult to define?
3. Why do Eastern religions appeal so strongly to many people in the West?
4. Do all "religions" have to involve belief in deities?
5. Can a set of beliefs and practices centred on extraterrestrial aliens be considered a "religion"?
6. What do you think are some of the factors that might attract some people to new religious movements?
7. How do new religious movements gain acceptance?
8. How do new religious movements tend to change over time?

Glossary

Bab The individual expected to appear as the "Gateway" to the new prophet in the **Baha'i Faith**.

Baha'i Faith The religious tradition of those who call themselves Baha'i, meaning "adherents of Baha ('u 'llah)."

bhakti Devotional faith, the favoured spiritual path in ISKCON.

Church of Jesus Christ of Latter-day Saints The formal name of the largest Mormon organization, abbreviated as "LDS."

cult Term for a new religion, typically demanding loyalty to a charismatic leader.

dianetics L. Ron Hubbard's term for the system he developed to clear mental blocks.

E-meter A device used in **Scientology** to detect mental blocks.

engrams The term for mental blocks in **Scientology**.

Falun Dafa The "law wheel" said to be acquired through Dafa practice.

Free Zoners Individuals or groups teaching Hubbard's thought independently of Scientology International.

Hare Krishnas Informal name for the members of **ISKCON**, based on their chant.

ISKCON International Society for Krishna Consciousness.

Kabbalah Traditional Jewish mysticism.

Komeito A Japanese political party loosely associated with **Soka Gakkai**.

Mormons Another name for members of the **Church of Jesus Christ of Latter-day Saints**.

millenarian Term used to refer to the belief that the current social order will soon come to an end.

Nation of Islam (NOI) An African-American movement that originated in Detroit in 1930. Its practice of Islam has become more aligned with the Sunni tradition in recent years.

New Age A vague term embracing a diversity of religious or spiritual movements providing alternatives to mainstream Western religions.

qi (or **chi**) Spiritual energy.

qigong Exercises to cultivate ***qi***.

Raëlian Movement A new religion originating in France in the 1970s, based on the belief that an alien revealed previously unknown information about the creation of life on Earth to a man named Raël.

Scientology A new religion devoted to clearing mental blockages; founded by L. Ron Hubbard.

sect A sociological term for a group that breaks away from the main religion.

Soka Gakkai A lay movement that originated in the 1930s among Japanese adherents of Pure Land Buddhism; now an independent new religion teaching the power of chanting homage to the *Lotus Sutra*.

spherot The 10 attributes of God in **Kabbalah**.

thetan Term for the soul or mind in **Scientology**.

Vaishnava A Hindu who worships Vishnu and related deities.

Wicca A name for witchcraft or the Craft.

Further Reading

Baha'u'llah. 1952. ***Gleanings from the Writings of Baha'u'llah*, rev. edn. Wilmette, IL: Baha'i Publishing Trust.** A good selection of Baha'i writings.

Barrett, David V. 2003. ***The New Believers: A Survey of Sects, Cults and Alternative Religions*. London: Octopus Publishing Group.** A good place to start on the topic of cults versus new religions.

Dan, Joseph. 2005. ***Kabbalah: A Very Short Introduction*. Oxford: Oxford University Press.** A useful introduction.

Drew, A. J. 2003. ***The Wiccan Bible: Exploring the Mysteries of the Craft from Birth to Summerland*. Franklin, NJ: Career Press.** An overview of Wicca.

Esslemont, John E. 1979. ***Bahá'u'lláh and the New Era: An Introduction to the Bahá'í Faith*. 4th edn. Wilmette, IL: Baha'i Publishing Trust.** The standard survey recommended by Baha'is.

Gallagher, Eugene V., William M. Ashcraft, and W. Michael Ashcraft, eds. 2006. ***An Introduction to New and Alternative Religions in America*. 5 vols. Westport: Greenwood Press.** Scholarly introductions to religious movements from colonial era to the present.

Headley, Marc. 2009. ***Blown for Good: Behind the Iron Curtain of Scientology*. Burbank: BFG Books.** The autobiography of a former Scientologist turned critic.

Hubbard, L. Ron. 1956. ***Scientology: The Fundamentals of Thought*. 2007. Los Angeles: Bridge Publications.** The basic introduction, by Scientology's founder.

Lewis, James R., and J. Gordon Melton, eds. 1992. ***Perspectives on the New Age*. Albany: State University of New York Press.** One of the best assessments of the New Age phenomenon.

Li Hongzhi. 2000. ***Falun Gong*. 3rd edn. New York: University Publishing Co.** Master Li's introduction to Falun Dafa.

Miller, William McElwee. 1974. ***The Baha'i Faith: Its History and Teachings*. Pasadena: William Carey Library.** An outsider's view of Bahai.

Muster, Nori J. 2001. ***Betrayal of the Spirit: My Life behind the Headlines of the Hare Krishna Movement*. Champaign: University of Illinois Press.** A former member's critical view of ISKCON.

Ostling, Richard, and Joan K. Ostling. 2007. ***Mormon America—Revised and Updated Edition: The Power and the Promise*. New York: HarperOne.** An overview of the issues.

Porter, Noah. 2003. ***Falun Gong in the United States: An Ethnographic Study*. N.p.: Dissertation.Com.** Argues against the "cult" label based on interviews and publications.

Seager, Richard H. 2006. ***Encountering the Dharma: Daisaku Ikeda, Soka Gakkai, and the Globalization of Buddhist Humanism*. Berkeley: University of California Press.** A scholarly overview.

Shinn, Larry D. 1987. ***The Dark Lord: Cult Images and the Hare Krishnas in America*. Philadelphia: Westminster Press.** An objective account, based on extensive interviews.

Starhawk. 1982. ***Dreaming the Dark*. Boston: Beacon Press.** One of many works by an important Wicca leader.

White, Vibert L., Jr. 2001. ***Inside the Nation of Islam: A Historical and Personal Testimony by a Black Muslim*. Gainesville: University Press of Florida.** Particularly interesting because the author was involved both in the NOI and in the organization of the 1995 March.

Wright, Lawrence. 2013. ***Going Clear: Scientology, Hollywood, and the Prison of Belief*. New York: Alfred A. Knopf.** A balanced but critical overview of Scientology, its leaders, and its celebrity followers.

Recommended Websites

www.bahai.org
Site of the Baha'i religion.

www.falundafa.org
Site of Falun Dafa.

www.finalcall.com
News site of the Nation of Islam.

www.internationfreezone.net
Portal for the Free Zoner alternative to Scientology.

www.iskcon.org
Site of the International Society for Krishna Consciousness.

www.kabbalah.com
Site of the Kabbalah Centre International.

www.lds.org
Site of the Church of Jesus Christ of Latter-day Saints, the Mormons.

www.komei.or.jp
Site of the New Komeito party, loosely affiliated with Soka Gakkai.

www.rael.org
Site of the International Raëlian Movement.

www.scientology.org
Site of the international Scientology organization.

www.sgi.org
Site of Soka Gakkai International.

www.wicca.org
Site of the Church and School of Wicca.

References

Amnesty International. "Human Rights in China." Accessed 10 March 2010 at www.amnesty.ca/ blog2.php?blog=keep_the_promise_2&page=7.

Book of Mormon, The. 1961. Salt Lake City: The Church of Jesus Christ of Latter-day Saints.

Dawson, Lorne L. 2006. *Comprehending Cults: The Sociology of New Religious Movements*. Toronto: Oxford University Press.

Erlanger, Steven. 2009. "French Branch of Scientology Convicted of Fraud." *New York Times*. Accessed 10 March 2010 at www.nytimes.com/2009/10/28/world/europe/28france.html? _r=1.

"Focus in Front." Accessed 10 March 2010 at www.kabbalah.com/newsletters/weekly-consciousness-tune-ups/focus-front.

Hubbard, L. Ron. 1968. *Dianetics: The Modern Science of Mental Health*. Los Angeles: Bridge Publications.

Huss, Boaz. 2005. "All You Need is LAV: Madonna and Postmodern Kabbalah." *Jewish Quarterly Review* 95, 4: 611–24.

Ikeda, Daisaku. 2008. "Toward Humanitarian Competition: A New Current in History." Accessed 10 March 2010 at www.sgi.org/peace2009sum.html.

"Introduction: What Is Falun Dafa?." Accessed 10 March 2010 at www.falundafa.org/eng/intro.html.

Kabbalah Centre. "Reincarnation." Accessed 10 March 2010 at www.kabbalah.com/node/434.

Lee, Martha F. 1996. *The Nation of Islam: An American Millenarian Movement*. Syracuse: Syracuse University Press.

Levi, Jerome M. 2009. "Structuralism and Kabbalah: Sciences of Mysticism or Mystifications of Science?" *Anthropological Quarterly* 82, 4 (Fall).

Lewis, James R. 2003. *Legitimating New Religions*. Rutgers: Rutgers University Press.

Li Hongzhi. 2000. *Falun Gong*. 3rd edn. New York: University Publishing Co.

Ljungdahl, Alex. 1975. "What We Can Learn from Non-Biblical Prophet Movements." In *New Religions*, ed. Haralds Biezais. Stockholm: Almqvist & Wiksell International.

Muhammad, Elijah. 1997. *Message to the Blackman in America*. Phoenix: Secretarius Memps Publications.

Nichiren. 1999. *The Writings of Nichiren Daishonin*. Vol. 1. Trans. Gosho Translation Committee. Santa Monica: Soka Gakkai.

Olyan, Saul M., and Gary A. Anderson. 2009. *Priesthood and Cult in Ancient Israel*. Sheffield: Sheffield Academic Press.

Ortega, Tony. 2009. "Tom Cruise Told Me to Talk to a Bottle: Life at Scientology's Secret Headquarters." *The Village Voice*. Accessed 10 March 2010 at http://blogs.villagevoice.com/runninscared/archives/2009/11/tom_cruise_was.php.

Palmer, Susan Jean. 1995. "Women in the Raelian Movement: New Religious Experiments in Gender and Authority." In *The Gods Have Landed: New Religions from Other Worlds*, ed. James R. Lewis. Albany: State University of New York Press.

Prabhupada, A.C. Bhaktivedanta. 1968. *Teachings of Lord Chaitanya: The Golden Avatar*. New York: The Bhaktivedanta Book Trust.

Sahib, Hatim A. 1951. "The Nation of Islam." Master's thesis. University of Chicago. Cited in Lee 1996: 23.

"72 Names of God, The." Accessed 15 March at www.kabbalah.com/node/432.

Starhawk. 1982. *Dreaming the Dark*. Boston: Beacon Press.

Walker, Dennis. 2005. *Islam and the Search for African-American Nationhood: Elijah Muhammad, Louis Farrakhan and the Nation of Islam*. Atlanta: Clarity Press.

White, Vibert L., Jr. 2001. *Inside the Nation of Islam: A Historical and Personal Testimony by a Black Muslim*. Gainesville: University Press of Florida.

Note

Parts of this chapter, especially in the sections on the Mormons, the Baha'i Faith, Wicca, and New Age movements, incorporate material written by the late Will Oxtoby for earlier editions of the work.

Credits

Page 37, excerpt: Reprinted with the permission of Scribner Publishing Group, a division of Simon & Schuster, Inc. from CUSTER DIED FOR YOUR SINS: AN INDIAN MANIFESTO by Vine Deloria Jr. Copyright © 1969 by Vine Deloria Jr. Copyright renewed © 1997 by Vine Deloria Jr. All rights reserved.

Page 66, excerpt: *Things Fall Apart* by Chinua Achebe. Copyright © 1959 by Chinua Achebe, used by permission of The Wylie Agency LLC.

Page 119, excerpt: Shlomo Pines (tr). *Guide of the Perplexed*. University of Chicago Press, 1963.

Page 124, excerpt: from A TREASURY OF JEWISH FOLKLORE by Nathan Ausubel, copyright © 1948 and copyright renewed © 1975 by Crown Publishers, an imprint of Random House LLC. Used by permission of Crown Books, an imprint of the Crown Publishing Group, a division of Random House LLC. All rights reserved.

Page 171, excerpt: © 1975, Sister Benedicta Ward, tr. A Cistercian Studies publication. Published by Liturgical Press, Collegeville MN

Page 255, excerpt: Menocal, María Rosa, Ten Years After: The Virtues of Exile, Scripta Mediterranea, Vols. XIX-XX 1998-1999, 55. Published by the Canadian Institute for Mediterranean Studies.

Page 293, excerpt: from THE BHAGAVAD-GITA by Barbara Miller, translation copyright © 1986 by Barbara Stoler Miller. Used by permission of Bantam Books, an imprint of Random House, a division of Random House LLC. All rights reserved.

Page 312, excerpt: Hawley, John S., and Mark Juergensmeyer, trans. 1988. *Songs of the Saints of India*. New York: Oxford University Press. 50-1. By permission of Oxford University Press USA.

Page 312, excerpt: Hawley, John S., and Mark Juergensmeyer, trans. 1988. *Songs of the Saints of India*. New York: Oxford University Press. 137. By permission of Oxford University Press USA.

Page 530, excerpt: as cited in Lee, Peter H., et al., eds. 1993. *Sourcebook of Korean Civilization. Vol. I.* New York: Columbia University Press page 24. Original source: "The Lay of King Tongmyong," from The Korea Journal, Vol. 13.7.

Index